Advance Praise for
Acts of Inquiry in Qualitative I

"At long last, the rich qualitative research resources of a decade of the *Harvard Educational Review* are together in one readily accessible volume. Not only will readers have important perspectives from critical social science disciplines, but the many theoretical arguments and case studies are now side by side. The value of *Acts of Inquiry* is not just as a collection of some of the most thoughtful and biting work of the field, but also as a timesaver for teachers and students. Who hasn't searched frantically for that *HER* article that addressed exactly the point a student raised in class? As required reading in qualitative methods classes, it will outshine many of the resources now available for its breadth and comprehensiveness."
— *Yvonna S. Lincoln, Texas A&M University*

"*Acts of Inquiry in Qualitative Research* provides the kind of examples I search for to use in my qualitative research methods class — diverse and thoughtful articles that will not only deepen students' understanding of (and questions about) research methods, but also stimulate their interest in and thinking about a variety of educational topics. *Acts of Inquiry* is a fine collection of articles and a valuable accompaniment to any qualitative research methods text."
— *Corrine Glesne, University of Vermont*

"This collection of articles succeeds in bringing together an unusual assortment of writers and ideas that further the conversation on the nature, issues, and uses of qualitative research. It is definitely a volume to use as a teacher, student, or practitioner in pursuit of insight and information about qualitative research. The many articles, divided into six sections, inform the reader not only by their content, but also by their often extensive bibliographies."
— *Alan Peshkin, Stanford University*

"In teaching qualitative research methodology, I give students articles and papers that explicate as well as illustrate the concepts I introduce. *Acts of Inquiry in Qualitative Research* does both, and it does them in one volume. Even better, it does them well! For those who do, read, and write interpretive research, *Acts of Inquiry* is a valuable and unique resource that offers both breadth and depth."
— *Sharon Rallis, University of Connecticut*

"Long overdue, this excellent collection of essays serves to bring qualitative research to the forefront of social science inquiry."
— *Norman K. Denzin, University of Illinois at Urbana*

Acts of Inquiry
in
Qualitative Research

BÁRBARA M. BRIZUELA

JULIE PEARSON STEWART

ROMINA G. CARRILLO

JENNIFER GARVEY BERGER

Editors

Harvard Educational Review

Reprint Series No. 34

Library of Congress Card Number 00-130103
ISBN 0-916690-36-9

Harvard Educational Review
Gutman Library Suite 349
6 Appian Way
Cambridge, MA 02138

Cover Design: Alyssa Morris
Editorial Production: Dody Riggs
Typography: Sheila Walsh

We would like to thank Stephanie Cramer for giving us permission to reproduce her painting "West" on the cover.

Dedication

*We dedicate this book to our families, friends, and colleagues
who support our work and our lives,
and to the spirit of collaboration and cooperation
that made the book possible.*

Contents

Introduction

Doing, reading, and writing qualitative research are part of the same complex craft.[1] Each is an act of inquiry that aims at making meaning of the world. Although people often perceive them as discrete and disconnected, these three acts are interrelated and require many of the same skills, approaches, and attitudes. In each, we construct meanings, understandings, and interpretations about others' behaviors or interpretations of events. Many think of *reading* qualitative research — a text — as a passive act. But done well, it requires our active engagement with that text and, ultimately, with ourselves. In this way, reading qualitative research becomes an integral part of the qualitative research process, for it often sparks the questions that drive other research. Similarly, many think of *writing* qualitative research as an activity that occurs once research is completed. We choose to think of it, along with reading and doing, as part of the research process, one of the ongoing acts of inquiry in qualitative research. Referring specifically to ethnographic research, Hammersley and Atkinson (1995) explain the relationship of doing research to reading it and writing it: "One cannot ignore the work of reading and writing in the construction of ethnographic research. It is now widely recognized that 'the ethnography' is produced as much by how we write as by the processes of data collection and analysis; equally how we write is linked directly to how we read" (1995, p. 239).[2]

In this volume, *Acts of Inquiry in Qualitative Research*, we invite readers to join us in reading about others who do and write qualitative research. It is not an invitation to take part in an easy or passive task. It requires, rather, a hands-on and "minds-on"[3] approach that connects reading to doing and writing qualitative research. Readers of *Acts of Inquiry in Qualitative Research* will engage in tasks similar to those that authors of the studies presented in this volume have carried out — that is, as readers, they will search for and construct their own meanings, understandings, interpretations, and questions of the texts they encounter. Readers will engage in a complex task of interpreting someone else's interpretation of what is often yet another person's interpretation of events. In so doing, they will confront and question the assumptions of writers and participants. But, as Denis Donoghue (1998) writes, in the process, readers must also ask what they themselves "assume goes without saying" (p. 36).

No single book can answer all possible questions about qualitative research. It is our hope, however, that this book will contribute to further acts of inquiry into the complexity that surrounds us. We also hope it will provoke us to ask even more questions in the ongoing quest to understand the world. Our intent is not to offer the penultimate answer to anything or to detail the penultimate qualitative methodology.

We four editors are students, teachers, and doers of qualitative research. We are all women, but we bring varied and complex professional and personal histories, interests, and habits of thought and work to writing this introduction. From various ethnicities, disciplinary backgrounds, and levels of experience in teaching, we are daughters, mothers, sisters, and individuals. In other words, we bring rich and various perspectives to this book and to this introduction. What we share is a belief in searching for meaning and constantly questioning what we see, read, hear, feel, and do. It is this belief and this quest that we hope to share in these pages.

We choose to model an act of inquiry on "Snow," a poem written by British poet Louis MacNeice in 1935.[4] We do so knowing that the idea of using literary skills to interpret the data of qualitative research studies raises questions that we and our readers might want to consider: How, for example, is reading a poem different from reading a research text? What does it mean to treat social science as literary studies? Are the social sciences and literature polarities, or do they coexist beside and inside one another? What would it mean to seek out their connections in the chapters of this book? What would be gained? What would be lost? How, even, could it be done? The point is that every supposed answer contributes to and creates even more questions. It is with this ongoing, reflexive inquiry in mind that we enter MacNeice's poem and this book.

The Complexity of "Things Being Various"

MacNeice describes the world as one in which discrepancies, multiplicities, and ambiguities abound:

> The room was suddenly rich and the great bay-window was
> Spawning snow and pink roses against it
> Soundlessly collateral and incompatible:
> World is suddener than we fancy it.
>
> World is crazier and more of it than we think,
> Incorrigibly plural. I peel and portion
> A tangerine and spit the pips and feel the drunkenness of things being various.
>
> And the fire flames with a bubbling sound for the world
> Is more spiteful and gay than one supposes —
> On the tongue on the eyes on the ears in the palms of one's hands —
> There is more than glass between the snow and the huge roses.
>
> (MacNeice, 1935)

MacNeice's poem immerses readers in a multiple and asymmetric world in which contrasting images abound. It is a world of snow and pink roses; a rich room with a blazing fireplace and snow outside the bay window; a world of cold and warmth, spring and winter, simultaneously. It is in this discrepant, plural, ambiguous, and multiple world that qualitative researchers work and in which they try to make meaning. As researchers, we, like MacNeice, feel "the drunkenness of things being various," and keep wondering what, besides glass, there is "between the snow and the huge roses." We try to make sense of MacNeice's world — one that is "soundlessly collateral and incompatible," a sudden world. We feel the discrepancy, plurality, ambiguity, and multiplicity of the world "on the tongue on the eyes on the ears in the palms of

[our] hands" — all simultaneously, with nothing but ourselves to help us begin to understand all those sudden, instantaneous, and simultaneous feelings.

Within this staggeringly complex world, we carry out the task of qualitative research. We *do* qualitative research — that is, we plan studies, gather data, conduct interviews, and observe. From our data, we try to understand, make sense, and construct interpretations and meanings. In the act of *doing* qualitative research, as Frederick Erickson (1986) recommends, we ask ourselves a series of questions: What is happening here, specifically? What does it mean? How do we make that meaning? We also ask these questions as we read and write qualitative research. They give us not a hard and fast formula for evaluation, but a way to think about and question the texts we read and a way to think about the texts we create.

Using MacNeice's poem as an example of a text, we may answer these questions in numerous ways. What follows is one possible response to these questions, a response based on our particular knowledge and experiences, yet rigorously grounded in what the poem says. While it offers a response, it also raises further questions and leaves others unasked and unexplored.

- *What is happening here, specifically?* There are many levels of responses to this first question. We might note that the poem is specifically set in a room with a bay window, a blazing fireplace, and an arrangement of pink roses. It is winter and is snowing outside, but inside the room it is warm. The juxtaposition of the roses and the snow on either side of the window causes wonder. The speaker is eating a tangerine and spits the seeds. The fire flares up, making noises as it does so. These observations leave many questions unsettled and ambiguous; for example, What makes the room "suddenly rich"? Who is speaking? To whom?
- *What does it mean?* It is essential to keep in mind that the response to this question is not *the* meaning; it is one *particular* meaning from a wide range of possibilities as constructed through a web of personal beliefs, fears, hopes, and knowledge. In making meaning, we, as readers, bring these elements to the act of reading the poem, yet scrupulously ground it in the data of the poem's text. To us at this time, the poem means that the world is "incorrigibly plural." It is at once "soundlessly collateral and incompatible" — an ambiguous and contradictory world in which roses and snow and warmth and cold coexist. And between the two extremes of "the snow and the huge roses," just as between many of the polarities we find in life, there is a vast range of possibilities waiting to be tasted, seen, heard, and felt. In our quest to make meaning of the poem, further questions arise. For example, what does "the fire flames with a bubbling sound" mean? And why a tangerine and not an orange?
- *How do we make that meaning?* MacNeice creates this ambiguous and contradictory world with asymmetric groupings of images — roses and snow, for example — that counter assumptions. He juxtaposes opposites — "soundlessly collateral and incompatible." In the phrase "incorrigibly plural," the poet plays on the multiple meaning of *incorrigible*. According to the third edition of the *American Heritage Dictionary*, it means "incapable of being corrected or reformed," "firmly rooted," or "difficult or impossible to control or manage." He thus makes meaning through his deliberate and asymmetric choice of language. But there are other questions. Why, for example, are there no commas between the phrases of the tenth line? In

fact, why is there little internal punctuation? Evaluating how the poem makes meaning then leads recursively to more questions about what is happening and what it means.

These are by no means all the questions that could arise from reading MacNeice's poem. Cultural, historic, and geographic contexts could give rise to other questions for the reader's consideration. In fact, the questions could go on and on because each reader could formulate questions based on particular contexts and personal assumptions. In doing, reading, and writing qualitative research, we go through a recursive process similar to the one we use with this poem. Through that process, we try to construct meanings and interpretations in our quest to understand various aspects of this incorrigibly plural world.

Part of that plurality can be found in the many interpretations of what qualitative research is. For example, is it art or is it science? Or is it both? If so, what does that mean for those who read, write, and do qualitative research? In using MacNeice's poem as a means to understand qualitative research, we have highlighted qualitative research as art, but, as MacNeice observed, the world is "more of it than we think." Researchers such as Sara Lawrence-Lightfoot (1994, 1997) and Annie Rogers (1995), both trained in the social sciences, practice and write their crafts as art and science. For Lightfoot, it is portraiture; for Rogers, it is poetics. Other qualitative researchers, such as Sonia Nieto (1998), move it even closer to narrative and novel; others, such as Raymond McDermott and Jeffrey Aron (1978), suggest ties with drama; Hammersley and Atkinson refer to ethnographic research as a "textual enterprise" (1995, p. 239). Yet the structure of most qualitative research studies is scientific. For example, Peter Johnston's "Understanding Reading Disability: A Case Study Approach" and Diane Holt-Reynolds's "Good Readers, Good Teachers? Subject Matter Expertise as a Challenge in Learning to Teach," among other chapters in this book, include traditionally scientific sections, such as introduction, literature review, methods, findings, and conclusions. Even the definition of what counts as qualitative research, of where its roots lie, is varied and multiple.

That multiplicity is further compounded by the fact that qualitative research takes place in a "soundlessly collateral and incompatible" world. As a result, in doing, writing, and reading qualitative research, we must consider the multiple roles and perspectives of researchers and participants, as well as the multiple contexts within which their work takes place. Given the multiplicity of qualitative research and the incredible varieties and possible permutations of human beings and what they do, interpretive researchers have little choice but to deal with complexity and variety.

Nor do researchers want to avoid it. In fact, this very complexity makes qualitative research necessary in our ongoing quest to make sense of the world. Because events and people are so varied, the primary concern of interpretive research must be, as Erickson writes, "particularizability, rather than generalizability" (1986, p. 130). Qualitative researchers seek to interpret what particular people in particular situations at particular times *do,* as well as what those particular behaviors *mean* to those who do them and to those with and to whom they are done. They try to make meaning of the actions of various human beings by holding to the data with systematicity and rigor, much as we held to the data of the poem in our analysis. While much qualitative research concerns everyday things such as observing events, talking to people, and trying to figure out what it all means, the care with which such processes are undertaken separates such research from everyday life. Unlike people who are simply going about their daily lives, qualitative researchers are mindful of the way each decision affects the data gathering — each interaction with participants, each decision about which data to gather, which questions to ask, each selection of pieces of data to analyze and explore.

We have designed this book to reflect the complexity and wide range of possibilities that are a part of qualitative research. It is divided into six subsections based on the following aspects of qualitative research: habits of thought and work, ethics and validity, the relationships between the researcher and the participants, data collection, data analysis and interpretation, and the uses of research. Each section focuses the reader's attention on one aspect of a study, and the individual chapters highlight the complexity and wide range of possibilities involved in each area. We ask readers to bring the questions we asked of MacNeice's poem, their own questions, and their skills of interpretation to reading the chapters in this book as part of their acts of inquiry.

"Habits of Thought and Work"

Researchers themselves are part of the complexity and variation in interpretive research. Norman Denzin writes that there are many "terrains of qualitative research" and within those terrains are "multiple interpretive communities" (1992, p. 511). Among those terrains using qualitative research methodologies to study education are the academic disciplines of anthropology, education, linguistics, psychology, and sociology.

As George Marcus notes, each discipline is built on particular "habits of thought and work" (1998, p. 203), and each has its own epistemology, conventions, and sets of questions that it seeks to address. Currently, the criteria for conducting and evaluating interpretive research in these disciplines are in flux, as seen in the myriad approaches within those disciplinary communities, including the multiple interpretive communities of feminism, literary theory, cultural Marxism, neo-Marxism, cultural studies, teacher research, sociolinguistics, psycholinguistics, cognitive psychology, and developmental psychology. The authors in this section explore the following questions: What has been the discipline's most important contribution to the general area of qualitative research? How has the discipline influenced the methods of qualitative research? How has the discipline influenced the central questions of qualitative research? Because qualitative research is an evolving area, how is change occurring and what is evolving? Their responses to these questions raise even further questions regarding what constitutes qualitative research: What, if any, are its boundaries and limitations? What are its commonalities across disciplines? Do other disciplines use qualitative methodology? What qualifies a researcher to do qualitative research?

Ethics and Validity

In any study, questions about ethics and validity arise, and the same complexity and plurality found in qualitative research's underlying habits of thought and work also shape these questions. Because qualitative research is particular rather than generalizable and because it is so shaped by the researcher and context (Erickson, 1986), no single set of ethics or criteria for validity applies across the board. Instead, as Laurel Richardson (1991) writes, ethics and criteria of validity draw from a particular and individual web of moral, practical, political, and personal beliefs and ideals that help researchers navigate complex and multiple roles between themselves, participants, and local contexts.

Faced with what MacNeice calls "the drunkenness of things being various," qualitative researchers begin their work with a reflection on their roles and identities and the effects that those elements may have on the research process and relationships. Because these elements change and shift during the course of a study, the researcher continues her examination of ethics and relationships throughout.[5] The process of reflection is thus an ongoing part of the research process in which ethics and validity are at the forefront of the qualitative researcher's concerns. In a sense, ethics and validity emerge from researchers' acts of inquiry as they revisit and question these issues and themselves throughout the research process.

So, what standard are researchers to use in determining the ethics and validity of their work? Does multiplicity then mean that anything goes in qualitative research, that questions of ethics and validity are simply too complex to tackle? On the contrary. The authors in this book, and particularly those in this section, suggest that these concerns are omnipresent in qualitative research. Elliot Mishler, for example, finds that there are "no rules" (p. 418) for assessing validity. He argues that " 'rules' for proper research are not universally applicable, are modified by pragmatic considerations" (p. 418). They must, in other words, be set in the context of the study itself. After reflecting on the particularities of his work, Mishler suggests that the new criterion for the validity of interpretive studies is trustworthiness — "the degree to which we can rely on the concepts, methods, and inferences of a study, or tradition of inquiry, as the basis for our own theorizing and empirical research" (p. 419).

While Mishler proposes "trustworthiness" as a new criterion for validity, Andrew Gitlin responds to the particularity of his work by proposing a different standard of validity for his study. Drawing on a Rawlsian vision of justice, Gitlin states that "one criteria for validity would be the degree to which the research process enabled disenfranchised groups to fully participate in the decisionmaking process; examine their beliefs, actions, and the school context; and make changes based on this understanding" (p. 446). For Gitlin and his study, change and the development of voice, rather than "truthfulness," become the primary criteria for the validity of a study. It is also noteworthy that he says that his idea represents only "one criteria for validity," suggesting that there are other such criteria that researchers can determine and explore in the particularities of their studies.

Our perspective — one that sees reading, doing, and writing qualitative research as parts of an ongoing process — also suggests that questions regarding what is valid and what is ethical drive all parts of this process. Readers of qualitative research must therefore constantly question the text to explore the authors' responses to these issues and to see where they themselves stand. Among the questions we as readers could ask are: What assumptions might the author not acknowledge? How might this effect validity?

The Relationships between the Researcher and the Participants

In examining relationships between researchers and participants, many who read, practice, and write qualitative research focus on issues of power; that is, they examine what separates and divides the researcher and the researched. From this perspective, questions of power assume a dichotomy of those who have it and those who don't. In contrast, the authors in this section question this arrangement. They reflect on power, but they also reflect on their relationships with those they study, on participants' voices in the research process, and the multiple identities of all the people involved. In other words, they look not only at what separates the researcher and participants, but also at what ties them together. For researchers, that process begins by reflecting on their own roles and identities and by examining their effects on the research process.

In exploring these concerns, Annie Rogers recognizes her power as a researcher and then questions the responsibilities that come with that recognition. She asks: To whom am I, as qualitative researcher, responsible? And how? What are those relationships when they are in flux and part of a work in progress? She also reflects on her voice and the role it may play in research relationships and the research process. Based on this reflective act of inquiry, she chooses to integrate her roles as analyzer and participant, weaving her own story with the stories of her participants. In addition, she considers the effects of her work on others outside her group of participants. The issue of ethics is thus present in this aspect of qualitative research as well, for her actions raise questions regarding the effects of such choices on ethics and validity. How, for example, might that decision affect her analysis of the participants? How does closeness affect vision?

Reflections on the roles of the researcher and the participants can also lead to redefinition. For example, Polly Ulichny and Wendy Schoener challenge the typical asymmetries of the relationship between researcher and researched and create a relationship of full collaboration in which both assume the role of researcher. Both women discuss Schoener's teaching, and both women participate in writing. Their work together shows the unpredictable complexity of the relationship between the researcher and the researched and the wide range of possibilities therein. Again, these decisions raise further questions for the researcher and the writer, and for the reader as well. In what ways does the blurring of roles shape analysis? Given that one author is a teacher and the other a researcher, is the relationship between Ulichny and Schoener a full and equal collaboration?

The multiple identities of both the researcher and the participants also contribute to the complexity of the research relationship. In her chapter, Joan Kernan Cone writes of her roles as teacher and as researcher, roles that are generally assumed to have some degree of power, over either students or participants. Yet Cone, like Ulichny and Schoener, recognizes the same thing that MacNeice does in his poem: that "there is more than glass between the snow and the huge roses." Her supposedly powerless students are concurrently her informants and the evaluators of her teaching. Like the world we are immersed in, the people in Cone's study are "incorrigibly plural," with multiple, often symbiotic and complementary, and occasionally competing roles.

As researchers, writers, and readers, we often look at the role of power in relationships. Issues of power are certainly present, but other forces also function in relationships between researchers and participants. Which other areas should we consider? To which other aspects of relationships does the power of power blind us?

Data Collection

Qualitative researchers begin with a question they want to answer, a problem they want to explore, or a situation they choose to change. That question, problem, or situation — which is open to modification or change throughout the research process — reflects the researcher, her interests and beliefs. It also drives the entire research process and determines how data is collected. In turn, the choices researchers make about data collection influence what they see. In reading qualitative research studies, readers might consider how researchers collect the data, why they choose to collect the data as they do, and what process led to those decisions.

Choosing to collect data in one way is also a decision not to do it in another way. Inevitably, there are costs and benefits to each choice. These choices are not about convenience or meaningless decisions; they reflect an intentional search to match data collection methods to the questions in which one is most interested. As with all acts, these decisions have effects on outcome — effects that the reader, as well as the researcher and the writer of research, must question.

Seeking to match his research aims and questions with the types of methods he chose for collecting data, Peter Johnston examines the psychological and social determinants of reading failure. He chooses to focus on "the cognitive, affective, social, and personal history" (p. 155) of the three men with whom he worked by using observational data and extensive verbal reports about their past and present experiences in learning to read. He argues that case studies are particularly well suited to his purposes because of the critical nature of the "substantial individual differences in experience and in important dimensions of behavior (both overt and covert)" (p. 155). Johnston's choice of method in data collection is thus deliberate. Among other possibilities, he could have carried out a group study or chosen younger disabled readers. As Johnston explains, however, learning strategies are "best studied at the individual level" (p. 154). On the other hand, "adult disabled readers have conscious access to more mental processes" (p. 155). Had he chosen to study younger disabled readers, how might the study have been different? How did his participants' "access to more mental processes" (p. 155) affect his work?

Sometimes the questions that researchers seek to answer require that they create new ways of responding to questions and understanding events. Adrienne Alton-Lee, Graham Nuthall, and John Patrick speculated about the hidden voices of children in classroom discourse. Their questions moved their research away from the typical focus on public statements, or those things that can be fairly easily overheard, and directed them instead to the whispers of children. To have access to those whispers, they used individual microphones to record children's private utterances to others and themselves. Even this innovative matching of data collection to research question leaves some unanswered questions: How did these microphones alter children's utterances? How does the act of listening to what was not meant to be heard influence what the children said? What effect does observation have on performance?

Data Analysis and Interpretation

Reading qualitative research, like reading literature, is not merely a matter of running one's eyes over pages and gathering facts. Readers consider what is happening specifically within the text, and then move from what is happening to what these events/ words mean. The story becomes the data, to be interpreted through the minds of the readers. Thus, as Erickson (1986) explains, the data in and of themselves do not tell researchers anything. Instead, the data are interpreted through the researcher's theoretical presuppositions and assumptions about the nature of schools, of teachers and teaching, and of children. In other words, the constant search for meaning is a recursive asking of the questions presented at the outset of this introduction — What is happening here, specifically? What does it mean? How does it make that meaning?

Readers of qualitative research remain open to possibilities and interpretations that are unexplored in a particular study. In this sense, the reader must enter the data of the text with the same openness and inquisitiveness that the researcher does. Donald Freeman illustrates the need for these qualities in the process of analysis and interpretation as he tries to understand the complexity of teacher knowledge. He argues for the use of methods other than those traditionally used in the interpretation and analysis of teachers' "words." He invites readers and researchers to think about how the lines between the different issues in qualitative research are blurred, how "the conventional distinction between data gathering and analysis [is] blurred as collection and interpretation of data [become] iterative and even symbiotic processes" (p. 743). He reminds us that the process of analysis and interpretation is ongoing and that even the first question — What is going on here? — is an analytic and interpretive one. He maintains that paying close attention to analysis even in the earliest data gathering stages is necessary for careful research and analysis. The same is true for readers of qualitative research who constantly analyze and reanalyze as they read.

Reba Page, Yvette Samson, and Michele Crockett go even further than Freeman. They suggest that interpretation does not simply continue the process of making meaning; it begins it. They present one interpretation, only to use it, along with the data that led to it, to construct yet other interpretations. As they reflected on their own process of data collection and analysis, they discovered many other possibilities of "meanings" in the data. By offering readers long streams of data and a range in their possible interpretations and analyses, the authors allow readers to entertain a wide variety of possible explanations and ultimately to make decisions and interpretations for themselves. Page and her colleagues thus begin with an act of inquiry that they continue beyond the doing and the writing of qualitative research. They invite readers to continue this act of inquiry by questioning and interpreting their data and their analyses.

The Uses of Research

The goal of qualitative research is the production of knowledge. One question that qualitative researchers confront is, What are the uses of the knowledge that we construct? Whether their goal is transforming society, improving teaching practice (their own or someone else's), shaping policy, evaluating current practices, or adding to or creating theories, qualitative researchers target their writing to a wide range of possible audiences and purposes. Those choices affect results.

Concha Delgado-Gaitan depicts her evolving role as an observer, active participant, and facilitator of community empowerment in Carpinteria, a predominantly

Mexican American community in California. Her narrative focuses on how what she learned about herself informed her role "in crafting the study and influencing change" (p. 392) within the community. In her case, the research study was "useful" as a reflection of her changing role. And in this process of reflection and change, her aims in terms of her relationships within the participant community also changed — from observer to facilitator and community advocate. But such choices, as noted previously, are not without consequence or price: Delgado-Gaitan's advocacy influenced the task of producing knowledge. This leaves the reader questioning her iterative process of advocacy and knowledge production, the way using the knowledge she produces to transform a community might have influenced the knowledge she produced.

That researchers make choices about how to use the data they collect — and can modify those choices — can be seen in Sonia Nieto's work. In 1992, Nieto collected data to create case studies of ten "successful" junior and senior high school students. In 1994, she reshaped the same data presented in "Lessons from Students on Creating a Chance to Dream" to another end: to challenge policymakers and educators interested in school reform to "hear" and analyze students' comments in order "to create environments in which all children are capable of learning" (p. 394). Nieto arranges the data against a backdrop of research literature to shed light on what she learned — and what readers could learn. In revisiting her data with this intention in mind, Nieto uses what Harry Wolcott calls "a heavy hand" (1983, p. 8). Her revisit of the same data shows that research can have multiple uses in multiple contexts; it also raises questions regarding the uses of research. For example, how do researchers balance what the data say and what they want the data to say? And how do the reader, the researcher, and the writer know what that balance is?

Diane Holt-Reynolds's chapter illustrates the use of one portrait — derived from a larger pool of data — to create a "counter-intuitive case" of knowledge of subject-matter expertise. Holt-Reynolds explores the role that knowledge of subject-matter expertise plays for a student teacher, and how that knowledge does not translate into an understanding of how to model and share that expertise with her students. By offering readers extensive data, Holt-Reynolds sketches an expanded "definition of subject-matter expertise [that] must include an awareness of concepts, ideas, and dispositions that must be actually taught to others" (p. 43). Her portrait of the student teacher offers heuristic insight, leads us to challenge traditional assumptions about disciplinary knowledge, and challenges teacher educators to consider the implications of this knowledge for their own work with prospective teachers. Yet this portrait also leaves questions unexplored. Readers will probably begin to consider issues of sampling in order to make a specific point. A purposeful selection of a single case offers a great deal to policymakers in terms of depth, but how would a more random or larger sample have changed Holt-Reynolds's message or its impact?

Conclusion

The multiple and complex ways in which we do and read qualitative research parallel the multiple and complex ways we choose to write our studies. The various ways we choose to "present" our studies seem to be especially linked to the uses we may want to give to our research — the audiences we choose, as in Nieto's case; the relationships we may want to establish with the community we are working with, as in Delgado-Gaitan's case; the reflections about policy and reform, as in Nieto's case; and even the intent of proposing different alternative analyses for the study, as in Page, Samson, and Crockett's chapter. The boundaries between data collection, analysis, uses of research, and choices about presentation of research begin to blur, as do the boundaries between doing, reading, and writing.

If there is any conclusion to draw about qualitative research, it is that its various aspects — among them ethics and validity, the relationship between the researcher and the participants, data collection, data analysis and interpretation, and the uses of research — are integrally related and require constant reexamination. The common thread among these various parts is the ongoing and systematic act of inquiry. As Brown and Dowling explain, "Research is properly conceived, not, primarily, as a sequence of stages, nor as a collection of skills and techniques, nor as a set of rules, though it entails all of these. Rather, it should be understood . . . as the continuous application of a particularly coherent and systematic and reflexive way of questioning, a mode of interrogation" (1998, p. 1).

We know that putting these chapters in a single book changes the context of each of them a little, highlighting some things that we have chosen (the aspects of the research process) while ignoring others (a shared context or content). To put them together creates one kind of conversation among these chapters; we welcome our readers into the conversation with these researchers and with one another. In the process of figuring out what "more than glass" there is "between the snow and the huge roses," qualitative researchers search for meaning as they grapple with the "incorrigibly plural" world in which we live. It is this quest for what seems unseen, perhaps even unseeable, that drives qualitative researchers to research, to comb through their data, to ask new questions, and to find new ways to understand these questions. It is this quest that we ask readers to join.

Bárbara M. Brizuela
Julie Pearson Stewart
Romina G. Carrillo
Jennifer Garvey Berger

Notes

1. Although many scholars and researchers use the term *qualitative* research, we will also refer to this form of research as *interpretive* research. In doing so, we adopt the terminology that Paul Rabinow and William M. Sullivan use in their groundbreaking book, *Interpretive Social Science* (1973). We do so for the same reasons Frederick Erickson cites: 1) interpretive research allows for inclusion of various forms of research such as case studies and ethnographies; 2) it avoids the quantitative/qualitative dichotomy that underlay the first decades of this form of research and allows inclusion of quantitative methods within a qualitative methodology; 3) it more precisely defines a key feature of the various approaches of this form of research — that is, a "central research interest in human meaning in social life and its elucidation and exposition by the researcher" (1986, p. 119).

2. Anthony Brown and Paul Dowling (1998) also recognize the relationship among these three acts, referring to them as the three Rs of research: Reading, pRoducing, and wRiting.

3. The term *minds-on* is borrowed from Duckworth, Easley, Hawkins, and Henriques (1990).

4. MacNeice, an Irish-born British poet, wrote primarily during the 1930s and 1940s. Although often categorized as a political poet, his primary concern was the ambiguity of experience.
5. We struggled with the pronoun forms to use throughout this text. It seems that even deciding which pronoun to use requires reflection. Using "her/his" places some distance between us,

References

Denzin, N. (1992). The art and politics of interpretation. In M. D. LeCompte, W. L. Millroy, & J. Preissle (Eds.), *The handbook of qualitative research in education* (pp. 500–515). San Diego: Academic Press.

Donoghue, D. (1998). *The practice of reading.* New Haven, CT: Yale University Press.

Duckworth, E., Easley, J., Hawkins, D., & Henriques, A. (1990). *Science education: A minds-on approach for the elementary years.* Hillsdale, NJ: Lawrence Erlbaum.

Erickson, F. (1986). Qualitative methods in research on teaching. In M. C. Wittrock (Ed.), *Handbook of research on teaching* (3rd ed., pp. 119–161). New York: Macmillan.

Hammersley, M., & Atkinson, P. (1995). *Ethnography: Principles in practice* (2nd ed.). London: Routledge.

Lawrence-Lightfoot, S. (1994). *I've known rivers: Lives of loss and liberation.* Reading, MA: Addison-Wesley.

Lawrence-Lightfoot, S., & Hoffman-Davis, J. (1997). *Art and science of portraiture.* San Francisco: Jossey-Bass.

MacNeice, L. (1972). "Snow." In H. Gardner (Ed.), *The New Oxford Book of English Verse, 1250–.* Oxford, Eng.: Oxford University Press.

Marcus, G. (1998). *Ethnography through thick and thin.* Princeton, NJ: Princeton University Press.

McDermott, R. P., & Aron, J. (1978). Pirandello in the classroom: On the possibility of equal educational opportunity in American culture. In M. C. Reynolds (Ed.), *Futures of education for exceptional students: Emerging structures* (41–64). Minneapolis: National Support Systems Project.

Nieto, S. (1998). Fact and fiction: Stories of Puerto Ricans in U.S. schools. *Harvard Educational Review, 68,* 133–163.

Rabinow, P., & Sullivan, W. M. (1987). *Interpretive social science: A second look.* Berkeley: University of California Press.

Richardson, L. (1991). Writing: A method of inquiry. In M. D. LeCompte, W. L. Millroy, & J. Preissle (Eds.), *The handbook of qualitative research in education* (pp. 516–529). San Diego: Academic Press.

Rogers, A. G. (1995). *A shining affliction: A story of harm and healing in psychotherapy.* New York: Viking.

Rossman, G. B., & Rallis, S. F. (1998). *Learning in the field. An introduction to qualitative research.* Thousand Oaks, CA: Sage.

Wolcott, H. (1983). Adequate schools and inadequate education: The life history of a sneaky kid. *Anthropology and Education Quarterly, 4,* 3–32.

We would like to thank Karen Maloney, Dody Riggs, Joan Razzante, Kelly Graves-Desai, Claire Scott, Kathy Gallagher, and the Editorial Board of the *Harvard Educational Review* for their help in shaping the concept and content of this volume.

"Snow," by Louis MacNeice, is used with permission of David Higham Associates Limited, London, England.

PART ONE

"Habits of Thought and Work"

The Turn Inward in
Qualitative Research

REBA N. PAGE

In the mid-1980s, my daughter, then a high school senior, put a bumper sticker on the family car that declared, "Question Authority." By the time my son graduated from high school at the end of the decade, some floodgate seemed to have opened, because one of the stickers on his beat-up Sirocco stated, "Question Everything." Both bumper stickers reiterated a theme that had achieved considerable salience, but was not expressed on stickers, when the children's ancient parents were in college in the early 1960s.

"Question Authority" and Question Everything" could be epigraphs for the broader context of the five essays in this section. The authority of the academic disciplines has been the subject of intense scrutiny during the past forty years. Everything about them has been questioned, from their theories, findings, and methods of inquiry, to the role and identity of scholars, their training and tenure, as well as the value and even the possibility of research in the human sciences. This scrutiny continues unabated as one dynamic in the modern struggle to define the proper relationship between an egalitarianism that honors all individuals' right to participate in setting a society's course and an expertise that elevates some people as being more knowledgeable (Hofstadter, 1962).

The five essays that follow evoke and recreate this struggle because they are written from the perspective of particular disciplines, and because their subject is qualitative research. Qualitative research has been at the center of the crisis in disciplinary authority. Its distinctive contribution has resided precisely in its emphasis on raising questions about ideas otherwise taken for granted and in its seemingly untutored means of locating these ideas and bringing them to consciousness. Qualitative research has challenged the "science" in the social sciences, and in the natural sciences too, even though science has long been the gold standard for knowledge and a source of disciplinary authority. It has secured a place in contemporary research publications, graduate curricula, and funding agencies. And even as qualitative research has gained currency in the now-familiar competition with positivism, its questioning has turned inward onto itself to produce an exhilarating and at times exhausting proliferation of types *within* the qualitative paradigm. That proliferation is one source of the present alarm that "anything goes" in educational research and of

Harvard Educational Review Vol. 70 No. 1 Spring 2000, 23–38

nostalgia for the large-scale, randomized experiments thought to provide unbiased and exact answers[1] (Miller, 1999; Mosteller, Light, & Sachs, 1996; Viadero, 1999).

In this essay, I introduce dimensions of the broader context in which the next five essays are set to suggest that the myriad forms of qualitative research are not the result of mindless inattention, but are instead a response to significant intellectual and material transformations. I also attend to context in order to place the essays in conversation with each other. Each by itself offers an intriguing perspective on the character and evolution of qualitative research, its contributions to education and schooling, and possible directions for the methodology's future. Read together, the essays are at least as provocative, expressing the similarities and schisms around foundational problems that now press the educational community: Are there core characteristics that distinguish qualitative methodology, despite its many varieties? Is training required to use such a seemingly artless mode of inquiry? Why is research methodology currently of such interest in education, and should it be? Of what value is qualitative research to school practitioners or policymakers? By what standards — and by whose — should its value be judged? The five essays that follow in this section evoke these questions and challenge us to take them up, to clarify purposes in our research, and, in the process, to renew the educational community.

The Context

The field of educational studies has participated in the developing uncertainties and self-consciousness experienced in other academic disciplines during the past half century, albeit at its own pace and with its own eccentricities.[2] In a particularly incisive review, Bellack (1978) describes the tumult that appeared in research on teaching in the late 1970s. His review captures the confidence in early challenges to the quantitative ideology and, equally important, foreshadows the internal challenges the qualitative ideology would itself encounter in the succeeding decades.[3]

Bellack begins by characterizing the "mainstream scientific ideology" as being defined chiefly by its methods. Derived from the natural sciences, the methods shaped how research into teacher effectiveness had largely been conducted since the 1950s. There are three steps to this research: first, describe teaching objectively and impartially, that is, numerically; second, correlate measures of teaching with measures of student learning (usually scores on academic achievement tests); and lastly, devise experiments to test the significant correlations in controlled settings. These methods imply that the purposes of teaching are transparent and, therefore, that the important questions are technical. The chief question is, What teaching practices most effectively produce student learning? Developing causal explanations, "scientific research" would then translate directly into rules for practice.

As Bellack describes, problems with the process-product model became increasingly apparent, as studies accumulated but produced persistently contradictory and ambiguous results.[4] Proponents responded by retouching the three-step method. Critical outsiders, however, having recovered the hermeneutic, or interpretive, orientation in social research, issued a fundamental indictment: Traditional research about teaching was conceptually vacuous because it pursued the wrong questions, and its reliance on correlational and experimental methods meant it couldn't imagine better ones.[5]

These critics shared in the cultural turn in the human sciences, in which the conceptual worlds people lived within seemed the focal point for a comprehensive system of analysis (Geertz, 1973; White, 1973). They saw the central research issue as conceptual clarification of teaching, including both its unintended and manifest effects, and its patterned variation. Therefore, rather than asking whether teaching "works," they asked what teaching "means" (including its tacit meanings), how people construct its meaning, and how meaning varies by context. Such questions require a different method, fieldwork, which includes such strategies as participant-observation, interviewing, and perusal of documents and other artifacts. Explanation is teleological rather than mechanically causal because, unlike balls rolling down inclined planes, people act based on what they think and intend (even when what they think is wrong).[6] The emphasis on meaning-making extends to the relationship between research and practice. Rather than rules, qualitative research provides ideas — what Dewey (1929) called "intellectual instrumentalities" or Cronbach (1975) referred to as "working hypotheses" (both cited in Bellack, 1978, pp. 18–20). Readers can use the ideas to recognize and interpret their own teaching or other teaching they know about (see also Greeno et al., 1999; Wehlage, 1981). Put bluntly, *readers*, rather than research, generalize.

Although Bellack is sympathetic to the early qualitative research, he identifies two serious problems.[7] First, however meticulous their descriptions of teaching, qualitative researchers were generally cavalier in describing their methods, their approach to data analysis, and the warrant for their claims. Second, while the researchers credited local particulars, they either ignored or finessed "frame factors" — that is, the wider social and historical contexts that presumably have some impact on, and are themselves influenced by, local instances of teaching (or learning, curriculum, etc.). Both problems raise questions about the authoritativeness of qualitative accounts by making it difficult for readers to assess their validity.

Bellack's two criticisms moved front and center *within* qualitative methodology during the succeeding decades to constitute what is now sometimes termed the *crisis in representation*. The crisis converged on the positivism lingering in the qualitative claim that researchers could document and explain, fully and accurately, another's life-world as it is. Limits in the methodology's ability to deliver objective, impartial close-ups became apparent as studies became more explicit about how qualitative research was conducted. Qualitative research, it turned out, is no less a social construction than the cultures it studies, and the mediating influence of the researcher is therefore ineluctable.

Material changes during the half century intensified the epistemological concern with representation. Empires dissolved, the Cold War ended, civil rights were extended, capital adopted transnational forms, and a revolution in communications put people everywhere in instantaneous contact, sometimes whether anyone wanted the contact or not. The structural mutations have dizzying implications for the academic disciplines. What is the demand for studies of "local knowledge" (Geertz, 1983) if the village is global? For "thick descriptions" (Geertz, 1973) or close reading if knowledge circulates in "flows"? Or for "research" if all truth is partial (Clifford, 1986), both in the sense of being limited and being motivated?[8]

The crisis in representation presented both an *aesthetic* challenge and a *political* challenge to conventions of qualitative research. In response to the first, scholars turned to literary theory, the visual and musical arts, and philosophy, particularly deconstruction, to borrow ways to think about the dilemmas of representation. For example, they reflected on the "surplus of difference" with which the language in any text marks the partiality and instability of its representations, no matter how "thick" the description or apparently universal the analytic categories.[9] Even an insider's story cannot close the gap between experience and its representation (Miller, 1998). Qualitative researchers also became cognizant of rhetorical conventions that shaped their purportedly objective accounts of social reality, and therefore appreciated more fully that research did not replicate worlds so much as it *made* them (Clifford & Marcus, 1986; Geertz, 1973; Van Maanen, 1988).[10] On both counts, the genre, "research," came under fire. After all, if rhetorical embellishments shape how research is reported and, therefore, what the research amounts to, where is science? The authority of social science would seem to rest merely on its ability to persuade others of that authority with words rather than on the new knowledge it proffers.

In response to the aesthetic challenge, scholars also began giving greater attention to reflexivity, including both the self-positing freedom of individuals and the sociocultural relations that constrain individuals.[11] They experimented with modes of reproduction that gave more prominence to their own meaning-making, the artfulness of accounts, and the diverse "voices" and alternate views of informants. Dialogic scripts (Simon & Dippo, 1986), collaborative authorship (Clifford, 1997), autobiographical ethnographies (Behar, 1996), even novels (Ellis & Bochner, 1996; Viadero, 1999) all seemed to promise more candid representations than conventional social science. At the same time, the experiments spawned more questions: Are reflexive accounts so focused on the researcher that the subject of study is neglected? Do the requirements of narrative override analysis? Is an ethnographic novel a contradiction in terms?

The crisis in representation also presented a political challenge to qualitative research, as concern centered not only on how knowledge is represented, but on how — and whose — representations become representative for others.[12] The focus of studies expanded beyond the practices and meaning of everyday life in particular locales to encompass the wider institutions, ideologies, and power structures that maintain lifeworlds and make them seem simply "the way things are."

One impetus for the political turn came from critical theory's inversion of traditional notions about knowledge and the state as a means to freedom. As Foucault (1981), Williams (1977), and others suggested, the modern state is not a disinterested arbiter for contending groups. It is intent on surveillance and control, and, toward those ends, funds and commandeers some knowledges while subjugating others. Hence, knowledge is not objectively warranted or innocent, but, rather, is determined by "regimes of truth." Another impetus — postcolonial, feminist, and critical race studies (Harding, 1987; Ladson-Billings & Tate, 1995; Martin, 1994; Reinharz, 1992; Spivak, 1988; Tate, 1997) — turned the discourse about the possibility of objective knowledge to the identity of researchers to suggest that the positions and institutional backing of scholars shape the questions they ask, the methods they use to study them, the representations they develop from their studies, and the dissemination of the representations as representative. Pressed further, some argued that cultures should be studied only by local peoples. Not only are outsider accounts inevitably tainted and limited in their ability to "give voice" to others (who already have voices), but subalterns know the language and customs firsthand and with a fluency and depth outsiders can never achieve (Marcus, 1998). Further, subalterns have local, practical interests at heart and pursue research that can inform action and critique.

Interest in the politics of representing knowledge fostered new interdisciplinary alignments, such as cultural studies and science studies, as scholars looked beyond single disciplinary traditions to the array of human sciences, perhaps most notably recovering history (Chartier, 1997; Hughes, 1975; Roseberry, 1989).[13] Intent on tracing symbolic action across local arenas, state politics, and transglobal economies, they began designing "multi-sited" research that "studied up" and would give as thick a description of policy elites, the state, or communication networks as had heretofore been provided for local, often marginalized, communities (Marcus, 1998). The new focus on explicating power also shifted fieldwork relations. As researchers found themselves as baffled and threatened as their informants by the new world order of monolithic capitalism, state surveillance, and standardizing media, they looked for complicity with subjects against "the third force" rather than relations of rapport or collaboration (Marcus, 1997).

Questions multiplied here too, however. The most difficult, perhaps: If power operates through research, should qualitative scholars become advocates for a particular "agenda"? And, if they do, how may advocacy compromise the equally important task of producing knowledge (Hammersley & Atkinson, 1995)? Further, *which* agenda should a researcher sponsor, given that people disagree both about what is important, and with the recommendations of academics and other elites? Agar (1996), for example, urges university scholars to pay more attention to informants' disdain for their proposals for social change.

Throughout the ferment, however exhausting, the developments in qualitative research have improved rather than destroyed the methodology by clarifying its distinctive contribution to human understanding. First, basic constructs in the human sciences have been reconceptualized and resurrected for contemporary use, particularly that protean entity, "culture."[14] Where culture was earlier theorized as a self-enclosed, coherent, and largely unchanging system of symbols and meanings, it is now also framed as a set of practices through which the meanings and symbols are continually reflected and recreated (Sewell, 1999). This shift brings change and difference to the fore. Looking at practices, scholars and subjects alike are now more conscious of the pervasiveness of hybrid rather than essentialist life-forms (Boon, 1998); they notice the moral ambiguities rather than straightforward choices that perplex the modern and postmodern world; and they track the fluidity with which subjects make and traverse worlds (past as well as present) as they strain against norms and are constrained by them (Varenne, 1995). At the same time, the attention to freedom and mobility is matched by an equal awareness of structures of oppression, and research works to specify the mechanisms and situations in which the center holds and a culture coerces and stabilizes (Varenne, 1986).

Second, the ferment has included a reconstruction of qualitative methodology (Agar, 1996; Erickson, 1986). It retains its earlier distinctive features, chiefly a research focus on "one human being trying to figure out what some others are up to" (Agar, 1996, p. 2), the ancient and seemingly ordinary method of fieldwork, and a research logic that is both empirical *and* imaginative as it works to portray how people are simultaneously unique and connected, often in ways they only partially comprehend. But other features of the methodology have changed in response to the representational challenges. More explicit attention is now given to how local and larger worlds are linked, to the basis for the authority of qualitative claims, to the odd conjunctions of fluid identities and stable structures, to disappearing distinctions between insider and outsider knowledge, and to the positioning of all inquiry, albeit more complexly than most theories have imagined.

In a sense, qualitative methodology can be portrayed as a work in progress and its practitioners as scribes in motion. The methodology encounters questions and advances new tactics and, in the process, produces other questions. Thus, some researchers acknowledge the empirical and theoretical value of individualistic *and* social explanations of education and develop analyses that tack self-consciously between the two (Erickson, 1986). Confronting the twin specters of objectivism and relativism that haunt Western philosophy (Bernstein, 1983), other scholars seek a middle ground between the discredited earlier claim that qualitative studies can produce objective truths and the equally troubling charge that qualitative studies are nothing but relative social constructions. Researchers are also interested in the sometimes uncomfortable middle between interpretive and securely scientific models of inquiry and representation. As Boon (1998) suggests, studies in culture increasingly "accent hybridity" (p. 141).

The Essays

Dewey (1916/1966) proposed that academic disciplines have to be continuously reconstructed if the knowledge they store and organize is to be useful in conditions that differ from the conditions in which the knowledge was originally produced. The conversation about reconstruction is again before the educational community and immanent in the five essays in this section.

The essay by George Spindler and Lorie Hammond illustrates the conversational difficulties. Spindler is rather querulous about educators' assessment that ethnography is one of anthropology's two most significant contributions to education. He writes that "method was of no particular interest" at one of the first gatherings of anthropologists and educators, held in 1954, because attendees were focused on substance — that is, on culturally defined problems and processes in education and schooling, particularly the import of diversity. Equally strange to Spindler is the fact that many educators today claim to do ethnography, yet they have taken no coursework in anthropology, are not conducting cultural inquiry, and don't even seem to realize that ethnography is not synonymous with qualitative research.

Perhaps as a reminder, Spindler directs his section of the essay to the core characteristics of "an ethnographic approach," a subspecies of qualitative research. This approach is distinguished by its interest in the diverse ways people act and in what they must know, often tacitly, that makes their actions sensible or understandable. To find out, researchers undertake extended, in-situ fieldwork in which they participate and observe as informally as possible, guided by hypotheses that evolve through their fieldwork rather than being tightly formulated beforehand. Eventually they translate what at first seemed exotic and render it "familiar," or human (see also Boon, 1998;

Ricouer, 1976). Although something is always lost in translation, those conducting qualitative studies seek to honor local knowledge *and* to recast it, using disciplinary constructs, so as to explicate its internal cohesion and its connections with knowledge from other locales.

Still, Spindler is less confident about the place of disciplines than Mary Metz and Shirley Brice Heath, who identify a similar set of core characteristics, although they place in the foreground the questions and analytic concepts of sociology and linguistics rather than anthropology. He wonders whether anthropology's emblematic concept, culture, can be insisted on as a core characteristic when anthropology "is in the throes of internal criticism and the culture concept has come in for its share." Moreover, he asks what *is* anthropology's distinctive contribution to understanding humanity when anthropologists disagree among themselves and people untrained in anthropology produce studies of culture, including literary critics, journalists, and filmmakers, not to mention local members of a culture? Spindler muses that perhaps anthropological ethnography has given "only its character" to qualitative research in education, but not its techniques or concepts.

If Spindler is indecisive about whether disciplinary knowledge is a prerequisite for conducting or using qualitative studies, Heath is not. A major point in her essay is that linguists have found qualitative methods to be a powerful means of tracing the "out of awareness factors" entailed in all language and learning and have used them to produce findings of practical import for schooling and education, although the research has been either ignored or misconstrued by educators. For example, programs in teacher education have not incorporated a theory of learning that credits diverse forms of knowledge display or various modes of teaching. Dissertations in education and language diverge similarly from the topics of most interest to linguists, produce little in the way of analysis, and instead sketch idiosyncratic cases of teaching, personal self-reports, or "agendas" aimed at proving the superiority of one method of teaching over another.

Heath attributes the problems in knowledge use and production to weak graduate programs in education. Courses in qualitative methodology, for example, emphasize techniques and give short shrift to theory or empirical studies, whether from linguistics or other disciplines. As a result, students come out knowing how to take field notes, but uninformed about what it might make sense to take notes about. But educators need to do more than absorb the "character" of a discipline, and simply being an educational "insider" presents problems for research rather than a guarantee of validity. Heath advocates training in at least two disciplines, and in fields other than education, so that educators can develop a "social science eye" focused on "basic research." She implies that this kind of research, although "basic," is eminently practical because knowing *how* situations are produced is a prerequisite to planning for different ones. It appears, too, that Heath's recommendations are meant for teachers as well as graduate students, not necessarily so that teachers can add research to their already long list of professional duties, but so they can be critical readers and astute users of research. Then, Heath suggests, the educational community will have members who, like Courtney Cazden, can move successfully between research and practice and bring the perspective of each to bear on the other.

Like Spindler and Heath, Mary Metz presents the value of the disciplines, but, more than they do, she argues the case for more systematic attention to methodology.

As she puts it, research is "a multifaceted dialogue among meta-theories about existence and knowledge, substantive theory, and information about the empirical world," and scholars in education need to be grounded in all three. Traditionally, however, in part because many scholars see method as implicit in and secondary to the theories and archives of disciplines, qualitative research has been taught offhandedly, as a kind of experiential practicum in which novices learn the method by doing it.[15]

In her essay, Metz begins by clarifying that qualitative research is *not* simply a collection of techniques, such as interviewing or participant-observation. It is a methodology and, as such, "a theory and analysis of how research is and should be done." Moreover, there are "competing qualitative methodologies," each with its own assumptions about the nature of knowledge that are "related to others about self, social interaction, culture, and society." From Metz's perspective, then, qualitative methodology is not a set of transparent techniques, nor is it only a sidebar to the more important substantive findings of research, because *how* a scholar studies and re/presents others will constitute *what* the scholar learns about them. Because of the often unappreciated complexity of qualitative research, explicit methodological training is especially critical. Training is also warranted, according to Metz, because if the qualities that distinguish qualitative and quantitative methodologies are left unaddressed, as well as those that divide "competing" versions of qualitative research, then any text can "co-opt" the qualitative label and the methodology's hard-won legitimacy will be jeopardized.

Metz specifies two threats to qualitative sociology. First, qualitative research is too often cast simply as description, storytelling as a means of "giving voice" to underrepresented others or documentation that things are done differently in some particular locale.[16] To be research, however, a qualitative account must develop a systematic, self-conscious *analysis*. This analysis will credit local perspectives *and* "put them in conversation with" an explicit, etic interpretation. In sociology, this analysis is focused on the roots, patterns, and consequences of group interactions and on the "larger societal system of which all are a part." Analysis presents a public, credible argument that identifies the crucial rather than incidental differences in a case, spells out how they matter for schooling, establishes the case's representativeness, and tests systematically the validity of core hypotheses. Readers may be persuaded that an analysis is authoritative or they may contest it, but, in either case, their response is possible because the researcher has provided an explicit analysis.

The second threat that Metz identifies derives from qualitative methodology's seeming simplicity and "the lack of technical sophistication" of many that use it. Some quantitative researchers, notably in policy studies, now routinely add qualitative components to their research projects. Other scholars "valorize the perspectives of insiders" and argue that only insiders can and should speak about their own situations because scholarly interpretations are "imperialist" or universalizing. In both cases, however, the qualitative data often serve only as human interest stories. Without understanding the assumptions of qualitative methodology, users may observe, participate, and interview, but give little attention to what a local perspective is in its own terms, how it arises and is maintained, or how it might alter the questions and analytic categories the users begin with. As Metz notes, combining research methods may be economically sensible but, given the different assumptions of the traditional and interpretive methodologies, combinations may also produce studies that are a hodge-podge of contradictions. And if subaltern studies arise because there *are* real problems with misinterpretations, and these are often grounded in power differences between researchers and participants, it may be wiser to call on researchers to improve their practices than to assume that communication across social differences is impossible.[17]

Of the five essays, Annie Rogers's presents the most optimistic assessment of the value of qualitative research, regarding it as a particularly potent means to reconstruct the discipline of psychology and to promote "socially responsible research." This optimism may derive from psychology's relative lack of experience with the methodology, particularly, as Rogers notes, because the field has "ignored" how much qualitative research figures in its history. The methodology may look radical, as it did to scholars in other disciplines in the 1960s and 1970s, while its divisive potential, as Spindler reports for anthropology, may be less apparent.

On the other hand, the ambivalence about and resistance to qualitative research among many in the field of psychology may allow the discipline to benefit from the critiques *within* qualitative research and avoid the extremes experienced elsewhere. For example, Rogers reports how psychologists have capitalized particularly on the poetic turn in the human sciences. Some now study the narratives people construct to give meaning to the world. Using the construct narrative, they refocus psychology on individuals and their unique ways of knowing *and* on what is common across stories. Narrative provides for reflexivity, too, enabling psychologists not only to convey the complex narratives that are their subject of study, but also to reflect on their own use of the form.[18] According to Rogers, qualitative research "integrates" traditional psychological findings with literary theory to point to a new epistemology in which human knowledge is posited as developing relationally, largely metaphorically and unconsciously, and with both biological and cultural wiring (see also Bruner, 1996; Shore, 1996).

Rogers's essay echoes the others in the importance it attaches to analysis in qualitative studies, and here, too, narrative is central. Although Rogers does not spell out the analytic process she and her students have developed, "interpretive poetics" intrigues as an attempt to account for both the researcher's and participants' subjectivity, the meaning of stories, the evaluation of divergent interpretations, and the accumulation of individual interpretations in "theoretically compelling stories of human development."[19] One wants more information about crucial issues and questions it raises: What criteria distinguish good and less satisfactory interpretations? How are divergent interpretations adjudicated? Does treating aesthetic productions as artifacts of human development risk "psychologizing" them; that is, muting what is ineffable or sublime in autobiographies and stories with disciplined interpretations whose purpose is, after all, to theorize (Berkovitch, 1998; Culler, 1997)? [20] This is a reminder of the limits of research and the dangers of reducing all forms of knowledge and human meaning-making to it.

The essays in this section written by educators — Maggie Lampert's essay and Lorie Hammond's contribution to the essay with Spindler — stand in sharp contrast to the others, particularly in their assessments of the value of and need for disciplinary training of educators. Hammond, for example, suggests that educators and researchers live in quite separate worlds. Educators are intent on solving practical problems, while anthropologists, for example, seek to understand and communicate cultural phenomena. Thus the two groups use qualitative research for different purposes. As Hammond notes, educators may borrow a "set of tools" from anthropology, but they will bend the tools to their own purposes, particularly the management of conflict that often appears in multicultural schools "because people don't realize that others don't see the world the way they do." Scholars who criticize educators for their "adaptations" of qualitative research are missing the point. Although what Hammond calls "friendly outsiders" from the university may be welcomed as consultants who can help schools apply qualitative research or offer them technical expertise in pursuing their own action research, schools rely rather minimally on the knowledge universities develop. In this respect, Hammond's assessment of the relationship between the worlds of school and university may be the most realistic among the essayists.

By contrast, Lampert envisions some mutually beneficial and, possibly, closer connections between schools and universities. In particular, she proposes that teachers conduct research on teaching, not just read or implement it. As she notes, the idea of teacher research (like subaltern studies) is a logical extension of qualitative methodology's emphasis on local meaning perspectives: teachers are best situated to know about the practice of teaching. Furthermore, the earlier hope that qualitative research on teaching would better speak to teachers than process-product research because it addressed issues teachers saw as relevant, considered life in classrooms, and wrote accessible, narrative reports seems not to have materialized. On both counts, therefore, adding teacher research to the store of information about teaching will fill the breach by providing practical knowledge of import to both scholarship and the profession. While teacher research may result in teachers being "formally added to the educational research community," Lampert casts the school-university relationship somewhat ambiguously. For instance, she sees teacher research fostering the development of a teaching profession able to set its own standards, without imposition from outside experts.

Despite these aspirations, Lampert nonetheless recounts numerous objections that others have raised to teacher research: calling for practitioner research subtly undermines the value of the work teachers already do; working conditions make collaborative, professional inquiry impossible; teachers, as school insiders, won't be able to see beyond the culture of the school and the taken-for-granted view of what and who schools are for; and idiosyncratic stories about teaching can't be theorized, or if they are, teachers elsewhere won't credit them.

One source of Lampert's hopes lies in her view that teachers are especially well-situated to capture the "strategic knowledge" that characterizes so much of teaching — the knowledge-in-action (Schwab, 1969) in classrooms where generic rules fail in application, principles are often contradictory, and simple choices are impossible. This kind of knowledge differs from both the single-minded, "propositional knowledge" promulgated by academic experts and the abstracted precedents established in qualitative case studies because it foregrounds the dilemmas that endure in teaching.

Another source of Lampert's hopes is the success she has experienced in using hypertext to more vividly represent the flow and complexity of classroom interactions. Representing the dilemmas of practice is itself a dilemma, as Lampert notes. Practice is particular, eclectic, and contingent. However, its representation, even in stories, can only proceed from a point of view that will necessarily formalize, focus, and delimit experience. Hypertext modulates some of the representational problems associated with written and spoken texts. Whether the medium also promotes analysis or mystifies the process may be an important question.

In sum, these five essays converge in agreement that qualitative research has contributed significantly to understanding education, although they differ on how practically useful the generated knowledge has been. The methodology has proved an apt means of capturing what is latent as well as manifest in classrooms, and it has provided for interpretations that have reconfigured some of the most sacred truisms of schooling. The essays also differ — most dramatically, perhaps — on what *research* is and, therefore, who should do it. These complexities make the essays a rich resource for deliberations within the educational community.

Notes

1. In 1986, Erickson's "family" of related approaches to qualitative research included ethnographic, qualitative, participant observational, case study, symbolic interactionist, phenomenological, constructivist, and interpretive. Today's "family" is bigger and might include critical ethnography, cultural studies, feminist studies, "new" ethnography (Agar, 1996), "multi-sited imaginaries" (Marcus, 1998), science studies, teacher research, postcolonial studies, and action and collaborative research. This is only a cursory selection from among the many approaches that could be mentioned.

2. As the five essays demonstrate, the questioning of conventional academic practices has developed unevenly across various disciplines (compare, too, Bonnell & Hunt, 1999; Marcus, 1998; Rowe, 1998).

3. Bellack (1978) uses "ideology" in connection with scientific practice to refer to "the constellation of beliefs, assumptions, and practices that influence the training and behavior of researchers representing contrasting research traditions" (p. 3). As Bellack also notes, his stark rendering of the two major traditions necessarily obscures and may even distort some of the complexity of educational research. Despite this, his review is invaluable for its sharp identification of points of contention between the methodologies, ranging from the problems deemed worthy of study to how to gather and interpret data to the relation between educational research and practice. Those who argue that quantitative and qualitative methodologies should be combined would do well to read the review.

4. The process-product model, with modifications, continues to dominate research on teaching; see Erickson's (1986) more recent, detailed inventory of its possibilities and limitations.

5. Bellack (1978) reviews only sociological variants of qualitative research: phenomenology, social interactionism, and ethnomethodology.

6. As Erickson (1986) clarifies, meaning is causal for human action.

7. Criticism of hermeneutics did not suddenly appear in the 1970s, nor was earlier scholarship unaware of the limits of representation. However, such concerns became increasingly salient in educational studies beginning in the late 1970s. See, for example, Mehan's (1978) critique of ethnography or the general introduction and essays in Spindler (1982) .

8. More detailed histories of the crisis of authority in the disciplines and from a variety of perspectives are available in Bonnell and Hunt (1999), Bruner (1996), Clifford and Marcus (1986), Geertz (1983, 1988), Marcus (1998), Rowe (1998), and Shore (1996). Crisis also threatens the idea of the university (Lloyd, 1998; Miller, 1998).

9. "Thick description," a phrase made familiar by Geertz (1973), is what ethnographers do. In fieldwork and in the texts they produce about that fieldwork, they describe and analyze sociocultural meaning, its contexts, and its import.

10. Studies of the rhetoric and practices of the natural sciences, particularly following Kuhn (1970), suggest that the natural sciences themselves do not live up to the ideal of Science. See LaTour and Woolgar (1979) and Traweeck (1988).

11. Hammersley and Atkinson's (1995) introduction to ethnographic research is organized around the topic of reflexivity. See also Seigel's (1999) essay, "Problematizing the Self."
12. I separate the poetics and politics of representing knowledge for analytic purposes. They are also often given different weight in critical and cultural studies. Rowe (1998) suggests, however, that earlier divisions between critical and cultural studies have become a dialectic in which both now acknowledge the dangers of essentialist categories and the importance of solidarity for politics.
13. Even though educational studies has long been an interdisciplinary venture, it is rarely included on lists of the new and exciting ventures in interdisciplinarity. Instead, it continues to be disparaged as only an amalgamation of approaches.
14. For changes in definitions of "social" and "society," see Bonnell and Hunt (1999). For changes in psychological constructs, see Bruner (1996) and Shore (1996).
15. It may be, too, that scholars object to methodological training because they are aware of education's past dalliances with method to the neglect of conceptual clarification.
16. Agar (1996) discusses the importance of not confusing all differences with those that are analytically and practically consequential.
17. See Page, Samson, and Crockett (1998) for a discussion of how the advantage is not all on the side of university researchers. Schools may appropriate research projects for their own internal purposes.
18. Rogers's (1995) own *A Shining Affliction* is a compelling example. Marcus (1998) proposes experimental meldings of art and science in ethnographies, but he cautions doctoral students to write dissertations that meet traditional standards so that students will be seen as having the legitimate credentials needed to land a job.
19. The clearest discussion of interpretive analysis is Agar's (1985, 1996) discussion of *abduction.*
20. The reverse move is equally problematic, as when cognitive projects are reduced to literature. Is Freud only a storyteller, history only metanarrative, or science only rhetoric? See Culler (1997).

References

Agar, M. (1985). *Speaking of ethnography.* Thousands Oaks, CA: Sage.

Agar, M. (1996). *The professional stranger: An informal introduction to ethnography* (2nd ed.). San Diego: Academic Press.

Behar, R. (1996). *The vulnerable observer: Anthropology that breaks your heart.* Boston: Beacon Press.

Bellack, A. (1978). *Competing ideologies in research on teaching* (Uppsala Reports on Education No. 1). Uppsala, Sweden: Uppsala University, Department of Education.

Berkovitch, S. (1998). The function of the literary in a time of cultural studies. In J. C. Rowe (Ed.), *"Culture" and the problem of the disciplines* (pp. 69–86). New York: Columbia University Press.

Bernstein, R. (1983). *Beyond objectivism and relativism.* Philadelphia: University of Pennsylvania Press.

Bonnell, V., & Hunt, L. (Eds.). (1999). *Beyond the cultural turn: New directions in the study of society and culture.* Berkeley: University of California Press.

Boon, J. (1998). Accenting hybridity: Postcolonial cultural studies, a Boasian anthropologist, and I. In J. C. Rowe (Ed.), *"Culture" and the problem of the disciplines* (pp. 141–170). New York: Columbia University Press.

Bruner, J. (1996). *The culture of education.* Cambridge, MA: Harvard University Press.

Chartier, R. (1997). *On the edge of the cliff: History, language, and practices.* Baltimore: Johns Hopkins University Press.

Clifford, J. (1986). Introduction: Partial truths. In J. Clifford & G. Marcus (Eds.), *Writing culture* (pp. 1–26). Berkeley: University of California Press.

Clifford, J. (1997). *Routes: Travel and translation in the late twentieth century.* Cambridge, MA: Harvard University Press.

Clifford, J., & Marcus, G. (1986). *Writing culture: The poetics and politics of ethnography.* Berkeley: University of California Press.

Cronbach, L. (1975). Beyond the two disciplines of scientific psychology. *American Psychologist, 30,* 116–127.

Culler, J. (1997). *Literary theory: A very short introduction.* Oxford, Eng.: Oxford University Press.

Dewey, J. (1929). *The sources of a science of education.* New York: Liveright.

Dewey, J. (1966). *Democracy and education.* New York: Free Press. (Original work published 1916)

Ellis, C., & Bochner, A. (1996). *Composing ethnography: Alternative forms of qualitative writing.* Walnut Creek, CA: Alta Mira Press.

Erickson, F. (1986). Qualitative methods in research on teaching. In M. Wittrock (Ed.), *Handbook of research on teaching* (3rd ed., pp. 119–161). New York: Macmillan.

Foucault, M. (1981). *Power/knowledge: Selected interviews and other writings, 1972–1977.* New York: Pantheon Books.

Geertz, C. (1973). *The interpretation of culture: Selected essays.* New York: Basic Books.

Geertz, C. (1983). *Local knowledge: Further essays in interpretive anthropology.* New York: Basic Books.

Geertz, C. (1988). *Works and lives: The anthropologist as author.* Stanford, CA: Stanford University Press.

Greeno, J., McDermott, R., Cole, K., Engle, R., Goldman, S., Knudsen, J., Lauman, B., & Linde, C. (1999). Research, reform, and aims in education: Modes of action in search of each other. In E. Lagemann & L. Shulman (Eds.), *Issues in educational research* (pp. 299–335). San Francisco: Jossey-Bass.

Hammersley, M., & Atkinson, P. (1995). *Ethnography: Principles in practice* (2nd ed.). London: Routledge.

Harding, S. (Ed.). (1987). *Feminism and methodology.* Bloomington: Indiana University Press.

Hofstadter, R. (1962). *Anti-intellectualism in American life.* New York: Vintage Books.

Hughes, H. S. (1975). *History as art and as science: Twin vistas on the past.* Chicago: University of Chicago Press.

Kuhn, T. (1970). *The structure of scientific revolutions* (2nd ed.). Chicago: University of Chicago Press.

Ladson-Billings, G., & Tate, W. (1995). Toward a critical theory of education. *Teachers College Record, 97,* 47–68.

LaTour, B., & Woolgar, S. (1979). *Laboratory life: The social construction of scientific facts.* Beverly Hills, CA: Sage.

Lloyd, D. (1998). Foundations of diversity: Thinking the university in a time of multiculturalism. In R. C. Rowe (Ed.), *"Culture" and the problem of the disciplines* (pp. 15–44). New York: Columbia University Press.

Marcus, G. (1997). The uses of complicity in the changing mise-en-scene of anthropological fieldwork. *Representations, 59,* 85–108.

Marcus, G. (1998). *Ethnography through thick and thin.* Princeton, NJ: Princeton University Press.

Martin, J. (1994). *Changing the educational landscape.* New York: Routledge.

Mehan, H. (1978). Structuring school structure. *Harvard Educational Review, 48,* 32–65.

Miller, D. (1999, August 6). The black hole of education research. *Chronicle of Higher Education,* pp. A17–A18.

Miller, J. H. (1998). Literary and cultural studies in the transnational university. In J. C. Rowe (Ed.), *"Culture" and the problem of the disciplines* (pp. 45–68). New York: Columbia University Press.

Mosteller, F., Light, R., & Sachs, J. (1996). Sustained inquiry in education: Lessons from skill grouping and class size. *Harvard Educational Review, 66,* 797–828.

Page, R., Samson, Y., & Crockett, M. (1988). Reporting ethnography to informants. *Harvard Educational Review, 68,* 299–333.

Reinharz, S. (1992). *Feminist methods in social research.* Oxford, Eng.: Oxford University Press.

Ricouer, P. (1976). *Interpretation theory: Discourse and the surplus of meaning.* Fort Worth: Texas Christian University Press.

Rogers, A. (1995). *A shining affliction: A study of harm and healing in psychotherapy.* New York: Viking.

Roseberry, W. (1989). *Anthropologies and histories: Essays in culture, history, and political economy.* New Brunswick, NJ: Rutgers University Press.

Rowe, J. C. (Ed.). (1998) *"Culture" and the problem of the disciplines.* New York: Columbia University Press.

Schwab, J. (1969). The practical: A language for curriculum. *School Review, 78,* 1–23.

Seigel, J. (1999). Problematizing the self. In V. Bonnell & L. Hunt (Eds.), *Beyond the cultural turn: New directions in the study of society and culture* (pp. 281–314). Berkeley: University of California Press.

Sewell, W., Jr. (1999). The concept(s) of culture. In V. Bonnell & L. Hunt (Eds.), *Beyond the cultural turn: New directions in the study of society and culture* (pp. 35–61). Berkeley: University of California Press.

Shore, D. (1996). *Culture in mind: Cognition, culture, and the problem of meaning.* New York: Oxford University Press.

Simon, R., & Dippo, D. (1986). On critical ethnographic work. *Anthropology and Education Quarterly, 17,* 195–202.

Spindler, G. (1982). *Doing the ethnography of schooling: Educational anthropology in action.* New York: Holt, Rinehart & Winston.

Spivak, G. (1988). Can the subaltern speak? In C. Nelson & L. Grossberg (Eds.), *Marxism and the interpretation of culture* (pp. 271–313). Urbana: University of Illinois Press.

Tate, W. (1997). Critical race theory and education: History, theory, and implications. In M. Apple (Ed.), *Review of research in education, Volume 22* (pp. 195–247). Washington, DC: American Educational Research Association.

Traweeck, S. (1988). *Beamtimes and lifetimes: The world of high energy physics.* Cambridge, MA: Harvard University Press.

Van Maanen, J. (1988). *Tales of the field: On writing ethnography.* Chicago: University of Chicago Press.

Varenne, H. (1986). *Symbolizing America.* Lincoln: University of Nebraska Press.

Varenne, H. (1995). The social facting of education: Durkheim's legacy. *Journal of Curriculum Studies, 27,* 373–389.

Viadero, D. (1999, June 23). New priorities, focus sought for research. *Education Week,* pp. 1, 33.

Wehlage, G. (1981). The purpose of generalization in field-study research. In T. Popkewitz & R. Tabachnick (Eds.), *A study of schooling* (pp. 211–226). New York: Praeger.

White, H. (1973). *Metahistory: The historical imagination in nineteenth-century Europe.* Baltimore: Johns Hopkins University Press.

Williams, R. (1977). *Marxism and literature.* Oxford, Eng.: Oxford University Press.

The Use of Anthropological Methods in Educational Research: Two Perspectives

GEORGE SPINDLER
LORIE HAMMOND

In an attempt to bring together anthropology and education, we have engaged in a collaboration on the relationship of these fields to qualitative research. The collaborators are George Spindler, an anthropologist, and Lorie Hammond, a teacher educator involved with practitioner research. We feel that anthropology has made two primary contributions to the field of education: the study of culture and the methodology of ethnography. In turn, educators and educational researchers have adapted these two contributions to their particular contexts and issues. To relate what we feel is a dialogue between anthropology and education, we have structured this article to reflect the multiple perspectives of educational anthropology.

An Anthropologist's Perspective

Today one scarcely refers to an anthropology of education, or educational anthropology, without mentioning ethnography in the same breath. Not only has ethnography become a major contribution of anthropology to education, but virtually anything resembling qualitative research seems to be called ethnography. This understandably upsets anthropologists, who think of themselves as having invented ethnography. It is what anthropologists have always done when they do fieldwork. It is part and parcel of *being* an anthropologist, rather than merely a method.

Forty-five years ago, when my wife, Louise Spindler, and I published *Anthropology and Education*, a report of the conference of 1954 on anthropology and education, we found occasion to index "ethnography" only once (Spindler, 1955). As twelve educators and a like number of anthropologists talked to each other for four days about the relations between anthropology and education, both groups realized the potential between the two fields, one a discipline, the other a massive conglomerate of approaches to the understanding and practice of education. Eight of the anthropologists had written papers to which the educators responded, and yet only one reference to ethnography! Instead, our discussions and writings focused on what became one of an-

Harvard Educational Review   Vol. 70   No. 1   Spring 2000, 39–48

thropology's primary contributions to education: the cultural perspective. Research methods, particularly the ethnographic approach, would not become an important contribution until later.

Almost thirty years later, Louise and I became so overwhelmed by the proliferation of the term ethnography that we found ourselves coining terms to cover various sectors of qualitative research being called ethnography. We came up with "anthroethnography" for anthropological ethnography, "socioethnography" for sociological ethnography, and "psychoethnography" for psychological ethnography (Spindler & Spindler, 1982). We never went so far as to refer to an "eduethnography," but it would have been a logical next step, particularly since ethnography had diffused so broadly into education. That diffusion sometimes had unanticipated results. For instance, as we came into contact with qualitative research projects in education, we found people claiming to be ethnographers who had never taken a course in anthropology, who were quite naive about culture and cultural process, and who were quite unaware that the term meant anything more than qualitative research.

Regarding the methodological contributions of anthropology to education, perhaps ethnography has given its character if not its techniques, tools, and conceptual orientation to educational qualitative research. However, the contribution of anthropological ethnography to qualitative research is more substantial than that statement implies.

Educational anthropology, the disciplinary seat of the ethnography of education, is as old in its origins as any other social discipline. It is usually held to begin with the writings of Edgar Hewett, in 1906. Actually, Hewett was preceded by others, such as Earl Barnes (1896) and Nina Vandewalker (1898), educators heavily influenced by anthropology (Eddy, 1997; Ford, 1997). Prominent anthropologists lent their prestige to writings about education for the next fifty years or so, but with virtually no attempt to do ethnography. Jules Henry was one great exception, and his *Culture Against Man* (1963) was a major breakthrough into the ethnography of education. My wife Louise and I followed with a series of articles beginning in 1955 that represented serious attempts to apply ethnography to the study of education (Spindler, in press). Today, writing about the ethnography of education abounds; for instance, the journal *Anthropology and Education Quarterly* publishes many ethnographic pieces.

Some ethnographic educational research is genuinely concerned with cultural attributes. Other research explains why it instead favors other social processes, but it may still use established ethnographic techniques and methodology to collect and analyze data. The works of Dell Hymes, Margaret Gibson, Diane Hoffman, David Fetterman, Frederick Erickson, Hugh Mehan, Shirley Brice Heath, Courtney Cazden, Jules Henry, Ray McDermott, Hervé Varenne, Alan Peshkin, George and Louise Spindler, Henry Trueba, Harry Wolcott, Karen Watson-Gageo, Concha Delgado-Gaitan, Fred Gearing, John Singleton, Jacquetta Burnett, David Smith, Elizabeth Eddy, Reba Page, Margaret Lecompte, and a legion of others are all genuinely ethnographic. How do you recognize it when you see it? There is considerably more involved than attention to cultural issues, and some of these beyond-culture attributes are shared with nonethnographic works in qualitative research. The attributes that make a research genuinely ethnographic are spelled out below.

The ethnographic approach includes a number of specifiable attributes, some of which I will attempt to delineate. The first feature is observation, which is frequently described as participant observation. It is a major approach in conventional anthropological field research; it is a way to get started. It is, however, not so easy in the settings in which most educational ethnographers work — classrooms, playgroups, peer groups, and other characteristic settings of behavior in schools — though some workers have done it with considerable success. In 1981, my wife and I tried it in a third-grade class in Schoenhausen Grundschule, in Schoenhausen, Germany. I tried to do all the work of the third graders, but gave it up after a few weeks because it was impossible to do proper ethnography and the work of a third grader simultaneously. Still, I went on school hikes, played games, and ate lunch with the children. The girls often crammed into our Volkswagen in the schoolyard, and Louise exchanged jokes and riddles with them. This kind of participation made us familiar and nonthreatening to the children and doubtless helped us to do good ethnography in the classroom and outside of it. We spent a lot of social time with the teachers that could be called participant observation. It was the only social life we had while doing fieldwork in Schoenhausen.

Another attribute of an ethnographic approach is that ethnographers usually work at their sites for long periods of time. Validity in anthropological fieldwork is largely dependent on time spent in study. A year is considered a short period for a whole community study, or the study of a band or a group, and most anthropologists spend more time than that. One must see things happen more than once, hear the same things said by people about themselves and others, and experience the same feelings about things people do repeatedly before these data can be regarded as the basis for valid observations. I find this to be a most distinguishing feature of anthropological ethnography. So-called ethnographic studies are done all too frequently in school sites in what most anthropologists would regard as inadequate time periods. School administrators as well as researchers themselves are impatient with studies that require long stretches of time in the schools and classrooms. An impasse is quickly reached, and the temptation to do a "quick and dirty" job is sometimes overwhelming.

Another feature worth noting is the volume of material that ethnographers tend to collect. One takes notes, records on audio and video tape, does time-lapse photography, and uses various stimuli, such as photographs, line drawings, word lists, and so on. The field ethnographer is also a collector of artifacts — drawings, documents, newspaper articles, editorials, memos, letters to the editor, essays, texts of speeches, and so forth. Louise and I always tried to scoop up everything that wasn't fastened down and that people would part with. Often one doesn't know specifically why a given item has been collected, and much of what is brought back is never used, but enough is used, and unpredictably, so that the collection is worthwhile.

In the initial phases of research, the ethnographer should not work out specific hypotheses or even highly specific categories of observation. And one should never prepare a specific list of questions, or any form of pre-codings, to be applied in interviews. The reason for this is to avoid predetermining what is observed or what is elicited from informants. The problem that one thinks one is going to investigate is not usually the one actually studied. Particularly in the first stages of fieldwork, the problem must be allowed to develop without predetermination, and the views of the natives must be allowed to dominate.

The ethnographer explores and tests hypotheses, but these hypotheses have evolved out of the fieldwork itself. A problematic context is entered, such as the observable fact that a given White female teacher does not seem to communicate effectively with the Black boys in her sixth-grade class. Observation leads to the conclusion that her style is seen as confrontational. One can then generate specific hypotheses about the features of that style that seem confrontational, and focus inquiry upon them. Yet other hypotheses may be generated as work continues.

One of the essential attributes of an ethnographic methodology is that it is the emic knowledge of the informant(s) that the ethnographer seeks. While the ethnographer brings etic knowledge to the study, it must be laid aside, at least temporarily, to allow the emic viewpoint of the "native" to be recorded and understood. However, the final ethnographic report cannot consist of this emic cultural content alone. The mere act of arranging it for an ethnographic report imposes an etic structure on it, and any interpretation the ethnographer places on the emic data forces it into an etic structure. But arrangement of emic data and interpretation are essential if the strange is to be converted to the familiar so that it can be understood in other contexts. Any publication by an author of any disciplinary identification that exhibits these attributes can be said to be genuinely ethnographic.

There are other attributes of the ethnographic approach that could profitably be explored in this article, but it is time to turn this discussion over to a different kind of ethnography, one in which people usually regarded as "informants" become interpreters of ethnographic information they themselves have collected. In such research, the ethnographer and the "native" are more equally empowered. This kind of research is often conducted by action researchers or, in education, through teacher research.

A Teacher Educator's Perspective

I first encountered educational anthropology as an elementary school teacher and graduate student. Later, as a teacher educator, I was looking for a research tradition that would 1) help my colleagues and me explain the dilemmas faced by our students in multicultural school settings, and 2) incorporate the voices of teachers and community members. The work of educational anthropologists stood out among the research genres to which I was exposed. Cultural explanations of minority school failure provided the missing link I sought between individualized psychological explanations that omitted contextual factors, and broad historical and political explanations that did not illuminate specific situations. A focus on culture through the methodology of ethnography provided a tool that explained how larger societal forces affected interpersonal interaction patterns in classrooms and communities. It was not until I dialogued with George Spindler that I began to realize how differently anthropologists and practitioner researchers like myself view the purpose and process of educational research. In this section of the article, I shall explain how and why ethnography has proved an appealing methodology for practitioner researchers like myself, and the particular dilemmas of methodology and power that arise when practitioners attempt to do ethnography.

Why Ethnography Appeals to Educators

Practitioner researchers approach research as a problem-solving device. This makes their work different in focus than that of many anthropologists, whose main purpose is to understand and explain cultural processes. While for an anthropologist explanation marks the end of an inquiry, for a practitioner researcher, explanation is an enlightening step in a problem-solving process. Once a problem is defined, sometimes through participant observation, practitioners are eager to try to remedy it. This creates a new research opportunity: the need to observe the treatment to see if it is effective. In both the case of defining a problem and of assessing the effectiveness of a treatment, ethnography is an appealing research method because it describes the interactions that occur. Whereas quantitative studies often focus on treatments and outcomes, they rarely provide a way of learning *how* a specific treatment actually looks as it is being applied. Ethnographic methods enable an observer to chronicle the course of a treatment and to voice the reactions of all participants through interviews.

Practitioners are also attracted to ethnography because it can equalize power by involving teachers and other community members in the analysis of problems and solutions. Teacher research is important partially because it allows insider knowledge from classrooms and communities to enter research circles so that their voices might influence a larger audience. Too often, in teachers' eyes, researchers define the problems of schools from the outside, then provide curriculum or pedagogical packages that embody solutions that may or may not fit the local context. Outside solutions disempower teachers, making them into transmitters of pre-packaged materials rather than inquiring professionals equipped to decide what their students need. Teacher research, on the other hand, encourages teachers to look at their own work from an etic perspective and to participate in dialogues beyond their school communities. It expands their role as reflective professionals. Ethnography seems an appropriate genre for teacher research because it allows people *within* the educational community to tell and interpret their stories.

Large numbers of practitioners in education and in other fields face levels of diversity in their daily activities that rival those experienced by only a handful of anthropologists and adventurers several decades ago. It is natural, then, that teachers facing this situation turn to the discipline invented to study cross-cultural situations: anthropology and, more specifically, ethnography, the branch of anthropology that enables researchers to understand the voices of the "other." Over the past decade some states, including California, have received large numbers of new immigrants; in many schools diverse minority populations have become the majority (Trueba, 1989). Over a quarter of California's students come from homes where not only are languages other than English spoken, but child-rearing practices and ideas about schooling may also diverge greatly from teachers' expectations. If school is seen from an anthropological perspective, as an institution of cultural transmission that links generations and maintains continuity (Spindler, 1997), then it is not surprising that the discontinuities between family and school cultures often disrupt the traditional function of schooling in profound ways. Anthropology can help teachers separate their personal cultural values from those of their students in order to see both themselves and their students more clearly.

Seminal works in educational anthropology such as Shirley Brice Heath's account of language use among Appalachian children (1983) provide cultural explanations for school failure among nonmainstream children. Similarly, George and Louise Spindler's work on Roger Harker (a pseudonym), a seemingly successful educator who unwittingly ignored the minority students in his classroom, illustrates how professionals can contribute to minority children's school failure while earnestly believing that they are helping all students (Spindler & Spindler, 1990). Both of these pieces of research and others like them (see Boggs, 1985; Philips, 1983) help educators see the effects of cultural context and teacher attitude on the success or failure of diverse students.

To an educator, the assumptions behind anthropology offer a productive lens for viewing cross-cultural educational settings because anthropologists assume that "everyone is active and making sense," yet "everyday life becomes invisible in its living" (Erickson & Christman, 1996, p. 151). These are inherently "no-fault" assumptions based on the notion that people make decisions because their decisions "make sense" within their cultural framework, whether they are teachers or parents, majority or minority community members. When viewed from this perspective, most conflicts arise because people are unaware that the invisible matrix of cultural values that govern their thinking does not match the values of the other party or group. Learning more about the other party is the first step in solving the problem. In schools beset with concerns about test scores and other measures that mark poor and diverse children as deficient or "at risk," an anthropological perspective provides a healthy reminder that diverse populations of children and families may do things in different ways not because they are making errors, but because they view the world through a cultural context that varies from that of the mainstream. "Funds of knowledge" projects, such as Moll's work with Arizona researchers, teachers, and families (Moll, Amanti, Neff, & Gonzalez, 1992), build curriculum on the strengths of minority communities, rather than seeing their differences as deficits. The assumption of cultural relativism central to anthropology makes positive interpretations of diversity possible, and ethnography overlaps with narrative genres — such as oral history — in which parents' and children's voices can be heard.

The above examples are only a few of the reasons why teacher researchers are attracted to qualitative research techniques, and specifically to ethnography. Even in settings that are not culturally diverse, school creates a culture in which the different positions occupied by administrators, teachers, parents, and students can create unspoken misunderstandings. Strategies that assist practitioners to gain distance from their own position and to understand the position of others can help to reveal hidden agendas not otherwise visible. However, while ethnography is appealing to educators, significant problems arise when the standards that Spindler would apply to ethnography become applied to the work of practitioners.

Challenges Practitioners Face in Doing Ethnographic Work

Earlier in this piece, Spindler describes several characteristics of good ethnography, some of which are better suited to practitioners' inquiries than others. The first is extended participant observation. Teachers seem, on the surface, well-positioned to do this task since they are truly "participants." However, teachers are also busy playing their role as emic members of the situation and may have trouble finding either the time or the perspective to observe their own work situation from enough distance to achieve an etic view. It is commonly stated that anthropologists must make the familiar strange in order to see the hidden agendas that are generally invisible to insiders. On the one hand, the beauty of teacher research is that it encourages practitioners to develop a reflective, outsider's view of their own work. On the other hand, anthropologists might argue that an insider cannot see the hidden agendas in his/her own situation. Erickson and Christman (1996) describe the importance of "taking stock," of assessing what is going on, before one attempts to make improvements. In their case, they advocate the role of the "friendly outsider" who works with practitioners to assist them in taking stock. While it could be questioned whether the power teachers gain by researching their own work is undermined when a professional ethnographer reveals hidden agendas they cannot see, teachers and researchers working together can share complementary skills.

Another feature of ethnography is long-term observation and data collection, involving many facets of a situation. Teachers are well-equipped to report on local knowledge since their familiarity with their situation is profound. However, they are also preoccupied with the pressures of their job and do not have time for extensive record-keeping. Video cameras, audio tapes, student portfolios, and the like provide possibilities for recording activities as they occur for future analysis. However, the analysis still takes time, and one might ask whether teachers have time to do the painstaking sorting and pondering of data in which anthropologists engage. In fact, not all successful teacher research leads to publication. For some teacher researchers, improved practice is the goal.

A third feature of ethnography is its openness. Spindler restates the tenets of grounded theory: that the observer should not begin with specific hypotheses or even highly specific categories of observation, but should let the cultural process reveal itself through immersion first in the environment, then in the data. This approach is central to the revelation of hidden agendas, since the important things "discovered" by anthropologists are previously unexplained cultural processes rather than easily observed events or activities. As suggested earlier, educators tend to take a more directed approach. Their purpose is to solve problems, not merely to describe. Yet in their anxiousness to solve problems, are educators likely to take a dispassionate view that enables hidden agendas to be revealed? In short, are they too close to the subject?

Are educators able to do good ethnography, as defined by Spindler and other anthropologists? Is it not possible that ethnographic techniques enable practitioners to understand their students and their own work better and hence to improve their practice? One of the major questions in practitioner research is whether basic research standards should apply. Various types of interviews and observations that derive from ethnographic methods are becoming a part of routine school practices, such as assessment and teacher education. These practices do not always result in research per se, but they may result in an enhanced school climate due to increased cross-cultural or cross-positional understandings.

While both ethnographers studying schools and practitioners reflecting upon their own work present dilemmas of methodology and power, these difficulties should not invalidate the importance of ethnography as a tool for understanding schooling. All forms of research present possibilities and limitations and are appropriate to some and not all situations. Cazden (personal communication, August 1999) and Erickson and Christman (1996) both point out the complementary possibilities created when basic researchers and practitioner researchers share their work. In this case, the voices of insiders and outsiders can be blended and processual understandings discovered by both types of researchers can be applied to the solution of problems by the only people who can really solve them: the practitioners who have the local knowledge necessary for action.

What is clear is that educators derive more from anthropology, as reflected in an understanding of cultural process and in the methodology of ethnography, than anthropologists generally understand or would have thought possible. The dialogue in this article is itself subject to ethnographic analysis. The misunderstandings between anthropologists and educators are partially cultural in themselves, since each set of researchers sees the world through a different lens. Anthropologists have a culture that, like all cultures, has its boundaries and gatekeepers. These are important for any academic discipline that develops through dialogue among insiders. (See Kuhn, 1970, on "normal science" for an explanation of this idea.) Yet anthropology is also a set of ideas and practices that educators and other professionals experience and sometimes adopt and/or adapt. It is natural that when educators co-opt ideas from anthropology they transform the field in ways that may not seem rigorous to anthropologists. That educators rarely become disciplined anthropologists does not mean than anthropology has not had an effect on qualitative research in education. Education, as an applied field, has different goals than anthropology, and many of its goals involve action as well as understanding. Educational research is often both reflective and active, whereas anthropological research is explanatory. As in most cross-cultural situations, an ideal solution would be the marriage of information from both fields, coupled with a recognition of what each contributes to the other and, most importantly, to our collective understanding of how to educate all children in an increasingly diverse society.

References

Barnes, E. (1896). *Studies in education* (vol. 1). Stanford, CA: Stanford University Press.

Boggs, S. T. (1985). *Speaking, reading, and listening: A study of Hawaiian children at home and school*. Norwood, NJ: Ablex.

Cazden, C. (1999). Discussion at Spencer Foundation Practitioner Research Conference, August 1999, held at Wingspread Conference Center, Racine, Wisconsin.

Eddy, E. M. (1997). Theory, research, and application in educational anthropology. In G. Spindler (Ed.), *Education and cultural process* (pp. 4–25). Prospect Heights, IL: Waveland Press.

Ford, R. (1997). Educational anthropology: Early history and educationist contributors. In G. Spindler (Ed.), *Education and cultural process* (pp. 26–27). Prospect Heights, IL: Waveland Press.

Henry, J. (1963). *Culture against man*. New York: Random House.

Erickson, F., & Christman, J. B. (1996). Taking stock/making change: Stories of collaboration in local school reform. *Theory Into Practice, 35,* 149–157.

Heath, S. B. (1983) *Ways with words: Language, life, and work in communities and classrooms.* Cambridge, Eng.: Cambridge University Press.

Hewett, E. (1906). Anthropology and education. *American Anthropologist, 6,* 574–575.

Kuhn, T. S. (1970). *The structure of scientific revolutions* (2nd ed.). Chicago: University of Chicago Press.

Moll, L. C., Amanti, C., Neff, D., & Gonzalez, N. (1992) Funds of knowledge for teaching: Using a qualitative approach to connect homes and classrooms. *Theory Into Practice, 31,* 132–141.

Philips, S. U. (1983). *The invisible culture: Communication in classroom and community on the Warm Springs Indian Reservation.* New York: Longman.

Spindler, G. (Ed.). (1955). *Education and anthropology.* Stanford, CA: Stanford University Press.

Spindler, G. (1997). The transmission of culture. In G. Spindler (Ed.), *Education and cultural process* (pp. 275–309). Prospect Heights, IL: Waveland Press.

Spindler, G. (Ed.). (in press). *Fifty years of anthropology and education: A Spindler anthology: 1950–2000.* Mahwah, NJ: Lawrence Erlbaum.

Spindler, G., & Spindler, L. (Eds.). (1982). *Doing the ethnography of education.* New York: Holt, Rinehart, and Winston.

Spindler, G., & Spindler, L. (1990). *The American cultural dialogue.* London: Falmer Press.

Trueba, H. (1989). *Educating the linguistic minorities for the twenty-first century.* Boston: Heinle & Heinle.

Vandewalker, N. (1898). Some demands of education upon anthropology. *American Journal of Sociology, 4,* 69–74.

Linguistics in the Study of Language in Education

SHIRLEY BRICE HEATH

A little-known play, *So it is (if you think so)* by Luigi Pirandello, captures well the state of those who study discourse or language use in context. In the play's conclusion, one character says to another: "I find you all exhausted from your search to find out who and what other people are, and how things are, as if other people or things were simply this or that particular way in their own right" (1995, p. 148). Qualitative researchers who study language in use pride themselves on their ability to search out the "how" of what is said or written, relying primarily on the immediate context of communication. Their conclusions can often make claims only about the single situation being studied, or what critics regard as "simply" one instance. Linguists know that their studies of language often reveal knowledge that any speaker sees as painfully evident once it is explicated: that teachers respond to student answers with an evaluative comment, or that middle-class parents often ask toddlers and infants to name things in their environments. Linguists argue that their work lays open how speakers operate with grammatical competence that lies beyond conscious awareness, and how a speaker chooses to use language in a "particular way," modifying tone, word choice, syntactical arrangement, and accompanying body language and props to accomplish certain communicative ends (for further discussion of this point, see Burowoy, 1991; Pelissier, 1981). Uncovering what we think of ourselves as already knowing is, however, not only the work of linguists, but of all social scientists who bring their analytical tools to bear on just "who and what other things are." Context and intentionality, as well as automatic self-regulation, shape human behavior, and understanding just how these work in communication should play a central role for educators interested in learning and teaching (Bargh & Chartrand, 1999).

My goal here is to ask what we know about linguistics and its contributions to qualitative research about language in education. Linguists come in many brands, some centered on formal grammars "in the head" and others on performance of language influenced by social factors. Those I consider here are of the latter type and include linguists who may think of themselves as sociolinguists, anthropological linguists, ethnomethodologists, or educational linguists; all focus on the immediate conditions of any utterance and the interrelatedness of components of the discourse. These researchers do so, however, with somewhat different ends in mind. To all these linguists, both social and linguistic cognition matter, as does the speaker's inner sense

Harvard Educational Review   Vol. 70   No. 1   Spring 2000, 49–59

of the role he or she is playing at a particular communicative moment, but getting at these often subconscious factors is no simple task. Language use is always more than it appears, and qualitative research methods offer some powerful ways to unravel Pirandello's "simply this." For example, the study of how children of certain sociocultural and situational family settings are socialized through language and taught how to use language reveals much about how they may respond to the expectations of those whose socialization differs. This work to uncover what goes on in and through language socialization advances our understanding of how formal education's requirements — that students show what they know in certain oral and written forms — may not tap students' customary ways of communicating their competence.

Key Contributions of Linguistics to the Field of Qualitative Research

The ways of language and learning and whether or not they ever work "in their own right" has been of special interest for formal education in Great Britain and the United States since the end of the 1960s. Before this time, linguists and psycholinguists had for decades studied early language acquisition, speech disorders, and the phenomenon of bilingualism. However, it was only when scholars in both nations faced up to the reality of children with diverse cultural, linguistic, and class backgrounds learning in the same classrooms that they turned to instructional settings to consider how learning and language worked interdependently. In Great Britain, Douglas Barnes and James Britton led this effort by linking up with teachers in classrooms to ask a basic question: "What's going on?" Together researchers and teachers listened to children in peer interactions of small-group work and compared this language with that of formal classroom discussion. They recorded the ways young children expressed their curiosity about the science of their everyday world, played with the poetic nature of language, and created metaphors of explanation for their theories. They explored how the extent and shape of what children knew showed up in different ways when they were encouraged to express themselves through a range of genres (Barnes, Britton, Rosen, & L.A.T.E., 1969; Barr, D'Arcy, & Healy, 1982).

In the United States, perhaps the most famous collaboration between a linguist and a classroom teacher came through Hugh Mehan's 1979 study of Courtney Cazden's year of teaching. This work introduced the concept of "teacher talk," an idea that dominated examinations of language in classrooms for another decade. The initiation-response-evaluation (IRE) pattern of such talk prompted tough questions about assumptions teachers and researchers made about the passivity of children; students, it seemed, were expected to respond to teachers by giving back what teachers already knew. Linguists recognized that classroom teachers were redirecting the interrogative nature of questions — generally accepted in child language studies as truly information-seeking or routinely game-linked. Linguists who were studying language socialization in other parts of the world and among different classes and ethnic groups in the United States showed how such redirection of questions in formal schooling bore almost no relation to ways that interrogatives worked in the early learning of children outside mainstream, literate, school-oriented families (Heath, 1982a, 1982b, 1983; Ochs, 1988; Schiefflin & Ochs, 1986). These scholars demonstrated across societies of radically different social organization and ideology how patterns of language be-havior — particularly around questions — varied greatly and were tightly linked with the distribution of roles and responsibilities within families. In response to my study of working-class Black and White children in their neighborhoods and at school (1982a, 1982b, 1983), which documented the wide gaps in language ideology and use, educators tried to redirect their thinking about the appropriateness of this type of questioning as the primary mode of assessment and interaction in classrooms. Soon thereafter, numerous studies emerged that compared spoken and written language practices within indigenous systems to practices preferred by formal schooling. These studies exposed some of the unexamined key assumptions about language and its role in learning (Briggs, 1986), as did several other studies in the 1980s (Au & Jordan, 1981; Borofsky, 1987; Spindler, 1982).

These examinations also brought together long-term fieldwork, immersion within other languages besides English, and careful audiorecording (and sometimes video-recording) of actual language structures and their extralinguistic features. This work showed how much the language of recitation, examination, and even discussion in classrooms or within authority-dominant situations lay in long-standing ideas about a transmission model of socialization in which teachers teach and students learn. Text-books and tests were for the most part structured around decontextualized discrete-point knowledge as the only type that can determine grade-level achievement. Getting at creative, independent thought that either went beyond expected answers or raised further questions had to be left largely to certain types of classroom activities and to the extra-credit sections of textbooks. Sociolinguists showed that the usual textbook questions called for straightforward answers, drawing inappropriate re-sponses from children whose early socialization and peer interactions had taught them to value heavy use of metaphor and sociodramatic bids that asked others to join in imaginative and hypothesized scenarios. The "logic" of these and other "nonstan-dard" ways of telling stories, arguing a claim, or illustrating generalizations did not fit the "standard" in classroom discussions or answers called for in many tests and the general end-of-chapter questions of textbooks (Labov, 1969, 1970; Shuy, 1965; for a review of these and related points, see Morgan, 1994; Rickford, 1997; Rickford & Rickford, 1995).

Influences on Educational Practice and Teacher Education

Ironically, few studies showed that this research on what happens with language in classrooms, textbooks, and texts had sustained and substantial influence on actual classroom practices, even though many courses in teacher education included read-ings from linguists concerned with learning. It was therefore not possible for linguists to carry out longitudinal research on the effects that systematic alterations in class-room practice based on linguistic studies might have on student performance (for fur-ther discussion of this point, see Rickford & Rickford, 1995). Few teacher education programs saw the need to inform teachers about how language works, how context matters, and how close examination of the interdependence of language, context, and socialization could matter in understanding learning. Sociolinguists such as Roger Shuy and William Labov attempted to infuse teacher training with linguistics, so that teachers could enter their classrooms with extensive knowledge about dialect differences, language variation, and ways of using linguistic criticism (Fowler, 1986) to interpret written texts. However, these efforts had little substantive influence on teacher training programs.

It was at this point — late in the 1980s — that Cazden (1988) published the most comprehensive work on classroom language. She not only motivated numerous other scholars to move their study of language into classrooms, but also kept up a steady stream of critique of this work. Drawing continuously from advances in cognitive psychology and social theory while remaining committed to teacher education, Cazden has kept a vigilant eye on classroom discourse. Her model of careful examination of data for theory-building influenced a cast of scholars including Sarah Michaels, James Gee, Deborah Hicks, Marilyn Merritt, and many others. These linguist-educators recognized how a range of research foci (e.g., from small-group interactions to national planning and policy questions to "new literacy studies" that examine workplace changes, including technology) may affect what we understand as "literacy."

The work of Courtney Cazden and these scholars bore the strong mark of Dell Hymes, who was perhaps the key voice in the United States calling for careful attention to language contexts. During the 1960s, his early reader, *Language in Culture and Society* (1964), was followed by numerous works stressing the value of ethnography in the study of different forms of communication. *Functions of Language in the Classroom* (Cazden, John, & Hymes, 1972) reflects the power of interdisciplinary collaboration: Cazden as linguist, Vera John as psychologist, and Hymes as anthropologist. Indeed, the fundamental question behind this volume and the authors' collaboration still persists in qualitative work on language and education: What exactly are the functions of language in the classroom or in any situation where we claim that learning is (or should be) taking place? Linguists still struggle in their thickly textured studies of language use to solve the riddle of the relation between observed language behaviors that come "out of the mouth" and mental processes that go on "in the head" (Zentella, 1997). For example, how much of what children learn about science is internalized and retained from a rich verbal debate recorded among a small group of students carrying out a science project? Another nagging worry in qualitative linguistic studies is whether or not any one-time linguistic performance represents internalized sociogrammatical rules that stick with the speaker.

However, our inability to solve this riddle in the nearly three decades since the 1972 seminal work of Cazden, John, and Hymes cannot detract from the foundations and subsequent exemplars these scholars have set out for thickly textured and qualitatively rich studies of language in use. They and their students have demonstrated the value of long-term participant observation, micro-analysis of specific genres highly valued by certain cultural groups, retrospective interviews with speakers, and documentation of oral and written language in interaction.

While these scholars worked primarily across the three fields of linguistics, psychology, and anthropology, scholars within ethnomethodology and sociology were simultaneously attending to language use, though with highly different definitions of context. These scholars (e.g., Aaron Cicourel, Harvey Sacks, and Emmanuel Schegloff) primarily used patterns of the moment, what sociologist Erving Goffman called "situation." Whereas early linguistics scholars had worked toward making evident the wide societal canvas on which language worked, those closer to the sociological tradition gave depth and texture to very small segments of this canvas. Through their work, the minutiae of paint, style of brush, number of brush strokes, and patterns of layering in the sequential steps of producing certain fragments of the canvas became clear. Examples of this work are myriad, but the coming together of all of these elements is perhaps best represented in the work of Schegloff (1988; see also Cicourel, 1974; Sacks & Schegloff, 1974). These scholars called attention to previously unnoticed rule-governed parts of language, such as how conversationalists "open up" closings of conversations and know the difference between a joke and a story opening. These and other scholars also helped call attention to the key components of *register* — a variety of language closely associated with its use within a particular association and most often under circumstances in which the speaker has a particular professional identity with respect to other interlocutors: physician, attorney, teacher, sportscaster, coach, and so on. Such research, though often focused at the micro-level of interaction, made qualitative researchers aware of the penetrating influence that professional socialization in appropriate ways of using language — oral and written — held for one's career identity. In other words, the use of a specific register in a single situation represents a layering of different language socializations within the same individual, enabling people to be secure in playing a variety of roles, including their chosen professional role.

The works and the scholars mentioned here represent the grounding of qualitative work on language in education. They reflect 1) an understanding of the "quality" of language as a matter of texture and grain, which requires substantial subject matter and knowledge across several disciplines; and 2) familiarity on either a sustained or structural basis with context (whether societal or situational) and the ways in which microstructural elements relate to organizational macrostructures. Primary methods of data collection center around audiotaping or videotaping, plus taking field notes in many cases, followed by discussion with speakers about the patterns appearing in the data. Central to this work is careful transcription, which linguists revealed as bearing within its own techniques certain orientations to theory (Edwards & Lampert, 1993). In other words, linguists pointed out that one's choice of the way to arrange transcribed data on the page (e.g., which speaker was viewed as the "first speaker") could reflect certain a priori assumptions or theory of power relations. This work fits well with the qualitative field notes and historical understandings that often overlook patterns of language use and their frequencies. Moreover, such transcription enables entry to the body of language, then easily facilitates analysis by various electronic means, including concordances. These electronic supports for quantitative analysis, often simple frequency counts of word usage, have the potential to enhance greatly certain behavioral or attitudinal issues. For example, if a frequency count of negatives turns out to be much higher for one teacher as compared with another, linguists are alerted to consider a host of contextual factors ranging from the type of lesson to the possibility of different ideological positions the two teachers may hold with regard to students' ability to handle the subject matter. As a further example of ways that qualitative analyses of language use may enhance quantitative work within youth-based organizations whose ethos flows from an understanding of young people as resources, coaches (both athletic and artistic) display certain frequency patterns in the structure of their questions, directives, and clarifications, and these, in turn, co-vary with particular times of each season. In a season's opening days and early weeks of practice, certain other patterns prevail and differ in their specific situational contexts; similarly, as playoffs or final performances draw near, these patterns shift (Heath & Langman, 1994). The constant interplay of rich descriptive materials from field notes and such simple quantitative steps as frequency counts or ratios helps researchers guard against rushing to select the "perfect" example from their qualitative data to illustrate a point. It is always wise to bear in mind that several different types of evidence should be used to support any single claim.

What about Classroom Research?

Since the early 1990s, highly specific attention to language situations in classrooms, as well as their settings and materials, has followed logically from the foundational qualitative work in the study of language and learning. Scholars have begun to consider small-group work, literature circles, peer conferences, and covert talk among students, as well as textbook language and forms of writing done by students under different conditions. Many of these concerns have been especially popular as dissertation topics within schools of education, for they do not involve costly fieldwork in distant locations, learning a new language, or undergoing the culture shock of living in a foreign environment. Methods within this work quickly began to diverge, however, from those used by the discipline-based scholars noted above. Most notably, researchers saw no need to pay detailed attention to time schedules or artifacts of situations already familiar to them. For example, already knowing the language, many scholars saw no need to keep close records of different labels or names that members of the group being studied might choose to refer to the same item when different listeners were present. Therefore, many of the time-consuming methods of record-keeping used by qualitative scholars studying language situations they did not know fell away when former teachers entered the familiar terrain of classrooms to carry out qualitative research on speaking and writing. Few, for example, have found it necessary to look in detail at the relations between written and spoken language used within the same lesson and the relative patterns of change over time for language in each medium (see Chafe & Tannen, 1987, for detailed examples of what can be discovered with close examination).

It is worth examining the reasons why this divergence came about for graduate work in education at the end of the 1980s and continues today. The first has to do with the fact that qualitative methods, and most particularly the study of discourse, have entered schools of education in the past decade. In doing so, however, the study of language has been approached through methods usually described as "ethnographic" and including a component on "discourse." It is rare that the teaching of such methods comes along with courses in linguistics, or substantial work in theories related to understanding language acquisition, structure, and use within the fields of anthropology, psychology, or sociology. Acquisition or language-development study often exists primarily as self-reporting in personal case histories, rather than a detailed following of context, frequency, and complexity of uses of certain structures of language. Structures of language and changes in language over time receive attention primarily in terms of where and how nonstandard varieties can work in classrooms. Examinations of language use tend to focus on those sanctioned in assessment tools — essays, class discussions, and question responses. Analysis of written texts depends primarily on coding and classifying, so that in the end we know a great deal about what to call types of language uses, but less about their co-occurrence features, and only a modicum about actual structures. When certain forms or structures (such as if-then clauses) of language occur, linguists attending to contexts of usage will pay attention to circumstances and characteristics of simultaneous or near-simultaneous factors or events. For example, will small-group talk intended to complete a joint project that is to be constructed or performed, but not written, include, on average, a greater frequency of if-then clauses than small-group sessions preparing for a whole-class discussion? This co-occurrence as a regular pattern is worth noting for follow-through inquiry. Questions typically asked in early-language-acquisition studies about particular language structures and changing constructions and contexts of usage do not tend to find their way into classroom studies of language. For example, now that cognitive psychologists have contributed a great deal to our understanding of strategy-building and planful thinking, it would seem to follow that discourse analysts will attend to classroom evidence of linguistic structures such as conditionals, modals, and mental state verbs in small-group work, particularly around project planning. These findings could, in turn, be considered in relation to changes not only in scores on performance-based tests, but also in frequency and quality of creative and exploratory extra-credit work undertaken by students.

The Future

The evolution of qualitative methods in the study of language in education will surely be more influenced by cognitive psychology than has been the case in the past three decades. Such a link will insist on more attention to learning over time and contexts and less to classifying what happens in highly specific classrooms or more generalizable classroom events, such as literature circles or peer conferencing. Necessary to this evolution, however, is substantial recognition that methods of research cannot sit totally in the service of advocacy of particular ideologies, teaching methods, approaches to assessment, or evaluation of school reform efforts. Much qualitative work on language by researchers from within education has had an agenda often linked to current debates over "best" methods of teaching writing or reading, or even departures from teacher–whole classroom patterns of interaction. Basic research on language development, altered patterns of learning in co-occurrence with different oral and written language structures in use, or correlations between oral and written developmental patterns, especially with regard to genre and register, is much needed. Currently, for example, no baseline exists for older children and adolescents of language development across genres or syntactic structures. This baseline is necessary to hypothesize a critical form of expression for high-end academic performance. However, if a student can reason hypothetically but has had few opportunities to hear or to generate the kinds of language forms needed to show this reasoning, then standard academic assessment would conclude that this student's inability to express this reasoning amounts to a lack of knowledge. It may well be the case, particularly for students for whom the classroom language is not their home or peer language, that these students know and understand what is being asked of them but have not yet developed the necessary linguistic means to express what they know. The same point holds for students whose home and peer talk have not provided abundant exemplars and occasions for arguing a point, debating an issue, or presenting support for both sides of an argument. Such criteria hold for academic language and that of many professions, but they have no value in households, for example, where music, visual arts and crafts, or gardening — generally accomplished through demonstration and practice rather than verbal explication — have been the primary joint family activities.

Similarly, an understanding of how texts of certain institutional origins (such as newspaper articles on educational issues or memos from the central offices of school districts) work goes unaddressed except by critical theorists (e.g., Caldas-Coulthard & Coulthard, 1996). Investigation of the discourse of varying origins and purposes could complement such work by enabling close examination of specific linguistic structures (e.g., Cook, 1992; Fowler, 1986).

But those who will carry out such work must have a grounding in linguistics and one or more of the other disciplines most related to understanding the context of language use. Schools of education that prepare education researchers will need to make room in their curricula for students to take such courses and alter the direction of traditional courses in methods. Such changes would provide education researchers with substantive disciplinary grounding for the study of language and would also make possible courses in education whose titles would move along the lines of "Language in Learning" rather than "Issues in Language Education." Qualitative research has an extensive future, primarily because it has the potential to answer previously unaddressed questions of language in education. Advancements in theory will come through work that stays tightly connected to the central concern in education — learning. But the lessons we have learned from qualitative work during recent decades cannot be lost in any advances that come; we cannot forget the extent to which we now understand the embeddedness of language in systems of meaning, situation, and ideologies surrounding teacher-student relations. Needed now is progress on using linguistics with qualitative methods to grasp change over time, in individual and organizational or social grouping.

This progress will move us beyond the problem that Pirandello's irreverent character finds in our exhausting search "to find out who and what other people are." It is when we are able to know not only "who and what" but also "how" through the medium most accessible to scrutiny — language — that we will find the right retort. In so doing, some of us have faith that we will advance our own theoretical understanding of how understanding works, and also how learning environments support language.

References

Au, K. H., & Jordan, C. (1981). Teaching reading to Hawaiian children: Finding a culturally appropriate solution. In H. T. Trueba, G. P. Guthrie, & K. H. Au (Eds.), *Culture and the bilingual classroom* (pp. 139–152). Rowley, MA: Newbury.

Bargh, J. A., & Chartrand, T. L. (1999). The unbearable automaticity of being. *American Psychologist, 54*, 462–479.

Barnes, D., Britton, J., Rosen, H., & L.A.T.E. (1969). *Language, the learner, and the school.* London: Penguin.

Barr, M., D'Arcy, P., & Healy, M. K. (1982). *What's going on? Language learning episodes in British and American classrooms, grades 4-13.* Montclair, NJ: Boynton Cook.

Borofsky, R. (1987). *Making history.* Cambridge, Eng.: Cambridge University Press.

Briggs, C. L. (1986). *Learning how to ask.* New York: Cambridge University Press.

Burowoy, M. (Ed.). (1991). *Ethnography unbound.* Berkeley: University of California Press.

Caldas-Coulthard, C. R., & Coulthard, M. (Eds.). (1996). *Texts and practices: Readings in critical discourse analysis.* London: Routledge.

Cazden, C. (1988). *Classroom language.* Portsmouth, NH: Heinemann.

Cazden, C., John, V., & Hymes, D. (1972). *Functions of language in the classroom.* New York: Teachers College Press.

Chafe, W., & Tannen, D. (1987). The relationship between written and spoken language. *Annual Review of Anthropology, 16*, 383–407.

Cicourel, A. (1974). *Language use and school performance.* New York: Academic Press.

Cook, G. (1992). *The discourse of advertising.* London: Routledge.

Edwards, J. A., & Lampert, M. D. (Eds.). (1993). *Talking data: Transcription and coding in discourse research.* Hillsdale, NJ: Lawrence Erlbaum.

Fowler, R. (1986). *Linguistic criticism.* Oxford, Eng.: Oxford University Press.

Heath, S. B. (1982a). Questioning at home and at school: A comparative study. In G. Spindler (Ed.), *Doing the ethnography of schooling* (pp. 102–131). New York: Holt, Rinehart & Winston.

Heath, S. B. (1982b). What no bedtime story means: Narrative skills at home and at school. *Language and Society, 11*, 49–76.

Heath, S. B. (1983). *Ways with words: Language, life, and work in communities and classrooms.* New York: Cambridge University Press.

Heath, S. B., & Langman, J. (1994). Shared thinking and the register of coaching. In D. Biber & E. Finegan (Eds.), *Sociolinguistic perspectives on register* (pp. 82–105). New York: Cambridge University Press.

Hymes, D. (1964). *Language in culture and society.* New York: Harper & Row.

Labov, W. (1969). *The study of nonstandard English.* Urbana, IL: National Council of Teachers of English.

Labov, W. (1970). The logic of nonstandard English. In F. Williams (Ed.), *Language and poverty* (pp. 153–189). Chicago: Markham.

Mehan, H. (1979). *Learning lessons: Social organization in the classroom.* Cambridge, MA: Harvard University Press.

Morgan, M. (1994). Theories and politics in African American English. *Annual Review of Anthropology, 23*, 325–345.

Ochs, E. (1988). *Culture and language development.* New York: Cambridge University Press.

Pelissier, C. (1981). The anthropology of teaching and learning. *Annual Review of Anthropology, 20*, 75–95.

Pirandello, L. (1995). *Six characters in search of an author and other plays.* London: Penguin Books.

Rickford, J. (1997). Unequal partnership: Sociolinguistics and the African American speech community. *Language in Society, 26*, 161–192.

Rickford, J., & Rickford, A. (1995). Dialect readers revisited. *Linguistics and Education, 7*, 107–128.

Sacks, H., & Schegloff, E. (1974). *Opening up closings.* In R. Turner (Ed.), *Ethnomethodology* (pp. 233–264). Hardmondsworth, Eng.: Penguin.

Schegloff, E. (1988). Discourse as an interactional achievement II. In D. Tannen (Ed.), *Linguistics in context: Connecting observation and understanding* (pp. 135–158). Norwood, NJ: Ablex.

Schiefflin, B., & Ochs, E. (1986). Language socialization. *Annual Review of Anthropology, 15*, 163–191.

Shuy, R. (Ed.). (1965). *Social dialects and language learning*. Champaign, IL: National Council of Teachers of English.

Spindler, G. (Ed.). (1982). *Doing the ethnography of schooling*. New York: Holt, Rinehart & Winston.

Zentella, A. (1997). *Hablamos los dos: Growing up bilingual*. London: Basil Blackwell.

Sociology and Qualitative Methodologies in Educational Research

MARY HAYWOOD METZ

Currently, both sociology and qualitative research are full of competing schools and perspectives. Amid such fluidity, I write from the perspective of one sociologist about the kinds of qualitative research in sociology I believe have had the most influence on the study of education. In this article, I describe contributions of qualitative sociology to a methodology that is being widely used in educational research. I then describe some substantive contributions of qualitative sociology to understanding social processes in education. Finally, I discuss differences between the methodology of qualitative sociology and that of two different kinds of qualitative research in education and make a few suggestions for a methodological détente.

Qualitative methods are tools in the service of research questions and the theoretical (or practical) bodies of knowledge they seek to expand. To define qualitative research as a collection of methods is to delineate an incoherent and far-flung entity. One cannot usefully discuss qualitative research without attending to the methodologies that underlie its methods.

A methodology is a theory and analysis of how research does or should proceed. Qualitative methodologies in education — and they are plural — carry assumptions or propositions about the nature of knowledge, the self, social interaction, culture, and society. Research is a multifaceted dialogue among meta-theories about existence and knowledge, substantive theory, and information about the empirical world.[1] Understandings of methodology grow in tandem with empirical investigation and the development of social theory (Harding, 1987). Defining qualitative research by the cluster of qualitative methodologies that claim the name makes it possible to sort out both similarities and differences among them and their alliances with differing disciplines, theories, and subjects for investigation.

The Research Methodology of Qualitative Sociology

The Chicago School

The roots of qualitative sociology in this country are many.[2] Still, the most direct and forceful influences on the tradition of qualitative research in sociology stem from U.S.

Harvard Educational Review   Vol. 70   No. 1   Spring 2000, 60–74

sociologists of the early twentieth century. George Herbert Mead, W. I. Thomas, Ellsworth Faris, and others, mostly at the University of Chicago, founded an American sociology that looked closely at the ties between society and the individual and emphasized the importance of meaning; they believed that all human understanding is highly interpretive and socially shaped. Chicago School theorists saw understandings of society, and also of the natural world, as socially constructed and constantly reconstructed by new generations through social interaction. While every participant holds a "definition of the situation," each actor's definition of a situation will be deeply colored by the definitions of those around him/her in his/her social context. According to W. I. Thomas, "if [people] define situations as real, they are real in their consequences" (Thomas & Thomas, 1928, p. 572). The ideas of socially and individually constructed meaning have resonated widely in qualitative sociology.[3]

Several of the early sociologists in the Chicago School, especially Robert Park and his students, were fascinated with the diverse life of the growing city around them. They fanned out through the city documenting and analyzing the perspectives and intra- and inter-group interactions of a broad range of social assemblages, such as the immigrant Polish community (Thomas & Znaniecki, 1927), the privileged Gold Coast juxtaposed to nearby slums (Zorbaugh, 1929), as well as a variety of deviant groups — for example, hobos (Anderson, 1923) and professional thieves (Sutherland, 1937). As Park's students and, in turn, their students took positions in sociology departments throughout the country and their writings became foundational readings in sociology, their work directly and indirectly formed much subsequent qualitative research in sociology.

Still, qualitative research methodology held a prominent position in sociology only briefly. For the last two-thirds of the twentieth century, sociology in general and the sociology of education in particular have been dominated by the logic and practice of a "scientific" sociology based on quantitatively measurable survey research. Survey research seeks to understand social processes underlying complex behavior by aggregating individual attitudes and behavior and studying their correlation with social characteristics of the actors, with their position in various social structures, or with other attitudes and behavior. That its generalizations may not apply in many individual situations or in certain social groups is often not a matter of concern; it seeks primarily to identify and measure the magnitude and direction of broad social influences. The processes that occur in interacting groups with localized shared meanings are neither of interest to, nor within the methodological reach of, proponents of large-scale survey methods.

Contributions of Qualitative Sociology to Research Methodology

The tradition of qualitative research has persisted despite marginalization within sociology. In my view, four critical elements in the methodology of qualitative research stem from the founding Chicago School. First, sociologists who want to understand a group must make a concerted effort to understand its worldview in its own terms. Deep understanding of insiders' views is critical, including the tacit assumptions and patterns of which they may not be articulately aware. A large body of qualitative work in sociology not directly connected to the Chicago School explores insiders' views in depth (for example, relevant to schooling, Rubin's 1972 study of pro- and antibusing groups and Lareau's 1989 study of middle- and working-class parents in relationship with their first graders' schools).

Second, qualitative researchers in this tradition in sociology discover insider perspectives by spending a long time in contact with a group: participating in their lives with them, and seeking to understand mundane routines, special celebrations and rituals, and unplanned critical incidents. Researchers must listen for the interpretations that members of the group give for their own actions, the actions of other members of the group, and the actions, real and imagined, of outsiders. They must both mark these as they occur in the flow of daily life and, eventually, elicit them more systematically to develop, test, and correct their own growing understandings. They must take careful note, captured in words or visual images, of the physical setting with all its culturally developed artifacts and must study all kinds of documents both formal and informal.

Researchers must compare and contrast all these pieces of data with each other and "triangulate" them in systematic ways in order to develop, question, refine, and/or discard interpretations of them and the underlying perspectives they reflect.

Third, sociologists bring their own sociological lens to their analysis. They do not simply describe what they see or become voices for insiders' perspectives. Rather, they analyze the roots, patterns, and consequences of those perspectives. As sociologists, they often pay particular attention to various kinds of social structures, and to the economic or technical infrastructure and interaction patterns, in a society and in smaller groups they study within it.

Finally, like the Chicago School, most qualitative sociologists study groups within complex, often urban, social settings. They are keenly aware that the groups they study both form social systems and cultural patterns of their own *and* accommodate their lives to the diverse groups around them and the larger societal systems of which all are a part. The groups studied by the Chicago School were simultaneously citizens of Chicago and the United States, or even of other nations. Members of any group were also simultaneously members of other groups within Chicago. They belonged at the same time to ethnic groups, to religious groups, to families, to occupational groups, to avocational groups, and to groups of age and gender peers. Such groups are not simply wholes to be studied as isolated entities, although understanding them as wholes is important. Rather, their members have multiple allegiances and the groups, as groups, have to negotiate with and adjust to other groups and to the social reality of the overarching social entitites of which they are a part.

These insights are critical for the study of education. Groups in education — classrooms, schools, peer groups, families, neighborhoods,[4] even administrative departments — can be studied as entities with meaning systems of their own. But one must also study their relationships with other groups in order to understand them fully.

Studies in this genre are conducted with such intense and extensive data collection in order to understand insiders' perspectives at a deep level, about which they themselves are not fully articulate. Such depth and intensity is also needed in order to confront researchers with enough material to enable them to capture understandings to which their professional and personal frameworks may make them insensitive. In good work of this kind, the research process helps first the researcher and then the reader to understand the coherence and value in a way of life they do not share, or to see with fresh eyes the dimensions of one of which they are a part. In either case, the research illumines how the social reality in a location is connected to, even partially forged by, the social structures and different cultural understandings that surround it. At the same time, such research ventures are simultaneously instruments for improving — whether by fine tuning or reorienting — the very theoretical tools with which they were undertaken.[5] Data and theory are in profound conversation; the final work interprets and reinterprets both data and theory in the light of the other.

I believe that at least the first three elements of qualitative methodology in sociology are fundamental to qualitative research that should be properly called "ethnography." Researchers doing such work must: 1) make a concerted effort to understand participants' perspectives in their own terms; 2) participate with the people they study on a prolonged basis, collecting multiple kinds of data from multiple sources and triangulating them; and 3) analyze with a lens that locates every study in a broader analytic and theoretical framework, if not of a discipline then of some other intellectual tradition, established or emerging. While attention to nested social systems and individual multiple allegiances that surround and crisscross research settings is important in complex industrial societies, and particularly so in education, it is not as critical to the definition of ethnography. It is perhaps an emphasis most important to sociologists.

Sociology and Anthropology

Anthropologists coined the term ethnography and many are legitimately possessive of it. Though the referent of the term is less than unitary (Agar, 1985; Geertz, 1973), for anthropologists it roughly indicates a holistic study of a culture, based on a methodology close to what I have just described. But that methodology need not be used only for the holistic study of a group and its culture — and in sociology often it is not. Thus, anthropologists might narrow the term even more than I have, rightly claiming that sociologists have broadened it, even if only slightly. In education, some authors use the term a great deal more broadly to refer to any research that uses non-quantitative methods. When used so broadly, it loses its meaning.

There is much commonality between qualitative sociology and anthropology. There was considerable mutual influence between anthropologists and the Chicago School of sociologists throughout the first half of the century (Bogdan & Biklen, 1992; Wax, 1971). That mutual influence between anthropology and qualitative sociology has continued.[6] As they share at least the first three elements of the methodology I have described,[7] together they provide roots for research based on these methodological elements conducted by scholars trained in education rather than in either sociology or anthropology.

Still, I do not mean to suggest that qualitative sociology and anthropology are interchangeable, despite considerable kinship and a mutually beneficial intellectual conversation that shapes both fields. There are important differences between them as well. For example, as I have suggested, anthropologists may put more emphasis on the culture of society as a whole or study smaller settings as if they were a cultural whole, although they also study intercultural contact. Sociologists, by contrast, are more likely to emphasize the ways that the settings they study are nested within other units. Anthropologists are more likely to work like clinicians, seeking the fullest possible description and analysis of one setting. Sociologists generally want to generalize from the settings they study to other settings; they analyze particular social processes within a given setting as affected by that setting, but do not attempt to explicate all aspects of the setting. In addition, some anthropologists probably attribute more causal force to culture, or less reified cultural dynamics, than do sociologists, who look more quickly to social structures, technical constraints, and the exercise of external power to understand the patterns they analyze.

Substantive Contributions of Qualitative Sociology to an Understanding of Education

In the United States, the method of studying education in sociology that has drawn the most attention and resources has been survey research. It has, until recently, treated schools as "black boxes" — that is, as unexamined intervening variables that do or do not create associations between the "inputs" and "outputs" that are being studied. Such studies have looked at the effects of schooling on (mostly male) status attainment (e.g., Featherman & Hauser, 1978; Grusky & Hauser, 1984) and at the effects of schools' resources on students' achievement (summarized in Burtless, 1996; Gamoran, 1992) with, at best, broad measures of activities inside schools, such as track placement.[8] However, more recent surveys and statistical methods have made it possible to get some rough measures of effects of intra-school processes common across many schools.[9]

By contrast, qualitative sociologists studying education in the United States have looked inside schools to understand their internal processes.[10] They have had an important influence on the study of teaching,[11] but have made their greatest direct contribution to the substantive knowledge base in education in the study of school organization.[12]

Sociologists have developed an enormous body of theory and research concerning organizations. Schools are distinctive organizations in several respects: their raw material and products are children, not things, and their well-educated workers must make constant on-the-spot decisions in ambiguous circumstances. Theorist Charles Perrow (1967) has offered a penetrating analysis of the relationship between the nature of the work that members of an organization do and the kinds of organizational control structures that are appropriate. Robert Dreeben (1973), using similar logic, has pointed out the consequences for schools. Along somewhat similar lines, Charles Bidwell (1965), in a classic article, showed how schools must struggle with inconsistent principles of organization because they are formally organized as strictly hierarchical bureaucracies, while the work of their teachers is professional and demands more autonomy.

In his early and seminal *The Sociology of Teaching,* Willard Waller (1932/1965) argued that schools are not only formal organizations but also small communities in which teachers and students spend a significant portion of their waking lives. Qualitative studies flowering in the 1950s showed that all organizations have both formal, official systems and informal systems that grow up spontaneously.[13] The informal system is a blend of the various subcultures (of social class, race, religion, region, and so forth) that workers bring into an organization and the patterns that arise as human beings adapt to, and make meaning in, the physical and social structures within which they find themselves. Actual practices in the daily life of organizations emerge as a synthesis of the formal and informal organizational systems. Individual organizations and their component parts develop their own semi-independent cultures — an insight recently taken up, but often trivialized, by U.S. business. In both sociology and education, the significance of informal systems and organizational culture seems to be alternately found, lost, and found again.

Fluid, partially informal social patterns contained within the frame of formal organizations are well-suited to be studied by qualitative methodologies and poorly suited to be studied by survey research. Sociologists (e.g., Gracey, 1972; McPherson, 1972; Metz, 1978, 1986, 1990; Noblit, 1979; Noblit & Dempsey, 1996; Swidler, 1979) have explored the operation of informal systems internal to schools and the interpenetration of surrounding communities with the internal lives of schools. Many other educational researchers, informed in various ways by sociology, have done equally interesting studies of a generally ethnographic kind along similar lines (Cusick, 1973, 1983; Grant, 1988; Ladson-Billings, 1994; Lesko, 1988; Lipman, 1998; McNeil, 1986; Page, 1991; Schofield, 1982).

The Future of Qualitative Research in Education

Currently, researchers representing a wide variety of disciplinary backgrounds, methodologies, and substantive interests are engaging in diverse forms of qualitative research in education. I will address two kinds of qualitative research, both of which have methodologies that are related to — but at odds with — the methodology associated with qualitative sociology. Both offer challenges to the continued legitimacy of that methodology.

There is a growing body of case study research based on qualitative methods pursued as part of large, mixed-methods projects grounded in a dominant, quantitative component. Policy researchers, but also quantitative sociologists, are more and more attracted to such designs as they increasingly appreciate the importance of interactive processes within schools.

Many researchers conducting these case studies pursue them with the deductive, individualistic logic appropriate to quantitative research. Most do not seek insiders' perspectives at a level beyond that of straightforward answers to questions generated from researchers' perspectives developed prior to the study. Such researchers rarely look for underlying coherence that might be inconsistent with their deductive premises or capture complexity and contradiction within the setting. They neither seek to, nor gather the information needed to, apprehend and reflect on the disjunctions between their own and insiders' perspectives that could lead them to alter their framework of analysis. Thus, while much of this work is to be applauded for descriptive enrichment of analysis of quantitative data, much of it must be treated with great caution, for both its lack of the technical safeguards for accuracy of more sophisticated qualitative research and its weakness in developing more than a surface understanding of insiders' perspectives.

There is a danger that this kind of qualitative research, which is less expensive and easier to conduct than ethnography and more easily assimilated to questions stemming from policy (Becker, 1983), will overwhelm and replace ethnographic methodology by co-opting the label of qualitative research. A primary source of this danger is a lack of awareness among the researchers doing it of how much they are importing assumptions and perspectives consistent with quantitative methodology, and of how fundamentally their qualitative studies differ from ethnographic research.

Holding a very different relationship to the methodology of qualitative sociology, an array of newer research methodologies, such as some forms of feminist research, postmodern research, and even some action research, valorize the perspective of insiders in the groups being studied. They are deeply suspicious of any analysis that studies insiders' perspectives from without, whether ethnographic or quantitative. While there is increasing internal debate in such circles on the meaning of being an insider and on the requisites for meaningful understanding of insider perspectives, disciplinary lenses and research by outsiders are at best skeptically examined for inauthentic imposition of an alien point of view (e.g., Collins, 1991; Fine, 1994; Lather, 1991).

These methodological arguments arise from legitimate concerns. There are many examples of both quantitative researchers and ethnographers who have either failed to consider insider perspectives or misinterpreted them in the light of some combination of Western, White, male, middle-class, or administrative perspectives woven into traditional disciplines or into the personal social formation of researchers.[14] To address such problems, rather than reject the possibility of a research conversation that can cross social differences and intellectual traditions, I find it more constructive to seek ways to make such a conversation more even-handed and accurate. There should be ways of making the "gaze" of the research community more reciprocal with regard to who interprets other groups and whose groups are interpreted. Already, as more women and people of color enter the research community, and as it becomes more legitimate both for them and for researchers with working-class origins to draw on their background experience, such researchers are bringing neglected perspectives to traditional disciplines. Further, these criticisms underscore the importance of "studying up," studying those with the same or more, rather than less, power than academic researchers. In addition, researchers should seek empathetically to understand the perspectives of the people they study — something that is at least enjoined, even if often imperfectly practiced, in ethnographic methodology.

The future of qualitative research in the sociology of education in particular is complicated by ambiguity about who counts as a "sociologist" in the contemporary world. Currently, qualitative research with a sociological bent is being done by young scholars from schools of education, though often they studied with professors whose own education took place in sociology or anthropology departments. Using a broad definition of sociology, one can point to a good deal of interesting work by young scholars using qualitative methods, a very large proportion of them women and many of them people of color. They tend to concentrate on issues of race, gender, and sometimes social class as they affect staff and students' actions and experiences in schools, the interface between home and school, and students' career paths.[15] Their sociological leanings are especially evident where they emphasize school organization and the effects of social structure.[16]

Despite its great value, neither ethnography, nor any other qualitative methodology, is the most useful methodology for all questions. The social world, even the enterprise of education, is far too complex to be captured by any single methodology. We need to clarify the assumptions and procedures of varied methodologies and to discourage wasteful struggles among them. If educational researchers explicitly matched their questions with the most appropriate theories, methodologies, and methods, it would be easier for all to see both the strengths and limitations of each approach and its associated studies.

Questions of quality — in the sense of excellence or worth — apply to all kinds of research; there is good and poor research in every genre. To separate issues of excellence from differences among methodologies, newer genres need to work out the criteria by which both their own practitioners and outside readers can judge worth within the genre. Further, if a variety of research genres are to bloom, we will need some people who will specialize in building bridges among research approaches and finding ways to articulate the cumulative significance of their disparate findings.[17] Academics will have to find language and socially shared understandings through which to legitimize a much greater variety of research approaches than have previously been accepted by the academy, the public, or the increasingly significant audiences at funding sources.

Notes

1. The word empirical has recently been widely misused to refer only to quantified data. Used correctly, it refers to information that has been gathered in any systematic way about the world around us as it is available through experience rather than through mere deduction. Qualitative data are profoundly empirical.

2. They crisscross in ways much too complex to recount in an article this short. I omit the important influence of German sociologist Max Weber's concern with meaning as a driving force in society and his methodological emphasis on understanding, or *Verstehen*. This theoretical line has been reenforced for some sociologists through the German philosopher and "phenomenologist" Edmund Husserl and his student Alfred Schutz, who came to the United States during the Nazi era. They, as much as or more than the Chicago School that I discuss, provided the grounding for Peter Berger's interpretation of the social construction of reality, which was influential both through his accessible textbook, *An Invitation to Sociology* (1963), and his more scholarly work with Thomas Luckmann, *The Social Construction of Reality* (1966), widely read outside of sociology as well as within it. I also omit the German Georg Simmel under whom Robert Park (discussed below) studied briefly, but consequentially. Most sociologists are also well aware of Marx's discussions of the relations of social structure and culture. Marx's understanding that culture or social meanings are with varying success imposed on the unfortunate many by the powerful few, as others have advanced and elaborated it, enjoys considerable current attention in education, including one important line of qualitative research (e.g., Fine, 1991; Foley, 1990; Valli, 1986; Weis, 1990; Willis, 1977). Although such understandings have much influence on work that may not be directly in its tradition — including my own more recent work — I say little more of neo-Marxism or critical theory in this article. While critical theory is an important continuing tradition in sociology, these sociologists have paid little attention to education. On the other hand, most important critical theorists concerned with education, including many who do qualitative research, are not sociologists, although some do use modifications of the research methodology I discuss.

3. There are forms of qualitative research in sociology that owe much less to the Chicago School than the work I highlight in this article. Ethnomethodology, which tries to achieve a radical skepticism that can make visible the construction of the social rules of everyday life, stems primarily from the work of European phenomenologists and existentialist philosophers. It follows a different methodology and therefore different practical research strategies from the qualitative sociology I highlight here. Despite some similarity in ideas with the Chicago

School, postmodern studies in education acknowledge more kinship with European philosophers than with the sociologists of the Chicago School who were contemporaries of, and in conversation with, the pragmatist John Dewey at Chicago.

4. Many modern urban and suburban neighborhoods are not groups and do not share a meaning system, but some do.

5. Some of my colleagues who use quantitative methodologies have been surprised to hear me say that if a student writing a qualitative dissertation does not emerge with the initial research question somewhat transformed, he or she probably was not paying sufficient attention in the field. Data and theo

6. In writing this article, I found myself going to my bookshelf to find out the disciplinary affiliation of some of my favorite authors. I received a number of surprises — and in some cases I was unable to find the answer! I have assigned labels according to scholars' formal training first, or, secondarily, the department in which they teach. Because careers are mobile with regard to discipline, I have probably made a few mistakes, for which I apologize in advance.

7. Anthropologist Fred Erickson, in a widely read statement on ethnographic methodology, includes the fourth (Erickson, 1986).

8. Ironically, perhaps James Coleman's quantitative studies should be counted among the important contributions of sociology to qualitative research in education. His 1966 study (Coleman et al., 1966) found that differences in the characteristics of schools he was able to measure with a large-scale national survey had little impact on student achievement, once students' race and class were factored out of consideration. This finding, repeated in other quantitative studies, has stimulated a good deal of qualitative research by nonsociologists trying to identify characteristics in the internal processes of schools that do make a difference for students.

9. Recently, advances in questionnaire constructions and analysis have made it possible to get richer indicators of within-school processes. More sophisticated sampling and statistical analysis, especially hierarchical linear modeling (Bryk & Raudenbush, 1992), have made it easier to study the effects of within-school processes that may vary with contextual conditions. Though much improved, these methods still are individualistic in their overall strategy and have only relatively blunt instruments for studying interacting influences affected by local settings.

10. There has been an unfortunate discontinuity between U.S. and British work in education and especially in the sociology of education. There has been and continues to be a large volume of qualitative research on classroom processes, as well as teaching and school organization by British sociologists. Names of British sociologists such as Stephen Ball, Sara Delamont, Martyn Denscombe, Ivor Goodson, Anthony Green, Martyn Hammersley, Andy Hargreaves, David Hargreaves, Colin Lacey, Lynda Measor, Peter Woods, and others, as well as that of Australian Robert W. Connell, ought to be household words to students who read qualitative studies of education, but most are not. Critical theorist Paul Willis, well-known to scholars in the United States, is an exception.

11. Willard Waller, who took a masters degree at Chicago under Robert Faris, anticipated many of the insights about teaching worked out more systematically by others through the rest of the twentieth century in his classic *The Sociology of Teaching* (1932/1965). Howard Becker, directly in the Chicago tradition, followed with a small study of Chicago teachers in the 1950s (1952, 1953). Gertrude McPherson (1972) used ethnographic techniques to write a dissertation, later published, based on full participation as a teacher in a small town. The research that followed on teaching as work has relied mostly on a mixture of survey research methods and open-ended qualitative interviews, in most cases with minimal, or no, observation. Dan Lortie's classic *Schoolteacher* (1975), which combined survey research with open-ended qualitative interviews, set the pattern for a considerable body of work by nonsociologists bearing some sociological influence, perhaps most obviously that by Marilyn Cohn and Robert Kottkamp (1993) and Susan Moore Johnson (1990). Recent work by sociologist Joan Talbert and policy analyst Milbrey McLaughlin emphasizes the multiple contexts of teaching and their differential effects on teachers' individual and collective experience and

meaning making (e.g., Talbert & McLaughlin, 1993). Their research methods are mixed ones of survey research and short-term field studies repeated longitudinally. Their Center for Research on the Context of Secondary School Teaching at Stanford has supported work by a variety of authors that highlights the importance of a range of interacting contexts for teaching (see Bascia, 1994; Cohen, McLaughlin, & Talbert, 1993; Little & McLaughlin, 1993; Siskin, 1994; Siskin & Little, 1995).

12. Until recently, sociologists have contributed little to the fertile qualitative literature in education on students and on cultural differences. There are a few qualitative sociological studies that connect student life to organizational settings (e.g., Bossert, 1979; Mehan, 1979). There are also many quantitative studies of student life, some with considerable practical implications and relevance to topics more often studied qualitatively. For example, see Elizabeth Cohen and Rachel Lotan's recent collection of articles in this tradition (Cohen & Lotan, 1997).

13. For example, Philip Selznick studied the Tennessee Valley Authority (1949), Alvin Gouldner studied a gypsum mine and board plant (1954), Peter Blau studied social workers in a bureaucratized office (1963), and Gresham Sykes studied a maximum security prison (1958).

14. This concern is not new, however. In writing for an education journal twenty years ago — in the very early stages of the current concern with this topic — about the ways in which the social and disciplinary background of a researcher can affect both what she can see and what those studied will let her see, I found a large body of literature on both topics by qualitative researchers in both sociology and anthropology (Metz, 1983). Such reflectiveness did not, of course, make these researcher authors able, or willing, to render the world exactly as insiders saw it. Furthermore, in a complex industrial society, overlapping group memberships of individuals and inescapable interactions between groups both make it difficult to define insiders and outsiders and make it necessary to consider both in order to understand the society in which insiders, outsiders — and readers — lead their daily lives. The difficulties lie much less in fundamental problems in the ability to understand groups not one's own than in the effects of unequal power on the ways such studies are conducted and interpreted.

15. In sociology other than the sociology of education, this kind of work emerged much earlier. I hesitate to give citations here, in part because it is so ambiguous who is to be included in the sociological fold. Still, there is much work of the kind described in the text by young authors, who are mostly just starting their careers. Many of these authors recently presented work at the meetings of the American Educational Research Association and American Sociological Association (see Bixby & Golden, 1997; Carter, 1999; Conchas, 1999; Horvat, 1999; Inoway-Ronnie, 1997; Lewis, Chesler, & Forman, 1999; Lopez, 1999; Perry, 1999; Tyson, 1999).

16. Again, only as examples, one might look at some of the following work (Hemmings, 1996; Kelly, 1993; Lipman, 1998; Pace, 1999).

17. There are some initial efforts being made in these directions. One occasionally sees reviews of the literature that attempt to cross genres (for example, Lee, Bryk, & Smith, 1993). The National Science Foundation convened a working group on ways to interpret and judge the quality of diverse kinds of research in 1998, reported in a symposium at the meeting of the American Educational Research Association in 1999 and summarized in a paper by the convenor (Suter, in press). In 1999, the Stanford University School of Education convened a conference on the topic as it pertains to teaching of research in graduate education programs (Kaminsky, 1999).

References

Agar, M. (1985). *Speaking of ethnography.* Beverly Hills, CA: Sage.

Anderson, N. (1923). *The hobo.* Chicago: University of Chicago Press.

Bascia, N. (1994). *Unions in teachers' professional lives.* New York: Teachers College Press.

Becker, H. (1952). The career of the Chicago public school teacher. *American Journal of Sociology, 57*, 470–477.

Becker, H. (1953). The teacher in the authority system of the public schools. *Journal of Educational Sociology, 27*, 128–141.

Becker, H. (1983). Studying urban schools. *Anthropology and Education Quarterly, 14*, 99–108.

Berger, P. L. (1963). *An invitation to sociology: A humanistic perspective.* Garden City, NY: Doubleday.

Berger, P., & Luckmann, T. (1966). *The social construction of reality.* New York: Doubleday.

Bidwell, C. (1965). The school as a formal organization. In J. March (Ed.), *Handbook of organizations* (pp. 972–1022). Chicago: Rand McNally.

Bixby, J., & Golden, B. (1997, April). *Race, social class, and student achievement: Differing perspectives of Black and White teachers.* Paper presented at the annual meeting of the American Educational Research Association, Chicago.

Blau, P. (1963). *The dynamics of bureaucracy.* Chicago: University of Chicago Press.

Bogdan, R. C., & Biklen, S. K. (1992). *Qualitative research for education: An introduction to theory and methods* (2nd ed.). Boston: Allyn & Bacon.

Bossert, S. (1979). *Tasks and social relationships in classrooms: A study of instructional organization and its consequences.* New York: Cambridge University Press.

Bryk, A., & Raudenbush, S. W. (1992). *Hierarchical linear models: Applications and data analysis methods.* Newbury Park, CA: Sage.

Burtless, G. (Ed.). (1996). *Does money matter? The effect of school resources on student achievement and adult success.* Washington, DC: Brookings Institution Press.

Carter, P. L. (1999, April). *What's school got to do with it? More explanation on the attitude-achievement paradox among low income minority students.* Paper presented at the annual meeting of the American Educational Research Association, Montreal.

Cohen, D. K., McLaughlin, M. W., & Talbert, J. E. (Eds.). (1993). *Teaching for understanding: Challenges for policy and practice.* San Francisco: Jossey-Bass.

Cohn, M. M., & Kottkamp, R. B. (1993). *Teachers: The missing voice in education.* Albany: State University of New York Press.

Cohen, E. G., & Lotan, R. A. (Eds.). (1997). *Working for equity in heterogeneous classrooms: Sociological theory in practice.* New York: Teachers College Press.

Coleman, J., Campbell, E., Hobson, C., McPartland, J., Mood, A., Weinfield, F., & York, R. (1966). *Equality of educational opportunity.* Washington, DC: Government Printing Office.

Collins, P. H. (1991). *Black feminist thought: Knowledge, consciousness, and the politics of empowerment.* New York: Routledge.

Conchas, G. (1999, August). *Surfing the "model minority" wave of success: Vietnamese youth and the construction of academic identity and ideology.* Paper presented at the annual meeting of the American Sociological Association.

Cusick, P. (1973). *Inside high school: The students' world.* New York: Holt, Rinehart & Winston.

Cusick, P. A. (1983). *The egalitarian ideal and the American high school: Studies of three schools.* New York: Longman.

Dreeben, R. (1973). The school as a workplace. In R. M. W. Travers (Ed.), *Second handbook of research on teaching* (pp. 450–473). Chicago: Rand McNally.

Erickson, F. (1986). Qualitative methods in research on teaching. In M. C. Wittrock (Ed.), *Handbook of research on teaching* (pp. 119–161). New York: Macmillan.

Featherman, D., & Hauser, R. M. (1978). *Opportunity and change.* New York: Academic Press.

Fine, M. (1994). Dis-stance and other stances: Negotiations of power inside feminist research. In A. Gitlin (Ed.), *Power and method: Political activism and educational research* (pp. 13–35). New York: Routledge.

Fine, M. (1991). *Framing dropouts: Notes on the politics of an urban high school.* Albany: State University of New York Press.

Foley, D. E. (1990). *Learning capitalist culture: Deep in the heart of Tejas.* Philadelphia: University of Pennsylvania Press.

Gamoran, A. (1992). Social factors in education. In M. Alkin (Ed.), *Encyclopedia of educational research* (pp. 1222–1229). New York: Macmillan.

Geertz, C. (1973). Thick description: Toward an interpretive theory of culture. In C. Geertz (Ed.), *The interpretation of cultures* (pp. 3–30). New York: Basic Books.

Gouldner, A. (1954). *Patterns of industrial bureaucracy.* Glencoe, IL: Free Press.

Gracey, H. L. (1972). *Curriculum or craftsmanship: Elementary school teachers in a bureaucratic system.* Chicago: University of Chicago Press.

Grant, G. (1988). *The world we created at Hamilton High.* Cambridge, MA: Harvard University Press.

Grusky, D. B., & Hauser, R. M. (1984). Comparative social mobility revisited: Models of convergence and divergence in 16 countries. *American Sociological Review, 49,* 19–38.

Harding, S. (1987). Introduction. In S. Harding (Ed.), *Feminism and methodology* (pp. 1–14). Bloomington: Indiana University Press.

Hemmings, A. (1996). Conflicting images? Being Black and a model high school student. *Anthropology and Education Quarterly, 27,* 20–50.

Horvat, E. M. (1999, August). *Understanding educational opportunity and the importance of habitus.* Paper presented at the annual meeting of the American Sociological Association, Chicago.

Inoway-Ronnie, E. (1997, April). *Signposts of success: How teachers in lower-income schools balance pressures to nurture yet challenge students academically.* Paper presented at the annual meeting of the American Educational Research Association, Chicago.

Johnson, S. M. (1990). *Teachers at work: Achieving success in our schools.* New York: Basic Books.

Kaminsky, A. (1999). Quality and methodology in education research and training: Learning through difference. In *Proceedings of the Spencer/SUSE RTG Working Conference on Methodology and Quality.* Stanford, CA: Stanford University School of Education.

Kelly, D. M. (1993). *Last chance high: How girls and boys drop in and out of alternative schools.* New Haven, CT: Yale University Press.

Ladson-Billings, G. (1994). *The dreamkeepers.* San Francisco: Jossey-Bass.

Lareau, A. (1989). *Home advantage: Social class and parental intervention in elementary education.* New York: Falmer Press.

Lather, P. (1991). *Getting smart: Feminist research and pedagogy within the postmodern.* New York: Routledge.

Lee, V. E., Bryk, A. S., & Smith, J. B. (1993). The organization of effective secondary schools. *Review of Research in Education, 19,* 171–267.

Lesko, N. (1988). *Symbolizing society: Stories, rites, and structure in a Catholic high school.* Philadelphia: Falmer Press.

Lewis, A., Chesler, M., & Forman, T. (1999, August*). "I'm not going to think of you as Black, I'll just think of you as my friend": Color-blind ideologies and exclusionary race relations on a predominately White campus.* Paper presented at the Annual Meeting of the American Sociological Association, Chicago.

Lipman, P. (1998). *Race, class, and power in school restructuring.* Albany: State University of New York Press.

Little, J. W., & McLaughlin, M. W. (Eds.). (1993). *Teachers' work: Individuals, colleagues, and contexts.* New York: Teachers College Press.

Lopez, N. (1999, August). *Race-gender high school lessons.* Paper presented at the annual meeting of the American Sociological Association, Chicago.

Lortie, D. C. (1975). *Schoolteacher: A sociological study.* Chicago: University of Chicago Press.

McNeil, L. (1986). *Contradictions of control: School structure and school knowledge.* New York: Routledge.

McPherson, G. H. (1972). *Small town teacher.* Cambridge, MA: Harvard University Press.

Mehan, H. (1979). *Learning lessons: Social organization in the classroom.* Cambridge, MA: Harvard University Press.

Metz, M. H. (1978). *Classrooms and corridors: The crisis of authority in desegregated secondary schools.* Berkeley: University of California Press.

Metz, M. H. (1983, January 4). What can be learned from educational ethnography? *Urban Education, 7,* 391–418.

Metz, M. H. (1986). *Different by design: The context and character of three magnet schools.* New York: Routledge.

Metz, M. H. (1990). How social class differences shape teachers' work. In M. W. McLaughlin, J. E. Talbert, & N. Bascia (Eds.), *The contexts of teaching in secondary schools: Teachers' realities* (pp. 40–107). New York: Teachers College Press.

Noblit, G. (1979). Patience and prudence in a southern high school: Managing the political economy of desegregated education. In R. C. Rist (Ed.), *Desegregated schools: Appraisals of an American experiment* (pp. 65–88). New York: Academic Press.

Noblit, G. W., & Dempsey, V. O. (1996). *The social construction of virtue: The moral life of schools.* Albany: State University of New York Press.

Pace, J. (1999, April). *Between order and engagement: Trying to win the consent of African American students.* Paper presented at the annual meeting of the American Educational Research Association, Montreal.

Page, R. N. (1991). *Lower track classrooms: A curricular and cultural perspective.* New York: Teachers College Press.

Perrow, C. (1967). A framework for the comparative analysis of organizations. *American Sociological Review, 32,* 194–208.

Perry, P. G. (1999, August). *White means never having to say you're ethnic: A comparative ethnography in high schools of the construction of "White" as "cultureless".* Paper presented at the annual meeting of the American Sociological Association, Chicago.

Rubin, L. B. (1972). *Busing and backlash.* Berkeley: University of California Press.

Schofield, J. (1982). *Black and White in school: Trust, tension, or tolerance?* New York: Praeger.

Selznick, P. (1949). *TVA and the grassroots.* Berkeley: University of California Press

Siskin, L. S. (1994). *Realms of knowledge: Academic departments in secondary schools.* London: Falmer Press.

Siskin, L. S., & Little, J. W. (Eds.). (1995). *The subjects in question: Departmental organization and the high school.* New York: Teachers College Press.

Suter, L. (in press). *Guiding principles for mathematics and science education research methods: Report of a workshop.* Washington, DC: National Science Foundation.

Sutherland, E. H. (1937). *The professional thief.* Chicago: University of Chicago Press.

Swidler, A. (1979). *Organization without authority.* Cambridge, MA: Harvard University Press.

Sykes, G. (1958). *The society of captives: A study of a maximum security prison.* Princeton, NJ: Princeton University Press.

Talbert, J., & McLaughlin, M. W. (1993). Understanding teaching in context. In D. K. Cohen, M. W. McLaughlin, & J. Talbert (Eds.), *Teaching for understanding: Challenges for policy and practice* (pp. 167–206). San Francisco: Jossey-Bass.

Thomas, W. I., & Thomas, D. (1928). *The child in America.* New York: Knopf.

Thomas, W. I., & Znaniecki, F. (1927). *The Polish peasant in Europe and America.* New York: Knopf.

Tyson, K. (1999, August). *Notes from the back of the room: How tensions between schooling goals for Black students undermine learning and other problems of cultural coaching.* Paper presented at the annual meeting of the American Sociological Association, Chicago.

Valli, L. (1986). *Becoming clerical workers.* New York: Routledge.

Waller, W. (1932/1965). *The sociology of teaching.* New York: John Wiley.

Wax, R. (1971). *Doing fieldwork: Warnings and advice.* Chicago: University of Chicago Press.

Weis, L. (1990). *Working class without work: High school students in a de-industrializing economy.* New York: Routledge.

Willis, P. (1977). *Learning to labor: How working-class kids get working-class jobs.* New York: Columbia University Press.

Zorbaugh, H. W. (1929). *The Gold Coast and the slum.* Chicago: University of Chicago Press.

When Methods Matter: Qualitative Research Issues in Psychology

ANNIE G. ROGERS

Although psychology is a field in which methods matter a great deal, we psychologists have had an ambivalent and resistant relationship with qualitative research methods, lagging behind the other social sciences in acceptance and knowledge of qualitative research (Zeller & Farmer, 1999). Many psychologists question whether or not qualitative methods have a place in the field, rather than focusing on what psychology may have to learn from or contribute to qualitative methods (Maracek, Fine, & Kidder, 1997). This resistance on the part of psychologists is rooted in historical traditions, as well as contemporary misconceptions and obstacles. However, knowledgeable practitioners of qualitative research in psychology pose critical questions and challenges to the field and have begun to propose new standards of socially responsible research for both qualitative and quantitative researchers, research that represents human beings as whole persons living in dynamic, complex social arrangements. At the end of this century, these challenges arise primarily from social, developmental, and clinical psychologists, and have little affected mainstream research funding and publications. Despite the bleakness of this picture, psychology is in a key position to impact real-world problems such as violence in schools through qualitative research methods in which ethical, social, political, and psychological dimensions of human relationships, institutions, and societies are entwined aspects of inquiry. From this perspective, psychology has something unique to offer qualitative methods, and qualitative methods can help psychologists create more socially responsive research. Such research is socially responsible to the extent that it highlights and serves the needs of participants in research and their communities.

I come to this article as a psychologist trained as a clinician in the 1980s who is deeply versed in developmental traditions of psychology, as well as in psychometrics and statistics. I have been a poet and painter for most of my life and found much of my training in psychology akin to learning a foreign language. For the past twelve years I have explored and written about existing qualitative methods with colleagues and students (Rogers, Brown, & Tappan, 1993; Rogers, Casey, Holland, & Nakkula, 1996) and have created a new method, an Interpretive Poetics (Rogers, Casey, Ekert, Nakkula, & Sheinberg, 1999), that seeks to account for unconscious and relationally

Harvard Educational Review   Vol. 70   No. 1   Spring 2000, 75–85

contextualized knowledge in life narratives. I have also taught courses on research interviewing, feminist methodology, and developmental qualitative research.

A Plurality of Perspectives on Qualitative Research

It would be misleading to discuss any specific contributions of psychology to qualitative methods without first providing an overview of different and sometimes dissenting views within the field. These perspectives range from those who are resistant to qualitative methods, to those who view qualitative methods as a complementary adjunct to quantitative methods, to those who view qualitative methods as a unique paradigm of research that calls for a reconsideration of all research practices. I believe that there is real value in carefully designed quantitative research studies and that we have little reason to fear that such research is endangered.

Despite recent intentions to open the field to a plurality of methods (Jessor, 1996), psychology continues to pose formidable obstacles to the practice and publication of qualitative research. Some of this resistance is rooted in a long history of logical positivism, behaviorism, and psychometrics as foundational to a view of psychology as a legitimate science. These traditions make it difficult for those trained in psychology to imagine, much less embrace, the particular challenges and practices posed by qualitative researchers. For example, any first-year psychology student in a graduate program is well-versed in the ideology that psychological research must involve the use of precise measurement, the manipulation of variables (preferably in an experimental design), the articulation of specific hypotheses with the goal of empirically testing theory, and the use of passive voice construction in writing. Qualitative research, which might include observations as well as informal discussions or interviews with participants, might be tolerated in pilot research, but would hardly be encouraged as a reliable and valid source of knowledge (Henwood & Pidgeon, 1994).

For example, the guidelines of the American Psychological Association (APA) style manual (1994) run directly counter to most practices of writing and reflecting on qualitative research. Given the intention of promoting methodological pluralism in psychology, one might expect to see changes in the most recent edition of the APA manual; to the contrary, the only notable change for qualitative researchers has been the switching of the word "subjects" to "participants." Otherwise, the APA manual retains its role as upholding codified guidelines for producing research articles consistent with positivist ideology and methods of research. Specifically, these include "1. the use of objective, third person point of view; 2. emphasis on precision, with mathematics as a model; 3. avoidance of metaphors and other expressive uses of language; and, 4. support of claims with experimental, empirical evidence from nature" (Bazerman, 1984, pp. 1–2). Given the gatekeeping function of the APA manual for journal editors and for prospective authors and the "tortoise-pace that attends even the most innocuous of changes" (Zeller & Farmer, 1999, p. 16), I agree with Ruthellen Josselson and Amia Lieblich (1996) that the APA manual is effectively "fettering the mind in the name of science" (p. 651). These constraints are experienced acutely by qualitative researchers for whom doing and writing research are entwined strands of a creative, as well as scientific, enterprise.

Although Robert Elliot (1997) has provided a forum for discussing standards of qualitative research in psychology for several years, many qualitative researchers still find that they "have to sneak their work past watchful, APA-bound editors" (Zeller & Farmer, 1999, p. 4). Recently, however, a consortium of editors, particularly editors of mental health and child development journals, has begun to push for the publication of more qualitative research in APA journals. Predictably, there is a mixture of dissent and endorsement among these editors concerning whether or not to publish qualitative research articles (Azar, 1999). Some editors wonder how to review such research, while others simply wish to continue to publish exclusively quantitative studies.

While this situation may appear grim — with journal editors, research funders, and psychology departments acting as gatekeepers for acceptable research and creating formidable challenges to qualitative researchers — some psychologists see qualitative research as a complementary, valuable addition to quantitative methods in psychology.

There are at least three ways that these psychologists view qualitative and quantitative methods as complementary to one another. First of all, while qualitative methods provide information about contexts, meanings, and power relationships in data collection and analysis (Maracek, Fine, & Kidder, 1997), quantitative methods lead to an accumulation of knowledge that is acontextual but empirically precise (Jessor, 1996). Secondly, some psychologists view qualitative methods as suitable for a process of discovery or hypothesis generation, while quantitative methods are seen as ideal for testing hypotheses through a process of verification (Grolnick, Cole, Laurenitis, & Schwartzman, 1990). In a third instance of a complementary understanding, some psychologists view qualitative methods as better designed to uncover individual psychological meanings, while quantitative methods, with their larger sample sizes and use of statistical procedures, are seen as the best choice for understanding group trends (Krahn, Hohn, & Kime, 1995).

Another group of psychologists, and I include myself here, see qualitative research not as a supplement, but as a separate paradigm that raises critical questions about what it means to conduct good and socially responsible psychological research, irrespective of whether the methods are primarily numerical or textual. Erica Burman (1997) specifically cautions against "using arguments for qualitative research that dilute its critical edge by allowing it to be assimilated into quantitative approaches" (p. 787). She argues instead that qualitative research methods do not simply extend or complement quantitative methods, but create different representations of the world and challenge some of the limits and sometimes abuses of positivist research studies.

Historical and Contemporary Trends of Qualitative Research in Psychology

Paradoxically, though the current dominant paradigm in psychology eschews qualitative research, it does so despite the fact that major historical contributions to the field were discovered through qualitative case studies. For example, William James captured the spirit of qualitative research in the fledgling field of psychology in terms of an attempt to understand "the varieties of the human mind in living action" (1901/

1994, p. 114). Clinical case studies were responsible for the founding insights of psychoanalysis (Breuer & Freud, 1885/1955), the description of psychosocial stages of human development and identity formation (Erikson, 1958, 1963), and the conceptualization of developmental structures in childhood play and moral thought (Piaget, 1948). From the 1930s to the 1960s, a major impetus to explore the psychology of individual lives came from the personology[1] of Henry Murray (1938) and his students such as Robert White (1952). Gordon Allport and his colleagues (1937, 1967) were similarly influential and productive during this time, with their interests in idiographic methods and personal documents. In the 1930s, John Dollard (1937) conducted qualitative field-based research on race relations in the South, and after World War II, Kurt Lewin (1948) studied group processes using qualitative methods. Muzafer and Carolyn Sherif and their colleagues (Sherif, Harvey, White, Hood, & Sherif, 1961) explored the rivalries of boys in summer camp in the 1950s and 1960s using qualitative methods of inquiry. In the 1970s and 1980s, psychology was challenged and influenced by qualitative work on individual lives, institutional and social structures, psychobiographies, and group histories (Block, 1971; Elder, 1974; Fine, 1983; Gilligan, 1982/1993; Josselson, 1973, 1978; McAdams, 1988; Runyan, 1982). This kind of work has grown so significantly during the 1990s, particularly in terms of feminist and multicultural challenges to psychological theory, that it is impossible to cite all the relevant literature (see, for example, from 1992 alone: Brown & Gilligan, 1992; Kidder, 1992; Wetherell & Potter, 1992). While this brief review is by no means definitive or exhaustive, the main point is that psychological theory has gained a great deal from qualitative methods historically, despite its ambivalence about such methods.

Recent Contributions to Qualitative Methodology
by Psychologists

In this section I have chosen to profile the work of seven oft-cited psychological researchers to show some of the ways that psychology has contributed to shaping qualitative methods.[2]

In contemporary psychology, Jerome Bruner (1986) authorizes a narrative approach to psychology through what he calls "narrative modes of knowing." He provides a crucial framework for the psychological study of individual autobiographies, stories, and lives. Narrative modes of knowing privilege the particular details of lived experience. In narratives, meanings are constructed through social discourse, and events or stories are situated in particular contexts. Narrative modes of knowing are constructed simultaneously on at least two levels in psychological research: by the individual who creates a story of her or his life, and by the researcher who bridges an understanding of this particular person's story with another narrative of interpretive analysis. For example, a child may tell an interviewer a story about an early memory, but a researcher might interpret that story by comparing it to other stories of early memories told by children of differing ages to understand how children construct memories developmentally.

Elliot Mishler (1996) further clarifies the importance of a narrative approach to the study of human development. Criticizing the overwhelming reliance on group means and trends used by developmental psychologists, he argues that such "inferences lead to an idealized, universal child" (p. 78). The child represented by a group mean is no child in particular, yet is "redefined as the real reality" (p. 78). Noting repeated disparities between the findings of individual case studies and population-based methods in developmental psychology, Mishler argues for the combined use of case-based methods with longitudinal analysis of temporally ordered sequences. Mishler sees case-based methods as a scientific form of inquiry that restores agency and respect to individuals by treating people as subjects with histories and intentions.

Louise Kidder and Michelle Fine (1997) highlight the merits of qualitative approaches for understanding human beings fully and accurately, and they emphasize the ethics of research in developing a critical psychology. They describe how qualitative methods have been used in their own research and by other researchers to show how race, class, and gender shape lived experience. Kidder and Fine also challenge qualitative researchers to assert interpretive authority over their data, rather than assuming that the voices of participants speak for themselves in some uncritical way. They, like other feminist and critical researchers, argue that qualitative research offers an opportunity to analyze "the nuanced strategies by which power operates through individual and collective psychologies" (Kidder & Fine, 1997, p. 37).

Carol Gilligan's (1982/1993) understanding of voice as central to the creation of a relational psychology provides an important framework for qualitative researchers interested in narrative and human development. Voice is relational by definition, because speaking depends upon being listened to and heard. Gilligan and her colleagues, particularly Lyn Brown, provide a voice-centered method for analyzing interview data, a *Listener's Guide* (Brown & Gilligan, 1992; Brown et al., 1988; Gilligan, Brown, & Rogers, 1989; Rogers, Brown, & Tappan, 1993), in which a researcher listens to an interview through multiple, overlapping layers of analysis, discerning multiple voices in a single text. This feminist method has provided a critical framework for reconsideration of gender and human development.[3]

Ruthellen Josselson (1994) elaborates on a way of working with narrative data that she calls "imagining the real" (p. 28). Drawing on the work of Martin Buber, who understood imagining the real as considering "what the other is wishing, feeling, perceiving, and thinking" (Buber, 1965, p. 70, cited in Josselson, 1994, p. 28), Josselson takes an active stance of empathy in her analysis of narratives. Using Mikhail Bakhtin's (1986) theory of the novel, a groundbreaking view of the individual as existing on multiple planes simultaneously, Josselson explicates her notion of "the dialogic self." To trace the growth or development of a whole person, she argues, "we must find those places in narrative where self is most clearly in dialogue with itself" (Josselson, 1994, p. 37). In contrast to the simple recitation of a known story, Josselson sees these dialogic moments in interviews as turning points in meaning-making that are part of a process of developmental unfolding.

Taken together, these methodological examples that contemporary psychologists bring to qualitative research point toward critical, careful, and rigorous analyses of narrative data that can empirically inform psychological theory, particularly developmental theory. These various approaches to narrative research locate agency and interpretive authority in research participants, reflect on the relationship between researchers and participants, and engage multiple readings and frameworks in data analysis.

Evolution in Qualitative Research:
A Personal Response and a New Method

I can identify a topography of change in four distinct concerns raised by qualitative researchers. Each of these concerns informs the development of a new method of qualitative analysis I created recently with a team of doctoral students, an Interpretive Poetics (Rogers, Casey, Ekert, Nakkula, & Sheinberg, 1999; Rogers, Casey, Ekert, & Holland, 1999), so I will discuss them together.

The first of these concerns is the subjectivity of *both* researchers and participants, commonly noted by qualitative researchers as though a critical recognition alone was a sufficient answer to this concern. Reframing subjectivity in qualitative research as common psychological processes through which both participants and researchers experience and interpret their worlds, my colleagues and I identify four "truths" derived from psychology about human experience. These truths shape the way we understand and problematize subjectivity: 1) human knowledge is relational in nature (Gilligan, 1996); 2) cognitive understanding is constructed almost entirely through figurative processes and metaphors (Gibbs, 1994; Lakoff & Johnson, 1998); 3) most of our knowledge is unconscious (Lakoff & Johnson, 1998) and our minds work through dynamic unconscious processes that can be traced in data; and 4) our interpretations are inherently embodied and reflect the ways the mind and memory work at a neurological level, as well as the ways gender, development, and culture shape everyday recollections and interpretations (Pillemer, 1998). Our Interpretive Poetics method draws on these four truths as we consider how language and research relationships are constructed in a process of psychological and developmental inquiry (Rogers, Casey, Ekert, & Holland, 1999).

The second area of change, the artistic potential of qualitative research, has been raised by an increasing number of qualitative researchers (for example, Lawrence-Lightfoot & Davis, 1997). Elliot Eisner's questions about qualitative methods and artistic process are particularly long-standing and incisive. In a recent address to the American Educational Research Association, he asked, "Can we have our evidentiary base and still maintain the sometimes imaginative and poetic quality of well-crafted qualitative research?" (Eisner, 1997, p. 269). My students and I asked ourselves this very question as we sat together reading rich and startlingly poetic children's narratives of memory, imagination, and relationships. Our answer to this question was to create an artistic method of analysis based on the variation and multiplicity of images and sounds characteristic of the best poetry. Our method is not merely artistic, but is comprised of multiple layers that specify explicit practices of analysis using evidence from language data for their construction. These layers include restorying, relational dynamics, languages of the unsayable, and figurative thought in language contrasts (see Rogers, Casey, Ekert, Nakkula, & Sheinberg, 1999, for a full description).

Both Eisner (1997) and Mishler (1996) raise critical questions about how researchers should critically evaluate qualitative interpretations, and I see this as a growing edge of concern among qualitative researchers, and also certainly a persistent question among editors of psychology journals who are friendly toward qualitative work but do not know how to evaluate it (Azar, 1999). In Interpretive Poetics, data analysis is continuously evaluated through evidence and alternative interpretations. Each layer of the analysis refines and potentially calls into question interpretations made when working within any previous layer, so that a viable interpretation builds over an intensive analytic process that is open to question and revision (Rogers, Casey, Ekert, & Holland, 1999).

For example, in the analysis of languages of the unsayable, those negations, revisions, erasures, and smokescreens that surround what is actually said in an interview mark everything ten-year-old David[4] conveys about his experience of family life. While this dimension of the Interpretive Poetics represents only one level of analysis, it builds upon the interviewer's earlier analysis of her relationship with David as connected and close, and both amplifies and modifies that description. This way of working allows the researcher to build and check interpretations carefully and invites artistry in writing. As David talks with his interviewer, Jenny, he uses a language of revision in two ways: to correct accounts of past events ("My uncle had to walk [my] dog[s], no, he had to feed them") and to undo previously expressed knowledge ("My dad and mom stopped hitting me like last year . . . [but] just, you see, my mom still hits me"). Tracing a language of revisions, one of the languages of the unsayable, through these excerpts helps to understand David's process of remembering and reconstructing events, of selecting details and impressions. This analysis also provides hints about knowledge that may be difficult, or perhaps impossible, for David to hold and to speak when he is ten years old, talking about life in his family, in a particular relationship.

Finally, in my conversations with psychologists doing qualitative research, we find ourselves asking increasingly about how to build theory from qualitative research, rather than allowing each qualitative study to stand alone, as if entire onto itself, too often lacking any coherent theory (R. Josselson, personal communication, March 1998). Working with an Interpretive Poetics requires a researcher to situate her or his interpretive questions (made explicit in each layer of the analysis) in relation to broader research questions, and in relation to a theoretical framework that may be challenged or modified in the process of using the method. Teaching this method at the Harvard University Graduate School of Education for the first time, I saw students learn to make linkages among research questions, the four layers of the analytic process, and an unfolding theoretical story about their own qualitative data. This method, itself in a process of evolution, seeks to clarify how cross-case analyses can be used to build theoretically compelling stories of human development.

The real promise of qualitative methods in psychology — why such methods must matter, despite current obstacles to publication — lies in the potential of a qualitative paradigm of psychological research to represent human beings as whole persons living in particular social and cultural contexts. People are unconscious of much of their experience, internally contradictory, embedded in relationships through which self and world are continuously interpreted and revised, sometimes overwhelmed by wordless suffering that researchers are challenged to hear, yet ultimately knowledgeable about their own lives and cultures. Qualitative research methods can accurately portray human beings engaged in and shaped by such complex psychological processes.

Notes

1. Personology was an attempt to understand how particular personality traits were influenced positively and negatively by social values and personal history, using methods specifically designed for the study of individuals rather than groups, such as the Thematic Apperception Test.
2. The selection of qualitative researchers is by no means exhaustive or exemplary of all contributions to qualitative methods in psychology, nor do I intend to review the whole of any person's work in qualitative methods.
3. While feminist methodology, a well-developed area within qualitative research, is beyond the scope of this brief review, the *Listener's Guide* functions as a feminist method by actively resisting traditional methods of categorizing girls' and women's narratives.
4. David, a Caucasian boy, is a participant in my longitudinal study of children's conceptions of memory and relationships, called "Telling All One's Heart."

References

Allport, G. (1937). *Personality: A psychological interpretation.* New York: Holt.

Allport, G. (1967). Gordon W. Allport. In E. Boring & G. Lindzey (Eds.), *A history of psychology in autobiography* (vol. 5, pp. 1–25). New York: Appleton-Century-Crofts.

American Psychological Association. (1994). *Publication manual of the American Psychological Association* (4th ed.). Washington, DC: Author.

Azar, B. (1999, February). *Consortium of editors pushes shift in child research method.* Available at <http://www.apa.org/monitor/feb99/qual.html>.

Bakhtin, M. (1986). *Speech genres and other late essays.* Austin: University of Texas Press.

Bazerman, G. (1984). Modern evolution of the experimental approach in physics: Spectroscopic articles in *Physical Review,* 1893–1980. *Social Studies in Science, 14,* 163–196.

Block, J. (1971). *Lives through time.* Berkeley, CA: Bancroft Books.

Breuer, J., & Freud, S. (1955). *Studies on hysteria.* In *Standard Edition 2* (J. Strachey, Ed. & Trans.). London: Hogarth Press. (Original work published 1885)

Brown, L., Argyris, D., Attanucci, J., Bardige, B., Gilligan, C., Johnson, K., Miller, B., Osborne, D., Tappan, M., Ward, J., Wiggins, G., & Wilcox, D. (1988). *A guide to reading narratives of conflict and choice for self and moral voice.* Unpublished manuscript.

Brown, L., & Gilligan, C. (1992). *Meeting at the crossroads: Women's psychology and girls' development.* Cambridge, MA: Harvard University Press.

Bruner, J. (1986). *Actual minds, possible worlds.* Cambridge, MA: Harvard University Press.

Buber, M. (1965). *The knowledge of man.* New York: HarperCollins.

Burman, E. (1997). Minding the gap: Positivism, psychology, and the politics of qualitative methods. *Journal of Social Issues, 53,* 785–801.

Dollard, J. (1937). *Caste and class in a southern town.* Garden City, NY: Doubleday.

Eisner, E. (1997). The new frontier in qualitative research methodology. *Qualitative Inquiry, 3,* 259–273.

Elder, G. (1974). *Children of the great depression.* Chicago: University of Chicago Press.

Elliot, R. (1997, March). Qualitative guidelines. Available at <fac0029@unoffol.utoledo. edu>.

Erikson, E. (1958). *Young man Luther.* New York: Norton.

Erikson, E. (1963). *Childhood and society* (2nd ed.). New York: Norton.

Fine, M. (1983). Coping with rape: Critical perspectives on consciousness. *Imagination, Cognition, and Personality: A Scientific Study of Consciousness, 3,* 249–264.

Gibbs, R. (1994). *The poetics of mind: Figurative thought, language, and understanding.* New York: Cambridge University Press.

Gilligan, C. (1993). *In a different voice*. Cambridge, MA: Harvard University Press. (Original work published 1982)

Gilligan, C. (1996). The centrality of relationship in human development: A puzzle, some evidence, and a theory. In G. Noam & K. Fischer (Eds.), *Development and vulnerability in close relationships* (pp. 237–261). Mahwah, NJ: Lawrence Erlbaum.

Gilligan, C., Brown, L., & Rogers, A. (1989). Psyche embedded: A place for body, relationships and culture in personality theory. In A. Rabin, R. Zucker, R. Emmons, & S. Frank (Eds.), *Studying persons and lives* (pp. 86–147). New York: Springer.

Grolnick, W., Cole, R., Laurenitis, L., & Schwartzman, P. (1990). Playing with fire: A developmental assessment of children's fire understanding and experience. *Journal of Clinical Child Psychology, 19*, 128–135.

Henwood, K., & Pidgeon, N. (1994). Beyond the qualitative paradigm: A framework for introducing diversity within qualitative psychology. *Journal of Community and Applied Social Psychology, 4*, 225–238.

James, W. (1994). *The varieties of religious experience: A study in human nature*. New York: Modern Library. (Original work published 1901)

Jessor, R. (1996). Ethnographic methods in contemporary perspective. In R. Jessor, A. Colby, & R. Schweder (Eds.), *Ethnography and human development* (pp. 3–14). Chicago: Chicago University Press.

Josselson, R. (1973). Psychodynamic aspects of identity formation in college women. *Journal of Youth and Adolescence, 2*, 3–52.

Josselson, R. (1978). *Finding herself: Pathways to identity development in women*. San Francisco: Jossey-Bass.

Josselson, R. (1994). Imagining the real: Empathy, narrative, and the dialogic self. *Narrative Study of Lives, 4*, 27–44.

Josselson, R., & Lieblich, A. (1996). Fettering the mind in the name of "science." *American Psychologist, 51*, 651–652.

Kidder, L. (1992). Requirements for being "Japanese": Stories of refugees. *International Journal of Intercultural Relations, 16*, 383–393.

Kidder, L., & Fine, M. (1997). Qualitative inquiry in psychology: A radical tradition. In D. Fox & I. Prilleltensky (Eds.), *Critical psychology: An introduction* (pp. 34–50). Thousand Oaks, CA: Sage.

Krahn, G., Hohn, M., & Kime, C. (1995). Incorporating qualitative approaches into clinical child psychology research. *Journal of Clinical Child Psychology, 24*, 204–213.

Lakoff, G., & Johnson, M. (1998). *Philosophy in the flesh: The embodied mind and its challenge to western thought*. Boston: Basic Books.

Lawrence-Lightfoot, S., & Davis, J. (1997). *The art and science of portraiture*. San Francisco: Jossey-Bass.

Lewin, K. (1948). *Resolving social conflicts: Selected papers on group dynamics*. New York: Harper & Row.

Maracek, J., Fine, M., & Kidder, L. (1997). Working between worlds: Qualitative methods and social psychology. *Journal of Social Issues, 15*, 631–644.

McAdams, D. (1988). *Power, intimacy and the life story*. New York: Guilford.

Mishler, E. (1996). Missing persons: Recovering developmental stories/histories. In R. Jessor, A. Colby, & R. Schweder (Eds.), *Ethnography and human development: context and meaning in social inquiry* (pp. 73–99). Chicago: Chicago University Press.

Murray, H. (1938). *Explorations in personality*. New York: Oxford University Press.

Piaget, J. (1948). *The moral judgement of the child* (M. Gabain, Trans.). Glencoe, IL: Free Press.

Pillemer, D. (1998). *Momentous events, vivid memories: How unforgettable moments help us understand the meaning of our lives*. Cambridge, MA: Harvard University Press.

Rogers, A., Brown, L., & Tappan, M. (1993). Interpreting ego development in girls: Regression or resistance? *Narrative Study of Lives, 2*, 1–36.

Rogers, A., Casey, M., Holland, J., & Nakkula, V. (1996). Developmental research as an intervention in children's lives. *Journal of Child and Youth Care Work, 11,* 95–104.

Rogers, A., Casey, M., Ekert, J., & Holland, J. (1999). *An interpretive poetics: A method for analyzing interview and written data in qualitative research.* Unpublished manuscript.

Rogers, A., Casey, M., Ekert, J., Nakkula, V., & Sheinberg, N. (1999). An interpretive poetics of languages of the unsayable. *Narrative Study of Lives, 6,* 77–106.

Runyan, M. (1982). In defense of the case study method. *American Journal of Orthopsychiatry, 52,* 440–446.

Sherif, M., Harvey, O., White, B., Hood, W., & Sherif, C. (1961). *Intergroup conflict and cooperation: The robbers' cave experiment.* Norman, OK: University Book Exchange.

Wetherell, M., & Potter, J. (1992). *Mapping the language of racism.* Hemel Hempstead, Eng.: Harvester Wheatsheaf.

White, R. (1952). *Lives in progress.* New York: Holt, Rinehart & Winston.

Zeller, N., & Farmer, F. (1999). "Catchy, clever titles are not acceptable": Style, APA, and qualitative reporting. *Qualitative Studies in Education, 12,* 3–19.

I wish to thank Lynn Sorsoli for her help in collecting many of the qualitative methods articles for this review, and Paula White for sending me additional references in Ireland. Thanks also to Ide O'Carroll for inspiration about the title.

Knowing Teaching:
The Intersection of Research on
Teaching and Qualitative Research

MAGDALENE LAMPERT

Educational researchers struggle incessantly with the relationship between knowledge and action. What does it mean to do scholarship in an applied field? What methodologies are appropriate to capture the problems of the field? Are these practitioners' problems? Are they problems worthy of scholarly inquiry? What is the relevance of the findings of scholarly research for improving practice? In wrestling with these questions, educational research and qualitative research have intertwined and influenced one another, raising issues that mix content questions with methodological problems. In the halls of academe, questions about voice, about the relationship between the researcher and the researched, and about the relevance of scholarship to the solution of social problems have always been high on the agendas of both qualitative research and educational research. In the corners where educational research attends to teaching, these questions have been particularly prominent.

What Is Research on Teaching?

I started teaching in the 1960s, inspired by contemporary commentaries about what was wrong with schools. Among the most influential of these commentaries were stories about teaching written in the first person by reformers who taught school to find out what was going on there and what could be done about it.[1] My experience as a teacher in an urban high school confirmed what I had been reading. But, when I turned from classroom teaching to the academic study of teaching in 1978, I discovered that books like these were not found on the assigned reading lists in my graduate school courses. Only in a history seminar did I encounter some writing about practice by teachers from the 1920s and 1930s, teachers who started schools, designed curricula, and studied children.[2] In the contemporary writing about teaching that I was assigned, the teacher's voice was not to be heard.

I am not the only one who has been puzzling about the teacher's role in research on teaching. In *Educational Researcher*, the monthly journal of the American Educational Research Association (AERA), the question of who in the research community speaks

Harvard Educational Review   Vol. 70   No. 1   Spring 2000, 86–99

appropriately of teaching and how they should go about studying practice has been raised repeatedly over the last decade.[3] Most recently, Gary Anderson and Kathryn Herr examined the problem of making room for "rigorous practitioner knowledge" in schools and universities.[4] They pointed to the classic relationship between professional knowledge and "systematic knowledge produced by schools of higher learning" as one of the sticking points in defining appropriate methods of research on teaching, as well as in determining who is qualified to do it. As scholars argue about both the purposes and the validity of research on teaching, the question of who should do research on teaching spills over into questions about method and mixes with assertions about appropriate genres for reporting research. Is research on teaching a scholarly effort to understand a complex practice? Is it only of interest if applying it produces student learning? Is it an instrumental project, identifying problems, proposing solutions, and testing them in practice? Is it meant to produce knowledge for teachers? Or for those who prepare teachers? Or for those who control teachers' working conditions?

In the midst of all these questions, not only paradigms but also products and venues for communicating findings have proliferated. The AERA established a new division (Division K) for research on "Teaching and Teacher Education" in June 1984. It quickly became the largest division in the association, with seven different sections. From a practitioner's perspective, the boundaries among the sections are somewhat puzzling: one deals with research on teaching "subject matter," one with research on "collaborative or partnership settings" for teaching, one with research on teaching in multicultural settings, and one with research on "teaching and learning in the contexts of teachers' work," which is further divided into a subsection for pedagogical aspects and a subsection for organizational aspects. A separate section is devoted to "self-study and practitioner inquiry and scholarship on teachers and teaching."[5] In all of the sections of Division K, research is "construed broadly to include but not be limited to, philosophical, historical, ecological, ethnographic, descriptive, correlational, or experimental studies." Research on teaching and qualitative research have grown and developed together, and the hodgepodge that has resulted from their interaction has become an institution.

Teacher Research

One element in this jumble of practice-focused inquiry stands out as especially worthy of commentary. The formal addition of practitioners to the community of researchers on teaching, indicated by their inclusion in the AERA as well as other scholarly institutions, seems to raise the most interesting questions for qualitative research. The shift from thinking of research as something that is done *on* teachers to a kind of work that is done *by* teachers could not have happened without the concurrent growth in appreciation of the contributions of qualitative research to the field of educational scholarship in recent years. In the 1970s, qualitative research helped to open educational research to questions of meaning, perspective, ownership, and purpose, and into this opening came teacher research.

Teachers have become participants in academic communities of research in several different ways. Some who make their living by teaching full time in K-12 schools conduct inquiry in their own and in one another's classrooms.[6] Others collaborate with university researchers while retaining their teaching positions, contributing the perspective of daily practice to the questions under study.[7] In a few cases, teachers regard inquiry to be part of their day-to-day work in classrooms. In other cases, it is one among many opportunities for "professional development," offered alongside summer institutes on subject matter, workshops on classroom management techniques, and conference sessions on new curricula. And then there are faculty members of colleges and universities who choose to teach in K-12 schools as a means to create a site for pursuing investigations of practice.[8] Some teach part of every day, others teach full time for a year or more. A multitude of books and articles are produced by this conglomeration of practitioners, some published in academic presses and journals, some in popular media. A few hybrid presses and journals have emerged that would be hard to identify as one or the other, and which count a majority of teachers among their authors. Conferences are devoted to teacher research, and funding agencies are making money available to support it.[9] The genres used to convey the findings of teacher research are as varied as the ways in which this work is structured.

Issues Raised for Qualitative Research by Teacher Research

Teacher research raises numerous issues for scholars who do qualitative research. Here I will consider only three: the potential for teacher research to change ideas about who is responsible for producing professional knowledge, the benefits and dangers of inserting the self into social science, and the challenges of presenting the problems of a practice from inside that practice.

Professional Responsibility

If teachers are doing research on their own practice, might they assume a central role in professional knowledge production? If teaching problems were considered to be the responsibility of the profession, rather than private trials for individuals to endure or mechanical defects for outsiders to repair, a great deal of expertise could be mustered in the service of improving practice. Such a move would redefine power relationships between practitioners and researchers, and raise questions about what nonpractitioners have to add to the "knowledge base." Practitioners doing research on practice could change the kinds of questions that are asked and the new understanding that is produced. If teachers write about their work from the inside, including both personal and professional perspectives on the problems of practice, their work could substantially alter what we now think of as appropriate conventions in the discourse of applied research.[10] As they communicated about their inquiry, teachers would develop a new syntax and a new semantics to add to those of the academic disciplines in the study of educational phenomena. Just as sociologists, anthropologists, and psychologists now both use and modify a variety of qualitative methods, practitioners would test and contribute to the development of these approaches to producing new knowledge.

Although appealing, looked at through an outsider's lens, this scenario is not without its problems. One of them has to do with where we draw the line between research and thoughtful practice. As Ken Zeichner has asked, "Is it proper to call it research when teachers examine their practice in a systematic and intentional manner?"[11] I will not take on that issue here, as Zeichner has already done so, and he is more qualified to give it adequate treatment than I. Another problem has to do with the social arrangements around teaching that tend to stifle inquiry. Creating a professional discourse in teaching has been a persistent challenge in the United States. In 1975, Dan Lortie wrote:

> The preparation of teachers does not seem to result in the analytic turn of mind one finds in other occupations whose members are trained in colleges and universities. . . . One hears little mention of the disciplines of observation, comparison, rules of inference, sampling, testing hypotheses through treatment and so forth. Scientific modes of reasoning and pedagogical practice seem compartmentalized; I observed this even among science teachers. This intellectual segregation puzzles me; those in other kinds of "people work" (e.g. clinical psychology, psychiatry, social work) seem more inclined to connect clinical issues with scientific modes of thought. This separation is relevant because it militates against the development of an effective technical culture and because its absence means that conservative doctrines receive less factual challenge; each teacher is encouraged to have a personal version of teaching truth.[12]

In the past twenty-five years, many questions have been raised about the value and character of "the scientific method." But the problem that Lortie calls "intellectual segregation" persists among teachers, as does the rarity of observation, comparison, rules of inference, sampling, and testing hypotheses through treatment.[13] What Lortie calls "a personal version of teaching truth" continues to exist for most teachers alongside of and often untouched by the "teaching truths" that are produced by university researchers.[14] No professional language for describing and analyzing practice has developed in the United States, even as teachers reject the descriptions and analyses of scholars.[15] This deficit is particularly alarming when it is considered in light of recent psychological and linguistic work on the relationships between shared language, the development of understanding, and problem-solving activity.[16] It is notable that teacher educators are not drawn from the ranks of accomplished teachers and that "practice teaching" is rarely conducted as the kind of apprenticeship that doctors and lawyers experience as they work on practical problems together with more experienced members of their intended profession. What this means is that the language of practice remains flat or nonexistent.

That teachers do not learn simply by engaging in collaborative professional inquiry has as much to do with the structure of their work as it does with a disposition toward privacy and intuition. Currently, few teachers in the United States have the time and space in their work lives to think about the dynamics of teaching, let alone the resources to document their work and study the problems of their practice. Collaborations among practitioners to work on the problems of practice are considered "luxuries," rather than essential components of the work, as they would be in other professions such as medical or legal practice.[17] In Japan, by contrast, the structure of professional development in teaching is built on the assumption that teaching is a collaborative process rather than a private enterprise, and that it is improved through teachers' collaborative inquiry, including peer planning of curriculum and instruction.[18] In K-12 classrooms, Japanese teachers regularly teach "research lessons" to their students that are designed, recorded, and discussed by groups of practitioners working together on a particular problem of curriculum and instruction. Such work — which occurs at the school and district level as well as in national professional organizations — is thought not only to improve classroom practice, but also to connect classroom practice to broader educational goals and to explore conflicting ideas. Similarly, in China, a decades-long tradition and a well-articulated structure has new and experienced teachers collaborating in inquiry and practical problem-solving.[19] In the United Kingdom, a strong tradition of "action research" by teachers began in the 1960s and continues today.[20] The teachers who produce and communicate knowledge of teaching in these cultures are not a special brand of "teacher researchers," they do what they do as part of their everyday practice, accepting the study of teaching and the solving of its problems as a professional responsibility.

Although the structural supports for it are still weak, teacher research on practice seems to be gaining ground. As teachers talk at conferences and write for their peers, they are beginning to create a genre of professional inquiry. As scholars who teach make their teaching experiments available for common investigation, they develop a shared text for analysis by others and a language of conceptual frames based in practice. This work is part of a modest but growing set of complementary institutional efforts, including teachers' collaborative assessment of student work, district-level teacher research groups, professional development schools, and the presentation of practice for assessment by fellow teachers in teacher portfolios, all of which might qualify as forms of "qualitative research." As these new professional venues become opportunities for teachers to conduct inquiry and communicate their findings, how will their work be regarded in relation to the larger picture of "knowledge production"? Should practitioners' research meet the same standards of method as scholarly research? If they invent their own methods, will these methods make their way into academic discourse? Should they?

Bringing the Self into Scholarly Activity

Writing academic texts in the first person is a current trend in many of the social sciences. Teacher research is but one small example of this phenomenon, but it gives qualitative researchers in education a context in which to examine the potential and the problems of this kind of writing. There are at least three issues of interest to qualitative researchers that arise from getting the self into a central position in research on teaching: the potential and pitfalls of autobiographical narrative as a scholarly genre; the capacity to uncover invisible, relational aspects of the work that have not been recognized by outsiders; and the mixture of responsibility and analysis that such work entails. In 1985, as a justification for writing about my teaching in the first person as a form of scholarship, I argued:

> Who the teacher is has a great deal to do with both the way she defines problems and what can and will be done about them. The academician solves problems that are recognized in some universal way as being important, whereas a teacher's problems arise because the state of affairs in the classroom is not what she wants it to be. Thus, practical problems, in contrast to theoretical ones, involve someone's wish for

a change and the will to make it. Even though the teacher may be influenced by many powerful sources outside herself, the responsibility to act lies within. Like the researcher and the theoretician, she identifies problems and imagines solutions to them, but her job involves the additional personal burden of doing something about these problems in the classroom and living with the consequences of her actions over time. Thus, by way of acknowledging this deeply personal dimension of teaching practice, I have chosen not only to present the particular details of [other] teachers' problems, but to draw one of these problems from my own experience.[21]

In the 1980s, research on teacher thinking expanded to include the teacher's voice alongside the researcher's, as scholars sought to understand why practitioners act the way they do. In naming the teacher thinking that this approach revealed as "practical knowledge," researchers like Freema Elbaz, Jean Clandinin, and Michael Connelly raised new epistemological questions, as well as new questions about what sorts of research methods were appropriate for the study of teaching.

Another way to bring teachers' voices into the research literature has occurred through the publication of autobiographical narratives, but several scholars have advised proceeding cautiously with this approach. In a keynote address to the International Study Association on Teacher Thinking in 1995, Ivor Goodson observed that it was dangerous to believe "that merely by allowing people to 'narrate' that we in any serious way give them voice and agency."[22] Goodson quotes Cynthia Chamber's review of Connelly and Clandinin's book, *Teachers as Curriculum Planners: Narratives of Experience:*

> These authors offer us the naive hope that if teachers learn "to tell and understand their own story" they will be returned to their rightful place at the center of curriculum planning and reform. And yet, their method leaves each teacher a "blackbird singing in the dead of night"; isolated, and sadly ignorant of how his/her song is part of a much larger singing of the world.[23]

He notes as well that Kathy Carter celebrated the insertion of teachers' voices into educational research in 1993, but she also observed:

> For those of us telling stories in our work, we will not serve the community well if we sanctify story-telling work and build an epistemology on it to the point that we simply substitute one paradigmatic domination for another without challenging the domination itself. We must, then, become much more self-conscious than we have been in the past about the issues involved in narrative and story, such as interpretation, authenticity, normative value, and what our purposes are for telling stories in the first place.[24]

Working in the fields of psychology and sociology, Louise Kidder and Michelle Fine have made similar critical comments about the celebration of the insider's narrative. They assert that is it is the responsibility of researchers who stand outside the context of practice to "assert interpretive authority," placing the actor's story in relation to other actors and the world of ideas. Citing Joyce Ladner's commentaries on race research, they observe, "For Ladner, the very point of conducting social research is to interrupt the 'common sense' frames, ideologically driven by social arrangements or what she calls 'the system,' and to provide alternative lenses for viewing social behavior."[25] Kidder and Fine suggest that multiple lenses of this sort are possible and desirable in researchers' interpretations of practitioners' stories: they call this work "kaleidoscopic."

How we regard the personal in teacher research is both a practical and a deeply epistemological question, forcing us back to the enduring puzzles educational researchers deal with about how to relate what is learned from a single "case" in all its complexity to other situations in which similar problems arise. What does it mean for problems that arise for particular people in particular contexts to be similar across settings? What additional skill or knowledge does a practitioner, or for that matter a scholar, need to have to take knowledge from one case into another?

The Problem of Representation

Once you know teaching from the inside, how do you communicate what you know so that there can be an accumulation of knowledge in the field? Writing about first-person teacher research in mathematics education, Deborah Ball goes beyond the importance of inserting the teacher's voice into the discourse of teaching and raises questions about the nature of autobiographical argument: on what basis are claims made by first-person writers, and on what evidence do readers accept them? Ball observes that teachers writing about teaching force us to ask what we mean by "truth" and to examine the writer's purposes as we define it. She draws on Ruth Behar's work, which describes the changing discourse of anthropology to emphasize that autobiographical scholarly writing is more difficult than more familiar academic argument. Behar issues a caution to which all who are involved in such projects would be wise to attend:

> As is the case with any intellectual trend, some experiments work out better than others. It is far from easy to locate oneself in one's own text. Writing vulnerably takes as much skill, nuance, and willingness to follow through on the ramifications of a complicated idea as writing invulnerably and distantly. I would say it takes greater skill.[26]

Why would the teacher researcher be "writing vulnerably"? What is it about this kind of writing that requires so much skill, given that it is the telling of one's own story? As a teacher writing about my own teaching, I certainly have access to special knowledge, but at the same time, I am constrained by the limitations of any medium to express the multiple aspects of what I know. Although it is my aim to retain the richness and complexity of what is going on in what I write about my teaching, being in the middle of it makes me painfully aware of the impossibility of telling the whole story. Language, even supplemented by other media, is simply inadequate to capture my experience and knowledge of teaching practice. It is inadequate even to capture all of the aspects of an event, to say nothing of representing the constellations of feelings and intentions imbedded in that event. That I can have more of a sense of the whole of what is going on than any observer is both a blessing and a curse when I try to write about it.

Practice is doing. As I have argued, the study of practice thus begins in the setting in which a particular practitioner acts. To study practice means that I cannot succeed by limiting the focus of my inquiry, since a limited focus hinders practical problem-solving. Yet, in the course of attempting to tell about any practice, even if the telling is in the first person, one necessarily formalizes what has been learned, leaving out some aspects of the experience and highlighting others. It is not only the outsider who can bring what Kidder and Fine call "kaleidoscopic interpretations." For any inquiry into one's own practice, there are many possible stories to tell. For every story that is told, there are many possible meanings to interpret. Stories about practice are not mirrors of experience: like all texts, they are constructed by the author with certain intentions in mind.[27] When one is writing about oneself, no description seems adequate to the experience, and yet without description, what is learned remains private and unexamined.

This judgment about the inadequacy of language to represent my multifaceted experience of practice is more than scrupulous self-criticism. My audience can hold me to a higher standard of verisimilitude than they would other authors of case studies of teaching because I am the teacher I am portraying. Other kinds of writers about teaching are excused for leaving out considerations of gender or political context or parental relations or subject matter because these are outside of their area of expertise. As a teacher, I cannot ignore any of these domains, and I am also expected not to ignore them as a self-referential writer. In 1987, I turned to video as a possible solution to the problem of representing the complex nature of my teaching to others. I reasoned that, with video, the viewer would have greater access to the complex interactions occurring in the classroom even if they were limited by my editorial selection of a few minutes of the lesson from a longer stream of activity or by the angle of the videographer's lens. Such representations of the practices of teaching and studying seem authentic because what is going on for the participants seems to be available to the viewer all at once, rather than filtered through the interests of a describer.[28] In contrast to writing, video makes it possible to have a running image of the teacher-student-subject interaction without isolating these into single elements that then need to be put back together in some way to convey the whole.

When I show a videotape of my classroom, the question of how much "background" I need to provide and what to tell people before showing the tape always worries me. I am never satisfied that I have figured it out. Invariably, I run up against the frustration of wanting to show and say more than I have time for, and wish I could say, "You had to have been there to understand what that was about." Once viewers start to comment on what they see me doing on the tape, the video seems to represent so little of what I know about what is going on. And what I know from "being there" has a lot to do with reasoning about the actions we are seeing on the tape. Speculating about why I did what I did and evidence of the reasonableness of those actions would need to be grounded in much more information than what was available. The possibility of real-time representations of teaching on video seems to exacerbate the problem of communicating about my practice rather than solving it.

My experiences with video pushed me to want to invent a better representation of teaching practice to serve as a basis for collaborative analysis and problem-solving. Working as elementary teachers, teacher educators, and researchers on teaching, Deborah Ball and I began to experiment in 1989 with multimedia. We assembled multiple records of our practice in an electronically accessible database that could be used by a teacher and her audience as the text to be interpreted in analytic discussions about practice. Although the promise of the technology has been greater than the reality, this representation of teaching continues to be both practically and conceptually appealing.[29] Multimedia technology has the potential to enable us to represent the kind of knowing that Ball and I find essential to our own teaching but lacking in research on teaching — what Lee Shulman has called "strategic" modes of knowing in practice.[30] Shulman's characterization of strategic knowing is strikingly similar to the rhetoric used by developers of multimedia technologies.[31] He observes that propositional knowledge is what is most conventionally delivered in academic settings to be "applied" in practice. He claims that case knowledge, with its vivid detail, makes the propositions it illustrates more memorable, but is still clearly distinguishable from strategic knowledge — knowledge as it is used in actual situations of practice:

> Both propositions and cases share the burden of unilaterality, the deficiency of turning the reader or user toward a single, particular rule or practical way of seeing. Strategic knowledge comes into play as the teacher confronts particular situations or problems, whether theoretical, practical, or moral, where principles collide and no simple solution is possible. Strategic knowledge is developed when the lessons of single principles contradict one another, or the precedents of particular cases are incompatible.[32]

It is precisely this sort of representation of practices of teaching that multimedia is supposed to make possible. It appealed to us because it could capture the complexity of practice that we saw from the inside, the strategic piece that required both thinking and doing but did not have a simple face. And perhaps it is this desire to understand the strategies teachers use in practice that drives the development of teacher research more broadly.

Where Next?

In 1990, the research team that I was working with conjured up the idea of a computer supported database called the "Investigator's Working Environment" (IWE), which would further the study of teaching by enabling the activities of browsing, organizing, annotating, and displaying records of classroom teaching and learning in multiple media, along with individual and group commentaries on these records. The IWE was to be designed so that classroom practitioners and educational researchers, as well as students, parents, school administrators, and policymakers, could have access to the same set of records and add their interpretations to those records for access by others in both synchronous and asynchronous conversations about the problems of teaching. In 1999, we are closer to the IWE becoming a reality than we were ten years ago, and perhaps it represents an idea of where qualitative research on teaching might be going. New technologies for recording and archiving video and audio data and increasingly sophisticated communications and database technologies have great promise for integrating broad sweeps with deep analyses. Decreased financial and cognitive costs of access means that communication between scholars and practitioners can be more readily established on a common base of information. Electronic communications enable participation in conversations about a common text among participants that are not limited by time and place. And new database technologies make possible links between primary sources and interpretations of those sources, opening up new ground on the old questions of how "results" of research are to be reported and their validity judged.

What research on teaching has become, particularly in the hands of teacher researchers, opens up new prospects and new puzzles for qualitative research. The new tools that practitioners and researchers have at their disposal will change both what kind of data can be collected and how analyses of that data can be carried out and communicated. As qualitative research on teaching evolves, practitioners and researchers will need to take account of the contributions of teachers who take on the responsibility of using these tools as a basis for generating context-specific professional knowledge. Practitioners and researchers will need to consider what counts as a "good" interpretation of events as the stories of practitioners about those events are placed alongside interpretive scholarship of various sorts. And practitioners and researchers will need to face the representational challenges of communicating about practice when it has been "known" from the inside. As we allow more voices into the conversation and enable the juxtaposition of their analyses, we will struggle with understanding the nature of practice, the nature of knowledge, and what knowledge is good for.

Notes

1. For example, George Dennison, *The Lives of Children* (New York: Random House, 1969); James Herndon, *The Way It Spozed to Be* (New York: Simon & Shuster, 1968); John Holt, *How Children Fail* (New York: Pitman, 1964) and *How Children Learn* (New York: Pitman, 1967); Herb Kohl, *36 Children* (New York: New American Library, 1967); Jonathan Kozol, *Death at An Early Age* (New York: Houghton Mifflin, 1967).

2. *The Dewey School,* written by teachers at Chicago Lab School (Katherine Camp Mahew and Anna Camp Edwards [New York: Appleton-Century, 1936]), is a particularly interesting example of this genre.

3. See, for example, Marilyn Cochran-Smith and Susan Lytle, "Research on Teaching and Teacher Research: The Issues that Divide," *Educational Researcher, 19,* No. 2 (1990), 2–11; Kathy Carter, "The Place of Story in the Study of Teaching and Teacher Education," *Educational Researcher, 22,* No. 1 (1993), 5–12, 18; Virginia Richardson, "Conducting Research on Practice," *Educational Researcher, 23,* No. 5 (1994), 5–10; D. Jean Clandinin and F. Michael Connelly, "Teachers' Professional Knowledge Landscapes: Teacher Stories — Stories of Teachers — School Stories — Stories of Schools," *Educational Researcher, 25,* No. 3 (1996), 24–30.

4. Gary R. Anderson and Kathryn Herr, "The New Paradigm Wars: Is There Room for Rigorous Practitioner Knowledge in Schools and Universities?" *Educational Researcher, 28,* No. 5 (1999), 12–21, 40.

5. See "2000 Annual Meeting Call for Proposals," *Educational Researcher, 28,* No. 4 (1999), 39.

6. See, for example, Joan Krater, Jane Zeni, and Nancy Devlin Cason, *Mirror Images: Teaching Writing in Black and White* (Portsmouth, NH: Heinemann, 1994); Karen Hale Hankins, "Cacophony to Symphony: Memoirs in Teacher Research," *Harvard Educational Review, 68* (1998), 80–95; and Karen Gallas, *Talking Their Way into Science: Hearing Children's Questions and Theories and Responding with Curricula* (New York: Teachers College Press, 1995).

7. See, for example, Sarah Warshauer Freedman, E. R. Simons, J. S. Kalnin, A. Casareno, and the M-CLASS Teams, *Inside City Schools: Investigating Literacy in Multicultural Classrooms* (New York: Teachers College Press, 1999).

8. See, for example, Timothy J. Lensmire, *When Children Write: Critical Re-visions of the Writing Workshop* (New York: Teachers College Press, 1994); Deborah Lowenberg Ball and Suzanne M. Wilson, "Integrity in Teaching: Recognizing the Fusion of the Moral and Intellectual,"

American Educational Research Journal, 33, No. 1 (1996), 155–192; Magdalene Lampert, "When the Problem Is Not the Question and the Solution Is Not the Answer," *American Educational Research Journal, 27,* No. 1 (1990), 29–64.

9. For example, "Voices from the Classroom," sponsored by The Center for Research on Evaluation, Standards and Student Testing (CRESS), Davis, CA; the teacher research section of the Ethnography Forum, University of Pennsylvania; The International Conference on Teacher Research, held annually by the National Writing Project; The Spencer Foundation; National Council for Teacher Education (NCTE).

10. See Susan Florio-Ruane, "Conversation and Narrative in Collaborative Research: An Ethnography of the Written Literacy Forum," in *Stories Lives Tell: Narrative and Dialogue in Education,* ed. Carol Witherell and Nel Noddings (New York: Teachers College Press, 1991), p. 247.

11. Kenneth Zeichner and Susan Noffke, "Practitioner Research," in *Fourth Handbook of Research on Teaching,* ed. Virginia Richardson (Washington, DC: American Educational Research Association, in press).

12. Dan Lortie, *Schoolteacher* (Chicago: University of Chicago Press, 1975), p. 230.

13. Michael Huberman, "The Model of the Independent Artisan in Teachers' Professional Relations," in *Teacher's Work,* ed. Judith Warren-Little and Milbrey McLaughlin (New York: Teachers College Press, 1993), pp. 11–50; Judith Warren Little, "The Persistence of Privacy: Autonomy and Initiative in Teachers' Professional Relations," *Teachers College Record, 91* (1990), 509–536.

14. Zeichner and Noffke, "Practitioner Research"; Michael Huberman, "Moving Mainstream: Taking a Closer Look at Teacher Research," *Language Arts, 73* (1996), 124–140.

15. The potential of National Board for Professional Teaching Standards (NBPTS), Interstate New Teachers Assessment and Support Consortium (INTASC), and National Council for the Accreditation of Teacher Education (NCATE) to support this development are described in *What Matters Most: Teaching for America's Future* (New York: National Commission on Teaching and America's Future, 1996). For a discussion of the difference and relationship between local and professional language, see Donald Freeman, "Renaming Experience/Reconstructing Practice: Developing New Understandings of Teaching," *Teaching and Teacher Education, 9* (1993), 485–497.

16. For an application of this idea to teacher development, see Mary K. Stein, Edward A. Silver, and Margaret Schwan Smith, "Mathematics Reform and Teacher Development: A Community of Practice, Perspective," in *Thinking Practices in Mathematics and Science Learning,* ed. James Greeno and Shelly Goldman (Mahwah, NJ: Lawrence Erlbaum, 1998), pp. 17–52,

17. See Deborah Lowenberg Ball and Sylvia Rundquist, "Collaboration as a Context for Joining Teacher Learning with Learning about Teaching," in *Teaching for Understanding: Challenges for Policy and Practice,* ed. David K. Cohen, Milbrey W. McLaughlin, and Joan E. Talbert (San Francisco: Jossey-Bass, 1993), pp. 13–42; Suzanne Wilson, Carol Miller, and Carol Yerkes, "Deeply Rooted Change: A Tale of Learning to Teach Adventurously" in *Teaching for Understanding: Challenges for Policy and Practice,* ed. David K. Cohen, Milbrey W. McLaughlin, and Joan E. Talbert (San Francisco: Jossey-Bass, 1993), pp. 84–129.

18. Catherine Lewis and Ineko Tsuchida, "A Lesson Is Like a Swiftly Flowing River," *American Educator, 22,* No. 4 (1998), 12–17, 50–51; N. Ken Shimahara, "The Japanese Model of Professional Development: Teaching as Craft," *Teaching and Teacher Education, 14* (1998), 451–462.

19. Lynne Paine and Liping Ma, "Teachers Working Together: A Dialogue on Organizational and Cultural Perspectives of Chinese Teachers," *International Journal of Educational Research, 19* (1993), 675–698.

20. See John Elliot, "School-Based Curriculum Development and Action Research in the United Kingdom," in *International Action Research: A Casebook for Educational Reform,* ed. Sandra Hollingsworth (London: Falmer Press, 1997), pp. 17–28.

21. I refer to "How Do Teachers Manage to Teach?" *Harvard Educational Review, 55* (1985), 180; see also footnotes to this article and its brief review of supporting literature.

22. This address was published as Ivor Goodson, "Representing Teachers: Bringing Teachers Back In," in *Changing Research and Practice: Teachers' Professionalism, Identity, and Knowledge*, ed. Michael Kompf, W. Richard Bond, Don Dworet, and R. Terrance Boak (London: Falmer Press, 1966), pp. 211–221. The quote is on pp. 215–216.

23. Cynthia Chambers, "Review of Teachers as Curriculum Planners: Narratives of Experience," *Journal of Educational Policy, 6* (1991) 353–354 (p. 354 quoted in Goodson, "Representing Teachers," p. 216).

24. Kathy Carter, "The Place of Story in the Study of Teaching and Teacher Education," *Educational Researcher, 22,* No. 1 (1993), 11 (quoted in Goodson, "Representing Teachers," p. 220).

25. Louise Kidder and Michelle Fine, "Qualitative Inquiry in Psychology: A Radical Tradition," in *Critical Psychology: An Introduction*, ed. Dennis R. Fox and Isaac Prilletensky (Thousand Oaks, CA: Sage, 1997), pp. 34–50.

26. Deborah Lowenberg Ball, "Working in the Inside: Using One's Own Practice as a Site for Studying Teaching and Learning," in *In Research Design in Mathematics and Science Education*, ed. Anthony Kelly and Richard Lesh (Amsterdam: Kluwer, 1999), p. 400.

27. For examples of multiple stories being told about the same teaching events, see Harriet Bjerrum Nielsen, "Seductive Texts with Serious Intentions," *Educational Researcher, 24,* No. 1 (1995), 4–12.

28. Katherine Merseth and Catherine Lacey, "Weaving Stronger Fabric: The Pedagogical Promise of Hypermedia and Case Methods in Teacher Education," *Teaching and Teacher Education, 9* (1993), 283–299; Gary Sykes and Tom Bird, "Teacher Education and the Case Idea," in *Review of Research in Education*, ed. Gerald Grant (Washington, DC: American Educational Research Association, 1992), pp. 457–521; Deidre LeFevre, "Why Video?" Unpublished manuscript, University of Michigan, 1999.

29. For a full description of this project and references to similar projects, see Magdalene Lampert and Deborah Ball, *Teaching, Multimedia and Mathematics: Investigations of Real Practice* (New York: Teachers College Press, 1998).

30. Lee Shulman, "Those Who Understand: Knowledge Growth in Teaching," *Educational Researcher, 15,* No. 2 (1986), 4–14.

31. See, for example, the essays in Sueann Ambron and Kristina Hooper, *Interactive Multimedia: Visions of Multimedia for Developers, Educators, and Information Providers* (Redmond, WA: Microsoft Press, 1988).

32. Shulman, "Those Who Understand," p. 12.

PART TWO

Ethics and Validity

The Colonizer/Colonized
Chicana Ethnographer:
Identity, Marginalization, and
Co-optation in the Field

SOFIA VILLENAS

It is not easy to name our pain, to theorize from that location.
> (hooks, 1994, p. 74)

Like a *mojado* [wetback] ethnographer, I attempt to cross the artificial
borders into occupied academic territories, searching for a *coyote* [smuggler]
to secure a safe passage.
> (E. G. Murillo Jr., personal communication, 1995)

What happens when members of low-status and marginalized groups become university-sanctioned "native" ethnographers of their own communities? How is this "native" ethnographer positioned vis-à-vis her own community, the majority culture, the research setting, and the academy? While qualitative researchers in the field of education theorize about their own privilege in relation to their research participants, the "native" ethnographer must deal with her own marginalizing experiences and identities in relation to dominant society. This "native" ethnographer is potentially both the colonizer, in her university cloak, and the colonized, as a member of the very community that is made "other" in her research.

I am this "native" ethnographer in the field of education, a first-generation Chicana born in Los Angeles of immigrant parents from Ecuador. Geographically, politically, and economically, I have lived under the same yoke of colonization as the Chicano communities I study, experiencing the same discrimination and alienation from mainstream society that comes from being a member of a caste "minority."[1] I share the same ethnic consciousness and regional and linguistic experiences. The commonly used terms "Hispanic" and "Latino" do not adequately describe who I am.[2] Racially and ethnically I am *indigena*, a detribalized Native American woman, descendant of the Quechua-speaking people of the South American Andes. Politically I am a Chicana, born and raised in the American Southwest, in the legendary territories of Aztlan.[3] This story is about how these identities came into play in the process of conducting research with an emerging Latino community located in the U.S. South.

Harvard Educational Review Vol. 66 No. 4 Winter 1996, 711–731

The Colonizer/Colonized Dilemma

Rethinking the political and personal subjectivities of researcher and ethnographer has in recent times pushed the boundaries of theorizing about the multiple identities of the researcher within the research context of privilege and power. Qualitative researchers in education have called for a reexamination of the raced, gendered, aged, and classed positions of the researcher with respect to the research participants (Fine, 1994; Lather, 1991; Roman & Apple, 1990). These researchers are also recognizing that they are and have been implicated in imperialist agendas (Pratt, 1986; Rosaldo, 1989) by participating in "othering" (Fine, 1994) and in the exploitation and domination of their research subjects (Roman & Apple, 1990).[4]

In the last decade, ethnographers and qualitative researchers have illuminated the ways in which the researched are colonized and exploited. By objectifying the subjectivities of the researched, by assuming authority, and by not questioning their own privileged positions (Crapanzano, 1986; Fine, 1994; Rosaldo, 1989; Van Galen & Eaker, 1995), ethnographers have participated as colonizers of the researched. Rosaldo (1989) uses the image of the "Lone Ethnographer" who once upon a time "rode off into the sunset in search of his 'natives'" (p. 30). After undergoing arduous fieldwork as his rite of passage, the Lone Ethnographer "returned home to write a 'true' account of the culture" (p. 30). In the texts of classic anthropology, people were depicted as "members of a harmonious, internally homogeneous and unchanging culture" (p. 31), and written about in a way that "normalizes life by describing social activities as if they were always repeated in the same manner by everyone in the group" (p. 42). Rosaldo reminds us that this manner of objectifying people's lives has been the classic norm of ethnography, and that researchers have rarely asked what the researched think about how their lives are being interpreted and described in text.

Researchers are also implicated as colonizers when they claim authenticity of interpretation and description under the guise of authority. In a critique of Geertz's description of the Balinese cockfight, Crapanzano (1986) exposes the ways in which the event described is subverted and sacrificed to "a literary discourse that is far removed from the indigenous discourse of their occurrence" (p. 76). This discourse, according to Crapanzano, is ultimately masked by the authority of the author, "who at least in much ethnography, stands above and behind those whose experiences he purports to describe" (p. 76).

As ethnographers, we are also like colonizers when we fail to question our own identities and privileged positions, and in the ways in which our writings perpetuate "othering." As Fine (1994) explains:

> When we write essays about subjugated Others as if *they* were a homogeneous mass (of vice or virtue), free-floating and severed from contexts of oppression, and as if we were neutral transmitters of voices and stories, we tilt toward a narrative strategy that reproduces Othering on, despite, or even "for." (1994, p. 74)

Moreover, we are like colonizers when, as Van Galen and Eaker (1995) point out, the professional and intellectual gatekeeping structures (e.g., university admissions to graduate studies, journal publication referees) from which we gain our legitimacy and privilege remain "highly inaccessible to those on whose behalf we claim to write" (p. 114).

For example, women teachers of working-class backgrounds are expected to consume a body of literature that emanates from elite universities from which they are excluded, and that thus excludes them from the production of material used for the teaching profession and their own training. Fine (1994) and Van Galen and Eaker (1995) urge ethnographers to probe the nature of their relationship to those they write about.

While we continue to push the borders of the multiple, decentered, and politicized self as researcher, we continue to analyze and write about *ourselves* in a unidirectional manner as imperialist researchers (Rosaldo, 1989) and colonizers (Fine, 1994) in relation to the research participants. Yet, what about the researcher as colonizer *and* colonized? Here is my own dilemma: as a Chicana graduate student in a White institution and an educational ethnographer of Latino communities, I am both, as well as in between the two. I am the coloni*zed* in relation to the greater society, to the institution of higher learning, and to the dominant majority culture in the research setting. I am the coloni*zer* because I am the educated, "marginalized" researcher, recruited and sanctioned by privileged dominant institutions to write for and about Latino communities. I am a walking contradiction with a foot in both worlds — in the dominant privileged institutions *and* in the marginalized communities. Yet, I possess my own agency and will to promote my own and the collective agendas of particular Latino communities. I did not even consider the multiplicity of self and identity and the nuances of what such consideration meant until I had to confront my own marginality as a Chicana researcher in relation to the dominant majority culture in the research setting. In the research context of power and domination, I encountered what it means to examine closely within myself the intersectedness of race, class, gender, and other conceptual notions of identity.

I am a Chicana doctoral student, and have been conducting research in a small rural community in North Carolina, which I have named Hope City. My research project involved the educational life histories of Latina mothers who were recent immigrants to Hope City. In the telling of their stories, the women defined education — how they experienced it in their lives as learners and teachers in families, communities, and schools, and how they constructed educational models for raising their own children. I spent over two years in Hope City, teaching English as a Second Language (ESL) at the local community college and in an after-school tutorial program for elementary-school-age Spanish-speaking children. I participated in family social gatherings, and in community and church events and meetings. I also had a lot of contact with the English-speaking community of professionals who were servicing Latino families in health care and education, joining them in meetings and informal gatherings. These professionals were also formally interviewed by other colleagues involved in the Hope City project. As a team, we were funded by a child development center to investigate the beliefs about education held by the agencies and schools serving the Hope City Latino community, and by the diverse Latino community members themselves. In my own research, I systematically analyzed the public sphere and the organization of relations of power in Hope City. Through a historiographic analysis of the town's newspaper and through my observations and participant observations within the community of school and agency professionals, I found that the Latino community in Hope City was being framed as a "problem."

At the beginning of the research project, I was aware of the politics and privilege of my researcher role and my relation to the research participants. I was eager to experience the process of constructing meaning with the research participants. By talking with these Latina mothers about their beliefs and philosophies of child rearing and education, as well as my own, I hoped to engage them in conversations about how they could create a dignified space for themselves and their families in a previously biracial community that was not accustomed to Latinos. I had vague ideas about community projects that I hoped would emerge from the research participants themselves. When I reflected later, these notions seemed arrogant, as if I thought I knew the hopes and aspirations of this Latino community. I realized I had to question all my assumptions about this southern Latino community, such as defining as problems certain aspects of their lives that, to them, were not problematic at all. I was certainly ready to learn from this Latino community, but in the process of seeking to reform my relationship with them, I failed to notice that I was being repositioned and co-opted by the dominant English-speaking community to legitimate their discourse of "Latinos as problem." In the course of working with Hope City's non-Latino school and service professionals, I discovered that while I engaged in a rethinking of my own politics and the processes of empowerment within the Latino community, I was hiding my own marginality in relation to the majority culture. I did not know then that I would have to scrutinize my own lived experiences as a Chicana daughter, mother, wife, and student in confronting the dominant community's discourses of "othering" and of difference.

In this article, I attempt to heed Fine's words in "unearthing the blurred boundaries between Self and Other" (1994, p. 72). Weis (1995) summarizes the discourse on colonialism, which takes as its central point the idea that the colonial "other" and the self (read the "Western White" self) are simultaneously co-constructed, the first being judged against the latter. Furthermore, Weis notes, "this process of 'othering' is key to understanding relations of domination and subordination, historically and currently" (p. 18). This article, then, speaks to the discourses of "othering" that jolted me out of my perceived unproblematic identity and role as a Chicana researcher in education, and into a co-construction of the "Western" self and the Chicana "other." This ongoing story involves my confrontation with my contradictory identities — as a Chicana researcher in the power structures of the dominant discourse of "other," and as a Chicana working with this marginalized Latino community. Through this story, I hope to recontextualize the ways in which qualitative researchers in education have theorized about identity and privilege to include the repositioning and manipulation of identities that can occur, particularly with native ethnographers. This recontextualization problematizes the ways in which qualitative researchers who seek to analyze privilege and the "situatedness" of each ethnographer fail to note that we as ethnographers of education are not all the same "We" in the literature of privileged ethnographers. My standpoint as a Chicana and my historical relation to Latino communities mediate and complicate my "privilege." Unveiling the ways in which the ethnographer is situated in oppressive structures is a critical task for qualitative researchers in the field of education. Even in new positions of privilege, the Chicana ethnographer cannot escape a history of her own marginalization nor her guilt of complicity.

Personal History

My encounter with discourses of difference and of "othering" as a child in Los Angeles neighborhoods and schools intensified my scrutinization of my own identity and role as a Chicana in academia. Growing up in Los Angeles, I was aware of racism. As a child, I acted out the effects of colonization, refusing to speak Spanish, emphasizing that I was South American and not Mexican, as Mexicans were relegated to second-class citizenship. I grew up knowing that my culture and language were not valued, but I did not suffer direct, blatant racism. I found safety in numbers, as there were many other Latinas, Chicanas, and Mexicans with whom I could hang out.

As I grew older, our peer group continually created and celebrated our Chicano/Latino cultures and languages. As an adult, I thought I had overcome the loss of self that comes with second-class relegation of the Spanish language and Latino cultures, and that I did not speak with the voice of a colonized person, one whose culture and language were devalued. Yet I was not as prepared for Eurocentric academia as I thought I was. In community, I had learned to manipulate my identities successfully and did not expect them to be manipulated by others. But such a manipulation is precisely what occurred when I began my professional university training in ethnographic research. At the university, I experienced the dilemma of creating my identity as a Chicana researcher in the midst of Eurocentric discourses of "other." Being an ethnographer made my contradictory position more obvious, complex, and ironic. I recognize this contradiction now, but at the university, the discourse of "othering" did not begin with my research study.

An awakening of sorts occurred for me when I attended a seminar on topics in education. On that particular day, the topic was whether public single-population schools should exist. The readings for that week centered on public and private schools for women only, for gays and lesbians, and schools based on Afrocentric or Chicano-centric curriculum. Most of my fellow classmates argued that people should not be separated, reasoning that students should be integrated so that everybody could come together to talk about societal inequities and find solutions together. They argued that single-population schools promoted separatism, and that through integrated schools, the Eurocentric curricula would be challenged. While I agreed that all people need to dialogue about oppression and work together to bring about social justice and therefore was in favor of integrated schools, I did not agree that Afrocentric or Chicano-centric curricula and schools promoted separatism. In trying to engage in the discussion, however, I began to feel uncomfortable. I tried to explain why I felt that disenfranchised groups had the right to these curricula if they wanted them and, furthermore, why I felt they were important and necessary. I argued that people who have been stripped of their cultures through public schooling need to come together and reclaim their cultures, histories, and languages, but although I believed this, I was nevertheless buying into the discourse of fear of separatism, saying that we needed to have separate spaces before coming together to be a part of the larger group. Of course, implicit in this argument was the idea that as people of color, we were going "to come together" to join the dominant culture and integrate ourselves within it, rather than challenge the notion of a single common culture.

The discourse of this group of fellow students and friends was so powerful that it disabled me. I explained my stance apologetically, acquiescing to the notion that we

would have to come back and join a mainstream culture and society rather than challenge it. Everyone else was speaking as if they were detached and removed from the
topic, rationalizing the logic of their arguments, but it was different for me. The topic
was personal and deeply embedded in my experiences. In this conversation, I was not
the subject anymore but the object, the "other." Using Cornell West's words, hooks
(1990) writes that people often engage in debates that "highlight notions of difference, marginality, and 'otherness' in such a way that it further marginalizes actual
people of difference and otherness" (p. 125). hooks likens these debates to reinscrib-
ing patterns of colonization: "When this happens . . . the 'Other' is always made object, appropriated, interpreted, taken over by those in power, by those who dominate"
(1990, p. 125).

In this same manner, I felt that my experiences as a Latina going through the Eurocentric curriculum of public schools was being objectified and appropriated through a
rationalized logical argument against Chicano- or Afrocentric schools. In the rational,
logical arguments in that seminar, no space existed for my deeply passionate personal
experience and voice, for me to argue for the right to choose to be with Latinas/os, for
us to be educated together and to center our curriculum in our diverse roots and history, to find out about ourselves and to claim ourselves in our own terms. My classmates and I talked against oppressed groups coming together to form their own
schools in a way that ignored the existence of race, class, and gender privileges among
the class participants. In this discussion, an aura of disinterested, detached, scientific
rationalism existed that rendered me voiceless and silenced. Ellsworth (1989) describes the oppression of rational argument as putting as its opposite the irrational
"other" — for example, women and people of color. In schools, she said, the rational
argument has become the "vehicle for regulating conflict and the power to speak"
(p. 303).

After the group dispersed, I was left feeling stripped of my identity and angry with
myself for betraying my own voice. I had fallen into the trap of the dominant discourse, trying to convince the group not to worry, that we would eventually come
around to integrating ourselves. But into what? I did not know, but it was implied
that we would integrate ourselves into some core set of shared social and cultural ideals and belief systems, a core that evidently was the White, middle-class lifestyle. I was
reminded again of Ellsworth's (1989) critique of critical pedagogy. She argues that the
dialogue emphasized in critical pedagogy assumes that we could all engage in dialogue
equally as if we were not raced, gendered, and classed persons with vested interests
and different experiences. The seminar participants (including myself) failed to see
how, in the process of discussing people of color, we silenced and marginalized the
very voices of those who were supposed to have been the subjects and authors of their
experiences — the voices of fellow Chicana and African American classmates.

I now realize that something else also occurred that afternoon in our seminar. The
topic, as well as the disinterested, detached way in which the discussion was carried
out, fueled what I wanted so desperately to express, but could not. I was the only
Chicana there, and had to think and speak individualistically rather than collectively.
I was without my Latino friends from home who shared the power of our activism in
defying the colonization of our identities and of our people. In the absence of that
collectivity, I changed my commitment and orientation from the visions my friends
and I had shared. Cut off from those who collectively sustained them, I lost those vi-

sions of activism and self-determination. Deep inside, I wanted to voice what I was experiencing at that moment — the disempowerment that comes from being cut off from your own. Perez (1991), a Chicana feminist, writes what I wanted to express at that time:

> You attempt to "penetrate" the place I speak from with my Chicana/Latina hermanas. I have rights to my space. I have boundaries. . . . At times, I must separate from you, from your invasion. So call me a separatist, but to me this is not about separatism. It is about survival. I think of myself as one who must separate to my space and language of women to revitalize, to nurture and be nurtured. Then, I can resurface to build the coalitions that we must build to make the true revolution — all of us together acting the ideal, making alliance without a hierarchy of oppression. (p. 178)

Only now, as I am writing these words, do I realize what was happening. It hit me and it hurt me. I felt it in my bones, but I could not articulate it until now. The coalitions referred to by Perez imply groups of empowered and self-identified peoples who do not have to pack neatly and put away their languages and cultures in order to comply with a "standard" way of being. To be Chicanas in the myriad and infinite ways there are of being, to come as we are, poses a threat to integrated schools and to mainstream society. In the absence of collectivity in my graduate seminar, I could not be true to my vision of a Chicana.

Revealing Tension in My Identity as a Chicana Researcher

As I look back, describe, and theorize about my seminar experience, I can articulate the elements that constituted my marginalization and my complicity in the discourses of difference and "othering." The power of the dominant discourse of "other," the objectification of my experiences as the "other" through detached, rational argumentation, and the severing of a collective vision and memory that disabled me and rendered me voiceless, all constituted marginalization and complicity. These elements resurfaced when I started the process of conducting qualitative research with the Latino community in Hope City, North Carolina. There, my dilemma of being a Chicana and a researcher became problematic in ways similar to my experiences in the seminar, that is, as an accomplice to the marginalization and objectification of my identity and experiences as a Chicana, which became embedded in the power structure of the dominant and the disenfranchised.

Going into the field, my intent was to gain access to the Hope City Latino community so that I could interview Latina mothers about their beliefs on child rearing and education, particularly as their narratives played out in the context of a changing rural southern town. Yet I did not want only to take their stories and leave. I also wanted to become involved in some way with their Latino community, either through bilingual tutoring for children with their mothers or through English-as-a-Second-Language (ESL) instruction. As I sought to gain access to the community, I had to speak with numerous English-speaking institutional representatives, including educators in the elementary school, community college, and health department. From the beginning, I felt uncomfortable in my conversations with these community leaders and with their cultural views of Latino families, and of the women in particular. They constructed Latino families as "problems" tending toward violence, sexism, machismo, and low educational aspirations. In their meetings, well-meaning providers talked about showing Latina mothers models of proper child rearing. A Hope City newspaper headline read, "Program Teaches Hispanics How to Be Better Mothers." Other articles about Latino families carried headlines such as "Literacy Void." Again, the dominant discourse concerning the "other" was powerful and overwhelming — so much so that I found myself, as in the seminar, participating in it as an accomplice. I began to talk the talk.

I remember accompanying an ESL instructor from the community college to the trailer park where he gave classes. We stood in the grassy area in the middle of the park, looking out at the individual trailers, some with children and families outside them. The instructor was giving me the rundown on their living conditions and other problems. I was nodding my head, all the while gazing at the people who looked back at us. I remember ducking my head, painfully aware of my awkward position. Whose side was I on? In participating in this manner with the instructor, I was, as hooks (1989) says, "one with them in a fellowship of the chosen and superior, [it was] a gesture of inclusion in 'whiteness'" (p. 68), affirming that I had been assimilated. I felt uncomfortable, yet I participated, as in the graduate seminar, by betraying my anger and remaining silent, and by not challenging the discourse. In conversations with Hope City professionals, I had to choose my alignment in the power structure of the community — either with the leaders who were in positions to make policy, or with the disenfranchised Latino community.

Choosing to align myself with the dominant English-speaking leaders entailed sharing the same discourse and language to talk about the Latino community. To do this, I had to distance myself from the Latino community and the experiences I shared with them, and speak as the subject about the object. I could do this in the eyes of the dominant English-speaking community because I was formally educated and spoke English as well as they.

In this southern community, there were no other Chicanas/os in leadership positions. I had no one with whom to share a collective vision for the empowerment of "our" community. The ESL instructor and I spoke in a detached manner about the problems of "these people," as if I had not been socialized in a Latino family and immigrant community. I spoke as if Latino families and friends had not been the most important people in my private life. I silenced myself so that I could have further conversations with the community leaders who were the key to my accessing the educational institutions of the community. By participating in their discourse, I had to disengage myself from my experiences as an intimate participant in Latino families and communities. The dominant discourse of difference was powerful, and my experiences were again nullified through my participation in detached and rational discussions of the problems of the "other."

My uncomfortable feelings soon turned to outrage and hurt. One particular discussion with a school principal startled me out of my perceived unproblematic role as a Chicana researcher. My adviser and I went to speak with the principal about my starting a mother/child class to teach children how to read and write in Spanish. The principal, who held blatantly racist views of Latino families, told us he would play the devil's advocate and point out some problems — for example, how were we going to get mothers to come? He went on to say that we had to understand the Hispanic family. The man, he said, dictates, and the woman is subservient: "The man will not let her out of the house. They do not care about education and so it's hard to get the mothers to come to the school." An ESL teacher who was also in the room explained that these were poor people, blue-collar workers who did not have education themselves. I later responded angrily in my field notes:

> How dare you say this to me. How is it that you are telling me what Latino families are like. I was so insulted. They were talking about my "raza" so negatively as if I were not Latina myself. This goes to show how easily I can "pass" and that in certain contexts, I am not identified as one of "them." With this conversation as in others, I have felt that I have had to put on a different persona in order to play along with well meaning racist discourse. I have felt very uncomfortable talking to benevolent people about the "other," the exotic poor people who need our help. "Our" referring to my complicity as researcher. (Field notes, March 1994)

After that incident, I began to question my identity and my role as a Chicana researcher. It was evident that the dominant English-speaking community did not consider me a Latina, like the women we were discussing, but a middle-class, educated woman of Spanish descent. How was I to relate to this dominant discourse of difference and "othering?"

I looked to recent works on the researcher's role in disenfranchised communities in which the researcher shares the same cultural background as the research participants. Delgado-Gaitan (1993) and Delgado-Gaitan and Trueba (1991) write about an ethnography of empowerment, a framework that "provides a broad sociocultural premise and possible strategy for studying the process of disempowerment and empowerment of disenfranchised communities" (p. 391). This kind of ethnography is based on a Freirean notion of self-awareness of the social and cultural context of the nature of oppression suffered by disempowered people (Delgado-Gaitan & Trueba, 1991). Such a framework calls for "the construction of knowledge through the social interaction between researcher and researched with the fundamental purpose of improving the living conditions of the communities being researched" (Delgado-Gaitan & Trueba, 1991, p. 392). Delgado-Gaitan (1993) emphasizes that the researcher shapes the research participants and their environment while, at the same time, the researcher is also shaped by the participants and the dynamics of their interactions. Delgado-Gaitan's (1993) own provocative story is of the transformation of her role with respect to her work on literacy practices in the homes and schools of a Latino community. As the parents mobilized to effect changes in the school, Delgado-Gaitan redefined her role as researcher to become involved as facilitator and informant in the process of community empowerment. As a result of her own unique experiences, Delgado-Gaitan, a Latina herself, built upon the notion of making problematic her relationship with Latino communities. By doing so, she put into practice qualitative researchers' call for the reexamination of one's identity and place within the research context of privilege and power.

My story extends this notion by problematizing the relationship between the marginalized researcher and the majority culture. The internalization of oppressive discourses relating to one's own people, especially as a product of institutionalized education and university training, can lead to a disempowerment of the researcher and the research process. The analysis can be extended then to include the empowerment of the researcher and the role of the ethnographer's culture, self-identity, and her/his raced, classed, and gendered experiences in the research process. In my case, while I naively looked for ways in which I could help Latina mothers "empower" themselves (see Le Compte & de Marrais, 1992, for a critique on the discourse on empowerment), I failed to realize that I needed to help myself become empowered vis-à-vis the dominant, English-speaking community. I needed to examine my own identity in the particular cultural arena that formed the context for my research study. Not having done so, I could not engage in the process of constructing knowledge with the research participants. I needed first to ask myself, How am I, as a Chicana researcher, damaged by my own marginality? Furthermore, how am I complicit in the manipulation of my identities such that I participate in my own colonization and marginalization and, by extension, that of my own people — those with whom I feel a cultural and collective connectedness and commitment?

For these reasons, researchers must examine how their subjectivities and perceptions are negotiated and changed, not only in relation to the disenfranchised community as research participants, but also through interactions with the majority culture. In most cases, the latter are the people who espouse the dominant discourse of difference and "other," that is, the cultural views of Latino families as a "problem" — poor, disadvantaged, and language deficient. In Hope City, Latina mothers are constructed as "at risk" in the discourse of the dominant community (i.e., professionals in education, health, and social services) so that the ways in which they raise and educate their children are devalued (Swadener & Lubeck, 1995). It is this "at risk" and "problem" discourse that I was being pushed hard to legitimate in Hope City. Yet this discourse concerned my own rearing, my own family, my own mother, and my own beliefs and those of my community. Through my engagement in the majority culture's "Latinos as problem" discourse, I was further marginalized and encircled in my own guilt of complicity.

Identity, Tension, and Power:
Interpreting My Insider/Outsider Perspective

I find it useful to appropriate Delgado-Gaitan's (1993) insider/outsider concept and apply it in a different manner to my emerging and changing identity as a Chicana researcher. In the process of conducting her study, Delgado-Gaitan (1993) learned that a researcher initially could only be an outsider to the community of research participants, but that with insight, the researcher could foster relational and reflective processes with their participants and in time become an insider. What are the particular behaviors and/or characteristics of the researcher that can make her/him an insider to the community of research participants? In a general sense, it is the sharing of collective experiences and a collective space with the research participants, such that the researcher is gradually accepted as a member of that particular community. As researchers, we can be insiders and outsiders to a particular community of research participants at many different levels and at different times.

In my case, I had two layers of communities to penetrate, at least on different terms. From my perspective at the time, the irony was that I was becoming an insider to the "wrong" community — the dominant, English-speaking community of leaders with whom I felt no familial, historical, or intimate relation. I was, in fact, the outsider to the Latino community of this town, since I was not *of* their community and did not share in their everyday experiences (I did not live in Hope City). Further, I was being recruited by the institutional representatives to become an insider in the legitimization of the dominant discourse of Latinos as "problem" and "victim." The effects on me of participating in the dominant discourse in a detached manner through rational dialogue were powerful. Consequently, I had to step back and negotiate internally the ongoing recruiting efforts of the dominant, English-speaking community leaders to their discourses of difference.

I began my fieldwork on-site at the beginning of the spring semester of the academic year. I discussed with my advisr ehow the White community might be cautious in talking with me about the Latino community, since I might be perceived as a member of this community. As I stated earlier, my adviser and I were soon proven wrong. The White community leaders were eager to talk to me about their perceptions of Latino families.

I had worked hard all semester to gain access to the Hope City Latino community and to find a niche in which to practice my profession of *maestra* (teacher), and to do research as well. My diligence paid off in that many opportunities were opened for me by English-speaking community leaders. I had received invitations to teach ESL and literacy in the churches (both the Catholic and Methodist churches), the elementary school, the community college, and the health department.

I decided to dedicate my time to teaching ESL to adults at the community college, a job in which I not only had experience but that I also thoroughly enjoyed. At the end of the semester, I looked to see what my story in terms of my research had been thus far. I had written in my field notes about my uneasy and uncomfortable feelings as I had conversations with English-speaking community leaders. Interestingly, I had also recorded my feelings of awkwardness when I talked to Latinas/os as a researcher researching "them." I was unconsciously documenting the power relations that defined the research context of which I, the dominant community leaders, and the Latino immigrant community each formed a part. Roman and Apple (1990) emphasize that a crucial task for the ethnographer should be the "elaboration of the structural power relations that formed the basis for conducting the field research and the study" (p. 60). The documentation of my feelings of anger and awkwardness formed the basis for the elaboration of my identity as a Chicana researcher in the community's power structure.

The power play in the recruitment efforts of the White power structure, and later in their efforts to appropriate me, was clearly evident. To recruit me to their discourse and narratives of difference, the community leaders had to view me as equal with them in the power structure. They appropriated my persona and appeared, at least initially, to welcome me as an equal.

I later understood this welcome to be a form of colonizing. They appropriated my persona by presuming shared assumptions of a body of experiences. For example, a community college instructor warned me about the dangers of the trailer park, implying that I shared his fear of poor people and of people of color. The community leaders also treated me as an equal by talking about Latinos as the "other" and including me in the distanced and detached conversations about the "problems of Latinos." Sharing our detached, rational observations of Latinos made me seem objective and scientific, and seemed to put us on equal footing with each other and in a superior position to the Latino community.

I felt powerful because I could discuss "their" problems. I was even in a position to negotiate power with the elementary school principal when I proposed Spanish tutoring classes for young children and their mothers. Not only did my credentials give me leverage in these negotiations, but my professional identity and language also met the criteria for inclusion and commonality with the institutional representatives. In more ways than one, I found it easier to be an insider to the community of dominant English-speaking leaders than to the Latino community.

The powerholders' recruiting efforts were intense precisely because they had a lot at stake in interpreting, structuring, and legitimating their cultural constructions of difference and diversity. The schools and agencies were interpreting Latino "cultures" and child-rearing practices. They were structuring the relationships between the Latino and English-speaking communities through the mediating force of agency bureaucracies (see Adkins, Givens, McKinney, Murillo, & Villenas, 1995). And they were legitimating the "at risk" and "problem" discourses.

Undoubtedly, as a "Hispanic" professional, I served to legitimate the "at risk" discourse and the definition of Latino child-rearing as a "problem." Sleeter (1995) argues that "the discourse over 'children at risk' can be understood as a struggle for power over how to define children, families, and communities who are poor, of color, and/or native speakers of languages other than English" (p. ix).

In later months, community leaders called on me to speak about and for the Latino community. In their eyes, I was the "expert" on the educational experiences of Latino families, not because I had begun talking with Latina mothers and could possibly articulate their points of view, but because I was seen as the professional who possessed formal education, teaching experience, and spoke both Spanish and English. Indeed, they would introduce me not only by name, but also by my academic credentials and past teaching experience. On one occasion, I was asked to speak to a group of community leaders from various social service agencies about Latino families and their educational needs. I chose to speak about the strengths of language and literacy socialization in Latino families. On another occasion, I was asked to translate for and represent the Latinas from my ESL class at a meeting to organize a county chapter of a council for women. At yet another meeting, called by the county migrant education office, about one hundred Latino parents met in the elementary school cafeteria where I spoke to them about strategies to help their children in school. On all of these occasions, I was serving as the broker for and the link to the Latino community for the professional community leaders. They called on me to participate in meetings and to give presentations. The stakeholders of this community clearly felt an urgent need to co-opt certain people, such as myself and other English-speaking town leaders, to represent the Latino community. It was as if in doing so, they did not have to handle the raw material. The Latino community was too foreign, too different, too working class, too brown; so they appropriated me, Sofia, the preprocessed package, wrapped in formal education and labeled in English.

Of course I did not want to be associated with the dominating power structure in the eyes of the Latino community. I had qualms about being perceived as the imperialist researcher. I felt tension with the Latino community when I was in my role as researcher, and when they saw me in company and complicity with the community leaders. I am reminded of two situations in which I felt these tensions most acutely.

It felt normal and comfortable, for example, when I visited Tienda Adrian (Adrian's Store), a Latino food store, with my husband and children. We spoke with the store owners in Spanish, asking about the town. However, the following week I felt uncomfortable when I revisited Tienda Adrian with my adviser and approached the store owners cloaked in my university researcher role to ask about the town. Similarly, I felt the tension of power in my researcher role when I began formal interviews with the women in the Latino community. The interviewing situation was uncomfortable for me, in contrast to the times we had engaged in informal talks about raising and educating children in Hope City.

I felt the tension of power and complicity even more directly when I engaged in social interaction with an English-speaking institutional representative and a Latina client at the same time. I felt this more acutely when service agency providers used English to talk about Latina clients in their presence. The Latina clients, who, for the most part, were new arrivals in Hope City, could not speak English. One particular service provider had the habit of introducing me to a Latina client and then giving me her personal life history right in front of her. In these situations, power was wielded through language, and English became the language of exclusion. The women's personal lives were presented to me like an open book in a language that they did not understand. In having to respond in English to the service provider, I was self-conscious and awkward about the exploitation and "othering" of the women. I did not want to be complicit with the "colonial administrator," but I was unaware that this was how I was being positioned.

My feelings of complicity and guilt, however, led me to engage in small, spontaneous, subversive strategies and acts of resistance. Any time a community leader spoke in English about a Latina client in her presence, I translated. Sometimes I would change the meanings somewhat so as not to cause embarrassment or hurt. On one occasion, for example, I said, "He's saying that you had gone through some rough times," even though the service agency provider said that she had had a nervous breakdown and had psychological problems. I began to translate into Spanish everything I said to community leaders when Latinos were present.

I also brought politics and subversion to the meetings at which I spoke for the community leaders. I did not always say what they wanted to hear, stirring controversy at one meeting and causing some Whites to react defensively at another. At one meeting at the elementary school, I disrupted the discourse of dominance by not accepting the seat they had saved for me in the front of the room facing the Latino audience. Instead, I took a seat among some Latino friends.

As an ESL instructor, a maestra, in the Latino community, I am more active in dialogue and discussions with my Latino students than with the community of school and agency professionals. In being able to name and identify the situatedness of my identities, I am beginning to react to my positioning and act toward a transformation of my identity and role as a Chicana educational researcher in a Latino community.

Negotiating Identities: Toward New Discourses

I am in the process of my own learning, and it is not my goal to arrive at a final resolution. Rather, I am in continual discovery. Identity and self are multiple and continually remade, reconstructed, reconstituted, and renewed in each new context and situation (Stone, 1992). When I left Los Angeles to attend graduate school in the South, I also left behind identities formed against the backdrop of a segregated city and against a historical context of the racial subordination and conquest of Native and Mexican peoples. In my limited and segregated experiences, I only knew Whites as living the middle-class lifestyle, and rarely as working-class people. I defined myself and was defined by this historical relationship.

In North Carolina, at first I believed I had encountered a place where a historically embedded antagonism did not exist between Mexicans and European Americans, as it exists in the Southwest. There is no territorial Alamo to remember, nor a U.S.-Mexico treaty that appropriated one-third of Mexico's land. I seemed to have forgotten the history of the genocide of American Indians and of the slavery and segregation of African Americans. Nevertheless, I believed space existed in which I could enter into new relationships with the majority culture and define new grounds and new terms. Because of this belief, I found it painful to go into the town where I was to conduct my research project, a town where a new immigrant community of Latinos were the objects of oppressive discourses. The old relationships and identities formed against these discourses were being reinscribed in me. In confronting these oppressive discourses of difference, I experienced domination and oppression, and was a party to the exercising of them.

This story demonstrates that some Chicanas/os do not move from marginalization to new positions of privilege associated with university affiliation, as if switching from one seat to another on the bus. We do not suddenly become powerful in our new identities and roles as university researchers. We do not leave one to get to the other. As Chicanas/os and ethnographers of color, we carry our baggage with us — a baggage of marginalization, complicity, and resentment, as well as *orgullo* (pride) and celebration. These are not easily cast away. No doubt it is not too difficult to embrace wholeheartedly the privileges of upward mobility, but to many of us the costs are great. Just as becoming raceless was a strategy for Black adolescents who, in Fordham's (1988) study, had to unlearn their racial identities and cultural behaviors in order to make it through high school and beyond, so must some Chicanas/os do the same. As bilingual, tricultural peoples, we "continually walk out of one culture and into another" (Anzaldúa, 1987, p. 77). In Anzaldúa's images, we are straddling multiple worlds, trying to break from colonized identities formed against White supremacy and male dominance and to form a new consciousness: "I am in all cultures, at the same time" (p. 77). We learn to tolerate contradictions and ambiguities of identities and to "seek new images of identities, new beliefs about ourselves" (p. 87).

While I recognize that part of my ongoing process is seeking, forging, and negotiating new images and identities, I am also raging against postmodern renderings of the White middle-class "discovery" that politically and socially situate the ethnographer as synonymous with colonizer, imperialist, and privileged researcher. In this view, it does not matter whether we are Chicanas/os or middle-class White male ethnographers. In the name of a postmodern understanding of identity and privilege, I am led to believe that I am now the same "researcher as colonizer," that I am now privileged, and that I share the same guilt for the same exploitation of the less privileged research participants. In a sense, I was not only being recruited to legitimate the majority culture's discourse of "Latinos as problem," but I am also symbolically being co-opted to legitimate academia's declaration of the postmodern ethnographer as the socially and politically privileged colonizer. In both instances, I am being co-opted to be like the colonizer, the oppressor, in ways that ignore my own struggle as a Chicana against subjugation and marginalization.

Thus, while I recognize my contradictory position and privilege (that come from university affiliation), and while I would gladly serve as a facilitator and translator for the voices of the Latina mothers of a small rural town in North Carolina (if they would have me), I must also see myself as going beyond the role of facilitator. I must see my own historical being and space. I must know that I will not "mimic the colonizers" (Perez, 1991, p. 177) and call myself the ethnographer/colonizer, for this insults my gendered, racial memory.

As I look back on my experience in the graduate seminar, I know that in the future I will not be silent, just as I could not be silent any more in the face of the dominant community's attempts to recruit me to their discourses about the Latino population in Hope City. I cannot continue to pretend that as a qualitative researcher in education, I am distanced from intimacy, hope, anger, and a historical collectivity with Latino communities. For these reasons, I cannot be neutral in the field, because to be so is to continue to be complicit in my own subjugation and that of the Latino communities. To take on only the role of facilitator is to deny my own activism. I must recognize that my own liberation and emancipation in relationship with my community are at stake, and that continued marginalization and subjugation are the perils.

I did not seek these confrontations and realizations. They came upon me while I was turned the other way, disengaging myself from the intimacy of Latina sisterhood. They came upon me as I convinced myself that I had to be careful because I was the privileged and thus the colonizer. I was attuned to seeking to reform my relationship with the research participants and to promote their empowerment, without realizing that *I* was being worked on and commodified, that *I* needed to be empowered. I suddenly found myself complicit in my own subjugation, vis-à-vis the dominant public discourse.

In the meantime, I find hope in Fine's (1994) narrative of the way her Latina niece, who was adopted into her middle-class Jewish family, moved in and out of identities as she fought a criminal case for sexual assault. Fine writes:

> Jackie mingled her autobiography with our surveilled borders on her Self and the raced and gendered legal interpretations of her Other by which she was surrounded. She braided them into her story, her deposition. . . . She slid from victim to survivor, from naive to coy, from deeply experienced young woman to child. In her deposition she dismantled the very categories I so worried we had constructed as sediment pillars around her, and she wandered among them, pivoting her identity, her self representations, and, therefore, her audiences. (1994, p. 71)

Herein I find the key: to resist "othering" and marginalization is to use our multiplicity of identities in order to tolerate and welcome the contradictions and ambiguities, as Anzaldúa (1987) writes, so that in our quest for liberation, we also dismantle the categories and the conquering language of the colonizer. In this manner, we "work the hyphen between Self and Other," as Fine (1994, p. 72) challenges us to do, yet we work from within ourselves as the Self/Other, Colonizer/Colonized ethnographer.

Thus, it is important to continue theorizing on the researchers' multiplicity of identities and the implications of this for qualitative research in education. As members of marginalized groups assume more privileged positions in the educational socioeconomic structures of hierarchy, people who were once merely the exotic objects of inquiry are now the inquirers — the ones formulating and asking the questions. As some enter the ranks of teachers, administrators, and scholars, we are becoming the enforcers and legitimators as well as the creators of official knowledge. Hence, as qualitative researchers in the field of education, we need to explore and understand the dilemmas created for Chicanas/os, African Americans, Native Americans, and scholars from other disenfranchised groups vis-à-vis the majority culture. We scholars/activists of color need to understand the ways in which we manipulate our multiple, fluid, clashing, and colonized identities and how our identities are manipulated and marginalized in the midst of oppressive discourses. Luke and Luke (1995) argue, "Only by describing and understanding how power works in oppressive social formations, how identity is shaped both through contestation and collusion with oppressive regimes of control, is it possible to lay down a systematic knowledge of marginal identities" (p. 376).

Further studies are also needed that capture the intricacies of marginalized teachers and scholars who are teaching and researching their own communities. Watson-Gegeo (1994) introduces a collection of articles that illuminate important questions dealing with "minority" teachers teaching "minority" students.[5] These excellent studies encourage further probing of the questions of resisting, negotiating, and tolerating identities in a context of power and privilege — in other words, to pay close attention to how we manipulate our identities and how our identities are manipulated by others. We need to see how Latino ethnographers, for example, become commodified in the process of research. At the same time, we also need to examine the gender, race, and class dynamics created in the university setting, where, for example, women of color, who are professors, and middle-class White students come together (see Vargas, 1996). These are critical questions that need further exploration.

Conclusion

This story is an attempt to untangle my own multiplicity of identities played out in the terrains of privilege and power in ethnographic research. With the new generation of "native" ethnographers, including myself, increasingly working within and writing about our own communities, we are beginning to question how our histories and identities are entangled in the workings of domination as we engage the oppressive discourses of "othering." In my case, while researching in a rural town in North Carolina, I had to confront both my own marginalization and my complicity in "othering" myself and my community, as I encountered the discourse that identified Latino family education and child-rearing practices as "problem" and "lacking."

At a time when qualitative researchers in education are questioning their own privilege in relation to the research participants, the "we" in the literature needs to be retheorized. My identity/role as a Chicana ethnographer cannot be collapsed in terms of "privileged" researcher in the same manner that other ethnographers are privileged in their relationships with their research participants. In failing to address the ways in which the ethnographer can be damaged by her/his own marginalization in the larger society, the literature has created a "we" that does not include my experience in the field as a Chicana ethnographer.

What might this story teach majority-culture ethnographers of education so that they too move beyond the "researcher as privileged" dilemma? I believe they also can confront their own multiplicities of identity and histories of complicity and mark the points of their own marginalization. Rosaldo (1989) and Patai (1991) write that ethnographers cannot escape their complicity in exploiting the "researched," yet I still need to ask, What is the nature of the space that I have found, and what are the possibilities for the Latino community in Hope City, North Carolina? My space is a fluid space of crossing borders and, as such, a contradictory one of collusion and oppositionality, complicity and subversion. For "Hispanos" in Hope City, surrounded by a historically violent and entrenched biracial society in which one is either Black or White, emancipatory possibilities lie in the creation of a dignified public space where they can negotiate new identities and break down the biraciality. Likewise, my challenge to majority-culture ethnographers is that they call upon their own marginalizing experiences and find a space for the emergence of new identities and discourses in the practice of solidarity with marginalized peoples.

My own journey moves me toward new transcendent discourses that are transformative and emancipatory. I hope to be, in Olson and Shopes's words, a "citizen-scholar-activist(s) rooted in the community" (cited in Van Galen & Eaker, 1995, p. 120). Recognizing our multidimensional identities as colonizers, colonized, neither, and in-between, we *camaradas* in struggle must work from within and facilitate a process where Latinas/os become the subjects and the creators of knowledge. My answer to the ethnographer-as-colonizer dilemma is that I will not stop at being the public translator and facilitator for my communities, but that I am my own voice, an activist seeking liberation from my own historical oppression in relation to my communities. We *mojado* ethnographers look anxiously to learn about the rich diversity of Latino communities in the U.S., and in doing so, create our own rich diversity of models, paradigms, and languages as we cross between our communities and "the artificial borders into occupied academic territories" (E. G. Murillo Jr., personal communication, 1995).

Notes

1. *Chicano* and *Chicana* are self-identified terms used by peoples of Mexican origin. They are political terms of self-determination and solidarity that originated in the Chicano liberation movement of the 1960s.

2. *Hispanic* is a U.S. government term used to classify Spanish-speaking peoples of Latin America living in the United States. *Latino* refers to a collective community of Latin Americans. Latino is my chosen term, which I use interchangeably with the emic term *Hispano*. I use Latino to refer to the very diverse Spanish-speaking community of Hope City (a pseudonym), North Carolina. *Latino* also refers to male members of the community, while *Latina* refers to the women. Members of the Latino community in Hope City usually refer to themselves in national terms: Mexican, Salvadoran, Guatemalan, etc. However, they have also adopted the term Hispanos to refer to themselves collectively as a community. It is also important to note

that people self-identify differently. For this reason, when I refer to my friends, I use the various terms with which they identify themselves. Also, an *Indigenista* or *Mesocentric* (Godina, 1996) perspective has spurred interest among Latinos and peoples of indigenous ancestry between themselves and tribal Native Americans. In essence, through this movement we (including myself) are saying that we *are* Native American people.

3. *Aztlan* refers to the mythical origins and ancient homelands of the Aztec civilization. Over the last thirty years, Aztlan has been popularized by the Chicano liberation movement and is linked to the vast northern territories of Mexico that were invaded and annexed by the United States in 1848.

4. *Othering* refers to objectifying people who are different than the Western White self in a manner that renders them inferior.

5. This edited collection includes articles by Foster (1994) on the views of African American teachers who counter prevailing hegemonic beliefs about African American children in reform efforts to improve their achievement in schools; Watson-Gegeo and Gegeo (1994) on the ways in which a history of colonization and modernization in the Solomon Islands serves to keep teachers' cultural knowledge out of the classroom; and Lipka (1994), who examined how Yup'ik Eskimo teachers in Alaska face administrative barriers when working to include their language and culture in their classrooms.

References

Adkins, A., Givens, G., McKinney, M., Murillo, E., & Villenas, S. (1995, November). *Contested childrearing: The social construction of Latino childrearing.* Paper presented at the meeting of the American Educational Studies Association, Cleveland, OH.

Anzaldúa, G. (1987). *Borderlands/La frontera.* San Francisco: Aunt Lute Books.

Crapanzano, V. (1986). Hermes' dilemma: The masking of subversion in ethnographic description. In J. Clifford & G. Marcus (Eds.), *Writing culture* (pp. 51–76). Berkeley: University of California Press.

Delgado-Gaitan, C. (1993). Researching change and changing the researcher. *Harvard Educational Review, 63,* 389–411.

Delgado-Gaitan, C., & Trueba, H. (1991). *Crossing cultural borders: Education for immigrant families in America.* London: Falmer Press.

Ellsworth, E. (1989). Why doesn't this feel empowering? Working through the myths of critical pedagogy. *Harvard Educational Review, 59,* 297–324.

Fine, M. (1994). Working the hyphens: Reinventing self and other in qualitative research. In N. Denzin & Y. Lincoln (Eds.), *Handbook of qualitative research* (pp. 70–82). Thousand Oaks, CA: Sage.

Fordham, S. (1988). Racelessness as a factor in Black students' school success: Pragmatic strategy or pyrrhic victory? *Harvard Educational Review, 58,* 54–84.

Foster, M. (1994). The role of community and culture in school reform efforts: Examining the views of African American teachers. *Educational Foundations, 8*(2), 5–26.

Godina, H. (1996, April). *Mesocentrism: Teaching indigenous Mexican culture in the classroom.* Paper presented at the annual meeting of the American Educational Research Association, New York.

hooks, b. (1989). Talking back: Thinking feminist, thinking Black. Boston: South End Press.

hooks, b. (1990). *Yearning.* Boston: South End Press.

hooks, b. (1994). *Teaching to transgress: Education as the practice of freedom.* New York: Routledge.

Lather, P. (1991). *Getting smart: Feminist research and pedagogy with/in the postmodern.* New York: Routledge.

LeCompte, M., & de Marrais, K. (1992). The disempowering of empowerment: Out of the revolution and into the classroom. *Educational Foundations, 6*(13), 5–31.

Lipka, J. (1994). Schools failing minority teachers: Problems and suggestions. *Educational Foundations, 8*(2), 57–80.

Luke, C., & Luke, A. (1995). Just naming? Educational discourses and the politics of identity. In W. Pink & G. Noblit (Eds.), *Continuity and contradiction: The futures of the sociology of education* (pp. 357–380). Cresskill, NJ: Hampton Press.

Patai, D. (1991). U.S. academics and third world women: Is ethical research possible? In S. Gluck & D. Patai (Eds.), *Women's words: The feminist practice of oral history* (pp. 137–153). New York: Routledge.

Perez, E. (1991). Sexuality and discourse: Notes from a Chicana survivor. In C. Trujillo (Ed.), *Chicana lesbians: The girls our mothers warned us about* (pp. 158–184). Berkeley, CA: Third Woman Press.

Pratt, M. (1986). Fieldwork in common places. In J. Clifford & G. Marcus (Eds.), *Writing culture* (pp. 27–50). Berkeley: University of California Press.

Roman, L., & Apple, M. (1990). Is naturalism a move away from positivism? Materialist and feminist approaches to subjectivity in ethnographic research. In E. Eisner & A. Peshkin (Eds.), *Qualitative inquiry in education: The continuing debate* (pp. 38–73). New York: Teachers College Press.

Rosaldo, R. (1989). *Culture and truth: The remaking of social analysis.* Boston: Beacon Press.

Sleeter, C. (1995). Foreword. In B. Swadener & S. Lubeck (Eds.), *Children and families "at promise"* (pp. ix–xi). Albany: State University of New York Press.

Stone, L. (1992). The essentialist tension in reflective teacher education. In L. Valli (Ed.), *Reflective teacher education: Cases and critiques* (pp. 198–211). Albany: State University of New York Press.

Swadener, B., & Lubeck, S. (Eds.). (1995). *Children and families "at promise."* Albany: State University of New York Press.

Van Galen, J., & Eaker, D. (1995). Beyond settling for scholarship: On defining the beginning and ending points of postmodern research. In W. Pink & G. Noblit (Eds.), *Continuity and contradiction: The futures of the sociology of education* (pp. 113–131). Cresskill, NJ: Hampton Press.

Vargas, L. (1996, April). *When the other is the teacher: Implications for teacher diversity in higher education. Paper presented at the annual meeting of the Eastern Communication Association, New York City.*

Watson-Gegeo, K. (1994). Introduction: What's culture got to do with it? Minority teachers teaching minority students. *Educational Foundations, 8*(2), 3–4.

Watson-Gegeo, K., & Gegeo, D. (1994). Keeping culture out of the classroom in rural Solomon Islands schools: A critical analysis. *Educational Foundations, 8*(2), 27–55.

Weis, L. (1995). Identity formation and the process of "othering": Unraveling sexual threads. *Educational Foundations, 9*(1), 17–33.

I am indebted to George Noblit for the conversations that enabled me to tell this story. I also wish to thank Amee Adkins and Lynda Stone for their insights on the manuscript and to Bernardo Gallegos for his encouragement. The research project in Hope City was funded by the Frank Porter Graham Child Development Center, with partial funding by the North Carolina Humanities Council.

Educative Research, Voice,
and School Change

ANDREW DAVID GITLIN

Over the last two decades, dramatic shifts have occurred in the research methods that can be legitimately employed in the field of education. Ethnography, once the primary method of anthropologists, for example, is now
widely used and valued by the educational research community. And, more recently,
it has been noted that "nothing about objective-quantitative research preclude[s] the
description and analysis of classroom practices with interpretive-qualitative methods" (Gage, 1989, p. 142). Although the use of ethnography has enabled educational researchers to pose questions and gain insights previously ignored in most objective-quantitative studies, and the move to a more pluralistic view of method has
some advantages, I will argue that these changes in educational research methods
have done little to alter the alienating relationship between the researcher and those
studied.[1]

Educational research is still a process that for the most part silences those studied,
ignores their personal knowledge, and strengthens the assumption that researchers are
the producers of knowledge. Building on this critique, I will briefly outline the theoretical underpinnings of an alternative methodological approach, educative research
(Gitlin, Siegal, & Boru, 1989), that attempts to transform the relationship between
researchers and school practitioners by developing the voice of teachers. Finally, and
most central to this article, I want to describe an initial attempt to translate educative
research into practice, including in that description the themes that guided the
project.

The Politics of Method

Most methodological debates focus either on the validity and reliability of the results,
or the degree of compatibility between approaches (Howe, 1988; Kirk & Miller,
1985; LeCompte & Goetz, 1982). In a recent article discussing shifts in social science
methodology, Gage (1989), for example, reviews the competing approaches by raising questions about the relationship between paradigms and the data they produce.
Ignored in this type of debate is an analysis of the way method structures relations between the researcher and those studied. This oversight leaves the impression that the

Harvard Educational Review Vol. 60 No. 4 November 1990, 443–466

central concern is how to fit the appropriate method with a particular question. In contrast, focusing on the relationship between method and actors illuminates a set of political concerns not raised in most methodological debates.

In experimental research, for example, subjects are excluded from the production of knowledge, except in a post hoc fashion. By setting up a laboratory-type situation from which generalizations can be made to determine a wide range of rules or laws, those studied are "subject to the dictates and whims of external authorities" (Belenky, Clinchy, Goldberger, & Tarule, 1986, p. 57) who claim to make sense of life in classrooms. In the case of teachers, research of this kind strengthens the assumption that practitioners do not produce knowledge, that their personal knowledge is not useful, and that researchers set policy.

The politics of objective-quantitative studies may not be surprising to some who have chosen to embrace a more interpretive-qualitative approach. However, a close look at these methods indicates that they often structure the relationship between the researcher and those studied in much the same way. In a previous article, with the help of some colleagues, I illustrated the way educational ethnographies act to silence and objectify the subject (Gitlin, Siegal, & Boru, 1989). In this paper I add to that analysis by drawing on two examples from recent scholarship that point to the politics of traditional ethnographic methods.[2] In doing so, my intent is not so much to criticize the individual researchers but rather to show how commonsense assumptions about method often act behind our backs in powerful and constraining ways.

In a recent issue of the *Journal of Curriculum and Supervision*, White (1989) "analyzes how a kindergarten teacher and her students use speech as they actively engage in the formation of knowledge in a social studies lesson" (p. 299). She bases her results on a four-year ethnographic study that includes extensive observations and interviews. After one observation she asked the teacher what she thought of the lesson. The teacher responded by saying that "the lesson went fine" and she had "met her objectives" (p. 315). In response to an expanded version of these statements, White concluded:

> I did not think the lesson was fine. Although the lesson bustled with activities — songs were sung, enriching materials were brought in for the children, and questions were cheerfully asked and answered — I did not think that much reaching or learning had occurred. I was troubled by how polite forms of discourse masked that lack of construction of substantial knowledge. (p. 315)

Clearly, the teacher and researcher viewed the lesson differently. In some sense, this disagreement provided an important opportunity for the researcher and teacher to examine their underlying assumptions and attempt to understand more fully the complexities of classroom life. Such a discussion, however, would challenge the established ethnographic norm that the researcher should influence the behavior and attitudes of the subjects as little as possible (Agar, 1980). White is apparently aware of this norm and defines her role accordingly:

> Since I was an observing researcher and not in a supervisory or collaborative relationship with her, I didn't think that discussing my questions with her was appropriate. But my vague sense of being troubled about this lesson has pursued me, ultimately compelling me to write this article. (p. 315)

Constraining the research process in this way reinforces the alienating relationship between researcher and practitioner; the teacher's explanation of the lesson is discounted, the researcher is assumed to have a better understanding of what was going on without hearing the teacher's response to her arguments. In this instance, research is a one-way process that is done to teachers; their personal knowledge is discredited, and the researcher assumes an expert role as one who produces knowledge. As a result, the teacher's understanding of the classroom is unchanged and the researcher is not able to benefit from the teacher's personal knowledge and insights.

In contrast to the above example, Fine (1987), in an article on silencing in the public schools, is more critical of the researcher's role and the types of relationships that can occur with the use of ethnographic methods.

> The process of conducting research within schools to identify words that could have been said, talk that should have been nurtured, and information that needed to be announced, suffers from voyeurism and perhaps the worst of post hoc arrogance. The researcher's sadistic pleasure of spotting another teacher's collapsed contradiction, aborted analysis, or silencing sentence was moderated only by the ever present knowledge that similar analytic surgery could easily be performed on my own classes. (p. 172)

Understanding the strained relation between researcher and those studied, however, does not necessarily lead to alterations in this relationship. Fine sees in the teachers she observed "the 'naturalness' of not naming, of shutting down or marginalizing conversations for the 'sake of getting on with learning' that demands educators' attention" (p. 172). She does not see as clearly the influence of research on these teachers.[3] Because these teachers were involved in the research process only in terms of responding to the researcher's report, research was done on them, and their knowledge was not considered in terms of the formation of the question or the interpretation of the results. Just as teachers may silence students to get on with learning, so may researchers silence those studied to get on with their research.

If research is going to help develop practitioners' voices, as opposed to silencing them, researchers must engage in dialogue with practitioners at both the level of question-posing and the interpretation of the findings. This change in the research process suggests the need for corresponding changes in definitions of validity and reliability. The "truthfulness" of the data can no longer be understood as something extracted by an individual armed with a set of research procedures, but rather as a mutual process between researcher and subject, that recognizes the value of practical knowledge, theoretical inquiry, and systematic examinations. The researchers' knowledge is not assumed to be more legitimate than the subjects', nor is their role one of helping the needy other. Rather, the researcher and subject attempt to come to a mutual understanding based on their own strongly articulated positions.

Questions of validity, however, must go beyond the truthfulness of the data. The influence of the research process on who produces knowledge, who is seen as an expert, and the resulting changes at the level of school practice are also part of an expanded and more political view of validity. For example, one criterion of validity would be the degree to which the research process enabled disenfranchised groups to fully participate in the decisionmaking process; examine their beliefs, actions, and the school context; and make changes based on this understanding.[4]

It should be noted that this type of catalytic validity is unlikely to occur by simply asking practitioners to read research, because their job is structured to make this difficult (Bullough & Gitlin, 1989); articles also are written in coded ways that limit accessibility.[5] Even if teachers do read the research, this trickling down of knowledge leaves in place the privileged position of the academic as the sole producer of knowledge, thereby preventing full participation of disenfranchised groups.

Traditional notions of reliability are also altered when the central aim of the research process is to develop voice. Within traditional methods, reliability is understood in terms of the ability of independent researchers to come to the same conclusions when the same procedures are used. In contrast, when the aim is the development of voice, it is undesirable and not expected that independent researcher-subject teams would come to the same conclusions. It is also undesirable for the procedures to remain unchanged from context to context. Procedures should not only be allowed to evolve within a particular research study, but also to change given the needs and priorities of a particular population. Reliability, therefore, cannot be based on duplicating procedures but rather must center on attempts to satisfy the underlying principle of voice and its relation to a particular type of school change.

Educative Research Theory

Given these arguments about the way method structures relations, it follows that those concerned with school change, the teacher's role, and the division of labor that tears at our educational community need to rethink traditional research methods. Efforts in this area have gained tremendous momentum in the last decade. Carr and Kemmis's work (1986), for example, has fostered a politicized form of action research that not only gives a say to practitioners but also exposes some of the myths surrounding scientific research. Lather (1986) and Weiler (1988), on the other hand, have championed the need for openly ideological research that is grounded in the recognition of the oppressed place of women in a male-dominated society. And Simon and Dippo (1986) have worked on forms of critical ethnography that attempt to make changes that contest schools' role in replicating societal race, class, and gender relations. While the alternative approach described in this article differs from these efforts in certain ways, its development draws heavily on these scholars' insights and the way they have enabled all of us to rethink what is legitimate educational research. Because the emphasis of this article is on the working out of this alternative, the primary assumptions will only be discussed in a cursory fashion.

Underlying most research methods is the assumption that knowledge is something that researchers extract from those studied; it is a one-way process that researchers use to put together a convincing story about the way things are or should be in school. Lost in this process is the notion that knowledge can also arise from dialogue involving the interaction between the speaker and listener within a particular context (Clark & Holquist, 1984). And it is this turn toward dialogue that helps distinguish the educative research approach. To consider the implications of this approach it is necessary to say a few words on what is meant by dialogue.[6]

Dialogue, as I am using the term, differs from talk or conversation in several important ways. People talk to each other all the time, but the talk often is not important to the participants. A good example of this is when two individuals greet each other in the hall and one asks, "How are you doing?" and the other replies, "Fine." Dialogue, on the other hand, is entered into because it presupposes a "tacit sense of relevance" (Bernstein, 1983, p. 2). A precondition for dialogue, therefore, is that all participants see the discourse as important and have a say in determining its course. Talk differs also from dialogue because talk is often used to try to sway someone to one's point of view. It doesn't matter if the topic is the weather, politics, art, or one's relationship with a friend, an attempt is made to convince the other in order to "win the argument." Dialogue does not pit one actor against another but rather enables participants to work together to understand the subject being discussed. Finally, dialogue requires that even if one person understands the situation more completely than the other, "the person with understanding does not know and judge as one who stands apart unaffected, but as one united by the specific bond with the other; [s/he] thinks with the other and undergoes the situation with him [her]" (Gadamer, 1975, p. 288). Neither does gaining an understanding require that all prejudices or prejudgments be removed, as this is clearly impossible. The aim of the dialogue is simply to make prejudgments apparent and to "test them critically in the course of inquiry" (Bernstein, 1983, p. 128). Such critical testing of prejudgments empowers actors to challenge taken-for-granted notions that influence the way they see the world and judge their practice.

This emphasis on dialogue suggests a shift in a number of epistemological concerns when compared to more traditional forms of research. In particular, the dialogical emphasis of educative research has implications for wider issues, such as who has the authority to produce knowledge, the methods of knowing, and the knowledge produced (Messer-Davidow, 1985).

In contrast to most inquiry where researchers "determine the research, conduct it, evaluate the subjects' behavior and present the findings " (Messer-Davidow, 1985, p. 13), educative research views traditionally excluded groups — including teachers, students, and parents — as having the authority to produce knowledge. This authority not only suggests a right to participate in research, but an opportunity to enter into a dialogical process where the researcher avoids imposing meaning and estranged groups can be changed from "reactive objects into society-making subjects" (Shor, 1980, p. 98). Because this switch can play an important part in confronting the division of labor between researchers and those studied — a division the educative research process attempts to challenge — it is unacceptable within this approach to silence and objectify those studied in the name of conducting research.

Methods of knowing are also altered within the educative approach. Whereas many methods attempt to determine an objective finding by having the researcher take a disinterested position, dialogical approaches assume that it is impossible to remove bias completely. The intent of dialogical methods, therefore, is not to come up with universal truths, but rather to identify and examine the normative truths that are embedded in a particular historical context. Because knowledge is viewed as a social construction, not only is the objectivity of dominant ideologies undermined, but experience can be seen as having truth value. In addition, instead of accepting a technical view of knowledge that allows inherently political, moral, and ethical questions to be reduced to "how to" concerns, educative research explicitly attempts to illuminate such concerns so that actors can further develop a political philosophy and a rationale for action. By including disenfranchised groups in this political process, a much more defensible understanding of the politics of schooling can be promised.

Educative research also differs from many traditional approaches by insisting that the research process have, where possible, a collective moment. If actions are to be taken that confront the school-wide structures and normative priorities that define educational relations and activities in narrow ways, then some form of collective action is necessary. The intent of this collective action is not to silence minority opinions or actions, but rather to enable ever-changing groups with common interests to act in concert on the limits of public education.

In sum, educative research expands the authority to produce knowledge beyond the researcher; attempts to restructure the researcher-subject relation such that both are involved in identifying and examining beliefs, practices, and normative truths; invokes the moral claim against silencing the other in the name of research; fosters a political view of knowledge; and attempts to encourage a more collective approach to research that can mobilize groups typically left out of educational policy discourse. Methods seen as appropriate parts of the educative research project cannot be imposed on a group of individuals without regard for cultural concerns, contextual situations, and individual differences. Instead, methods and persons must be in a dialectical relation such that the individuals can alter the procedures as the procedures inevitably will alter the experience. When such a relation occurs, participants can not only correct contradictions and limitations in the methods, but also alter the methods in ways that enable individuals to build on what they know, as opposed to becoming subject to a new but still dominating set of procedures (Belenky et al, 1986).

Building on these underlying assumptions of educative research, the section that follows provides an overview of the events that helped shape this method. This overview begins with an account of how the educative research project began.

Educative Research Practice

The cooperative Masters program at the University of Utah gave me the opportunity to engage in educative research. In this program, twenty elementary and secondary teachers from a particular district go through the coursework as a group. Classes meet in the schools and teachers have a say in determining the direction and content of the program. While the length of the program varies, it usually lasts two years and results in a Masters of Education degree for participants.

Because this type of program has a history of collaboration between teachers and university faculty and provides a tremendous amount of freedom in terms of course structure, I decided to explore the possibility of having the cooperative focus on educative research. Toward this end, in my initial meeting with the teachers in September 1988, I laid out my sense of the dominant relationship between university researchers and practitioners, why this relation was problematic, and a possible avenue to confront this relation — namely, educative research. The teachers all agreed to accept this theme, and many appeared enthusiastic. In retrospect, however, it is clear that they really didn't have a choice, that some were less than excited about the direction, and that I was acting in the role of an expert who knew what the teachers needed. At the time, however, I felt enough support to develop a program based on the assumptions of educative research. What follows is a very brief overview of the types of activities in which we engaged over the first year.

The educative research project (ERP) started with the writing of a school history. For the school in which they worked, all teachers were asked to identify common school structures — such as curriculum programs or staffing patterns — and to interview teachers, parents, and administrators to get a sense of the structures, beliefs, behaviors, and traditions of the school. Teachers were also encouraged to collect other information of interest to them. Teachers used this data to compare their current school situation with the recent history of the school and with changes found in our system of public education. To illuminate some of these issues, I suggested the following set of readings: Eisner's (1979) *The Educational Imagination*, Sarason's (1971) *The Culture of the School and the Problem of Change*, Apple's (1979) *Ideology and Curriculum*, and Kliebard's (1987) *The Struggle for the American Curriculum*. Once the data had been collected, teachers could use these readings to further their analysis of the school history.

When the school histories were close to completion we switched from a focus on the structure and culture of schooling to an exploration of the self. To facilitate this exploration teachers wrote personal histories. The teachers could pose any questions they wanted, but I did suggest that they consider the following questions:

Why did I choose teaching as a career?
What shaped me as a teacher?
What is my philosophy about teaching?
What, if any, changes have I seen in my teaching philosophy and practice?

I chose these questions because I believed they had the potential to illuminate the politics of schooling by exposing the influence of context on teaching and schooling, cultural norms, and one's teaching philosophy. As was true of the school history, I did not take a neutral position but explicitly chose readings that would illuminate political issues often obscured in discussions of schooling. In particular, I suggested Apple's (1986) *Teachers and Text*, Leach's (1988) "Teacher Education and Reform," and Spencer's (1984) "The Home and School Lives of Women Teachers." The teachers could substitute other texts or utilize these readings in any way they desired.

Up to this point the research was still primarily individualistic. If a more collective approach to research was to occur, we had to find ways to share, compare, and analyze what was common and different about the school and personal histories. Toward this end, I decided to introduce the teachers to a set of procedures that would further discussion on these texts as well as other future concerns. I told them they could use any dialogical model they wanted, but I only introduced the approach I developed over the last decade, horizontal evaluation (Gitlin & Goldstein, 1987; Gitlin & Smyth, 1989). To acquaint them with the model, I gave them a brief overview of the assumptions underlying this approach, asked them to read anonymous transcripts of others who had used the model, and encouraged them to try horizontal evaluation with a trusted colleague.

Suffice it to say, all the teachers decided to use this approach. As was true of the initial decision to center the cooperative Masters program around educative research, it is now clear that the teachers really didn't have a choice. I had used my privileged position to structure the experience, and in so doing, lost an opportunity to challenge the dominant relationship between researcher and practitioner.

To understand how horizontal evaluation influenced the educative research process, it is important to explain the procedures in some detail.[7] Horizontal evaluation is a process in which teachers start out by collaboratively analyzing the relationship between their teaching intentions and their practices in ways that point to living contradictions (Whitehead & Lomax, 1987). This is another way of saying that they are searching for the gap between what they desire to do in their teaching and what they actually end up doing. Where there is not this mismatch between intention and practice, teachers think through why it is they want to achieve the particular ends they have identified, as opposed to unquestioningly accepting them. Intentions can be stated in advance or can emerge from discussion. When stated in advance, they become a text for analysis. A teacher, for example, might have the intention of integrating life within schools with the experiences outside the classroom. Instead of simply observing the extent to which his or her practice reflects this intent, it is important that participants discuss why this integration is important, and under what conditions and for which groups it might be most appropriate. Once issues like this can be clarified, their desirability can be examined and debated in relation to a normative framework.

To become clearer about the relationship between educational means and ends, horizontal evaluation draws primarily on the work of Gadamer (1975) and Habermas (1976). In particular, their arguments have helped shape three methods, "communication analysis," "historical perspective," and "challenge statements," which can be utilized to enhance and deepen the dialogue between the teacher and observer.

Communication analysis. Communication analysis makes it possible for participants to understand how the prejudgments they hold about teaching frame their teaching and shape interactions. For example, if a teacher regards chaotic student behavior as being caused by the "low abilities" of the students, the question, "What do you mean by low abilities?" could be posed. Implicit values that lie behind statements and practices like this, therefore, can be made explicit and thus reconsidered by the participants. Reconsideration of these values can amount to a transformation in the way teachers make and remake school reality in small ways on a daily basis. If teachers realize that the grouping of students authorized by the school is inappropriate because it penalizes those who differ from the dominant culture, then classroom structures and pedagogy can be reorganized to reflect a more egalitarian view of the way students should be treated.

Historical perspective. Adopting a historical perspective with respect to particular teaching strategies allows apparently commonsense notions and actions to be seen not as natural and immutable, but rather as choices that are part of a historical tradition that serves particular interests while denying others. For instance, if a teacher regards teaching as a process of depositing information in the heads of students, adopting a historical perspective can encourage discussion about what factors have historically encouraged this kind of pedagogy. The interests embedded within such a view can then be more fully analyzed.

Challenge statements. Where discussion between teacher and colleague about in-class activity has become stilted, stalled, or bogged down, and cannot go beyond clarifying values and prejudgments, then either of the parties can initiate a challenge statement designed to get discussion moving again. For example, if a teacher holds to the view that students should obey his or her classroom rules in all circumstances, questions can be raised about students' and teachers' rights and about the role and purpose of adult authority. The resulting conversation might seek to investigate the legitimacy of adult authority and the implications this holds for the education of students in a democracy.

Alternatives. In addition to these methods, horizontal evaluation asks participants to link the insights gained through dialogue to the realization of alternative teaching practices. The alternative is not an end point, an unalterable part of the teachers' repertoire, but rather a turning point for further discourse on the relation of intentions to practice. In other words, while the dialogue may end with a suggested alternative, this alternative then becomes part of a new set of practices that are then examined by the participants. Alternatives are an important part of the dialogical process because new insights are linked to practice, thereby avoiding action without reflection or reflection without action (Freire, 1985).

Using this process where possible, teachers were asked to get together in groups and look across school and personal histories to identify common themes, problems, dilemmas, or concerns. These collective histories were then shared with everyone involved in the project and put in written form. To facilitate this discourse, I suggested we read a series of articles on what might be broadly termed the politics of schooling. These readings included Grant and Sleeter's (1988) "Race, Class, and Gender and Abandoned Dreams," Weis's (1988) "High School Girls in a Deindustrializing Economy," and Perry's (1988) "A Black Student's Reflection on Public and Private Schools." In particular, the focus was on how issues of race, class, and gender influenced the problems we pose and what is taken for granted in the classroom.

I chose these readings to address the importance of understanding schooling as a political process, and also because the issues raised in the school and personal histories focused on gender, race, and class. While the teachers didn't always use these terms, it was clear that the personal and school histories addressed race discrimination, oppression of women, and the hierarchical divisions between certain groups. We, therefore, were able to look across school and personal histories and to name the themes and problems identified. Further, because the political side of their histories was sometimes hidden, the readings acted to point out broader implications or questions that the teachers could ask about their areas of interest.

In an attempt to continually link our discussions to classroom practice, we also observed each other using horizontal evaluation in an attempt to capture any recurring concerns or problems. Because these concerns or problems were articulated in writing, they became texts that could be related to school and personal histories as well as to the collective histories. Two factors were important in making the horizontal evaluation experience more helpful for those involved in the project: the teacher who was observing had a paid substitute, and the audiotaped discourse that followed the observation was transcribed and given back to the teacher. The funds for these activities were diverted from those normally allotted by the university to support the researcher.

At this point, teachers were asked to utilize their personal and school histories and the horizontal evaluation experiences to pose a research question. Some teachers worked individually while others worked in groups to identify an issue of importance. This question or concern could be tentative in nature, but it had to be defined with enough specificity to enable them to go to the library and search for relevant literature. When a group or an individual felt they had explored an issue in some depth, they were asked to restate their problem and put together a plan for a pilot study that would give them additional insights and some experience with collecting and analyzing data. One teacher, for example, centered her problem on the question of what it means to be a successful teacher. With this in mind she then tried to design a study that would help her refine the question of success and collect some data on this issue.

As these pilot studies were completed, teachers shared with other members of the project their results and questions. At the end of these presentations the teachers were asked to write a "First Look" paper that reported their findings. When the school year ended, we started an intensive period of writing that captured the first year's journey. As the teachers and I wrote, we shared parts of our papers with other members of the project to get feedback.

In total, these events suggest the need for some dramatic changes in the way research is conducted and the roles particular participants play. In the sections that follow I will try to illuminate how the ERP can shape the relationship between researcher and those studied, so that those silenced begin to develop their own voices. I will also discuss how voice can contribute to school change. To do this, I will rely on the texts the teachers produced as part of the ERP. Because I am weaving these texts together and developing a set of constructs, this is my story. This story differs from many others because the researcher is included in the text. I did not abstract data from teachers, but rather, through a process of mutual understanding, tried to give meaning to a set of events based on the knowledge the teachers produced.

Question Posing

One way most traditional research reproduced the hierarchical and alienating relationship between practitioners and researchers is by centering the process of question posing in the hands of the university researcher. Practitioners, as a result, do not have an opportunity to address issues they feel are important and, given the authority of those who conduct research, are expected to comply with their recommendations. A first step in altering this relationship is to encourage teachers to be involved in the process of question posing. This shift in the locus of control creates a less alienating situation for the teachers involved and increases the likelihood that theoretical concerns will be linked to those associated with practice. Simply altering the locus of control, however, remains limiting in some dramatic ways. In particular, this type of change does little or nothing to challenge the way dominant views of teaching and schooling constrain our understanding of educational problems. This is so for several reasons.

The questions we ask are never simply our own. Instead, they reflect an ongoing negotiation among the influences of material conditions or contexts, cultural norms, and self. If a teacher states, for example, that his or her biggest concern is how to get control of the students, this question or problem is related to, among other things, a set of cultural norms about the legitimate authority of teachers, a personal philosophy about teaching, and the influence of material conditions, such as the teacher-pupil ratio found in the school. However, while the teacher-pupil ratio in the classroom and the cultural norms concerning the question of legitimate authority inevitably influence an individual's philosophy of teaching, this philosophy cannot be reduced to these influences in any sort of exact manner. In other words, a teacher's perspective on educational problems or issues can never be either completely determined by or transcend material conditions or cultural norms. And it is this tension between a set of values grounded in the self and what Bakhtin refers to as an official ideology "that is in relatively close accord with the socially approved values of the culture as a whole and that is shaped by the 'law of surroundings' [the material conditions]" (Clark & Holquist, 1984, pp. 183–184) that complicates the process of question posing. If educative research simply alters the locus of control such that the teacher determines the research question, because the material conditions under which teachers work give them few opportunities to reflect on the relationship between their values and those of the official ideology, the power of what is taken for granted pushes the negotiation process to the side of the dominant worldview.

Given that this sort of result would dramatically constrain the types of questions addressed, educative research not only tries to give teachers a say in question posing, but — importantly — encourages them to examine the values they hold and the culture in which they work, including both the material realities of this culture and wider societal influences. The examples that follow trace this process of question posing.

For Kate, a teacher in the educative research project, this type of inquiry became possible during the writing and analysis of her school history.[8] The starting point was an examination of the math program used at her school.

> The math program fosters what is referred to as an implicit curriculum by Eliot Eisner (1987). It stresses competition as students are aware of which group they are in and what grade level most of their group is in. The implicit importance placed on math at Highland Park is also in the timing; it is designed for efficiency, not comfort, as students must move to different locations with all their materials. Because there is a need for improved math skills in our society, Highland Park's emphasis on measurable objectives and efficiency in the program strives to meet that need. The teacher's role in the math program is to provide efficient instruction. (Kate, school history)

Kate has uncovered the way a math program fosters competition among students and strengthens a constrained role where teachers spend a great deal of time making sure students learn the ideas and concepts determined by others. She also added to this analysis by considering the relation between school norms and those held by the wider society.

> One assumption of the [math] curriculum is that schools are similar in aims to industry, so the schools are set up in a similar manner. However, the ultimate goal of industry is not increased productivity but to make money, or simply stated to in-

crease personal gain. This would certainly limit the potential of education to develop humans to their full capacity. (Kate, school history)

Once the official ideology of individualism and profit had been identified, Kate reflected on its relationship to her personal values.

> I question the premise that schools should adopt this value of our society or indus-
> try. I feel that many District policies operate on the assumption that our society's
> needs are synonymous with the needs of our corporate structure. There's not much
> poetry in that assumption. (Kate, school history)

The importance of this example is not that Kate got the issue "right" in some sense
of the word, or understood the situation completely, but rather that through the writing of her school history she could consider the context of schooling and its relation
to societal influences. She was, therefore, less likely to be constrained by the official
ideology. When operating within the official ideology, for example, one might accept
the notion of achievement as the criterion by which to measure success. Kate, on the
other hand, considers some of the values that underlie this position, such as competition, efficiency, and individualism, and analyzes these values in relation to a set of personal beliefs and the influence of context. By doing so her concerns include the need
to alter school structures that reinforce a particular view of schooling.

For other teachers involved in the educative research project, the question-posing
process was strongly influenced by the writing of personal histories. Beth's personal
history recaptured the normative assumptions that encouraged her to be a teacher in
the first place.

> Having grown up in a very traditional and conservative family, teaching, or any
> other "public servant" position was in my parents' eyes, a suitable, but no doubt
> temporary career for me. Of the women in my family (grandmothers, aunts, cous-
> ins) who had careers, five were teachers and one was a nurse. I believe it was par-
> tially these familial expectations that both repelled and later induced me to become
> a teacher. (Beth, personal history)

By articulating why she entered teaching, Beth has shown that the choice was not
simply her own but rather involved an uneasy compromise between a set of personal
values and cultural norms connected to issues of gender. By illuminating this tension,
Beth could see that part of her struggle with teaching was also the struggle of a bright,
talented woman doing a type of "women's work" that is commonly devalued by the
society at large.

Reflections on her student teaching experience furthered this analysis by pointing
out how the cultural norms found in the school reinforced the notion that others
should determine the aims of schooling.

> At the conclusion of the student teaching experience, my earliest assumptions about
> life in the classroom had been formed. . . . But it was more than just what I observed
> in the classroom. It was the pervasive feeling that I sensed about schools in general:
> places where little bodies come to be filled up with knowledge that someone else,
> often not the teacher, has determined would be good for them. It was this assump-
> tion, that while not wanting to be a part of it, I was also willing to condone as nor-
> mal and let it go unchallenged. (Beth, personal history)

Beth does not agree that teachers should defer to others in determining the educational good for students; she is, however, at this time in her career, willing to let this hierarchy go unchallenged. By engaging in such an analysis, she has illuminated some of the normative priorities that narrow the institutional role of teacher. At the same time, further dialogue clarified how her reluctance to challenge these norms helps legitimate this constrained role.

When Beth examined her most recent teaching experiences, she also found that, as was true of her analysis of the cultural norms, the material conditions of the school, in the form of a behavioral management system, led her away from her personal values and beliefs.

> The use of Assertiveness Discipline and the constraints of teaching in a district which emphasizes the curriculum as technology orientation has made me feel that my own philosophy of teaching is continually getting lost and failing to solidify. (Beth, personal history)

The articulation of these tensions between self, cultural norms, and context enabled Beth to see that the "culture of teaching and . . . school structures have played a powerful role in shaping me as a teacher," and that she longed to find a way to better express the values and priorities she believed in as a teacher: "What I wanted to do was to shift the focus of my classroom from being teacher centered, to student centered, and to assume more of a cognitive process approach to curriculum" (Beth, problem paper). In a general sense, the challenge Beth has set before her is how to alter the relationship between the official ideology and her personal beliefs. She has laid out a terrain for discourse in which questions about the teacher's role and assumptions about teaching, both those held personally and those widely accepted, could be debated and included in the formation of her problem.

My involvement in the ERP also helped me reexamine the focus of educative research. At the beginning of the project my problem was framed primarily in terms of the other — namely, the teacher. Specifically, I was interested in seeing if the educative research process would enable teachers to view their classrooms in a way that reflected concerns about race, class, and gender. To facilitate this result, I put together a set of readings that had a particular political bent. However, as we discussed these readings, several teachers found them inappropriate and formed their question in technical terms. Conna Lee is a case in point. For Conna Lee, a kindergarten teacher, the problem was how to share ideas that "worked" with other teachers. Questions of bulletin boards and music lessons were some of her main concerns.

My first response to Conna Lee's problem was disappointment. This project, I remember thinking, isn't going to challenge anything and is likely to reinforce the notion that teachers think in terms of means, even if given the opportunity to do otherwise. But as I talked with Conna Lee I could see the connection between her material conditions and her questions, and I realized that forcing a change in her research focus would impose a new but still official ideology on her. Further, as I reflected on my personal history, the ties between my work context and the questions I was asking also became apparent. What I learned from Conna Lee is that the problem of educative research cannot simply be directed at the practitioner and that instead, both practitioner and researcher need to examine and reexamine how context and cultural norms influence the questions we ask. When I understood this, my question became: How can researchers and practitioners enter into a research process that *honors* the questions asked but enables *all* participants to rethink those questions without reproducing the division of labor that privileges academics while silencing practitioners?

Dialogical Understanding

The process of posing questions helps clarify the complex tensions that influence the issues we choose to research. It may not, however, enable participants to critique and challenge the values they hold and their view of culture and contextual influences. As a consequence, although research is no longer imposed on practitioners, it could end up being nothing more than a solipsistic endeavor. Through her examination of school and personal histories, for example, Beth brought to her research an understanding of cultural norms, context, and self. Up to this point, however, she had not had an opportunity to engage in dialogue on one of her key assumptions: that success as a teacher involved a change to a more student-centered approach. To foster such an analysis Beth used the horizontal evaluation approach with a peer.

Horizontal evaluation was used by many members of the project to rethink the positions held in their personal and school histories, to look across these projects, to reconsider the questions they posed, to gain insights from students and others, and to interpret the research process and findings. The examples that follow focus specifically on how dialogue influenced question posing and the interpretation of the research process.

For most teachers the initial experience with horizontal evaluation was rather uncomfortable and far from productive because a level of trust had not been established that would encourage the participants to see evaluation as something more than a game imposed from above. But over time many began to trust each other as well as the process.

> Eeva and I decided to meet at her home to do the post-conference. It was then, perhaps in a more relaxed atmosphere, that my focus began to change, and I began to trust in the process. For me, this was a shift in perspective that evaluation could be something other than "judgment" from some external locus of control. (Karen, horizontal evaluation paper)

This trust, in turn, allowed these teachers to be more critical of their educational views and practices. As Karen writes, "By the third lap [the third time the teachers had engaged in dialogue about their teaching] we were more comfortable with making challenge statements [a horizontal evaluation procedure] which caused us to rethink our practices."

Through this type of critical analysis, the core of what would later become a research question started to take shape. Karen, for example, came to the realization that her stated intentions about *success* were more an attempt to justify what she already did than to seriously consider its meaning in a classroom context.

> On a day to day basis I strive to address "success" in a rather routinized way. There is an element of justification when I look at my intentions. For me, I reluctantly admit, when I am asked to state my intentions they are most often designed to indi-

cate the "rightness" or "well-groundedness" of my choices to someone outside myself and my students, as though my statements about intentions are a way to absolve
me of the guilt of knowing that my practices do not always match my intentions.
(Karen, problem paper)

Part of Karen's research question, therefore, was to gain "more personal clarity on
what my teaching principles are in an effort to fill in some blanks in my own professional language." She also wanted to explore the types of influences that had shaped
her meaning of success. A first attempt at such an analysis was evident when she identified a tension between her training as a special education teacher, with its emphasis
on measurable results, and the questions her colleague raised about whose interests are
served by this orientation.

> As a special education teacher, I have been trained to some extent, to be a behavior-
> ist, someone who must have a tangible management system with measurable re-
> sults, but when asked what interests are served and for whom, I have blanks in my
> dialogue and experience some real cognitive anxiety. (Karen, problem paper)

Karen's dialogue with a colleague enabled her to pose a question about her work and
consider some of the influences on it. She also planned to expand this concern to consider the association between her identified and evolving notions of success and classroom practice. Again, this understanding of the relationship between practice and intentions will depend largely on a continuing dialogue with a trusted colleague.

For other teachers dialogue was used to reflect on the types of intervention strategies they were using to confront the questions they had posed. Robyn, for example,
started her journey with the realization that many of her decisions about teaching, including the choice of teaching as a career, had actually been made by others.

> My story begins with my mother. My mother always insisted that I get a college ed-
> ucation and teach school. She believed it to be the ideal profession for a woman.
> Often, I would hear, "You're in school when the children are in school, and you're
> home when the children are home." She regretted the fact she didn't finish college
> and go into teaching. Despite a few moments of rebellion, I did what she wanted.
> (Robyn, personal history)

She also concluded that her passive attitude conflicted with her beliefs about teacher
professionalism and the need for school change.

> When given a choice, my first inclination is to keep quiet and do what I want later,
> regardless of what I was told. . . . It is this attitude of passive, seeming agreement
> that permits the continuation of the system. If change is to take place, if teachers are
> to gain in power and professionalism, we each need to say what we believe. . . .
> Taking risks is not easy for me, but I want to learn to do it. I want to be able to say
> what I believe, not hide behind my closed classroom door. (Robyn, problem paper)

Born out of this tension between the assumption that teachers should voice their
opinions and participate in the process of school change and the tendency to keep
quiet and do what they want came the identification of a question: What types of actions can be taken that will enable teachers to express what they believe and participate in a process of school change? Toward this end, Robyn decided to hold a series of

teacher support group meetings. Instead of just collecting observation and interview data on these meetings, as is typical of most approaches to research, Robyn engaged in dialogue with a member of the teacher support group and used these insights to analyze the meetings. This dialogue produced some dramatic and stunning findings, not the least of which is that Robyn's role in the support meeting may have contradicted her intention to develop teachers' voices.

> I continue to question my level of direct intervention. Teachers complained of attending meetings where the agenda is determined and manipulated by the administration. How different can it be if the agenda is determined and manipulated by me? Probably a minimal difference. The intention of the project is to give teachers a forum to develop their voices, in whatever direction that might be. How can that happen if they cannot have a voice in how the meetings are organized? If I perceive my position as one who is more knowledgeable because I have experienced or read more, am I again any different than the administration? No. (Robyn, first look)

This insight produced quite a bit of frustration on Robyn's part. It did, however, move her to rethink her role and raise questions about her beliefs and practice. Because educative research is a process, not just a product, these types of rethinking can be continually raised and linked to practice.

Voice

Up to this point my arguments have centered on the way the ERP enables participants to enter into a complex process of reflection and critique. In this section I want to view these developments in relation to a more fundamental change related to the development of voice — a change that is pivotal in reconstructing both the researcher-practitioner relationship and schools.

When fully developed, voice is a form of political action that is both an articulation of one's critical opinions and a protest (Hirschman, 1970). The protest is not simply a gripe but a challenge to instances of domination and oppression. Although the meaning of oppression and domination is always defined within a particular historical context, this focus "reinserts back into the language of schooling the primacy of the political" (Giroux, 1989, p. 136). Members of the educational community are encouraged to examine relations where there is an unjust exercise of power or authority, including the analysis of structures that unnecessarily elevate particular groups and stereotype and constrain others. In an educational context, the development of voice has implications for both the roles of those involved in schools and the structure of schooling.

For those traditionally disenfranchised from schools, the development of voice means attaining the right to tell their stories. The telling of these stories allows these groups to enter into policy debates and challenge the authority of others — such as university researchers, business people, and district and state policymakers — to tell *the* educational story. This is so because the telling of a story is not the rendering of facts, but rather the putting together of a plot that imposes meanings on the events reported (Tappan & Brown, 1989). By determining the plot, these groups assert their authority to give meaning to educational events and their right to be involved in educational policy.

The process of giving meaning to educational events benefits from an examination of the assumptions about teaching and schooling that underlie those events. The development of voice, therefore, reshapes roles so that disenfranchised members have the right to tell their stories and the opportunity to examine underlying assumptions relating to teaching and to schooling. Teachers, for example, took the opportunity to investigate assumptions such as those concerning gender and work and the practitioner-student relationship.

Finally, the development of voice requires that school structures be altered to encourage political action and protest. In contrast to a set of structures that primarily limit action to the physical and/or psychological withdrawal from the school, what Hirschman (1970) calls "exit-structures" would be put in place. These would make it possible for members of the educational community to influence and reconstruct the school through criticism and protest. Put differently, structures would be in place to enable groups to tell their stories and have those stories make a difference, instead of the present situation — teachers and others leaving a school when concerns arise or staying at that school but only going through the motions.

The examples that follow focus on the possibilities for the development of teachers' voices within current school structures. They also suggest that, if the role of the researcher and those studied is to be reconstructed in fundamental ways, the ERP must be expanded beyond teachers, and schools must be altered to allow voice to make a difference. Under these circumstances it is possible to see how the alteration of the politics of research could also have significant implications for school change.

For Kathy, the process of developing her voice began with writing her school history. In the articulation of this story it became apparent that many of the current school structures remained unchanged not so much because of thoughtful consideration but rather tradition. As Kathy writes, "Through the school history I came to realize what structures had been imposed on the staff and students purely because that's the way we've always done it." By seeing that these structures were in place more because of what others didn't say than because of arguments for their existence, Kathy was able to challenge their legitimacy. When she did so, she realized that the longevity of these structures resulted in part from teachers' inability to articulate alternatives and, therefore, their willingness to accept the status quo.

> I was better able to deal with these structures knowing which ones were in place because of tradition, with no educational basis, others because alternatives had not been investigated and still others because teachers were either satisfied with the status quo or feared the process of conflict and change. (Kathy, first look)

As Kathy continued to tell her story, it became clear that school structures (such as the division of students into ability groups) not only left her with fifteen students who were "hostile toward school, and physically attacked each other," but also encouraged her to take on a somewhat oppressive role through which she tried to command their attention and force them to learn.

> I chose to teach them as a group, hoping to command their attention and in so doing force them to learn. Discipline was strict, attention was demanded. Everyone was miserable. Reading skills were not improving. I knew that everything I was doing was in opposition to my philosophy. For three and one half hours

> Monday through Thursday, I hated what I was doing but saw no way out. (Kathy, first look)

Telling this story enabled Kathy to see the contradictions between her philosophy and practice and convinced her to seek some sort of alternative. Because ability grouping was "imposed by the school district and strictly enforced," Kathy's protest was not directed at this structure but rather at alternative ways to teach within the structure.

> The possible alternative was born out of my own experience in writing and examining my personal and school history and through the process of exploring my intentions in the horizontal evaluation post-conference. I posed this problem and challenge for myself: can the use of student personal histories promote further understanding of self and others, build trust and develop a sense of community in the elementary classroom? (Kathy, first look)

Now that Kathy has researched this alternative, she has not only told her story but has also attempted to rewrite it, albeit with a new ending. As her voice developed, she confronted a set of practices that were used to control and dominate students.

Pat's story is also one of protest. Its beginning, however, had little to do with the political. Instead, it exposed a passion and commitment to computers.

> I spent hours trying to figure out very simple programs. The challenge and frustration did not deter me from spending significant time after school in a small crowded room where the computer was kept. What developed was a very personal interest in the mechanics of the technology. (Pat, first look)

As the story unfolded, doubts arose in the form of what was not asked about computers at in-service sessions.

> There were few issues raised by the instructors in the in-services which questioned the promotion of computing. There were some questions raised at workshops concerning the selection of user friendly software but no other issues were raised about any problems which might be associated with the ubiquitous promotion of computing. (Pat, personal history)

These concerns grew stronger as Pat dialogued with others about the interests served by computers: "The discovery of a diverse range of opinion concerning computers was alarming and discomforting to one who was convinced that this technology could only be criticized by the uninformed and the techno-phobic." In the telling of this story Pat came to a startling realization: Computers might work against women's rights and minority equality, issues to which she was strongly committed. Computers, she saw, have the potential to further dominate, while she had thought they would surely be advantageous, if not downright progressive.

> While I questioned some of the literature, I began to see the significance of what for me were personal political beliefs concerning women's rights and minority equality. Could it be that the technology which I pursued with such enthusiasm was another obstacle to rights which I held dear? (Pat, first look)

By examining her assumptions about teaching and schooling, including questions about who has access to computers, what jobs would result, and who was likely to fill them, Pat strengthened her voice and used that strength to question the use of computers.

As was true of Pat's story, the beginning of Laurence's story was anything but political. In fact, his story began with a deep cynicism about all foundational types of educational literature.

> This was my gut feeling [about the classroom]. I could not, and did not want to explain this position in any philosophical or psychological pedagogy. This was my understanding from the experience that I had working with students in the classroom. (Laurence, first look)

In particular, Laurence was interested in finding more experiments to fill the holes in his biology curriculum. To begin such a quest, he asked me what I thought he should do. Unfortunately, having not yet read his story, my response was far from satisfactory.

> The first resource that I explored was Andrew. He suggested starting with the writings of John Dewey and his laboratory school because of its emphasis on using hands-on activities for learning. This suggestion was the last thing that I wanted to hear! It brought back all of the loathing and resentment that had built up inside me during my undergraduate educational studies. (Laurence, first look)

We spent some time discussing the pros and cons of reading foundational literature, but in the end Laurence refused to let the educative project slip away from his control; it was his question and his project.

> I rejected Andrew's argument; it did not persuade me to pursue a philosophical approach. This educative research was not going to be turned into a game. Andrew was not going to set up the hoops and I was certainly not going to jump through them. This was my project and I knew what I wanted to study. (Laurence, first look)

In many ways, Laurence was arguing for the right to tell his story. In particular, he decided to search for, in his words, "cookbook"-type activities. During this review of the literature, Laurence came across an article that used the word *inquiry* as a synonym for experiment. What attracted Laurence to this article was that it was directly related to the story he was trying to tell. It also asked questions that went beyond the scope of this problem — namely, why should inquiry be used in the classroom?

> This article appeared to ask a question that related to my problem: "why isn't inquiry used more in the classroom?" My problem involved what and how to include inquiry while the authors of this article asked why should inquiry be used. (Laurence, first look)

These new questions led Laurence in a different direction — to study the learning theory of Piaget and consider how it related to his gut feelings about his classroom. Where Laurence had initially rejected this type of literature because it silenced his gut feelings, it took on a new importance when he felt that it was related to the story he was beginning to tell. As Laurence's voice became stronger, he was able to integrate this new array of arguments into his understanding of teaching.

Laurence's story is also a protest. In contrast to Kathy and Pat, who directed their protest inward at their commitments and teaching practices, Laurence directed his protest at the researcher-practitioner relationship. It is unclear what this protest will mean for his relations with students, but at the very least he has challenged the long history of domination that has left teachers silent.

Laurence's story, as well as those of the other teachers, influenced my voice. What I learned from Laurence and Pat is that voice is a developmental process that has many starting points. The role of the researcher in this regard is to enable a further examination of the story, not to impose a particular beginning. From Pat and Kathy I learned how voice could challenge the traditional researcher-subject relationship while also enabling protest in an oppressive teacher-student relationship. The courage of the teachers to look critically at their role contrasted sharply with my past actions, which had focused on identifying theories of oppression without considering my part in the process.

Confronting Individualism

An individual can challenge and expose relations of domination, but this is unlikely to alter these relations. Instead, such a fundamental type of change requires, at the very least, a collective protest. To encourage this result, I asked those involved in the project to create collective school and personal histories that could identify common points of struggle. There can be little doubt that during the first year of the project these common concerns resulted in very few examples of collective protest. This is so, in part, because I retained and utilized the privileged position of the university researcher, thereby encouraging teachers to direct their attention to finding out what I wanted. However, as time went on, we learned more about our histories and could see places where we remained trapped in taken-for-granted traditions. And from this analysis traditional roles started to fade. By the end of the first year the teachers were leading the group sessions and selecting the articles we were to read. The conversation focused on their concerns and reflected their voices. I still expressed my opinion as a member of the group, but as the example of Laurence indicates, many teachers felt comfortable with viewing my arguments as one story — not the story they had to follow.

This change seemed to set the stage for more collective action. As Karen put it, the dialogical process reached the point where "the ice had broken sufficiently to allow us to see that we were in the same boat and could actually see that we had common concerns and patterns." The dialogue, however, was not limited to the discussion of common and differing concerns, but also linked personal issues with argued positions. This type of connected knowing (Belenky et al., 1986) is apparent in Valerie's description of a weekend retreat she went on with several of the other participants in the project.

> We read papers, talked about problems we encountered collecting data, and difficulties in understanding how to proceed. We also shared a knowledge of the desire of each of our mothers for us to receive an education . . . and the love of fathers who had exhibited weaknesses and strengths and had in their own way left experiences of legacy and pain. The sharing of our humanness was strengthening. (Valerie, first look)

By linking the personal with the positions argued, these participants honor who they are and what they know as they work together in a process of reflection that helps them examine the assumptions and ideas that guide their practice and ideology.

At the beginning of the second year of the project, the modest foundation for a collective approach to research started to show some real promise. As part of an attempt to enable teachers to be heard, I invited the superintendent and assistant superintendent to a seminar at which several members of the ERP told their research stories. At the end of the seminar one of the teachers asked the superintendent about the possibility of a collective project. She wanted to know, in particular, if he would support such an endeavor, what types of problems they could work on, and if he would take the results seriously. In response to these questions the superintendent not only pledged his support and willingness to listen, but also suggested that the teachers choose the research question that the seminar focused on: namely, how to restructure the teachers' school day to allow them to examine assumptions about teaching and schooling. It is important to note that this project will begin after the master's coursework is finished and will involve as many as half the teachers in the ERP.

Conclusion

Educative research takes a dramatic departure from many traditional methods of research by challenging the privileged position of the university researcher to produce knowledge, changing the focus of research from problem solving to question posing, and fostering teachers' voices by enabling those who work in schools to tell and retell their stories based on a critical examination of teaching and schooling. When successful, research of this kind is no longer a one-way process from researcher to subject but a dialogical process that brings researcher and subject together in the quest for an understanding of teaching that recognizes the political moment. As the educative research process spreads, it becomes possible to imagine a type of community that utilizes protest and political action to restructure schooling.

Unfortunately, the working out of this view of research is far from easy. In many instances, as this description of the project indicates, my strong commitment to illuminate the politics of schooling blinded me to teachers' personal knowledge and to the importance of building on this understanding. Several teachers in the project also found the process frustrating. Those teachers who had a vast amount of experience and had learned to trust their gut feelings, for example, felt anger at the beginning of the project, if for no other reason than that the determination of a question or concern was seen as an affront to their experience as teachers. As Diane said in one of our final meetings, "[When the project started,] I didn't have any problems; why should I find one?"

Furthermore, because the project was part of a Masters program, the work generated by the project had to be done on top of all the other teaching responsibilities. For some teachers, especially those who had families, this further intensification of their work made it necessary either to withdraw from the project or simply try to get through. And even for those who, through huge expenditures of time and energy, fully participated in the project, there was no structure in place at the school level that would allow their voices to be heard. While there have been some promising developments concerning the continuation of the project after the Master's coursework is finished, some sort of major support will be necessary if teachers are going to continue to develop their voices and expand the process to other members of the educational community. These limitations and internal contradictions need to be confronted if educative research is to alter the relationship between researchers and those studied and, in the process, foster a type of school change based on protest.

ERP has not so much altered the relation between practitioner and those studied or focused school change around political protest as it has created a text that raises questions and explores a range of possibilities that can further discourse on the politics of method and the impact of alternative methods on school change. Unless we develop and debate alternative processes of inquiry that attempt to change the relationship between researcher and those studied, research will continue to legitimate the privileged position of the researcher while silencing those studied.

Notes

1. Because the emphasis of this paper is on methods, the way institutions structure the researcher-subject relationship is not discussed. However, there can be little doubt that transforming this relationship in fundamental ways would require, in addition to changes in methods, dramatic alterations in the structure of the university and public schools.
2. I use the word *traditional* to distinguish these methods from a number of promising approaches that fit under the rubric of critical ethnography.
3. Fine's latest work challenges many of the assumptions found in the noted manuscript on silencing. In particular, she argues for a type of research that is participatory, with researchers and participants working together, and in which activist knowledge is gathered in the midst of social change projects. For a complete discussion of these issues, see Fine (1992).
4. I am drawing on Pateman's (1970) notion of full participation to indicate that participants would have a say in decisionmaking and, importantly, the power to influence this process. (For a further description of full participation see Pateman, 1970.)
5. It is often thought that teachers don't read academic research because of deficits in their knowledge and background. I want to suggest instead that the problem is not what teachers lack, but is rather a result of the use of a set of codes that are specific to the academic research culture.
6. The section that follows on dialogue can be found in a revised version in Gitlin, 1990.
7. The section that follows is taken from an article coauthored with Karen Price that appeared in the 1992 *Association of Supervision and Curriculum Yearbook.*
8. My decision to reference these texts by the teacher's first names is clearly contradictory. On the one hand, I am supporting the hierarchical distinction between researchers and teachers that the project is trying to challenge. On the other, this is the way I know these people and it would be a type of forgery to rename them.

References

Agar, M. (1980). *The professional stranger: An informal introduction to ethnography.* New York: Academic Press.

Apple, M. (1979). *Ideology and curriculum.* London: Routledge & Kegan Paul.

Apple, M. (1986). *Teachers and text: A political economy of class and gender relations in education.* New York: Routledge & Kegan Paul.

Belenky, M. F., Clinchy, B. M. Goldberger, N. R., & Tarule, J. M. (1986). *Women's ways of knowing: The development of self, voice and mind.* New York: Basic Books.

Bernstein, R. (1983). *Beyond objectivism and relativism: Science, hermeneutics and praxis.* Philadelphia: University of Pennsylvania Press.

Bullough, R., & Gitlin, A. (1989). Toward educative communities: Teacher education and the quest for the reflective practitioner. *Qualitative Studies in Education, 2,* 285–298.

Carr, W., & Kemmis, S. (1986). *Becoming critical: Education, knowledge and action research.* London: Falmer Press.

Clark, K., & Holquist, M. (1984). *Mikhail Bakhtin.* Cambridge, MA: Harvard University Press.

Eisner, E. (1979). *The educational imagination.* New York: Macmillan.

Fine, M. (1987). Silencing in public schools. *Language Arts, 64,* 157–174.

Fine, M. (1992). Passion, politics, and power: Feminist research possibilities. In *Disruptive voices: The possibilities of feminist research.* Ann Arbor: University of Michigan Press.

Freire, P. (1985). *Culture, power and liberation.* South Hadley, MA: Bergin & Garvey.

Gadamer, H. G. (1975). *Truth and method.* New York: Seabury Press.

Gage, N. L. (1989). The paradigm wars and their aftermath. *Teachers College Record, 91,* 135–150.

Giroux, H. (1989). Schooling as a form of cultural politics: Toward a pedagogy of difference. In H. Giroux & P. McLaren (Eds.), *Critical pedagogy, the state and cultural struggle* (pp. 125–151). Albany: State University of New York Press.

Gitlin, A. (1990). Understanding teaching dialogically. *Teachers College Record, 91,* 537–564.

Gitlin, A., & Goldstein, S. (1987). A dialogical approach to understanding: Horizontal evaluation. *Educational Theory, 37,* 17–27.

Gitlin, A., Siegal, M., & Boru, K. (1989). The politics of method: From leftist ethnography to educative research. *Qualitative Studies in Education, 2,* 237–253.

Gitlin, A., & Smyth, J. (1989). *Teacher evaluation: Educative alternatives.* Philadelphia: Falmer Press.

Grant, C., & Sleeter, C. (1988). Race, class, and gender and abandoned dreams. *Teachers College Record, 90,* 19–40.

Habermas, J. (1976). *Communication and the evolution of society.* Boston: Beacon Press.

Hirschman, A. (1970). *Exit, voice and loyalty.* Cambridge, MA: Harvard University Press.

Howe, K. (1988). Against the quantitative-qualitative incompatibility thesis, or dogmas die hard. *Educational Researcher, 17*(8), 10–23.

Kirk, J., & Miller, M. (1985). *Reliability and validity in qualitative research.* Beverly Hills, CA: Sage.

Kliebard, H. (1987). *The struggle for the American curriculum.* New York: Routledge & Kegan Paul.

Lather, P. (1986). Research as praxis. *Harvard Educational Review, 52,* 255–277.

Leach, M. (1988). Teacher education and reform: What's sex got to do with it? *Educational Foundations, 58*(3), 4–14.

LeCompte, M., & Goetz, J. (1982). Problems of reliability and validity in ethnographic research. *Review of Educational Research, 52,* 31–60.

Messer-Davidow, E. (1985). Knowers, knowing, knowledge: Feminist theory and education. *Journal of Thought, 20*(3), 8–24.

Pateman, C. (1970). *Participation and democratic theory.* New York: Cambridge University Press.

Perry, I. (1988). A Black student's reflection on public and private schools. *Harvard Educational Review, 58,* 332–336.

Sarason, S. (1971). *The culture of the school and the problem of change.* Boston: Allyn & Bacon.

Shor, I. (1980). *Critical teaching and everyday life.* Boston: South End Press.

Simon, R., & Dippo, D. (1986). On critical ethnographic work. *Anthropology and Education Quarterly, 17,* 195–202.

Spencer, D. (1984). The home and school lives of women teachers. *Elementary School Journal, 84,* 283–298.

Tappan, M., & Brown, L. (1989). Stories told and lessons learned: Toward a narrative approach to moral development and moral education. *Harvard Educational Review, 59,* 182–205.

Weiler, K. (1988). *Women teaching for change: Gender, class and power.* South Hadley, MA: Bergin & Garvey.

Weis, L. (1988). High school girls in a deindustrializing economy. In L. Weis (Ed.), *Class, race and gender in American education* (pp. 183–208). Albany: State University of New York Press.

White, J. (1989). The politics of politeness in the classroom: Cultural codes that create and constrain knowledge construction. *Journal of Curriculum and Supervision, 4,* 298–321.

Whitehead, J., & Lomax, P. (1987). Action research and the politics of educational knowledge. *British Educational Research Journal, 13,* 175–190.

Validation in Inquiry-Guided Research: The Role of Exemplars in Narrative Studies

ELLIOT G. MISHLER

The reason why only the right predicates happen so luckily to have become well entrenched is just that the well entrenched predicates thereby become the right ones. (p. 98) . . . The line between valid and invalid predictions (or inductions or projections) is drawn upon how the world is and has been described and anticipated in words. (Goodman, 1979/1983, p. 121)

Rules are only rules by virtue of social conventions: they are social conventions. . . . That is the sociological resolution of the problem of inductive inference. . . . It is not the regularity of the world that imposes itself on our senses but the regularity of our institutionalized beliefs that imposes itself on the world. (Collins, 1985, pp. 145–148)

Acceptance or rejection of a practice or theory comes about because a community is persuaded. Even research specialists do not judge a conclusion as it stands alone; they judge its compatibility with a network of prevailing beliefs. (Cronbach, 1988, p. 6)

The individual scientist tends to assume that data replicated by certain of his colleagues are more likely to prove reliable and representative than those of other colleagues. Although there is no logical basis for such decisions, they represent accumulated, practical scientific experience. (p. 108) . . . The fact is that there are no rules of experimental design. (Sidman, 1960, p. 214)

When I speak of knowledge embedded in shared exemplars, I am not referring to a mode of knowing that is less systematic or less analyzable than knowledge embedded in rules, laws, or criteria of identification. Instead I have in mind a manner of knowing which is misconstrued if reconstructed in rules that are first abstracted from exemplars and thereafter function in their stead. (Kuhn, 1962/1970, p. 192)

Validation: A Reformulation

Those of us in the social sciences who do one or another type of inquiry-guided research have long been aware that the standard approach to validity assessment is

Harvard Educational Review Vol. 60 No. 4 November 1990, 415–442

largely irrelevant to our concerns and problems.[1] This is not surprising, since the prevailing conception of and procedures for validation are based on an experimental model whereas our studies are designed explicitly as an alternative to that model, with features that differ markedly and in detail from those characteristic of experiments.

These differences in the design of experimental and inquiry-guided studies have not prevented the mis-application of experiment-based criteria and methods of validation to other types of studies, resulting in their being evaluated as lacking scientific rigor. With failure built in from the start, they are systematically denied legitimacy, and the dominance of the experimental model is assured. A new approach to validation is required that takes into account the distinctive features and problems of inquiry-guided studies and, at the same time, provides alternative, applicable methods for researchers. This article is directed to that task.[2]

Like the fabled Gordian Knot, validation is a mess of entangled concepts and methods with an abundance of loose threads. Sophisticated, technical procedures pulling out and straightening each thread, one at a time, seem to leave the knot very much as it was. The apparent increase in rigor and precision of successive advances in methods have brought us no closer to resolving the special problems faced by inquiry-guided researchers. Alexander the Great's decisive cut through the intractable Knot — a move that dissolved the problem by doing away with it — suggests that we might do better to begin at the beginning with a radical, conceptual recasting of the problem.

In sketching out a new perspective, I will begin by reformulating validation as the social construction of knowledge. With this reformulation, the key issue becomes whether the relevant community of scientists evaluates reported findings as sufficiently trustworthy to rely on them for their own work. I ground this perspective in recent historical and sociological studies of scientific practice. Further, I suggest that this reformulation is compatible with a growing recognition among mainstream validity theorists of the centrality of interpretation in validation, which poses intractable problems for the standard model. Using Kuhn's analysis of the role of exemplars in science, I then examine several instances of how validity claims are made and may be assessed in inquiry-guided, interpretive studies.

Recent studies in the history, philosophy, and sociology of science have seriously damaged the "storybook image of science" (Mitroff, 1974) — an image that has served to legitimate the dominant conception of validation. These new studies, which focus on actual practices of scientists rather than on textbook idealizations, reveal science as a human endeavor marked by uncertainty, controversy, and ad hoc pragmatic procedures—a far cry from an abstract and severe "logic" of scientific discovery. Validation has come to be recognized as problematic in a deep theoretical sense, rather than as a technical problem to be solved by more rigorous rules and procedures. An extended review of these developments is beyond the limits of this paper, but the quotations with which I began may evoke the tenor and thrust of the argument.[3]

Further encouragement for an alternative approach may be found in recent views of some of the principal architects of our current governing conception. A new understanding of validity has evolved gradually over the last 35–40 years, from the first codification of standards by the American Psychological Association (APA, 1954) and the influential paper by Cronbach and Meehl (1955). One of the central features of both statements was the partitioning of validity into four types: content, predictive, concurrent, and construct.[4] This was followed by successive efforts to revise the model, without altering the assumption of different specifiable types, by proposing other typologies.[5]

Each new proposal underscored the fundamentally flawed nature of this model. It became clear that validation, the touchstone of scientific inquiry, could not be achieved by applying a formal algorithm to assess each type of validity. Campbell and Stanley's (1963; see also Cook & Campbell, 1979) elegant and influential analysis of different quasi-experimental designs and their respective threats to one or another validity has turned out, in retrospect, to be a death-blow to the typology approach. There are two reasons for this unanticipated consequence, both reflecting Campbell and Stanley's clear understanding that validity assessments are not assured by following procedures but depend on investigators' judgments of the relative importance of different "threats." First, no general, abstract rules can be provided for assessing overall levels of validity in particular studies or domains of inquiry. Second, no formal or standard procedure can be determined either for assigning weights to different threats to any one type of validity, or for comparing different types of validity. These assessments are matters of judgment and interpretation. And these evaluations depend, irremediably, on the whole range of linguistic practices, social norms and contexts, assumptions and traditions that the rules had been designed to eliminate. To Sidman's (1960) statement that there are "no rules of experimental design," we may now add that there are "no rules" for assessing validity. Investigators, of course, follow accepted procedures in their domains of inquiry. However, as will become clear, these "rules" for proper research are not universally applicable, are modified by pragmatic considerations, and do not bypass or substitute for their nonrule-governed interpretation of their data.

Recognition of these unresolvable problems has led to a new perspective in which validity is viewed as a unitary concept with construct validation as the fundamental problem.[6] This, of course, makes issues of meaning and interpretation central. Thus, Cronbach (1984) states that the "end goal of validation is explanation and understanding. Therefore, the profession is coming around to the view that *all* validation is construct validation" (p. 126). Messick (1989), reviewing the history of changing conceptions, argues that validation is essentially a type of "scientific inquiry," and that a validity judgment is an "inductive summary" of all available information, with issues of meaning and interpretation central to the process. He also expands the validation framework to include social values and social consequences of findings as contexts for validity assessments.[7]

This emergent consensus is good news. It acknowledges, albeit implicitly, that the traditional approach has failed and offers an opportunity for exploring alternatives. The new emphasis on interpretation, and on social contexts and values, resonates closely with the detailed findings of historians and sociologists of science. Both developments encourage us to view all types of research as "forms of life" (Wittgenstein, 1953; see also Brenner, 1981) rather than technical exercises governed by an abstract logic of methodological rules. With this understanding, we may be able to move toward a conception of validation that is more relevant not only to inquiry-guided studies but to experimental modes of research as well.

Trustworthiness: Grounds for Belief and Action

As a first step, I propose to redefine validation as the process(es) through which we make claims for and evaluate the "trustworthiness" of reported observations, interpretations, and generalizations.[8] The essential criterion for such judgments is the degree to which we can rely on the concepts, methods, and inferences of a study, or tradition of inquiry, as the basis for our own theorizing and empirical research. If our overall assessment of a study's trustworthiness is high enough for us to act on it, we are granting the findings a sufficient degree of validity to invest our own time and energy, and to put at risk our reputations as competent investigators. As more and more investigators act on this assumption and find that it "works," the findings take on the aura of objective fact; they become "well-entrenched." (Goodman, 1983).

This definition and criterion depart in critical ways from standard doctrine. First, by making validation rather than validity the key term (see Messick, 1989), they focus on the range of ongoing activities through which claims are made and appraised rather than on the static properties of instruments and scores. Second, by adopting a functional criterion — whether findings are relied upon for further work — rather than abstract rules, validation is understood as embedded within the general flow of scientific research rather than being treated as a separate and different type of assessment.[9] In this way, this definition and criterion emphasize the role played in validation by scientists' working knowledge and experience, aligning the process more closely with what scientists actually do (Collins, 1985; Latour, 1990; Latour & Woolgar, 1979; Lynch, 1985; Ravetz, 1971; Sidman, 1960) than with what they are assumed to be and supposed to do.

Further, focusing on trustworthiness rather than truth displaces validation from its traditional location in a presumably objective, nonreactive, and neutral reality, and moves it to the social world — a world constructed in and through our discourse and actions, through praxis. Since social worlds are endlessly being remade as norms and practices change, it is clear that judgments of trustworthiness may change with time, even when addressed to the "same" findings. Finally, truth claims and their warrants are not assessed in isolation, but enter a more general discourse of validation that includes not only other scientists but many parties in the larger community with different and often conflicting views. (See Latour's 1988 account of shifting conflicts and alliances in the "validation" of Pasteur's microbial theory of infection; also Richards, 1979, on the reception of non-Euclidean geometry in nineteenth-century England.)

Reformulating validation as the social discourse through which trustworthiness is established elides such familiar shibboleths as reliability, falsifiability, and objectivity. These criteria are neither trivial nor irrelevant, but they must be understood as particular ways of warranting validity claims rather than as universal, abstract guarantors of truth. They are rhetorical strategies (Simons, 1989) that fit only one model of science — experimental, hypothesis-testing, and so forth. Used as proof criteria, they serve a deviance-sanctioning function, marking off "good" from "bad" scientific practice. (See Gieryn, 1983, and Prelli, 1989, for case studies of the rhetoric of exclusion.)

Bazerman (1989), reviewing Collins's (1985) studies of replication and induction in science, observes that "experimentation is so embedded in forms of life that compelling experimental results are compelling only to those who have already entered in the form of life which generates the result" (p. 115). These warrants have less "rightness of fit" (Goodman, 1978) for interpretive and inquiry-guided forms of research that, in turn, may only be compelling to those who have entered that form of life.[10]

Conflict and controversy are as much a part of "normal science" (Kuhn, 1970) as the shared concepts, procedures, and findings dutifully inscribed in textbooks. All scientific reports — from spare accounts of methods and findings to philosophical analyses — are partisan forays into contested terrain. Nonetheless, the "truths" of normal science are embedded in complex networks of concepts, linguistic and technical practices, and an established framework of norms and values (Collins, 1985; see also Campbell, 1979, on the "tribal model" of scientific knowledge), and it is not surprising that they are markedly resistant to change. New approaches or new discoveries cannot easily be absorbed, nor can their potential threat to the whole system be defused by tinkering with minor details.

For these reasons, I would not expect easy assent to this new formulation of validation. However, by showing that experimentalists are in the same boat as inquiry-guided researchers in that we all rely for the validation of our work on contextually grounded linguistic and interpretive practices, I hope to gain a hearing and perhaps enlist "allies" (Latour, 1988). As Collins (1985) points out, the possibility of changing current practices depends on putting forward "an interpretation of data which has the potential to create some contradictions and reverberate through the social and conceptual web . . . [but] must not appear to be completely unreasonable" (p. 151).

Exemplars: Resources for Inquiry

If validity claims cannot be settled by appeal to abstract, standard rules, or algorithms, what would be a useful alternative approach? The indeterminateness of such claims is not a matter of the imprecision of technical methods. Rather, definitions of evidence and rules and criteria for their assessment are embedded in networks of assumptions and accepted practices that constitute a tradition. Recommending new rules for inquiry-guided studies would confront us with the same uncertainties that, as we have seen, undermine the canonical approach. The utility of alternative rules would be limited — as are the standard ones — to their pragmatic function as accounting practices that help researchers monitor, arrange, and order their data in some methodic way.[11] Rather than proposing yet another list of rules and criteria, I will rely on Kuhn's (1970) analysis of "exemplars" to suggest an approach to the problem of how claims for trustworthiness may be made and evaluated.[12]

Kuhn's (1962/1970) concept of paradigms and the role they play in "normal science" has had considerable influence in studies of the history and sociology of science. Responding to criticism about ambiguities in the referents of this term, he replaced it with "disciplinary matrix" for the full set of assumptions, theories, and practices shared within a community of specialists. A critical element of this matrix is the "exemplar":

> By it I mean, initially, the concrete problem-solutions that students encounter from the start of their scientific education, whether in laboratories, on examinations, or at the ends of chapters in science tests . . . [and] at least some of the technical problem-solutions found in the periodical literature that scientists encounter during

their post-educational research careers and that also show them by example how their job is to be done. More than other sorts of components of the disciplinary matrix, differences between sets of exemplars provide the community-fine structure of science. (Kuhn, 1970, p. 187)

Kuhn views "knowledge embedded in shared exemplars" as a "mode of knowing" no less systematic or susceptible to analysis than that of "rules, laws, or criteria" (p. 192), and also recognizes that these "modes" of doing and acting are not acquired simply by "encounters" with textual descriptions. Skilled research is a craft (Ravetz, 1971; see also Polanyi, 1966, on "tacit knowing"), and, like any craft, it is learned by apprenticeship to competent researchers, by hands-on experience, and by continual practice. It seems remarkable, if we stop to think about it, that research competence is assumed to be gained by learning abstract rules of scientific procedure. Why should such "working knowledge" (Harper, 1987; Mishler, 1989) be learned any more easily, or through other ways, than the competence required for playing the violin or blowing glass or throwing pots?

Technical descriptions of methods in themselves, however detailed and precise, are insufficient for replication, the prescribed route to validation. Sidman (1960) observes that it is "common practice in biological science" for researchers to make personal visits to the laboratories of competent users of an experimental procedure to "learn the required skills firsthand" (p. 109). Replication is a routinely uncertain endeavor and, as Collins (1985, pp. 29–78) argues, the usual notion is misleading and does not correspond to how scientists use other studies as springboards for their own work rather than "replicating" them.

Collins documents the "capricious nature" of the transfer of knowledge and concludes that such knowledge "travels best (or only) through accomplished practitioners," that "experimental ability is invisible in its passage," and that the only evidence of the "proper" conduct of an experiment is the "proper" experimental outcome — not the precision with which the work was done. Finally, he observes that although successive failures to replicate might lead scientists to temporarily suspend their belief that following "algorithm-like instructions" make carrying out an experiment a "formality," this belief "re-crystallizes catastrophically upon the successful completion of an experiment" (p. 76). Thus, by concealing their skills and artfulness from themselves — their own craft and tacit knowledge — scientists reaffirm the "objectivity" of their findings and reproduce the assumptive framework of "normal science."

In sum, knowledge is validated within a community of scientists as they come to share nonproblematic and useful ways of thinking about and solving problems. Representing the "community-fine structure of science" (Kuhn, 1970, p. 187), exemplars contain within themselves the criteria and procedures for evaluating the "trustworthiness" of studies and serve as testaments to the internal history of validation within particular domains of inquiry.[13] Developing new exemplars is a complex social process, over which individual investigators have only modest control. To move toward this goal, those of us engaged in inquiry-guided and interpretive forms of research have the task of articulating and clarifying the features and methods of our studies, of showing how the work is done, and what problems become accessible to study. Although they cannot serve as "standard" rules, a context-based explication is required of how observations are transformed into data and findings, and of how interpretations are grounded.

In the remainder of this article, I will focus on studies of narrative, one branch of interpretive research, and propose three different approaches as candidate exemplars. My immediate aim is to demonstrate alternative ways to do such studies that may be useful to other investigators. My broader aim is to promote a dialogue about ways of doing inquiry-guided research so that together we can develop a community with shared exemplars through which we confirm and validate our collective work.

Candidate Exemplars for Interpretive Research

There may be several exemplars, each with its own variants, that achieve legitimacy within a community of specialists sharing a perspective and methodology — "search cells" or "language communities" in Koch's (1976) terms. Together they constitute normal practice — the ordinary, taken-for-granted, and trustworthy concepts and methods for solving puzzles and problems within a particular area of work. Legitimacy cannot be legislated in advance. Neither abstract rules nor appeal to an idealized version of the scientific method will suffice. Rather, the defining features of exemplars are inferred from the actual practices of working scientists. Like the inductive categories of "natural" objects studied by cognitive psychologists, experiments and types of inquiry-guided studies are both "fuzzy categories" (Mervis & Rosch, 1981; Rosch, 1973, 1978; Rosch & Mervis, 1975). Each includes prototypes — for example, the model experiment, and a range of variants, such as "quasi-experiments."

As a context for discussing the approaches that I am nominating, tentatively, as candidate exemplars, I will first briefly outline some features of the dominant research exemplar as it has been applied to the study of narratives. All of the studies I will examine, though differing in content and theoretical orientation, share certain characteristics that make for useful comparison: each 1) focuses on a piece of "interpretive discourse," 2) takes this "text" as its basic datum, 3) reconceptualizes it as an instance of a more abstract and general "type," 4) provides a method for characterizing and "coding" textual units, 5) specifies the "structure" of relationships among them, and 6) interprets the "meaning" of this structure within a theoretical framework. Interpretive discourse (White, 1989) refers to researchers' understandings of the texts as representing efforts by speakers/authors themselves to describe and interpret their experiences.

As will be seen, the three proposed alternatives share features distinguishing them from the standard approach. Each "displays" the full texts to which the analytic procedures are applied, in contrast to the typical presentation of decontextualized fragments illustrating a coding manual. Further, rather than defining coding "dimensions" that are independent of and isolated from each other, these studies focus on analytic "structures" of relationships among textual features, which then become the basis for theoretical interpretation.

Normal Science and Narrative Research

Many critics of the positivist-based experimental model argue that its assumptions — about, for example, causality and objectivity — are inappropriate for the study of language and meaning (see footnote 2). Their argument would apply to research on "narrative modes of knowing" (Bruner, 1986). Investigators, however, are not governed in their practices by philosophical analyses of their epistemological and ontological assumptions. Skilled researchers working within the standard framework can find ways of adapting and applying their methods to any phenomenon that catches their interest, and narratives have not escaped their net.

Two recent studies (McAdams, 1985; Stewart, Franz, & Layton, 1988) illustrate how this is done. Both use life history narratives to examine issues of personal identity. I will focus on their research practices — on some of the ways they make the dominant exemplar "work" on apparently unsuitable material. Although they warrant their validity claims by an explicit reliance on "standard" methods, it turns out that their success in carrying out their analyses depends fundamentally on their pragmatic modifications of these methods. This is their "practical accomplishment" (Garfinkel, 1967) as researchers. Although I emphasize their research practices in this section, the inappropriateness of their conceptual models for narrative research is an equally important problem that will be addressed at various points. The aim of this brief review of their work is to set the stage for discussion of more appropriate approaches.

These investigators face a difficult task. They must convert voluminous, multidimensional, and variable language samples into the types of objects that allow them to apply standard procedures — sampling, measuring, counting, and hypothesis-testing through statistical analysis. To make the problem reasonably tractable, they begin deductively, relying on general theories to specify a few dimensions — power and intimacy motives for McAdams, based on McClelland's model; themes of identity, intimacy, and generativity for Stewart et al. from Erikson's (1950/1959) model of ego development. These concepts — motives and themes — are converted into coding categories that are applied to the original texts: responses to interviews from samples of respondents in McAdams's case and from letters, diaries, and autobiographical memoirs of one person in Stewart et al.'s study. The resultant "scores" are the data for successive stages of description, analysis, and interpretation.

Their competence as researchers is displayed by their success in accomplishing this transformation — from the messy and diffuse narrative texts with which they begin to the quantitative measures that now represent and stand for those texts. The reduction and transformation of source data — that is, initial observations and descriptions — is a necessary feature of all research. However, different rules and strategies of reduction lead to different re-presentations of the phenomena. These new "objects," constructed by researchers, include and emphasize only some features of the originals and exclude others as irrelevant to their interests. Interpretive researchers view the transformations achieved by the standard model as deeply flawed distortions in that they exclude precisely those features of the phenomena that are their essential, defining characteristics. Thus, with reference to narratives, representing them as scores for separate motives or themes, as is done in these two studies, excludes both their structural and sequential features, which are specifically what makes them "narratives" rather than some other type of text.

A principal claim of researchers who follow an experiment-based model is that their use of standard methods and procedures allows others to replicate their studies. Thus, Stewart et al. assert the generalizability of their codes: "The coding definitions were designed for use in coding any verbal text for preoccupation with self-definitional issues" (p. 49). Studies in the history and sociology of science, reviewed earlier, make it clear that "standardization" is not easily achieved and that replication is a function of local, situated practices. The problem may be seen in the ways that "standard" methods are modified in these two studies so that they can be applied to the particular and contingent features of their data.

For example, Stewart et al.'s coding units are "meaningful phrases" defined by the presence of a "codable image" (p. 57), which can include any length of text. Adequate understanding and use of this code depend on this particular study's coders' subculture (Mishler, 1984, p. 37) and, in a strong sense, the coding procedure could not be transferred directly to another research context. McAdams found it necessary to alter coding definitions of power and intimacy for individuals' accounts of their "earliest memories," since these were "rather banal and lacking in feeling tone." Categories were "broadened to include events and actions similar, though perhaps not identical, to the original characterizations" (pp. 173–174). Broadening or narrowing coding categories is, of course, an option open to other researchers, and the question of whether or not they had "replicated" the procedure would then be unanswerable.

Sometimes inconsistencies or contradictions, appearing at one or another stage in an analysis, require a mid-stream change in methods. Looking at summary scores for the "same" themes in different types of documents referring to the same time period, Stewart et al. found themselves "faced with the dilemma that we had not only different accounts of the period, but accounts in which the scores were in fact uncorrelated" (p. 59). Rather than taking this finding as a test of their hypotheses, they decided to "treat these media as alternative expressions" and "took the higher score for a given month, for all subcategories of that stage, regardless of which medium produced it" (p. 59). McAdams found that "the four main themes for power and intimacy did not appear relevant for the coding" of "negative nuclear episodes." He "settled inductively on four new themes for each of the content categories of power and intimacy. In some cases, the new themes bear some resemblance, typically as an opposite, to the original themes used in the analysis of positive nuclear episodes. In other cases, any similarity is lacking" (p. 158).

Similar observations might be made about the situated practices through which any investigator assures the success of his or her work. The main point is that standard methods are poorly standardized, allowing great latitude to researchers in how they specify them, and specification is contextually grounded in the idiosyncrasies and exigencies of particular studies. All investigators have to adapt, convert, and translate "standard" methods to solve their practical problems.

McAdams's and Stewart et al.'s online, pragmatic decisions are as much a part of normal scientific practice as their use of a coding manual and statistical tests. However, they highlight the problematic nature of their validity claims. Standard procedures — for sampling, coding, and quantifying — are weak and insufficient warrants because when they are actually applied they turn out to be context-bound, nonspecifiable in terms of "rules," and not generalizable. Close examination of the procedures used in any study would reveal a similar gap between the assumption of standardization and actual practices. Other investigators would be unable to determine whether their own versions, or adaptations, of their procedures represented a reasonable equivalent of them. Replication, rather than being assured by these procedures, would be essentially indeterminate.

Alternative Models for Narrative Research[14]

The three studies I will review below depart in significant ways from normal practice. They do not escape the thorny and unavoidable problems of validation. Nonetheless, I hope to show that they provide reasonable grounds for and ways of assessing their claims for trustworthiness, and, also, that they are more adequate and appropriate models for the study of narratives as a type of interpretive discourse.

—Life History Narratives and Identity Formation

A life history interview with one artist-furniture maker provides the narrative text that I analyze in my study of adult identity formation (Mishler, 1992). Reviewing my work in the context of the preceding discussion of standard studies that also focused on issues of identity will help to clarify differences in our respective research strategies and methods.

Informing and guiding my study is the question of how craftspersons sustain their commitments to and motivations for nonalienating forms of work in an inhospitable sociocultural and economic environment. Drawing on William Morris's (1883/1966) concept of the "craftsman ideal," which assigns a high value to craft work as creative, varied, and useful, I try to understand how craftspersons balance that "mode of being" with economic, social, and family demands. I define identity formation as the process by which these problems are resolved over the life course.

The concepts of alienated and nonalienated work are not used to derive testable hypotheses but as issues to explore with respondents to learn whether and how they might be relevant to them in their work. My inductive approach contrasts with McAdams's and Stewart's deductive one, and leads to different methods for collecting, describing, analyzing, and interpreting the interviews. For example, my research interviews are relatively unstructured, with respondents controlling the introduction, content, and flow of topics. Informing them of my interest in how craftspersons live and work, I ask them to talk about how they came to be doing the work they're doing and "what's involved in the kind of life you lead that's related to being in the crafts." Within this frame of a research interview, we have a shared task and purpose: to understand how they came to do and how they view their current work. The personal narrative that emerges is a solution to this task, representing the individual's general solution to the task of making sense of his or her life.

I take it for granted that the account produced during the interview is a reconstruction of the past, shaped by the particular context of its telling. A respondent's reinterpretation of his or her work history is the basic "text" for analysis and interpretation. The problem of "distortion" that troubles Stewart et al. — that is, whether the account corresponds to the "real" past — does not arise since I do not rely on a correspondence model of truth, where the earlier "objective" reality serves as a validity criterion for what is being told now. This is not a weakness, but rather a hallmark of interpretive research in which the key problem is understanding how individuals interpret events and experiences, rather than assessing whether or not their interpretations correspond to or mirror the researchers' interpretive construct of "objective" reality. A concern with distortion places the burden of validity claims on the wrong shoulders — it is the investigator's problem, not the respondent's. Instead of assuming a past reality as a criterion, a potential warrant for the validity of my interpretation is whether it makes sense to the respondent.

My text-sampling procedure does not follow a statistical model, but reflects successive steps of the inquiry: interviews with a small, varied group of artist-craftspersons, repeated listenings to taped interviews and readings of transcripts, discovery of parallel trajectories in their work histories, development and refinement of a model of work history narratives, selection of this respondent as a representative case, and specification of the episodes and structure of his narrative for detailed analysis and interpretation. Thus, the text samples were not drawn randomly but inductively, and chosen as representative of patterns I was finding in the full data set.

Clearly, this form of inquiry-guided or "grounded theory" research (Glaser & Strauss, 1967; Strauss, 1987) involves a continual dialectic between data, analysis, and theory. Its steps are no more mysterious or less attentive to the data than statistical procedures. The latter, as we saw in McAdams's and Stewart et al.'s studies also require online adjustments. This process-dependence of research decisions, though usually viewed as a methodological weakness and a source of contamination and error, is a necessary part of any study.

I view the "personal narratives" that emerge during the interviews as retrospective accounts whose function is to provide a sense of coherence and continuity through life transitions (Cohler, 1982), that is, as representing the formation of a craft identity. My analytic model focuses on respondents' reports of their shifts between types of work, of the reasons for these changes, and of how they achieved their current work identity. It distinguishes between and then links together the two essential dimensions of any narrative — the "non-chronological" or structural one, and the "chronological" or temporal one (Ricoeur, 1981). The structural component locates work identities within social and cultural contexts that define alternatives and limit choices among culturally available types of work for artist-craftspersons: Art, Craft, Type of Craft, and specific Mode of Craft work. Each succeeding choice is constrained by the previous ones. The second component focuses on the temporal ordering of respondents' actual choices within this structure of general categories, which serve as a "code" to classify the narrative episodes, or "units" of the interview.

The structure of hierarchically ordered categories was empirically rather than theoretically derived. Using it as a framework to locate the "identity relevance" of particular choices led to the discovery that the achievement of a current work identity was neither linear nor progressive. In shifting from one job to another, individuals sometimes made moves within the same category and sometimes moved back to a prior one before going on to succeeding ones. I refer to these shifts as "detours," as off the straight path to their achieved identity. Further, they are recognized by the respondents themselves, from their current vantage point and achieved identity, as functioning in this way. This is one criterion for assessing the trustworthiness of the model and my interpretation of the identity relevance of job changes.

For example, my analytic distinction between Art and Craft derives from and can be tracked directly back to respondents' ways of talking about their different types of work. For example, the furniture-maker refers to the distinction as present in "this endless discussion that goes on and on and on in schools and between professionals and all that." As to himself: "I don't consider myself just a craftsperson. I consider myself a designer committed to craftsmanship." For him, "a craftsperson and an artist are synonymous if you're looking at those that you respect as good craftspeople. Not people who are just churning out objects, but people who are doing personal work, and doing progressive work." And further, "It has to do probably with their input into creating the object, rather than being given a design or being given something to copy and produce and just giving with their manual skills as — as opposed to their intellect and creativity."

Further, the episodes that are the plot of his work history narrative, which I constructed from the full interview, include all of the different jobs and transitions that he describes. Thus, he specifies a sequence of changes from entering college as a "chemical engineer," switching to train as an "architect," when he first "became involved in the design world" (an Art choice), and changing again to become a "landscape architect." His first postcollege job was as an architect (Art), but then he began to work with a "third-generation craftsman" and "really started to do woodworking" (a Craft choice). After two years, feeling that he was "being locked into Milltown, Indiana, for the rest of my life" and was "wasting" his training in landscape architecture, he moved and "started working as a landscape architect" (a detour back to Art).

He stayed at this for five-and-a-half years, and then, realizing that "it just wasn't what I wanted to do for the rest of my life," he "did a search and, uh, decided to go" to graduate school for training in furniture making: "totally investing myself in — in, ah, the furniture world as a craftsman" (a switch back to Crafts). It is his own evaluation of his work as a landscape architect as off the path to his current work identity that grounds my interpretation of it as a detour. He received a degree in "crafts, treating furniture as an art form," and then began "teaching" furniture making, and setting up a "shop" and "doing some shows and commission work" (his move to his current Mode of Work and his achieved identity as an artist-furniture maker). Note that his transitions between types of work are explicitly marked by such locutions as: "I decided I wanted to do something else," "so at that time . . . I started working as," "so I did a search and, uh, decided to go," "I ended up, um . . . opting to go."

The view of validation that I have advanced suggests that the questions to be asked about my study, and of any study within any research tradition, are: What are the warrants for my claims? Could other investigators make a reasonable judgment of their adequacy? Would they be able to determine how my findings and interpretations were "produced" and, on that basis, decide whether they were trustworthy enough to be relied upon for their own work? I believe these questions have affirmative answers. The primary reason is the visibility of the work: of the data in the form of the texts used in the analysis, with full transcripts and tapes that can be made available to other researchers; of the methods that transformed the texts into findings; and of the direct linkages shown between data, findings, and interpretation.

I am not arguing that my methods and procedures "validate" my findings and interpretations. That would be counter to my basic thesis that validation is the social construction of a discourse through which the results of a study come to be viewed as sufficiently trustworthy for other investigators to rely upon in their own work. Nor does my study escape the difficult problems of "knowledge transmission," of how others might learn how to do this type of work and of what criteria they could use to determine the degree of equivalence between our respective studies. I am arguing, however, that they would be able to make a reasoned and informed assessment about whether or not my validity claims are well warranted.

I used my own study to contrast one type of narrative research with examples of standard practice. Parallels between the studies, particularly their shared focus on identity and their analysis of texts, allowed me to highlight and clarify differences between them in methods for collecting, displaying, analyzing, and interpreting data. The next two candidate exemplars differ from my own in aims, methods, texts, and models of narrative analysis.

—Narrativization in the Oral Style

A seven-year-old Black child tells a story about her puppy during "sharing time" in her second-grade class (Michaels, 1981). It does not match her teacher's expectations, lacking the standard story structure of sequentially connected episodes. (Michaels refers to it as "topic-associating" rather than "topic-centered.") Finding it difficult to understand and missing the point, the teacher treats it as a sign of the child's inadequate language skills. (See Riessman, 1987, on an interviewer's similar difficulties with a respondent's nonstandard narrative.)

Gee (1985, also 1986) reexamines the story as an instance of an "oral" rather than a "literate" style (Heath, 1982, 1983). Starting with the assumption that "one of the primary ways — perhaps *the* primary way — human beings make sense of their experience is by casting it in a narrative form" (p. 11), Gee tries to explicate how this child does that. His stylistic analysis reveals that her narrative "shares many features with narratives found throughout the world in oral cultures" (p. 9), with its structure achieved through such "technical devices" as "repetition, parallelism, sound play, juxtaposition, foregrounding, delaying, and showing rather than telling [that] are hallmarks of spoken language in its most oral mode, reaching its peak in the poetry, narratives, and epics of oral cultures" (p. 26).

His route to a description and understanding of the "structures behind her narrative performance" begins with his observation/hearing of a "characteristic prosodic pattern." Her extended stretch of speech consists of "a series of relatively short sequences of words, each sequence having a continuous intonational contour" (p. 12). A fall in pitch does not come until after several such sequences. This contrasts with literate speech, where falling contours tend to mark ends of sentences. Gee suggests that her falling contours have discourse-level rather than syntactic-level functions, and serve to mark the ends of episodes rather than sentences.

Displaying the text in terms of the "'lines' that L is aiming at," the "idea units" that she expresses as short clauses, "it becomes apparent that L groups her lines together into series of lines — often four lines long — that have parallel structure and match each other in content or topic" (p. 14). Gee calls these groups of lines "stanzas." Using the stanza as the basic structural unit in his analysis, he finds that the sequence of stanzas in her narrative, each representing an episode, are grouped together: there are three main parts to her story, each of which has two subparts. The following excerpts illustrate Gee's structural analysis (1985, pp. 34–35).

Part 1: INTRODUCTION
    Part 1A: Setting
        1. Last yesterday in the morning
        2. there was a hook on the top of the stairway
        3. an' my father was pickin me up
        4. an I got stuck on the hook up there
        5. an' I hadn't had breakfast

6. he wouldn't take me down =
7. until I finished all my breakfast =
8. cause I didn't like oatmeal either //

Part 1B
9. an' then my puppy came
10. he was asleep
11. he tried to get up
12. an he ripped my pants
13. an' he dropped the oatmeal all over

Part 3: RESOLUTION
Part 3A: Concluding Episodes
. . .
36. an' last yesterday, an' now they put him asleep
37. an' he's still in the hospital
38. (an' the doctor said . . .) he got a shot because
39. he was nervous about my home that I had

Part 3B: Coda
. . .
41. an' he could still stay but
42. he thought he wasn't gonna be able to let him go //

The first part of her story takes place in the child's home, the "setting" described first in two four-line stanzas followed by another two four-line stanzas that introduce her puppy and father. The second part involves going to school and being followed by her puppy, "complicating actions" consisting again of two four-line stanzas, with a brief non-narrative "evaluation" section. The last part takes place in a hospital, the "resolution" of the story in two four-line stanzas and a concluding two-line "coda." By using terms for the story components — "setting," "complicating actions," and so forth — from a model for standard, temporally ordered narratives (Labov, 1972; Labov & Waletzky, 1967), Gee is arguing that this story has a structure that serves the usual functions of narratives despite its different surface appearance.

Gee's close analysis of this structure and features of the child's speech uncovers an underlying theme: her sense of being "counterpoised between the world of the puppy and the adult world," where "she must deny her own longings and those of the puppy in turn, so he will not disrupt the discipline of that world" (p. 20). Although her story was not "well-received by her teacher" who found it "inconsistent, disconnected, and rambling," Gee refers to it as a "tour de force" (p. 24). In a "quite sophisticated way" she makes sense of her world through narrativization that both states her problem and its resolution: "why she doesn't have her puppy, why he didn't work out, and ultimately why she must belong to the world of home and school" (p. 24).

Gee's elegant analysis is an important contribution to narrative studies. Further, it provides what we need to assess its trustworthiness— the full text is displayed, as are its "re-presentations" in terms of stanzas and narrative functions: the technical devices that make it work are clearly defined and visible; the underlying structure is specified; and his interpretation is tied directly to the data. These are essentially the same grounds I proposed earlier in describing my study of a life-history narrative as strong warrants for the validity claims that may be made in alternative types of narrative study.

—Proust's Narrative Strategy

White (1989) explicates the "narrative strategy" used by Marcel Proust in his *A la récherche du temps perdu* by a close textual analysis of one paragraph from this multivolume novel. He "frames" this brief extract by observing that it appears, on first inspection, as a "descriptive pause" or "interlude" in the action (p. 4). The paragraph relates four successive "characterizations" of a fountain by the narrator, Marcel, as he walks toward it in a garden of the Guermantes' palace where he has been attending a soiree. The text is presented in French because, White argues, translations other than his own blur distinctions that are important for his analysis.

A novel differs in many respects from the narrative texts usually studied by social scientists, such as the life history interviews and stories of personal experience in, respectively, my own and Gee's studies. (However, see Bruner's [1986] argument for studying great works of fiction.) Nonetheless, although White's terms may be unfamiliar, his analysis is generally applicable to other types of texts since he follows a sequence of steps that closely parallel those of more typical "empirical" studies: theoretical formulation of interpretative discourse, selection of a sample text, definition and application of coding categories, redescription of the text in terms of the categories, finding a sequential order of categories, analytic restatement of this finding as a structural model of narration, interpretation of the function of the text in the larger narrative, generalization of the interpretation into a theory of narrative strategy.

White begins by distinguishing "interpretive discourse" from both explanation and description. He refers to interpretation as a "preliminary stage" in efforts to understand an object or event when we are uncertain as to how to "properly" describe or explain it. It is an "effort of deciding, not only *how* to describe and explain such an object, but *whether* it can be adequately described or explained at all" (p. 1). This is White's theoretical category in which he locates Marcel's sequence of descriptions — the passage that is the object for his analysis. He then proposes that the characteristic "modality of discursive articulation" in interpretative discourse is "more *tropical* than logical." That is, it is organized in terms of the meanings and functions of the different tropes and their relation to each other rather than by a series of propositions that are logically or causally connected. It departs from literal or technical language and from relations of "strict deducibility," "giving itself over to techniques of figuration" (p. 2). His analysis focuses on Proust's use of four such "techniques" — familiar tropes of literary criticism: metaphor, metonymy, synecdoche, and irony.[15]

The analytic function of these tropes is the same as the "codes" for self-preoccupations, motives, work spheres, and poetic devices found in the studies described earlier. Although they may be unfamiliar to social scientists, they are drawn from a comprehensive category system, refined through a long tradition of literary criticism and textual analysis. As is true of any coding system, an adequate comprehension of what the tropes "mean" requires more than their definition. We must also understand the conceptual framework within which they are located; that is, we must understand them as linguistic practices within a type of discourse. For White, their significance lies in their relationship to each other as they are deployed in an orderly sequence. Thus, he presents a structural model for the analysis of this passage as a narrative, much as Gee and I did in our respective studies.

These tropes are omnipresent in both fictional and nonfictional narrative accounts. Pointing them out, or counting them, would not tell us very much about Proust's "narrative strategy," which is White's primary concern. To this end, he focuses on their specific sequential placement relative to each other and on the overall function of this "tropical" order. (Note the resemblance between this approach and Gee's emphasis on the discourse — rather than the syntactic-level functions of narrative devices.) White summarizes the "model" of narration, displayed in this passage, as a successive movement of the narrator through the four tropes, as alternative descriptions of the fountain: from an initial "metaphoric apprehension" of it, through a "metonymic" characterization as a "dispersion of its attributes," to a "synecdochic comprehension of its possible 'nature,'" to, finally, "an ironic distancing of the process of narration itself" (p. 6).

This "passage" through the four tropes parallels the actual movement of the narrator toward the fountain, with each stage marked explicitly in the text. From afar, the narrator's impression of the fountain is captured in a metaphor as a "pale and quivering plume." Closer, the fountain is "revealed to be 'in reality as often interrupted as the scattering of the fall,'" with new jets of water producing the effect of the "single flow," a metonymic description. At the third stage, the "form" and "content" of the spray are "'grasped together' as a whole indistinguishable from the parts that constitute it," "in the manner of a synecdoche." The last characterization is

> by turns lyrical-elegiac and playful in tone . . . at once ironical in its structure and radically revisionary with respect to all three of the preceding descriptions. . . . It both radically alters the semantic domain from which its figures of speech are drawn and abruptly, almost violently, undercuts the very impulse to metaphorize by its reminder that the fountain is, after all, *only* a fountain. (pp. 7–11)

The passage ends in this ironic mode.

White observes that the fourth description is not the "most precise, correct, comprehensive, or appropriate" one. The other three cannot be "adjudged in some way inferior." Rather, it gives us, as we near the end of the passage, the "crucial bit of information that allows us suddenly to grasp 'the point of it all.' . . . to discern something like the kind of 'plot' that permits a retrospective correlation of the events of this 'story' as a story of a particular kind — a specifically 'ironic' story" (pp. 11–12).

He then proposes that the trope-sequence structure of this passage, "considered as a *narrational unit* . . . is related to the three scenes of interpretation that precede it by the four figurative modes which constitute the substance of its own form," and, further, that "as a *model of interpretation* itself, the fountain scene provides a paradigm for how to read the three more extensive scenes of interpretation that precede it" (p. 20). That is, each of the preceding scenes and the relationship among them and the key paragraph reveals the same structure of successive tropes — metaphor, metonymy, synecdoche, and irony — with the fountain scene functionally related to each of the others through the same forms of figuration.

Finally, bringing his argument back to the distinction between interpretation and either explanation or description, he states that there is no "logical connection" between the scenes. The relation is "only tropical, which is to say that it is unpredictable, unnecessary, undeductible, arbitrary and so on but, at the same time, functionally effective and retrodictable as a narrative unit *once its tropical relationship to what comes before (and what comes after) it is discerned*" (p. 13). This is his answer to the question of how narration and interpretation

> can be endowed with a coherence quite other than the kinds of coherence it may possess at the level of the sentence (grammatical coherence) and the level of demonstration or explicit argument (logical coherence). Obviously, my answer to this question is "figurative coherence," the coherence of the activity of (linguistic) figuration itself. (p. 19)

Can we make a reasonable assessment about the trustworthiness of White's analysis? I think we can, and for the same reasons I gave for the preceding two studies, namely, the visibility of his analysis. That is, he presents the full text of the passage, explicitly defines and links the coding categories to specific words and phrases, and shows us the location and sequential ordering of the different tropes, that is, the structure of the paragraph.

One advantage of choosing a relatively unfamiliar "literary" approach as a candidate exemplar for narrative analysis is that it highlights the problematic nature of validation. Although White has shown us what he did, the "rules" that inform his analysis cannot be applied mechanically. We must have some level of specialized knowledge and skills to assess its adequacy and potential range of application. Minimally, of course, it would be useful to have more than high school mastery of French as well as an understanding of tropes. However, that would only scratch the surface of what we have to know to understand White's research practice as a form of life and, from that understanding, be able to decide whether it would be a productive direction to pursue in our own work. The same requirement applies, of course, to our efforts to assess the validity claims of any study. Since White displays the evidence for his claims, this problem is not his but ours.

I have focused only on the first level of White's analysis — his description of the structure of the paragraph as a sequence of tropes and his interpretation of this structure as a narrative strategy. He expands his interpretation to the larger narrative context of the core paragraph, the three preceding scenes in this chapter, and then to the novel as a whole. How far we would wish to pursue our assessment of his work depends on the aims and scope of our own studies. Different criteria might come into play, depending on our theoretical interests and the range of inferences that we intend. We would, however, have a place to begin these extended explorations.

Conclusion

In this article, I have proposed an approach to the critical assessment of inquiry-guided research that is more appropriate to the features of such studies — ethnographies, case studies, textual analyses — than the standard experiment-based model. These studies, comprising a significant sector of the theoretical and empirical enterprise in psychology and the social sciences, are not designed as experiments, and do not "test" hypotheses, "measure" variation on quantitative dimensions, or "test" the significance of findings with statistical procedures. Criteria and procedures based on the dominant experimental/quantitative prototype are irrelevant to these studies in the literal sense that there is nothing to which to apply them.[16] When the standard model is misapplied, as it often is, inquiry-guided studies fail the test and are denied scientific legitimacy.

Recognizing this problem, other investigators engaged in these studies have proposed alternative validity criteria and procedures that parallel the standard ones, but take into account the special features of inquiry-guided research. Although these efforts have been useful, particularly in their critique of the standard model, I believe that they do not go far enough. By retaining the dominant model as the implicit ground against which alternative approaches are evaluated, the latter continue to be viewed as inadequate, temporary expedients — useful, perhaps, but only until the time that "real" scientific methods are found.

My proposal moves in a different direction. As a point of departure, I argued that the dominant research model is an abstract idealization that does not correspond to how the work of science gets done. I suggested replacing the "storybook image of science" with an empirically based description of scientific practices, of the ways that working scientists produce, test, and validate their findings. When closely observed, as in studies by historians and sociologists of science, research scientists turn out to resemble craftspersons more than logicians. Competence depends on apprenticeship training, continued practice, and experience-based, contextual knowledge of the specific methods applicable to a phenomenon of interest rather than on an abstract "logic of discovery" and application of formal "rules."

Further, the knowledge base for scientific research is largely tacit and unexplicated, learned through a process of socialization into a particular "form of life." The discovery, testing, and validation of findings is embedded in cultural and linguistic practices. Transmission of the necessary knowledge for replicating other work is an uncertain process, depending primarily on personal contact with researchers and observation of their practices. Even this does not guarantee comparability, as one of Collin's (1985) respondents indicates:

> It's very difficult to make a carbon copy. . . . But if it turns out that what's critical is the way he glued his transducers, and he forgets to tell you that the technician always puts a copy of the *Physical Review* on top of them for weight, well, it would make all the difference. (p. 86)

Within this perspective on science as practice, I proposed a reformulation of validation as the social construction of scientific knowledge. It is evident that the model to which inquiry-guided researchers have been held accountable has little if any reality. Experimental scientists proceed in pragmatic ways, learning from their errors and failures, adapting procedures to their local contexts, making decisions on the basis of their accumulated experiences.

This resemblance between experimental and inquiry-guided studies becomes clear when we shift our attention from single studies to research programs. The typical way of doing experimental work is to conduct a series of successive studies, each building on preceding ones, and this progression is clearly inquiry-guided. The analogue in complex nonexperimental studies is the sequence of different stages — from initial observations, through preliminary coding, through further observations, revisions of coding, and so on — which may be viewed as substudies building progressively on each other. (This is, of course, an insight we owe to "grounded theory"; see Glaser & Strauss, 1967; Strauss, 1987.)

This discovery — of the contextually grounded, experience-based, socially constructed nature of scientific knowledge — should be cause for celebration rather than despair. It does not dispense with methods for systematic study but locates them in the world of practice rather than in the abstract spaces of Venn diagrams or Latin Squares. Assessments of the validity of any single study are provisional. Following *the* rules of experimental design, quantification and statistical analysis are not truth tests but methodic accounting procedures, and a researcher's documentation of their use is part of the rhetoric of a particular form of scientific life. This perspective does not lead to an empty relativism or to Feyerabend's (1978) anarchic program of an "anything goes" science. Methods are still assessed for their consistency and utility in producing trustworthy findings, and trustworthiness is tested repeatedly and gains in strength through our reliance on these findings as the basis for further work.

The recent convergence among some prominent validity theorists on the primacy of construct validity adds support to the argument I advanced based on studies of scientific practice. Their emphasis on the fundamental importance of theory and interpretation in validation puts the problem beyond the reach of "technical" solutions. Again, this shift away from formal rules and procedures does not mean a retreat from systematic and methodic ways of inquiry. But it does mean that more is involved in these ways (that is, these practices) than was captured by explicit and elaborate lists of types of and threats to validity.

If standard rules will not serve for experiments, neither will they serve for inquiry-guided studies. As an alternative approach, I adopted Kuhn's (1962/1970) concept of exemplars, the "concrete problem-solutions" that show researchers "by example how their job is to be done" (p. 187). In experimental sciences, laboratory exercises do this job. Learning from them depends on more than following a series of outlined steps: heat "x" to 80°C and add "y." Ravetz (1971) remarks that "one of the things that every schoolboy knows about science is a general property of scientific equipment, which has been given the name of the 'fourth law of thermodynamics': no experiment goes properly the first time" (p. 76). Making an experiment work requires attention to various idiosyncratic features of the laboratory, of instrument errors and artifacts, of the ambient temperature and humidity, and many other factors too numerous and cumbersome to list but easily recognized in practice. Thus, learning from exemplars is a process of contextually grounded practice, which brings us full circle to what we have come to understand as scientific research.

An important task for the less well established areas of scientific inquiry is to develop a collection of relevant exemplars.[17] I proposed three studies as candidate exemplars for narrative research, recognizing that they are only a few of the many potential ones. They vary in types of texts, concepts, aims, and methods and were chosen to suggest a range of alternative approaches. However, they are similar in several important respects that I believe make them strong candidates, and, at the same time, differ from the standard model in ways that make them more appropriate for studies of narratives. These are the display of the primary texts; the specification of analytic categories and the distinctions in terms of discernible features of the texts; and, theoretical interpretations focused on structures, that is, on relations among different categories, rather than on variables.

In each study, the text is available so that other researchers can inspect it and assess the adequacy with which the methods and interpretations represent the data. Further, the availability of the primary data allows for a reasonable judgment, albeit a preliminary one, of whether and how representative it might be of other texts. That is, the question may be addressed, in an empirically grounded way, of the possible generalizability of findings and interpretations, of the "projectibility" (Goodman, 1979/1983) of inferences based on the analyses. Our assessments of trustworthiness are as firmly grounded as those we might make of studies relying on the standard research model.

The central theoretical aim in each of the selected studies is to describe, analyze, and interpret a pattern of relationships within a set of conceptually specified analytic categories. I refer to these patterns as structures, and the studies are instances of different types of structural analysis. These structures represent a significant characteristic of the texts at a more abstract level. Their general theoretical significance depends upon whether or not the particular texts are representative samples of a general class of texts. For example, in my study of an artist-craftsman's narrative, the double structure of hierarchically ordered possible choices among types of work and the temporal ordering of actual choices is viewed as a model for analyses of the work histories of other craftspersons. Gee relates the stanza structure of a child's story, and her use of technical poetic strategies to achieve meaning and coherence, to the typical form of narratives in oral cultures. And White's discovery of the sequential structure of tropes in one paragraph of Proust's novel — from metaphor, to metonymy, to synecdoche, to irony — is interpreted by him as an instance of a general narrative strategy.

In these studies, theory and analysis are in a continuing dialectic with each other and with the data, and the process is open to us. This does not mean that we would necessarily be compelled or persuaded by the findings of any particular study, or agree with a proposed interpretation. But, as I have repeatedly stressed, we are given sufficient information to make a judgment of their trustworthiness and can then decide whether or not to depend on them for further work.

This paper was written for, and from the perspective of, researchers engaged in inquiry-guided and interpretive studies. As a member of that new but growing research community, I have tried to show that we can make a strong claim for the scientific legitimacy of our work. Our collective task, to which I hope this paper has contributed, is to engage each other in vigorous debate about issues of validation as we move toward an alternative form of scientific life.

Notes

1. I use the term *inquiry-guided* research for a family of approaches that explicitly acknowledge and rely on the dialectic interplay of theory, methods, and findings over the course of a study. This includes many variants of "qualitative" and interpretive research — ethnographies, case studies, ethno-methodological and grounded-theory inquiries, and analyses of texts and discourses — that share an emphasis on the continuous process through which observations and interpretations shape and reshape each other. This feature marks their departure from the dominant model of hypothesis-testing experimentation.

2. Frustrated by the misunderstanding and devaluation of their work associated with the standard approach, many nonexperimental researchers either dismiss or ignore issues of validation. Kvale (1989b), for example, notes that discussion of the validity of results in qualitative research is "an exception rather than the rule" (p. 73). Nonetheless, my attempt to deal with

the special features of such studies is only one of a number of such efforts, which include Cherryholmes, 1988; Katz, 1983; Kvale, 1989a; Lather, 1986; Lincoln & Guba, 1985; Reason & Rowan, 1981. There are parallels among our approaches, particularly in our respective critiques of the experiment-based model of validation, as well as differences in our proposals. Detailed comparisons of the epistemological and ontological assumptions of the positivist tradition underlying experimental models and alternative "post-positivist" perspectives are provided by several of these authors (see also Carini, 1975; Mishler, 1979; Polkinghorne, 1988) and will not be repeated here.

3. Among the instructive studies and analyses of scientific practice that bear on issues of validation are Collins, 1985; Gilbert & Mulkay, 1981, 1984; Goodman, 1978, 1979/1983; Kuhn, 1962/1970, 1970/1974a, 1970/1974b; Latour, 1988, 1990; Latour & Woolgar, 1979; Lynch, 1985; Mitroff, 1974a, 1974b; Ravetz, 1971. Useful collections of sociological studies of science are Barnes & Edge, 1982; Barnes & Shapin, 1979; Knorr, Krohn, & Whitley, 1981; and Simons, 1989.

4. Both "predictive" and "concurrent" validities are "criterion-oriented": the first refers to the relation between a test score and a criterion measure obtained "some time after the test is given," the second to a criterion measure "determined at essentially the same time" (Cronbach & Meehl, 1955, pp. 281–282). Content validity, "ordinarily to be established deductively," involves a systematic sampling of test items from a universal of interest (p. 282): "Construct validation is involved whenever a test is to be interpreted as a measure of some attribute or quality which is not 'operationally defined.' . . . Construct validity is not to be identified solely by particular investigative procedures, but by the orientation of the investigator" (p. 282).

5. Among these revisions are: Campbell and Stanley's (1963) external-internal contrast pair, updated by Cook and Campbell (1979) to statistical conclusion, internal, construct, and external; Katz's (1983) reliability, representativeness, reactivity, and replicability; Lather's (1986) triangulation, face, construct, and catalytic; Levy's (1981) communicability, plausibility, generalizability, and interpretability; Lincoln and Guba's (1985) credibility, transferability, dependability, and confirmability. Rather than partitioning validity, some investigators parse the research process into different steps, each requiring its own validity assessment; for example, Brinberg and McGrath's (1982, 1985) "network of validity concepts," Huberman and Miles's (1983) rules for data display and reduction. Lincoln and Guba's (1985) "audit," and Tagg's (1985) "facet" analysis.

6. This view had early proponents. For example, Cronbach and Meehl (1955) viewed construct validity as the fundamental issue, and Loevinger (1957) asserted that "since predictive, concurrent, and content validities are all ad hoc, construct validity is the whole of validity from a scientific point of view" (p. 636). However, as Angoff (1985) points out, this view did not become generally accepted until the late 1970s. Consensus on this position is, nonetheless, hardly universal. For example, Messick's (1989) proposal of construct validation as a "unifying theme" is harshly criticized by another prominent methodologist who finds this approach "questionable" and his solution unsuccessful since "there is no agreed upon method for determining construct validity" (Green, 1990, p. 850).

7. Cherryholmes (1988), in a parallel expansion, locates validation within larger systems of sociopolitical discourse: "Construct validation is a pragmatic and socially critical activity because clear-cut distinctions among social research, social theory, and social practice cannot be sustained" (p. 421); "Decisions about construct validity cannot be disentangled from ethico-political decisions" (p. 440).

8. Trustworthiness is the key term in Lincoln and Guba's (1985) analysis of validation in "naturalistic inquiries." They pose the basic issue as: "How can an inquirer persuade his or her audiences (including self) that the findings of an inquiry are worth paying attention to, worth taking account of?" (p. 290). We share that view of the researcher's task, but I place more emphasis on other researchers' willingness to act on the basis of, as well as pay attention to, a study, and on the continuing social process through which claims are contested, assessed, and warranted.

9. This gives primacy to the "pragmatic" conception of truth in contrast to "correspondence" or "coherence" conceptions, although the latter also enter into our assessments (Enerstvedt, 1989).

10. Only a strong faith in experiments could account for their compellingness, since they are so difficult and time-consuming, and so often fail. Collins (1985) points out that "experiments hardly ever work the first time; indeed, they hardly ever work at all" (p. 41). Even the apparently rapid spread of a new experimental procedure or piece of equipment requires trial-and-error and modification to meet local conditions and problems. For example, examination of widespread "replications" of studies of vacuums after Boyle's invention of the air pump shows "that no two pumps are the same and that each transportation through Europe means a *transformation* of the pump" (Latour, 1990, p. 154; see Shapin & Schaffer, 1985). See also Ravetz (1971) on the many "pitfalls" involved in any experiment.

11. Other critics of the standard model are more sanguine about the value of substitute rules tailored to the specific features of inquiry-guided research. For example, Huberman and Miles (1983) provide detailed procedures for data reduction and display, and Lincoln and Guba (1985) offer an elaborate set of axioms, characteristics, and guidelines for "naturalistic inquiries," parallel to those used in experimental studies. Salner (1989) avoids rules but lists nine "qualities and abilities [that] the human researcher needs" (pp. 65–68).

12. The value of exemplars for clarifying and comparing alternative research models has been recognized by, among others, Bredo and Feinberg (1982) for educational research; Dervin, Grossberg, O'Keefe, and Wartella (1989) for communication studies; and Morgan (1983) for organizational research.

13. The social production of knowledge is more visible in the histories of initially marginal lines of inquiry that managed, though their methods deviated from established tenets and prescriptions, to carve out niches in the ecological space of science. Prime examples are psychoanalysis, cognitive stage theory, experimental behaviorism, and ethnomethodology — associated respectively with the names of their originators: Freud, Piaget, Skinner, and Garfinkel. Each made problematic a previously taken-for-granted or ignored phenomenon, respectively, dreams and slips of the tongue, the orderly development of cognitive structures, the dependence of stable behavior on the frequency and timing of contingent reinforcements, and the relationship between social norms and actions as practical accomplishments of actors' routine practices. Further each provided an alternative methodology for its study: free association, process observation and interview, schedules of reinforcement and baselines, norm-violation procedures, and conversation analyses.

    Experimental designs, quantitative scales, and tests of significance are notably absent. Learning these new approaches required apprenticeship through, for example, psychoanalytic training, or at the Geneva Institute, in the Pigeon Lab, or in intensive workshops and seminars. With their paths blocked to establishment journals, proponents of these schools of thought founded their own or circulated unpublished documents through their networks, as was the case, for example, with Harvey Sacks's lecture notes on conversation analysis, many of which were published posthumously (Jefferson, 1989). Facing resistance and rejection in their home disciplines, they found allies in others: in literature and history, among teachers and educators, and in the ranks of anthropologists and linguists.

14. The study of narratives has emerged in recent years as a large and diverse area of inquiry. The three models suggested here as candidate exemplars do not and are not intended to represent the variety of approaches. There are many others that might serve as well and that merit attention. For an appreciation of the range of work, see Bruner, 1986, 1990; Labov, 1972; Labov & Waletzky, 1967; Langellier, 1989; McAdams & Ochberg, 1988; Mishler, 1986a, 1986b, 1992; Paget, 1983; Polanyi, 1985; Polkinghorne, 1988; Riessman, 1990; Rosenwald & Ochberg, 1992; Sarbin, 1986a, 1986b; White, 1987; Young, 1984, 1987; and two issues of *Critical Inquiry:* Vol. 7, 1980, and Vol. 7, 1981.

15. These tropes are "fuzzy categories." Burke (1945) refers to them as the "master tropes," and observes that they "shade into one another. Give a man but one of them, tell him to exploit its possibilities, and if he is thorough in doing so, he will come upon the other three" (p. 503). Briefly, a metaphor involves describing or characterizing something in terms of something

else, a metonymy describes a whole by one of its parts or aspects, a synecdoche represents the relationship between the parts and the whole, and irony brings together all the terms or "sub-perspectives" so that they interact with and influence one another in a "total form" (Burke, p. 512).

16. My conjoint term *experimental/quantitative prototype* reflects the prevailing view of an intimate and inherent linkage between statistics and experimentation, a position I have not challenged in this paper. However, the relationship is problematic, and it is worth noting that there is a viable, critical perspective that sees these two "methods" as antithetical to each other. It is expressed forcefully by Lewin and Skinner, who are poles apart on most other issues, but share a negative view of the assumed equivalence between experimental and statistical "controls." Thus, Lewin (1931/1935), observing the "commanding significance of statistics in contemporary psychology," argues that reliance on frequencies of occurrences cannot lead to theoretical "laws," which depend instead on the study of the individual case in all its "concreteness." And Skinner (1961), commenting on "The Flight from the Laboratory," attributes it to a deficiency in graduate school training: "They have taught statistics in lieu of scientific method. Unfortunately, the statistical pattern is incompatible with some major features of laboratory research" (p. 247). He goes on to point out various "destructive" effects of the emphasis on statistics, such as their leaving the psychologist with "at best an indirect acquaintance with the 'facts' he discovers" and the "inimical" effect on laboratory practice of statisticians' recommendations. A recent, related critique of the tendency in sociological research to assume that statistical controls can be substituted for experimental controls in causal analyses may be found in Lieberson (1985).

17. Many inquiry-guided studies differ not only from the experimental prototype, but from the structural analysis of narrative texts that I have examined. The specific features of, for example, ethnographies or studies of social institutions require different criteria and procedures for assessing their trustworthiness. I hope that other researchers will undertake the task of explicating their methods so that we can build a corpus of exemplars for various types of research.

References

American Psychological Association. (1954). Technical recommendations for psychological tests and diagnostic techniques (Part 2). *Psychological Bulletin, 51*(2).

Angoff, W. H. (1988). Validity: An evolving concept. In H. Wainer & H. I. Braun (Eds.), *Test validity.* Hillsdale, NJ: Erlbaum.

Barnes, B., & Edge, D. (Eds.). (1982). *Science in context: Readings in the sociology of science.* Cambridge, MA: MIT Press.

Barnes, B., & Shapin, S. (Eds.). (1979). *Natural order: Historical studies of scientific culture.* Beverly Hills, CA: Sage.

Bazerman, C. (1989). [Review of the book *Changing order: Replication and induction in scientific practice*]. *Philosophy of the Social Sciences, 19,* 115–118.

Bredo, E., & Feinberg, W. (Eds.). (1982). *Knowledge and values in social and educational research.* Philadelphia: Temple University Press.

Brenner, M. (1981). *Social method and social life.* New York: Academic Press.

Brinberg, D., & McGrath, J. E. (1982). A network of validity concepts within the research process. In D. Brinberg & L. H. Kidder (Eds.), *Forms of validity in research.* San Francisco: Jossey-Bass.

Brinberg, D., & McGrath, J. E. (1985). *Validity and the research process.* Beverly Hills, CA: Sage.

Bruner, J. (1986). *Actual minds, possible worlds.* Cambridge, MA: Harvard University Press.

Bruner, J. (1990). *Acts of meaning.* Cambridge, MA: Harvard University Press.

Burke, K. (1945). *A grammar of motives.* New York: Prentice-Hall.

Campbell, D. T. (1979). A tribal model of the social system vehicle carrying scientific knowledge. *Knowledge: Creation, Diffusion, Utilization, 1,* 181–201.

Campbell, D. T., & Stanley, J. T. (1963). Experimental and quasi-experimental designs for research. In N. L. Gage (Ed.), *Handbook of research on teaching*. New York: Rand McNally.

Carini, P. F. (1975). *Observation and description: An alternative methodology for the investigation of human phenomena* (North Dakota Study Group on Evaluation Monograph). Grand Forks: University of North Dakota Press.

Cherryholmes, C. H. (1988). Construct validity and the discourses of research. *American Journal of Education, 96,* 421–457.

Cohler, B. J. (1982). Personal narrative and life course. In P. B. Baltes & O. G. Brim, Jr. (Eds.), *Life-span development and behavior.* New York: Academic Press.

Collins, H. M. (1985). *Changing order: Replication and induction in scientific practice.* Beverly Hills, CA: Sage.

Cook, T. D., & Campbell, D. T. (1979). *Quasi-experimentation: Design and analysis issues for field settings.* Chicago: Rand McNally.

Critical Inquiry. (1980). On narrative. Vol. 7, 1–236.

Critical Inquiry. (1981). Critical response. Vol. 7, 777–809.

Cronbach, L. J. (1984). *Essentials of psychological testing* (4th ed.). New York: Harper & Row.

Cronbach, L. J. (1988). Five perspectives on validity argument. In H. Wainer & H. I. Braun (Eds.), *Test validity.* Hillsdale, NJ: Erlbaum.

Cronbach, L. J., & Meehl, P. E. (1955). Construct validity in psychological tests. *Psychological Bulletin, 52,* 281–302.

Dervin, B., Grossberg, L., O'Keefe, B. J., & Wartella, E. (Eds.). (1989). *Rethinking communication: Vol. 2. Paradigm exemplars.* Newbury Park, CA: Sage.

Educational Testing Service. (1980). *Test use and validity.* Princeton: Author.

Enerstvedt, R. T. (1989). The problem of validity in social science. In S. Kvale (Ed.), *Issues of validity in qualitative research.* Lund, Sweden: Studentlitteratur.

Erikson, E. H. (1950). *Childhood and society.* New York: Norton.

Erikson, E. H. (1959). *Identity and the life cycle* [Monograph No. 1]. New York: International Universities Press.

Fehr, B. J., & Stetson, J. (1990). A bibliography for ethnomethodology. In J. Coulter (Ed.), *Ethnomethodological sociology* (vol. 1). Aldershot, Eng.: Edward Elgar.

Feyerabend, P. (1978). *Against method.* London: Verso.

Frankel, R. M. (1983). The laying on of hands: Aspects of the organization of gaze, touch, and talk in the medical encounter. In S. Fisher & A. D. Todd (Eds.), *The social organization of doctor-patient communication.* Washington, DC: Center for Applied Linguistics.

Garfinkel, H. (1967). *Studies in ethnomethodology.* Englewood Cliffs, NJ: Prentice-Hall.

Gee, J. P. (1985). The narrativization of experience in the oral style. *Boston University Journal of Education, 167,* 9–35.

Gee, J. P. (1986). Units in the production of narrative discourse. *Discourse Processes, 9,* 391–422.

Gieryn, T. F. (1983). Boundary-work and the demarcation of science from non-science: Strains and interests in the professional ideologies of scientists. *American Sociological Review, 48,* 781–795.

Gilbert, G. N., & Mulkay, M. (1981). Contexts of scientific discourse: Social accounting in experimental papers. In K. D. Knorr, R. Krohn, & R. Whitley (Eds.), *The social process of scientific investigation.* Boston: Reidel.

Gilbert, G. N., & Mulkay, M. (1984). *Opening pandora's box: A sociological analysis of scientists' discourse.* Cambridge, Eng.: Cambridge University Press.

Glaser, B. G., & Strauss, A. (1967). *The discovery of grounded theory.* Chicago: Aldine.

Goodman, N. (1978). *Ways of worldmaking.* Indianapolis: Hackett.

Goodman, N. (1979/1983). *Fact, fiction, and forecast* (4th ed.). Cambridge, MA: Harvard University Press.

Green, B. F. (1990). [Review of the book *Educational measurement*]. *Contemporary Psychology, 35,* 850–851.

Harper, D. (1987). *Working knowledge: Skill and community in a small shop.* Chicago: University of Chicago Press.

Heath, S. B. (1982). What no bedtime story means: Narrative skills at home and school. *Language in Society, 11,* 49–76.

Heath, S. B. (1983). *Ways with words: Language, life, and work in communities and classrooms.* Cambridge, Eng.: Cambridge University Press.

Heritage, J. (1984). A change of state token and aspects of its sequential placement. In J. M. Atkinson & J. Heritage (Eds.), *Structures of social action.* Cambridge, Eng.: Cambridge University Press.

Hernadi, P. (Ed.). (1989). *The rhetoric of interpretation and the interpretation of rhetoric.* Durham, NC: Duke University Press.

Huberman, A. M., & Miles, M. B. (1983). Drawing valid meaning from qualitative data: Some techniques of data reduction and display. *Quality and Quantity, 17,* 281–339.

Jefferson, G. (1978). Explanation of transcript notation. In J. Schenkein (Ed.), *Studies in the organization of conversational interaction.* New York: Academic Press.

Jefferson, G. (Ed.). (1989). Harvey Sacks: Lectures 1964–65 [Special issue]. *Human Studies, 12*(3–4).

Katz, J. (1983). A theory of qualitative methodology: The social system of analytic fieldwork. In R. M. Emerson (Ed.), *Contemporary field research.* Boston: Little, Brown.

Knorr, K. D., Krohn, R., & Whitley, R. (Eds.). (1981). *The social process of scientific investigation.* Boston: Reidel.

Koch, S. (1976). Language communities, search cells, and the psychological studies. In W. J. Arnold (Ed.), *Nebraska symposium on motivation, 1975.* Lincoln: University of Nebraska Press.

Kuhn, T. S. (1962/1970). *The structure of scientific revolutions* (2nd ed.). Chicago: University of Chicago Press.

Kuhn, T. S. (1970/1974a). Logic of discovery or psychology of research? In I. Lakatos & A. Musgrave (Eds.), *Criticism and the growth of knowledge.* Cambridge, Eng.: Cambridge University Press.

Kuhn, T. S. (1970/1974b). Reflections on my critics. In I. Lakatos & A. Musgrave (Eds.), *Criticism and the growth of knowledge.* Cambridge, Eng.: Cambridge University Press.

Kvale, S. (Ed.). (1989a). *Issues of validity in qualitative research.* Lund, Sweden: Studentlitteratur.

Kvale, S. (1989b). To validate is to question. In S. Kvale (Ed.), *Issues of validity in qualitative research.* Lund, Sweden: Studentlitteratur.

Labov, W. (1972). The transformation of experience in narrative syntax. In W. Labov (Ed.), *Language in the inner city: Studies in the Black English vernacular.* Philadelphia: University of Pennsylvania Press.

Labov, W., & Waletzky, J. (1967). Narrative analysis: Oral versions of personal experience. In J. Helms (Ed.), *Essays on the verbal and visual arts.* Seattle: University of Washington Press.

Lakatos, I., & Musgrave, A. (Eds.). (1974). *Criticism and the growth of knowledge* (3rd ed.). Cambridge, Eng.: Cambridge University Press.

Langellier, K. M. (1989). Personal narratives: Perspectives on theory and research. *Text and Performance Quarterly, 9,* 243–276.

Lather, P. (1986). Issues of validity in openly ideological research: Between a rock and a soft place. *Interchange, 17*(4), 63–84.

Latour, B. (1988). *The pasteurization of France.* Cambridge, MA: Harvard University Press.

Latour, B. (1990). Postmodern? No, simply Amodern! Steps towards an anthropology of science. *Studies in the History and Philosophy of Science, 21*(1), 145–171.

Latour, B., & Woolgar, S. (1979). *Laboratory life: The social construction of scientific facts.* Beverly Hills, CA: Sage.

Levy, P. (1981). On the relation between method and substance in psychology. *Bulletin, British Psychological Society, 34,* 265–270.

Lewin, K. (1931/1935). The conflict between Aristotelian and Galilean modes of thought in contemporary psychology. In K. Lewin, *A dynamic theory of personality: Selected papers.* New York: McGraw-Hill.

Lieberson, S. (1985). *Making it count: The improvement of social research and theory.* Berkeley: University of California Press.

Lincoln, Y. S., & Guba, E. G. (1985). *Naturalistic inquiry.* Beverly Hills, CA: Sage.

Loevinger, J. (1957). Objective tests as instruments of psychological theory [Monograph Supplement No. 9]. *Psychological Reports, 3,* 635–694.

Lynch, M. (1985). *Art and artifact in laboratory science: A study of shop work and shop talk in a research laboratory.* Boston: Routledge & Kegan Paul.

McAdams, D. P. (1985). *Power, intimacy, and the life story: Personological inquiries and identity.* Homewood, IL: Dorsey.

McAdams, D. P., & Ochberg, R. L. (Eds.). (1988). Psychobiography and life narratives [Special issue]. *Journal of Personality, 56*(1).

McClelland, D. C. (1984). *Human motivation.* Glenview, IL: Scott, Foresman.

Mervis, C. B., & Rosch, E. (1981). Categorization of natural objects. *Annual Review of Psychology, 32,* 89–115.

Messick, S. (1989). Validity. In R. L. Linn (Ed.), *Educational measurement* (3rd ed.). New York: Macmillan.

Michaels, S. (1981). Sharing time: Children's narrative styles and differential access to literacy. *Language in Society, 10,* 423–442.

Mishler, E. G. (1979). Meaning in context: Is there any other kind? *Harvard Educational Review, 49,* 1–19.

Mishler, E. G. (1984). *The discourse of medicine: Dialectics of medical interviews.* Norwood, NJ: Ablex.

Mishler, E. G. (1986a). *Research interviewing: Context and narrative.* Cambridge, MA: Harvard University Press.

Mishler, E. G. (1986b). The analysis of interview narratives. In T. R. Sarbin (Ed.), *Narrative psychology: The storied nature of human conduct.* New York: Praeger.

Mishler, E. G. (1989). [Review of the book *Working knowledge: Skill and community in a small shop*]. *American Craft, 49*(2), 22.

Mishler, E. G. (1992). Work, identity, and narrative: An artist-craftsman's story. In G. Rosenwalk & R. Ochberg (Eds.), *Storied lives: The cultural politics of self-understanding.* New Haven, CT: Yale University Press.

Mitroff, I. (1974a). Norms and counter-norms in a select group of the Apollo moon scientists: A case study of the ambivalence of scientists. *American Sociological Review, 39,* 579–595.

Mitroff, I. (1974b). *The subjective side of science: A philosophical inquiry into the psychology of the Apollo moon scientists.* Amsterdam: Elsevier.

Morgan, G. (Ed.). (1983). *Beyond method: Strategies for social research.* Beverly Hills, CA: Sage.

Morris, W. (1883/1966). Art under plutocracy. In M. Morris (Ed.), *The collected works of William Morris: Vol. XXIII. Signs of change: Lectures on socialism.* New York: Russell and Russell.

Paget, M. A. (1983). Experience and knowledge. *Human Studies, 6,* 67–90.

Polanyi, M. (1985). Conversational storytelling. In T. A. van Dijk (Ed.), *Handbook of discourse analysis* (vol. 3). London: Academic Press.

Polanyi, M. (1966). *The tacit dimension.* New York: Doubleday.

Polkinghorne, D. E. (1988). *Narrative knowing and the human sciences.* Albany: State University of New York Press.

Prelli, L. J. (1989). The rhetorical construction of scientific ethos. In H. W. Simons (Ed.), *Rhetoric in the human sciences.* Newbury Park, CA: Sage.

Ravetz, J. R. (1971). *Scientific knowledge and its social problems.* New York: Oxford University Press.

Reason, P., & Rowan, R. (Eds.). (1981). *Human inquiry: A sourcebook of new paradigm research.* New York: Wiley.

Richards, J. L. (1979). The reception of a mathematical theory: Non-Euclidean geometry in England, 1868–1883. In B. Barnes & S. Shapin (Eds.), *Natural order: Historical studies of scientific culture.* Beverly Hills, CA: Sage.

Ricoeur, P. (1981). *Hermeneutics and the human sciences: Essays on language, action, and interpretation.* New York: Cambridge University Press.

Riessman, C. K. (1987). When gender is not enough. *Gender and Society, 1,* 172–207.

Riessman, C. K. (1990). *Divorce talk: Women and men make sense of personal relationships*. New Brunswick, NJ: Rutgers University Press.

Roberts, R. M. (1989). *Serendipity: Accidental discoveries in science*. New York: Wiley.

Rosch, E. (1973). On the internal structure of perceptual and semantic categories. In T. E. Moore (Ed.), *Cognitive development and the acquisition of language*. New York: Academic Press.

Rosch, E. (1978). Principles of categorization. In E. Rosch & B. B. Lloyd (Eds.), *Cognition and categorization*. Hillsdale, NJ: Erlbaum.

Rosch, E., & Mervis, C. B. (1975). Family resemblances: Studies in the internal structure of categories. *Cognitive Psychology, 7,* 573–605.

Rosenwald, G., & Ochberg, R. (Eds.). (1992). *Storied lives: The cultural politics of self-understanding*. New Haven, CT: Yale University Press.

Salner, M. (1989). Validity in human science research. In S. Kvale (Ed.), *Issues of validity in qualitative research*. Lund, Sweden: Studentlitteratur.

Sarbin, T. R. (1986a). *Narrative psychology: The storied nature of human conduct*. New York: Praeger.

Sarbin, T. R. (1986b). The narrative as a root metaphor for psychology. In T. R. Sarbin, *Narrative psychology: The storied nature of human conduct*. New York: Praeger.

Schegloff, E. A., & Sacks, H. (1973). Opening up closings. *Semiotica, 7,* 289–327.

Schenkein, J. (Ed.). (1978). *Studies in the organization of conversational interaction*. New York: Academic Press.

Shapin, S., & Schaffer, S. (1985). *Leviathan and the air pump: Hobbes, Boyle, and the experimental life*. Princeton, NJ: Princeton University Press.

Sidman, M. (1960). *Tactics of scientific research: Evaluating experimental data in psychology*. New York: Basic Books.

Simons, H. W. (Ed.). (1989). *Rhetoric in the human sciences*. Newbury Park, CA: Sage.

Skinner, B. F. (1961). *Cumulative record*. New York: Appleton-Century-Crofts.

Stewart, A. J., Franz, C., & Layton, L. (1988). The changing self: Using personal documents to study lives. *Journal of Personality, 56*(1), 41–74.

Strauss, A. L. (1987). *Qualitative analysis for social scientists*. New York: Cambridge University Press.

Tagg, S. K. (1985). Life story interviews and their interpretation. In M. Brenner, J. Brown, & D. Canter (Eds.), *The research interview: Uses and approaches*. London: Academic Press.

Wainer, H., & Braun, H. I. (Eds.). (1988). *Test validity*. Hillsdale, NJ: Erlbaum.

White, H. (1987). *The content of the form: Narrative discourse and historical representation*. Baltimore: Johns Hopkins University Press.

White, H. (1989). The rhetoric of interpretation. In P. Hernadi (Ed.), *The rhetoric of interpretation and the interpretation of rhetoric*. Durham, NC: Duke University Press.

Wittgenstein, L. (1953). *Philosophical investigations* (3rd ed.). Oxford, Eng.: Blackwell.

Wooton, A. J. (1988). Remarks on the methodology of conversation analysis. In D. Rogers & P. Bull (Eds.), *Conversation: An interdisciplinary perspective*. Clevedon, Eng.: Multilingual Matters.

Young, K. (1984). Ontological puzzles about narratives. *Poetics, 13,* 239–259.

Young, K. G. (1987). *Taleworlds and storyrealms*. Boston: Martinus Nijhoff.

This article reflects an extended dialogue over the past few years with members of my research seminar about problems of validation in inquiry-guided and interpretive research. They responded seriously and constructively to earlier efforts in what may have appeared to them as a quixotic activity. For their fine blend of support and criticism, I wish to thank Jane Attanucci, Darlene Douglas-Steele, Rosanna Hertz, Roque Mendez, Catherine Riessman, and Stephen Soldz; and Vicky Steinitz for her patient, skeptical, and close readings of various drafts. Although I could not always follow their recommendations, I would like to acknowledge the detailed comments of Phil Brown, Stuart Hauser, Dorothy Hollingsworth, Robert McCarley, Mike Miller, and the editors of the *Harvard Educational Review*.

PART THREE

The Relationships
between the Researcher
and the Participants

Voice, Play, and a Practice
of Ordinary Courage in Girls' and
Women's Lives

ANNIE G. ROGERS

Introduction: A Poetics of Research

> Artistic form is congruent with the dynamic forms of our direct sensuous life; works
> of art are projections of "felt life," as Henry James called it, into spatial, temporal,
> and poetic structures. They are images of feeling that formulate it for our concep-
> tion. (Langer, 1942, p. 159)

The language of empirical "science," the language of formal propositions, of tests and
proofs, Suzanne Langer (1942) tells us, cannot take the press or imprint of inner life,
the life of feeling. To convey this life, the language of the arts is required. When the
inner life, the "direct sensuous life" (Langer, 1942, p. 159), *is* the subject of empirical
research, as it is in this article about courage, the form of research and of writing about
research itself must become artistic. Writing in an artistic, subjective voice is not an
impediment to theory building, but allows me to build theory and use theory to make
suggestions for educational practice. In this article, I have created what I call a poetics
of research, finding the "spatial, temporal, and poetic structures" (Langer, 1942, p.
159) necessary to convey what I have learned about courage in the lives of individual
girls and women. The "poetics of research" I present here involves changing not only
the voice of research, but also its practices. The particular practices of research I rely
on throughout this article are drawn from an overlapping theoretical model much like
Russian nesting dolls. Since this model guides my entire project, I will briefly explain
it. At the broadest level, I am guided by feminist epistemology and methodology;
then, nested in that framework is the voice-centered, relational approach to research
developed by the Harvard Project on Women's Psychology and Girls' Development;
nested in that approach is the subjective model of writing for social scientists outlined
by the sociologist Susan Krieger (1991); and, finally, nested within that subjective
model is the last "doll," the philosophical poetics of Gaston Bachelard (1958/1969).
While I cannot explain the details of each part of this model within the scope of this
paper, I will touch on each of its components.

Women scholars have criticized the portrayal of girls and women as objects of social construction, and have made efforts to correct research practices accordingly for

Harvard Educational Review   Vol. 63   No. 3   Fall 1993, 265–295

nearly two decades, though this work is still relatively unknown (see Collins, 1989; Harding, 1987; Nielsen, 1990). Feminist epistemology, a set of theories about the nature of knowledge, has challenged many tenets of classical androcentric epistemology. Women scholars have questioned those tests of legitimacy required of "knowledge" and of the "knower" that historically have been defined by men in Western patriarchal societies and cultures. Specifically, they have challenged the existence of abstract, objective, and universal truths, laws, or principles defined as "knowledge" and derived by a "knower" through male-defined practices of argumentation or experimentation. Feminist methodology is a theory or set of guidelines about how to conduct research in the face of disbelief in such an epistemology. A feminist methodologist, for example, rejects the belief that one can separate the "subjectivity" of the researcher from the "object" of her research and, in fact, creates research practices that close the inevitable distance between the researcher and the participants in the research (see also Cook & Fonow, 1990; Ladner, 1987). Feminist methodologists also reject the belief in universal laws or truths and seek out ways to limit the power of researchers to make global generalizations. Resisting the "objectification" of the research process, a feminist methodologist might criticize the omission of the researcher as a protagonist in the research, as well as its interpreter and author, and seek ways to include her or him as a "subjective" presence throughout the research process. These concerns guided me in the design of my research, particularly what I chose to define as legitimate "knowledge," as well as the ways in which I formed relationships in various contexts in the course of this research and the manner in which I have represented those relationships in this article.

More specifically, the practice of research I present is based on a voice-centered, relational approach to psychology and education pioneered by myself and other members of the Harvard Project on Women's Psychology and Girls' Development. This approach entails listening to girls and women as authorities about their own experiences and representing their voices in a written text, rather than replacing their words with psychological interpretations that cannot be questioned by the reader. Listening to girls and women in this way requires us to bring ourselves into relationship with another subjective voice, a real presence, a living girl or woman who may or may not be able to recognize herself in our descriptions of her. Knowing the power of making psychological interpretations, which includes our power to make ourselves invulnerable by revealing only the lives of others, my colleagues and I have tried to reveal our own lived experience in our work, so that our readers might understand the basis for our interpretations. A voice-centered, relational approach to research entails representing verbatim the voices of girls and women, including the voice of the researcher. The presence of two voices, two perspectives, which may or may not be in harmony or agreement, allows a reader room to agree or disagree with the researcher's interpretations. This voice-centered, relational way of conducting research, I believe, is vital to educational research and educational practice — because it reveals human differences and limits the power of the researchers' interpretations and generalizations.

To reveal myself in my work means to bring the self, the psyche, soul, mind, spirit — that peculiarly structured inner world that makes each of us who we are — directly into my work. This means that when I go into a school or community or clinical setting in the course of my research, I form relationships, expecting both to influence others and to be influenced and changed myself. If I participate in authentic relationships, how could this be otherwise? Moreover, like Susan Krieger (1991), who argues against the commonly held belief that the self is a "contaminant" in social science research (to be held out of research relationships and, even more critically, to be circumvented in making interpretations), I believe that the self is a researcher's finest and most valuable "touchstone" for making relationships and creating interpretations throughout the research process. Many common practices of ethnographic and interview research, however, are concerned with ways to keep track of or reflect upon one's social position and deeply held beliefs, with the goal of "bracketing" or "putting aside" what one knows as oneself. I think that these practices, particularly for women and others who have been marginalized in academic discourse, muffle one's voice, knowledge, and originality.

Another increasingly common practice among researchers, including feminist researchers, involves naming one's social location — one's gender, race or ethnicity, social class, and (sometimes) one's sexual orientation — and the social location of the research participants, and saying little more. Such information has been withheld in social science research far too long, to the detriment of knowing anything at all about researchers or the participants in their research. But the naming of social locations in a given society or culture, though important information, does not begin to replace the details of subjective experience. The individual voices of researchers and participants reveal the complexity of inner life when it is not robbed of its own subjectivity.

Finally, the last Russian nesting doll of this model, the concept most central to this work, though clearly embedded or nested in other, larger practices and frameworks, is the concept of a "poetics" as defined by the French philosopher Gaston Bachelard (1958/1969). His poetics joins the mind with the soul, and the imagination with "dreaming consciousness," in the act of writing itself. The poetics he creates as a philosopher is meant to be a "reverberation," a "resonance," a "re-percussion" — of time, space, and memory — that arises in the reader in response to the imaginative speech of the writer. This particular poetics, a sensitivity and responsiveness to the emergent images and the associative logic of poetry, is central to the way I interpret and write about courage throughout this article.

In addition to presenting this nested theoretical model, the "poetics of research" that guides my work throughout this article, I want to describe briefly the contexts of my research, myself, and the girls and women who were participants in my research.

I went to many places over the course of five years (1987–1991) to learn about courage in the lives of girls and women. The different contexts of my research included several schools: a private girls' school, a coeducational public elementary school, and a small and innovative coeducational community school. It also included my clinical consulting room, a women's oral history project, and an acting workshop for women and men from all over the world. I came to each of these places as a researcher, as a participant, or as a therapist, and quickly became a part of a community.

The voices of girls and women, including those of my colleagues and myself, that I draw upon in this article include the following groups:

1. Eighteen preadolescent and adolescent girls and three adult women who were involved in a longitudinal research study and pilot program to prevent pervasive losses of voice and knowledge among girls. I directed this project, entitled "Strengthening Healthy Resistance and Courage in Girls," for four years. We called the pilot program

the "Theater, Writing, and Outing Club." The women who were part of this program were Carol Gilligan, principal investigator for the study, Normi Noel, a director and voice teacher from Boston's Shakespeare & Company, and myself. We are European-American and European-Canadian women, diverse with respect to sexual orientation and class, ranging in age from our thirties to our fifties. The girls we met with in two groups came from two different schools. One group of ten girls attended a coeducational public elementary school, the Tobin School in Cambridge, Massachusetts, and was diverse with respect to class, race, ethnicity, and socioeconomic status. These girls were fourth and fifth graders with whom we met weekly after school for three years. The second group of eight girls attended a small, innovative coeducational community school, the Atrium School in Watertown, Massachusetts. This school, founded by Virginia Kahn and a group of interested parents, was designed to be responsive to the educational and emotional needs of elementary-aged children. They were all European-American girls from the sixth-grade class. We met with them intensively for short periods over three summers.

2. Two girls I interviewed as participants in the Laurel-Harvard study, a longitudinal study of girls' development between the Harvard Project on Women's Psychology and Girls' Development and the Laurel School, a private girls' school in Cleveland, Ohio. This study was directed by Lyn Mikel Brown, with Carol Gilligan as the principal investigator. Eighty-six percent were European-American girls, and 14 percent were girls of color, primarily from upper-middle-class homes.

3. One adolescent European-American girl I have seen in my private psychotherapy practice.

4. Seven European-American women, some of whom are immigrants to this country, ranging in age from thirty to eighty years old, from differing socioeconomic and ethnic groups, who came together to talk about their lives. These women formed the Intergenerational Women's Oral History Group at the Erikson Center in Cambridge, Massachusetts.[1]

5. Two women, diverse in nationality and sexual orientation, who were engaged in an intensive, month-long acting workshop for professional male and female actors from all over the world offered by Shakespeare & Company in Wellesley, Massachusetts.

Although the girls I present in this article attended both private and public schools and are diverse in ethnicity, race, and class, I have chosen to present detailed interviews with an Asian-American girl and an African-American girl to address the continuing silence of these girls' voices in the research literature on human development. I make no claim to generalize from my interviews with these two girls, nor from the larger studies I draw upon here, to the experiences of all girls and women. I have not set out to test hypotheses about human development here. The purpose of writing this article, rather, is to explore my theoretical understanding of girls' and women's development based on limited empirical studies and my efforts to prevent and treat psychological difficulties. The girls whose voices I bring into this article illustrate a pattern, a loss and regaining of courage. I hope my poetics of writing and research will be useful to educators, as well as to educational and psychological researchers, in understanding what these girls are saying.

I begin with an ordinary scene from girls' lives in school.

Play, Invention, and the Embodiment of Courage

And did you ever tell me
how your mother called you in from play
and from whom? To what? These atoms filmed by ordinary dust
that common life we each and all bent out of orbit from
to which we must return simply to say
this is where I came from
this is what I knew . . .
(Rich, 1981, p. 22)

On a Friday afternoon, I wait for a play to begin.[2] Eve, a slim eleven-year-old girl with straight brown hair pulled back in a ponytail, jumps up with a red plastic container and dumps shells along the edge of the audience, to indicate a "shoreline." Amy gets up and faces the audience, her black-and-white composition book in hand. The room grows quiet. Amy's red bangs touch her eyebrows. She begins, "Stories and poems about life on Plum Island." In a flash, Joan, Eve, and Rachel gather behind her. The girls hover in a circle, backs rounded as they lean in with extended arms. "I live on an island called Plum Island," Amy reads, and glances over at her "island." "I live next to the ocean," she continues, as the girls spin and scatter out, making the motion of waves with their bodies, leaning forward, pulling back. "I wake up to the sound of wind in the trees. In other islands you wake up to the sounds of birds." The girls begin to make gull sounds. The audience bursts into laughter.

I, too, am caught up in the girls' playful inventiveness in this drama that involves their entire bodies. Amy's voice comes clearly into the room. She takes me to the island, and in the school auditorium, the ocean breaks against a shoreline.

The play seems, at first glance, a bit silly, a delightful little piece, but nothing worth noting — in fact, one of the most ordinary experiences in children's lives. Yet, as I watch this scene, I am struck by a quality of boldness in the girls' play. Other girls come to mind: A ten-year-old sitting in the back seat of my car says, "I know all about lies. My house is wallpapered with lies," in a heated discussion about when it is not good to lie. A twelve-year-old girl, wary and sad, suddenly looks directly into my eyes and says, "My dad is really a violent man. You wouldn't know it meeting him on the street, but at home he just crushes my mother down like an aluminum can that you, that you would just step on."[3] I listen to girls' voices late in childhood, and I hear a natural courage, an edge into truth-telling that is potentially disruptive and troubling. But what do I mean by courage?

I begin with the life history of the word *courage*, its etymology in the English language.[4] Courage came from the Latin word *cor*, meaning "heart," and from a common Romanic word, *aetaticum*, or "age." In its original English form, in 1051, courage meant "the heart of an age." Yet by 1300, courage had lost its association with age, and therefore with time and with development. Taken out of time, courage meant simply "heart." In 1300, courage was also linked very closely with speaking. One definition of courage was "to speak one's mind by telling all one's heart" (Simpson & Weiner, 1989, p. 1051). At this time, the definition of courage drew speaking into relation with mind and heart, intellect and love.

In the year 1386, Chaucer wrote, "And smale foules maken melodie . . . so pricketh hem nature in hir corages" in the Prologue to *The Canterbury Tales* (Baugh, 1963). In modern parlance, the music of small birds pricks the traveling pilgrims in their very natures, or hearts; that is, in "hir corages." Courage, then, meant "a responsive heart," as well as "a spirit or liveliness."

By 1490, however, courage was commonly used to mean "that quality of mind which shows itself in facing danger without fear or shrinking, bravery, boldness, valour" (Simpson & Weiner, 1989, p. 1051). At this point in time, courage became cut off from the heart, the seat of feelings. No longer embodied, courage was defined as a "quality of mind" revealed through the absence of fear. The verb forms "take courage" and "pluck up courage" came into common usage and were associated with the spoils of the warrior: stealing, pillaging, and sometimes rape.

One way to understand the etymology of courage is to consider its history as a series of losses. Over the course of five centuries, from 1051 to 1490, courage was cut off from its sources in time, in the heart, and in feelings. In other words, courage was slowly dissociated from what traditional Western culture considers "feminine" qualities, and came to mean "that quality of mind that shows itself in facing danger without fear or shrinking," a definition associated with the bravery and heroism of boys and men. The pattern of losses in the history of the word courage seems to reflect an increasing invisibility of girls' and women's courage in Western culture. This historical pattern interests me because it also seems to reflect losses girls experience as they come of age in contemporary times. Girls we have studied show a tendency to be vulnerable to certain psychological losses as they move from childhood into adolescence: the loss of clarity, of self-confidence, of voice itself (Brown, 1989; Brown & Gilligan, 1992; Rogers & Gilligan, 1989).

I sit in a small music room with Marcia — one of the participants in the Laurel-Harvard study — a thirteen-year-old European-American eighth-grade girl wearing a plaid skirt and green sweater, her legs crossed. Dark, curly hair frames her face. I have come to interview her. I want to learn from Marcia about the lives of girls. She studies me in swift glances, her face closed, as I set up my tape recorder. During this interview I listen to the cadence of Marcia's quick sentences, punctuated by the phrases: "I don't know" and "this doesn't make any sense." We hear these phrases sharply increase in our longitudinal interviews, marking a repression of knowledge as girls enter early adolescence (see also Brown & Gilligan, 1992). I feel Marcia slipping away from me; her confusion and the dismissal of her knowledge resonates with the voices of girls her age whom I have interviewed over several years. I begin to wonder if girls lose not only clarity, self-confidence, and voice — but also their courage — as they come of age in androcentric cultures.

But I remember Amy at eleven, her voice coming straight out into the room as she stood reading, and the three girls playing to one side of her. I remember these girls on the beach at Plum Island, where we took them one day — running and twirling in their strong little tadpole bodies, the sudden shifts in feelings — pleasure to impatience to anger and back to pleasure — how their voices carried these feelings easily on the wind. The historical, layered meanings of courage live in these girls' bodies. Courage — "the heart of an age," "to speak one's mind by telling all one's heart," to have a "responsive heart," as well as a "spirit or liveliness" and a quality of "boldness." I discover that by restoring the word courage to its original meanings, the ordinary experiences of the eight- to twelve-year-old girls I have observed and known suddenly become coherent to me.

From Ordinary to Transgressive Courage

Reading the bones, wetting a fingertip
to trace archaic characters, I feel
a breeze of silence flow up past my wrist,
icy. Can I speak here? The bones say I must.
(Ponsot, 1988, p. 72)

My observation about a loss of courage in the lives of girls is embedded in a newly emerging psychology of women based on empirical studies of girls. As a number of recent studies document, adolescence is a time of psychological risk and vulnerability for girls (see Ebata, 1987; Elder, Nguyen, & Caspi, 1985; Petersen, 1988; Petersen & Ebata, 1987). In particular, the move into adolescence affects girls' self-conceptions. Adolescence marks a sharp increase in episodes of depression (Rutter, 1986) and eating disorders among girls, and a sharp drop in self-esteem and self-confidence, at least in White and Latina girls (Block, 1990; Greenberg-Lake Analysis Group, 1991; Wellesley College Center for Research on Women, 1992). In addition, girls tend to lose ground in their assessments of their academic achievement and in their aspirations during adolescence. Girls begin to separate their feelings and intellectual experiences at this time (Debold, 1990), and to show a striking loss of intelligence and capacity to think critically, as measured by standardized tests (Bernardez, 1965; Burks et al., 1930; Hoffman, 1975; Lueptow, 1980). There is clearly a need to understand what is happening in the lives of girls inside and outside of schools, and why adolescence is a time of psychological distress and risk.

In their work together, Lyn Mikel Brown and Carol Gilligan (1992) provide an explanation for the appearance of psychological distress in girls' development. As late childhood falls into adolescence, many of the twelve- and thirteen-year-old girls at the Laurel School began to live under the "tyranny" of the "perfect girl," a mythological (but oh so real!) icon of the culture — the girl that everybody loves because she has no bad thoughts and feelings, but is always "kind" and "nice." Her power was so real to the girls themselves that they began to lose a full range of feelings, and seemed quite suddenly confused (see also Brown, 1991a). Brown and Gilligan (1993) describe one possible outcome of this struggle as a "series of dissociations girls must make between psyche and body, between self and relationship, between the inner world of thoughts and feelings and the outer world of public knowledge — if they are to enter, without disrupting, the world they live in as young women." Another possible outcome would be for girls to resist these disconnections, and in doing so to change the order of their relationships in the world. In calling attention to the costs of girls' dissociations, Brown and Gilligan also theoretically explain how the psychological problems that some girls experience during adolescence — eating disorders and depression — are rooted in the politics of girls' relationships (see also Gilligan, 1990a).

I come back to the observation of courage among younger girls.

What happens to the ordinary courage of these girls as their bodies begin to change, as nubs of breasts emerge and hips begin to form the contours of a woman's body? To tell a coherent story about even a single girl's development and the fate of her courage, I must enter another's psyche, take time to know another "self," someone like myself and also different from myself. But what concept of self can hold the embodied meanings of a girl's courage? I turn to Pamela Hadas, a poet who describes the "self" as "any true I in a story" (1987, p. 190). Similarly, the psychologist Lyn Mikel Brown (1989) sees a connection between the development of self and story as she describes girls' willingness to trust the authority of their own experience, at least until the edge of adolescence (1991b). Brown notices, however, that to speak with authority about one's own life, a girl must resist "the cultural story of female becoming" (1991b, p. 2).

I have begun to articulate a concept of self that is inseparable from courage, the determination to speak truthfully, with integrity, to tell a story that has not been welcomed in the world. What I mean by the "true I" is the self who describes her experience courageously, rendering a story in detailed transparency, voicing a full range of feelings.

Two girls and one woman come to my mind, come into the room, three voices, three muses, each with a story about her relationship with her mother. Together they illustrate one pattern in women's development: a move from "ordinary courage" to what I call "transgressive courage."

Helen — a fourth-grade European-American girl from the Atrium School — is nine years old. She wears a green corduroy dress and white tights, her dark hair caught back in a barrette. She sits on a folding metal chair, swinging her feet, in a small room in her elementary school. It is early afternoon, just after lunchtime in her school day. She tells me about a time when her mother left the house after an argument with her father. "No one was doing anything about it, and so I knew where she was and I called her up, and asked why did you leave us like that? I told her to come home. I said, I am mad at you for leaving us. You can talk to Daddy now, . . . so please come home. And she did." In straightforward terms, Helen tells her mother what she thinks and feels, and effectively brings her home. She describes this phone exchange in the same matter-of-fact tone of voice she uses to tell me about playing croquet with her dog: "I usually win and she doesn't like that, but what can you expect?"

Karen — a depressed fourteen-year-old girl I have seen in my clinical practice — sits with one leg crossed over the other, fingering the edges of her gray sweatshirt, looking out of the window into the twilight. "I don't want to tell my mother a lot of things anymore," she begins:

> If I ever said to her, you know, why don't you fight back? I am really mad about you giving in to dad all the time, my mother would think she did something wrong and she would feel bad about it. I think she wants to think she knows a lot about my true feelings because she is afraid that if she doesn't, she will know she doesn't and she will be afraid that, you know, she's just not important in my life, we are just not as close anymore, which isn't true.

As if walking through a room where all the mirrors are hung crooked, I get dizzy trying to find my way through this statement. "But if you were to say that you are mad?" I ask. "Why should I make her life sadder by telling her, by saying that? I mean, she doesn't need to know, it is just better that she does not know all of me."

Karen's voice is uncertain, small, but her face is set, daring me to inquire any further. She looks away, and comes back to meet my eyes. Her sadness is immense.

Susan turns toward me, light brown hair falling away from her face. Susan, a woman in my Psychology of Women Seminar at Harvard, recalls a conversation with her mother when her father was hospitalized:

My senses were trained to listen closely to the strain of voice, to hear the meaning of breath, to catch the deflections, to push gently. . . . My mother's voice is not coming from her body. She's struggling to make up answers that she thinks are acceptable for me to hear. She doesn't want me to worry. She doesn't want me to know that she is worried. . . . From years of training I know how to push the anger aside and gently press for more information.

I can read the signposts of Susan's knowledge, for she reads, as I read and decipher, a coded knowledge of relationships between women. This recognition swiftly passes back and forth between us.

As I listen to Helen, Karen, and Susan, I hear a struggle for courage in relationships in a society where speaking about what one knows as a girl or a woman is not simple. What was ordinary and natural questioning of her mother for nine-year-old Helen has become a dangerous set of questions for Karen at fourteen. Karen herself senses this and calls her unspoken questions "kind of like trespassing, you know, going where you are not supposed to go." And Susan, who secretly trespasses into forbidden knowledge about her mother's feelings, carries this unspeakable knowledge around like a bomb. Karen's and Susan's courage has become transgressive insofar as they have each dared to know what they are not supposed to know about their mothers and voiced their knowledge with me. Transgressive courage involves going beyond the strictures of forbidden knowledge of relationships, including cultural conspiracies of silence that surround women's knowledge.

These three muses represent not only individual girls and women I have spoken with and known variously as a clinician, teacher, and researcher; they also represent a broader pattern of girls' and women's development within a repressive culture. The loss of an ordinary, embodied courage — a "boldness, spirit and liveliness," the capacity to "speak one's mind by telling all one's heart" — is a loss many girls experience at the edge of adolescence, a loss that leaves in its wake unspeakable longing and rage, as well as a struggle for courage in relationships — the sense that speaking as a "true I" is transgressive and dangerous. What is unspeakable and unspoken in the public world then becomes a feminine "underground" (Gilligan, 1990b), a private world where the "unpaid-for education" of women takes place (Woolf, 1938/1966), where women's knowledge of relationships is buried or kept under wraps in any androcentric culture.

Listening to Narratives of Courage

I'm on my way running
I'm on my way running
Looking toward me is the edge of the world . . .
>   — Traditional song for a young girl's puberty ceremony,
>   Papago tribe (cited in Reese, Wilkinson, & Koppelman, 1983, p. 1)

In order to understand a loss of ordinary courage in women's lives, I have had to go back to girls who have yet to experience such a loss. I listen to preadolescent girls speaking about themselves and their relationships and reenter my questions about courage from the point of view of an "insider," a woman remembering her girlhood and the moments when, running ahead, "looking toward me is the edge of the world." As I listen to girls from different social classes and ethnic groups in various school settings within this culture, I know that there are things I do not hear or fully understand, there are lines I am not able to cross, and there are some questions I do not even think to ask.

In this section, I present the voices of two girls, an eleven-year-old African American girl, and a ten-year-old Asian American girl.[5] The girls come from middle- and upper-middle-class families. As an American woman of Irish ancestry who grew up in a lower-class home, I am different from these girls in two fundamental ways: 1) I have not been exposed to the racism that they and their families face every day in this society and culture; and 2) I grew up less privileged than they in terms of socioeconomic status. Because these realities are by no means simple, and because describing sociological differences without clearly understanding individual voices may be misleading, I present the girls' voices in some detail, so that any reader can agree with or reject my interpretations. I also include the ways that the girls spoke or behaved in other contexts wherever that might shed further light on my interpretations.

The method of analysis I use is based on the *Listener's Guide* (Brown et al., 1988; Brown & Gilligan, 1992; Rogers, Brown, & Tappan, 1993), a way of listening to girls in interview texts developed by members of the Harvard Project on Women's Psychology and Girls' Development. The method entails listening for multiple voices within a text through differing interpretive frameworks. Using this method, I have learned to become a "responsive" and "resisting" reader of interview texts, to hear girls speaking both against and within cultural prescriptions about their lives, reading between the gaps I feel between lived experience and the dominant culture's conventions of femininity (see Brown & Gilligan, 1990).

As I read to understand girls' narratives as stories about courage, I am not asking girls to agree or disagree with my concept of "ordinary courage." I developed this concept over a period of years in response to listening to many girls and women, and I am relying on the older definition of the word, as described earlier. In order to discern what I call ordinary courage — "the capacity to speak one's mind by telling all one's heart" — I listen to several voices with a single text in mind. I attend first to the "true I" speaking, that is, the self who describes her experience with a full range of feelings in detailed transparency. Then I listen again for the "feminine not spoken," that is, for a subtext of unspoken meanings or messages (see also Rogers, 1992). Finally, I piece together an interpretation of each girl's struggle for courage by turning to a text written by an older woman; a woman who shares each girl's race and class, as I do not share this experience or understanding with them. Often I hear a resonance between their voices, a haunting harmony, as if listening to singing. This way of listening opens into an acoustical space between girls' and women's voices, where I join as a third voice speaking about what I recall, what I know, and what I do not understand. The purpose of working this way is not to present a "final" or "true" or even classically "valid" interpretation of data. (Such a goal assumes that by employing certain strategies I could put aside all potential differences in interpretation and come to the "right" interpretation.) I do not think this is possible. Therefore, by bringing together multiple voices — the voice of a girl telling a story about relationships, the voice of a woman like the girl drawn from literature, and my own voice as a researcher — I seek to highlight and hold differences in voice and in perspective alongside one another and, in so doing, not to override or overwrite any single voice.

Let me now introduce eleven-year-old LaTanya, a middle-class African American girl who attends a small community school. She is a lively, humorous girl, her voice clear and strong. Asked to tell a story about a relationship, she tells the following story about her father:

> Jokewise and things like that my dad's fun to be around. Like when we go down and get pizzas he likes to make me embarrassed. He says the greatest thing is watching daughters being embarrassed by their dads. So he had his slippers on and we went down to get pizza and I said, "I will go in and get it dad," and he said, "No, I'll come," and I said, "Please dad, stay in there," and he said, "No, I'm coming," and I gave him the money and said, "I'm going back to the car," and then he said, "No, come." So I came with him and we went in and got the pizzas and everything and we come back and he started dancing around in the street and really, really, he was dancing up and down and twirling around and I almost dropped the pizzas it was so funny. And we got in and he started, you know, accelerating (she makes accelerating noises) like that, and it was so funny, and so I was laughing and when we got back home and so he does lots of crazy things.

I read first for the narrative "I" of this story; focusing on the self-statements in the text: "I said I will go in . . . I said please dad, stay in there . . . I gave him the money . . . [I] said I'm going back to the car . . . I came with him . . . I almost dropped the pizzas . . . I was laughing." LaTanya tells her interviewer about giving her father a series of commands, of protesting, then suddenly giving in and almost dropping the pizzas. I identify the self speaking here as a "true I" because she creates a drama of detailed transparency. As I listen to the tape of her interview, I can hear peals of laughter. As LaTanya tells about teetering between going and staying, she clearly enjoys being teased. In her story, she creates a dialogue or play that is fundamentally two-sided. If I listen for what LaTanya knows about relationships, how she considers her father through this story, here is how she describes him: "My dad's fun to be around . . . he likes to make me embarrassed . . . he says the greatest thing is watching daughters being embarrassed by their dads . . . he had his slippers on . . . he said no, I'll come . . . he said, no, I'm coming . . . he said no, come . . . he started dancing . . . he was dancing up and down and twirling around . . . he started, you know, accelerating like that . . . he does lots of crazy things." As I listen to her, I get the impression that LaTanya knows her father as a man who plays with her and does not placate her, but who instead holds his own in this argument about his own silliness.

What is unspoken here? What questions are whispered between the lines of this funny little story? Of course, I cannot know with any certainty, as LaTanya was not directly asked these questions. But, I have learned that there are commonly unspoken messages and questions in girls' stories that remain muffled, enfolded in silence. I listen between the lines of LaTanya's story about playing and teasing with her father from other sections of the interview in an attempt to understand her unspoken messages, questions, and silences. LaTanya tells a companion story about her fourteen-year-old sister and her father: "He makes her change clothes from skimpy stuff to clothes he likes better before she goes out [on dates], and he doesn't really listen to her like he does with me. . . . When they fight, they do that a lot these days, he usually wins. He wins with me too, but I mean, I can just tell, I can tell, that he really embarrasses her sometimes." I hear questions LaTanya does not speak directly: Will my dad ever really embarrass me? For how long will he play with me as he does now, when I am eleven? For how long will I be able to hold my own in arguments with him, even when he "wins"?

In my attempt to understand LaTanya's story, I turn to a poem by Nikki Giovanni:

> a poem is pure energy
> horizontally contained
> between the mind of the reader
> of the poet and the ear of the reader
> if it does not sing discard the ear
> for poetry is song
> if it does not delight discard
> the heart for poetry is joy . . .
> (Giovanni, cited in Webber & Grumman, 1978, p. 192)

This poem, together with LaTanya's narrative, speaks to me about her ordinary, embodied courage, linking LaTanya with many other girls of this age. Eleven-year-old LaTanya tells a story about the possibility of listening too, listening in a relationship — and LaTanya's capacity to dwell in possibility, to live between the lines of argument and play with her father, *is* the poetry of her story. Her courage comes from her connection with a "true I" who understands her father's intentions and can argue playfully. In fact, LaTanya's capacity to play her part in this scene depends upon her seeing through her father — seeing that he wishes to tease her, make her embarrassed, and beyond this, sensing that his pleasure in the game revolves around her playing her part by giving him commands about what he may and may not do, by protesting what she will and will not do. LaTanya's story of how she plays in the street with her dad, almost dropping the pizzas, is Nikki Giovanni's poetry of song and delight.

In the next excerpt, I am interviewing a girl I have observed in the classroom, so that she knows who I am before I begin to interview her. Her voice plays against my voice in the following dialogue.

Meyee is ten years old and in the fourth grade in her small community school this year. She is a second-generation Chinese American girl with straight black hair, pulled back in a ponytail today. She has dark eyes that light up as she speaks and an easy smile. She sits on a small sofa in a cozy office in her private school, tugging on the ears of a stuffed Eeyore. We have been talking for about forty minutes, and we are in the section of the interview protocol where I ask girls about relationships in which others were not listening to them.

"Can you tell me about a time when you felt you were not being listened to?" I ask her.

Meyee pauses, thinking this over. "When my mom and dad make decisions without consulting me and I feel like 'But mom, you never ask to hear me . . . But MOM!' It makes me really mad and I hate it and I feel that they are taking advantage of me just because I am younger."

"Can you tell me about a certain time?"

"I don't remember any, but I just feel it," she replies, looking off.

"When you say, 'they are taking advantage of me,' can you imagine that you might have a little bit of power?" I ask.

"Well, my parents consult me about my birthday, what kind of party would I like, what kind of cake would I like?" she says with a rising inflection. She tilts her head and raises one shoulder.

"So some decisions they might include you?"

"Not very often," she says wryly.

"Okay. When you are not being listened to, how do you get people to listen?"

"I shout," Meyee says, very matter of fact.

"Does that work?" I wonder out loud.

"Sometimes." Ruefully, she adds, "I also get sent to my room. But, oh well."

Meyee looks at me and grins conspiratorially. "I also do a very mean, practical joke on them. Like if my mom is talking to my dad, this is a good idea, I haven't done it yet, I could just go to one of the upper extensions, we have a ton of them [in our house], I could just go up and like burp, a real loud burp, and that would get their attention or something." We laugh.

"Do you think *that* would work?" I ask her.

"Maybe. It would get them very mad, but it would also get them to listen to me. And if they ask for an explanation, I'll tell them."

I begin by listening to the narrative "I," the self who responds to my questions. "I feel like, 'But mom, you never ask to hear me'. . . I hate it . . . I feel that they are taking advantage . . . I am younger . . . I don't remember . . . I just feel it . . . I shout . . . I also get sent to my room . . . I also do a very mean practical joke on them . . . I haven't done it yet . . . I could just go . . . I could just go up and like burp . . . I'll tell them." As I listen to the "I" clauses in this order, I hear a "true I," a girl who feels her thoughts and trusts her feelings, even when she doesn't have a memory of a particular incident. This ten-year-old girl speaking about herself also feels "taken advantage of" and not listened to, but she cares enough, or has enough courage perhaps, to disrupt her family a bit on her own behalf — by shouting, or by planning "a very mean practical joke."

As I listen to what Meyee does not say, what she perhaps knows but doesn't say to me, I feel the edge of her daring. She calls a loud burp a "very mean practical joke." The joke and how "mean" it is depends, of course, on the disruptiveness of her act, on catching her parents off guard to get them to listen to her. She implies that this behavior may require an explanation: "If they ask me for an explanation, I'll tell them." But she has also spoken about making her parents angry, and about getting sent to her room. Meyee implies that her plan is risky, that she may be punished for it. What remains unspoken is that she must continually gauge what she can and cannot do and say because she is, in fact, younger and relatively less powerful than her parents.

What Meyee can and cannot say aloud is affected, to some extent, by my questions and responses to her. They are the questions and responses of an adult woman who grew up as an Irish American girl in a family where she often felt powerless. I am also her interviewer here — and therefore more powerful than she is in this situation. When Meyee says, "They are taking advantage of me," I ask, "Can you imagine that you might have a little bit of power?" I wanted to align myself with her daring through that question, but perhaps I dismissed her feeling of powerlessness, not wanting to recall my own feelings. She tells me then that her parents consult her about her birthday. In a rising inflection she gives examples: "What kind of party would I like, what kind of cake would I like?" — as if to say, "Is this what you want me to say?" The back and forth dance of what can and cannot be spoken about we create together. When I ask, rather hopefully, "So some decisions they might include you?" she replies, "Not very often," bringing me back to her reality and to my questions about not being listened to.

I listen next to Nelly Wong, a Chinese American writer, and bring a fragment of one of her poems to Meyee's story, to my own questions about courage:

> When I was growing up, I was proud
> of my English, my grammar, my spelling
> fitting into the group of smart children
> smart Chinese children, fitting in,
> belonging, getting in line
> (Wong, cited in Reese, Wilkinson & Koppelman, 1983, p. 171)

I have observed Meyee in her school, "fitting in, belonging, getting in line," yet I hear Meyee as a resistor of conventions. She does not fit the image of the "good girl" of a dominant White culture — she is too outspoken, too mischievous. And she does not fit the image of a "good Asian girl" either — she is too strong, too bold. "And if they ask for an explanation, I'll tell them," she says, thinking about her experiment with a "loud burp." But I wonder what she can tell her parents, her teachers, and me, her interviewer. It seems to me that Meyee's plan for the practical joke of a loud burp requires some foresight and courage; but if she is to continue to say what she knows aloud — to trust her own feelings and knowledge as a Chinese American girl growing into a woman in this culture and learning about herself and the world in our educational system — she will need much more foresight and courage. I wonder what she will know as a young woman, this girl of ten who is now so strong and brave.

In reading the interview transcripts of these two girls, LaTanya and Meyee, I noticed that I did not directly ask them about their experiences as African American and Asian American girls, as children who stand outside the dominant culture by virtue of both race and gender. In retrospect, I wish that I had asked this question, because I might have learned something critical about their different experiences of courage. I mark this gap in my knowledge and skill so that others might see the gap and wonder about it too.

The Recovery of Courage: Through Voice and Play

What is a practice of courage in relationships that makes it possible for women and girls, and for women of different generations, to stay with one another, rather than abandoning one another at the edge of difficult and vital truths? I think again of Amy, Helen, Meyee, and LaTanya, girls at ten and eleven — their ordinary courage, their outspokenness, and their insistence on real or authentic relationships. Living just at the edge of adolescence, these girls conducted profound experiments in relationships — experiments to sustain their courage. But to continue to do so is anything but easy. Adolescent girls and women who risk their truths in relationships risk a great deal. Courage may be in fact dangerous at times — when knowledge is new and fragile; when reaching out for a desired connection may lead to a painful repudiation; when

speaking without any real possibility of being heard may lead to betrayal or abandonment. But the ways girls and women, and women of different generations, negotiate
these difficult issues together mark the fate of female courage in families and schools,
and in the culture at large.

The recovery of ordinary courage in women's lives is nothing short of extraordi-
nary, because it depends upon finding a voice to speak what has been unspeakable.
Often this process begins in a safe, playful, and challenging relational context among
women or among women and girls together. Women of all ages then begin to remember and reexperience that lively and playful and knowing younger self that Emily
Hancock calls "the girl within" (Hancock, 1989).

"Finding a voice" is not a metaphorical phrase, but a literal, psycho-physical finding of voice. The voice, played on breath and linked with real feelings, reveals the self
— and is therefore vital to authentic contact and to the recovery of courage. Kristin
Linklater, who has extensive experience training actors, describes in her book *Freeing
the Natural Voice* (1976) a voice that carries every nuance of human thought, a voice
connected with breath and with feelings: "The natural voice is transparent — revealing, not describing, inner impulses of emotion and thought, directly and spontaneously" (p. 2).

Linklater's "natural voice" is, in my terms, the voice of ordinary courage. Muscular
tension, or any inhibition of the free flow of breath in the body, distorts this voice and
protects us from being known. But when an adolescent girl or a woman begins to
speak in a natural or transparent voice, bringing herself into relationships as a "true I,"
and living courageously in the sense of "speaking her mind by telling all her heart,"
she may be in danger. Within some contexts, women can expect to be heard only if
they learn to "modulate" their voices. A loud or strong voice in a woman tends to be
associated with rudeness, anger, and aggression. The effort to modulate the voice, to
be quiet, involves going "off" one's voice. It is not unusual for adult women in Western cultures to sound somewhat "breathy," which results in a diminishment of clarity
and power, as well as a narrowing of the full octave of pitches available for speaking.
Perhaps once these physical changes have affected the voices of adolescent girls, it is
easier for girls to adapt to living as women within men's knowledge and traditions —
in our educational system and in our society.

The range of self-protective compromises — including the unconscious covering
of voice — that diminishes a girl's courage and knowledge of herself, seems endless.
Are these self-protective compromises really necessary, or might the ordinary, embodied courage of girls somehow remain intact? And if self-protective compromises at adolescence are unavoidable to girls in this culture, can ordinary courage be recovered
later in life?

These questions became acute in my developmental and preventive work with girls
and women in three different contexts: a) in the Theater, Writing, and Outing Club
for Girls from the Atrium School conducted by myself, Carol Gilligan, and Normi
Noel; b) in the Shakespeare & Company's month-long acting workshop in which I
was a participant; and c) in the Intergenerational Women's Oral History Group at the
Erikson Center, in which I was also a participant. In each of these settings, women
and girls experienced ordinary courage — through voice and play. Three distinct but
overlapping stories that emerged from the contexts described clarify the process of
coming into courage for girls and women at different times in their development.

In the first instance, both the ease of calling forth the ordinary courage of preadolescent girls and the fragility of their courage became clear to me.

The members of the Theater, Writing, and Outing Club for Girls sit in a circle in an empty school auditorium. Eight eleven- and twelve-year-old girls have gathered with three women: Carol Gilligan; Normi Noel, a director and voice teacher from Boston's Shakespeare & Company; and myself. Normi is leading the group in theater exercises this rainy Wednesday morning. She tells us that to be actors first we must be entirely honest about our feelings, because our feelings will become the "stuff" of theater. We go around the group. Joan begins: "If I say my feelings, they will keep changing," observing at age twelve, just at the edge of adolescence, the fluidity of her own emotional life. We speak around this circle, each intent, without evaluations.

Then Normi introduces a game, "Stories: One-word-at-a-time." The girls want to create a story about witches. They will create the story word by word. Normi takes on the role of group "scribe." There is little or no time to think. Here is the story about "witches" composed on the spot:

> Witches. There are disgusting witches. Broomsticks. Bugs owls eat, like crawly insects. Witches tend to want everything. They tend to think of anything that you love. But they can magically transform into production hats. Eat chicken and never eat fried pickles. They are going home soon so that they can disguise themselves as rabbits with leaves. Feelings I feel: gross disgusting sick mad witches. Crazy women eat toilet paper and barbaric hair. They're very indigestous, overwhelming like antidisestablishmentarianists, or weird people. Hair spray smells like witches' breath. Garbage smells like farts. Murals feel revolting, like cats and sardines. Anyway, people tend subconsciously to throw up.

Here is a story about forbidden feelings, a story about greed, love, disguise, disgust, and about what cannot be digested. It may also be read as a rather rude, banal story about witches told by eight young girls. But I listen to this story from another vantage point, from the point of view of a woman who listens for a story of courage. What is spoken and what is unspeakable in this story? What do girls know about women, when women are disguised as witches? I hear the girls naming an unspeakable longing and vulnerability in women: "Witches tend to want everything. They tend to think of anything that you love." I hear a struggle to see through disguise and not to be taken in by the mystifying ways women cover themselves: "They are going home soon to disguise themselves as rabbits with leaves." The girls touch on the subject of women's madness; their voices join in with a chorus of voices condemning women: "Feelings I feel: gross, disgusting, sick, mad, witches. Crazy women eat toilet paper and barbaric hair." The girls also actively resist female conventions of beauty: "Hair spray smells like witches' breath." In quick succession, "witches' breath" is associated with "garbage," "farts," and "cats and sardines." The girls reject the entire list, framing this line of associations with the phrases, "they're very indigestous" and "people tend subconsciously to throw up."

Listening to and watching the girls perform their story with these thoughts flying through my mind, I double over in laughter as they play out, in lively mimed movements, each phrase of their story, and "freeze" to hold their outrageous poses on Normi's command.

What Carol, Normi, and I are doing here seems quite simple. Through the avenue of play and theater, we call girls' voices out into the room, we listen to them and enjoy them, and we delight in their ordinary courage — played through their voices and physical poses. We hear ourselves through the girls' voices, ourselves speaking a bit more clearly and courageously. But what we are doing is also dangerous. When we perform this for the girls' mothers and teachers, for example, the bad feelings, all the madness and ugliness held in this fanciful story, go flat. The fragility of the girls' courage becomes apparent only when it disappears in front of this audience.

Yet I know that I could not stay with the girls' feelings and know the full range of my own responses without Normi and Carol, without all our conversations about how the girls affect each of us. Being with the girls brings to the surface my questions about courage, and their ordinary courage soaks into my body, straightens my spine. When Normi commutes from New York to work with us, she gets dizzy on the long train rides back and forth as she comes and goes from experiencing her own courage with girls and women in this way. For a few weeks after our summer session with these eleven- and twelve-year-old girls, I can look at Carol standing straight in one of her sundresses, her long hair falling in a different way, and I can tell that she is thinking of one particular girl who also stands that way. I ask her and find that I am correct. The girls connect with each of us beyond the time we spend with them — they come into our bodies, they enter our dreams, they join us on our train journeys, they speak to us when we sit down to write. Witches indeed!

We three, all adult women, remember ourselves vividly as girls in their presence. During this period of our work with the girls, Carol had recently returned from participating in a month-long acting workshop conducted by Shakespeare & Company. She had discovered, she told us, "the mechanism of dissociation in girls' voices at adolescence." What she learned was "the way girls dissociate is to stop breathing, hold their stomachs in, and in this way, girls cut off breath and feelings from their voices." I was intrigued by this idea, and still more intrigued as I watched Normi work with the eleven- and twelve-year-old girls in our Theater, Writing, and Outing Club. Normi noticed that "the girls' voices come straight out from the center of their faces." She added, "These little creatures naturally speak on their voices most of the time! Women do not do that." I did not know what the phrase "on their voices" really meant, but I wanted to find out because that phrase seemed intricately linked with ordinary courage.

In the second context, Shakespeare & Company's acting workshop, I came to understand this linkage between voice and courage more fully. "What am I doing here?" I ask myself, looking around the dim room, which gradually grows lighter. Of course I know. Encouraged by Carol and Normi, I have come to this acting workshop to explore the links between voice and courage, beginning with my voice and a search for my own courage.[6] The fear is familiar enough. I feel uncannily light-hearted, however. Restless, unable to sleep more than five hours the night before, I have returned to the place I began my voice class. I button my sweater up to my chin, remembering: The room lit up with lamps. Seven people, men and women, sitting in a semicircle of folding chairs at one end, my "basics" group. For me, unlike the others who are professional Shakespearean actors, this is my first voice class. Each one has stood and performed one of Shakespeare's monologues or sonnets, but I have chosen to begin with a poem, one of my own (Rogers, 1990), not daring to start with Shakespeare.

"From the porch / when dark / stole the colors of childhood / from the very sky . . ." I begin. "Where are you?" asks Kristin, my basics teacher.[7] "On the porch," I answer, as if this were a perfectly obvious place to begin. "No, no!" she says, striding toward me, her brown eyes sharp. "First you have to come into this room!" I look around thinking, "What could be simpler?" But it wasn't simple at all to come into my body in that room. Over the next thirty minutes, Kristin had me perform a "three-act play." "Here is how it goes," she said, "Act I: I am, Act II: here, Act III: in this room." Stomping on the carpet in bare feet, pounding the walls with my hands, whispering, shouting, I cajole and finally convince myself, Kristin, and my small audience of my presence in the room.

Kristin pulls one of the folding chairs out from the semicircle and places it backward. "Sit," she says, "and begin your poem."

"From the porch / when dark / stole the colors of childhood from the very sky . . ." "What? What are the colors of childhood?" Kristin asks. "You know, feelings, ordinary things, play." "What are you feeling?" "Nothing in particular." She pulls me up from the chair and begins a clapping game, dancing around me in her gray high-top tennis shoes, in her black sweatsuit with moons and stars, her short gray hair standing up on end. She sticks her tongue out at me and encourages me to give chase around the chair. Laughing, I chase her and sit again, and still laughing, begin — "From the porch / when dark / stole the colors of childhood from the very sky / and I'd lost a shoe-box-full of / myself . . ." "Of what? Not of things." "Of myself." "Say it again." "Of myself," I whisper. "Again." "Of myself," I say aloud, and feel the fresh loss of my whole lively self. "Go on." "The voices came. / They were in the loosening bud of my body / they came like blue rain / like angels from the dark." Kristin stands next to me, one hand on my belly. "Breathe," she says, as I stop breathing. "What did the voices say to you? Did you like them? Did they frighten you? What does blue rain feel like? Who were the angels? Where were you standing on the porch? How old were you? What were you seeing and hearing from the porch?" Her questions come into my body with each intake of breath.[8] Images, voices, feelings, the view from the back porch flood me, in my thirteen-year-old body. "Keep going," Kristin says softly. "They came from everywhere / snowing down, they swirled and settled on a white wooden table . . ." Kristin pummels my chest, moves my arms up and down, "Just ignore me," she says, "I'm helping you." And she was! My words came clearly into the room. I heard myself saying, "They said: Go and lick the white metal ice / that tears ragged / a layer of tongue . . ." "Like that? The voices just asked you like that?" Kristin says, incredulous. "Well no, they were a little meaner," I admitted. "Meaner? I bet they were downright sadistic!" She grabs me by the hand and takes me back to the couch at the far end of the room. She looks back at my basics group. "Don't move until you feel terrified. Then raise one finger," she instructs them. "Here, stand up here and try it again — to them." I stand in silence. Kristin shouts, "Off you go!" Caught off guard, I shout, "Go and lick the white metal ice / that tears ragged / a layer of tongue." I yell it over and over, my throat dry. At the other end of the room, no one budges. Kristin is up on the couch with me in a flash. "I want you to send them terror. I want you to make them want to get out of this room — fast," she whispers to me. Suddenly, my voice, filled with hatred and suppressed rage, comes from deep within my abdomen, from a place I've never heard before. "Go and lick the white metal ice / that tears ragged / a layer of tongue!" "Good. . . . Now go on," Kristin says, laughing.

"I tried to hold them in my very hand; / they evaporated, as if endangered things / and my fingers lay / as in a bell that lay above a clapper. / They rang out cracking from the sky / like ink left in a blotter too long. / At day's end / each one of them would make up / for me / the deepest crib / of doubt / black me in."

The white ceiling became a dark sky, filled with cold stars, then black — and the voices, once cut off from me, came back to me. My own voice came from within my body, resonated through the tiny bones of my face. My lips and arms tingled from the vibrations. And my small audience sat still, as if suspended in time. "Like that?" I asked, turning to Kristin, who had climbed down from the couch and was now grinning like the Cheshire Cat himself.

Reliving this work, I stood and looked out into the falling snow and felt wetness on my cheeks. My small voice, not so very small after all, lived in my body. I had struggled for understanding, for words, for voice itself, at the edge of the sofa, at the edge of the unspeakable — as a "true I." I wanted more of this, much more, for myself — and for other girls and women.

It is not coincidental that the poem I chose for my voice work reveals a story about a loss of voice so complete as to mean a loss of "myself" at age thirteen. "When dark stole the colors of childhood from the very sky . . ." ushers in a time of crisis in many girls' development when cultural darkness and psychological repression lead to a loss of ordinary courage. Once my own courage was endangered in this way, the "true I" became fragmented and "the voices came from everywhere." Carrying my dissociated hate and rage, they said, "Go and lick the white metal ice that tears ragged a layer of tongue." These voices echoed cultural messages to forget what I knew, to stop speaking. Yet, once these voices came back into my body, released on sound, their repression was no longer necessary. Courage seemed, at least momentarily, ordinary again.

Voice, played on breath in the body, is, I discovered, a powerful way for women to recover memory and courage. Kristin is a Scottish woman a generation older than I, and I experienced myself in the position of the daughter in this playful and powerful scene with her. The process of recovering ordinary courage involved crossing a full generation in relationship with a woman, and with traveling back in time through the psycho-physical experience of the voice work. I wondered about the intergenerational possibilities for extending this work. Was it critical to cross a generation in order for women to experience the recovery of memory and of courage? Was the structure of the voice work critical? How would elderly women experience themselves in a relational context with younger women?

I had the chance to explore some of these questions in a third context, a structured six-week-long Intergenerational Women's Oral History Group at the Erikson Center in Cambridge, Massachusetts. The group was created and facilitated by Vicki Magee and Lisa Sjostrom, who had joined me in writing a year-long ethnography at the Erikson Center (see Rogers, Fradin, Magee, & Sjostrom, 1992). I was invited to participate in this group, as well as to act as an adviser. We met weekly in a large sunny room with many windows. Sitting in a circle with teacups in hand, we were a group of seven women ranging in age from thirty to eighty. Each week we prepared to talk about a different topic or time period in our lives, guided by questions created by the two facilitators, who were also full participants in our conversations.

I arrived a little late at the Erikson Center one early spring day. The others had already gathered in the circle. The tape recorder picked up the overlapping voices and laughter of the group as we settled in. The topic of the week was adolescence. Some of us brought pictures and mementos to share. Nora pushed back a few gray wisps of hair, sat up straighter, and began:

> The worst moment of my adolescence was, I was probably twelve, and you see I was a tomboy. It was a matter of great pride that I could do anything my older brother could do, and my friends were tomboys too. After school, um, this was in the twenties, after school, we would change out of our dresses into what would nowadays be called shorts, but they were our bloomers and middies, and we'd put on our sneakers. I was a year younger than my friends, because I'd skipped first grade. And just about this time, a new girl moved into our neighborhood. She was not like us, she was from Boston . . . and she was kind of glamorous. All the time I was becoming more and more jealous of Emily, she was growing closer and closer to my best friend Faith. . . . We would be going to this tea-dance, that was the plan. I would, of course, come home and climb trees and ride my bike, going about what I'd always done with great determination, but Faith wasn't interested in doing these things any longer. She was too busy making plans with Emily for the tea dance. And one day everything just rolled up inside me in this great tremendous surge of anger, and I turned to Faith and I pounded her on the chest just as hard as I could. And then I ran home, crying. To have hurt my friend. She was totally bewildered by my attack. It was terrible. Somehow my mother seemed to know and to understand, I didn't expect that from her, but she didn't think it was so terrible, what I'd done. But everything just stopped. My whole world stopped. It was the end of everything. We didn't play after school. It was the end of an era.

Listening to the tape of this conversation, I hear, as Nora moves into the memory of herself at twelve, her voice shift and become more vibrant and full. Her voice drops down and catches the edge of her rage as she says, "And one day everything just rolled up inside me in this great tremendous surge of anger, and I turned to Faith and I pounded her on the chest just as hard as I could." There is no one present working with Nora to help her come onto her voice — this spontaneously happens as she enters the memory of herself at twelve. As she continues to speak, her voice becomes "transparent — revealing inner impulses of emotion and thought directly"; in other words, she comes onto Linklater's "natural voice" (p. 2).

When Nora continues and says, "But everything just stopped. My whole world stopped. It was the end of everything. We didn't play after school. It was the end of an era," her voice changes again. I hear her bewilderment and her sadness, also familiar to me, and to all of us in the room as we sit in rapt silence. I hear within her bewilderment the confusion of the girls I have listened to: "I don't know . . ." What can be known? What is understood? Nora says her mother knew and understood, "Somehow my mother seemed to know and to understand," yet this was not enough, because "everything just stopped." As I hear Nora's voice change, carrying every nuance of feeling so that we, her listeners, enter her story moment by moment with her, I hear the ordinary courage of the girls I have known. This quality of courage, "the capacity to speak one's mind by telling all one's heart," comes into her body and into her voice at eighty as she lives within the memory of herself at twelve.

What is the relational context in which this happened? The context is intergenerational, and it is with women that Nora chooses to tell this story. I have known Nora and been with her in a community setting for nine months — making music, doing artwork, cooking, talking, eating, and planning the program of our activities together.[9] I was drawn to Nora initially when I discovered that she was an impossible tease, playful and quick. That playful and courageous girl clearly lived just below the surface and could be quite easily called out to play with me.

As we continued to talk about our adolescence in the group that day, the familiar pattern emerged: each of us entered a time of loss during adolescence, loss of voice and of self, and each of us in different ways struggled hard to hold onto ourselves and harder still to remember and live within our resistance and our courage as women. In our thirties and forties and sixties and eighties, this was clearly an ongoing, life-long struggle.

Nora and the conversation about her story stay with me. What is the practice of relationships that might sustain girls' courage and help women to recover those memories of themselves as courageous girls? Could a practice of courage come into schools, where women and girls might join together most readily? And with what implications for girls' development and education, for women's knowledge, creativity, and power?

Looking Back — Toward a Practice of Courage

You're beside me at the window,
Shivering sympathetically. Together
we go over the details. Each telling begins
my education again. I want to know
nothing less than I know . . .
(Mazur, 1986, p. 16)

The "we" of this poem becomes you and I — you, the reader of this article, I, its author — looking back through the window of the text toward a practice of courage among girls and women. Together we go over the details.

When courage is linked to one of its oldest meanings in the English language, "to speak one's mind by telling all one's heart," the embodied or ordinary courage of eight- to twelve-year-old girls becomes readily visible and audible. Yet the courage of girls has been rendered all but nonexistent over the centuries as the word came to signify the bravery and heroic valor of men, so that neither men nor women were likely to discern the courage of girls. This cultural loss is reflected by a developmental loss of ordinary courage that occurs in many girls' lives in early adolescence.

At this time in their development, some girls begin to forget the ordinary courage they experienced in relationships as children. In early adolescence, these girls invent a "cover story" and a "cover girl" to go with their stories — the girl who has no bad thoughts or feelings, but who is always nice and kind (see Brown, 1989; Brown & Gilligan, 1992). At this time in their lives, these girls speak about feeling abandoned or betrayed by women and stop saying what they really think and feel. Girls who give up authentic relationships try to sustain an anemic shadow of these relationships in the service of becoming good women: women who are "sensitive," "caring," women who would never "hurt anyone." They enter conventions of feminine goodness by cutting off the breath in their bodies, effectively disguising their feelings when they speak. These girls also silence themselves, deliberately choosing not to speak about what they know. This self-silencing, used at first as a political strategy of self-protection, slips over into a psychological resistance — the disconnection of one's own experience from consciousness (Gilligan, 1990a; Rogers et al., 1993). Then the silence or amnesia of the unconscious erases the memory of the struggle for voice and conscious knowledge. Although these girls convincingly appear to be doing quite well in schools — they report getting good grades, becoming less impulsive and more mature, and acquiring more "self-confidence" — they also report "losing weight," feeling "depressed" or "numb" or "out of touch." Moreover, at times they seem unable to know and name their feelings and thoughts clearly (see Brown & Gilligan, 1992; Rogers et al., 1993).

Girls who show this pattern are not simply victims of a society and a school system that undermine their belief in the reality of their own experience. These girls actively struggle to protect themselves. When they no longer feel welcomed as themselves in their relationships — with all their love, anger, and authenticity intact — then, in order to preserve some vital connection with themselves, the girls make a move to prevent a kind of self-murder. The "true I," the self who spoke a full range of feelings in detailed transparency, begins to see and hear double — to watch and listen to herself in her own terms, while at the same time comparing this knowledge of herself with what is named "reality" in her family and school. This fragmentation and muffling of voice means a loss of embodied feelings, the loss of a sense that courage can be quite ordinary. Yet the strategies that many girls growing into women adopt to live in androcentric culture are deeply self-preservative, for the deliberate move into hiding actually protects against the death of the "true I." The "true I" becomes an elusive, ephemeral, imprisoned self. Held away from public scrutiny, this hidden self speaks to the self who acts in the world. "But when the self speaks to the self, who is speaking?" Virginia Woolf asks. "The entombed soul, the spirit driven in, in, to the central catacomb; the self that took the veil and left the world — a coward perhaps, yet, somehow beautiful, as it flits with its lanterns restlessly up and down the dark corridors" (Woolf, 1921/1944, p. 19). From the "dark corridors" of women's diaries, dreams, and half-finished thoughts, the "true I" may potentially be recovered.

How is it possible, then, for adolescent girls and women who show this pattern of loss to recover voice and courage, to live whole, and to speak again in the world? This is a difficult process. The adolescent girls seemed to forget the memory of themselves as courageous and create another story, recalling themselves at ages from nine to twelve as "rude" or "inappropriate," "bad" or "disturbed." These are the very words some teachers and therapists also use to describe girls who stand outside the culture's conventions of the "good girl." But the process of recovering voice and courage involves remembering another story, recalling a girl-self who was in the oldest sense of the word courageous — able to "speak her mind by telling all her heart."

Beyond the bounds of childhood, many girls and women are also understandably reluctant to bring themselves authentically into their relationships. Their courage seems suddenly treacherous, transgressive, dangerous. But the "true I" lives on in an underground world, waiting and hoping for a sign that she may emerge, whole, and open herself again. This wish is nothing short of terrifying, for it reawakens the fear of another abandonment, another shattering loss. Girls, astute observers of their mothers and teachers, seem to know when women can and cannot face squarely into a struggle with them. Unfortunately, women's reluctance to experience another loss becomes a powerful psychological defense. When women cannot enter deeply into girls' struggles for a real relationship, women are effectively saying to girls, "No, I'll not risk being truthful with you; I will distance myself from you because I can't stay close to you any longer." Thus the defense — the story of inevitable loss and betrayal designed to protect from repeated losses — repeats itself generation after generation, handed down unconsciously from women to girls, from mothers to daughters.

But as difficult as it may be, I think that women can recover their courage with one another and find ways to preserve the courage of girls in the next generation. In my personal experience, this work has involved uncovering memories of myself in late childhood in relationships with older women and with girls. I have also seen women like Nora in the Intergenerational Women's Oral History Group recover voice and courage as they remember themselves at the edge of adolescence. Emily Hancock (1989) also found that women speaking to her about their lives spontaneously re-called themselves as young girls, and repeatedly uncovered memories of themselves as children. Through their "rediscovery of the true self" (p. 1), women found the touch-stone of their adult identity, "the girl within." I have also seen teachers in another act-ing workshop designed specifically for teachers discover the power of their voices and come into vivid memories of themselves as girls.[10]

But what of the girls who are living in the world now as they are coming of age and facing a real crisis of courage? In my collaborative preventive and clinical work with girls, the hope of sustaining girls' courage is present moment by moment in the strug-gle for real relationship. This is what I call a practice of courage. This practice involves the art of being playful and outspoken, and of being a vulnerable and staunch fighter — someone who transgresses the conventions of feminine goodness. To engage in this practice would upset the structures of formal education that preserve the status quo of our society. If girls and women were to say in school what they know to be true, the inequities and the neglect of girls in our educational system would become much clearer, and also more poignant and disturbing.

Discovering this practice of courage is not a matter of good intentions. Instead, it seems to require a skilled listening, a way of listening now supported by empirical studies of girls' experiences. When I speak and listen to girls I am always seeking to get under the surface of what is being said — listening for the "true I," the voice of the girl who knows and describes her experience through a full range of feelings, who can tell the story of her life and her relationships in detailed transparency. This listening is difficult because a girl's voice may suddenly shift into indirect, coded speech that is hard to follow, or may get quickly covered over by conventions she wants to believe and may want me to believe too. When I ask a hard question or miss a critical point, she falls into an awkward silence. Sometimes she does not wish to reveal herself to me at all. To listen for courage then means to listen between sudden shifts in voice and si-lence, and to track my own feelings and responses in the moment-by-moment rela-tionship. I find this activity, which is central to my research, teaching, and clinical work, frightening and exhilarating. To invite a girl to reveal herself in my presence, I have found it necessary to make an opening for her courage through mine, revealing myself as someone who struggles as she struggles, breaking conventions of standard teaching, research, and clinical practice to do so (see also Rogers, 1991a).

To learn this practice of courage with girls and women we need time and space to breathe freely, to be vulnerable, to speak honestly with one another. This means having time in the structure of our work as teachers or as psychologists to engage in this kind of relationship. It also means breaking traditional and time-honored conventions of feminine goodness to create a new order or logic of relationships between women and girls.

Engaging the artistic imagination and providing intergenerational interaction between girls and women are two ways to reveal what girls and women know from their own experience. The three stories presented, which emerged respectively from the contexts of the Theater, Writing, and Outing Club, the Acting Workshop, and the Intergenerational Women's Oral History Group attest to this possibility.

Central to my learning a practice of courage has been the continued presence of girls in my life and my deepening friendships and collaboration with women. These relationships have been a catalyst for remembering myself as a girl. As I began to sift though these memories in relation to my clinical work and teaching and writing, I created a girl-woman, an amalgam of myself and the girls I have known. She is twelve years old, no longer entirely a child, not yet a woman. Finding strength in her presence, I look toward a practice of courage I hope will be useful to teachers and therapists, women and men, and to girls themselves.

TWELVE

She perches on a flat rock in the rain
dances about on curled tongues of seaweed, barefoot,
careful of barnacles. She leaps down into warm waves, scoops
water, splashes, scoops and sprays warm salt water over
the rock to see if tiny white slits will open,
will tiny white mouths feed from her splashing hands?

She curls up in an old blue bathrobe, in a big wing
chair, balancing chocolate, diary, her tilting tea and doll.
Who would ever discern her courage, watching her?

Snow is falling. It's started. Each flake moves
upward in the night whispering about indirect questions
her mother's averted eyes. In her unblinking need to know
her heart can hear wicks sputtering golden words
the silver tongues of snow on every ledge.
No one will ever be able to translate this inscrutable
new language, the letters and characters
of an ingenious layered grammar
a whole and private music of her own tuned inside to
the air outside turns
the scrub oaks turn the cranberries turn red.
She bleeds but who will ever see this?
The time is coming
when she will turn tilting the world away
from diary and dolls poems and paintings.

But now she is still at home
still rock-leaping
she is of a whole
at the kitchen door listening out into love.

It is eight o'clock. It is still twilight and shore slapping
sounds travel about darkness innocent of grammar.

She comes back to me now with the story of how she forgot
her fossils and snake, left her mother without a kiss —
already she was homesick
when she climbed on the bus for summer camp, leaving
her mother's timeless scent and recent lap;
already she was homesick for all the lost collections.
The way I welcome her back she is in pieces
she etches images carefully if only it will stop somewhere
then crosshatches them out eye and ear and hand
cannot join the pieces now missing
depth will she slip off will she see the edge?

I am going back for her the way I remember her
standing on a rock in the rain, her head tilted back
rain pouring into her wide open mouth,
running down her upturned face.[11]

Notes

1. The Intergenerational Program at the Erikson Center, directed by Dorothy Austin, is a program for vital elders, adults, teenagers, and children. It was designed and is run by resident artists, elders, and Center staff. I am a resident artist and have directed an ethnographic study of the project.
2. The group I am observing here are sixth graders at the Atrium School, who are members of the Theater, Writing, and Outing Club for Girls, a program designed to strengthen and preserve girls' voices during a developmental period when their voices are clearest. The names presented in this text are all pseudonyms, with the exception of the names of the researchers.
3. One of the girls was a member of the Tobin School Theater, Writing, and Outing Club group, and the other girl I saw in private practice.
4. Judith Jordan has also written about courage, emphasizing "courage in connection" within the context of a relational practice of psychotherapy. See her paper, "Courage in Connection: Conflict, Compassion, Creativity" (1990).
5. These girls were part of the Strengthening Healthy Resistance and Courage in Girls longitudinal study, but were not members of the Theater, Writing, and Outing Club.
6. Tina Packer, the director of the company, invited me to attend.
7. Kristin Linklater is the director of training of this acting workshop. She is the author of *Freeing the Natural Voice* (1976), a widely used voice method, and has trained actors at theater companies and universities throughout the world.
8. .Linklater's voice and text work here is designed to bring an actor's feelings and life experiences to bear directly on his or her performance. The method of asking a rapid succession of questions in rhythm with the actor's breathing is called "Dropping-In," a way to get a text "into the body" pioneered by Packer, Linklater, and a core group of master teachers at Shakespeare & Company.
9. Nora is a member of the staff. I am a resident artist and have directed an ethnographic study of the project.
10. This workshop, funded by the National Endowment for the Humanities, brought teachers together for voice and acting training, so that they might be more effective teachers of Shakespeare. Beatrice Nelson, the project director, and Kristin Linklater asked me to attend and write an ethnography of this workshop.

11. This poem has also been published separately in a special issue of *Women's Studies Quarterly* (Rogers, 1991b), entitled "Women, Girls, and the Culture of Education."

References

Bachelard, G. (1969). *The poetics of space*. Boston: Beacon Press. (Original work published 1958)

Baugh, C. (1963). *Chaucer's major poetry*. Engelwood Cliffs, NJ: Prentice-Hall.

Bernardez, T. (1965). The feminine role: Case report. *Bulletin of the Menninger Clinic, 29*, 204.

Block, J. (1990, October). Ego resilience through time: Antecedents and ramifications. In *Resilience and psychological health*. Symposium of the Boston Psychoanalytic Society, Boston, MA.

Brown, L. (1989). *Narratives of relationship: The development of a care voice in girls ages 7 to 16* (Monograph No. 8). Cambridge, MA: Harvard Project on Women's Psychology and Girls' Development.

Brown, L. (1991a). A problem of vision: The development of relational voice in girls ages 7 to 16. *Women's Studies Quarterly, 19*(1/2), 52–71.

Brown, L. (1991b). Telling a girl's life: Self-authorization as a form of resistance. *Women and Therapy, 11*(3/4), 71–86.

Brown, L., Argyris, D., Attanucci, J., Bardige, B., Gilligan, C., Johnston, K., Miller, B., Osborne, D., Tappan, M., Ward, J., Wiggins, G., & Wilcox, D. (1988). *A guide to reading narratives of conflict and choice for self and relational voices* (Monograph No. 1). Cambridge, MA: Harvard Graduate School of Education, Center for Study of Gender, Education, and Human Development.

Brown, L., & Gilligan, C. (1990, August). Listening for self and relational voices: A responsive/resisting reader's guide. In M. Franklin (Chair), *Literary theory as a guide to psychological analysis*. Symposium conducted at the annual meeting of the American Psychological Association, Boston.

Brown, L., & Gilligan, C. (1992). *Meeting at the crossroads: Women's psychology and girls' development*. Cambridge, MA: Harvard University Press.

Brown, L., & Gilligan, C. (1993). Meeting at the crossroads: Women's psychology and girls' development. *Feminism and Psychology, 3*(1), 11–35.

Burks, B., Jensen, D., Terman, L., Leahy, A., Marshall, H., & Oden, M. (1930). *Genetic studies of genius: Vol. III. The promise of youth: Follow-up studies of a thousand gifted children*. Stanford, CA: Stanford University Press.

Collins, P. H. (1989). The social construction of black feminist thought. *Signs, 14*, 745–773.

Cook, J., & Fonow, M. (1990). Knowledge and women's interests: Issues of epistemology and methodology in feminist sociological research. In J. Nielsen (Ed.), *Feminist research methods: Exemplary readings in the social sciences* (pp. 69–93). Boulder, CO: Westview Press.

Debold, E. (1990, November). *The flesh becomes word*. Paper presented at the Conference on Diversity in Ways of Knowing, Association for Women in Psychology, Western Massachusetts and Vermont Region, Brattleboro, VT.

Ebata, A. (1987). *A longitudinal study of distress during early adolescence*. Unpublished doctoral dissertation, Pennsylvania State University.

Elder, G., Nguyen, T., & Caspi, A. (1985). Linking family hardship to children's lives. *Child Development, 56*, 361–375.

Gilligan, C. (1990a). Joining the resistance: Psychology, politics, girls and women. *Michigan Quarterly Review, 29*, 501–536.

Gilligan, C. (1990b). Teaching Shakespeare's sister: Notes from the underground of female adolescence. In C. Gilligan, N. Lyons, & T. Hanmer (Eds.), *Making connections: The relational worlds of adolescent girls at Emma Willard School* (pp. 6–29). Cambridge, MA: Harvard University Press.

Greenberg-Lake Analysis Group. (1991). *Shortchanging girls, shortchanging America: A nationwide poll to assess self esteem, educational experiences, interest in math and science, and career aspirations of girls and boys ages 9–15*. Washington, DC: American Association of University Women.

Hadas, P. (1987). Because it hath no bottom: Self, narrative and the power to die. In P. Young-Eisendrath & J. Hall (Eds.), *The book of the self: Person, pretext and process* (pp. 186–221). New York: New York University Press.

Hancock, E. (1989). *The girl within: A groundbreaking new approach to female identity*. New York: Fawcett Columbia.

Harding, S. (Ed.). (1987). *Feminism and methodology: Social science issues*. Bloomington: Indiana University Press.

Hoffman, L. (1975). Fear of success in males and females: 1965 and 1971. In M. Mednick, S. Tangri, & L. Hoffman (Eds.), *Women and achievement: Social and motivational analyses* (pp. 221–230). Washington, DC: Hemisphere.

Jordan, J. (1990). *Courage in connection: Conflict, compassion, creativity* (Work in Progress, No. 45). Wellesley, MA: Stone Center Working Papers Series.

Krieger, S. (1991). *Social science and the self: Personal essays on an art form*. New Brunswick, NJ: Rutgers University Press.

Ladner, J. (1987). Introduction to tomorrow's tomorrow: The black woman. In S. Harding (Ed.), *Feminism and methodology* (pp. 74–83). Bloomington: Indiana University Press.

Langer, S. (1942). *Philosophy in a new key*. Cambridge, MA: Harvard University Press.

Linklater, K. (1976). *Freeing the natural voice*. New York: Drama Book.

Lueptow, L. (1980). Gender wording, sex, and response to items on achievement value. *Psychological Reports, 45*(1), 140–142.

Mazur, G. (1986). *The pose of happiness*. Boston: Godine.

Nielsen, J. (Ed.). (1990). *Feminist research methods: Exemplary readings in the social sciences*. Boulder, CO: Westview Press.

Petersen, A. (1988). Adolescent development. *Annual Review of Psychology, 39,* 583–607.

Petersen, A., & Ebata, A. (1987). Developmental transitions and adolescent problem behavior: Implications for prevention and intervention. In K. Hurrelmann, F. Kaufmann, & F. Losel (Eds.), *Social intervention: Potential and constraints* (pp. 167–184). Berlin: Walter de Gruyter.

Ponsot, M. (1988). *In the green dark*. New York: Alfred Knopf.

Reese, L., Wilkinson, J., & Koppelman, P. (1983). *I'm on my way running: Women speak on coming of age*. New York: Avon Books.

Rich, A. (1981). *A wild patience has taken me this far*. New York: Norton.

Rogers, A. (1990). *From the porch*. Unpublished poem.

Rogers, A. (1991a). A feminist poetics of psychotherapy. *Women and Therapy, 11*(3/4), 33–53.

Rogers, A. (1991b). Twelve. *Women's Studies Quarterly, 19*(1/2), 29–30.

Rogers, A. (1992). Marguerite Sechehaye and Renee: A feminist reading of two accounts of a treatment. *Qualitative Studies in Education, 5,* 245–251.

Rogers, A., Brown, L., & Tappan, M. (1993). Interpreting ego development in girls: Regression or resistance? *Narrative Study of Lives, 2,* 1–36.

Rogers, A., Fradin, D., Magee, V., & Sjostrom, L. (1992). *The Erikson Center: An ethnography of an intergenerational arts program*. Unpublished manuscript, Harvard Graduate School of Education.

Rogers, A., & Gilligan, C. (1989). *Translating girls' voices: Two languages of development* Unpublished manuscript, Harvard University, Project on Women's Psychology and Girls' Development.

Rutter, M. (1986). The developmental psychopathy of depression: Issues and perspectives. *Depression in young people: Developmental and clinical perspectives* (pp. 3–30). New York: Guilford.

Simpson, J., & Weiner, E. (1989). *The Oxford English dictionary* (2nd ed., vol. III). Oxford, Eng.: Clarendon Press.

Webber, J. L., & Grumman, J. (1978). *Woman as writer.* Boston: Houghton Mifflin.

Wellesley College Center for Research on Women. (1992). *The AAUW report: How schools shortchange girls.* Washington, DC: American Association of University Women and National Education Association.

Woolf, V. (1944). *A haunted house and other stories.* New York: Harcourt, Brace & World. (Original work published 1921)

Woolf, V. (1966). *Three guineas.* San Diego: Harcourt Brace Jovanovich. (Original work published 1938)

The research I draw upon in this article has been supported by Joan Lipsitz and the Lilly Endowment; by Lawrence Cremin, Marion Faldet, and Linda Fitzgerald and the Spencer Foundation; by Benjamin Barber and the Walt Whitman Center for Democracy; and by the American Association of University Women. I am grateful to Ginny Kahn, Dan Vorenberg, and Ted Mermin at the Atrium School, and to the Tobin School girls and their parents. My research and writing also draw from a feminist research collaborative, the Harvard Project on Women's Psychology and Girls' Development at the Harvard Graduate School of Education. The students who worked most closely with me — Kathleen Curtis, Kathryn Geismar, Amy Grillo, Heather Thompson, Sarah Ingersoll, and Kate O'Neill — listened and supported my interest in courage. Thank you to Kate O'Neill and to Sarah Hanson for help in editing and proofreading this article. I also want to acknowledge and thank Kathryn Geismar, Carla Rensenbrink, Sally Middlebrooks, and Gladys Capella Noya for working with me on behalf of the *Harvard Educational Review* Board. I have been inspired by the ongoing work of Lyn Mikel Brown and Carol Gilligan. A particular thanks to Carol Gilligan and Normi Noel, the women directly involved in the Theater, Writing, and Outing Club for Girls, and to the girls themselves.

Teacher-Researcher Collaboration
from Two Perspectives

POLLY ULICHNY
WENDY SCHOENER

This article tells the story of qualitative research that evolved into a collaborative project between the two of us: Wendy, a teacher, and Polly, a researcher. Collaboration for us came to mean determining mutual goals for the research, sharing responsibility for the research product, and building a trusting relationship that permitted interdependence and mutuality between teacher and researcher.

This story is told from both of our perspectives. Polly details the process of establishing rapport in qualitative research and describes the elements of discourse and relationship that contributed to an evolving collaboration between the researcher and the teacher. She frames her understanding of conducting collaborative qualitative inquiry within a feminist methodology. Wendy describes her journey through the project, from the misgivings and fears that surrounded her initial participation in the "researcher's project" to her insights and professional development as an English-as-a-Second-Language (ESL) instructor and teacher-researcher.

Collaborative Research and the Role of Rapport

Traditional qualitative research acknowledges the centrality of rapport between researcher and informant. Most references to establishing rapport discuss the need to establish trust in the field with informants, and at the same time to remain detached and "neutral" in order to avoid biasing the data collected. The title of Agar's text on ethnographic methods, *The Professional Stranger* (1980), captures the role that many mainstream qualitative researchers advocate for students of ethnography or in-depth interviewing methodologies. Glesne and Peshkin (1992, p. 98) illustrate the advice most textbooks and manuals give to novices in qualitative research methods:

> When a distinction between rapport and friendship is made in qualitative literature, the overwhelming tendency is to warn against forming friendships because of the hazards of sample bias and loss of objectivity. These hazards are linked to over identification, also called "over-rapport" and "going native" (Gold, 1969; Miller, 1952; Shaffir, Stebbins, & Turowetz, 1980; Van Maanen, 1983).

Harvard Educational Review   Vol. 66   No. 3   Fall 1993, 496–524

Recently, however, feminists, critical ethnographers, and postmodern qualitative researchers have critiqued the traditional, detached stance of conducting participant observation precisely because it leads to objectifying and "othering" the informant of the research while hiding the identity of the much implicated researcher (Fine, 1994; Lather, 1991; Lincoln, 1995; Lykes, 1989; Oakley, 1981; Reason, 1994; Reinharz, 1984; Van Maanen, 1988).

A simple schematic delineates the possible research stances available to qualitative researchers along two continua — one of action and one of relationship:

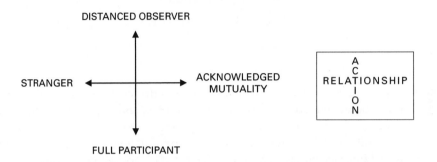

The action continuum ranges from distant observer — the researcher as a potted plant or fly on the wall observing social behaviors without any participation in the activity under way — to complete involvement — experience of and coparticipation in the events of the field. The relationship continuum offers the researcher a range of connections to informants in the field, from relative stranger to acknowledged mutuality as friends, confidants, facilitator-facilitated, or even informal therapist and client.[1]

The informants in qualitative research have similar continua along which they may situate themselves. The action dimension for them, however, refers to the research project and not to engagement in the field under study. As the informants become more engaged along either the action or relationship continuum, the research project is transformed into one of collaboration.

As with descriptions of possible researcher relations in the field, the literature on collaborative research offers an array of definitions for what is considered collaborative. These range from inviting informant input into the researcher's research questions or process, to requiring, in the case of some action research advocates, that the researcher investigate only what the host or informant community defines as the research focus (Oja & Smulyan, 1989; Reason, 1994; Reinharz, 1992; Stenhouse, 1975). As mentioned above, our definition of collaboration extends beyond the process of determining the focus of the research to creating a mutuality and interdependence between teacher and researcher in all phases of the research project. By mutuality we mean that the relationship that evolved between us was one of equal status based on mutual respect and concern. Since we each provided unique contributions to the project, interdependence meant that data collection, interpretation, and even communication of the results were activities we jointly participated in, albeit with differing contributions based on our roles, which we explain in detail below.

Relatively little has been written from the standpoint of the researched participant on the nature of relationship and involvement in the research process (see Florio and

Walsh, 1981, and Florio-Ruane and Dohanich, 1984, as exceptions). The more volu-minous literature that discusses the benefits and pitfalls of collaborative research comes, not surprisingly, from the researcher side of the interaction (Campbell, 1988; Gibson, 1985; Jacullo-Noto, 1984; Johnston, 1994; Reinharz, 1984; Wallace & Louden, 1994). Much of it discusses the difficulties of collaboration and the chal-lenge of producing research that benefits the teacher participants in the collaboration. Florio-Ruane (1991), for example, tells of the disappointing reaction that teacher col-laborators had to the researchers' final report of a lengthy joint investigation of writ-ing instruction:

> When we showed our teacher informants the technical report we had produced, . . . we were a bit nervous. We hoped at best to interest the teachers, at worst, not to of-fend them. . . . We were not at all prepared for their response. The teachers read our text carefully . . . [and] returned with little to say. Too polite to admit it, we later learned that they had found the report, not offensive, but frankly, dull and disap-pointing. They wondered that we had spent so much time with them and their stu-dents and noticed so little of what they thought important. . . . Additionally, our antiseptically third person accounts disappointed the teachers because they left out personal details of what we as researchers had learned or felt while sharing the class-room with them for a year. (p. 8)

Because of this disjuncture, some have claimed that the foundation of teacher-researcher collaboration is exploitation of teachers (Ladwig, 1991), and others have advocated that the academic researcher be replaced by teachers who investigate their own practice, thereby not only permitting the teacher's voice to be heard, but also to establish a new set of parameters defining teacher knowledge (Berthoff, 1987; Cochran-Smith & Lytle, 1990). We are sympathetic to both of these positions, but we take them as cautions rather than blueprints for conducting research on teaching. Researchers and teachers often see things from different perspectives, and it is true that the researcher's perspective has been the more credible in academic settings. But rather than eliminating the researcher from the enterprise of creating knowledge about teaching, the model we present is one in which both teacher and researcher have a voice, because in our study, we have profited from a successful collaborative ef-fort that has provided knowledge that we both value. Neither of us on our own would have been able to produce the study that emerged through our collaboration.

Our presentation here describes the evolution of this collaborative research project in the voices of both the researched and the researcher. We describe the conditions that existed for each of us upon entering this study, and how they affected our respec-tive expectations of the research process and its outcomes. As the study evolved, so did our positions along the continua of action and relationship. How we managed the shifts, what they felt like for each of us, and how they determined the direction of the research itself are the subjects of this article. Our intention here is not to prescribe a particular method of collaborative research, even though the results of this project, both in substance and process, were valued by both of us. We found that the detached position of participant-observer in a qualitative single-subject case study is not desir-able, and may not even be feasible. To make our case, we present a two-part narrative in which we chronicle how recognizing and dealing with whole persons in the research endeavor affected both of us, as well as the results of the research. While a prescription for relationships in the field is neither possible nor desirable, researchers and informants cannot escape the fact that, whatever their nature, relationships do exist and therefore require the attention of both researchers and researched.

Polly: Purposes of the Study

From my researcher's point of view, this project had two sources. First, as an educator interested in teaching and learning among diverse populations, I wanted to investigate how a teacher manages to instruct students from diverse cultures and linguistic backgrounds, students who presumably construct academic knowledge differently. I wanted to look at a "successful" resolution of these differences, and therefore chose to study an adult ESL classroom.

My experience in K–12 public school settings with ESL students, as a staff development instructor, researcher, and coordinator of an ESL teacher certification program, informed me of widespread teaching and learning that was less than ideal. This was due to many factors, including marginalization of ESL populations within the schools, a general lack of relevant training and experience among teachers assigned to ESL classes, and a common practice of pullout ESL instruction. My experience with adult ESL classes, which students attended voluntarily, was quite the opposite. Teachers in these classrooms were specially trained, and the students, who were eager to learn, rarely experienced misunderstandings and cultural mismatches that interfered with their learning. This seemed quite different from numerous examinations of K–12 classrooms, where culture and language differences between students and teachers caused widespread school failure (Cummins, 1986; Delpit, 1988; Heath, 1983; Nieto, 1994; Ogbu & Matute-Bianchi, 1986; Philips, 1972).

I was also interested in discovering how a teacher manages to interpret and respond to diverse learners, particularly when, at best, very few of them share common assumptions or a common language. Although most qualified ESL teachers speak another language, it is inconceivable that one would speak all the languages of the students she teaches in multilingual ESL classes. Much has been written about how an ESL teacher *should* teach linguistically and culturally diverse students, but very little research has investigated exactly how a teacher goes about it: how she plans, implements, and accommodates her instruction to meet the diverse and often extreme needs of her students (Ulichny, 1996). Thus, my reason for conducting this research was to examine closely an ESL teacher's practice by observing, audio-taping, and carrying out a discourse analysis of the classroom interaction.

Second, although I had embraced ethnography as a way of deepening my understanding of face-to-face interactions among linguistically diverse speakers, my initial experiences in the field were less than satisfactory. It seemed to me that understanding the context of the interactions and how they developed over time among the participants offered a deeper, and hence better, explanation of interactions than merely examining carefully transcribed linguistic data (Corsaro, 1981; Hymes, 1980; Watson-Gegeo & Ulichny, 1988). Nevertheless, one particular instance left me with serious questions about my role and responsibilities to informants of ethnographies.

Fieldwork Disaster

I had negotiated entry into a college-level ESL classroom through the teacher I wanted to investigate. I explained one of my purposes to her — to undertake a discourse analysis of the classroom interaction in order to explore how teaching and learning happens in an ESL environment — and she agreed to have me attend her classes weekly, talk informally to both her and the students as time permitted, and to tape-record interactions. I further explained to her that I had no preconceived notion of the categories I would be looking at. Rather, as an ethnographer, I was committed to letting the data drive my questions and the explanations for the interactions I observed. Within three weeks, however, I sensed a growing tension that eventually resulted in my leaving the class prematurely. Although the teacher never really asked me to leave, when the discomfort with my tape-recording caused her to suggest that I might be "stealing" her method, I offered to disband my study, and she readily agreed.

As I reflected on what the teacher's reasons might have been for wanting me to discontinue my observations and recordings of her classroom, I came to understand how naive my researcher's stance had been. My silent observations, private field notes, and analyses seemed to make this teacher extremely uncomfortable. It wasn't that I had criticized what I was seeing in her classroom; the very fact that I was there offered her a different vantage point from which to view her own practice. Furthermore, I left each lesson I attended with a record of the interaction and provided no accounting for it. Through my silent observations she viewed herself as she thought I must see her — conducting a less-than-perfect lesson and making mistakes. The more uncomfortable she became with her own practice, the more critical she was of her interactions with the class, and the more intolerable my silent scrutiny became.

Eventually, I abandoned my ethnography with the disconcerting feeling that I had somehow violated the principle that had drawn me to it in the first place — respect for the whole person within the context of practice. What right did I have as a researcher to interfere in her relationship with her students and her practice? None, I concluded. But I also concluded that remedying the situation in future studies would require some action, rather than the nonaction I had negotiated in this study.

In order to understand what action would be necessary to put at ease a research subject who was undergoing close scrutiny of her professional behavior, I considered aspects of the research situation that may have led to the disaster. I believe four features of the teacher-researcher relationship, enumerated below, serve to exacerbate teacher discomfort.

1. Invasive Design   My reflection on this situation led me to a number of insights about the design of participant-observer research. A qualitative single-subject case study of a professional practice can be a very invasive design. While the researcher is not manipulating the setting by imposing experiments or contrastive experiences, in-depth observations of one person's practice for the purpose of analysis intrudes on a most intimate component of the informant's identity — the relationship between personal and public identities in one's practice. In multisite studies or institution-wide investigations, the same degree of invasiveness may not be present. Observing many subjects engaged in similar behaviors focuses the researcher's attention on aspects of the social context and regularities of practices. Observing a single subject, however, shifts that attention to the way that a particular individual enacts her profession and why. I don't believe my initial negotiation into the teacher's classroom, which merely asked her to allow me to sit in and tape-record some lessons as a basis for a written report on an as yet unidentified question, prepared her for the feeling of intrusion into her secrets that she would experience.

2. Doubtful Benefits of the Research to the Informant   The potential benefits of the research to the practitioner are remote, because the ethnographer enters the field without a clear research question and with no prediction about the results of the study. Given the intimate view that the informant permits the researcher, shouldn't the subject expect something positive to emerge from the experience? For a practitioner, something positive usually means an enhancement of her own practice. Feeding back insights gained from the research is normally what the researcher expects to give back to the field. Current textbooks that introduce researchers to qualitative methods underscore the importance of payback, and suggest that researchers either give of their time (often difficult in the midst of a demanding academic life) or offer information gleaned from the study that would "improve" the field (Bogdan & Biklen, 1992; Ely et al., 1991). Ethicists and feminist social science researchers have gone further, suggesting that information about informants belongs to the informants as much as, if not more than, to the researcher (Deyhle, Hess, & LeCompte, 1992; Lather, 1991; LeCompte & Preissle, with Tesch, 1993; Lincoln, 1995). However, it is common knowledge among both researchers and teachers that the reports researchers produce rarely find their way into schools and classrooms (Cochran-Smith & Lytle, 1993). As Cochran-Smith and Lytle (1993) claim, "[researchers] fault teachers for not reading or not implementing the findings of [their] research even though teachers often view these findings as irrelevant and counterintuitive" (p. 10). The abstractions researchers struggle to produce seem removed from day-to-day experience and provide little direction for dealing with particular students and situations (Bickel & Hattrup, 1995).

On the other hand, practitioners who undergo the researcher's scrutiny are likely to be interested in the individualized feedback a participant-observer can provide, especially if the researcher presents herself as a nonjudgmental seeker of new knowledge. In the early stages of fieldwork, this request for feedback, whether explicit or implicit, can be difficult to manage. In my own experience, striving for neutral language to describe behaviors and censoring interpretation as much as possible in the data collection process made it difficult to say anything worthwhile to the practitioner about her work. The level at which I was operating — *what's going on here?* — would seem completely trivial to the practitioner, who is more interested in knowing *what does what's going on here mean for me and my students?* In reality, however, the participant observer is less likely to be able to answer that question during the initial stages of fieldwork than is the practitioner herself, a point to which I will return later.

3. Researcher as Critical Evaluator and the Issue of Trust   The third feature that can lead to teacher discomfort, a feature related to the previous two points, is the fact that the participant observer is obtrusive in the field. In spite of assurances and precautions to the contrary, the researcher alters the context of the situation by her very presence (see Labov, 1972, p. 209, for a discussion of this issue, which he has labeled the "observer's paradox"). Teachers are normally accustomed to being scrutinized by two types of observers — supervisors and apprentices. In both cases, but particularly in that of the supervisor, the object of the scrutiny is to judge the teacher's performance of professional duties. When teachers experience a researcher's intrusion into their profession and no feedback is forthcoming, they are likely to interpret the silence around issues of practice as implicit criticism. A reasonable inference from an observer's silence, then, is negative evaluation of practices.

This presumed critical stance of the researcher leads to the lack of trust that teachers often exhibit toward researchers. This distrust emerges, in my experience, from the distanced stance of the silent researcher-observer. Even though the process of conducting field research is intended to be nonjudgmental, the researcher needs to work to achieve this position, particularly in ethnographies of familiar settings and social institutions. Even though the researcher pushes beyond her initial judgments to achieve a deeper understanding of the informants in their contexts, the ultimate goal of educational research is to provide information that can promote better educational experiences for all. Thus, the educational researcher is likely to have an opinion about good and bad practices and is, furthermore, expected to discuss education in evaluative terms. It is doubtful, then, that the assurance of nonjudgmental research can be upheld.

Discussions of ethics and of the researcher's responsibilities to the field deal with this delicate contradiction by advocating anonymity in the reporting of research (Agar, 1980; Bogden & Biklen, 1992; Deyhle et al., 1992; Glesne & Peshkin, 1992; LeCompte et al., 1993; Stainback, 1988). This is intended to protect the informants from disapproving readers, as well as from identification by those who may influence their lives and livelihoods. Anonymity can protect them from the former, but it is unlikely to be totally successful in protecting them from the latter. It has been my experience that the informants of intensive qualitative research projects are far more concerned with what the researchers/experts think about them than with what anonymous readers of a scholarly journal will think. Anonymity as a protective device means little since it cannot be applied in the face-to-face encounters with the researcher.

A second source of informants' distrust — which was true in my particular case — comes from a history of research abuses in the university town in which the study was conducted. A particularly virile "town-gown" antagonism exists in educational settings that have been the targets of negative research reports. Less destructive, but nonetheless damaging to the teacher-researcher relationship, are the many examples of "rip-and-run" research, where both qualitative and quantitative researchers leave the field to publish their studies and are never heard from again by their hosts. Both the personal and professional contexts of conducting intensive observational research make for an uneasy alliance in the qualitative single-subject case study research design.

4. Power and Knowledge Differential   Finally, perhaps the most critical feature of the teacher-researcher relationship, and the feature underlying all that I have described so far, is the power/knowledge differential between researcher and teacher. Within the dyad, the researcher has more power while the teacher has more knowledge. This creates a contradiction in the research process that requires resolution.

The power of the researcher derives from the differential status that the wider academic community gives to the researcher's work — producing knowledge about teaching — versus the status accorded to the teacher. In the educational context, the researcher's version of a classroom or instructional practice is seen as more "objective" and convincing than the teacher's version. There is an assumption that the researcher, through rigorous methods, can see more, and more accurately, than the teacher. Moreover, with respect to the wider issues under investigation in the project, the researcher is believed to know more than the teacher. Power chits in the educational world are accumulated on the basis of the size of one's knowledge base within a formal, academic context. Thus, the researcher *appears* to the outside world as the more credible knower, which implies a knowledge of what should and shouldn't be done in the educational setting. Finally, through writings and public presentations, the researcher has access to a wider audience than the teacher. The written words of professionals in their scholarly formats establish generalized knowledge. It is difficult for informants of the particular to compete (Cochran-Smith & Lytle, 1990).

While the power and the knowledge appear to reside with the researcher vis-à-vis the broader educational community, it is, however, the teacher who has the most knowledge of the setting under investigation. The teacher knows what happens in her own classroom and why it happens more intimately than the researcher. The tension that results from intimately knowing one's own classroom, yet feeling that one's knowledge can legitimately be challenged by the researcher, creates a vulnerability that may shake a teacher's confidence in both teaching and knowing how to teach. This is, in essence, the wedge that inserts itself in the practitioner's concept of self as a professional. It separates professional practice from the professional and, hence, alienates the person from her work activity.

These aspects of the relationship between researcher and teacher evince the need to establish the teacher as the primary knower in the research project. As a result of that adjustment in the design and, therefore, in the relationships in the field, the power differential that exists between researcher and researched might also be diminished.

Wendy: To Engage or Not to Engage in the Research

I had been teaching ESL at the university level for just over a year when my office mate, Polly, asked me a favor. She was teaching graduate courses at the same school, and we knew each other, though not well, through the forced acquaintance of shared offices at the university. The favor had to do with the other part of her life — completing a research project on ESL teachers. My sincere impulse was to say no, thank you. A whole school semester? My blood pressure rose when supervisors came in to observe for a mere twenty minutes.

Nevertheless I said yes, though with misgivings. My primary motivation was, as I told her, to learn something about how to teach. I imagined that Polly would work as a supervisor in observing my teaching, with the object of making sure nothing was going too wrong and perhaps offering suggestions to improve my classroom work. My secondary motivation was to avoid disappointing the director of our center, who was always enthusiastic about teachers' involvement in research.

A researcher, for me, was simply and inevitably the stranger, the distant observer. Distance and nonaffiliation were required, I felt, to achieve the objectivity needed in research. I supposed that Polly's observations would give her the opportunity to discover problems that would be hurtful to hear about, and that she was honor-bound to reveal this hurtful news publicly, while preserving my anonymity.

I was concerned about how I could avoid feeling paralyzed in my practice if Polly gave me feedback that I was doing poorly. I was aware of the crisis of confidence in the teaching profession, that is, the public emphasis on "accountability," which suggested that teachers had somehow been less responsible than they should for student learning. I was also not very self-confident. I perceived that there were legitimate conflicting viewpoints on teaching ESL, and yet also believed that if I were a smarter person, I would have already learned the "right" answers to my teaching problems from existing research. I did not know Polly's orientation in this contentious area of education, but I did know that she was a researcher and that researchers had access to specialized knowledge frequently not available to practitioners. I decided I could resolve my predicament by preparing "extra hard" for the class she observed.

I did not express these views directly to Polly because I could not blame her for simply fulfilling her function as researcher, but I did verbalize them with peers, who agreed with me. I discussed the proposed project with one of the other teachers Polly hoped to observe, and this teacher's fearfulness about possible outcomes confirmed my own. We joked nervously about how Polly would inevitably compare us and then decide which one was better. If we were lucky, we reasoned, we would never find out her conclusions. Then, right before the new semester began, I learned that the two other teachers Polly had asked to participate in the project had said no and that my class would be the sole focus of her work. While this meant that I would not be compared with my colleagues, I imagined that the intensified focus on my teaching would yield its own dangers. Perhaps I would seem less talented under the close examination she would now have time to do.

There was nothing Polly could have said before we worked together to dispel my fears. She had been her usual approachable self through our initial negotiation for the project, the same friendly office mate that I had known for a semester. But her simple suggestion that we step into roles of observer and observed was enough to make me feel more wary. I imagined that the research situation could degenerate over the semester and leave me wishing I had never revealed myself. In the past, my anxiety about classroom observers had been visible enough to register with my students. What if I made my own students anxious by putting myself in a difficult position? Even without a watchful presence in my classroom, I regularly had moments of feeling that other teachers (and certainly researchers) would know intuitively how to do my work better than I did.

Over semester break, I prepared for the class Polly would observe, a noncredit ESL reading class recommended to students who were considered not yet ready for mainstream freshman courses. All the while I anticipated her reaction to my plans. Were the lessons too simplistic? Too demanding? I imagined both criticisms applying to the same lesson. I was working with a colleague to design a course based on individual chapters from college texts used on campus: a chapter on the family from a sociology text, one on language acquisition from a psychology text, another on developing world economies from an economics text, and one on Mendel's early genetic research from a biology text. We were doing this partially in reaction to the fact that the previous semester's course, based on social movements of the 1960s, had seemed to interest the students a good deal less than it had interested us. We were hopeful that changing topics and offering readings from a variety of sources would at least interest some of the students some of the time. Still, I would be trying an entirely new and different course in front of someone whose sympathy was hardly guaranteed, in my eyes, by virtue of her role.

Polly: Adjustments to the Method

At the end of my negative field experience, I decided to establish a research stance that would not be distant from and seemingly critical of a teacher's practice. After several months, I reinitiated negotiations with three ESL teachers at my university, thinking that observing three teachers instead of one might make them feel less threatened, as I would spend less time in each individual's classroom. I explained my intent — to study classroom interaction — and told them I wanted to minimize the discomfort that my presence might cause by speaking openly with each of them during the course of the study. Two of the three felt uncomfortable about having a researcher in their classrooms because both were trying out a new syllabus and were unsure about the results. They did not want to be observed as they worked through potential problems. Only one of the teachers, Wendy, agreed to have me study her class, and yet, as I discovered later, she was less than enthusiastic about my presence. What she indicated at the time, however, was that she was enthusiastic about participating in the study because she "thought she would learn something from it to improve her teaching." This added to my fears: I was already concerned about building trust; now I had to be concerned about what benefit the research might have for Wendy.

Wendy and I shared an office at the same university because we had schedules that rarely coincided. We also taught in different programs and had minimal knowledge of each other's work. Thus, although we shared our work space, we had not established much of a relationship prior to my entering the field of her classroom. The shared office might be an advantage, I reasoned, since we would have some opportunity to discuss the research and the classroom informally if we chose to. On the other hand, having to deal with each other in and out of the classroom might make us even more self-conscious. It was clear she expected me to give her feedback about her teaching. Would I have anything significant to tell her? And, more importantly, how would I handle situations in which my understandings of her practice were not positive? A researcher who has the luxury of observing interactions without the pressure of decisionmaking can see things that might be uncomfortable to report back to the teacher. This is particularly true when the researcher slows down the transcription process. Her privileged position allows her to listen carefully and reflect on what is happening at any given moment. For example, I might understand a student's question or contribution differently, not right or wrong, from the teacher, and see how the teacher may have misread or inadvertently silenced a student who was attempting to participate. While it might be useful for a teacher to be aware of such situations, a researcher-observer could easily jeopardize her relationship in the field if she communicated this information without sufficient regard for the teacher's self-esteem.

Erickson (1986) has illustrated this difficult situation in the form of a two-by-two matrix. Researchers can communicate news to their informants that is either known or unknown, good or bad. The good news is easy to hear, especially when it is unknown to the subject. It is the kind of information that overcomes the lack of trust an informant can experience. Known bad news is somewhat easy to hear and, with careful attention to the teacher's vulnerable position, can be shared in a way that does not undermine the fragile trust between researcher and informant. The greatest problem occurs in communicating bad news — what the researcher's privileged position reveals that has escaped the practitioner's awareness. At the beginning of this research endeavor, I had no experience and little confidence in being able to deal with that area.

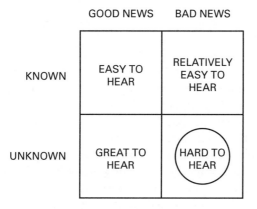

Just before I entered the field, but after I had negotiated entry into Wendy's classroom, I reached a solution, after consulting with Morimoto (personal communication, 1988), to my dual dilemma of dealing with feedback and establishing Wendy as the primary knower of the classroom meanings. I decided to let the seeing come from her, that I would access her knowledge and simultaneously reduce my power by taking a back seat in the interpretation of what transpired in the classroom. By doing so, I hoped the research would also be more likely to produce benefits that Wendy desired. This did not mean that I was eliminating the possibility of sharing bad news with Wendy, but rather that its introduction would come from her rather than from me. In the words of Morimoto (personal communication, also stated in Morimoto, Gregory, & Butler, 1973), researchers can most benefit a teacher when they lend an ear, not a remedy. What teachers need is the time and space to reflect on their practice so they can come up with their own solutions to problems.

Borrowing a method developed by Erickson and Shultz (1982), I decided to tape-record the classroom interactions I observed and subsequently interview Wendy about them, using the tapes as a stimulus for her recall. Contrary to recommendations for doing qualitative research, I would put off taking detailed field notes and carrying out an ongoing analysis of the classroom data, preferring to follow Wendy's lead. With my major difficulty resolved in this adjustment to the design, I was left with only one last hurdle: convincing Wendy to spend even *more* time on what was essentially *my* research project. I presented the idea, which I framed by relating my uneasiness with conducting single-subject observational research. It was my intention to impose my views on the research as little as possible, which was a very naive plan. I had justified my removal on the action continuum, but I had not anticipated the effects of this design on the relationship continuum.

When I asked Wendy to meet with me weekly to discuss the tapes, she expressed her reluctance. Too many of her waking hours were already dedicated to her profession and she felt that she needed to protect her minimal free time. I offered to meet her at her convenience in a non-work setting, and persuaded her to try it on a biweekly basis. If at any point she thought it was too time-consuming or not useful, she could call an end to the interviews.

Wendy: Reactions to the Adjustment

Before the semester started, Polly proposed that we meet weekly to discuss the class, in language that should have reassured me. She told me in several ways that she wanted to understand the classroom interaction from my point of view and that she had something to learn from me. But my general feelings about research were fatalistic enough then that I did not see the value of such work; it simply represented another risk. My first response to this request was that I didn't have the time for such interviews, which was true. I was the only full-time teacher on campus who had sixteen teaching hours per week. I made assignments at a rate that left me with stacks of papers to grade each week. But my greater fear, without doubt, was of the additional anxiety such meetings would cause. I told Polly I didn't have time to be so involved, rather than admitting to patent cowardice, but we negotiated. In the end, I agreed to less frequent meetings and the option to discontinue altogether if I wished. The problem of demands on my time had been addressed; the problem of risk had not been because I had not raised it.

Polly: Doing the Research

Wendy and I began the project wary of each other's reaction to our individual practices. I was concerned that I would make her feel uncomfortable or, worse, invalidated. Nonetheless, we began meeting every other week for several hours to listen to and comment on the audio tapes of the class. I tape-recorded each of these sessions, which included pieces of classroom interaction, and transcribed them. The following comments on the nature of the talk and its development are based on these data.

In the first interview we mainly listened to the tape and had short discussions of what Wendy found interesting. She framed most of what she chose to discuss in terms of crisis management in the classroom. She pointed out weaknesses in the way things were going and talked about how she might improve them. Attached to that were longer, free-flowing segments in which Wendy discussed why addressing the weaknesses was difficult, if not impossible. She seemed to me to be critical of her teaching. Her initial remarks after stopping the tape were prefaced with a version of "I could have done that better." In fact, in the first interview session, she did not stop the tape even once to comment on something positive. In addition to being critical, however, her talk demonstrated that she thought deeply about how to teach her classes. Her negative judgment made me wonder if it was a reaction to what she thought I must be thinking. If she pointed to the flaws, I would not have to. But her voluminous comments on the context of the classroom, student backgrounds, and reflections on practice encouraged me to think that the interviews might, in fact, be useful for her to consolidate her thinking. In a Vygotskyan sense, she was problematizing her practice, making it richer and truly complex through the talk. Reifying her practice at this reflective level seemed to hold her interest. I was not aware of struggling to keep the talk going, and we were both surprised when two hours had slipped by without our noticing the time.

The following example from that first interview demonstrates Wendy's tendency toward negative self-appraisal, as well as her deference to my more power-imbued understandings:[2]

(Wendy turns off the tape to comment.)

Wendy: Oh . . . uhm . . . a couple of things. Ugh! Do I really sound like that? My voice sounds ten octaves higher than what I think.

Polly: Tapes tend to do that, but I think that it sounds higher because you [normally] hear [your voice] in the cavity of your own head.

Wendy: I don't want . . . I'm so aware of not wanting to sound like a nursery school teacher (uh hm) with them. So it strikes me to hear my voice so high. I had a couple of other . . . I don't know actually. I'm almost more interested in hearing what you think about a couple of things. I wonder about sometimes simplifying things so much that I might not say precisely what I want to say.

Polly: Like what?

Since I was particularly sensitive to her negative feelings about her practice during the first listening session, I tried to curb them. I sometimes offered an explanation that was less negative than her own, as in the case of her voice in the example above, or rephrased her concerns in the form of dilemmas she was facing. This seemed to me to take the focus off of conducting a lesson badly and put it on the pressures that she felt caused her to respond in practice in a less than desirable way. By directing the talk to dilemmas and probing them with Wendy, I was not the passive listener I had intended to be. I introduced topics of discussion by naming dilemmas that previously had not been part of Wendy's meaning-making of her teaching practice. What was intended to be a mitigating contribution on my part turned out to be a significant role in introducing the essential themes of the analysis:

(Wendy has just commented negatively on her tendency to oversimplify text ideas for the students.)

Polly: Do you have any sense of why you do that? I mean is it . . .

Wendy: I guess it's my way of compensating for thinking that even the way I do it. . . . Oh how can I put it? Even the way I do it is gonna be pretty hard for some people and so predigesting it, simplifying it very drastically, is a way of not frightening those people. At the same time, what am I there for except to present something that's a little bit tough.

It seemed from Wendy's responses to my comments that she frequently interpreted them in evaluative terms. She heard them as suggestions for action, as well as frameworks for interpreting her classroom activities. During the interviews, I frequently stated that I was not evaluating her teaching or advocating for a particular practice over another:

Polly: You keep mentioning the schedule. Where does that come from?

Wendy: I know, I know uhm maybe it's not that important.

Polly: I mean I don't know, but it's something (uh hum) that you've mentioned several (uh hum) times about getting through the material and staying on schedule.

Wendy: Yah, yah, it's that I don't . . . I think for one thing, in spite of the fact that we haven't gotten very far in this chapter . . . maybe it's just my sense but I kind of feel that we've started to beat [the family chapter] to death and that it might be just as well to go on to the next thing. But I do that to myself a lot actually (uh hm). I'll think, oh boy, they're not ready and I really underestimated what it was going to take, and I'll put things off but I don't like it (laugh). You know it's kind of silly. I should really think about that.

Polly: So do you think, let me just play around with this, if you had a different kind of organization to your course, where every week you were working on a different reading and you were doing, I mean that's not a suggestion because you'd be throwing away all sorts of other advantages to this program, but would that allay your fears of getting through it faster? If you were not looking at the same content all the time?

We openly addressed Wendy's tendency to take all of my comments as suggestions. It became a topic of our talk as we explored the perceived differences in our power and knowledge bases. Although she persisted in hearing "suggestions" throughout the data collection period, she could also stand back and see what she was doing and take a more confident stance:

(We are trying to arrange my observations during the last weeks of the class. I asked when she will discuss the text reading next so I am sure to be present.)

Wendy: . . . when is the next time [we discuss biology]? Probably Monday, with the film.

Polly: Oh, 'cause you're going to discuss *Raisin in the Sun* the whole time. You're going to see the second part of it?

Wendy: The film requires two hours.

Polly: Oh, so you'll just show it part on Wednesday and show it again on Friday.

Wendy: Maybe I *should* stagger it. Somehow. You're right. Maybe we shouldn't be away from biology that long. I have to think about that.

Polly: I didn't, I didn't suggest that. I'm just . . .

Wendy: No, I know. (We both laugh.) I know, but you're making me think, I should say.

My talk, particularly during the first interviews, indicated a desire to shed the authority, the "seer" role Wendy seemed willing to give me. I joined her talk about the complexities of teaching, as well as the fact that there were no easy, textbook answers to most of them. I also showed a preference for responding to her negative comments with probing questions. I neither acknowledged nor disclaimed her judgment by asking her for more information. As the interviews progressed, it became somewhat more comfortable for me to address the known bad news she brought up. I was careful, however, not to initiate a bad news topic that could have placed me in the unknown-bad-news box (see figure, p. 187). If I did evaluate, I was generally positive in my assessment. I generally chose to voice only my positive assessments, of which there were many. During the initial phases of data collection, in particular, when Wendy and I were establishing our relationship and building trust, I chose to avoid commenting on my interpretations of classroom activities that seemed to limit student participation or show a misunderstanding of a student's meaning. I did not want to interfere with Wendy's interpretation of the classroom by steering the talk to mine. I planned to introduce my understandings, as necessary, in the discourse analysis of the classroom interaction that I intended to carry out after the conclusion of the class:

> *Wendy:* . . . Do you, do you get a feeling that, I mean it is kind of funny that I insisted on (laugh) having this done to myself in the time that I planned, but do you think that it seemed a little rushed?
>
> *Polly:* No.
>
> *Wendy:* 'Cause I don't want to give them that [impression].
>
> *Polly:* No, I've seen three extremely well designed lessons that you've presented that began and finished within the time period. I mean (uh hum) for each of those different kinds of lessons you had an agenda and you carried it through and it was completed . . . uhm . . . I don't feel like it was either too rushed or too slow.

A form of interaction that seemed to reduce the power differential by taking me out of the role of evaluator or expert was matching stories. Some of the problems Wendy identified in her classroom were ones that I could relate to my own teaching. When she wondered, for example, if she had allocated turns at talk in a way that encouraged participation rather than squelched it, I offered parallel reflections that revealed my own dilemmas on this issue.

Perhaps the most significant step I took in my attempts to reduce the power and knowledge differential, however, was to directly address the issue of how I envisioned it. In a form of matching story I revealed my own reservations about how to successfully conduct this type of research, much in the same way Wendy was opening up to me about her teaching. As we see in the following excerpt, it allowed us to talk frankly about some of the issues that had festered undercover in my previous experience. I could make clear that I didn't view myself as any more of an expert on how to manage the dilemmas than she was:

> *Polly:* (telling the story of being advised to listen as a researcher) . . . she is sharing her experience and talking to me and I said I know I'll want to jump in and say "oh, why don't you do this and why don't you do that," because it makes me feel helpful, you know, in some way (uh hum) because then that way there's some kind of ex-

change going on. But I don't have any right answers, I don't think I know how to do something. I mean that's precisely my point is that there is no expert knowledge about how to do these things. It's all by the seat of your pants and putting together your experience with what you think is going on and your background, whatever . . . And [Morimoto] said if you just listen and you give that attention . . . she's the expert of her expertise and what [conclusions] she draws, that's what you can give her (uh hum). And he said that's what you can (yah) give, attention, so that she can find out her own understanding (uh hum). And that made so much sense to me, I mean I just felt that unlocked it (uh hum). But I think that that's exactly what, you know, if you get anything out of this (uh hum) that's what it's going to be. It's all from you (uh hum).

Wendy: These dialogues are different from going home and thinking why do I do this (uh hm). It's so much personality too, you know. I mean I'm the first person who, when it comes time to make a decision, my first feeling is I'm going to make the wrong one (laugh) or it's not going to be good (laugh). So I think if I have that a little bit I can't reassure myself as much as you can assure me that well, gee, this is complicated or how many things go on (uh hm) and that puts a different face on things, it's interesting.

In spite of the fact that I had intended to be a good listener, which in my mind meant letting Wendy do all the talking, I had unconsciously taken an active role in the initial interviews. When I transcribed the interviews, I was very uncomfortable with the amount of substantive talk in which I had engaged. Nearly all the discussions of interview technique cautioned against this type of interaction, claiming it would either unduly influence the interviewee or shut down her opportunity to communicate (Davis, 1984; McCracken, 1988; Seidman, 1991). In an examination of the transcripts, however, Wendy seemed more encouraged to speak freely about her reflections on her teaching as a result. I believe that the initial establishment of a more mutual relationship during our talks was crucial to the success of the interviews. As a result of my greater participation in the talk, we advanced significantly along the relationship continuum in our first meetings, which made Wendy a more open and willing participant in the interviews. This type of interview technique, which involves greater interviewer disclosure, has been promulgated by some, but not all, feminist researchers. Oakley (1981), for example, suggests that the feminist researcher has an obligation to participate openly in talk with her subjects. To do otherwise is to use subjects as distanced objects to be merely studied.

The other caution of the methodologists, that too much talk by the interviewer would unduly influence the interviewee, was more probably the case. As I mentioned earlier, assuming I would take a back seat to the analysis was a naive position on my part. By naming dilemmas, recapitulating what I thought Wendy was saying, adding my own stories to confirm her experience, and complimenting her efforts, I was very influential in shaping the direction of the interview talk. I helped lay the terrain for reflective problem-solving, and Wendy began to use our sessions to do just that.

By adjusting my relationship in the field to a more collaborative stance by reducing the social distance that traditionally exists between researcher and teacher, I also got more involved in the activity of Wendy's teaching. Throughout her reflections and problem-solving, I functioned as a friend/counselor, ready to listen and to offer my reflections. As Wendy describes it, our talk was instrumental in the changes she underwent during this study and later. I had moved, therefore, along the action continuum from mere observer to active participant in the reflective process.

Wendy: Doing the Research

Polly and I both put great effort into making the first interviews succeed. I offered the thoughts I had about the classes we reviewed as frankly as possible. Dissembling and defensiveness seemed unfair when Polly showed such interest and never gave me reason to feel defensive. We also made the interviews partly a social time in which we could get to know each other better. But while we both made efforts, Polly shouldered the larger burden of making the first meeting work. She had to renegotiate virtually all of my ideas about researchers' and teachers' roles, and the goals of the project. Early interview transcripts indicate a degree of vulnerability on my part that surprised even me when I read them several weeks into the project. My talk was filled with doubts and criticisms of my work as a teacher. I was, as Polly imagined, trying to outrace her in finding my errors so that I would not have to hear them from her. I felt that, at any rate, being critical of practice was what we were supposed to do in research, however collaborative.

Polly responded in ways that blunted my worst fears. In the first of these moves, she made it clear that she was working with me as a colleague, not a supervisor, and she genuinely wanted to know how I saw my practice. I sometimes criticized my practice in the areas where I felt vulnerable — wondering, for example, why I could not glibly make up good definitions when students asked about unfamiliar vocabulary. That I chose this rather superficial issue underlines the anxiety I felt about Polly's evaluation of my performance. In response to such a trivial concern, Polly honestly said that she knew these issues made one feel vulnerable, but that she did not regard them as important problems in practice. In addition, she shared with me her own uncertainties about how to do her research, relating a talk she had had with an adviser who had suggested that a researcher needs to simply listen to a teacher/informant, and that this would offer the teacher a forum for finding her own solutions. At the time, the very idea that Polly dealt with uncertainty, too, came as a revelation and had a moderate leveling effect on the vast differences I imagined between us. Such reassurances occurred frequently in the first few weeks of our project, as Polly acted consistently on her belief that the person with more power must work to level the differences felt by those with less.

Outside of the interviews, Polly conveyed enthusiasm and warmth. More than in the past, we shared anecdotes from our teaching and our everyday lives when we crossed paths at the office. Polly once recounted her stepdaughter's having referred to me as "Polly's teacher," to which she replied that I *was* her teacher, not in the sense of her teacher/informant, but in the sense that I was teaching her things. These early interactions brought more clarity to the abstraction of Polly's wanting to hear my point of view, and I grew to give this notion some credence.

In the weeks of interviews that followed, I gradually became more confident and far more eager to talk about what had happened in class and the issues about which I had thought. My own talk took up a great deal more interview time, frequently interrupting Polly's. Her handling of our conversations affirmed my treatment of the interviews as my time to talk. Her questions were straightforward: "How many of [the students] do you think have any knowledge of biology at all? I mean, do you feel like . . . their background knowledge in biology is weaker than it was in, say, in psychology or economics or sociology?" In the transcripts, my answers to such questions, and my digressions from them, frequently ran three-quarters of a page. I began to look forward to sessions with Polly; my lack of time was no longer an issue. To my friends, I described my sessions with Polly as "therapy for teachers."

Although reluctant to be cast as my teacher, Polly made it possible for me to learn from our project in a manner similar to that observed by Schön (1983) in his research on training in professional schools. Schön notes, in the cases of both the architect and the psychotherapist studied, when the professor sees a student "stuck" in practice, the professor "attributes the student's predicament to his/her way of framing the problem" (p. 129) and helps the student to reframe the problem. While Polly always insisted that she did not have the answers to what I should do in my practice, she did offer a new, more distanced, and ultimately more merciful framing than my own of my practice: it was not, she argued persistently, that I "didn't have the right answer," but that teaching was rife with dilemmas that one managed as best one could. As our mutual trust deepened, our talks delved into the attitudes and beliefs I brought to my teaching, the institutional context in which I worked, and even the life history that led me into my career. Our talks helped me see that all of these factors contributed to how I framed and attempted to resolve problems in my teaching. By articulating my beliefs about what needed to happen in my class, I began to affirm the way I thought and to criticize constructively less superficial aspects of what I was doing.

Through this "therapy" process, I began to articulate a sequence of changes that I wanted to make in my teaching. Some problems could be solved quickly (such as allowing oral rehearsal time in small groups when students were still struggling with the material); others required a change in the syllabus and a new start (which I will discuss later); others I wryly called the "congenital" problems, those that hung on my own personality. This framework helped me to see that the fruit of my work with Polly could, and had to, extend beyond the semester; she was not expecting me to solve all my issues in the following weeks, nor was I.

Among my congenital problems was my tendency to "do the work" for the students, as we put it in interview shorthand: I favored making the work of comprehending the text easy for them (by offering a substantial foundation for that comprehension myself) rather than difficult (by letting them grapple with text) in the hope of helping them believe that they could produce what I modeled. The problem was that my ultimate goal for the course — for students to engage in what we called "seminar talk" based on texts — was defeated by my own methods. I sacrificed opportunities for students to struggle to make meaning because I did not want them to feel frustrated in their attempts to understand text. Students' frustration seemed to me proof of a teacher's failure to recognize their needs and lend help; it was the emblem of inexperienced teaching. Still, how would we get from struggle-free learning to seminar talk?

The real power of seeing my issues through the lens of Polly's interpretations was that I could get a little healthy distance from them. I could begin to say about myself, I do X, with these positive and negative results; I could change in these ways. A far cry from my embarrassed, somewhat helpless affect in our first talks.

But more pertinent than my own improved comfort was the accompanying higher level of clarity about my teaching practice, and how that clarity helped me to work with my own students. After discussing issues with Polly, solutions of startling simplicity came to my mind. I decided, for example, to provide for a more even share of turns per student, even though it meant violating other precepts of mine, such as not pressuring quiet students to speak and not interrupting the more willing speakers.

Also, Polly and I noticed the range of responses I got when I asked students only one broad question about a topic (Why are some countries rich and some poor?), rather than many questions, and I started thinking about using more such "key questions." I continued to grapple with the feedback I got from the class: questions that invited students to talk about their experience provoked answers that revealed their capacity for defining and analyzing. But questions that asked them to apply what they knew to a text were not as successful in bringing out that same capacity. They were capable, for example, of explaining causes of poverty in their own countries but less able to see where the arguments of the economics reading differed from their own. I could not readily assign causes to these areas of difficulty: were students confused by the text or less interested in text than in sharing their own ideas? Were the stakes too low for any individual to struggle through a critical reading of the text? As Polly observed, the higher stakes involved in arguing for the correctness of their answers to test questions had inspired many students to work carefully at articulating their interpretations of text.

Polly: The Place of an Independent Analysis and Unknown Bad News

The place of the researcher's independent analysis of the classroom data and how to broach the topic of unknown bad news are two remaining issues related to the emergent collaborative research we conducted. In our collaboration, the two were related.

While we both valued the richness of the reflective talk that took place during the interviews, as a discourse analyst I also valued the information a micro-analysis of the classroom interaction would provide. In many ways, Wendy's reflective analysis of the interaction, as well as the naming of her dilemmas, directed the micro-analysis. I chose to examine with an independent analytical lens passages of interaction that exemplified the development Wendy chronicled in our talks. I hoped to discover, in the talk itself, elements that confirmed her judgments and intuitions about the class. In addition, I expected my analysis to shed some light on events in the classroom that continued to perplex Wendy. I did wonder privately, and in conversation with Wendy, however, if that level of analysis would be useful or even interesting to Wendy.

Themes emerged from the micro-analysis similar to those Wendy had laid out. The analysis also provided more subtle information about how she managed to teach a group of students with diverse English ability and cultural differences. In other words, while she could name her dilemmas during the reflective stimulated-recall discussions, the discourse analysis indicated how she actually managed them. Some of this information was new to Wendy.

I first shared my interpretations with Wendy in conversation and later in writing. The analysis provided an in-depth look at what a teacher actually does during a class, and revealed how she interprets the class's contributions and what "in-flight" decisions she makes on that basis (Ulichny, 1996). There was one instance, however, in which the analysis provided what I worried would be the unknown bad news normally so difficult to convey. In the final stages of analysis, which took place during the writing of the research report, I discovered, contrary to Wendy's assumptions at the time of the occurrence, that the students had, in fact, progressed in their ability to understand and discuss expository text. I also discovered that Wendy's management of the classroom discourse prevented the students from displaying the ability effectively. I believe, however, that the strength of our relationship and the shared goal of making the research project useful first and foremost to Wendy helped us progress through the analysis.

Wendy: Reacting to the Research Report

Though I eagerly anticipated reading Polly's written report, which contained a microanalysis of the classroom talk, enriched by information gained during our taped conversations, I sensed that it might not always feel comfortable to see my semester reflected back at me alone. Ever since those early interviews, I had not imagined that Polly would write anything like the reports we had shuddered at during our talks — reports that were harshly critical of teachers or that failed to take into account why they behaved the way they did. Still, she would be writing for an intended audience much larger than me. Unlike the interviews, the report could not focus so intensely on my possible reactions and hurt feelings.

I did feel sheepish reading parts of the report — but not because of how Polly expressed her findings. Instead, I cringed a little at the difference between my best guiding intuitions applied during that semester and ways I now made sense of teaching — knowledge I gained from the project. I read certain ideas I had stated with conviction and wondered how I could have been so narrow in my thinking. I winced at my awkward phrasings in the interview transcripts, frankly doubting Polly's earlier comment to me that everyone's conversations sound incoherent in transcription.

Writing obliged Polly to use phrases she did not have to when speaking directly with me (reporting, for example, that "to Wendy's mind" a particular event meant X), and this caused me to think more about some of the areas in which she might well have disagreed with my interpretations but had chosen not to say so. As I had initially suspected, the micro-analysis revealed information about some of the difficult periods in the semester. In the last part of the course, the class and I studied the biology chapter I had selected, which proved to be the most problematic part of the course. I had never taken a college-level biology course myself, and I had seen during my planning that most of the chapters in the text, including those on cell physiology, were beyond my ability to teach. I had chosen the chapter on the Mendel flower experiments, basically a narrative, because I understood it best. Choosing readings on subjects in which the teacher has no college-level experience may seem quite foolhardy, but I had chosen them knowing that there is a movement in ESL that encourages just that. The ESL teacher, so the argument goes, "remains the language expert" in this situation while her students are "the sources of information from the various disciplines" (Braine, 1988, p. 702).

During this part of class, activity bogged down in ways that I did not understand clearly. Polly listened sympathetically to my concerns about the torpid pace of the class and the seeming regression of some students. Was this text really more difficult than the others? Was their background in biology possibly weaker than it had been in the other subjects? Had my other, competing commitments taken up so much time that I was inadequately prepared? With final exams on the horizon, had students simply stopped working on this not-for-credit course?

My own lack of background in this area caused me difficulties I had not anticipated, and student "sources of information" on biology never materialized in this class. Interestingly, a graduate student in biology attended the other section I taught, an unusual situation that reflected his difficulties functioning in English. While his knowledge of biology was infinitely superior to mine, even he was not in a position to save me from my own reading. He could clarify minor uncertainties I had, for example about vocabulary, but this barely addressed the difficulties I had in teaching an unfamiliar subject area. This left me questioning the assumptions of teaching across the curriculum: despite predictions, an excellent student source in biology and a teacher clearly proficient in English had added up to a whole far less than the sum of the parts.

I felt that if the material were less difficult for me, it would be for the students, and that they knew this, too. I realized that I was uncertain at best whenever students asked me questions outside of the text ("Is the 'pollinate'. . . for the flower or for the animals?" My answer: "Only flowers, I think. And maybe other plants. Maybe other plants.") My attempt at a pep talk yielded the information that the students thought the text was hard.

I chose to revert to very simple work with the Mendel text, asking questions designed to prompt student paraphrasing of the text, virtually sentence-by-sentence. After many weeks during which students had seemed better equipped to negotiate meaning, I was back to "doing the work" for the class. They had been successful earlier because they had been working on easier materials, I concluded. I was discouraged by my backtracking, but it seemed necessary. The semester ended with my regretful declaration to Polly that perhaps students did not think the course had helped their reading skills very much.

During the summer, Polly and I talked about her analysis of the tapes from this part of class. Her analysis revealed something that I had not really suspected at the time: the students had learned a great deal about how to participate in class and draw meaning from text, but they had probably been confused by my downshifting to simple questions and requests for paraphrasing. There were times on the tapes, Polly reported, when a student offered a correct answer that I did not recognize as such, since I was relying on students to focus on the same bit of text that I myself was using. My requirement that students go through the text with me in locating answers had been an impediment to class work rather than a support for dealing with "hard" text. In other words, the students were demonstrating more skill in handling the Mendel reading than I was.

It is true that I had a little distance from the course by the time Polly told me this news: the semester was over, the students had done well on a final test, and I was on to planning a completely different reading course for the next semester. But my warm reception of this information indicates more than anything else the value of Polly's and my work on our relationship in the project. I was more rueful than embarrassed at Polly's revelation and what it said about my own tactical errors. I felt cheered by the thought that the students had learned much more than we had thought. Polly also pointed out that these findings supported my decision not to teach subject material with which I was not familiar. My trust in the project already established, I was able to hear in her words the useful information they conveyed.

After reading the whole report, I felt very much respected in Polly's analysis. She had written with care and sympathy about every factor in my thinking and teaching experience that might explain some of my less felicitous choices. Also, she gave me the opportunity to respond to anything I wanted, and she added my comments to the report, as well as a long letter I had written about the effects of the project on me.

However, beyond my positive response to the written report lay the immense detail and the observer's perspective from which to draw important conclusions. The intensive work of the micro-analysis yielded the most thorough review of a course that I suppose I will ever have. It helped me appreciate, in a very different way than did the rest of our work, the intricacy of ESL teaching and learning. It crystallized my understanding of the unintended effects of the various strategies I employed. For example, the discourse analysis revealed the quick "online" decisions I made unconsciously in class. Polly spoke about the "fine tuning" of my practice; in close parallel, Schön writes of a "knowing-in-practice [that] tends to become increasingly tacit, spontaneous, and automatic, thereby conferring on [the practitioner and clients] the benefits of specialization" (Schön, 1983, p. 60). Polly pointed out many instances of such knowing, for example, my quickly cycling through questions designed to get at where students were troubled. While the questions depended upon the subject at hand, analysis revealed that they always functioned as a systematic probe: was unfamiliar vocabulary causing a problem, or was it disagreement with the text or a cultural misunderstanding?

Reading the report brought to mind, again in highly significant detail, ideas for how I might do better. It helped me to see with much greater clarity what strategies students employ in learning and how I might encourage the most constructive of these.

Polly: The Researcher Concludes

The form of collaborative action research that emerged in this project grew out of my concerns about controlling the damage that a researcher can inflict as a result of the higher status normally accorded her role as compared to a teacher's. It also developed from the way Wendy and I naturally evolved in our working relationship. This evolution was unpredictable at the start of the project and no doubt was greatly influenced by our respective personalities, interests, and interactive styles. I believe, however, that an essential ingredient to forging that relationship was overtly paying attention to it, voicing the difficulties inherent in teacher/researcher relationships, and, on my part, constantly monitoring how we were doing on that account. I have come to understand that wishing power and status differentials did not exist between researcher and informant is not enough to reduce them. Active participation in creating mutual structures in the research is required. These structures need to be created not only in the research design, but also in the everyday interaction that takes place between researcher and participants in the field.

This is not to say that researcher and teacher need to do everything together to create mutual structures in the research. Not only is this unrealistic, it is probably not desirable. There are different roles that each of the participants needs to assume during the project. Wendy needed to focus her energies on her teaching and I on the contribution this study would make to understanding teachers' practices in multilingual, multicultural classrooms. Acknowledging this difference helped give me license to talk about Wendy, not only to talk with her. The "covenantal" that guided my research, however, required that in talking about her I acknowledge the special responsibility I accrued toward her as a result of our relationship (Deyhle et al., 1992).

While Wendy and I had different agendas for the research on one level, we also shared a joint commitment — to further our collective knowledge about the complexity of the teaching task. We both saw this as a needed corrective to methodology handbooks and teacher manuals that reduce the work of teaching to scripts and strategies.

What emerged for us as a way of realizing that commitment can be expressed as a feminist approach to doing qualitative single-subject case studies (or any ethnographic work, for that matter, although the parameters of relationship will obviously change with increased numbers of participants). While there is no one definition of feminist research methodology, I agree with Reinharz's (1983) description as summarized by Neilson (1990). She describes it as "contextual, inclusive, experiential, involved, socially relevant . . . open to the environment, and inclusive of emotions and events as experienced" (p. 6). Moreover, most feminist researchers would agree with Roman (1992) that they are unified in rejecting "the subject-object dualism, or what feminist philosopher of science Harding (1986, 1987) calls, 'objectivism.' By objectivism, Harding means the stance often taken by researchers in attempts to remove, minimize, or make invisible their own subjectivities, beliefs, and practices, while simultaneously directing attention to the subjectivities, beliefs, and practices of their subject as the sole objects of scrutiny" (p. 556).

The feminist methodology that I engaged in to investigate my original question involved a number of precepts. The first one involved paying primary attention to the relationship and connection between people involved in the research. The report to an external audience was of secondary importance. In the end, we were both pleased with the results of the research as well as with our relationship. Had the data revealed a story that was critical of Wendy's teaching, or had I observed lessons and discovered mostly what was going wrong in the teaching and learning, I would not have published this account. The addition of this study to the published accounts of classroom research would not, in my opinion, have warranted the damage to Wendy's professional persona that publication would have entailed.[3] This is quite different from many ethnographies of classrooms that focus on what *could* be, under better circumstances, and often concentrate on the defects of the context under investigation.

I feel that my attention to going through or beyond the disaster tales that Wendy was anxious to lay out actually improved the results of this analysis. My ethic of relationship forced me to push the analysis to deeper levels in order to find significant patterns that explain both the interview and classroom data.

A second precept underlying the methodology was an interest in incorporating voices of traditionally unheard, undervalued members of the educational community into published research. The academic community of education professors and researchers has consistently ignored and undervalued the perspective of teachers in attempting to understand social context and cognition in schools. Valuing a teacher's voice raised my awareness of the wealth of information and insight that is untapped by most educational research.[4]

A third precept of my methodology was paying attention to power differences and leveling them when they appeared. This included the empowerment of the informant and her subjectivity. By this I mean that Wendy's interpretation of the classroom was the springboard from which I began my micro-analysis of the discourse. Her meanings and her subjectivity were, therefore, incorporated into the account of the classroom. Wendy's intimate involvement in providing the interpretation of the classroom activities altered the underlying priority of the researcher: as we conducted the study, we were both more interested in making the immediate situation — Wendy's classroom — the primary beneficiary of our activity, rather than the academy.

I shifted my attention from the eventual results of the research to the process of conducting it. This move made entry more acceptable to both of us and eased our dealing with the unknown bad news that emerged. Since all information we learned from the project was intended to support Wendy's instructional practice, it was easier to discuss bad news, even unknown bad news, without it being perceived as a researcher's exposé of problematic interactions. By discussing problems with the priority of instruction in mind, Wendy felt less vulnerable than she had imagined she would by a published report of a less-than-perfect practice.

Another underlying precept of the methodology was the transformational characteristic of the research. It was not a hands-off, neutralized view of a teacher and her classroom. With Wendy's implicit permission, we both engaged in change. Empowerment of the teacher was the precondition, as well as the outcome, of the transformative process.

Finally, we experienced, as a result of how we engaged in this project, an extension of the traditional boundaries of research. As our friendship, which began through the research, developed, the boundaries of public and private space blurred. In addition to our interviews there was a great deal of off-record talk. Some of this talk also, inevitably, became data for the analysis.

What resulted from this purposefully collaborative and feminist methodology was a way of conducting research that does not fit the usual description of participant observation. A more accurate term for it — Temporary Affiliation — was coined by Reinharz (1984). She describes this method as one of experiencing the subjects' world firsthand. While I was not a coteacher with Wendy, we coconstructed the reflective environment that provided much of the data. Reinharz calls this "affiliation" to underscore the making of personal commitments to people in the field, which more adequately describes our involvement, although our continued involvement in each other's lives years after the research project causes us to question the notion of *temporary* affiliation. Can partners in intense action and relationship in the field ever lose their affiliation with one another?

Wendy: The Teacher Concludes

My teaching and my views on teaching have changed markedly as a result of this project. I have abandoned the idea that I can give students a taste of many subject areas and choose materials for single-theme courses from areas with which I have only passing familiarity. My reading courses, since working on the project, have been grounded in American studies, English literature, and history, areas I know best. With another teacher, I have developed a course on the 1920s and 1930s in U.S. history. Another course features novels and autobiography by immigrants, Native Americans, and African Americans, and focuses on the possibility (important to my students as much as to me) of personal growth resulting from adversity. I have decided that my goal of giving students the opportunity to participate in text-based, classroom talk should take priority over other criteria, such as a selection of readings from "across the curricula." I exercise a more practiced eye in choosing texts by using readings that in some way parallel students' realities. I define the success of my classes in terms of full, articulate student participation. I act on greater faith that students can struggle together with text and direct our discussion if I give them the opportunity. I find ways of allowing the class itself to establish some shared understanding of texts without dragging students through the detailed "quiz-show" questions I had previously employed in teaching less familiar subject matter.

All of these tactical changes in my teaching have helped to produce courses closer to my ideal. If I were asked to identify the most important shift in my practice after this project, however, I would probably point to my willingness to share my own dilemmas with students, as Polly had with me. When composition students clamored for more intensive grammar correction ("Tell me every mistake I make"), I was not sure what course of action I thought best. But rather than hide my concerns from students and pick a strategy on my own, I suggested we experiment with different forms of feedback on their papers. One involves smattering student papers with symbols indicating every grammatical error I find; the other provides in letter form comments on and examples of a few types of errors found in a given composition and invites the writer to find more instances of such errors in the same paper. Then I polled the students themselves on their preferences: almost unanimously they decided the focus on fewer errors was more helpful. One student confessed that she treated the draft with many corrections as a secretarial exercise in which she decided on and plugged in correct answers without even rereading her draft. In such moments I am impressed again and again at the seriousness students display toward their endeavors: they are looking for situations in which they know they are truly engaged and learning.

This shift in my view of teaching reflects the two professional stances described by Schön: the defensive "expert" stance and that of the "reflective practitioner." The first feels she is "presumed to know and must claim to do so," either hiding or ignoring her own uncertainty. The second feels that she might not be the only one to know something relevant to the situation and that her "uncertainties may be a source of learning" (Schön, 1983, p. 300). In my experience, it is only by shedding the "expert" attitude that a teacher has the opportunity to treat relationships with students as real ones in which "right" answers are no longer the primary focus.

The psychological benefits of the project have proven nearly incalculable. When I started our work I did not believe that it could be collaborative at all, because I did not understand that my own, sufficient role was to do what I did. Instead I felt I was failing to do my share because I could not do Polly's part. Her task in the early weeks lay in convincing me that we each had something to contribute. I also believed that I was the wrong teacher for the right project: I recognized that I was often hurt, even by opinions I did not respect. I was not sure I could withstand the effects of having someone whose opinions I respected find fault with my professional performance. My own research experience with observing other ESL teachers, accrued since the end of this project, has helped me to see that most teachers, however excellent, experience the same sense of vulnerability that I did in research situations. Whatever their particular personalities, they, too, are subject to the effects of their marginal status in the university, the common perceptions of the hierarchy in which teachers and researchers are placed, and their lack of opportunity to see other teachers confronting the same dilemmas. Another positive result of my work with Polly is a "shifting of the debt," where I pay her back with my support of the talented teachers whose classrooms I observe.

Polly would argue that the learning I managed in her project came not from her but, as Morimoto predicted, from me. I am nevertheless grateful that she was there while I learned it and that we continue the rich dialogue that began with our project. I know now that I cannot divorce who I am from how I teach, but that something constructive can be made of this situation. And I have learned that I will always have dilemmas in my profession and that my greatest possibilities lie in paying attention to them.

Notes

1. The schematic presented here seemingly offers a static view of relationship and action possibilities. The reality of fieldwork, however, is dynamic. The evolution of a research project often involves shifts over time along these continua.

2. The transcripts are minimally edited to ease reading. Some hesitations and false starts have been eliminated and bracketed words inserted or substituted to make the meaning clearer. Both Wendy and I gave agreement feedback (uhm hmm) at regular intervals throughout the interviews. These are inserted in the conversation when they occurred. Punctuation in the transcripts respects conventions of written language. It is not intended to signal prosodic information. However, the following notations signal aspects of speaker performance: . . . — pause or hesitation; [] — candidate hearings of unclear utterances.

3. Cazden (personal communication) tells the story of early work on classroom discourse in which researchers revealed to a participating teacher that she tended to favor the White students in her class with nonverbal cues such as eye contact and body positioning. The teacher was so distraught at the thought of being racist in her instruction that she wanted to quit teaching.

4. Subsequent work in which I have been involved has focused on this point. A growing national network of urban teachers has been conducting research in their classrooms and disseminating this information as part of the Urban Sites Network of the National Writing Project. University-based researchers are primarily consultants in the research undertakings of the teachers (Muncey, Uhl, & Nyce, 1994; Peterson, Check, & Ylvisaker, 1996).

References

Agar, M. (1980). *The professional stranger.* New York: Academic Press.

Berthoff, A. (1987). The teacher as researcher. In D. Goswami & P. R. Stillman (Eds.), *Reclaiming the classroom: Teacher research as an agency for change* (pp. 28–38). Upper Montclair, NJ: Boynton/Cook.

Bickel, W. E., & Hattrup, R. A. (1995). Teachers and researchers in collaboration: Reflections on the process. *American Educational Research Journal, 32*(1), 35–64.

Bogdan, R., & Biklen, S. (1992). *Qualitative research for education: An introduction to theory and methods* (2nd ed.). Needham Heights, MA: Allyn & Bacon.

Braine, G. (1988). Two commentaries on Ruth Spack's "Initiating ESL students into the academic discourse community: How far should we go?" *TESOL Quarterly, 22,* 700–708.

Campbell, D. (1988). Collaboration and contradictions in a research and staff development project. *Teachers College Record, 90*(1), 99–121.

Cochran-Smith, M., & Lytle, S. L. (1990). Research on teaching and teacher research: The issues that divide. *Educational Researcher, 19*(2), 2-11.

Cochran-Smith, M., & Lytle, S. L. (1993). *Inside/outside: Teacher research and knowledge.* New York: Teachers College Press.

Corsaro, W. A. (1981). *Communicative processes in studies of social organization: Sociological approaches to discourse analysis. Text, 1*(1), 5–63.

Cummins, J. (1986). Empowering minority students: A framework for intervention. *Harvard Educational Review, 56,* 18–35.

Davis, J. (1984). Data into text. In R. F. Ellen (Ed.), *Ethnographic research: A guide to general conduct* (pp. 295–318). London: Academic Press.

Delpit, L. (1988). The silenced dialogue: Power and pedagogy in educating other people's children. *Harvard Educational Review, 58,* 280–298.

Deyhle, D. L., Hess, A. G., Jr., & LeCompte, M. D. (1992). Approaching ethical issues for qualitative researchers in education. In M. D. LeCompte, W. L. Millroy, & J. Preissle (Eds.), *The handbook of qualitative research in education* (pp. 597–642). San Diego: Academic Press.

Ely, M. et al. (1991). *Doing qualitative research: Circles within circles.* Bristol, PA: Falmer Press.

Erickson, F. (1986). Qualitative methods in research on teaching. In M. C. Wittrock (Ed.), *Handbook of research on teaching* (pp. 119–161). New York: Macmillan.

Erickson, F., & Schultz, J. (1982). *Gatekeeping in counseling interviews.* New York: Academic Press.

Fine, M. (1994). Working the hyphens: Reinventing self and other in qualitative research. In N. K. Denzin & Y. S. Lincoln (Eds.), *Handbook of qualitative research* (pp. 70–82). Thousand Oaks, CA: Sage.

Florio, S., & Walsh, M. (1981). The teacher as colleague in classroom research. In H. T. Trueba, G. Guthrie, & K. A. Au (Eds.), *Culture and the bilingual classroom* (pp. 87–101). Rowley, MA: Newbury House.

Florio-Ruane, S. (1991). *A conversational interpretation of teacher/researcher collaboration, George Mason University.* Manassas: Fairfax County, Virginia, Public Schools.

Florio-Ruane, S., & Dohanich, J. (1984). Communicating the findings: Teacher/researcher deliberations. *Language Arts, 61,* 724–730.

Gibson, M. A. (1985). Collaborative educational ethnography: Problems and profits. *Anthropology and Education Quarterly, 16,* 124–148.

Glesne, C., & Peshkin, A. (1992). *Becoming qualitative researchers: An introduction.* White Plains, NY: Longman.

Gold, R. (1969). Roles in sociological field observations. In G. McCall & J. L. Simmons (Eds.), *Issues in participant observation: A text and reader* (pp. 30–39). Menlo Park, CA: Addison-Wesley.

Harding, S. (1986). *The science question in feminism.* Ithaca, NY: Cornell University Press.

Harding, S. (1987). Introduction: Is there a feminist method? In S. Harding (Ed.), *Feminism and methodology* (pp. 1–14). Bloomington: Indiana University Press.

Heath, S. B. (1983). *Ways with words: Language, life, and work in communities and classrooms.* Cambridge, Eng.: Cambridge University Press.

Hymes, D. H. (1980). *Language in education.* Washington, DC: Center for Applied Linguistics.

Jacullo-Noto, J. (1984). Interactive research and development: Partners in craft. *Teachers College Record, 86,* 208–222.

Johnston, S. (1994). Is action research a "natural" process for teachers? *Educational Action Research, 2*(1), 39–48.

Labov, W. (1972). *Sociolinguistic patterns.* Philadelphia: University of Pennsylvania Press.

Ladwig, J. G. (1991). Is collaborative research exploitative? *Educational Theory, 41,* 111–120.

Lather, P. (1991). *Getting smart: Feminist research and pedagogy with/in the postmodern.* New York: Routledge.

LeCompte, M. D., & Preissle, J., with Tesch, R. (1993). *Ethnography and qualitative design in educational research* (2nd ed.). New York: Academic Press.

Lincoln, Y. S. (1995, April). *Standards for qualitative inquiry.* Paper presented at the annual meeting of the American Educational Research Association, San Francisco.

Lykes, B. (1989). Dialogue with Guatemalan women. In R. Unger (Ed.), *Representations: Social construction of gender* (pp. 167–184). Amityville, NY: Baywood.

McCracken, G. (1988). *The long interview.* Beverly Hills, CA: Sage.

Miller, S. M. (1952). The participant observer and "over-rapport." *American Sociological Review, 17,* 97–99.

Morimoto, K., Gregory, J., & Butler, P. (1973). Notes on the context for learning. *Harvard Educational Review, 43,* 245–257.

Muncey, D., Uhl, S., & Nyce, J. (1994). *An evaluation of the Urban Sites network* (Evaluation report submitted to the DeWitt Wallace-Reader's Digest Foundation). New York: Urban Sites Network of the National Writing Project.

Neilson, J. M. (1990). Introduction. In J. M. Neilson (Ed.), *Feminist research methods: Exemplary readings in the social sciences* (pp. 1–37) Boulder, CO: Westview Press.

Nieto, S. (1994). Lessons from students on creating a chance to dream. *Harvard Educational Review, 64,* 392–426.

Oakley, A. (1981). Interviewing women: A contradiction in terms. In H. Roberts (Ed.), *Doing feminist research* (pp. 30–61). Boston: Routledge & Kegan Paul.

Ogbu, J. U., & Matute-Bianchi, M. E. (1986). Understanding sociocultural factors: Knowledge, identity, and school adjustment. In California State Department of Education Bilingual Education Office (Ed.), *Beyond language: Social and cultural factors in schooling language minority students* (pp. 73–142). Los Angeles: California State University, Evaluation, Dissemination and Assessment Center.

Oja, S. N., & Smulyan, L. (1989). *Collaborative action research: A developmental approach.* London: Falmer.

Peterson, A., Check, J., & Ylvisaker, M. (Eds.). (1996). *Cityscapes: Eight views from the urban classroom.* Berkeley, CA: National Writing Project.

Philips, S. U. (1972). Participant structures and communication competence: Warm Springs children in community and classroom. In C. Cazden, D. Hymes, & V. P. John (Eds.), *Functions of language in the classroom* (pp. 161–189). New York: Teachers College Press.

Reason, P. (1994). Three approaches to participative inquiry. In N. K. Denzin & Y. S. Lincoln (Eds.), *Handbook of qualitative research* (pp. 324–339). Thousand Oaks, CA: Sage.

Reinharz, S. (1983). Experiential analysis: A contribution to feminist research. In G. Bowles & R. D. Klein (Eds.), *Theories of women's studies.* London: Routledge & Kegan Paul.

Reinharz, S. (1984). *On becoming a social scientist* (2nd ed.). New Brunswick, NJ: Transaction.

Reinharz, S. (1992). *Feminist methods in social research.* New York: Oxford University Press.

Roman, L. G. (1992). The political significance of other ways of narrating ethnography: A feminist materialist approach. In M. D. LeCompte, W. L. Millroy, & J. Preissle (Eds.), *The handbook of qualitative research in education* (pp. 555–594). New York: Academic Press.

Schön, D. A. (1983). *The reflective practitioner.* New York: Basic Books.

Seidman, I. E. (1991). *Interviewing as qualitative research.* New York: Teachers College Press.

Shaffir, W. G., Stebbins, R. A., & Turowetz, A. (1980). *Fieldwork experience.* New York: St. Martin's Press.

Stainback, S. B. (1988). *Understanding and conducting qualitative research.* Dubuque, IA: Kendall/Hunt.

Stenhouse, L. (1975). *An introduction to curriculum research and development.* London: Heinemann.

Ulichny, P. (1996). What's in a methodology? In D. Freeman & J. C. Richards (Eds.), *Teacher learning in language teaching* (pp. 178–196). Cambridge, Eng.: Cambridge University Press.

Van Maanen, J. (1983). The moral fix: On the ethics of fieldwork. In R. Emerson (Ed.), *Contemporary field research* (pp. 269–287). Boston: Little, Brown.

Van Maanen, J. (1988). *Tales of the field: On writing ethnography.* Chicago: University of Chicago Press.

Wallace, J., & Louden, W. (1994). Collaboration and the growth of teachers' knowledge. *Qualitative Studies in Education, 7,* 323–334.

Watson-Gegeo, K. A., & Ulichny, P. (1988). *Ethnographic inquiry in second language acquisition and instruction* (Working Paper). Manoa: University of Hawaii at Manoa, Department of ESL.

Appearing Acts:
Creating Readers in a
High School English Class

JOAN KERNAN CONE

T hey're never going to read Dickens. . . ."
    One Saturday evening in mid-November, during a conversation about teaching, a friend of mine — a computer genius and Tom Clancy fan — said to me, "You're having your kids read the wrong books. They're never going to read Dickens when they get out of school. You need to introduce them to authors they *will* read."

At first I was irritated by his words. What did he know of the books I was teaching? What did he know of my commitment to expand the canon, to bring new writers into my classroom who represented the cultural and racial backgrounds of my students? Yet, as much as I wanted to dismiss his suggestion as another example of everyone-knows-how-to-teach-better-than-teachers, I could not. He had touched a nerve.

For all of the attention I pay to literature in my classes, I am not producing readers: that is, students who choose to read on their own for pleasure and for knowledge. That saddens me. A friend of mine tells her students a truth I've known since I was five: "If you don't read, you can only live one tiny life" (a paraphrase of an S. I. Hayakawa idea). I want my students to share my experience of living many lives through reading. I, a wife, a mother, and a veteran teacher, have become Antonia Shimerda, Franny Glass, and Jing-Mei Woo; have traveled to Mahfouz's Cairo, Gordimer's Johannesburg, and Vargas Llosa's Milaflores; and have discovered the identity of Mr. Rochester's first wife, the intricacies of Willie Stark's politics, and the political intrigues of Deep Throat.

The habit of reading not only opens a world of vicarious adventure to students; it also encourages them to weigh ideas, take informed stands, and think deeply. Reading offers them insights into themselves and their worlds — private, national, global — insights that allow them to speak intelligently, vote wisely, rear kind children, counsel, lead. What happens to students who graduate from high school barely literate, reading only books assigned in class and having neither the skill nor the confidence to read a book on their own? Just as important, what happens to students who *can* read but do not; who go to college, perhaps to professional schools, and yet read only the daily newspaper, an occasional weekly newsmagazine, or the *New Yorker* in the dentist's of-

Harvard Educational Review Vol. 64 No. 4 Winter 1994, 450–473

fice? My friend's words challenged me to examine the way I was teaching literature, challenged me to find a way to lead students to become readers.

Creating Readers: Was Choice the Answer?

The next Monday I went to class, told my first- and second-period seniors what my friend had said about my teaching "the wrong books," and then gave them a reading assignment. If they wanted to earn an A for the semester, they had to read a novel of at least five hundred pages (or two of 250 pages) written since 1985, that had no Cliff Notes and had not been made into a film. I gave them two opportunities to take a test on the books. The first, two days before winter vacation; the second, one week before the end of the semester. The students immediately posed questions: Was a "novel" a fiction or nonfiction book? Did they have to buy the book, or could they check it out of the library? What if they chose a book with 480 pages? Would I be assigning other homework at the same time?

After answering their questions, I posted the deadline for finishing the book in large letters on my front chalkboard and moved on to *Othello*. A week before the independent reading book was due, I asked students to write a letter telling me how they were doing in each of their classes and how they thought they would do on their upcoming progress report, a written evaluation of their grade up to that point in the semester. In terms of English class, I asked them to discuss their independent reading book.

As I read over their papers, I grew uneasy. Some students, like Tassie, were excited about the assignment: "The outside reading is a wonderful idea. I love it! It gives me options. I can read eighty pages in two days or three pages in one day. It's up to me." Some, like Wilson, were moving along with the assignment: "I'm determined to finish my outside book since it tells a lot of things about China and I want to see how the student movement began." A few students had already finished their books. But the majority of the responses were not promising. Many students gave me what I felt were teacher-pleasing responses. Danielle wrote, "My independent reading book is *Misery* by Stephen King [no apology for reading a book made into a film]. Everything about this book is a mystery. I find myself really committed to this book." Others were even less specific — they had praise for the book, or they were doing fine with the reading, but they did not include the name of the book nor discuss its plot or characters. As Jeff commented, "My outside book is easier than I thought it would be because I barely have time to take a leak. I found something I could relate to and in turn it caught my attention."

My uneasiness about students' progress with their independent reading was confirmed the day I gave the first test. When asked to retell the ending of the book from the main character's point of view and to discuss why the ending was satisfying or unsatisfying, only nine students of thirty-four in first period and eleven of thirty-five in second period could do so in a way that demonstrated that they had read their book thoroughly and thoughtfully. A few tried to fake their answers. Craig wrote of *Remains of the Day*, "Well, in the end, Mr. Stevens drove off and was excited to show his employer all that he had learned on this interesting journey of his." What had happened to Jeff and Danielle, who had written only a few days before of being "really into" their books? "The book got boring and I didn't have time to start a new one." "I'll read a 500-page book next time." Others made no excuses or promises.

What had gone wrong? I had given students a choice of books, homework time to read, and, in the last few days before the test, class time for reading. Yet the majority of the students had not finished a book.

Despite the disappointing results, I was not willing to give up on the independent reading idea. Over the December vacation, I thought about what I could do. Clearly, I needed to check that students were reading books that fit the previously established criteria (such as no Cliff Notes, no books made into movies). My leniency with the first book had led to students "fudging": they had reported about novels that had been turned into films ("But I didn't see the movie"), books that were used in other classes, and autobiographies of current star athletes that bore a close resemblance to articles I had read in recent sports pages. In addition, I realized that waiting until close to the assignment deadline to give students in-class reading time was not a good idea. I needed to allocate time early in the term so that students had read enough of their books to complete the assignment.

When school reconvened in January, I was determined to make the next independent reading assignment a success. After handing back the December tests, I talked about the results and asked students to write about, and then discuss as a class, why they had read or not read the first book. I hoped that by forcing them to reflect first in writing and then aloud, I would help them take responsibility for reading and thereby inspire more of them to finish the next book. Several students said they had trouble finding a book. "I went to [a chain book store]," Kema announced, "and asked the lady to recommend a book written by an African American after 1985 and she said there weren't any." Students who were taking an elective class in African American literature were horrified — at the saleswoman's ignorance as well as at Kema's believing her. "What are you talking about?" they asked her. "What about Toni Morrison and Alice Walker? You need to go to another bookstore." Those comments created an opportunity for me to mention the names of bookstores easily accessible in nearby Berkeley — bookstores with readers as salesclerks and tables laden with books by African Americans, Asian Americans, Latinos, Native Americans, women, gays, new writers. Students who knew of other sources for books offered suggestions to those who didn't want to buy books. Next we talked about the criteria for choosing the books. The page limit this time was determined by what they had done on the previous independent reading assignment. If they had read a 500-page book, they had no further independent reading requirement; if they had read a 250-page book, they had to read another book of at least 250 pages; and if they had not read a book, they needed to choose a book of five hundred pages. The students stated that the 1985 publication date was too limiting and asked that it be changed to at least 1980 — I agreed. I restated my insistence on novels, not biographies or books from which movies had been made. The students asked if I had any suggestions, which I did. I had lots of books to lend and encouraged them to come in to talk with me so I could help them find books that were right for them.

I set aside the first three days of the following week for in-class silent reading. On Monday, several students came without books: they had forgotten their book at home, they hadn't had time to buy one or go to the library, or they couldn't find anything interesting. I handed out anthologies of short stories to these students and we all settled down for silent reading. The next day, every student had a book. During this time, I did not allow students to do other homework — despite their promises to read at home if they could just do their biology in class or protests about not being able to read without listening to music. If a student dropped her head in her arms for a nap, I sent her out to get a drink of water; the second time it happened I threatened to mark her absent.

At the end of the third day of reading, I asked students to write about their books: What is the title? What has happened so far in it? Do you like or dislike it? Why? What is it going to take for you to finish it by the due date?

In late January I tested students on their second independent reading book. Students who had read a 500-page book the first time and students who had not finished the second book used the test period as a study hall. Again, because I had not read all of the books my students had chosen, I wrote a generic prompt:

PART 1: Due at the end of the period.
— Give the title and author of your book. Summarize what happened in it in such a way that I will understand the plot.
— Choose the most unforgettable scene, describe it fully, and tell why that scene affected you as it did.

PART 2: Due at the beginning of class tomorrow.
— Tell me in detail why you chose the book.
— Thoroughly describe your process of reading this book: When did you read, for how long? When did you finish? How did you feel as you were reading it?

The results were better this time. In first period, seventeen out of thirty-four students had read books; in second period, twenty out of thirty-five had. For the second test, some students chose new books and some finished books they had started for the previous assignment. More significant than the results on the Part 1 recall and analysis sections were the comments on Part 2 about choices and processes:

> *Craig:* I grabbed this book because I knew I could finish it fast. What can I say? I was in the mood for some cheese-ball action.
>
> *Jeannine:* I chose *The Temple of My Familiar* because I like Alice Walker.
>
> *Kandi:* My aunt told me about this book — she read it two times.

Whatever the reason for choosing a book, once students were into it, most of them finished. Students, like Tachia, who had not read the first book, finished the second one:

> I loved *The Street* because it related to the streets around where I live. It's interesting to learn about the struggle of some Black poor people trying to go somewhere in life. . . . I read the book daily when possible, usually after I had done my other homework. I finished early.

As I read these comments and listened to the discussion in my classroom, I was filled with excitement. Changes were taking place in students' knowledge about and enthusiasm for reading. Students were recommending books to each other and were asking each other for recommendations:

Tassie: If you don't read any other book this year, read *Disappearing Acts!*

Kema: Jalaine, do you know a good book for me — not one you'd like, one I'd like.

They were also asking me for books to read. "Now don't get me wrong," Kandi said one day after class, "but are there *any* Black books that aren't about slavery?" I discovered they were even asking other teachers for books: "I hope it's okay with you that I told Rebecca to read an Anne Rice," a science teacher told me one morning. "I'm a total science fiction freak and Anne Rice is my favorite."

Along with my excitement came questions: What had brought about the change in Kema? In December she had written, "I have not read my independent book like I'm supposed to. I think to have an independent book was a burden on me and it makes me feel guilty." In January she was writing, *"Mama* is so good. I got it yesterday and I can't believe I'm on page 53. This book has 260 pages so I'll be able to finish it by Wednesday because of the long weekend." Why was Nikki, a University of California –bound student, not reading? In December she had selected *Beloved* because "schools should teach more works by African American writers" and in January she chose *Mama* "because I've heard a lot about it being a quality novel and it is written by an African American woman," and yet she had finished neither book. Why was it that some students had read several independent books and some, like Nikki, had trouble finishing any?

Looking for Answers

Assuming that what happens to children early in their school careers affects them as learners, I found some insights into my students' reading habits in university research on young children. Work by Rosenholtz and Simpson (1984) suggests that a determining factor in my students' success or failure on the independent reading assignments was their self-perception. In their seminal study on the formation of ability constructions, Rosenholtz and Simpson found that children's conceptions of their intellectual ability were "socially constructed during their early school experiences" and that schools "typically 'reproduce' institutionalized ability conceptions because their 'deep structure' produces patterns of performance and performance evaluation that make it logical for children to interpret their academic abilities unidimensionally" (p. 55). Research on self-fulfilling prophecy by Weinstein (1986) stressed the cumulative effect of differential teacher treatment of students. "What begins as small differences in student skills, grows due to coverage differences and to accompanying changes in children's behavior, self-esteem, and motivation" (p. 30). In their work with upper-grade elementary school students labeled "poor readers," Brown, Palinscar, and Purcell (1986) found that students who have formulated a negative diagnosis of their ability to succeed in school display "a typical pattern of learned helplessness" and "often develop compensatory coping strategies for preserving their self-worth" — strategies that include "devaluation of academic tasks, goals, and desired outcomes, and the justification of a lack of effort" (pp. 123–124).

My own work as a classroom teacher supports the connection between students' self-perceptions about ability and their school performance. For years I have watched students assigned to remedial classes wither, while students in "gifted" classes blossom. I have observed students in low-track classes act out, drop out, misbehave, and "give up and withhold effort . . . because failure given high effort inevitably will imply low ability and generate subsequent feelings of shame" (Rosenholtz & Simpson, 1984, p. 54). Students become nonlearners as a result of teachers' and their own low expectations. Was my students' success or failure with independent reading a result of their perceptions of themselves as readers? I needed to find out, and so I asked them to write an extended definition of a *reader,* and how they defined themselves in terms of that definition.

How "readers" saw themselves:

Students who identified themselves as readers saw reading as an opportunity to learn, to escape, to experience an adventure. Andrew wrote, "A reader is someone who can pick up a book and be transported to a new place, a place where the writer is in control but the reader is free to fill in the blanks, to view the scene as he wishes to." Students who identified as readers wrote about reading constantly and widely. "A reader," reflected Sarah, in e.e. cummings's style to capture the need for eclecticism, "is someone who reads — books novels plays newspapers magazines poetry prose, fiction and non-." "Readers," students said, read everywhere — waiting in lines, on the BART (Bay Area Rapid Transit) train, in classes when they finished assigned work, late at night. Students wrote of finishing a book and starting another immediately, of reading two books at the same time, of getting lost in reading. These "readers" finished books — even books they did not like. They knew where to get books: they wrote of libraries and bookstores and people they could rely on for suggestions. They had lists of books they wanted to read. They read some books more than once. They knew when they had become readers. "When I was in fourth grade," Keesha said, "I started reading Judy Blume books. That's how I became a reader. I read one of her books and decided it was good and she had to have more books that were just as good. One book from an author is all it takes."

How "nonreaders" saw themselves:

Not surprisingly, students who identified themselves as nonreaders also saw that being a reader was a matter of action. "They read when they have to and when they don't," commented Freddie. Karen noted that "readers don't read by chapters — they just read." According to these students, readers read fast, readers read long books, readers understand what they read, readers don't quit books. Many students who labeled themselves as nonreaders wrote of a change in their lives as readers:

August: When I was in the fourth grade, I was in a class for the gifted or whatever. Our teacher read us a book called *Never Cry Wolf* which she thought was so good. This was my first taste of literature and I hated it. I didn't want to hear about some man in the freezing cold, studying some wolves. That turned me off from books.

Lan: In my freshman year, I loved all the books [my English teacher] introduced us to, especially *Jane Eyre.* But now, it seems that every time we read a book, we have to analyze it. No matter how easy or hard the book is, we have to analyze what the author is saying.

What did these students do when assigned books for school? "If the book starts out boring, then I'll just pass and hopefully they'll have a movie out on it so I can watch it," wrote Freddie. "I always put off reading it until the last minute," Sean said. "It's funny how I work it out. If I start today, I have to read 80 pages a day and if I start next week, I'll have to read 150 pages a day. I procrastinate until my pages per day ratio is at my personal maximum. Time pressure gets me motivated."

Self-designated nonreaders were adamant about being *able* to read. They saw a real difference between reading habits and reading ability. As Laura commented, "Just because you don't read book after book, doesn't mean you can't read." In fact, these students' sixth- and eighth-grade scores on the California Achievement Test supported that distinction in most cases. That is, their scores indicated that in junior high, they were reading close to, at, or above grade level. The scores of ten self-designated nonreaders, however, did reflect reading problems. One, a special education student, scored in the eighteenth percentile, two scored in the high twenties, one in the thirty-first, and the rest in the fortieth percentiles in total reading. These students defined the act of reading quite differently from their "reader" and other "nonreader" classmates. For them, reading was not a comprehension activity, but a decoding skill or a performance opportunity. Nate wrote, "My life as a reader has been hell!! Don't get me wrong I can read, but it's just I hate doing it. I seem to have a little studdering [*sic*] problem and there's nothing more embarrassing when you're reading is to studder [*sic*]."

From my reading of students' reflections on themselves as readers and on the work they did in class, I drew the following general conclusions:

1. High grades did not necessarily correspond with the students' self-designation as a reader. Among those who saw themselves as readers were students who had earned straight A's or close to straight A's and students whose grade point averages were as low as 2.0 and 1.97. Low grades and self-designation as a nonreader, however, did correlate.
2. High SAT scores did not necessarily correspond with a student's self-designation as reader. Some students with combined SAT scores as low as 470 saw themselves as readers and others with scores as high as 1400 labeled themselves non-readers.
3. Among high-achieving students, both readers and nonreaders, no relationship existed between self-perception and performance on the independent reading assignments. Whatever label they gave themselves, high-achievers completed the independent reading. Among low-achieving students, however, a relationship did exist. That is, low-achievers who labeled themselves as nonreaders did not do the reading. The only exception to this self-perception/performance association was a group of five low-achievers who said they were readers but did not finish one independent book. These students, all young women, typically wrote statements about the place of reading in their lives using language that suggested that sounding like a reader and knowing the names of writers and works were as important as actually doing the reading. Alice, for example, declared, "I go through stages where I live, breathe, eat, and sleep with a book in my hand." Jalaine, a high-achiever, was the only example of a deflation rather than an inflation of self-perception: she identified herself as a nonreader, when a

good deal of evidence pointed to the contrary. Jalaine wrote that although she reads, she does not see herself as a reader because "I can't really get into books until I read a really good one. Once I do, I hunt for as many books by that author as I can. If I can't find any, I listen to what other people (mostly college students) are saying about books they're reading and then I go read those. . . . If I like a book, I read until I'm done with the entire book." The fact that she had so many books that she liked highlighted a seeming contradiction in her refusal to identify herself as a reader. Among her favorites: *I Know Why the Caged Bird Sings, The Color Purple, The Joy Luck Club, Wuthering Heights, Crime and Punishment.* When interviewed about her seeming self-mislabeling, Jalaine grew adamant. "No, I am not a reader. I read but I am not a reader. You want me to change what I wrote and I don't want to. I AM NOT A READER!" Her insistence on differentiating between reading a lot and being a reader intrigued me. What was she telling me that I couldn't hear?

4. School labels related to reading ability — "remedial," "average," and "fast" — did not necessarily affect the labels students used for themselves. While some students attributed their being nonreaders to school, the majority of the self-designated nonreaders did not blame school. Clifton stated, "There are two things that make me the reader I am: procrastination and laziness. . . . Reading is a bit like having a foreign accent. If you don't use it, you lose it."

In fact, several students saw themselves as readers despite a school label to the contrary. Frank identified himself as a reader, even though "in elementary and junior high I always, I mean *always,* scored below average in reading" and was "*always* assigned to below average reading groups and English classes." Rahima adamantly declared herself a reader despite being labeled a remedial student in seventh grade. "When I was in fourth grade, I read a lot and they wanted to skip me up to fifth grade but my mom didn't want me to do that. In seventh grade they put me in a dumb class, a reading class, with kids who couldn't read. I kept telling them I was in the wrong class, but they didn't believe me. So I just sat and read by myself. Then one day I got into a fight and when the principal called me in to suspend me, she checked my records. She asked me why was I in that reading class and I *told* her I had told them it was a mistake. The next day they moved me to the right class."

Another category — a "somewhat" reader:

While most students designated themselves as readers or nonreaders, several students were not comfortable with either label. "I think I am almost a reader," wrote Rebecca. "It wasn't until this year that I realized I liked reading and that reading doesn't have to be a task — it can be fun." Antoinette noted, "I believe I am becoming a reader. I am a beginning reader. I am beginning to read books on my own with pleasure." "I am somewhat of a reader," said Rob.

As I studied what these students had to say about readers and reading, I saw that they were indeed in between the two categories of reader and nonreader. This group of students had a hard time finding books, they procrastinated about starting books, and they often chose to watch TV rather than read, but once they got into a book, they read it. They also read newspapers and periodicals regularly and saw reading as valuable. "I know that if I was encouraged to read," Patty said, "I would read more."

Creating Readers: Was the Answer a New Curriculum?

As helpful as the research and student reflections were, they did not answer my question about how to transform students into readers. I needed to look further. I decided to focus on my second-period English class, a broad mix of students who had not elected to take Advanced Placement (AP) English Literature or AP English Language and Composition, or who had not completed the required summer work for those classes. Of the thirty-five enrolled in my second-period class, eight were labeled "certified gifted" and three were labeled "special ed." Students' academic interests and achievement levels varied widely: there were students who were taking calculus and those who had never taken algebra; students who were in French V and students assigned to social studies classes for English-as-a-Second-Language learners; students who were headed to UC Berkeley and students taking night classes to make up for lost credits so they could graduate with their class in June. Grade point averages ranged from 3.84 to 1.06. Two of the students cut class almost daily, and two others were absent at least once or twice a week. The twenty-three females and twelve males in the class represented almost all of the major racial and ethnic groups at our school, and students were from both the most affluent and poorest parts of our school district.

I chose this class for a variety of reasons. First, it included six "somewhat" readers, a group that intrigued me. What was it that held them back, made them tentative? What would it take for them to become real readers, students who would choose to read on their own for pleasure and knowledge? Second, of my four classes of seniors, second period had the widest range of students in terms of academic achievement. What I learned from studying them might help me in other classes and in my advocacy to end tracking schoolwide. And finally, unlike my AP English Language and Composition class, where the curriculum almost demanded I spend the third quarter preparing students for the national AP examination, the curriculum in English 4 was open. We had completed our school district's required readings and had practiced writing the required discourse modes. I was free to experiment, free to try out my belief about the role written reflection might play as a tool to affect students' perceptions of themselves as learners.

I decided to make independent reading the focus of the second semester and then to arrange all other reading and writing activities around it. Since many "readers" had expressed pleasure in reading books by and about people who shared their race or ethnicity, I thought that "somewhat" readers and "nonreaders" might enjoy these writers too. The first day of the third quarter, I gave out a new independent reading assignment: read a book written by or about someone in an ethnic or racial group with which you identify. I gave students three days to find a book and then allowed them two days for in-class silent reading.

My new curriculum plan called for alternating whole-class activities with independent reading activities. When students were working on an independent book, homework assignments were mostly limited to that book; I did not ask them to read two novels at the same time or ask them to write at home the essay forms we studied in class. In addition to studying plays and short stories, we spent a good deal of time working on argumentation through discussing current political events — the Rodney King verdict, the national election, the family values issue — and reading and writing argumentative essays on a wide range of topics. We also watched and discussed films, practiced a variety of writing activities — scholarship essays, letters to next year's seniors, and personal credos — and prepared a piece for the end of the year literary magazine. Along with these activities, I regularly asked students to tell me in writing about their independent reading book. This practice kept me informed of their progress and encouraged them to continue reading at a steady pace. When I felt that students were falling behind, I talked with them about the importance of keeping up with the assignment, helped them get connected to the book, or found them a different book. Occasionally I called parents to enlist their support.

For the second independent reading assignment of the quarter, I asked students to choose a book written by or about someone from a racial or ethnic group of which they were not a member. Again, I allowed a few days of in-class silent reading for them to get into the book, and I gave homework assignments related to the independent reading.

At the end of the third quarter, I had mixed feelings about the results of the independent reading assignments. I was heartened by all the book talk I was hearing in the room and delighted with the quality of the books students were reading: *Mama, Animal Dreams, Tracks, Praisesong for the Widow, The Joy Luck Club, Family, Migrant Souls, Tar Baby, Winter in the Blood, Spring Moon, Vampire Lestat, Macho, Gather Together in My Name, Jasmine, Lucy, Ceremony, Yellow Raft in Blue Water, How the Garcia Girls Lost Their Accents, Slave Girl, You Can't Keep a Good Woman Down, Cider House Rules, Iron and Silk, Manchild in the Promised Land, Black Elk Speaks.* Students' eclectic tastes moved me to ease my rule about novels written in the last ten years. I made exceptions easily, allowing students to read older books, books of short stories, biographies, and nonfiction works. Reading was what mattered, not genre or publication date. Dimming my excitement, however, was the worry that for all of my encouragement and allowances, not all students were reading. Nineteen students finished the first book, eighteen the second. I was particularly concerned about the six students who had read neither book. What would motivate them?

Creating Readers: The Emergence of Talk as an Answer

The first day of the fourth quarter was unusual. About one-third of the students in second period were absent, out of class to set up for a school carnival. Rather than begin a new lesson, I told students they could use the period as a study hall. But as I looked around at who was present, it occurred to me that there were several students who had done all of the independent reading assignments. Why not use the period to interview them? I escorted them into a small workroom adjacent to my classroom and said I wanted them to talk about themselves as readers — their history as readers, their process of reading, and whatever else that came up about reading. Because I did not want to lead or impede their discussion, once I got them started talking, I left them alone — with the tape recorder on. When I returned forty minutes later, they were involved in a lively sharing of most loved and most hated books. In the last few minutes of their discussion, I asked them for ideas about where we needed to go during the rest of the year with independent reading. They wanted to read books that they hadn't read in high school, "missed classics" that they thought would be expected of them as college freshmen. *And* they wanted to discuss the books. I laughed when I heard this — why hadn't I thought of adding "talk" to the independent reading project? Talk had been the main focus of the books we had studied as a class, and I had forgotten its importance when I moved to independent reading.

That night, as I listened to the tape, I was moved by my students' passion and the breadth of their reading:

Jalaine: When I was in tenth grade, I read this book called *Wuthering Heights*. And at first I would've never . . . just, just, picked that book up. But it was — I don't know — it was weird. Because the teacher was like "Well, read it and you'll understand it." And I did. And I thought that was kind of neat because, you know, I wouldn't never just read it myself . . . because it was . . . like a fifteenth century book.

Phillipa: I always wanted to read that book.

Jalaine: It was, it was hecka good, it was . . .

Phillipa: It's a love story, isn't it?

Jalaine: Yeah, yeah, and when you pick it up and stuff you wouldn't think it was good. And there's scandal in there and . . .

Phillipa: It's not filled with that Shakespeare stuff?

Jalaine: No, it's not really a lot of Shakespearean language. It's just — at times it will be . . . but it's hecka good.

Phillipa: I'm about to read it then. What's it called?

Jalaine: Wuthering Heights. I forgot who wrote it, though, but she has a sister.

David: Brontë.

Jalaine: Brontë! Brontë! And she has a sister who writes books, too, and . . . uh . . . I think my tenth-grade English teacher . . . Mr. Martin . . .

Antoinette: I remember him.

Jalaine: The one who used to ride a bike all the time . . .

Phillipa: Yeah, with a backpack.

Jalaine: Yeah, introduced us to them. The Brontë sisters — and that was when I started really reading a whole lot of stuff. Now I even read science fiction books.

They talked about becoming readers:

Antoinette: It was last year when I got into Black literature and started reading books that I enjoyed. Because at first I didn't think I was a reader because the books we read, I couldn't . . . relate to things and it was . . . I don't know . . . but after I started reading books that I liked . . . I could . . . I went back to read those same books and I could read them with an open mind. I didn't think I was [a reader] because I didn't think I was getting the point that everyone else was and because I felt I was reading books just for the class — which I was — but now I read things on my own, instead of just for the class.

Rob: I haven't been a reader all that long. A couple of years ago — even last year — I wasn't. I wasn't really. I couldn't be called a reader. I didn't read the books really. I just scammed through.

Antoinette: Aren't you afraid to take the test though?

Jennifer: What happened when the teacher picked the wrong place — the part you scammed through?

Rob: Well, you know, see, you've just got to play it off. See, well, I'd just read a little bit of it. I'd always be . . . the night before the test, I'd always be somewhere around page 50 of the book so I'd know some of the characters, you know. You know, I could wing it through because a lot of the time the books were old books that I already knew something about. I just didn't read 'em. I was on the wrong side of the tracks. But, but . . .

Jalaine: What changed you over then?

Rob: I really, I really can't say. I came into this class and I think I just had a different mentality, a mentality of . . .

Antoinette: Because we're *seniors*. [Laughter]

Rob: Something — I wanted, you know, I wanted to work hard and uh, uh, I guess, uh, I just wanted to . . . I knew I could do it. I just didn't 'cause I was being lazy. So I said, "this is, like, the time to just go all out" and I s'pose . . . I mean, I've read all the books in the class and took all the tests and, uh, so I'm just now becoming a reader, really. I s'pose. But see, it's still different, because I might watch — if given the choice, you know, I might still watch the news instead of reading the newspaper or something.

They talked of books — their favorites, *Catcher in the Rye, Beloved, Cider House Rules, The Bluest Eye;* books they wanted to read or reread, *1984, Animal Farm, Crime and Punishment, Hamlet* ("Is that the 'to be or not to be' one?"); books they had not understood, *Woman Warrior, Crime and Punishment, The Joy Luck Club.*

Jennifer: Another hard book is *Beloved.*

Jalaine: That's weird. Because I picked that up and read it straight through. I don't know. It was good — to me. I had read other Toni Morrison books and I kind of understood her style. I had read *The Bluest Eye* and then I read something else, I can't remember . . .

Phillipa: Sula?

Jalaine: Yeah, *Sula.* And then I said, "Well, I'm going to read *Beloved* now." It was different, but it was the same. She, like, used her style — the normal style that she did in the other two books — but she added stuff, like with the baby character, the ghost spirit — whatever you want to call it. That was different. You could understand why. I liked the book myself. And then I was listening to an interview she did on TV with that guy on Channel 9 [Bill Moyers on PBS] and she was kind of explaining it and I was, like, "Yeah, that's true, that's true." You know, it was, to me, it was, *Beloved* was easy to read. And I read it in like in a weekend. I read it while I was eatin' dinner and in the tub. All weekend.

They asked each other questions: Can you read anywhere? Can you read a book in one night? What do you do when a book starts out boring?

They talked about the "gaps" they saw in their reading education:

Phillipa: When I was in ninth grade we had this crazy teacher and we didn't get to read much. The lady was crazy! Miss _____. Remember her? Remember her? She was crazy. The only book I remember reading was *Animal Farm*. And I feel like I've missed out on a lot of ninth-grade reading — that everyone else, that ninth-grade classes read, that I still didn't get to read. I still haven't read *Mice and Men*. There was another book I wanted to read and I haven't read it.

[*Here I returned to the room and, because I couldn't resist, entered the discussion.*]

Cone: So, sometimes teachers don't hit on books you think you should read because . . . they're a part of the "conversation"? Like everyone has read *Of Mice and Men* so you should read it? But sometimes students don't want to read those books — the books that you're "supposed" to read.

Jennifer: But even though you don't want to read them, you need to be exposed to them, or you feel left out. . . . I mean, like she [Phillipa] says — she might not like *Mice and Men* but now she's regretting not having read it because she can't be part of the conversation. And she feels neglected. Even if you don't like a book at least it helps to be exposed to it and make the choice from there, you know, instead of not knowing whether you would have liked it or not.

As I listened, I also discovered the reason Jalaine had labeled herself a nonreader. "I signed up for AP," Jalaine began. "I read the first book. I read it to the best of my ability. So my [required summer] paper on this book was like fifteen pages. I sent it to Ms. Cone's house and about a week later I got this postcard saying, 'You did not read this book thoroughly. Pleeeeassee rewrite the summary.' I said, 'Oh, no. I spent fifteen dollars for this book and she's telling me to read it and write again — oh, no, I'm not.' I said, 'I'm not reading it over again.' And, um, I just got really discouraged when she said I didn't read it. I read it and she said I didn't read it." Reflecting on Jalaine's comments, it's little wonder that when I asked her to label herself, she wrote "nonreader": my rejection of her paper was a rejection of her as a reader.

The next day in class I suggested the "missed classic" idea for their next book. I said it was fine with me if they didn't all want to read the same book, but that whichever book they chose, they needed to read it well enough to discuss it in a group. The assignment that night was to think of a book they had always wanted to read, bring their suggestion to class the next day, and persuade a group of classmates to read it with them and discuss it. The titles they came back with were revealing. No one proposed *Jane Eyre, Animal Farm,* or *Brave New World* — not even the students who had suggested on the tape that they wanted to "fill in the gaps" in their reading history. They did not suggest books on the basis of what might impress a college. They wanted to read more current literature: *Disappearing Acts, Slaughterhouse 5, Her, The Color Purple, Speaker for the Dead, The Autobiography of Malcolm X.* Students made their choice and agreed to get a copy of the book they had selected. Four days later they met with their group leader (the student who had suggested the book) to decide how they wanted to begin the reading. The next two days in class, students met in their groups — in the classroom or in an adjacent empty classroom — either to read aloud or silently.

I joined the science fiction group, mainly to show the leader of that group that I wasn't as narrow-minded about science fiction as he had accused me of being. As I read the book, I found myself procrastinating, falling asleep, resisting rereading parts I was confused about, hating what I judged as silly pseudo-scientific language, disliking the characters, not caring about the action. I was irritated with myself for choosing the book and wished that I could find an audiotape of the book to listen to on my drive to school so that I didn't have to waste reading time on it. When I realized what was happening to me, I laughed out loud: my resistance to a book I did not want to read had turned me into a Freddie, a Karen, an August. I had taken on the characteristics of a nonreader.

The date for the book discussion arrived, and I was filled with apprehension, not for the students, but for me. Not because I hadn't finished my book — the achiever in me had pushed me through it — but because two visitors were coming. Carol Tateishi, director of the Bay Area Writing Project, University of California at Berkeley, and Richard Sterling, director of the Institute for Literacy Studies, Lehman College, City University of New York, wanted to observe the class as part of their study of the work of teacher researchers. The source of my apprehension was the largest independent reading group, the students reading *Disappearing Acts.* The day before, the leader of the group, Keesha, had told me that she and two other strong discussants in the group were going to miss the next day because of a field trip.

"What about the discussion?" I asked them. "Who's going to lead it?"

"Clifton says he'll do it," they told me.

My heart sank. Clifton has not finished one book all year.

"Clifton," I moaned. "Isn't there anybody else?"

"Don't worry," they reassured me, "he's reading the book."

When class began the next day, we moved into our discussion groups. Tateishi joined the *Malcolm X* group, Sterling went to Clifton's group, I went to my group. Occasionally, I looked around: all was going well. Every group was involved in animated talk. Clifton's group seemed the most excited. I relaxed.

At lunch I met with the visitors who were full of praise for the students' choice of books and the quality of their talk. When I shared my fears about Clifton's leading the group, Sterling assured me that Clifton had met the challenge. He knew the book, he was engaged with the characters, and he insisted that everyone participate in the discussion. When one girl tried to get out of answering by saying she felt the same as the last student who had spoken, Clifton said, "You know you can't get away with that in here — what do *you* think?"

For their last book, I asked students to read *Walkabout,* by James V. Marshall. The book, a story of racial and cultural misunderstanding and tragedy, seemed a fitting final project after our reading of books from the many cultural, ethnic, and racial groups in our class. This time I allowed no in-class reading and gave students a deadline of one week to finish the book. I wanted to give them practice in reading a book on their own in a short amount of time and I wanted to see what they would do with a book of my choosing. Twenty-nine out of thirty-five read the book.

Instead of a final examination, I asked second-period students to do a series of writings based on the reading they had done over the course of the year. I was particularly interested in their views about the place of independent reading in a high school curriculum and what suggestions they had for me that would improve my teaching. Students who had not done the independent reading — any or all of it — did not want the independent assignments. The great majority of students, however, found real value in it. Amaka wrote, "Independent reading should be a requirement for each grade level in high school." "If I were a teacher, I would make it mandatory to read at least three independent books a semester to pass my class," commented Phillipa. And

Jalaine observed, "Independent reading should be a class in itself. It gets you motivated to read."

Among their suggestions for the next year:

Keesha: Let the class have more of their own picks on books they want to read and less of the requirements. Every student cannot get into Shakespeare's thou's and art's and thee's. Why should we have to be required to know them? Less requirements will make a lot of difference.

Angel: I think that independent reading should divide equally with chosen reading — meaning, we should read independently as much as we read in school. The reading we did this year in and out of class let me know that I am a diverse reader, that I can read many different styles of literature and like them.

Jenna: Add Stephen King.

Wilson: Let students read nonfiction.

David: I hereby suggest to English teachers that they drop the hatred they have for science fiction. The prejudice I see of the medium of science fiction is annoying.

Creating Readers by Creating Community: "C'mon, Girl, You Got to Read It"

By the end of the year, most students in second period wrote about positive changes in their perceptions of themselves as readers. Kema's written reflections illustrate the kind of change that took place:

September 16th: The only book I have read on my own was *Daddy Cool* by Donald Gaines and *Heart of a Woman* by M. Angelou. . . . When and if I have an assignment to read a book, I do all my other homework first because I know if I pick that book up I would get restless especially if I don't want to do it. I know it's sad, but that how I feel.

January 27th: No! I do not see myself as a reader because I'm very picky about what I read. . . . I don't consider myself a reader especially in this class where I'm compared against students who have been on honor roll all of their lives. I would never take the chance to read or do any other things they do. Why? because that's how it is. [I chose the last book] because it is written by a female which happens to be black. She's telling my story. How I feel inside. What I see in life. What I'm going to get out of life. Terry McMillan is a powerful writer.

February 24th: Most of the books I have read in the past were fairy tales. I wanted to read something that I can apply to my life that might help me in the future — especially if it is by an African American writer. I stated [at the beginning of the year] that there is not a lot of them out there but boy was I wrong. At first I hated this book assignment. Now I'm getting used to it. I'm finding me in each one of the books I read. I don't like how things end sometimes but that's part of life. I read when I have time. Like when I'm not working or not at school. With these last two books I've read, I hate to put them down because they didn't bore me. I just had other things to do.

April 9th: I don't consider myself a reader yet. I'm getting there though. It's probably because I couldn't find something to read written by a true black woman until I
read books by Terry McMillan. That's when I found myself trying to read more and
more. . . . Until this year I hated reading with a passion until I learned how to pick
out books that interested me.

May 24th: I didn't think I'd make it with *Walkabout.* I couldn't get into that book.
Keesha kept telling me, "C'mon, girl, you got to read it — it's good." But I kept
asking, "Why I can't see how good it is?" But then I got to the part where the boy
died and it was good — just like Keesha said. . . . I still feel intimidated with some
kids in here — kids like Keesha and Jalaine and David, especially David. He is
never without a book. But I read all my books this year, every one of them. The
other day Keesha and me were at the mall and we saw this bookstore and we
thought we saw you in there. Keesha said, "There's Joan, let's go in." But it wasn't
you. We saw Toni's new book and Keesha want to buy it but it's too expensive so
she'll wait 'til it comes out in paperback.

What had brought about the change so clearly in Kema and in other students' perception of themselves as readers? As I made sense of what had happened over the year,
I saw that it was not the freedom to choose books, not the independent reading assignments themselves, not the students' reflections on themselves as readers that had
brought about the change. It was the combination of all those things — choice, assignments, reflections — in a community of readers that had brought about the
change. The secret was creating the community in which students could chose books,
read them, talk about them, and encourage each other to read.

I realize now that creating that community had started early in the year with my
belief in talk as a way to create an environment where students of all ability levels
could succeed, something I had worked on with AP students but had experienced
only limited success with in other classes (Cone, 1992). From the first book we read
in second period, I stressed the need for students to assist each other in making meaning together. We started with *Sula.* The first day, Melissa asked, "What's up with
Shaddrack — are his fingers really growing or is he freaking out?" She asked what
other students were afraid to ask and thereby set an example for them. As we made
our way through books, students asked questions of each other, cleared up confusions, defended their analysis, reinterpreted the text with each other — and in doing
so, taught each other how to read and analyze literature. "Did Sula plan to kill
Chicken Little?" "That's not right — Sula doing that with Jude — didn't she know it
would hurt Nel? Why'd she come back in the first place?" "What did it mean when it
said at the end that it was Sula Nel missed and not Jude?" And so it went — with novels like *Woman Warrior* and *One Flew over the Cuckoo's Nest* and short stories like "The
Tree" and "The Handsomest Drowned Man in the World." The emphasis was always
on asking questions, looking back at the text for substantiation, trying out interpretations, coming to agreement or living with disagreement. Students were creating
meaning together and teaching each other. And always, it was writing begetting talk
and talk begetting understanding.

On the second day of our study of *Othello,* for example, I asked students to write
down everything they knew about the characters from Act I. Phillipa said she knew
nothing. "Then write about what you don't know," I told her, "and then we'll talk."
She wrote:

I know I hate Shakespeare. I know I don't understand this play. I know nothing about this stupid play. And I hate it.

Okay, so I know there's this guy named Othello who is a famous soldier and he fell in love with this young girl. Another guy's in love with her, too. I forgot his name. Her name is Desdemona and she eloped with Othello. And there's this other guy who is jealous of Othello and mad at him. He works for Othello, I think. I can't remember why he's mad. Anyway this guy is setting out to destroy Othello. Who is black but Desdemona's dad, who is white, doesn't like him because he's black.

In fact, Phillipa knew a good deal about the play, which she discovered in the course of writing. When she shared that writing with her classmates, they learned from her and she learned from them. They explained the conflict between Iago and Othello, and they filled in the gaps of her understanding just as she had filled in gaps for them. Once they had gotten the first act straight, they could move to the second act. With each piece of literature, students wrote about what they knew and didn't know and then talked about it in a way that cleared up confusion and deepened understanding. With each piece students learned that saying they were confused wasn't going to get them off the hook. "What is confusing?" I'd ask. "What don't you understand?" "If you could ask a question of your classmates, what would you ask?" Gradually they came to see that asking questions was not a sign of stupidity, that getting lost in a book did not mean they had to reread or discard it or cut class until the book was finished, and that when students taught each other, they often explained material in a more accessible way than when teachers explained it. When the time came for the independent reading project, a sense of community had been established along with a sophisticated model for how to read a book.

The extent of our sense of community as readers is reflected in our connection to writer Terry McMillan. Early in the year, Tassie lent me *Disappearing Acts.* "You have *got* to read this. My sister-in-law gave it to me last Friday and I finished it this weekend. Now I'm reading her first book. Don't be shocked by the language." When I finished the book and gave it back to Tassie, she lent me *Mama.* Other girls in first and second period heard of the books, and began reading and recommending them. I bought copies to lend. Gradually a McMillan fan club developed. Kandi wrote, "*Disappearing Acts.* Everywhere I go I hear people talking about that book. I'll read it again right after my aunt is finished with it. It was so good I just gave it to her and told her to read it and that she'll love it. Sure enough she's in the middle of it and can't put it down. Just last week in my church a woman was reading the book (not in church, at choir practice). She told me that they are going to make a movie out of it. I can't wait to see it." After so much talk about McMillan's work, little wonder that *Disappearing Acts* was one of the books chosen as a group discussion book.

A few days after Clifton had led the discussion on the book, a notice came out in the newspaper advertising McMillan's new book, *Waiting to Exhale,* and a reading by her at a San Francisco bookstore. I told my students I planned to go to the event and said I was going to write a note inviting McMillan to visit our class. "You shouldn't write," Clifton said, "we should." And so they did; they wrote notes and letters to tell her of their admiration. Clifton did not have enough time in class to finish his letter, so he brought it to me at the end of the day, two pages long: "Truthfully I planned to dog-out your book just as I've done everyone else's. I just don't know what happened. As I started to read your book (I do start all the books I'm supposed to read) I found myself unable to leave it alone or put it down. It was almost as if I was addicted to this book. *Disappearing Acts* not only moved me but it became a part of me. Me, a person who doesn't by a long shot consider himself a reader knocked out your masterpiece of writing in less than seven days. I have now started on the book prior to *Disappearing Acts, Mama*." His postscript: "Thank you for changing my life. It was a change well needed."

I went to the reading with one of my second-period students and gave McMillan the packet of letters and my classroom phone number. The next morning, at 9 o'clock, she called. "I'd love to visit your class. I've got to meet Clifton." As it worked out, McMillan could not come — she was leaving the next day on her book tour and would not arrive back in the Bay Area until the day before graduation, too late to visit the class. The fact that she had wanted to visit, however, impressed my students. An author was interested in them.

A postscript to the independent reading assignment came with a visit from Kema in October 1992. She came to visit on Back-to-School Night to tell me of the books she is reading in community college. "I'm waiting for *Waiting to Exhale* to come out in paperback." I told her I'd lend her my copy of it — she could send her younger sister by the next day to pick it up. A month later I got the book back with the following note:

Mrs. Cone,

Thank you for sharing yet another piece of important literature with Kema, Keesha, and I.

Terry McMillan is really a gifted author and we all shared the book with our mothers. We even had a discussion group. I can't thank you enough.

Love,

Your former students,

Jalaine
Kema
Keesha

Creating Students as Readers: Principles for Change

By the end of a year of asking students to write and reflect, I had gotten to know my students as readers — their reading tastes, habits, problems — in a way I had never known them before, and I had come to know high school reading instruction in a way that would dramatically change the way I teach. I reached the following conclusions:

1. High schools can create readers.

In their study, "Poor Readers: Teach, Don't Label," Brown, Palinscar, and Purcell (1986) argue that the "effects of inadequate early experiences with the types of knowledge that clarify, elaborate, and extend knowledge can be overcome by providing the missing experience with explicit intervention" (p. 138). My study of senior English students corroborates those findings. Once students learned how to summarize, formulate questions about what they were reading, and discuss texts in an environment that encouraged collaborative meaning-making, they gained confidence as readers.

Beyond classroom instruction, other things also encouraged students as readers. Primary among these was the personal connection teachers made with individual students — finding a "match" between writers and students or subject matter and students. Jalaine wrote, "When I was in Black lit, I started reading a whole bunch of different stuff because that's the kind of teacher Mr. Greene is. He was like, 'Read Malcolm X,' *The Autobiography of Malcolm X,* and then 'Read somebody else's opinion of the book' and stuff like that. That happened in the tenth grade and then during that year I had Ms. Gocker and I started reading poetry."

The use of literature related to students' lives is also an important element in encouraging students to become readers. Teachers can make these connections by helping students see themselves in books, by choosing books that mirror their experience, and by helping them see the relevance of other people's stories to their own:

> *Jennifer:* As a child, I never found reading difficult, it just wasn't enjoyable. We were always forced to go the library, pick out our favorite book, take it home, and that's all I'd do. Pick out a book, take it home, and return it when it was due. I never found reading could be an enjoyable experience because it was never taught to be fun or interesting, just a lot of words on several pieces of paper. Then as I grew older and entered junior high school, we were assigned books and given more pages to read. This was also not enjoyable because to me it was hard, painful work. Each day we would be assigned a certain number of pages to read, then the following day we would be tested. In my opinion this was not an encouraging or accurate way to get students, like me, to read because there were always other ways of getting the answer to the test. Then finally as I entered high school, reading slowly became more enjoyable. Not because we were forced to read thousands of pages but just because we were being taught how to read and how to make meaning out of what we were reading. I no longer felt inferior to the texts. One of my most favorite books is *Black Boy.* It was my understanding of his triumphs and struggles through life that made the book enjoyable. Finally I was reading something that I felt like I could relate to and most of all understand.

2. High school literature programs need to include independent reading as an integral part of the curriculum.

With very few exceptions, the students in my second-period class who labeled themselves "nonreaders" had not been expected to read independently or encouraged by teachers to develop the habit of independent reading. The literature they had previously studied was read in class — mostly aloud — with short reading assignments for homework. When lengthy independent reading was assigned, it was usually for extra credit, an inducement that had little attraction for most of them.

Just as students who were taught in early elementary grades that reading was comprehension had an advantage over students taught that reading was decoding (Brown, Palinscar, & Purcell, 1986), students who were expected to read independently in high school had an advantage over those who were not expected to read on their own. Students who were assigned independent reading matured as readers. Again, Jennifer comments: "I've learned to speed read and I know for a fact it will help me in college. When

I used to read, I would examine every book, word for word for meaning. Now I know how to scan paragraphs and make meaning out of them — although I must admit that sometimes I reread parts to make sense. Now that I have learned to read faster, reading has become more enjoyable for me because it doesn't take me so loooonnnnngggg."

Asking students to read independently was not new to me. For years I had assigned "outside books." I took my students to the library, helped them find books, set a deadline for the book to be finished, and tested them with some kind of writing task. But independent reading was not an important part of my curriculum, mainly because readers read the books, and nonreaders did not — students who needed no motivation to read got A's, the rest got F's. Since independent reading was not a successful activity, I had (except for AP students) nearly discarded it in favor of having all students read the same book together according to a set schedule. That was not such a bad option: I chose books carefully, making sure I mixed complex works and not-so-complex ones to address the reading levels of my students, selected books that reflected the racial and ethnic background of my students, and brought in complementary films, essays, and short stories.

My study of the reading habits of students pointed out what was wrong with my avoidance of independent reading for all students: the longer I chose the books and assigned the pages, the more I reinforced my students' reading dependence on me, the teacher. More importantly, in not setting aside time for independent reading, I was not encouraging students to practice the comprehension skills they were learning in class, skills that I was carefully scaffolding with discussions and writing assignments. When I did not ask students to use those skills on their own, I was, in effect, implying that they either could not apply the skills on their own or they did not need to read independently — both messages that potentially reinforced their negative self-perceptions as learners.

3. High school literature programs need to provide an opportunity for students to choose texts.

For five students in second period, choice made no difference: with or without the right to choose a book on their own, they did not read. As Nina explained, "I didn't really choose not to read a book. I just never got around to reading one. I really don't know what your [*sic*] looking for in a book for us to read. I would like to read one by a Hispanic author, but I have no idea how to really find one. I know if I tried I could but I really didn't." For a few others — readers, nonreaders, somewhat-readers — choice was of little consequence. "Actually I preferred having no choice at all. I read what I'm assigned. I'd much rather read books that were already chosen. For the next year, less choice," wrote Sam. But most students saw choice as essential in getting students to read. Rebecca was enthusiastic: "Reading in class and out of class this year has let me explore a part of my world I never knew. It has given me a great sense of pride and accomplishment. I never really read until this year and I like it. I've read all the books except the last independent one. I've read more books this year than in my whole life put together. I've read from mysteries to vampire books to romances — a wide variety. I know now I can develop a good habit, reading. I can do it!"

For some students, choice provided the opportunity to pursue an interest in a specific genre, author, or issue. Jennifer was one of these students: "I hate to limit myself right now, but I'm going through a phase. An Alice Walker phase. All the books that I have read have been from Black writers because I find those interesting and I like to see how each writer is different." And Angel explained her preference: "I am really into reading books that involve a struggle of some type. Sometimes it makes me sad to read these kinds of books, but at the same time I can't keep my hands away from them."

For others, choice built confidence. "After I finish a book," wrote Kandi, "I feel as if I'm a whole different person. I don't know how to explain it, but I feel powerful, like I'm getting smarter or something." "When I didn't have to read the same thing as the person in front of me, I didn't have to worry about whether or not I got behind in the assigned reading. I took a chance with reading *House of Spirits* because it was really long and political which intimidated me a little. But I read it and I enjoyed it," Tassie wrote.

Advocating that students be given a choice of literature does not imply that books traditionally taught as part of the canon should be eliminated. Readers, somewhat-readers, and nonreaders alike often chose traditionally taught books as well as other, more contemporary, stories as their favorites. Common favorites included the following: *Grapes of Wrath, The Great Gatsby, One Flew over the Cuckoo's Nest, Where the Red Fern Grows, Their Eyes Were Watching God, Lord of the Flies, Cider House Rules, The Autobiography of Malcolm X, 1984, Catcher in the Rye, Sula, Black Boy, Disappearing Acts, The Color Purple.* Most students saw a need to balance teacher-selected books and student-selected books. Angel summed up her feelings: "I think it was a good idea [to have a choice] because we got to read books that the teacher liked and felt we should read, plus what we liked. In class we read books like *Sula, Woman Warrior, Othello, Pygmalion,* and *A Doll's House,* all of which were pretty good reading but honestly speaking, I wouldn't have picked those books up at the library. But I'm glad we read them."

4. Literature teachers need to make talk an essential part of reading.

Besides assisting students with understanding sophisticated text, talk inspired by writing can create a classroom atmosphere in which the most and least able reader can collaborate in making meaning and can learn from each other by sharing their insights, experiences, questions, and interpretations:

> *Phillipa:* I don't think I could read [*Romeo and Juliet*] by myself because I don't like Shakespeare and . . . and it's easier when you do in class because you can talk about it and . . . Like a person like Shakespeare — you can understand it better if, you know, if you talk about it.
>
> *Jennifer:* And make it interesting like when we read *Othello.*
>
> *Jalaine:* You know how she'd [the teacher] say like, "Othello, what's up with you?" And, "Cassio, what's up with you?"
>
> *Phillipa:* Really, really. I wouldn't have understood at all if we didn't review.
>
> *Jennifer:* She'd say, "Desdemona, what happened?" and I'd go like "Uh, uh," and Jalaine'd say, "Remember — " then something would trigger in my mind and I'd say, "Oh, okay," and I could go on and expand from there. But just off the bat if she'd say, "Here's a test," everyone would be going, "What's number one?"

Creating Readers:
Inviting Everyone into the Conversation

Rob wrote at the end of the year about his transformation into a reader, "I now consider myself a reader. Before I didn't read books. I did not consider myself a reader. But I've read every book assigned this year, class book and independent reading book. After I finished my last book I saw a book lying on my shelf. *A Summer Life* by Gary Soto. I don't know how it got there or who put it there but I picked it up and I began reading it. I began reading a book for no ulterior motive. I can't remember the last time I did that. I wanted to read for no one but myself, my own quest for further knowledge, my own enjoyment. I am a reader and I owe it all to this class. I've unlocked a chest full of hidden desire and emotion toward reading that I didn't know was there. Who knew?"

As successful as Rob's final reflection made me feel, I knew that for every Rob and Kema there were also Cliftons and Amakas graduating from high school, just beginning to see themselves as readers, as well as Nikkis and Nates who were leaving high school not having read a single book on their own. And that continues to sadden and concern me.

The issue of reading instruction, like most pedagogical issues, is a political one. Who are the students taught early on that reading is meaning-making, and who are the students taught that reading is decoding? Which students are asked to read on their own and which are not given independent reading assignments? What are the consequences when an education system invites one group of students to see themselves as independent thinkers and another to remain dependent on teacher instruction and teacher motivation?

If teachers intend for students to leave school as readers — to say nothing of leaving with positive perceptions of themselves as learners — then teachers must make dramatic changes in reading and literature instruction in ways that assist students in reading thoroughly and thoughtfully, encourage them to read on their own, and help them to develop the habit of reading.

At the end of the school year, Jennifer asked, "Ms. Cone, do you teach ninth graders the same as us?"

I replied, "After this year, yes."

References

Brown, A. L., Palinscar, A. S., & Purcell, L. (1986). Poor readers: Teach, don't label. In U. Neisser (Ed.), *School achievement of minority children: New perspectives* (pp. 105–143). Hillsdale, NJ: Lawrence Erlbaum.

Cone, J. K. (1992). Untracking AP English: Creating opportunity isn't enough. *Phi Delta Kappan, 73*, 712–717.

Rosenholtz, S., & Simpson, C. (1984). The formation of ability conceptions: Developmental trend or social construction? *Review of Educational Research, 54,* 31–63.

Weinstein, R. (1986) The teaching of reading and children's awareness of teacher expectations. In T. E. Raphael (Ed.), *Contexts of school-based literacy* (pp. 232–252). New York: Random House.

PART FOUR

Data Collection

Reframing Classroom Research:
A Lesson from the Private
World of Children

ADRIENNE ALTON-LEE
GRAHAM NUTHALL
JOHN PATRICK

In this article we explore children's public and private experiences during a lesson in an intermediate (sixth-grade) classroom in Aotearoa New Zealand. In the *Handbook for Research on Teaching,* Courtney Cazden described "two interpenetrating worlds: the official world of the teacher's agenda, and the unofficial world of the peer culture" (1986, p. 451). Although children in the classroom experience both of these worlds simultaneously, the unofficial, private world has been largely hidden from teachers and researchers. By exploring both the official and public, and the unofficial and private utterances of individual children, we can open a window onto the child's experience of both worlds.

We are unlikely to come to such a window with open minds. In both educational practice and research, children's talk in the unofficial world has frequently been "considered a nuisance; literal noise in the instructional system" (Cazden, 1986, p. 448). Children's talk, even when it involves engagement with curriculum content, may be judged off-task because it contravenes the rules of order in a classroom. The "official world" of the teacher's agenda has become not only the focus of classroom research, but also the lens through which children's behavior is observed and judged.

The unofficial children's talk that occurred during the class lesson we focus on in this article would have been categorized as off-task in most classroom observation schedules. There is now evidence, however, that observer judgments about children's "on-task" behavior are not a valid index of children's engagement with content (Blumenfeld & Meece, 1988; Peterson, Swing, Stark, & Waas, 1984), and that children's spontaneous talk during time "off-task" can contribute to their intellectual development (Dyson, 1987).

A fundamental challenge for educational researchers has been the inaccessibility of the learning processes that take place in the mind of the child. The early behaviorists resolved the issue by denying the significance, or even the existence, of internal processing. In contrast, more recent research in cognitive science and artificial intelli-

Harvard Educational Review Vol. 63 No. 1 Spring 1993, 50–84

gence has attempted to develop functional models of these internal processes. In the field of classroom research, techniques such as stimulated recall (Peterson et al., 1984) and eliciting children's reports of their own internal processing strategies (Blumenfeld & Meece, 1988) have been used to provide insights about classroom learning. These techniques, however, depend on children's conscious and selective recall of their mental processing. In the study reported here, we have employed a new technique, in which children's utterances are recorded by individual broadcast microphones during the course of classroom activities. These utterances provide a unique and concurrent source of data about children's learning processes and allow us to identify individual children's responses to curriculum content, their use of prior knowledge and experience, their existing misconceptions, and their strategies for engaging with curriculum.

In our larger research program, the Understanding Learning and Teaching Project, we have traced children's learning during their interaction with specific test-item content in the course of instructional units (Alton-Lee & Nuthall, 1992a; Nuthall & Alton-Lee, 1991, 1992).[1] We have explained knowledge acquisition in classrooms as a developmental process in which children generate specific knowledge constructs as they participate in the enacted curriculum. We define the enacted curriculum as the actual ways in which students encounter curriculum content as they participate in individual, group, and whole-class activities and tasks.

Utterance data can be a rich source of information about the ways in which children experience and negotiate the instructional, social, and cultural contexts of the classroom. If the purpose of educational research is to improve classroom practice, then we need to understand how teachers influence these contexts. Children's utterances, when triangulated with other data, can illuminate the hidden cognitive and cultural processes that mediate their learning and well-being.

In this article, we use several data sources from a single class lesson to demonstrate the interplay between instructional, social, and cultural contexts that influence children's experience. In particular, we focus on cultural processes mediating gender and race. We report a detailed analysis of four case-study children's experience of one lesson, using multiple sources of data: transcripts of the public enacted curriculum and of children's private utterances (transcribed from audio recordings); continuous observational records of case-study children; tests of short- and long-term learning outcomes; and interviews with the teacher and with the children. We explain how the utterance data helped in the development of a model of classroom learning. Finally, we consider the implications of our analysis for developing an understanding that takes into account both the psychological and sociocultural dimensions of classroom learning processes.

Gathering Utterance Data in the Classroom

We began each of the studies in our project by finding a teacher who was aware of the nature of the research and was eager to participate. Each teacher decided which curriculum unit we would study. We negotiated prior permission with the local education board and the principal and obtained written permission from the children's parents. The purpose of the research was explained to the children, and they were given the opportunity to decide whether or not to participate.[2]

The Understanding Learning and Teaching Project now comprises a series of six studies of children's learning in schools selected for racial and social-class contrasts in student population. This article focuses on an introductory lesson taught in a sixth-grade classroom in a suburban intermediate school (sixth- and seventh-grade students only) serving a predominantly *Pakeha* (White) middle- to upper-middle-class population.[3] Four case-study children in the classroom were selected from those who had parental permission, wanted to participate, and were easily accessible to the video camera. Any child the teacher believed might be adversely affected by the intensive observation was not chosen as a case-study student.

Individual broadcast microphones were used to record the private and public utterances of the children. Public utterances were those audible to the teacher and the class, including comments and exclamations that were called out during the lesson and recorded on the public transcript of the lesson. Private utterances included private conversations between children and the whispers and comments that children made to themselves. Each private microphone and transmitter was encased in a small plastic box and hung by an elastic band around the child's neck and under his or her sweater. Each day the children put on their microphone transmitters at the beginning of the unit and switched on the transmitters. The children were shown how to turn off the transmitters if at any time they wished to keep their conversation entirely private. All the children in the class who wished to participate wore the microphone transmitters, but only the transmitters worn by the case-study children were live. The children rarely switched off the microphone transmitters during teacher-directed lessons. There is evidence that they often forgot they were wearing the microphones but monitored their behavior when they did remember. For example:

> *Child (talking to peer): Don't give me that shit! — Nice little microphone.*

The children appeared to disregard the recording process after the familiarization period, perhaps because they did not receive any reactions from the researchers to what was recorded.

The Lesson

To illustrate the value of utterance data in revealing the processes that mediate children's experience in both the official and unofficial worlds, we selected a thirty-six-minute introductory whole-class lesson from a social studies unit entitled "New York City: A Study in Cultural Differences."[4] One of the teacher's goals in teaching the unit was for the children to develop more tolerance and appreciation for different races as they learned about the cultural mix in New York City. The teacher was a *Pakeha* (White) male.

Throughout the lesson the children were seated in a semicircle around the teacher, who used an overhead projector and a map as visual aids. During the first two minutes the teacher introduced the unit topic, and then the lesson itself began. The teacher began with a brainstorming activity, asking the children to respond to the question, "What does New York make you think of?" His purpose was to get "a word, a reaction, just to tune them in . . . getting them to bring to their awareness what they think about New York." The task difficulty increased slightly when he then asked, "What do you know about New York?" The teacher recorded the children's public responses on the overhead projector. The children were then asked to reflect on their re-sponses and to consider a third question, "What would it be like to live in New York?"

After this brainstorming activity, which lasted nine minutes, the lesson continued with teacher-led discussions about New York's European settlement, its geography, the reasons for its growth, and the location of boroughs, landmarks, and prominent buildings. While discussing the European settlement, the teacher emphasized key dates as "coat hangers or signposts" to help the children with the concept of time. He made frequent comparisons between New York City and Aotearoa New Zealand in order to relate the new information to the children's prior knowledge. Throughout the lesson the teacher interspersed brief reviews in which he asked the children to re-call factual details from the foregoing introductory lesson. At the end of the lesson he provided instructions for two follow-up map-labeling tasks to be done individually by the children.

Utterance Data as a Window on Children's Experience of the Lesson

We focused on four case-study children in order to trace the ways in which individual children participated in and were influenced by classroom processes.[5] The case-study children were selected to include children of different achievement levels and both boys and girls: Ann (average), Joe (low), Jon (high), and Mia (high).[6] All four children came from families in which both parents were in paid employment. Mia and John came from upper-middle-class families in which both parents were professionals (teacher and lawyer, teacher and scientist); Ann's and Joe's parents were in middle-class occupations (small business management, sales, and nursing). All were *Pakeha* (of European descent). The only Maori child in the class, Ricky, was not chosen for the case study because he was one of the children the teacher thought would be unset-tled by the observational process.

We classified each utterance of each case-study child according to whether it was public or private and whether it was related to the curriculum content.[7] Public utter-ances were then classified in relation to the teacher's designation within the enacted curriculum: that is, whether the child was publicly answering the question when called upon ("public nomination"), calling out the answer without being called on ("call out"), responding in chorus with other children ("choral response"), or reading with the group ("unison reading"). Private utterances were initially classified by audi-ence: whether the child was speaking or listening to a peer, talking to his or her self, or, in the case of one child, singing.

During the 36-minute lesson, the four case-study children produced 318 utterance strings, 86 percent of which occurred in the unofficial or private dimension of the children's experience of the lesson (see Table 1). For Ann, Joe, and Jon, public utter-ances comprised only 12 to 13 percent of their total utterances during this time. Mia engaged in much less private talk: 41 percent of her comparatively infrequent utter-ances were public.

Table 1 also shows the number of private utterances that were unrelated to curricu-lum content: 16 percent for Ann, 11 percent for Jon, and 10 percent (one utterance) for Mia. Mia's private utterance that was unrelated to curriculum content concerned the task, as did half of Ann's and a third of Jon's. Private utterances that were unre-

TABLE 1
Frequency of Public Talk, Peer Interaction, and Talking or Singing to Self for the Case-Study Children (36 Minutes)

	Number of Utterances			
Utterance Type/Audience	Ann	Joe	Jon	Mia
Public Talk				
Public nomination	2	3	7	3
Call out	5	11 (1)	3 (1)	1 (1)
Chorus response	2	0	1	1
Unison reading	2	0	2	2
Table				
Talks to peer	23 (14)	36 (17)	26 (10)	1 (1)
Listens to peer	3	18 (11)	8	1
Talks to self	49	37	53 (1)	8
Sings	0	0	10	0
Total	86 (14)	105 (29)	110 (12)	17 (2)

Note: The number of utterances in each category that were unrelated to curriculum content are indicated in parentheses.

lated to either the curriculum content or to the ongoing tasks were infrequent, except for those by Joe; even for Joe over two-thirds of his private utterances were related to curriculum content.

Beyond "Off-Task"

A comparison of the audio recordings and the observers' records revealed that fewer than a quarter of the private utterances recorded by the children's microphones were apparent to the observers. The simple finding that children's hidden classroom talk was far more prevalent than was apparent to the observers, who were each continuously watching one case-study child, reflects the children's expertise in hiding their private interactions. This is not surprising, given that private pupil talk is officially "off-task" during a teacher-directed lesson because it contravenes the rules of order. Doyle (1986) noted that in both secondary and elementary classrooms, quiet, private talk between peers, although permitted in other task contexts, contravened the rules for teacher-directed lessons.

Indeed, the common assumption in the official classroom world is that during a lesson children should talk only when they participate publicly, and the teacher should nominate who talks publicly. Classroom research, however, shows a discrepancy between the official rules and actual behavior patterns. Doyle (1986) reviewed a series of studies that found that teachers are not always consistent in enforcing rules against "call-outs," and Cazden (1986) noted that in the course of curriculum enactment the rules of turn-taking are relaxed as the momentum of a lesson increases. Kounin (1970) explained that teachers risk sacrificing the instructional flow and momentum of a lesson if they engage in too many reprimands to achieve rule enforcement.

During the lesson we studied, the teacher did not consistently reprimand children for the private talk he appeared to notice. We should note that, because the teacher was attending primarily to the instructional flow, he noticed much less of the private talk than did the observers. However, the teacher enforced the rules of order when he found private talk disruptive.

The data in Table 1 indicate that much officially "off-task" talk was not only actually task-relevant, but also directly relevant to the children's engagement with the curriculum content.

Before we move on to consider the children's curriculum-relevant utterances during the teacher-directed lesson, we briefly consider a further problem with the use of "on-task" and "off-task" classifications of children's talk. This problem is the prevalence of "on-task" talk that shows preoccupation with task organization or presentation (for example, printing headings and coloring maps) but that displaces the academic work the teacher intended the task to involve.

For example, in the map-labeling tasks that followed the lesson we described earlier, the teacher had asked the children to locate New York City on a map of the world and to identify and label the Hudson River, the Atlantic Ocean, Mexico, and Canada. The second task involved labeling the boroughs and key landmarks on a map of New York City. Compare Jon's and Ann's utterances over a parallel time period while working at these tasks:[8]

Ann:

Ann (talking to peer): Mine [felt-tipped pen] hasn't been used that much . . . it goes a bit funny.

Ann (talking to peer): Can I use your navy? Can I use your navy please? Are you going around the edge in navy blue? What are you going to do there?

Peer (talking to Ann): Blue. But not with blue felt. Blue pencil.

Ann (talking to peer): In pencil. Yeah! Can I use your green or are you using it? Rose, have you got a blue-green?

[Two minutes later]

Ann (talking to peer): Are you definitely using pencil? I'll tell you which blue I did. I'm not going to take long. Remember we had to do the map in social studies. It's not going to take as long as that.

[Two minutes later]

Ann (talking to peer): That blue works marvelous. My blue works hopeless.

Jon:

Jon (singing to self): New York! Hot in the city! Hot in the city tonight!

Jon (talking to self): New York. Hudson River. Atlantic Ocean is here.

[Two minutes later]

Jon (talking to self): Mexico. Mekiko. Mehico.

Peer (talking to Jon): Statue of Liberty, eh?

Jon (singing to self): Mehico Ga-la-la!

Jon (talking to peer): Do you like Canada? Do you like Canada, the place?

Peer (talking to Jon): Do you know their cops are the worst in the world?

Jon (talking to peer): They're nasty.

Jon (talking to self): Mounties? . . .

Jon (talking to peer): Man, I've lost track of this map. That must be the Bronx up there. Bronx, Queens. Aw man, this map's hard to follow. It's badly drawn.

Peer (talking to Jon): No it's not. It's easy . . .

Jon (talking to peer): Well, that's your opinion, Mark. New Jersey! New Jersey man [attempts accent].

Peer (talking to Jon): That's the Bronx, isn't it?

Jon (talking to peer): Yeah. That's the Bronx . . . uh, Queens is across from the Bronx.

Peer (talking to Jon): That big bit down there. Queens, Manhattan, Brooklyn, it's down there.

Jon (talking to self): Brooklyn . . .

Jon (talking to peer): Staten Island. That's it. Here it is.

These examples reveal that during the map-labeling task, Ann was largely preoccupied with the coloring process, while Jon systematically attempted to locate and label each place specified by the teacher in his instructions. A pattern found across our classroom studies is that children often become preoccupied with task presentation rather than engaging with the curriculum content. From our detailed records of children's experience of curriculum in the classrooms we studied, it is clear that off-task behavior played a relatively minor role in inhibiting learning, as compared with on-task behavior that did not involve engagement with curriculum concepts.

We now turn to the case-study children's public and private utterances during the teacher-directed lesson, a high proportion of which were directly relevant to the curriculum content (Ann, 84%; Joe, 72%; Jon, 89%; and Mia, 88%). We cannot know whether these utterances were facilitating or even mediating learning processes; some utterances may simply reflect some of the thinking processes used by the children during the lesson. Alternatively, verbalization in itself may facilitate children's learning.

Interpreting the Utterance Data

We needed to develop a framework for interpreting the educational significance of the children's utterances. The prevalence of children's private talk that was not directed at *any* audience led us away from a traditional view that utterances are always a form of communication. Much of the children's talk did involve communication, but a significant proportion involved the children's personal and hidden verbal responses to the classroom processes.

We developed a framework within which utterances are interpreted as a source of information about the ways in which children are responding to the classroom context (see Figure 1). The framework is grounded in our data and evolving theoretical work in the Understanding Learning and Teaching Project (Alton-Lee, 1984; Alton-Lee & Nuthall, 1990, 1992a; Nuthall & Alton-Lee, 1990, 1991, 1993) and derived from a process of theoretical triangulation with the work of Doyle (1983) and Apple and Weiss (1983) and with recent information-processing theory (Howard, 1987). Central to our framework is a concern with the children's process of knowledge construction; this process we frame not only within the larger classroom context, but also within the wider sociocultural context of which the classroom is a part.

In this framework, the four major dimensions of official classroom culture are the rules of order, the task routines, the curriculum, and the criteria by which children's performance is evaluated. As in any culture, many elements of these dimensions are implicit. The participants are enculturated over time (Berwick-Emms, 1989); it is the language, content, and perspectives of the curriculum that shape the classroom culture. For any particular classroom task, the task routines used by the teacher moderate the rules of order and shape the evaluative climate, creating particular contextual demands to be negotiated by the children (Doyle, 1983, 1986). The official agenda is that all children should acquire the same skills and knowledge through their participation in the classroom tasks. The teacher and children, however, have their own cultural perspectives, shaped by their gender, class, and race. These cultural perspectives influence their negotiation of the classroom culture and their public and private participation in curriculum enactment. The outcomes for children include not only how much they are able to learn from the official curriculum, but also what they learn about their own identity, value, and capability. The process of curriculum enactment itself is critical because children experience and learn culturally specific ways of participating that influence their learning and their well-being.

Our framework allows us to interpret the functions of children's utterances during a class lesson. Whether or not children talk privately is in itself significant, because private utterances contravene the rules of order in the lesson context. Accordingly, it is necessary to interpret the significance of silence. How a child negotiates the classroom culture during any lesson will influence the likelihood that she or he will participate, publicly or privately, in the lesson. Children's participation is also constrained by the evaluative dimension of classroom lessons. There is risk involved in responding publicly and failing. Individual children are more or less likely to be able to lower the risk and accomplish tasks successfully because of differences in their prior knowledge, experience, and the particular skills and resources available to them both within and outside of the classroom. For children, participation in classroom lessons involves negotiating risk publicly and managing the social consequences of succeeding or failing.

In addition to whether or not a child talks publicly or privately, we must pay particular attention to the audience of an utterance. Even within the private utterance data for this lesson, there were three distinct audience categories. At the most private level, the case-study children engaged in whispers to themselves that were inaudible to peers; the second level involved private interactions with a single peer that were hidden from other peers and the teacher; and the third level involved verbalizations accessible to a few peers but not public. By identifying audience, we can learn much about the way a child negotiates the culture of the classroom and sociocultural processes.

FIGURE 1

*A Framework for Interpreting the Contextual Influences on a
Child's Experience of a Classroom Lesson*

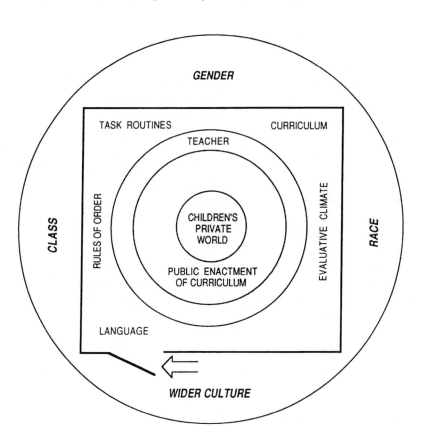

Using this framework, we explain a child's experience during a lesson as a unique process involving three concurrent strands: 1) responding to curriculum content, 2) managing the classroom culture, and 3) participating in sociocultural processes.

Responding to Curriculum Content: Developing Knowledge Constructs

Our understanding of the way children acquire knowledge in the classroom is that they generate specific knowledge constructs as they engage in the process of making meaning out of curriculum content. The term *knowledge construct* is used to refer to a unit of knowledge that is constructed in memory as the child interprets classroom experience in relation to prior knowledge. It is less generic than a schema (see Howard, 1987) and more general than a mental model (Johnson-Laird, 1983).

We developed a model of the processes by which children generate specific knowledge constructs during instructional units by comparing the developmental progression of children's experience of curriculum content they learned with that for content that they failed to learn. Elsewhere we have described the model (Nuthall & Alton-Lee, 1991, 1992), the success of that model in predicting children's learning in three studies with children of different ages studying different curriculum areas (Nuthall & Alton-Lee, 1993), and the rationale for the methodology used (Alton-Lee & Nuthall, 1992b).

According to our model, in order to generate a specific knowledge construct, a student needs to be exposed to a sequence of appropriate, topic-relevant information within a limited period of time. Knowledge-construct generation involves the child in a series of cognitive processes: obtaining information, creating associative links, elaborating the content, evaluating the truth and consistency of information, and developing metacognitive awareness (Nuthall & Alton-Lee, 1993).

The utterances recorded during the teacher-directed lesson in this study illuminate the ways in which the case-study children created associative links to their existing knowledge, evaluated the truth of their emerging understandings, and elaborated the content. It should be noted that, because the lesson we focus on in this article was only an introductory one (almost seven hours of class time were spent on the New York City unit), the utterances often reflect the preliminary stages of the children's knowledge-construct generation.

Creating associative links between new information and prior knowledge   The following utterances are examples of the ways in which the case-study children made connections with their prior knowledge and experience as they responded to the content of the enacted curriculum:

Teacher: . . . a whole 102 stories high. Imagine running up the stairs.

Mia (whispers to self): Cross country.

. . .

Teacher: . . . and the Dutch people under a Mr. Peter Stuyvesant, who of all things had a wooden leg.

Pupil (calls out): Smokes!

Teacher: If that helps.

Joe (talking to Ricky): Smokes! Ciggies!

. . .

Teacher: . . . Staten Island sometimes called Richmond.

Ricky (talking to Joe): I used to go to that school.

Joe (talking to Ricky): Richmond School.

. . .

[Teacher asks question about subway routes on map]

Ann (talking to self): Streams. Boats. In Lyttelton they have those boats.

. . .

Teacher: It's on . . . a little wee island. What is it, Jon?

Jon: Statue of Liberty.

Bart (talking to Jon): See that island there. That's where they dump their rubbish at the tip.

Jon (talking to Bart): I know 'cause they put rubbish barges down the Hudson River.

The teacher's invitation to imagine climbing the Empire State Building by the stairs reminded Mia of the school cross-country race scheduled for later in the day. Joe associated the name of Peter Stuyvesant with cigarettes (the brand his father smoked) after the teacher publicly validated another child's use of the association as a memory device. Joe realized that Ricky was making an association between Richmond Borough and Richmond School, which Ricky had attended previously. Ann's prior experience was insufficient to help her identify the subway route on the map, but she guessed, from her knowledge of a local seaport, that the symbols represented some kind of transport route. Jon's response to the teacher's question about an island near Manhattan was not only a public answer, but also a private display (to Bart) of extraordinarily specific prior knowledge about the use of barges for Manhattan rubbish disposal.

By identifying and making associations with personal experience and knowledge, children connect the new with the familiar in order to make sense or meaning out of the curriculum. Children's success at this process depends on the extent and availability of their general and topic-specific knowledge. The following excerpt illustrates the critical role that general knowledge can play in enabling a child to make sense of curriculum content:

Teacher: Brett?

Brett: The average stay for a visitor is two days.

Julia (talking to Ann): Are you only allowed to stay for two days?

Ann (talking to Julia): No that's an average. How long they do stay.

Although not every association made by the children occurred in response to a direct cue from the teacher, these associations were more likely to occur following the teacher's questions, cues, and hesitations. When reviewing the video record of the lesson, the teacher commented, "I'm pleased to see that I'm not only getting a pause, a 'wait-time,' but also that I was consciously doing it. . . . I'm asking them to think."

In addition to the logical associations the children made between their prior knowledge and the curriculum content, they also made idiosyncratic, playful, and joking associations; this was particularly true of the boys. These associations were sometimes linked to the meaning of curriculum material and sometimes to the sound of a name or an alternative meaning. For example:

Teacher: Manhattan.

Joe (talking to self): Madhattan!

. . .

Teacher: . . . sitting right on a fault line.

Joe (talking to self): Yeah! The line going across the motorway.

Jon's singing also illustrates this process:

Teacher (introducing the unit): We'll be handing out a map of New York . . .

Jon (singing to self): Cool, New York, hot in the city! Hot in the city! Hot in the city, to-night!

Teacher: Can you have a look [at map of New York City]?

(Jon singing to self): . . . from Central Park to Shanty Town . . . New York . . . do do!

The process of making links to the curriculum content is not always consistent with the public curriculum. Inappropriate links lead to misconceptions. The utterance data showed not only children's extant misconceptions, but also the development of misconceptions during the lesson. For example, Ann inappropriately linked the notion of East Indies (where the English explorers were intending to go when they "found" New York) and the Indians who lived in New York. As a result, she mistakenly generated the name "Eastern Indians" to refer to the Manhattan Indians.

Evaluating and validating emerging understandings   The children's utterances also demonstrated that they were integrating curriculum content. This involved identifying the implications of the new material and checking its coherence and validity in relation to their existing knowledge. In this monitoring process, they might identify their own misconceptions and explore evidence or reasons to support their emerging understandings. For example:

Teacher: 1664? . . . Charles?

Ann (talking to self) : American Revol –

Charles: Ah, um the English took over from the Dutch . . .

Ann (talking to self): Oh!

. . .

Teacher: Where did we start prior to 1600?

Jon (provides sound effects of gun fire): K.K.K.K.k.k.k.k.k . . .

Jon (talking to self): No machine guns . . . wouldn't have even been pump-action muskets.

. . .

Teacher: Yes, it [New York City] grew to a million people. It grew to more than . . .

Mia (talking to self): Eighty million.

Pupil: Eight million.

Teacher: What made you say eight million?

Ann (talking to peer): I guessed that because I just thought that New Zealand is three million and New York's bigger than that.

· · ·

Teacher: 1609?

Mia (talking to self): The Dutch [precedes the correct answer in public lesson by half a minute].

There is evidence to suggest that this monitoring and integration process is an internalization of the model of teacher-student interactions that the children experience in the public discussion. This cycle of question-answer-reaction has been well documented as the traditional pattern of teacher-student verbal interaction in the classroom (Aschner, 1959; Bellack, Hyman, Smith, & Kliebard, 1966). Empirical evidence indicates that students who participate publicly in the discussion cycle do not learn more than students who only listen to the cycle, and that listening to a discussion cycle is more effective than listening to a teacher lecture (see Hughes, 1973; Nuthall & Church, 1973). The utterances in this study suggest that the children are not only learning how to respond in an acceptable manner, but also that they are learning the teacher's role of reacting to responses. In their private utterances, both Mia and Ann responded to the teacher's cues and reacted like the teacher to their own covert utterances and to other children's overt responses. The evaluative climate of the lesson became their own internal evaluative process.

Developing and extending knowledge constructs   Once children have generated a specific knowledge construct, they develop and extend its content. Because the lesson we selected was the introductory session to the unit, the children were interacting with primarily new information; thus this process was only infrequently evident in their utterances. There was one example in Ann's utterances:

Teacher: What did they use the river as?

Ann (talking to Julia): Exporting.

Teacher: Neil?

Neil: A road.

Teacher: Thank you. They used the river as a road.

The notion that the Hudson River had been used to transport people was discussed in the public lesson, but the idea was not developed to include the commercial function that Ann privately suggested to Julia.

Jon had the most relevant prior knowledge of all the case-study children (he already knew the content of over three-quarters of the items in the pretest), so it is not surprising that his utterances frequently involved comments that developed, extended, and provided his personal perspective on the curriculum content:

Teacher: The English took over from the Dutch, and they said, "We'll blow you up if you don't give us the island!"

Jon (talking to self): Threatened them!

· · ·

Pupil (in response to first question, "What does New York make you think of?"): Nukes.

Jon (talking to self): Nuclear. There's none in New York. They're all in Washington.

As the unit progressed, these comments became more frequent. For example, in a later lesson about reasons for early immigration to New York, Jon found the teacher's explanation ironic:

Teacher: So wars meant that some folks said, "Let's shift from Europe and go to where there are no wars," so they went to America.

Jon (talking to self): Now America's king of war.

While there is danger in overinterpreting the utterance data, there are reasonable grounds for believing that, because they are spontaneous and private, they represent an externalization of normally covert processes; that is, that they represent spontaneous thinking aloud.

Jon's utterances during the introductory lesson reflected his higher prior knowledge: his utterances involved associative links, elaborations, evaluations of the truth and consistency of information, and metacognitive processes.[9] Ann's utterances were mainly concerned with monitoring her own misconceptions and emerging understandings. Joe frequently related the new curriculum content to his own knowledge, but he did little monitoring or integrating of the new knowledge. Mia was very quiet, but her characteristic response was to monitor her own answers.

It may be that these differences between the children reflect differences in their ability to organize their experiences and generate relevant knowledge constructs. But what constitutes "ability" here? What the utterances do reveal is the critical role of cultural capital in enabling the children to engage in the process of generating constructs.[10] This is apparent in both the topic-specific and general knowledge that the children brought to the lesson, or which they gained access to by interacting with peers and with the teacher during the lesson.

The utterances also reveal a difference between the children in the extent to which they incorporated into their processing a teacher-like role of monitoring the validity of their emerging understandings. Evidence of monitoring is least apparent in the utterances of Joe, the low achiever, suggesting that monitoring one's own understandings may be particularly critical to the knowledge-construct generation process.

It is important to remember, however, that with our focus on this one lesson we have opened only a partial window on the processes with which children generate knowledge constructs. Our studies indicate that such constructs are generated across a number of occasions throughout the course of a unit (Nuthall & Alton-Lee, 1992, 1993).

Managing the Classroom Culture

As is apparent in the section above, the children's ability to make meaning out of curriculum content was dependent on the extent to which they could draw upon relevant prior knowledge, skills (such as map interpretation), and experiences. When a child lacks these resources, she or he finds it difficult to manage the evaluative climate. In the following accounts, we consider what the utterances reveal about the ways in which the teacher and the case-study children managed the evaluative climate. Our findings should be interpreted with the proviso that our presence as observers almost certainly heightened the children's perception of the risk of replying.

Ann   Ann appeared to manage the evaluative climate with accurate judgment about the adequacy of her answers. Her public answers were consistently correct or appropriate and her eleven wrong answers were kept private. She was able to draw on considerable relevant prior knowledge during the lesson, including her recent television viewing of a news item about the Statue of Liberty. Almost 10 percent of Ann's utterances involved her friend Julia in a shared process of interacting with the curriculum content. When Ann was overwhelmed by new curriculum content and no longer able to engage in making associations to relevant prior knowledge and experience, she used an apparently deliberate strategy of repetition of key words:[11]

Teacher: The Dutch . . .

Ann (talking to self): The Dutch.

Teacher: . . . started a town on Manhattan; they called it New Amsterdam.

Ann (talking to self): New Amsterdam.

. . .

Teacher: There are three buildings I would like you to identify: United Nations, Empire State, and World Trade Center.

Ann (talking to self): World Trade, World Trade, Empire State, United Nations, Empire State.

Ann's style of participation in the lesson indicated almost total continuous involvement in the tasks or with the content. Of all the case-study children, she was most often observed to be focused on the teacher or on a relevant resource. Ann received no positive feedback from the teacher for her two publicly nominated responses, and she appeared frustrated in her desire to participate publicly more frequently. Of the four children, she was least likely to elicit teacher nomination with her hand raises: her fifteen hand raises during the lesson only elicited two teacher nominations. Ann responded by calling out her answers five times and by talking privately at a rate of two to three utterances per minute. A third of these utterances involved cooperative interactions with her friend, Julia. This private peer interaction appeared to play an important, mutually supportive role in both girls' management of the evaluative climate during the lesson. Julia sought Ann's help with strategies to remember the dates presented by the teacher. Ann shared her misconceptions with Julia. This talk was hidden, enabling Ann to give and receive peer support during the lesson, yet allowing her to avoid being seen by the teacher as contravening the rules of order.

Her management (masking) of her contravention of the rules of order was so effective that even when the teacher reviewed the video (long after the unit), Ann's private utterances were hidden, and he commented that "Ann doesn't offer as much as some of the others in terms of an active type of learning. . . . She learns just sitting and soaking it up."

Joe   Joe did not appear to manage the evaluative climate as carefully as Ann: his only two wrong answers were public responses. This can be explained partly by the absence of self-monitoring in Joe's interaction with curriculum content during the lesson; he did not appear to check the validity of his own answers.

Both Joe's utterances and the interview with Joe reveal that his free associations drew extensively on his prior knowledge and experiences, particularly on his television viewing: "Oh yeah! 'The Equalizer' program. The one just starting, there was this . . . picture of a subway and there was all this yukky stuff and rubbish." His background knowledge, however, was insufficient to enable him to answer public questions correctly:

> Teacher: Can you think of any city, say in New Zealand or anywhere else, that has got this type of [name]?
>
> *Joe (talking to self): No, damn!*

When another boy, Sean, gave information about the average stay for a visitor to New York being two days, Joe's retort was a scathing, "How do you know that?" But when the teacher then acknowledged Sean's prior reading as a valuable source of information, Joe grabbed a book from a nearby display. Throughout much of the rest of the lesson, Joe attempted to use the book to find answers to the teacher's questions:

> Teacher: What else is there in New York?
>
> Joe (calling out): Yeah, I know! I know! It's in this book!
>
> . . .
>
> Teacher: What did they use the river as [in the context of discussing the commercial growth of New York City]?
>
> *Joe (talking to self): It said canoeing here.*

Joe's determination to get right answers preoccupied him to the point that he failed to follow the meaning of the public discussion; hence his response of "canoeing" in the instance above. The process finally became public after a sequence when Joe called out and pleaded with the teacher to choose him to participate:

> Teacher: Why did New York grow, whereas the cities at the time that were a bit down there didn't grow nearly as much?
>
> Joe (calling out): I know!
>
> Teacher: You've got everything you need, Joe. Go!
>
> Joe: Well it says in this book. It may not be right, but it says that European settlers had a habit of pulling it out — of pulling something out.
>
> Teacher: Well! [pupils laugh] Let's just say you pulled it out of a book and I'm not certain what it is, but just leave it there, Joe.

The consequences of his public mistake did not seem to worry Joe excessively, and the teacher later commented, "I think it was a general humorous laugh and Joe was laughing as well. I don't think it was a ridicule laugh."

Though the social consequences of public failure were not serious for Joe, his inability to provide right answers seemed both to frustrate him and to motivate him to copy an effective strategy used by his peer — reading a book. Not only did Joe contravene the rules of order by getting the book, he also flicked through it in an attempt to get answers during the lesson. This strategy reduced the possibility of his making meaning of the ongoing curriculum content according to the teacher's agenda. During the lesson, Joe focused on the teacher or a relevant resource less than half as frequently as did both girls, though unlike them, he appeared to take great pleasure in the lesson, making jokes, word plays, and humorous free associations. He was the only case-study child to engage in more peer interactions than talking to himself.

Although a large proportion (41.5 percent) of Joe's social interactions involved a shared process of interacting with curriculum content, he also used the private world to abuse his peers. He engaged in serious breaches of the rules of order — kicking and name-calling. He was, however, very skilled at hiding his contraventions and was never individually reprimanded by the teacher. Actually, early in the lesson he was rewarded for breaking the public participation rule:

Teacher: That is, homework as opposed to what you do while you are?

Joe (calling out before the teacher opened up the turn to other children): At school!

Teacher: I want to hear a voice — "at school." Brilliant!

Joe's public response during the brainstorm, "Oh, what is, yeah . . . lots of violence," was rewarded with the affirmation, "He thinks, he does!" Joe made ten more public call-outs during the lesson.

Mia   Mia appeared to be the case-study child most concerned about the evaluative climate and the rules of order. Her private utterances were rare and mostly inaudible to her peers. Mia's only comment to a peer, "He always says 'Brilliant!'," concerned the teacher's feedback to other children and revealed Mia's sensitivity to the evaluative climate. He never said "brilliant" to Mia. Mia watched or glanced at the teacher or appropriate visual resource at least three times per minute, but she also glanced around at a rate of twice a minute. She appeared to be very attuned to other children's private talk — particularly to Jon's evaluative comments, even when he was not directing them to peers.

Mia contravened the rules of order for public participation only once, when she called out to the teacher that she and the other girls around her could not see the visual resource. Her desire to see the screen overcame her characteristic reticence.

When Mia raised her hand, she was less likely to elicit a teacher nomination than were the boys. However, she gave two publicly nominated responses. The teacher's response to her contribution to the brainstorm indicated that he was using a more stringent criteria for Mia than for the other case-study children. Unlike the other case-study children, Mia (for both public responses) used an interrogative intonation, suggesting that she was attempting to diminish the risk. This was surprising, given the apparently low-risk status of a brainstorming session. However, her anxiety was justified. Instead of accepting the response, the teacher probed further, thereby changing the level of risk when Mia was already the focus of public attention:

Mia: The Empire State Building, Sir?

Teacher: Something about the Empire State Building. Can I just ask another question? What do you know about the Empire State Building?

Mia: Um, it's the tallest building in the world, isn't it?

Teacher: Ah, no; it's not.

Mia (talking to self): I thought it was.

The public correction of her incorrect response was remembered by Mia a year after the New York City unit:

Interviewer: Do you remember quite well when you said something in class?

Mia: Yeah, 'cause I was wrong (laugh) so I remember that. . . . I always thought what I said was the highest building, so I was surprised when he said to me I was wrong.

Jon   Of the four case-study children, Jon was the one who, when he raised his hand, was recognized most often by the teacher: approximately one out of four times that he raised his hand he was called on. He was nominated publicly seven times and called out on three occasions. Jon appeared to be less constrained by the evaluative climate and more at ease than the other case-study children:

Teacher: What's his name?

Pupil: Oh, I'm not sure.

Teacher: I should have written it down. I'm being a wee bit nasty asking you to remember these things.

Jon: Starts with a C. Was it Cooligan or something?

Neil: I know! Peter Stuyvesant.

Jon (talking to self): Oh yeah!

Jon (talking to Neil): How did you know it was a cigarette, Neil? Ooohhh!

In the example above, Jon was prepared to take the risk to give a public response that he knew he was unsure about. When Neil gave the correct response, Jon's self-monitoring was private. Within the unofficial peer culture, he mocked Neil for having knowledge of cigarettes, suggestively implying that his knowledge may have been acquired illicitly. Jon effectively took the evaluative focus off himself.

Of all the case-study children, Jon had the most specific topic-relevant knowledge, much of which came from television. His most frequent private utterance response to the lesson was to give an answer. Out of sixteen of Jon's private answers, only one was incorrect.

The contribution of television to Jon's learning was extraordinarily specific. The mystery of his knowledge of Manhattan's barge rubbish disposal was revealed in an interview when he explained how he knew about the Hudson River:

Interviewer: How did you learn that?

Jon (laughing): "Yogi Bear" and "Top Cat"!

Interviewer: Tell me more. Educate me about "Yogi Bear" and "Top Cat."

Jon: Oh no! I don't think it was "Yogi Bear." I think it was "Top Cat." And one day he wanted to take a cruise down the Hudson River and the only way he could do that was on a garbage boat, and he got put in a garbage can or something and by accident he got taken away by the garbage man, and at the end all his friends sort of say, "Oh well, you got what you wanted T.C.! A cruise down the Hudson!" or something like that!

Another source of topic-specific prior knowledge, a magazine, was revealed in the interview with Jon:

Jon: . . . in the magazine (*Mad Magazine*) where . . . on a deserted New York subway at 3:00 in the morning . . . there's three dark figures creeping up behind with knives . . .

Jon's confidence about his own prior knowledge was reflected in his next-most frequent utterance type, which involved an evaluative commentary on the adequacy and shortcomings of public answers offered by other pupils. For example:

Pupil: It's [New York] sitting on a fault line.

Jon (talking to self) : It's not. That's San Francisco.

Teacher: OK. What did they name New Amsterdam?

Jon (talking to peer): New York. Everyone tends to forget that.

He was confident enough of his own topic-relevant prior knowledge to qualify information given by the teacher:

Teacher: The very first people who may have lived in this area would have been?

Pupil: Indians.

Jon (talking to self): Red Indians actually.

Jon's response to Charles's challenge to the teacher about historical inaccuracy in the curriculum indicated that he himself was evaluating his peers and the teacher:

Charles: The Vikings were there [America] first because they saved all those copies of bits of paper and they said the Vikings were there in 1300.

Teacher: Yes. So, what?

Charles: So you said they were there first but they weren't.

Jon (talking to self): Guilty, man!

Jon not only evaluated peer responses and the teacher's information, he also argued about public information with a male peer:

Mia: It's [Empire State Building] the tallest building in the world.

Jon (talking to self): No, it's not. It's the second tallest.

Frank (talking to Jon): It's not the second highest.

Jon (talking to Frank): I know what the highest is.

Frank (talking to Jon): There are lots of buildings higher than the Empire State. It was a few years ago it was.

Jon (talking to Frank): It's the second highest.

[Argument continues]

Jon (talking to Frank): It's got eighty-six floors!

Jon, like Mia, was prepared to contravene the rules of order in order to interact with curriculum content. He directly contravened the teacher's direction not to use any other resource to solve a subway route problem by using a map key to locate the requisite answer.

Toward the end of the lesson, Jon complained to a peer that he wanted to be getting on with his own agenda — writing his own story about New York. However, overall he appeared to derive great enjoyment and entertainment from the lesson:

Jon (talking to self, attempting American accent): West of the Mississippi.

[Teacher discusses reasons for expansion of New York City]

Jon (talking to peer): It also became big because it's a seaport. . . .

Jon (talking to peer): Because the Bronx Warriors were doing good!

Jon's private utterances gave us the impression that he was covertly directing his own movie version of the lesson, providing his version of a vocal sound track, relevant sound effects, and a commentary with corrections and modifications when he judged the enacted curriculum to be falling short of the needs of the topic.

The differences in the case-study children in their management of the classroom culture reflect not only differences in the resources they were able to bring to their participation, but also differences in the ways in which the teacher operated the official agenda for different children. Irrespective of achievement level, the case-study boys were more easily able to participate publicly, were more likely to be praised, and more likely to take the risk of offering answers of which they were uncertain. The girls were careful to keep answers they were unsure of covert. Mia's strategy of remaining comparatively silent contrasted with Ann's strategy of managing much of the lesson through hidden supportive interactions with her friend Julia.

Participating in Sociocultural Processes: Learning within the "Lived Culture" of the Classroom

Children's responses to curriculum occur within a cultural context that is also shaped by the wider society. This cultural context is described by Apple and Weiss as the "lived culture" of the classroom: "Lived culture refers to culture as it is produced in ongoing interactions and as a terrain in which class, race, and gender meanings and antagonisms are played out" (1983, p. 27). The records of the enacted curriculum and the children's utterance data provided us with a unique perspective on the specific processes through which the lived culture was produced by the teacher and the children and influenced the children's interaction with curriculum content during this lesson.

Cultural bias in the curriculum   Because teachers' agendas have shaped our perspectives on classroom practice, the unofficial world of the students has been invisible; in addition, the cultural dimensions of classroom processes in the official world have been invisible. Spender (1982) argued that the school curriculum is strongly biased toward a White male perspective. The content of the enacted curriculum of the lesson we studied included not a single mention of a female, but fifty mentions of males (for example, Peter Stuyvesant, Henry Hudson, the Duke of York, Englishmen, Englishman, the "man in charge").[12] Pronounced gender bias is not uncharacteristic in the enacted curriculum of the social studies units we have studied in the Understanding Learning and Teaching Project. For the entire New York City unit, references to females comprised only 2.4 percent of the references to people. In the enacted curriculum for a study of the Middle Ages, references to females comprised only 3.9 percent of the references to people (81.7 percent were references to males) in more than fifty-two hours of class time (Alton-Lee, Densem, & Nuthall, 1991; Alton-Lee & Densem, 1992). The few women mentioned in the New York City unit were characteristically derogated or marginalized.[13] Clearly, if particular groups of people are omitted from curriculum content or characteristically marginalized or derogated, the curriculum conveys a message about relative cultural valuing of those groups.

The role of the teacher   How does bias become so pronounced in the enacted curriculum? The school resources available to teachers and historical reference books contribute to this bias, but the teacher is instrumental in shaping the lived culture of the enacted curriculum beyond the initial selection of lesson content and resources.

During the lesson studied, the teacher unconsciously structured the children's experience of curriculum by race and gender as he identified with a particular cultural group — White men of European descent. Although he began by calling each group of people or men who lived in New York City "they," as the momentum of the lesson increased, he began to use "we" occasionally. The following examples, spread over a six-minute period, show the teacher's use of "we" when referring to White people:

Teacher: The very first people who may have lived in this area may have been?

Child: Indians.

Teacher: They gave their names to one of the islands because they spoke of the Manhattan Indians . . .

. . .

[Forty-five seconds later]

Teacher: When White men first came they found Indians. . . . They were called Manhattan Indians. Because White people, Europeans, we were . . .

Teacher: Before we, or the Dutch people could get this island where we wanted to build our city . . .

. . .

[Five minutes later]

Teacher: Wouldn't that have been lovely if we had have owned it [New York City]?

The teacher's use of pronouns conveyed not only his own unconscious identification with the European men who colonized New York, but also an implied positioning of the children in the class as "White people, Europeans, we." He went on to mention the Treaty of Waitangi, which was the original (broken) agreement between the Maori and Europeans (*Pakeha*) in Aotearoa New Zealand, but he did so from the perspective of a White (*Pakeha*) male strongly identified with English settlers:

Teacher: In terms of Christchurch, what is the approximate date the first lot of boats, the first four ships — the big ones — where all of our ancestors came from? You know we all came . . .

This evidence illustrates the claim made by Apple and Weiss (1983) that "what counts as school knowledge . . . tends to embody the interests and culture of the group or groups who have power to distribute and legitimate their worldview through educational institutions" (p. 28). The teacher plays an unknowing but critical role in the hegemonic cycle, and the White male bias becomes so customary it seems normal. In this lesson, the teacher's intention was to increase the children's appreciation of cultural diversity, but his unconscious assumption of "we" to refer to White males in the official enacted curriculum was in conflict with his overall aim. Although his conscious intent was to convey tolerance and cultural inclusiveness, the teacher inadvertently excluded Maori from "our ancestors . . . we all came" (a reference to the English settlement of Christchurch) during the process of curriculum enactment.

Cultural bias can also influence the enacted curriculum through the teacher's split-second decisions about who can contribute to the enacted curriculum through public participation. If a teacher unwittingly favors the participation of a particular group of children, then that group's knowledge, experiences, and cultural perspectives shape the curriculum content. Marked gender bias was apparent in who was nominated to participate and in who participated in the lesson. The boys' perspectives on New York City were twice as prominent as the girls' in the enacted curriculum. Eighty-five (70 percent) of the public contributions were made by boys compared with thirty-six (30 percent) by girls. There were fourteen girls and fifteen boys in the class, making the average public participation rate for a girl 2.6 responses, and for a boy 5.7 responses. Our analyses of the experiences of the case-study children suggest that this imbalance occurred partly because the teacher was more likely to nominate boys. Also, the evaluative climate was more stringent for the girls with respect to the responses of both the teacher and their male peers. We consider that the bias in the curriculum content may itself contribute to the imbalance through affirming and supporting the participation of those children who are White and male.

Like curriculum-content bias, gender bias in public participation, although not usually so pronounced, has been shown to be characteristic of much educational practice (Kelly, 1988; Sadker, Sadker, & Klein, 1991). Research in Aotearoa New Zealand has uncovered pronounced gender bias even in the practice of feminist teachers (Newton, 1988) and has shown patterns of cultural bias, with White (*Pakeha*) girls participating publicly more than Polynesian girls (Jones, 1985), and teachers giving more attention to both White (*Pakeha*) and Samoan children than to Maori children (Clay, 1985).

The curriculum enactment was not structured by gender just in the content and public participation. The children were physically segregated by gender, with the boys in a semicircle at the front and the girls in a semicircle behind. Such segregation was normal in this classroom, and the teacher appeared to keep the boys close as a means of proximity control. After his introduction, the teacher began the lesson proper with the comment, "Let's boot off!" — a football analogy close to the heart of male culture, both *Pakeha* and Maori, in Aotearoa New Zealand. Although the analogy is used by the teacher inclusively — "Let [u]s" — the prior experience of the children will have been influenced by gendered practices in sporting participation. For the boys, the analogy cued prior experience as active participants. For the girls, who were most unlikely ever to have played on a football team, the analogy cued either their experience as spectators or their lack of experience.

The role of popular culture in classroom learning   The utterances highlighted the ways in which images from and associations to popular culture and the media were integral to the children's classroom learning processes and their generation of knowledge constructs. For this particular topic, the children drew extensively on prior knowledge they had gained from their television viewing. For example, in the postunit interview, Jon described a documentary that he had watched before the unit:

> *Jon:* It [a documentary] was about the poor side and the rich side of New York, and that there was a street down the middle that divided them, 49th Street or something. Oh yeah, it was called "The Streets of New York" and it was all about crime and everything in New York.

The children did not focus only on television programs about New York City. Television advertisements and general programs also provided a common source of general prior knowledge that they linked to new curriculum content.

This background knowledge was also predominantly male focused (for example, with references to male cartoon characters, male television stars, male police, male baseball teams, male basketball players, male gangs, male brand names). There was also a difference in the television-viewing patterns of the female and male case-study children. For example, the boys reported watching more late-night American police shows than did the girls. Mia explained:

> *Mia:* Well, from the television I thought all of New York was like "Diff'rent Strokes." I thought it was all very posh and things. I had no idea about all the sort of slum areas and things.
>
> *Interviewer:* Have you ever seen anything on television about crime in New York?
>
> *Mia:* Crime in New York?
>
> *Mia:* Mmm . . . I don't think so . . . no . . . Dad doesn't like television much and especially he doesn't like American programs, so we don't watch them.

Children's responses to cultural bias in the curriculum   How did the children respond to the teacher's unconsciously positioning them by using the pronoun "we" to mean White and male? During the following interview, the female researcher was startled when Mia showed her unconscious identification with White males in the curriculum by using the pronoun "us." This occurred when she was asked about the early settlement of New York City:

Mia: I think it's the Indians. I think they were the first people to have it.

Interviewer: Mm.

Mia: 'Cause they just, see you don't um Indians came before sort of today sort of wearing, wearing all them facepaints and things and you sort of think of them being first there because they're before us. You can tell sort of. You think of Indians and you think of long hair and headbands and weapons . . . and . . .

Interviewer: Yeah. And you say, you don't think of them — you think of them being there before us?

Mia: Mm.

Interviewer: And do you feel, when you say us, do you mean that the people who came to settle New York after the Indians were people like us?

Mia: Mm. Mm. [nods]

Interviewer: How were they like us?

Mia: Well, they didn't wear um, war paint and carry weapons around. They just sort of had, they wore clothes like us, sort of [laugh] civilized clothes.

Interviewer: When you say us do you think of women or men?

Mia: I think of men really 'cause like, sort of early Canterbury you have visions of people wearing sort of long suits and things. You know I don't really, yeah, that's right! I only think of the men. [giggle] I don't think of the women. [giggle]

Mia's identification with White colonists contrasted with the perspective taken by Ricky, the only Maori boy in the class. Ricky also remembered the men who colonized New York City, but spoke of them as culturally distant — "they" as opposed to "we" or "us":

Ricky: Oh well, first it was the Indians and then I think it was Englishmen, and ever since they have lived there, I think.

Interviewer: And you say Englishmen. Who are you thinking of? What sort of people?

Ricky: Well they were a bit greedy and more advanced than the Indians, so they just made towns and that started from there. They got rich and that.

The utterance data revealed that Ricky's exclusion from the White male "we" in the enacted curriculum also influenced Joe during the lesson:

Teacher: Because White people . . .

Joe (talking to Ricky): Honkies.

Ricky (talking to Joe): Shut up!

Teacher: Europeans, we were . . .

Joe (talking to Ricky): Nigger!

Teacher: Watch this way please, Ricky! — were often wanting to get things . . .

Joe (talking to Ricky): Black man! Samoan!

. . .

Teacher: East Indies.

Joe (talking to peer): Ricky, they're going to play cricket![14]

. . .

Joe (talking to Ricky): Shut up! Prove it! Get stuffed, Ricky!

. . .

[Joe kicks Ricky]

Joe (talking to Ricky): Ricky hurt his foot!

Teacher: . . . the English took over from the Dutch and . . .

Joe (talking to self): They built a ship.

. . .

Ricky (talking to Joe): Idiot! You get out!

Joe (talking to Ricky): You kicked me first you, nigger!

Ricky (talking to Joe): Did not you honky honk. I'm not a nigger you flippin' honky honk!

. . .

Joe (talking to Ricky): Shut up!

Teacher: Ricky, could you try and watch here please?

. . .

Joe (talking to Ricky): Ow! You kicked me!

Ricky (talking to Joe): I haven't! I haven't! Prove it! Prove it!

Joe (talking to Ricky): God, you're dumb! Now I'll prove that you're dumb!

Ricky (talking to Joe): Prove it! You don't know!

. . .

Joe (talking to Ricky): All right! I will! . . . What's fifty-nine divided by sixteen . . . ?

Joe immediately responded to the teacher's inadvertent exclusion of Ricky from "White people, Europeans, we" and compounded the teacher's positioning of Ricky as "other" by directing racist abuse — *"Nigger!"* — at him. His provocative challenge after he first kicked Ricky — *"Prove it!"* — suggests that he felt inviolable even from the rules of order in the classroom. Joe's confidence was well placed. The teacher reprimanded Ricky repeatedly. The victimization experienced by Ricky culminated in a crisis when a group of White (*Pakeha*) boys, including Joe, went to the teacher after school to ask him to remove Ricky from the class because his "bad behavior" was "interfering" with their work. From the teacher's perspective, Ricky was always the child associated with trouble, since Joe was particularly skilled at hiding his racist provocation. Neither the teacher nor the observers ever heard instances of the racist abuse revealed later in the broadcast microphone transcripts, and in a later interview Ricky appeared to be surprised that the interviewer was aware of the racism.[15] When asked about the abuse he had experienced, Ricky attributed the cause of the racism to himself and revealed his solution to the problem:

> *Ricky:* Well sometimes people be racist to me 'cause I annoy them. Sometimes they . . . That's how I know. . . . Sometimes I just get up and hit them and they stop.

Although physical abuse contravened the rules of order in the classroom, the message that superior violence prevails was conveyed by the colonial perspective on history in the curriculum content. For example, the history of New York City provided in the enacted curriculum was a military history in which the English were seen as triumphant and superior conquerors of the Dutch. Ricky referred not only to the New York City unit, but also to other social studies units as the source of his definition of "advanced" meaning possessing superior military strength:

> *Interviewer:* You say they [the English] are more advanced?
> *Ricky:* Oh well, the Indians just had bows and arrows I think, and they had guns.

We suggest that the cultural bias in the curriculum enactment created a climate wherein the White (*Pakeha*) boys used their culturally privileged position to speak out more, contravene the rules of order more frequently, and derive more pleasure and entertainment from the lesson. When the teacher used the football term to initiate the lesson, Jon repeated the phrase and laughed. Mia watched Jon laughing.

The cultural climate triggered Joe's *private* racial abuse of Ricky, but it allowed the boys to engage in *public* sexist behavior involving sexual innuendo and verbal harassment of the girls. One girl in the class, Sarah, had high status among the children because she was a class councillor.[16] This status appeared to enable her to respond publicly more frequently than any other girl in the class, thereby breaking the pattern of male dominance. During the brainstorming session, however, when she responded that New York made her think of break dancing, Joe called out, labeling her "New Zealand Knickers!" (referring to underpants), making her the focus of a sexual innuendo and silencing her: she stopped participating after he made that remark. The introduction (by boys) of information involving sexual content or sexual innuendo was the major threat to orderliness during the lesson and gave rise to much joking among the boys while the girls watched. When one of the boys gave the response "flashers" (men who expose themselves) to one of the brainstorming questions, the ensuing disturbance brought the lesson to a halt. Although the teacher attempted to go on with the brainstorming session, his attempts failed, and he introduced a disciplinary measure — asking the boys to stand and sit down again. The football analogy appeared apt, as the teacher managed the behavior of the boys while the girls were spectators.

The low status of women in the curriculum was also reflected throughout the unit in the private utterances of both case-study boys. For example, during the introductory lesson, Joe responded "prostitutes" to the teacher's question about the first people to settle in New York, and "prostitutes" was the first public mention of women on the second day of the unit.

The language as well as the content and perspectives of the enacted curriculum play a powerful role in structuring cultural norms in the classroom. Who is included, how they are portrayed, and how the children are positioned in relation to them convey to the children messages about who is valued in society. The consequences for the well-being of children who are not White and male are profound. Mia accommodated to the norm by identifying as a White male at the cost of her own cultural identity as a White (*Pakeha*) female. Ricky admired the White male cultural norm, but became victim to it while blaming himself for the victimization. We do not have data to explain the ways Maori girls experience the enacted curriculum. However, in a lived culture featuring a curriculum in which White and male is valued and privileged, Maori girls are confronting bias against both their race and their gender.

The process worked both ways: the lived culture in the classroom contributed to the focus on male experience and interests in the enacted curriculum, and the curriculum significantly influenced power relations in the lived culture. Though the teacher intended to increase the children's tolerance of cultural differences, the hidden curriculum of differential cultural valuing was more powerful in the lesson we selected than his official agenda.

The Effect on the Teacher

In our experience, teachers who are prepared to open up their classrooms to the intensive audio and video recording and observational processes that these studies entail do so because of their deep commitment to children and to improving their educational practice. The experience, however, can be deeply disturbing when the evidence that is uncovered shows the impact of destructive cultural processes on individual children. The teacher involved in the New York City unit said that the data had a "devastating" effect on him, and that it was

> heart-rending because I would have liked to have thought that I was tuned in to what was happening in the class. . . . I just didn't know. . . . Prior to doing this research . . . I would've said "Yes, you know, I'm fully aware of all these things whether it's the race issue or the gender issue, whatever." . . . It comes as a real blow to find that in actual fact you're not necessarily doing things that are in line with what you believe. . . . You're faced with this discrepancy.

This teacher worked with us to disseminate the early findings and to make the research integral to his and our continuing work in teacher education; he has since taken up issues of gender and race in his own in-service teacher education courses. The following quotation describes his perception of the influence of the research on his practice:

> The important things in the long run are the outcomes. . . . The outcomes for me of taking part in this research are not what we originally [foresaw]. I believe that they're extremely positive because they've increased my level of awareness. They've altered my action. . . . It's altered the things that I think are important when I'm devising a curriculum. . . . It's altered the way I treat other people too.

He has also discussed the implications of involvement in the research with the teachers who have chosen to participate in two subsequent studies. They, in turn, have used the opportunity to evaluate their own curriculum reforms that address issues raised by earlier research.

Toward a Constructivist Perspective on Curriculum Learning

There are profound questions to be addressed about the value of curriculum knowledge. Traditional classroom research has bypassed the question of the value, asking instead questions about quantity and efficiency. Sociologists have framed the curriculum content children learn as a commodity (Apple & Weiss, 1983) of which children get more or less — as if it is external, material, and given. But the constructivist view of learning we have taken here renders the concept of curriculum as commodity inappropriate. The findings from our analyses suggest that children do not *receive* various proportions of that commodity. Rather, they construct their own knowledge as they struggle to make sense of the enacted curriculum within the lived culture of the classroom. Unless they resist, they learn to construct a worldview that undermines their gender if they are female and their race if they are non-White. In the kind of contexts we have studied, the knowledge they construct is a Trojan horse for those children who are not White and male. Those children who fail do not receive the certification that allows them a better chance of paid employment in the mainstream of society. Those who achieve do so by coming to construct within their own minds a worldview that legitimates White male power and their own subordination.

While cultural bias in the classroom context is framed by the curriculum, it permeates the entire classroom culture. We cannot adequately explain how cultural bias influences children's experience and learning unless we include the critical role of social class in mediating classroom processes. The role of social-class membership has been extensively documented in input-output studies of educational achievement and in studies showing how parental education and out-of-school access to curriculum-relevant cultural resources and experiences advantage upper-middle-class children (Apple & Weiss, 1983; Bowles & Gintis, 1976; Densem, Wilton, & Keeling, 1988; Lauder & Hughes, 1990). Shirley Brice Heath's (1982) study of the match between children's experiences of language and books at home and at school revealed the importance not just of resources, but also of culturally specific (by race and social class) ways of linking written material to experience. Heath explains that "the *culture* children learn as they grow up is, in fact, ways of taking meaning from the environment around them" (p. 49).

Although the social-class differences between the case-study children in this study were small relative to the range of social-class differences in Aotearoa New Zealand, these class differences were reflected in the children's curriculum-appropriate prior knowledge, experience, and resource access (cultural capital), and in the ways in which they interacted with the curriculum content. When we take into account the complex ways in which class, race, and gender mediate classroom processes, we have the potential for a more coherent explanation for the contradictions and conflicts in children's experiences in classrooms.

Although Mia's race and class privileged her in the classroom, and she learned more as measured by the unit test than the other case-study students, her secondary status as a female within the classroom culture shaped her reticent way of participating and her identification with male experience. Joe was generally perceived as a low achiever by the teacher, and his long-term learning as measured by the unit test was lowest. In spite of his privileged position participating as a White male in the classroom culture, he did not have access to sufficient prior knowledge or ways of monitoring his own cognitive processes to succeed in the class discussions. He was able, however, to use his powerful position to abuse privately his Maori peer and to harass publicly his female peers with no official consequence. Ricky experienced private abuse and unjust public reprimands, but he was engaged by Joe in a shared male culture, revealing the contradictions that arose from his being both male and Maori. Jon's participation in the lesson from a position of class, race, and gender privilege seems to have afforded him both freedom from the kind of anxiety evident in the girls' behavior and obvious pleasure as he sang and joked, impatiently correcting his peers. Ann's attempts to participate publicly were least successful and least rewarded, even though her private answers revealed that she successfully grappled with much of the new curriculum content, despite having less prior knowledge than Jon. She participated instead by talking privately with her friend Julia, taking refuge and offering support in a shared and hidden female world.

A child's class, race, and gender have a powerful and often contradictory effect on the way the child negotiates the sociocultural context of the classroom and they shape the child's experience in the lived culture. These cultural dimensions also have a profound effect on the way the enacted curriculum is translated into the child's personal beliefs and knowledge. Our model of the way children acquire knowledge through a process of generating knowledge constructs is based on the premise that children are more or less constantly engaged in trying to make sense of the curriculum. But making sense of curriculum content in the classroom is itself a cultural process. It involves the child in making links to prior knowledge and personal experience, and in integrating and evaluating new experiences to conform to his or her developing understanding of what constitutes coherent and valued knowledge.

It is critical to understand not only the extent to which classroom learning is culturally constructed, but also the consequences for some children when they attempt to manage the problem this cultural construction may pose for them. Some children may reject the enacted curriculum as alien, as belonging to "them," and not "us," to be kept at a distance from personal understandings and beliefs. Other children may respond to the enacted curriculum as something to be memorized or circumvented to avoid public humiliation. Still other children may actively engage in accommodating to the enacted curriculum by identifying with "them" and learning to be dismissive of their own experiences and perspectives. Some children may feel "at home" and able to pursue a model of "truth" that empowers them to evaluate and be critical of even the teacher's knowledge.

We have demonstrated that children's utterances in the private world raise fundamental questions about bias in research. To focus on the instructional dimension without attending to the lived culture of the classroom context makes invisible some of the most significant questions about both the learning and the well-being of children in classrooms. Our approach promises to allow the detailed records of children's experience to speak directly to teachers, to illuminate teaching practice, to lead to more adequate theoretical perspectives on classroom learning, and to inform theories about the role of schools in our society.

Notes

1. Our project, the Understanding Learning and Teaching Project, consists of a series of six studies of children's learning from integrated instructional units in fourth, sixth, and seventh grades (Alton-Lee, 1984; Alton-Lee & Nuthall, 1990, 1991, 1992a, 1992b; Nuthall & Alton-Lee, 1991, 1992, 1993). An instructional unit is a series of lessons and tasks through which students experience curriculum content relevant to a particular topic. The term *integrated* is used when different subject areas are integrated into the unit. For example, language, reading, and social studies were integrated into the New York City unit taught in the sixth-grade class we studied.
2. In this article and in all our research reports, the names of the children are changed.
3. *Pakeha* is the Maori term for White New Zealanders. We use the term as a mark of respect for the right of the indigenous people to name those who came after them. The term *Pakeha* is widely used in Aotearoa New Zealand. *Aotearoa* is the Maori word for New Zealand.
4. For the sake of simplicity, we use the term *lesson* to describe the 36-minute teacher-directed task sequence.
5. Although this article focuses predominantly on the four case-study children's participation in a single lesson, we traced their experience of the enacted curriculum throughout the entire unit in order to investigate their learning from their total in-class opportunity to learn specific item content (Alton-Lee & Nuthall, 1992b).
6. The achievement levels were determined using a variety of measures, including the teacher's prior assessment of each child's general achievement level and scores on the New Zealand Council for Educational Research standardized achievement tests (administered in schools at the beginning of each school year). The teacher's assessments of the case-study children's achievement levels were consistent with the children's performance on the standardized tests and with the children's actual learning from the unit, as measured by the unit test. However, the case-study children's prior knowledge, as measured by the unit pretest, indicated a possible gender difference rather than a general achievement difference. Out of 99 items, Jon scored 76 on the pretest, Joe scored 57, Ann scored 54, and Mia scored 53.
7. Utterances were defined by speaker and topic. Where the topic of an utterance string remained constant within a quarter-minute interval, the utterance string of a single speaker was counted as one utterance. We located the continuous data in quarter-minute intervals because they were the smallest practical time intervals for the synchronized transcriptions and observational data in the Understanding Learning and Teaching Project. When the topic of an utterance changed within a quarter-minute interval, the number of topics determined the number of distinct utterances counted. When utterance strings (for example, peer conversations) persisted across quarter-minute intervals, they were counted as additional utterances with the same topic. We use the term *utterance* rather than "utterance string" for simplicity. When the same utterance served more than one function, the content-relevant meaning took precedence in the coding. For example, Joe's utterance, "Hi Mom," was a response to the video camera and a free association to the U.S. usage of "Mom"; this utterance was categorized as content-relevant, whereas an utterance such as "look at the camera" would have been classified as relevant only to our observational procedures (in substance, off-task).
8. Throughout the article, private utterances are shown in italics and public utterances are shown in regular type.
9. On the unit pretest, consisting of 99 items, Jon already knew 19 items more than Joe, 23 items more than Ann, and 24 items more than Mia.

10. See Bourdieu (1977) for early arguments about cultural capital and habits. There is cultural bias in the cultural experiences that are publicly linked to new information in the enacted curriculum.

11. Our exploratory analyses of the relation between occurrence of utterance type and learning outcome revealed that Ann's repetition strategy was used more frequently during the time she spent on content she did not learn (Nuthall & Alton-Lee, 1990).

12. There were 112 mentions of people in which gender was not specified.

13. The first mention of a woman in the unit, and the only mention of a woman given in response to the teacher's question about occupations of New Yorkers, was "a prostitute." Another female mention was of a girlfriend of a boy who was the subject of a picture-book story set in New York City. The children suggested that the problems of children living in poverty in New York could be caused by bad mothers. One child explained that young mothers needed to be confined to their apartments because of the violence in the city, and a joke was made about men's ability to be more successful than women, even when they attempt suicide. By contrast, White men such as Henry Hudson and Peter Stuyvesant, portrayed as intrepid and conquering, were central throughout the main lessons in the unit.

14. Male sports teams in Aotearoa New Zealand have traditionally played cricket against West Indian teams. The topic of cricket plays a significant role in social communication throughout the country.

15. Both the school principal and the teacher agreed to allow us to interview Ricky because of their concern about the abuse he had experienced. When Ricky initially expressed reservation about participating, he was assured by the principal that he could choose either not to participate, or to participate with the option to end the interview at any time. Ricky did choose to be interviewed, and when he was answering a question about how he learned the concept of racism, he referred to his own experience. At this point the White (*Pakeha*) interviewer acknowledged that she knew about the abuse because of the audio recordings. Ricky appeared to be deeply surprised that an adult believed him, but then began to talk openly about his feelings about the racist abuse. He prolonged the interview through a recess period (a request unprecedented in our studies) and asked that he be allowed to continue in the long-term interview.

16. Sarah received more votes than any other child in the class on a sociometric questionnaire we designed to identify the children's status among their peers.

References

Alton-Lee, A. G. (1984). *Understanding learning and teaching: An investigation of pupil experience of content in relation to immediate and long term learning.* Unpublished doctoral dissertation, University of Canterbury, Christchurch, New Zealand.

Alton-Lee, A. G., & Densem, P. A. (1992). Towards a gender-inclusive school curriculum: Changing educational practice. In S. Middleton & A. Jones (Eds.), *Women and education in Aotearoa* (Vol. 2, pp. 197–220). Wellington: Bridget Williams.

Alton-Lee, A. G., Densem, P. A., & Nuthall, G. A. (1991). Imperatives of classroom research: Understanding what children learn about gender and race. In J. Morss & T. Linzey (Eds.), *Growing up: Lifespan development and the politics of human learning* (pp. 93–117). Auckland: Longman Paul.

Alton-Lee, A. G., & Nuthall, G. A. (1990). Pupil experiences and pupil learning in the elementary classroom: An illustration of a generative methodology. *Teaching and Teacher Education: An International Journal of Research and Studies, 6*(1), 27–46.

Alton-Lee, A. G., & Nuthall, G. A. (1991). *Understanding Learning and Teaching Project: Phase Two* (Report to the Ministry of Education). Wellington: Ministry of Education.

Alton-Lee, A. G., & Nuthall, G. A. (1992a). Challenges in developing a methodology to explain "Opportunity to Learn." *Classroom Interaction Journal, 27*(2), 1–9.

Alton-Lee, A. G., & Nuthall, G. A. (1992b). A generative methodology for classroom research. *Educational Research Methodology, 24*(2), 29–55.

Apple, M., & Weiss L. (Eds.). (1983). Introduction. In M. Apple and L. Weiss, *Ideology and practice in schooling* (pp. 3–33). Philadelphia: Temple University Press.

Aschner, M. J. (1959). *The analysis of classroom discourse: A method and its uses.* Unpublished doctoral dissertation, University of Illinois, Urbana.

Bellack, A., Hyman, R., Smith, F., & Kliebard, H. (1966). *The language of the classroom.* New York: Columbia University Press.

Berwick-Emms, P. E. (1989). *Classroom interaction patterns and their underlying structure: A study of how achievement in the first year of school is influenced by home patterns of interaction.* Unpublished doctoral dissertation, University of Canterbury, Christchurch, New Zealand.

Blumenfeld, P. C., & Meece, J. L. (1988). Task factors, teacher behavior, and students' involvement and use of learning strategies in science. *Elementary School Journal, 88*(3), 1–9.

Bourdieu, P. (1977). Cultural reproduction and social reproduction. In J. Karabel & A. Halsey (Eds.), *Power and ideology in education* (pp. 487–511). New York: Oxford University Press.

Bowles, S., & Gintis, H. (1976). *Schooling in capitalist America.* London: Routledge & Kegan Paul.

Cazden, C. B. (1986). Classroom discourse. In M. Wittrock (Ed.), *Handbook of research on teaching* (3rd ed., pp. 432–463). New York: Macmillan.

Clay, M. (1985). Engaging with the school system: A study of interactions in new entrant classrooms. *New Zealand Journal of Educational Studies, 20*(1), 20–38.

Densem, P., Wilton, K., & Keeling, B. (1988). Community, residential and family indicators of psychosocial retardation. *Mental Handicap in New Zealand, 11*(4), 4–26.

Doyle, W. (1983). Academic work. *Review of Educational Research, 53,* 159–199.

Doyle, W. (1986). Classroom organization and management. In M. Wittrock (Ed.), *Handbook of research on teaching* (3rd ed., pp. 392–431). New York: Macmillan.

Dyson, A. H. (1987). The value of "time off task": Young children's spontaneous talk and deliberate text. *Harvard Educational Review, 57,* 396–420.

Heath, S. B. (1982). What no bedtime story means: Narrative skills at home and school. *Language in Society, 11,* 49–76.

Howard, R. W. (1987). *Concepts and schemata.* London: Cassell.

Hughes, D. C. (1973). An experimental investigation of the effects of pupil responding and teacher reacting on pupil achievement. *American Educational Research Journal, 10,* 21–37.

Johnson-Laird, P. N. (1983). *Towards a complex science of language, inference and consciousness.* Cambridge, Eng.: Cambridge University Press.

Jones, A. (1985). Which girls are "learning to lose"? Gender, class, race in the classroom. *New Zealand Women's Studies Journal, 1*(2), 15–27.

Kelly, A. (1988). Gender differences in teacher-pupil interactions: A meta-analytic review. *Research in Education, 39,* 1–23.

Kounin, J. S. (1970). *Discipline and group management in classrooms.* New York: Holt, Rinehart & Winston.

Lauder, H., & Hughes, D. (1990). Social inequalities and differences in school outcomes. *New Zealand Journal of Educational Studies, 25*(1), 37–60.

Newton, K. (1988). *Gender differences in classroom interaction.* Unpublished master's thesis, University of Auckland, New Zealand.

Nuthall, G. A., & Alton-Lee, A. G. (1990). Research on teaching and learning: Thirty years of change. *Elementary School Journal, 90,* 547–570.

Nuthall G. A., & Alton-Lee, A. G. (1991, April). *Making the connection between teaching and learning.* Paper presented at the Annual Meeting of the American Educational Research Association, Chicago.

Nuthall, G. A., & Alton-Lee, A. G. (1992). Understanding how students learn in classrooms. In M. Pressley, K. Harris, & J. Guthrie (Eds.), *Promoting academic competence and literacy in school*. San Diego: Academic Press.

Nuthall, G. A., & Alton-Lee, A. G. (1993). *Understanding learning and teaching: A theory of student knowledge construction in classrooms*. Unpublished manuscript.

Nuthall, G. A., & Church, R. J. (1973). Experimental studies of teaching behavior. In G. Chanan (Ed.), *Towards a science of teaching* (pp. 9–25). Slough, Eng.: National Foundation for Educational Research.

Peterson, P. L., Swing, S. R., Stark, K. D., & Waas, G. A. (1984). Students' cognitions and time on task during mathematics instruction. *American Educational Research Journal, 21*, 487–515.

Sadker, M., Sadker, D., & Klein, S. (1991). The issue of gender in elementary and secondary education. *Review of Research in Education, 17*, 269–334.

Spender, D. (1982). *Invisible women: The schooling scandal*. London: Readers & Writers.

We acknowledge the Social Science Research Fund Committee, the University of Canterbury, the Ministry of Education, and the New Zealand Employment Service for providing funding for this project. We are deeply grateful to Roger Corbett for creating the broadcast microphone transmitters and to Greta Bowron, Anthea Warren, and Kerry Hancock for their meticulous work in assisting with the transcription and coding of data.

Understanding Reading Disability:
A Case Study Approach

PETER H. JOHNSTON

These are the words of an adult disabled reader and his wife:

Mrs. Wilson: I can remember one night our then little girl, who's now a teenager —
we were taking her to the emergency room . . . OK . . . on the way to the emergency
room, though — as sick as she was — she was reading the billboards to him, saying
different things, "Oh Daddy, look at," and so on and so forth. And when we got her
situated that night and came home, he said, "You know I cannot believe that this
little first grader can read words off of those billboards and I can't." And he said to
me, "How am I going to explain that to her when she comes home and says, 'Daddy
what's this?' "

Mr. Wilson: And I was totally . . . I never . . . and it's only happened to me once. I
was jealous of my own child . . . jealous so bad that I was . . . really felt it . . . in my
whole life. The jealousy that I felt for her . . . and of course it was over with in a second, but . . .

Jack Wilson went to school through the eighth grade, has normal intelligence, and
as a mere infant mastered the extraordinarily complex task of learning the English language. Why is it that he, along with roughly 14 million other Americans like him,
cannot read? (Weber, 1975) Does he, as most current theories argue, have a fundamental processing deficit that stands between him and literacy but did not prevent
him from learning spoken language? In this paper, I will use three case studies to argue
that there are more likely interpretations that have been systematically ignored because of an essentially reductionist approach to the investigation of reading failure. I
will argue that case studies involving examination of the individual's goals, motives,
and situations should play a much larger role in research into reading failure.

Theories of reading failure currently center on two major differences between good
and poor readers. The first is that people with reading problems process verbal information more slowly than others. Models based on this difference are represented, for
example, by the work of Sternberg and Wagner (1982), Vellutino (1983), and Wolford (1981). The second difference is in the area of higher mental processes such as
strategic and metacognitive (conscious and planful) behavior. Models that fall into
this category are in a substantial minority (Crowder, 1983) and have been described
by Ceci (1982), Clay (1979b), and Johnston and Winograd (1983).

Harvard Educational Review Vol. 55 No. 2 May 1985, 153–177

Major differences exist between the underlying assumptions and the nature of the research from these two schools of thought and in their educational implications. The theories based on differences in processing speed involve characteristics that are resistant to alteration through education, whereas the models based on differences in higher mental processes describe characteristics that potentially can be changed with education.

These differences are similar to the state/trait tension in personality psychology. The trait notion places a stable and internal characteristic at the root of the problem; the goal of researchers, therefore, is to explain between-subject variability and differences in average performances between groups. The alternative to this, represented by the "state" notion, seeks to explain the variability of individual performance across situations. In this case, the expected cause is less long-term and more amenable to instruction than when the trait notion is the guiding one.

Processing limitations and neurological factors as explanations of reading failure are based on a trait orientation that accepts inappropriate strategies as unchangeable and tries to work around them. Alternative explanations stress learning strategies, which are thought of as hypotheses and methods used by learners in different learning situations. These models suggest that the source of reading problems is a lack of strategies, inadequate strategies, and inappropriately generalized strategies. Other problems relate to a deficient or discrepant knowledge base on which the strategies operate. The educational solution, then, is to modify or teach learning strategies and discourage the use of ineffective approaches. By contrast, trait-oriented analysis accepts inappropriate strategies as unchangeable and tries to work around them.

The learning strategies approach, because it allows for individual diversity, is best studied at the individual level. This argument in favor of case studies over group studies has arisen in several different areas of psychology and education. In clinical psychology, for example, the argument has focused on the problem of the individuality of the client versus the generality of the syndrome (see, for example, Allport, 1962, 1966; Bern & Allen, 1974; Browning & Stover, 1971; Mischel, 1984). Behavioral psychology has made extensive use of single-subject research procedures, but until recently cognitive psychologists have generally avoided the use of case studies.

There has always been some support for the case studies in reading. The first one reported was by Morgan (1896), who described "a case of congenital word blindness." In 1938 Olson made the following two statements about case studies in the *National Society for Studies in Education Yearbook:* "From the point of view of prediction and control of the growth and the behavior of an individual, the case study is the most scientific method now known. . . . The case study in relation to education is a method with a respectable past and a promising future" (Olson, pp. 329–332). However, forty-seven years later, this "future" has not been realized. Clinical reading programs still have a slender research base (Arter & Jenkins, 1978). With few exceptions (for example, see Coles, 1984), cognitive scientists in the field of reading have not accepted case studies as sources of data for expanding theory and practice. *Reading Research Quarterly,* the major research journal in the field, has not published a single case study in its entire history. This amounts to a gross imbalance in methodology.

This article explores the nature of reading disability through the use of case studies of adult disabled readers. Case studies were used on the assumption that there can be substantial individual differences in experience and in important dimensions of behavior (both overt and covert) that are as critical as the commonalities between individuals. Adult disabled readers were selected rather than younger disabled readers because they have an important advantage: adult disabled readers have conscious access to many more mental processes than do younger reading-disabled children (Brown & Day, 1983). Thus they can partially overcome the problem frequently noted in the literature, that less mature readers are less aware of and less able to report on their own mental activity (for example, Gambrell & Heathington, 1981; Hare & Pulliam, 1980; Winograd & Johnston, 1982). Reading-process data and the subjects' reports about their present and past experiences learning to read are presented as data sources to suggest non-neurological explanations for reading failure and the difficulties encountered by adults learning to read.

I suggest that some proportion of adult reading disability results from a combination of conceptual difficulties, rational and irrational use of self-defeating strategies, and negative affective responses. Further, since adult disabled readers represent the maturity of reading failure, we might use these behaviors as indicators of the final form of younger disabled readers' behavior. Employing Vygotsky's (1978) perspective on psychological research, I will argue that an understanding of reading failure cannot be gained through fragmented analyses of the speed of performance of various isolated mental acts out of the context of their social and motivational environment and antecedents.[1] Rather, a useful understanding will only emerge from an integrated examination of the cognitive, affective, social, and personal history of the learner.

Method

Subjects

The subjects in this study were adult males, here called Jack, Bill, and Charlie, ages 45, 26, and 43 respectively. According to the Analytical Reading Inventory (Woods & Moe, 1981), their approximate reading levels at referral were second grade (Jack), third grade (Bill), and early kindergarten (Charlie). Jack and Charlie remained in school until eighth grade, while Bill continued until eleventh grade. Although no formal intelligence tests were administered, the occupational levels to which these men had risen, in spite of their reading failure, were evidence of their functioning within the normal range of intelligence.[2]

Procedures

Individual instruction sessions with each of these people were tape-recorded with his permission. Sessions ranged from forty-five minutes to two hours, and the data presented in this paper are largely drawn from eight sessions with each person. Sessions involved interactive assessment, spontaneous and elicited introspection and retrospection, and elicited think-aloud reports and oral reading performance. The conclusions made in this paper are drawn from a combination of all these sources from comparable information produced by more than one person.

Verbal reports remain a controversial source. Recent work, however, suggests that under certain conditions such reports can yield important, valid information (for example, Afflerbach & Johnston, 1985; Ericsson & Simon, 1980, 1984). It is particularly important to note that the retrospective accounts reported here describe traumatic experiences, like the one described at the beginning of this article. For such recollections it is likely that the recollection of the basic event is valid, while the details of the event may or may not be. In any case, these subjects' retrospective reports are unlikely to have been distorted in line with specific theoretical orientations such as might be the case with some previous work (for example, Simpson, 1979).[3]

Results and Discussions

The data relate to a variety of different theoretical frameworks, each of which can be used to help explain why intelligent and otherwise socially adept adults have failed to learn to read. Implicit are some suggestions for prevention and remediation of reading failure. The data have been organized within the general categories of 1) conceptual problems, 2) strategies, 3) anxiety, 4) attributions, and 5) goals and motivation. Each section contains data along with a discussion of their relevance to theories of and remedies for reading failure.

Conceptual Problems

Several types of data suggest that some of these readers' difficulties arise from or are compounded by misconceptions or missing conceptions about various aspects of reading. A minor but interesting example is Bill's pronunciation of "dwindle" as "windle." Did he simply not see the first letter? When asked to repeat it and explain, he noted that the *d* looked as though it ought to be silent. Another example is that Charlie was unable to perform phonemic segmentation of words, a difficulty that must have caused severe conceptual problems as he worked his way through the phonic worksheets with which he was supplied in an earlier adult education remedial program, since knowledge of phonemic segmentation is a prerequisite for analyzing letter/sound relationships.

Other examples are found in retrospective accounts of early reading experiences:

> *Bill:* Through first and second grade I can remember memorizing the books. I didn't read the stories, I would memorize them.
>
> *P. J. (Peter Johnston):* Did you know that wasn't really reading?
>
> *Bill:* No.
>
> *P. J.:* Or did you think that was what it was all about?
>
> *Bill:* At the time, yes.

Similarly Jack comments:

> I can remember first grade. . . . I couldn't figure out what they were doing and it never really caught up with me. . . . I never really could understand. . . . How do these kids know these letters? I know those letters made words, but how do they know them?

And again later:

I had learned symbols . . . and 1 and 2 and 3, which were symbols . . . and 1 is one, 2 is — even two numbers together will make a number. . . . But that just . . . you know . . . so I wanted that for five-letter words . . . yet . . . like I had this idea that . . . I was going to know just by looking at it, you know. . . . But there's no way you could possibly take all the words in the dictionary and just learn them by sight. Of course the teacher would hold these flash cards out and everybody would be hollering the words, and I don't know what the heck is going on, you know, what's she doing, you know. . . . How do they know the word?

Suppose that intelligent individuals such as Bill, Jack, and Charlie developed the notion that reading is largely remembering. They may continue to be at least moderately successful until the second or third grade, by which time the materials would be too difficult for them. To reveal their ignorance at that point would be socially stressful. Additionally, because the erroneous beliefs sometimes seem related to success, they are difficult to give up, much the same way that gambling beliefs and behaviors are difficult to erase. Merritt (1972) has noted this potential for partial reinforcement to make erroneous reading behaviors and concepts about print difficult to eliminate.

That reading difficulty can arise from, and be maintained by, conceptual errors is suggested by Downing's (1972) work on cognitive clarity and is very much in line with the work of Canney and Winograd (1979), Horn, Powers, and Mahabub (1983), and Massaro and Hestand (1983), which show substantial conceptual differences between more and less able readers. An important example of such difficulty is provided by Charlie. In our initial session, Charlie consistently recognized all but four letters of the alphabet and about twenty words. Quite quickly he eliminated the remaining letter confusions *b-d, q-b, d-b,* and *h-r* and learned another fifteen self-selected words. He could not, however, distinguish two of these words from each other — *street* and *sewer.* Since these were the only words beginning with *s,* his identification of them seemed heavily reliant on the first letter. In one session, these two words were placed one above the other and Charlie was asked, "In what ways are these two words different? How do they look different from one another?" He stared at the two words for fourteen seconds before responding, "This one's got five and this one's got six." His response suggests at least two particular *conceptual* difficulties: inattention to spatial orientation and to letter sequence. This conceptual interpretation differs from the more frequent perceptual interpretations. Although both explain the failure to detect stimulus differences, the perceptual explanation blames physical or physiological differences while the conceptual explanation attributes the problem to differences in knowledge of what is important and, hence, the allocation of attention. Several writers have noted the fact that both of these conceptual difficulties represent developmental discontinuities (Clay, 1979a; Merritt, 1972). Neither concept is salient for most of children's learning prior to their encountering print.

Clay's (1979b) work on the prevention and remediation of reading failure fits well with a conceptual interpretation. Clay strongly suggests the importance of early detection of erroneous or restricted development of concepts about print and print processing. Once an inappropriate concept is learned or an appropriate one not learned, further instruction that presupposes an understanding of that concept may be not only wasteful but also destructive because of the resultant experience of failure and its emotional consequences (Abramson, Garber, Seligman, 1980; Dweck, 1975; Johnston & Winograd, 1983; Merritt, 1972).

Retrospective accounts of schooling practices, as in Bill's "flash card" story, suggest that such conceptual difficulties may have been at the root of the problem for these readers. Consider also Bill's response to the question, "How did they teach you to read in the beginning?"

> That was Mrs. X. Stories were repetitious. It was easy. We just memorized them. Any time I used to have to stand up in class, I read great. Y'know . . . I got great marks and stuff. I remember that.

Thus, in this instance, the reading failure was possibly linked to early instructional practices and to the failure to detect a defective concept about reading.

Strategy

Another source of reading difficulty may be the strategies used by these individuals. These can be divided into two categories: general coping strategies used to "get through the day," and strategies used exclusively when reading is required.

General coping strategies. Society places a strong emphasis on literacy. This emphasis is not so much a high, positive value as an expectation that people will be literate. Adults who are not literate are painfully aware that they are considered inadequate. Bill, Jack, and Charlie each said that if people learned about his reading problems they would think of him as stupid. This social stigma has several ramifications, some of which are affective and will be discussed later. One ramification that is relevant here, however, is that these adults' behaviors are strongly motivated by the immediate problem of avoiding exposure as "stupid." This behavior reinforces the unsuccessful and unrewarding behaviors noted previously and ensures that any reading skills they do have receive little, if any, practice. As a result, skills do not become automatic and there is little experimentation with strategies that create flexibility in reading.

Unlike some cognitive difficulties, reading failure cannot be ignored because the demands for literacy are too pervasive. Disabled readers have two choices for dealing with their problem. They can try to fix it, or they can accept it and try to cope with it. Even in their early school years, Bill, Jack, and Charlie were all very good at devising coping strategies that used their strengths to compensate for their weaknesses. This approach began, at least for two of them, quite early. These are some of the coping strategies that they remember using:

> *Bill:* Oh you . . . sit there scared that the teacher's going to call on you. You become a class clown. . . . You can . . . either that or I could . . . I remember a lot of things I used to do, especially in eleventh grade. I had one teacher. . . . I used to walk her out to the car and everything. I'd proposition her all the time. She loved it. I got a . . . I walked out of it with a B average and I didn't do any homework and I didn't do anything in class. . . . But also you sit right up the front of the class too; you don't sit in the back . . . back is . . . They pick on the kids in the back. Since about third or fourth grade I haven't even done anything.
>
> *P. J.:* But you've had to read some stuff.

Bill: Any teacher who teachers her class says verbally what has to be learned. All you have to do is pay attention.

P. J.: Can you remember a point where you realized that memorizing wouldn't work anymore?

Bill: Yes, quite a few of them . . . I was afraid to say anything. It was easier to bluff.

Listening for oral instructions and bluffing are effective only for attaining short-term survival goals but are self-defeating in terms of the long-term goal of learning to read.

As these individuals became adults, they adopted several other coping strategies. One such strategy was to find alternative, nonprint information sources. For example, Bill participates in business meetings for which and at which he must read material. His strategy is to be sure to spend some time "shooting the breeze" with other participants before the meeting to pick up the gist of things. At the meeting he says nothing until asked for his opinion, by which time he has been able to gain enough information to respond. He reported that this also makes him appear conservative and thoughtful. Charlie reads the prices on gas pumps to get the right gas in his car and truck. He cannot read the words but uses the price hierarchy as his information source. Unlike many readers for whom the price is not so relevant, he always remembers the current prices. This method is not without risk, since diesel fuel has thrown him off a couple of times and he has put some diesel in his truck.

This avoidance of print is frequently supported by family and friends. Each of the people referred to in this paper had such support. For example, Jack's wife typed reports and read occasional reports to him. Bill noted that in school "I had a lot of girls who helped me . . . even in class . . . if I didn't know what was going on and all of a sudden I'd be called on, the answer would be there. Someone would be there to help me."

In general, Jack, Bill, and Charlie took a preventive approach to the problem, which involved systematically excluding print from their lives. The goal of their behavior was never to be caught in a situation in which they might be expected to read. This meant avoiding print at all costs in any potentially social situation. Thus, even though they may have wanted to learn to read, they systematically missed opportunities to practice decoding. This avoidance of print must be taken into account in explanations of reading failure that place causal emphasis on speed of processing and on automaticity differences between more and less able readers (see, for example, Sternberg & Wagner, 1982).

Reading strategies. For some, there are practical constraints on print avoidance. For example, two of these people had reached career positions — one in management — that required them to read. Invariably, the material that they were required to read was extremely difficult for them — far beyond their available reading skill. In order to handle such material, they were forced to invoke a different pattern of reading strategies from those used by normally developing readers.

The two men who could read to some degree dealt with the problem of having to read in similar ways. The next section will document their dominant strategies in this situation and contrast them with strategies used by younger, competent readers.

Both Jack and Bill make extensive use of their general knowledge and the context of a given word or phrase in order to figure it out. These context-driven strategies are characteristic of high-progress readers. Most important, they predict and they self-correct; however, the big difference between these adults and younger, high-progress readers is that more able readers use a balance of context and text when they arrive at a word they do not understand. Jack and Bill, on the other hand, rely excessively on context-utilization strategies that they have overdeveloped to the point that their strengths have become their weaknesses. That is, often these strategies are relied upon even when the context and their general knowledge are totally inadequate, and when they actually are capable of using a more efficient print-driven strategy, such as making use of the letter-sound relationship.

There are numerous ways to combine strategies to figure out words not instantly recognized. Forms of phonic analysis can be combined with forms of context strategy such as rereading the previous context or reading ahead to the end of the sentence. When mature efficient readers reach an unfamiliar word, they tend to use some form of phonic analysis, usually in conjunction with prediction (Holdaway, 1979). Rereading or reading ahead are usually tried only upon the failure of the other more efficient methods. Rereading is a particularly expensive strategy because it disrupts the flow of thought (Collins & Smith, 1982).

Bill's response, when confronted with an unknown word, is to use approximately the following sequence:

- read (or skim) to the end of the sentence (or several sentences);
- reread the sentence (or smaller or larger segment);
- consult memory for association (sometimes the first strategy used);
- and use letter/sound relationships (last resort).

This sequence of strategies is likely to be the reverse of that used by efficient readers; the least efficient strategies are used first. But although inefficient, they frequently give the reader enough to continue. For example, when Bill encountered the word *Charlene*, his thinking went as follows:

Bill: Charlotte — Charlene [long pause].

P. J.: Is it Charlotte or Charlene? How would you know? How would you figure it out?

Bill: It's Charlene?

P. J.: How did you know?

Bill: Because I have a Charlene . . . ah . . . working for me at work.

P. J.: OK. But how would you be able to figure it out from the letters?

Bill: l-e-n-e /ēn/ it looks to me.

P. J.: What would Charlotte end with?

Bill: e-t.

The text-driven strategies — his weakness — are avoided, even when they are available. The strategy he used here was to fall back on memory.[4]

Sometimes strategy implementation is less systematic. For example, Jack might simply look at different words for a clue:

Jack: Yeah . . . because know what? I wanted to bounce off those other words, to get that word without trying to sound the word right, without even realizing it. Why do I do that to myself? I do, though. You know, I do it self-consciously. But that's just what I was doing . . . trying to make these words tell me what this word is.

Again, this avoidance of text-driven strategies ensures that they will not be developed and certainly will not become automatic.

The extent to which this use of strengths to compensate for weaknesses dominates and distorts the reading process can be demonstrated by examining running records of Bill's reading. His reading bore many of the characteristics of what Coltheart, Patterson, and Marshall (1980) have called "deep dyslexia," in which readers frequently substitute synonyms while reading, allegedly because of neurological factors. For example, in one instance he substituted *cab* for *taxi* in the first sentence of a story. Other substitutions in that story were *tires/wheels, motor/engine,* and *walked/stepped.* The explanation for this behavior turned out to be more straightforward than "deep dyslexia." While Bill's *taxi/cab* substitution appears to have been done with insufficient context, the context was in fact more than sufficient. When he "read" the word *taxi,* his eyes were halfway down the page. There are two forms of evidence for this. The first is from his own reports, which suggest that Bill's problem is strategic rather than neurological.

I scan ahead to where I'm going to have trouble with . . . I often . . . I'm reading the sentence, but my mind is deciphering that word before I get to it. Or trying to figure out what that word is.

I've got to slow down when I read because my eyes will go faster than my mind. That's another thing I've had to learn to do. When I first started trying to get myself to read, I'd read over something; then, when I'd stop and read over it slow, it would be totally different.

The second form of evidence comes from analysis of oral reading with and without an intervention to prevent the use of this read-ahead strategy. An index card was prepared with a 1/4" by 3/4" piece cut from the top left corner. Bill was asked to read using this card to mask all but the word being read. This intervention was alternated for brief periods of time with normal reading without the card: a few minutes without the card, a few minutes with the card, then a few minutes without the card again, and so on. This type of design produced the pattern shown in Figure 1.

Forcing Bill to focus his attention on the print detail of the word being read increased his accuracy, decreased both the number and extent of his repetitions, and increased his self-correction rate. Bill normally did not decode even those words that he could readily figure out, a behavior that hampered the development of automatic decoding. Thus, his distorted reading strategies were self-perpetuating. Indeed, the order in which he used strategies seemed to be automatic. It was only with great determination and considerable frustration that Bill was able to resist rushing the masking card along to the end of the line. Often he was not able to resist. As he noted when asked how far ahead of his voice his eyes had traveled:

Bill: I used to be way ahead. I'm making myself slow down. Wherever my eyes are looking I try and read the words. That was a . . . that's very hard for me to do.

FIGURE 1

The Effects of a Self-Controlled Masking Card on Oral Reading Behaviors

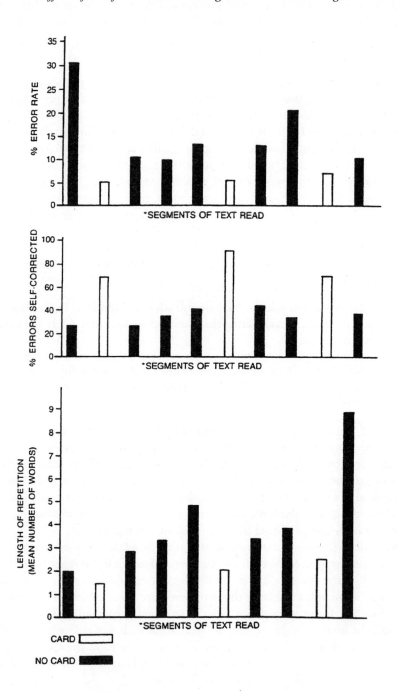

Segments of text were read with and without the use of a card masking all but the work being read. These text segments were not identical in length. Longer segments were broken into smaller units of similar length. The average number of words per segment was 134.

P. J.: OK. So you knew that before you were actually reading about . . . saying . . . this, you were looking here.

Bill: My eyes were about at least four words ahead all the time.

One consequence of Bill's approach to reading was that his attention was divided. He allocated some of his attention to the difficult word well before his voice arrived at the problem. This is very similar to efficient readers' eye-voice span, except that Bill seemed to allocate a far greater proportion of attention to the impending problem than would a normal reader who uses the eye-voice span largely to plan articulation of already-read text. Apparently, the competing demands on Bill's cognitive resources caused increasing interference with oral reading, evidenced by increasing pauses between words as the difficult word was approached (see Figure 2). He also noted this verbally:

> *Bill:* I was concentrating on that word [*mantel*] before I got to it. I was reading, but that's the word I was going to stumble on.
>
> *P. J.:* Do you know where you started worrying about it?
>
> *Bill:* I think when I hit *scientists* I already glanced back down to *mantel*. . . . I know I hit it back up in here someplace, too, when I was worried about it. There was *mantel* someplace else in here.

This voice print supports the verbal report. When Bill's voice was at point A, his eyes had already reached point B (the problematic word *mantel*). As his voice approached the word that he was still working out, the processing conflict between oral production of the words already read and the difficult word to be decoded produced increasing hesitations between words. As noted in the verbal report, a similar pattern of hesitations preceded the first use of the term *mantel* (Point C), including a false start at the word. Also worth noting is Bill's substitution of *heavy* for *deep* in a segment produced orally while presumably attending to the upcoming problem word.

Upon further inquiry it became apparent that Bill was very strong in what Sternberg (1984) would call "global planning." Upon turning a page his first step was to scan the page for difficult words so that he knew where they were located and could allocate attention appropriately ahead of time. Next, he began reading the page to himself before uttering the first word. Thus, there was a marked pause after each page was turned. I checked this on several occasions by turning the page and covering it within seconds, asking how many problem words were on the page and where they were. Bill was able to respond quite accurately. He also described this behavior.

> I initially started. . . . I would take something and look at it. . . . I've got to read this. I'd look down the whole thing and say, "Holy shit! I've got about six of them I'm going to run into" . . . and . . . in my mind I'd be worrying about those six as I started to read down.

Jack, too, had extremely well-developed predictive skill through the use of context. This sometimes led him into trouble because he maintained his view over that of the author. Consider his comments on his (mostly silent) reading of a book:

> Stone Fox . . . did not like the illustrations in that book at all. It didn't do me . . . these illustrations . . . I ignored them totally because I wanted my own visual idea of

FIGURE 2

Voice Print Showing the Location and Extent of Pauses
between Words as Read by Bill

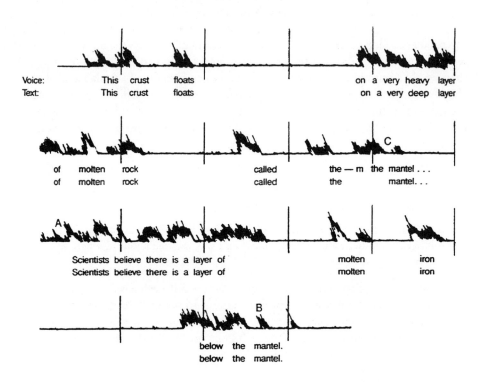

Voice: This crust   floats   on a very heavy layer
Text: This crust   floats   on a very deep layer

of   molten   rock   called   the — m the mantel . . .
of   molten   rock   called   the   mantel. . .

Scientists believe there is a layer of   molten   iron
Scientists believe there is a layer of   molten   iron

below   the   mantel.
below   the   mantel.

Note: When Bill's voice is at point A, his attention is already focused on point B. Similarly, his attention is focused on point C some time before his voice arrives at that point. The substantial hesitations preceding points B and C (the problematic word *mantel*) are apparently caused by interference between the demands of voice production and decoding.

who the characters were and I don't know if that's wrong. . . . But, see, that sometimes gets me messed up, though, with reading. Well, I get so involved with my visual . . . in my thoughts of what's going on . . . and then projecting ahead that I get overwhelmed and I shut down on reading . . . because everything's forced at once and I can't concentrate on decoding, see? So what happens to me . . . I've got to calm myself down and say, "Forget now what's going to happen two pages from now."

Jack's comments are very similar to Bill's, and the pattern of reading performance obtained with and without the masking card (shown in Figure 1) was also very similar to Bill's. From observation and self-report, it seems that silent reading differed from oral reading largely because neither Jack nor Bill read line by line down the page. Their eyes skipped back and forth, and more sections of the text were missed.

This overuse of meaning-driven strategies is interesting in the light of findings on the differences between more and less able readers, and more and less intelligent stu-

dents. That the individuals described here are intelligent is attested to by their considerable ability to use partial information (see, for example, Resnick & Glaser, 1976;
Sternberg & Wagner, 1982) and their extensive global planning (Sternberg, 1984).
Indeed, it is their intelligent response to a perceived problem that appears to prevent
them from developing normal reading behaviors. These data, at least for these particular readers, speak against the explanation of reading failure posed by Wolford
(1981), which lays the blame on failure to use partial information. On the other
hand, these data lend support to a model of reading failure such as that presented by
Ceci (1982), which emphasizes problems with higher-level processing and differences
in purposeful, rather than automatic, processing. Although Crowder (1983) notes
that such a model is at variance with most other models of disability, it may deserve
greater consideration.

A further problem with Bill, Jack, and Charlie's reported or observed reading
strategies is in their specificity. Some of their strategies were devised for certain tasks
and are of no use beyond those tasks. For example, Bill had trouble with the word
were, often confusing it with *when*. He expressed his solution strategy: "Is, was,
when, were — I just say that and I get it." He used this same strategy on three different occasions during the sessions. Its success, however, is restricted to the one task
and cannot be generalized to other problems. It is not clear how it works, but its
continued operation prevents the development of more functional, more widely applicable strategies.

Consider also the case described earlier of Charlie attempting to describe the differences between the two words *street* and *sewer*. His response was "This one's got five
and this one's got six." Charlie was then shown that street had two *e*'s next to each
other — which he indicated he had not detected — as well as some other characteristics. Subsequently he reliably distinguished between the two words and consistently
reported that the *ee* was the basis of his discrimination (after *s* for the initial distinction). The task confronting this intelligent and otherwise successful man required
that he combine knowledge that he already had — distinguishing letters and patterns
— with comparative skill that he already had in an essentially nonverbal task, the diagnosis and repair of pumps and related mechanical and electrical equipment. He was
simply not seeing the words. While motivated to learn to read, he typically did not
apply his available knowlege and skill to the task, and even when he did he used in-
flexible and restrictive problem-solving strategies, strategies that are uncharacteristic
of this generally resourceful person.

Thus, Charlie has developed isolated knowledge about a number of things. For example, he knew that adding an *s* to his Christian name resulted in a friend's surname,
and he could write this. However, he could not apply the principle of adding an *s* to
other words to produce new or altered words. Generalizing such a simple example requires practicing independently, taking the risk of applying it in a new context, and
having rich sources of feedback to define the limits of generalizability.

Anxiety

As discussed earlier, the risk of being seen as stupid caused Charlie, as it probably
causes other adults like him, to systematically avoid practice and feedback. There may
be other explanations of this behavior, too, such as anxiety.[5]

Charlie: j-a . . . uh . . . *j*'s . . . ah . . . getting nervous now.

P. J.: Can you write it?

Charlie: Oh boy . . . had it down last night. Ain't that something. I just had it in my head; that's why I brought it up. Boy, I can't believe this. . . .

Bill: I started sounding it out and stuff, but I started saying, "Hell, I know what this goddamn word is, how come I can't say it?"

In my view, the effect of anxiety in reading difficulty cannot be overestimated, although its circular causal properties are difficult to demonstrate. Charlie, the most severely reading disabled of the three discussed here, is a very fit and healthy forty-three-year-old who had been taking medication for high blood pressure since he was thirty-two. My first session with him is illustrative. His wife had made the initial contact for him to see me. I was to meet him at an appointed place. He arrived ten minutes early, left, and called his wife to tell her I had not shown up. When we later met, his anxiety was apparent in several ways. When I gave him the preprimer word list from the Analytical Reading Inventory (Woods & Moe, 1981), he could read only two words. He was flushed and wringing his hands under the table. Later in the session, after some success with words like *stop*, he was able to recognize, one at a time, more of these words. However, additional specific occurrences provided further evidence that anxiety caused problems. When asked to write *men's* he wrote *mem*, immediately scribbled it out, then wrote *me*, scribbled that out even more quickly, and then wrote *m*, and with trembling hand, admitting to nervousness, he was unable to write any more. Later, after experiencing some success, he was able to write this word unprompted. The next time his performance deteriorated in this manner, he noted his nervousness and indulged in extensive self-recrimination. His wife told me the next day that he had gone to a bar on his way home and "got smashed — he's never had to expose himself like that before."

The debilitating nature of such anxiety can also be seen in the self-reports, where Jack finally works out a word.

P. J.: That was fairly hard work.

Jack: Yes, it was.

P. J.: Because it's not that long, really. You've got much harder words up there.

Jack: I know it.

P. J.: Why do you think you had trouble like that?

Jack: I know one thing. I was getting . . . for some reason something triggered me off before this that I was starting to get tense . . . and I could see, I could feel myself shutting down. Like when I get this way I can feel my whole self tense . . . and I'm not absolutely, not even been . . . I'm not even . . . at one point there I wasn't even being able to . . . I had to force myself to concentrate because everything was going.

This stress may be greater for adult poor readers than for younger poor readers or for other adults facing difficult tasks because they have a longer history of stressful associations. For example:

Jack: What it is, it's the old feelings. It's like, y'know, well . . . something will trigger it. Like when I was a kid in school and they would ask me the first day, I would be in a first . . . say, a new class, and they would ask me to read, and the teacher didn't know that I couldn't read. Well, those feelings still can come back to me, and it's like a feeling . . . never . . . I can't even begin to explain. It's like you completely feel isolated, totally alone, and when that sets in . . . course, I don't get it now like I did then . . . but it's still that quaint feeling will come over me, and if I . . . if it over-whelms me . . . it . . . it . . . it takes you right up . . . you know, and you do, you shut right down.

I think it's more my emotions and my feelings, and, of course, it's a catching-up part. You know, it's like everything that has happened to me through the years all of a sudden comes all floating back, and it's like a crash. You know, your mind can go back and reach out and grab all those terrible, terrible. . . .

If I took . . . if . . . you know . . . like, I would have to take my time. It wouldn't come automatically, but if I was . . . kept myself calm . . . I could read it. Get myself . . . the least bit nervous . . . could not read it. If you wrote it in script, forget it [al-though he can write script letters].

Everything would go blank. I could not pull . . . I could not get anything out of it. It would just completely . . . could not function . . . could not function . . . could not organize my mind to make it, to read it.

These comments reflect a very severe form of anxiety, severe enough to be called a neurosis. Indeed, Merritt (1972) has described reading failure in just these terms. He notes the similarity between the characteristics of reading-disabled children and the behavior of animals who have suffered experimentally induced neurosis (although such research would no longer be acceptable). These include resistance to entering the learning situation, fear responses (trembling, hiding, attempting to escape from the learning situation), inability to resist making incorrect responses, compulsive re-sponding, regressive behavior, loss of the ability to delay a response, and changes in social behavior, such as symptoms of suspicion, aggressiveness, and refusal to join the flock (Hilgard & Marquis, 1964; Masserman, 1950).

The general level of anxiety with which these adults must live is evident from com-ments throughout this article, but for some it is exacerbated by having to deal with in-dividuals who take pleasure in tormenting them.

Bill: He [previous immediate superior] used to like to go through the dictionary to find words to drive me nuts. It drove me nuts because I couldn't even pronounce half of them and that was his specialty . . . so he'd write up the log at night. . . . There'd be important things I had to know, and he'd sit there for half an hour going through the dictionary, so that means I had to sit there for an hour and a half. [Bill talks about the "Webster."] It's fantastic, the words and stuff that are in there . . . it's not that . . . but you can go through it and find words that will drive you nuts, you know. Well, he used to sit there and do it. . . . Well, he's a coordinator now. [laughs] He used to always tell me, "You just remember you're number two," and I just used to laugh.

That such stress was also present in their school experiences is evidenced in these retrospective descriptions:

Charlie: You'd have to stand up and read your book or something, and if I couldn't read or something I'd just pass it on to the next kid.

. . . . .

Bill: I never learned anything through the whole class because two kids used to sit in back of me and beat on me all the time. Whenever I told the teacher she would . . . this is what sticks in my mind. . . . When I would go up to the teacher crying she told me I was a crybaby and go sit down or go in the corner. So I got punished, which I never understood, for being hurt.

. . . . .

Jack: Last week of school vacation was my traumatic week, thinking about how I had to go back into the new grade with my old classmates but with a new teacher, and have to tell her that I don't know how to read. Oh . . . it was terrible . . . so . . . I was cubbied in that little spot in my desk and there I can remember it; and it was like the third day and it was my turn to read and everybody said, "He doesn't know how to read." And she just says "next" and all . . .

If they didn't say "test" I could do it. I know it. If, you know . . . because that was another thing. Tests . . . tests to me . . . tell me that it was a test . . . you know . . . that would devastate me. . . . You'd have to tell me that . . . the word "test" . . . and my heart beats in my throat. . . . Now th . . . uh . . . this [present tutor] that I have now, I think she was aware of that and never would say "test." "We'll do this today," and I think my little trigger in my mind . . . course, I'm always thinking beyond, you know. I would say, this is a test, I know it is . . . to myself.

As noted above, these anxiety reactions seem almost literally to shut down the reader's mind. Interestingly, this same kind of reaction can be brought on by success.

Jack: I would start reading, and I would have to be very careful that all of a sudden I would get this flash on my mind: "My God, you're reading." The minute that happened — shut down.

It also seems that this effect can be quite general:

Jack: I was getting physically tired from reading. . . . Like, I'll start reading and this tiredness comes right over my mind. I almost feel that if I read another word it's going to break. You know . . . the eyes get heavy and I start shutting down, and if I just take a break when that happens — put the book down for awhile, maybe get a glass of water, just do something — then go back to it, it'll come back.

However, there appears to be an additional effect, which is

. . . and I hate even telling you this, but I need to learn the sounds of syllables and to be able to construct . . . and I was avoiding it so much because I'm afraid of it . . . you know . . . you get these little . . . I don't understand why I'm afraid of it.

Further evidence of this avoidance of print detail is provided by this comment from Jack about television credits:

I have actually witnessed myself . . . though . . . in the last few weeks . . . I can turn that right off . . . I have the . . . I don't know it's control or what, but I can actually . . . I can either make myself read it or look at it just like it is.

Together, these reactions — a general avoidance of print detail and a shutting down of processing under stress — could produce a condition of almost literal "word blindness" when reading is required. This would make learning to read a very difficult feat indeed.

Attributions

While anxiety seems very important, at least as important are the causes to which these individuals attribute their failure. Their attributions represent helpless (Dweck, 1975) or passive (Johnston & Winograd, 1983) responses to learning failure. These examples are illustrative:

Charlie: And I went to some program, too. I was in the special class up there for reading and writing, and it seemed the same way there. I was . . . just couldn't pick it up in my head or learn or anything. So I don't know what . . . ah . . . myself . . . I said to myself, I know I'm not going to . . . ah . . . I'm not going to know anything on that sheet because I'm full blank.

P. J.: Mmmm.

Charlie: Just like an idiot.

. . . . .

Bill: Because you feel stupid . . . because they're smarter than you, and if you say anything then you're lower than them . . . idiot can't read, y'know.

. . . . .

Jack: I worry that people will think I'm stupid.

P. J.: Do you think to yourself, maybe I am?

Jack: Yes.

Consider the consequences of these attributions. They imply a stable, internal, global factor beyond the learner's control: low intelligence. This attribution is highly unmotivating and is probably the most detrimental to learning (Dweck, 1975).

Where do these attributions come from? These comments suggest some possible sources:

Jack: Everyone . . . you know . . . [who] didn't bring in their homework would be punished. "Jack, it's all right." They didn't do nothing if I didn't have my home-work, there'd be nothing said to me. So then finally it was like a knife — it was al-most like a piercing pain in my head when she said it to me, "Jack, you don't have to worry about doing your homework anymore."

The boys [Jack's sons] started to have the trouble, I blamed myself for their prob-lem . . . which . . . figuring that it was hereditary . . . you know . . . dunce-o-me.[6]

An interesting change occurred in Jack's attributions as his reading improved. The following two statements represent a shift from helpless, unmotivating attributions to more active, motivating ones with some consequent side effects.

Jack: [initial interview] What's wrong with me that I have this problem?

Jack: [after considerable improvement] I don't know if I should say this or not, but the last few months I felt a little resentment towards my mother because of the instruction, and that bothers me. I sort of at some point say, "Well, why didn't she intervene or why didn't she do whatever she could have done to make this not happen to me?" Because . . . see . . . prior to now I have always felt that there is a possibility that something was wrong. You know, maybe I was retarded. I think that was always in the back of my mind and that's a hard thing to live with.

According to the extensive literature on teacher-student interaction reviewed recently by Allington (1983), Brophy (1983), Hiebert (1983), and Johnston and Winograd (1983), teachers treat less able students quite differently from more able students and, in doing so, implicitly tell the less able students that they are *constitutionally* less able. This attribution of failure to a cause for which there is little hope of a cure is profoundly unmotivating.

These attributions also follow from society's equating literacy with intelligence. Bill's awareness of this is evident when he finally admits his problem to some coworkers. The evidence lies in his attempts to legitimate his problem as a real entity separate from intelligence. Note in the following quotation his use of the term "dyslexia," which has now had considerable public exposure, and his reference to the university and the term "doctor."

Bill: It's funny . . . you start to . . . a lot of people . . . I says, "I'm going to [university name] . . . for . . . I've had some problems reading." I say "dyslexia" . . . just . . . y'know. They say, "Well, what's the problem?" and I say, "Well, I skip lines and sentences and, y'know, I get lost after about a page or so." There's a lot of people . . . it's . . . I always thought that . . .

P. J.: Oh, you thought you were alone?

Bill: Yeah! It . . . ah . . . *Doctor* — "I get the title in there — I go up and see Doctor Johnston," y'know. "Well, what's it cost anyway?" And I says, "Well, he's doing it for free." Y'know . . . and . . . ah . . . you hear the same problem I had. "How can I get help?" and "Jeez . . . you think he'd take me in?" I didn't realize it was that . . . ah . . . y'know . . . these guys are . . . well, I'm in supervision and that's probably crazy, them looking up at me and having problems, but these are maintenance men who have to read the manuals to fix the equipment, and they're stumbling through the manuals.

Bill: Like this weekend — the weekend before — is when I started talking to people. Well, once I talked to about three of them and got the same answer. We're all standing in a group. I was . . . y'know . . . when you throw out "dyslexia," well, that opens it up, y'know . . . and I don't feel bad talking about it.

These comments highlight the extreme loneliness felt by these individuals. Each thinks that he is virtually the only person with the problem. The comments also reveal a legitimate function for the term "dyslexia." While of little functional use in the scientific description of reading failure, it has a liberating social value in separating the concepts of literacy and intelligence.

Goals and Motivation

Charlie had considerable motivation for learning to read. He was being pushed at his primary job to accept a promotion that would pay more but add paper work, and at his part-time job his excuses for not reading — "forgot my glasses," and so on — were wearing thin. His army reserve friends had given him a very difficult time for missing all the promotion tests and hence never being promoted. Why, then, did he not seek assistance in solving his problem? There are several overlapping reasons for this. First, he noted the importance of secrecy. If people were to know that he could not read, they would think him stupid and not value his opinion. His desire to avoid being considered "marginal" to society, and his conflict between concealing his reading problem versus accepting and revealing it have been likened to the dilemma of the homosexual "coming out" (Charnley & Jones, 1979). (The psychology of such decisions has been described by Musgrove [1977].) A second reason behind Charlie's failure to seek assistance was his view of learning to read as a long-term goal, and, given his attributions, potentially an unattainable one. In the meantime, he had more immediate pressures from his two jobs and his social commitments.

Goal conflicts such as these cause these adults to feel constantly ambivalent about striving to learn to read. At different times, depending on the context, different goals assume different priorities, but usually the shorter-term goals take precedence. The aggregate effect on learning to read is generally negative. For example, Bill commented:

> I tried going to [a reading clinic]. Before I even went down and talked to them and . . . ah . . . I just . . . I don't know why . . . I just . . . I was on my way to it . . . do the rest of the stuff . . . just . . . ah . . . never went back.

Bill is not alone in this. The dropout rate from adult basic education courses in the United States is about one-third (Hunter & Harmon, 1979). Cook (1977) also notes that even the threat of loss of welfare payments for failure to attend such courses produced a turnout of only 2.6 percent of those affected.

Nicholls (1983) describes a distinction between motivation in ego-involving and task-involving situations. The distinction hinges on whether the central goal is to protect or enhance one's ego, or to complete a task, or solve a problem. Since the consequence of demonstrating an inability to read is highly ego-involving, the response is often self-defeating. For example, the shift from task-involvement to ego-involvement can be seen in this example from Bill:

> Your eyes have to move in a certain way on the paper so that when I started . . . you'd actually try to read it and you'd stumble through the paper and you notice they're staring at you. So then all of a sudden you're not reading. . . . Your eyes are just moving through the lines down the paper.

Nevertheless, Bill wanted so much to read that he tried several strategies on his own:

Bill: At work I had to learn to read.

P. J.: How did you do it?

Bill: Wasn't easy. I had to use the dictionary. I had to look up words.

P.J.: In order to look up in the dictionary you had to know how to read some.

Bill: That's where my biggest problem was . . . finding out where the words were in the dictionary. I had to look up . . . well, that isn't right . . . but it sounds like this . . . so if that sounds like this, then it should be over on this page in the dictionary. You know, it sort of breaks up the words for you.

In the dictionary a lot of definitions are hard because I couldn't read what the definition of the word was. But in the Webster, the one I have . . . it's what . . . the college dictionary . . . it usually has four or five meanings. If somewhere during the paragraph I can find one of the meanings to figure out what the word is, or pretty much. So, if I couldn't sound it out I could get a rough meaning of what the word was. Another thing I did in the last two years . . . *Sesame Street* . . . watch that with my kids. You see that? Mr. /ch/ or whatever.

On the satellite I'd find a lot of French movies, or whatever, that I could really not give a shit about, that had American on the bottom, and I'd go through them until I'd get real lost in the movie.

These efforts are all self-imposed, task-involving situations. This same intelligent and persistent person, in an ego-involving situation, reacts differently, as can be discerned from Bill's reaction to the suggestion that he read to his own children, ages five and eight.

I actually tried that but my eight-year-old started pointing out my mistakes, so that was that — never did that again.

Others' reactions to one's success can also affect motivation.

Bill: That one [book] I struggled through. I haven't read in a long time. Reading . . . the first time . . . my wife was in . . . I says, "Well, I've finished the book." She says "Well, OK." I says, "You don't understand. That's the first time I've read through a whole book." [laughs] She goes . . . she . . . she didn't think it was any big deal, she didn't. Well, that bothered me a little bit. But then after that I picked up this one. I read that in one night because . . .

P. J.: Was it easier going, or motivation was high, or . . .

Bill: Motivation was high.

Success in this case had a greater effect on motivation than the external feedback. The extreme emotional impact of realized success was expressed by Jack after he had been in the program for a considerable time and was reading at a seventh-grade instructional level:

P. J.: I thought of you when watching *Return of the Jedi.* It has subtitles.

Jack: [excited] You know . . . you know, I saw that and you know what? I realized after a while that I was reading them. I wasn't always finishing before they took it off the screen, but I was reading them. I used to avoid looking at the words, and I couldn't watch foreign movies. But I got such an incredible feeling . . . it was like . . . it's hard to explain. I get the same feeling when they play the Star Spangled Banner — sort of choked up.

Jack's motivation to learn was heightened by his perspective on the free tuition he was receiving in the university reading clinic.

Jack: I think it's a fantastic thing for the simple fact you got two people that are meeting for the same purpose. We're both there to learn . . . um . . . there's no pay involved. The teacher wants to get something out of this as well as the student.

P. J.: But is that what you think helped you best?

Jack: Yes . . . because . . . we're on the same level and I have to achieve for her as well as myself because if I don't achieve I'm gonna make her look like she's failing. . . . Like, see, I have went through the game at work of your paying somebody and I don't want to sound like . . . but it's monetary, when you're paying them, so, you know, do you really have to do it? I don't have to do it then . . . because you're paying them to do it for you. I think it's a fantastic thing.

On the other hand, there were frequent motivational conflicts. For example, these men occasionally expressed concern over the increased responsibility that improved reading skill might engender. If they were to improve they might be *expected* to read, even by those who are close to them and know that they have difficulty. Some of these motives may be quite subtle and difficult to gather evidence for. For example, after making good progress in the clinic, Jack reached a plateau at a sixth- to seventh-grade level where he has remained for nearly two semesters. The reasons for this have not been caught on tape and cannot be presented verbatim. However, conversations suggest that they include the fact that to an unemployed male, regular contact with a concerned female tutor is not something to be given up easily. Additionally, Jack seems to have deduced that if, after 45 years, he finally does become literate, then he always could have become literate. To admit this would force him to contemplate what might have been, and his struggle with this is not an easy one.

Conclusion

In this article I have tried to present a multifaceted yet integrated picture of adult reading failure. The complex set of conditions within which these individuals operate is inextricably interwoven with their cognitive activity. As noted earlier in footnote 1, this perspective is more in line with the work of Vygotsky and of Activity Theory than with the bulk of current research on reading failure. For example, with rare exceptions, the affective and motivational dimensions of reading failure are conspicuous mainly for their absence from current research and causal explanations.

Past attempts at explanations of the differences between good and poor readers have tended to dwell on the minutiae of mental operations without considering either the psychological or social contexts within which they occur. Diverse reader goals have also been given short shrift. Consistent with Activity Theory, in this paper I have argued that such impoverished models are dangerous in that diagnoses that follow from them will favor factors less modifiable through education than those described here. Rather than the neurological and processing deficit explanations currently in vogue, we need to consider more seriously explanations that stress combinations of anxiety, attributions, maladaptive strategies, inaccurate or nonexisting concepts about aspects of reading, and a huge variety of motivational factors. Although these aspects are most likely to exist in combination, I suspect that each alone is powerful enough to engender some degree of reading failure. Given the structure of teacher-student interactions (Allington, 1983; Brophy, 1983; Hiebert, 1981) and the present competitive social context equating literacy with intellect, it is perfectly reasonable to suppose that these factors are likely to cause or catalyze problems for many children.

The consequences of such an emphasis on educationally modifiable components strongly suggest, in contrast to most current models of reading disability, that reading failure can be prevented. Indeed, we have evidence that this is the case. Clay (1979b) has shown that children whose reading development is not proceeding normally can be identified after they have been in school for six months to a year. Intensive one-to-one instruction to clarify their misconceptions and accelerate the development of independent reading processes allows them to return to the regular instructional program in thirteen to fourteen weeks on the average. These students need no further assistance (Clay, 1979b and 1982). The interpretation also suggests that the longer a reading problem goes undetected the more difficult it will be to remedy. Thus, the emphasis is on early detection of reading difficulty, a suggestion that runs counter to some current practices that focus assessment at the end of schooling in an accountability model.

Most current explanations of reading difficulties focus on the level of operations, devoid of context, goals, motives, or history. While some work has focused on the context of reading failure rather than mental operations (McDermott, 1977; Mehan, 1979), there has been little effort to integrate these two dimensions. The consequent explanations of reading failure are sterile and have resulted in more or less terminal diagnoses of reading failure. Until we can integrate the depth of human feeling and thinking into our understanding of reading difficulties, we will have only a shadow of an explanation of the problem and ill-directed attempts at solutions.

Notes

1. This approach to the study of cognitive processes has previously been suggested by the Activity Theory model of cogitive research (Leontiev, 1979; Vygotsky, 1978; Wertsch, 1979; Zinchenko & Gordon, 1979). Activity Theory allows for three levels of activity — activities, actions, and operations — each of which is distinctive yet inseparable from the other two. In this model of human behavior, complex patterns of activities are considered to be the highest level of analysis. Motives and emotions are the major concern at this level of investigation because they drive the activity. At the second level of analysis (action), behavior is seen as organized around goals that are devised to be compatible with the motives. Operations are the third and lowest level of analyses. These more isolated component behaviors are selected to attain goals under particular conditions. Thus, operations are defined with respect to the context in which a goal is given.

2. I based this assumption on Sternberg's model (1984) of intelligence and on the American Association of Mental Deficiency adaptive behavior criteria.

3. Compare these individuals' naïveté with the personal recollections of Simpson (1979). Prior to writing her book, Simpson studied psychology at both undergraduate and graduate levels and had read a substantial amount of literature on the topic from a particular theoretical orientation. It would be hard to avoid distortions in these recollections to fit the subsequent understanding of the problem. Nonetheless, Simpson's work is excellent in its use of cases to build an understanding of the difficulties faced by individuals with literacy problems.

4. These observations should not, indeed cannot, be interpreted as suggesting a need for intensive phonics instruction as the remedial technique. For a relevant discussion the interested reader should refer to Holdaway (1979).

5. See references to attribution theory literature (for example, Butkowsky & Willows, 1980; Dweck, 1975; Johnston & Winograd, 1983; Weiner, 1972) discussed later in this paper.

6. Jack's blaming himself could increase anxiety over the children's reading, which might then be translated into stress on them.

References

Abramson, L. Y., Garber, J., & Seligman, M. E. P. (1980). Learned helplessness in humans: an attributional analysis. In J. Garber & M. E. P. Seligman (Eds.), *Human helplessness: Theory and applications* (pp. 3–34). New York: Academic Press.

Afflerbach, P., & Johnston, P. (1985). On the use of verbal reports in reading research. *Journal of Reading Behavior, 16,* 307–322.

Allington, R. L. (1983). The reading instruction provided readers of differing reading abilities. *Elementary School Journal, 83,* 559–568.

Allport, G. W. (1962). The general and unique in psychological science. *Journal of Personality, 30,* 405–422.

Allport, G. W. (1966). Traits revisited. *American Psychologist, 21,* 1–10.

Arter, J. A., & Jenkins, J. R. (1978, January). *Differential diagnosis — prescriptive teaching: A critical appraisal.* (ERIC Document Reproduction Service No. ED 150 578)

Bem, D. J., & Allen, G. (1974). On predicting some of the people some of the time: The search for cross-situational consistencies in behavior. *Psychological Review, 81,* 506–520.

Brophy, J. E. (1983). Research on the self-fulfilling prophecy and teacher expectations. *Journal of Educational Psychology, 75,* 631–661.

Brown, A. L., & Day, J. (1983). Macrorules for summarizing strategies: The development of expertise. *Journal of Verbal Learning and Verbal Behavior, 22,* 1–14.

Browning, R. M., & Stover, D. O. (1971). *Behavior modification in child treatment: An experimental and clinical approach.* Chicago: Aldine-Atherton.

Butkowsky, I. S., & Willows, D. M. (1980). Cognitive-motivational characteristics of children varying in reading ability: Evidence for learned helplessness in poor readers. *Journal of Educational Psychology, 72,* 408–422.

Canney, G., & Winograd, P. (1979). *Schemata for reading and reading comprehension performance* (Tech. Rep. No. 120). Urbana, IL: Center for the Study of Reading. (ERIC Document Reproduction Service No. ED 169 520)

Ceci, S. J. (1982). Extracting meaning from stimuli: Automatic and purposive processing of the language-based learning disabled. *Topics in Learning and Learning Disabilities, 2,* 46–53.

Charnley, A. H., & Jones, H. A. (1979). *The concept of success in adult literacy.* Cambridge, Eng.: Huntington.

Chi, M., & Koeske, R. (1983). Network representation of a child's dinosaur knowledge. *Developmental Psychology, 19,* 29–39.

Clay, M. M. (1979a). *Reading: The patterning of complex behaviour* (2nd ed.). Auckland, New Zealand: Heinemann.

Clay, M. M. (1979b). *The early detection of reading difficulties: A diagnostic survey with recovery procedures* (2nd ed.). Exeter, NH: Heinemann.

Clay, M. M. (1982). *Observing young readers: Selected papers.* Exeter, NH: Heinemann.

Coles, G. S. (1984). Adult illiteracy and learning theory: A study of cognition and activity. *Science and Society, 47,* 451–482.

Collins, A., & Smith, E. (1982). Teaching the process of reading comprehension. In D. K. Detterman & R. J. Sternberg (Eds.), *How and how much can intelligence be increased?* (pp. 173–185). Norwood, NJ: Ablex.

Coltheart, M., Patterson, K., & Marshall, J. (1980). *Deep dyslexia.* London: Routledge & Kegan Paul.

Cook, W. D. (1977). *Adult literacy education in the United States.* Newark, DE: International Reading Association.

Crowder, R. G. (1983). *Psychology of reading: A short survey.* New York: Oxford University Press.

Diener, C., & Dweck, C. (1978). An analysis of learned helplessness: Continuous changes in performance, strategy and achievement cognitions following failure. *Journal of Personality and Social Psychology, 36,* 451–462.

Downing, J. (1972). The cognitive clarity theory of learning to read. In V. Southgate (Ed.), *Literacy at all levels* (pp. 63–70). London: Ward Lock Educational.

Dweck, C. S. (1975). The role of expectancies and attributions in the alleviation of learned helplessness. *Journal of Personality and Social Psychology, 31,* 674–685.

Ericsson, K. A., & Simon, H. (1980). Verbal reports as data. *Psychological Review, 87,* 215.

Ericsson, K. A., & Simon, H. (1984). *Protocol analysis: Verbal reports as data.* Cambridge, MA: MIT Press.

Flower, L., & Hayes, J. (1978). The dynamics of composing: Making plans and juggling constraints. In L. Gregg & I. Steinberg (Eds.), *Cognitive processes in writing* (pp. 31–50). Hillsdale, NJ: Erlbaum.

Gambrell, L. B., & Heathington, B. S. (1981). Adult disabled readers' metacognitive awareness about reading tasks and strategies. *Journal of Reading Behavior, 8,* 215–222.

Hare, V., & Pulliam, C. (1980). College students' metacognitive awareness of reading behaviors. *Yearbook of the National Reading Conference* (pp. 226–231). Washington, DC: National Reading Conference.

Harris, K. R. (1982, March). *The effects of cognitive training on private speech and task performance during problem solving among learning disabled and normally achieving children.* Paper presented at the annual meeting of the American Educational Research Association, New York.

Hiebert, E. (1983). An examination of ability grouping for reading instruction. *Reading Research Quarterly, 18,* 231–255.

Hilgard, E. R., & Marquis, D. G. (1961). *Conditioning and learning.* London: Methuen.

Holdaway, D. (1979). *The foundations of literacy.* New York: Ashton Scholastic.

Horn, M. D., Powers, J. E., & Mahabub, P. (1983). Reader and nonreader conceptions of the spoken word. *Contemporary Educational Psychology, 8,* 403–418.

Hunter, C., & Harman, D. (1979). *Adult illiteracy in the United States.* New York: McGraw-Hill.

Johnston, P., & Winograd, P. (1983, December). *Passive failure in reading.* Paper presented at the annual meeting of the National Reading Conference, Austin, TX.

Leont'ev, A. (1979). The problem of activity in Soviet psychology. In J. V. Wertsch (Ed.), *The concept of activity in Soviet psychology* (pp. 37–71). Armonk, NY: Sharpe.

Massaro, D. W., & Hestand, J. (1983). Developmental relations between reading ability and knowledge of orthographic structure. *Contemporary Educational Psychology, 8,* 174–180.

Masserman, J. H. (1950). Experimental neuroses. *Scientific American, 182,* 38–43.

McDermott, R. P. (1977). Social relations as contexts for learning. *Harvard Educational Review, 47,* 198–213.

Mehan, H. (1979). *Learning lessons.* Cambridge, MA: Harvard University Press.

Meichenbaum, D. (1977). *Cognitive behavior modification.* New York: Plenum Press.

Merritt, J. E. (1972). Reading failure: A re-examination. In V. Southgate (Ed.), *Literacy at all levels* (pp. 175–184). London: Ward Lock Educational.

Mischel, W. (1984). Convergences and challenges in the search for consistency. *American Psychologist, 39,* 351–364.

Morgan, W. P. (1896). A case of congenital word-blindness. *British Medical Journal, 2,* 1378.

Musgrove, F. (1977). *Margins of the mind.* London: Methuen.

Nicholls, J. (1983). Conceptions of ability and achievement motivation: A theory and its implications for education. In S. Paris, G. Olson, & H. Stevenson (Eds.), *Learning and motivation in the classroom* (pp. 211–237). Hillsdale, NJ: Erlbaum.

Olson, W. C. (1938). General methods: case study. In G. M. Whipple (Ed.), *The scientific movement in education* (The 37th Yearbook of the National Society for the Study of Education, Part II, pp. 329–332). Bloomington, IL: Public School Publishing.

Resnick, L. B., & Glaser, R. (1976). Problem solving and intelligence. In L. B. Resnick (Ed.), *The nature of intelligence* (pp. 205–320). Hillsdale, NJ: Erlbaum.

Sidman, M. (1960). *Tactics of scientific research.* New York: Basic Books.

Simon, H. (1980). Problem solving and education. In D. Tuma & F. Reif (Eds.), *Problem solving and education* (pp. 81–96). Hillsdale, NJ: Erlbaum.

Simpson, E. (1979). *Reversals: A personal account of victory over dyslexia.* Boston, MA: Houghton Mifflin.

Sternberg, R. J. (1984). What should intelligence tests test? Implications of a triarchic theory of intelligence for intelligence testing. *Educational Researcher, 13,* 5–15.

Sternberg, R. J., & Wagner, R. K. (1982). Automatization failure in learning disabilities. *Topics in Learning and Learning Disabilities, 2,* 2–11.

Torgeson, J. K. (1977). The role of nonspecific factors in the task performance of learning-disabled children: A theoretical assessment. *Journal of Learning Disabilities, 10,* 27–34.

Vellutino, F. (1983). Childhood dyslexia: A language disorder. In H. R. Myklebust (Ed.), *Progress in learning disabilities* (vol. 5, pp. 135–173). New York: Grune & Stratton.

Vygotsky, L. S. (1962). *Thought and language.* Cambridge, MA: MIT Press.

Vygotsky, L. (1978). *Mind in society* (M. Cole, V. John-Steiner, S. Scribner, & E. Souberman, Trans.) Cambridge, MA: Harvard University Press.

Weber, R. M. (1975). Adult illiteracy in the United States. In J. Carroll & J. Chall (Eds.), *Toward a literate society* (pp. 147–164).

Weiner, B. (1972). *Theories of motivation.* Chicago, IL: Rand-McNally.

Wertsch, J. (1979). The concept of activity in Soviet psychology: An introduction. In J. Wertsch (Ed.), *The concept of activity in Soviet psychology* (pp. 3–36). Armonk, NY: Sharpe.

Winograd, P., & Johnston, P. (1982). Comprehension and the error detection paradigm. *Journal of Reading, 14,* 61–76.

Wolford, G. (1981, April). *Reading deficits: Are they specific to reading?* Paper presented at the meeting of the Society of Research in Child Development, Boston.

Woods, M. L., & Moe, A. J. (1981). *Analytical reading inventory* (2nd ed.). Columbus, OH: Merrill.

Zinchenko, V. P., & Gordon, V. M. (1979). Methodological problems in the psychological analysis of activity. In J. V. Wertsch (Ed.), *The concept of activity in Soviet psychology* (pp. 72–133). Armonk, NY: Sharpe.

I am indebted to "Bill," "Charlie," and "Jack" for their extensive contributions to my understanding of reading failure. This paper has also benefited from comments by Richard Allington, James Fleming, Rose-Marie Weber, and Peter Winograd.

PART FIVE

Data Analysis
and Interpretation

"To Take Them at Their Word": Language Data in the Study of Teachers' Knowledge

DONALD FREEMAN

Framing the Issue: "The desire to believe in a metaphor"

In his poem "The Pure Good of Theory," Wallace Stevens (1982, p. 329) writes about the ways we represent the world to ourselves. Describing the relationship between the world we experience and the world we make in metaphor, Stevens says:

> . . . If we propose
> A large-sculptured, platonic person, free from time,
> And imagine for him the speech he cannot speak,
> A form, then, protected from the battering, may
> Mature

This creation of ours becomes the thing itself and, as Stevens points out, we become used to it. Thus we replace what we live with stable images that enable our work to proceed. Stevens continues:

> Yet to speak of the whole world as metaphor
> Is still to stick to the contents of the mind
> And the desire to believe in a metaphor.
> It is nicer to stick to the nicer knowledge of
> Belief, that what it believes is not true.
> It is never the thing, but the version of the thing

The drive to make stable, predictable, and accessible images creates a tension, as Stevens puts it, between "the desire to believe in a metaphor" and the fact that "It is never the thing, but the version of the thing."

This tension in words as idealized metaphors for the worlds they capture is widespread in human experience. In educational research, the tension lies at the heart of the study of teachers' knowledge. In the study of teachers' knowledge, I include the domains of teacher thinking, teacher learning, teacher socialization, and any study that focuses on what Walberg (1977) called "teachers' mental lives." In these areas, us-

Harvard Educational Review Vol. 66 No. 4 Winter 1996, 732–761

ing Stevens's phrase, "the nicer knowledge of Belief" has provided both a theoretical foundation and a rationale for the practices of inquiry. Researchers have assumed certain unexamined relations between language ("the world as metaphor") and participants' thinking ("the contents of the mind") in order to capture the inner worlds of teachers in the language they use to express those worlds.

This article examines how the field of teachers' knowledge came to take language for granted, how it came to view language data as a world of metaphor for what participants know and think, and how these assumptions can be recast by drawing on linguistic theory. The argument has three parts. I begin with the status quo: how the treatment of language data evolved in research on teachers' knowledge. Against this backdrop, I introduce the linguist's stance: an alternative view that results in a fuller and more complex treatment of language in data analysis. Drawing on concepts from linguistic theory, I suggest ways in which language data can be analyzed in order to reveal more about individual users in relation to social context, the ways in which their thinking changes and evolves, and the role that the research process plays in shaping the data as it is gathered and analyzed. Finally, I illustrate this integrated approach with data from two studies on teacher change and conceptual development.

Double Meanings: "To take them at their word" and "language data"

The study of what people know generally turns on an analysis of what they say they know. Words are taken as providing a vehicle for thought, and people are usually "taken at their word." But this phrase can be read in two quite different, yet potentially complementary, ways. In the first and most common reading, to "take them at their word" means to believe in what people — in this case, teachers — say about themselves. Thus, teachers' words are taken for their capacity to reveal what is in the users' minds and therefore to *represent* their thinking. Using Stevens's phrase, this leads to "the nicer knowledge of Belief."

The other reading of the phrase gives a very different view. To "take them at their word" can mean to believe — or "take" — what the words say about themselves. From this perspective, language in general, and teachers' words in particular, *present* meaning in words that can be taken apart through careful examination and analysis. Here teachers' words are taken for their capacity to reveal how the words themselves are put together, through internally systematic contrasts and relationships, to present the users' thinking.

The two readings are not mutually exclusive; one depends on the other. They do, however, illuminate basic assumptions about the nature of language and how it is used as data in the study of teachers' knowledge. These assumptions bear serious reexamination. To date, research on teachers' knowledge has assumed, perhaps intuitively, that words can represent thought. In this *representational* view of language data, teachers' words are taken as isomorphic to their mental worlds: their words are assumed to capture their thoughts, beliefs, knowledge, and feelings. Thus, what teachers think can be seen in the language they use in oral interviews, in the written documents they produce, and in the language that comes from other data-gathering tasks and procedures, ranging from questionnaires and surveys to stimulated recall and policy capturing.[1] This tacit view that language represents thinking has dominated research on teachers' knowledge, influencing both research methodologies and the development of theoretical constructs. More importantly, it has served in critical ways to anchor the establishment of teachers' knowledge as a field of study and it has shaped the body of research findings.

The phrase "language data" itself helps distinguish between the "representational" and "presentational" approaches to its analysis. In the representational view, "language data" is treated as "data" or information first, and "language" second. It is studied for *what* it says and not necessarily *how* it says it. This assumption is problematic, given what has been understood about language in linguistics and related disciplines since the turn of this century, and for this reason bears close scrutiny. While treating language as thought may have served an important purpose as the study of teachers' knowledge emerged as a field, it is no longer appropriate to ignore what is known about the nature of language, and how those understandings can shape data analysis.

Research on teachers' knowledge can benefit from work in linguistics on the nature, form, and social dimensions of language and its relation to thought. This linguistic perspective returns some of the focus in data analysis to the "language" in "language data." It offers an alternative way to "take teachers at their word," one that preserves the cognitive and sociopolitical foundations of such research while, at the same time, working more fully with the complex nature of language data as language. This contribution from linguistics, called here a *presentational* approach, allows language data to be studied for the relationships it embodies.[2]

The representational and presentational approaches to language data are entirely complementary; in fact, they are largely inseparable. Their integration enhances and deepens data analysis and the understandings that result. Such integrated analyses accomplish two important goals. First, they allow researchers to examine the processes of teachers' thinking, self-definition, and change that are evident in the language itself. Presentational data analysis contributes tools for looking at the language itself and how it is conveying meaning through the use of words. When teachers' language is taken simply at face value as representing their inner worlds, researchers often assert that these thought processes have occurred, while presenting little direct evidence for the processes themselves. Thus, the outcomes are claimed, but the actual processes of learning, self-definition, and change are not identified.

Second, presentational analysts reframe questions of validity in such research. Validity, in a representational approach, becomes a matter of trusting the meanings that are represented in the data, and the speakers are "taken at their word." This permits little room for differences in analysis or interpretation of data, since these can become attacks on the veracity of individual participants in the research process. To challenge data or interpretation in representational analysis is to argue that someone must not be telling the truth; it amounts to *not* taking them at their word. With the addition of presentational analysis, language itself becomes the locus of study. Such analyses can show evidence of the processes of teachers' self-definition, learning, and change. The integration of representational and presentational analyses reveal not only *what* is being learned or is changing, but also *how* it is being learned or is changing. On this broader basis, discussions of validity can be shifted to matters of inter- and intra-linguistic analysis.

The Status Quo in Language Data: "World as metaphor"

To understand the integration of the two approaches, it is important to review how the representational approach to language evolved into a dominant framework in the study of teachers' knowledge. While neither explicit nor planned, this evolution came about through a mixture of principled commitment to an aim and an intuitive approach to reaching that aim. On the whole, language has been overlooked in the study of teachers' knowledge; when it is considered, it is from the perspective of power and participation, and the relationship between researcher and teacher (see Britzman, 1991; also Connelly & Clandinin, 1986a). Researchers have acknowledged the compelling ability of language, through the categories it creates, to shape the conceptual architecture in research. The argument has been both epistemological and sociopolitical. Bowers, a post-structuralist theoretician (1987, cited in Elbaz, 1991), claims that "language provides the conceptual categories which organize thought into predetermined patterns and set the boundaries on discourse." Elbaz notes, "The ability to determine these conceptual categories constitutes power" (1991, p. 116).

In its wider sociopolitical and epistemological dimensions, the debate diverts critical attention from the foundational assumption that language data, from whatever source, "represents" thought. Regardless of who determines the categories, this representational approach to data assumes that the language in those categories refers to aspects of the teachers' inner worlds. But what are the roots of this assumption? Where did it come from? And how did it develop?

Establishing the Terrain of Teachers' Knowledge: "A form, then, protected from the battering, may mature"

Throughout its development in this century, educational research has generally focused on student learning and achievement, and teaching has been almost exclusively examined through that lens (Clark & Peterson, 1986; Dunkin & Biddle, 1974; Suppes, 1978). The evolution of the accompanying process-product research paradigm cast teaching in terms of behaviors and activities that could be studied and assessed via learning outcomes. In summarizing these models of teaching, Shulman cites Gage to identify four common elements:

> These were (a) the perceptual and cognitive processes of the teacher, which eventuate in (b) action elements on the teacher's part. The teacher's actions are followed by (c) perceptual and cognitive processes on the pupil's part, which in turn lead to (d) actions on the part of pupils. (Gage, cited in Shulman, 1986, p. 5)

In this basic paradigm, teachers' thoughts motivated their actions, which triggered students' thoughts, which motivated students' actions. Through examination of the impact of these processes on one another, teaching could be related to learning:[3]

> A major goal [of process-product research] was to estimate the effects of teachers' actions or teaching performances on pupil learning. The assumption was made that differences among teachers in how they organize instruction, in the methods and materials they use, and in how they interact with pupils would have different

effects on how much children learned. (McDonald & Elias, quoted in Shulman, 1986, p. 10)

Within the process-product paradigm, teaching was framed in terms of the learning outcomes it produced, and, as such, its lived social complexity was overlooked. In the study of teaching, this paradigm faced some serious challenges in the 1960s and 1970s, most particularly in high-profile committee reports in the United States and in England, and in the publication of two studies that became highly influential, Jackson's (1968) *Life in Classrooms* and Lortie's (1975) *Schoolteacher: A Sociological Study.* These studies argued for recentering educational research on the classroom, as Lortie noted in his Preface:

> It is widely conceded that the core transactions of formal education take place where teachers and students meet. Almost every school practitioner is or was a classroom teacher; teaching is the root status of educational practice . . . *But although books and articles instructing teachers on how they should behave are legion, empirical studies of teaching work — and the outlook of those who staff schools — are rare.* (p. vii; emphasis added)

Lortie's view of the primacy of teachers drew upon Jackson's (1968) study of elementary schools. Jackson focused attention on schools and classrooms as contexts in which to examine and understand teaching. However, he extended assumptions about stability, regularity, and predictability that grew out of process-product research to the classroom, observing, "Not only is the classroom a relatively stable physical environment, it also provides a fairly constant social context. Behind the same old desks sit the same old students, in front of the familiar blackboard stands the familiar teacher" (Jackson, 1968, p. 7). From this outside perspective, there appeared to be great regularity in the public world of teaching. Perhaps for that reason, the teacher's mental world was perceived to be minimally sophisticated as well. Noting the "absence of technical terms in teachers' talk," Jackson commented, "Not only do teachers avoid elaborate words, they also seem to shun elaborate ideas" (p. 144).

These substantive shifts in how teaching was viewed were accompanied by movements in research methodology that centered on the interpretative worlds that were being overlooked in process-product research (Shulman, 1986). However, even as the concepts and methodologies of qualitative research took hold in educational inquiry, the basic focus remained on the acts of teaching and learning. Behavior was no longer the exclusive area of attention; instead, researchers examined classrooms as realms of meaning, and as social and interpersonal domains that included teachers' cognitive worlds and meanings. Despite this major shift in methodology and conceptual framework, teachers continued to be viewed as one element within the ecology of the classroom.

In focusing on meaning and interpretation, the qualitative paradigm opened the research process to questions of proprietorship. With regard to data collection and analysis, the issue was not only meaning, but *whose* meaning. The place of the teacher in research forced these questions to be addressed. Clear articulations of the issue began to take hold within the educational research establishment in the mid-1970s, when a panel convened by the National Institute of Education (NIE) outlined directions in research on teaching:

The Panelists took seriously the value of *the teacher's own description of how he or she constructs the reality of his [sic] classroom,* of what was done and why, and of who the students are, and how he or she feels about them. (National Institute of Education, 1975, p. 3; emphasis added)

Simultaneously, a 1976–1977 report by the Working Group on Classroom Decisionmaking of the Social Science Research Council (SSRC) in England made a similar argument in favor of teachers' views of their work (Eggleston, 1979; Sutcliffe, 1977). The increasing interest of the educational research community in the contexts of teaching and in the person and life experiences of teachers, as reflected in Jackson's and Lortie's work, combined with the reports from these two panels, helped to formulate the area of inquiry that came to be known variously as teacher thinking, teacher learning, or teachers' knowledge.[4]

The aim of such research was relatively clear from the outset, perhaps because its focus was easily identifiable. In the 1983 proceedings of the first meeting of the International Study Association of Teacher Thinking, Halkes and Olson (1984) stated:

Looking from a teacher-thinking perspective at teaching and learning, one is not so much striving for the disclosure of *the* effective teacher, but for the explanation and understanding of teaching processes as they are. After all, it is the teacher's subjective school-related knowledge which determines for the most part what happens in the classroom, whether the teacher can articulate her/his knowledge or not. (p. 1; original emphasis)

Comparing teacher cognition to its antecedents in process-product research, Halkes and Olson concluded, "Instead of reducing the complexities of teaching-learning situations into a few manageable research variables, one tries to find out how teachers cope with these complexities" (1984, p. 1).

Elbaz (1991) outlines the conceptual categories into which this area of inquiry has developed, suggesting that the areas of "teacher thinking, the culture of teaching, and the personal, practical knowledge of teachers" now comprised research on teachers' knowledge. The aim was still to provide within the research process a means and forum for the expression and examination of teachers' views and experiences of their worlds. Elbaz (1991) explains this aim in terms of voice:

Students of teacher thinking have all been concerned to redress an imbalance which had in the past given us knowledge of teaching from the outside only; many have been committed to return to teachers the right to speak for and about teaching. (p. 10)

This stance significantly altered the terrain of educational research. Inquiries into teachers' knowledge made a clear and convincing case for the need to include the perspectives and knowledge of teachers in understanding teaching, helping to broaden and refocus the ways and means of understanding education. However, from the outset, the field lacked commonly agreed-upon methodological procedures or a shared conceptual framework. While this ill-defined pluralism was an asset in many ways, it obscured the assumptions that undergird the methodological choices made in this research. Most crucially, it led to an intuitive approach to language data that overlooked its nature as language.

The Basic Methodological Dilemma: "To stick to the contents of the mind"

The strength of researchers' commitments to teachers and their worlds shaped a new basic methodological challenge: to "get inside teachers' heads," as Feiman-Nemser and Floden (1986) put it, to gain access to their views, perceptions, and understandings. Access to this interior landscape of teachers' "mental lives" depended on an intrusive research methodology. Since the interior landscape was as yet undefined, it was difficult to know how to gain access to it. Further, given the commitment of many researchers to the hermeneutic approach of qualitative methodologies and to "grounded theory" (Strauss, 1987), there was some hesitance to posit anything a priori.

This led to the basic dilemma: How could one work to establish teachers and their "mental lives" as the core of a research agenda while, at the same time, avoiding a definition of what those "mental lives" comprised? It was difficult to launch a field of inquiry, especially one with such a clearly defined allegiance to the individual teacher, without some notion of what one was examining. Some sort of a bridge was needed, one that could offer access to the teacher's world while leaving open what might be found within that world. In other words, it seemed reasonable as a starting point to posit what one was looking *at*, while leaving open what one was looking *for*, to suggest the form without defining its content. What was needed was an a priori conceptual framework that was essentially content-free. This bridge was initially and formally supplied by the notion of decisionmaking; more fundamentally, it was supplied by language as the form of data.

The Teacher as Decisionmaker: "If we propose a large-sculptured, platonic person . . ."

In the mid-1970s, the notion of teacher as decisionmaker gained ascendancy as the dominant construct in research on teachers' knowledge. Known variously as "decisionmaking," "clinical" or "data-based decisionmaking," or "information processing," the construct allowed researchers to conceive of teachers' internal worlds as complicated yet rational, intuitive yet purposeful realms. The two major literature reviews (Clark & Peterson, 1986; Shavelson & Stern, 1981) that cover the first decade of the field treat decisionmaking and the distinction between preactive and interactive decisions (originally noted by Jackson, 1968, pp. 151–152) as their organizing conceptual frameworks.[5]

The strength of the decisionmaking construct seemed largely imported from studies on medical diagnosis (see Kagan, 1988).[6] Shulman and Elstein explained the connection this way:

> The teacher's role is compared to a physician's role — as an active clinical information processor involved in planning, anticipating, judging, diagnosing, prescribing, problem-solving. The teacher is expected to function in a task environment containing quantities of different kinds of information that far exceed the capabilities or capacities of any human information processor. (p. 35)

Insofar as the aim of the research effort was to establish the place of the teacher in understanding classroom teaching and learning, it seemed logical — at least in retrospect — to borrow from a professional community in which the practitioner plays a central and uncontested role. Medicine offered the vision of such a community.[7]

The construct of decisionmaking provided an accessible point of departure for research, as well as a workable methodological map. Since early research paid a great deal of attention to teachers' planning processes and to how those plans played out in practice — an interesting correlate to physicians' procedures of diagnosis — the framework fit, by and large (see Clark & Peterson, 1986, pp. 260–268). Documented through stimulated recall (Bjerstedt, 1969), reportorial grid, interviews, or simulated tasks (Clark & Peterson, 1986, p. 260), decisionmaking served a dual purpose as a framework. First, it established the complex rationality of teaching, as well as the importance and validity of teachers and their worlds, as central concerns of this domain of research. Second, it also introduced a group of methodologically workable procedures through which to pursue these topics, procedures that allowed for both quantitative and qualitative analyses. Decisionmaking met the initial test of creating a form for looking at teachers' inner worlds (the decisions that seemed to structure those worlds) while, at the same time, leaving relatively open the content (what those decisions comprised).

The extended use of the decisionmaking construct in the first decade of the field was not entirely benign. Whereas the construct grew out of the twin needs to put teachers' "mental lives" at the heart of the enterprise and to invoke some methodological direction and coherence, it also contained certain key assumptions. Decisionmaking inherited and extended the process-product research view of the world as separated into thought and action. Within this dichotomy of inner and outer, teachers' thinking and their private inner worlds were revealed to the researcher through the skilled use of hermeneutically oriented methodologies. Teachers' decisions were put into words via the research process, thus making their inner worlds publicly accessible. Teachers were taken at their word because those words were seen to represent their thinking.

Language provided the key medium for creating an external map of this internal landscape. Teachers could tell, explain, confirm, reflect, and represent their thoughts, judgments, decisions, and ideas in words to the researcher, who could then, in turn, study and analyze their words in order to make sense of the internal worlds they represented. Decisionmaking as a construct began to separate teachers' thoughts from the language used to document those thoughts, and it was through words that teachers conveyed to researchers what was in their minds. Language data was data, and the research process came to mean "taking them at their word."

Narrative and Story: "Is still to stick to the contents of the mind"

By the mid-1980s, decisionmaking as an a priori construct was no longer central in research. Voicing increasing discomfort with the formulaic cognitive structures inherent in such work, Lowyck (1986) noted:

> We divide complex teaching activity into a chronological dissection without attention to more meaningful categories. We emphasize isolated variables within the preactive, interactive, and post-interactive phases without great concern for the interaction between phases. Now it seems to be time to focus on the integration of the research work already done. (p. 184)

While acknowledging that decisionmaking as a construct offered a useful focus for a young field in search of some initial coherence, Lowyck pointed out that the key relationship between thought and action — or decisionmaking and teaching behaviors — had been overlooked in the push to identify and examine teachers' cognitive worlds.

The concern for research strategies that integrated teachers' cognitive worlds and their actions became central to the next generation of research in teachers' knowledge. Under the rubric of "personal practical knowledge," researchers began to pursue the use of narrative (Clandinin, 1986; Clandinin & Connelly, 1987; Elbaz, 1983) and biography (Butt & Raymond, 1987) in work with teachers. Among other things, the aim was to redress some of the dichotomies that had surfaced in the first generation of work, dichotomies between teachers' cognitive world and their classroom practice, between researcher and teacher as research subject, and between thought and action.

Elbaz (1991) summarized the integrated view of the second generation of research on teachers' knowledge as a commitment to the teacher's story:

> For this work [on narrative and biography], the story is not that which links teacher thought and action, for thought and action are not seen as separate domains to begin with. Rather, the story is the very stuff of teaching, the landscape within which we live as teachers and researchers, and within which the work of teachers is seen as making sense. (p. 3)

The use of narrative and biography as research vehicles largely resisted the dichotomous approach to thought and action inherent in the decisionmaking framework. However, these methodologies did not alter the basic assumptions about language. Advocates of narrative continued to emphasize the representation of teachers' worlds through language data, although the form of these representations changed from decisions to stories (see Carter, 1993; also Hargreaves, 1996) or collaboratively developed narratives (Connelly & Clandinin, 1986a, 1990).

In the second generation of research, as in the first, there continued to be an interesting affinity among what was represented in language data, the form of that representation, and the relative status of that form in the wider world of educational theorizing. When teachers' knowledge was viewed as decisionmaking, some status accrued indirectly to both teachers and to the research community through connecting the construct to medicine and to physicians' decisionmaking. The form of language data was posited a priori as decisions, expressed as statements, while the content was supplied by the teacher/participant. In the use of narrative, biography, and story as research forms, the form was argued to be a natural one (Bruner, 1990), expressed in extended passages of language. Content and form developed together, often through researcher-teacher collaboration (Connelly & Clandinin, 1990). This form of language data also drew upon unrecognized and undervalued forms of knowledge and knowing (Belenky, Clinchy, Goldberger, & Tarule, 1986; Carter, 1993; Gilligan, 1982). Narrative diversified the nature of the landscape to be studied, introduced new means of doing so, and created different relationships between researchers and teachers. But the emphasis on language as a form that transmitted content remained unchanged. Narrative thus furthered the representational approach by emphasizing voice as a means to represent, or create, the teacher's story.

Important methodological differences emerged, however. In studies of decisionmaking, language served to represent the teacher's decisions, the rationale for them,

TABLE 1

Content, Form, and Frame of Reference of Language Data in the Study of Teachers'
Knowledge (1975 to Present)

"Generation" of Research	Content	Form (form of thought worded as linguistic form)	Frame of Reference
"First generation" (1975–1985)	Individually discrete descriptions of thought — planning, explanations of activity, etc.	"Decisions" — preactive/interactive worded as brief descriptive or propositional statements	Refers to medical diagnosis and clinical decisionmaking (see Kagan, 1988)
"Second generation" (1985–)	Integrated passages merging teacher's background and present practice, thinking, and classroom activity, also researcher and teacher/participant	"(Collaborative) narratives"; "stories"; "biographies" worded as extended passages of language	Refers to underrecognized and undervalued forms of knowledge and knowing (see Carter, 1993; Elbaz, 1991; and others)

and to a certain extent the mental context in which they were made. The role of the researcher was to gain access to and document those decisions, even if the notion of decision itself may have been an a priori construct. In studies conducted through narrative and biography, language became a vehicle for collaboration between teacher and researcher, out of which were said to emerge co-constructed accounts of the teacher's world or aspects of it (Connelly & Clandinin, 1986a, 1986b).

There were significant differences in data analysis as well. In decisionmaking studies, decisions were categorized as propositions about the teacher's inner world, and their development and interrelation were traced: data gathering and analysis were separated into sequential activities. Narrative, on the other hand, emphasized coherence and integration. There was increased attention to devices such as images (Clandinin, 1986; Elbaz, 1983) and metaphors (Munby, 1986), and to the collaborative process between researcher and teacher in developing and analyzing data. These devices were intended to integrate the teacher's words, actions, and classroom environment into a jointly interpreted whole (Connelly & Clandinin, 1990). The devices were not exclusively verbal, and, in fact, often drew on interpretations of the teacher's behavior, use of teaching materials, and classroom environment (as, for example, with teachers' images). However, the interpretation continued to depend heavily on language as a shared means of expressing the teacher's inner world. Likewise, the conventional distinction between data gathering and analysis was blurred as collection and interpretation of data became iterative and even symbiotic processes.

The underlying assumption that language data — field notes, interviews, journals, or co-constructed and co-analyzed narratives — can represent teachers' worlds continues to be basic to these areas of research in teachers' knowledge. In commenting on Clandinin and Connelly's (1987) review of studies of teachers' personal practical knowledge, Elbaz notes: "What we know of [a teacher's] practice is actually researcher assertion: *we have access to practice only through the language we use to formulate what we have seen*" (1987, p. 501; emphasis added). Therein lies the basic dilemma of researching what teachers think and know. As Wallace Stevens observed, "It is never the thing, but the version of the thing." The commitment to this representational view of language as data arose out of two basic impulses: the driving concern to recenter research on teachers' understandings and experiences in order to counter the process-product emphases in educational inquiry; and the commitment, which logically followed, to hermeneutic methodologies that could reach into that internal world.

I do not wish, however, to leave the impression that research on teachers' knowledge has been ill-served by this representational approach to language data. To the contrary, the study of teachers' knowledge has achieved the important twin aims of featuring teachers centrally in research and creating the beginnings of a shared framework for such inquiries through this approach. It is, in fact, due to these successes that we are now in a position to reconsider the nature of language data itself, to expand the methodological approaches used in its analysis, and to truly "take teachers at their word" by considering language data as language.

The Linguist's Stance:
"It is never the thing, but the version of the thing"

The linguist brings a number of tools and perspectives to the study of language data. This stance hinges on meaning and, specifically, on the question, *how does the data mean?* The response to this question elaborates a different view of what language is and how it is used. In the representational approach to language, the emphasis is on individuals whose words are taken to represent their thinking. A presentational approach repositions individuals within language, to see users as participants in wider social systems. Language is a function of that participation. Words are not expressions of individuals, but rather statements of connection to and within these social systems. Language provides a map of these relationships. As research data, it offers entry into the interrelation of an individual user and the world. To gain entry, however, language data must be studied for what it is — language — and how it is presenting the world, rather than simply for what it says about that world.

The antecedents of this presentational approach grow out of work in linguistics that began early in this century with the structural analysis of language pioneered by Swiss linguist de Saussure (1916/1978), the translinguistic analysis of Russian literary critic Bakhtin (1981), and the recent work in social linguistics by the U.S. linguist Gee (1990) and others. These theorists approach language as a social system in which individuals participate and through which they are defined. Thus the study of language — and, by extension, of language data — focuses on its systematicity, the relationships created within and through it, and the sources from which it is drawn. The following section presents these three central tenets — systematicity, relationship, and source — to help to unravel Wallace Stevens's riddle that language data is "never the thing, but the version of the thing."

The Individual and the Systematicity of Language

Structural linguists investigated the ways in which language makes meaning through two primary contrasts: what is said in contrast to what is not said, and what is said in contrast to what precedes and follows it. The former are referred to as paradigmatic or associative contrasts; the latter as syntagmatic ones. So *"Joe is talking to Maria"* gains some of its meaning through the implicit contrast to other potential subjects such as *"Maria is talking to Joe."* As potentials, these paradigmatic contrasts always stand outside the given statement in tension or contrast to one another. Syntagmatic contrasts, on the other hand, unfold through time, as the speaker is speaking or the writer is writing. In the example above, "Joe" is linked to *"is talking"* so that each element is governed by those that precede it and, in turn, governs those that follow. A paradigmatic change forces a syntagmatic one: if "Joe" changes to "I," then "is" changes to "am talking."

The implications of this interdependent connection of paradigmatic and syntagmatic contrasts are critically important. By attending to the systematic nature of language, structural linguistics helped to redefine how language could mean. Instead of reference — words representing things in the inner or outer world — the focus is on contrasts, specifically the boundaries between them, which de Saussure called the concept of linguistic value. These contrasts gain and hold their meaning through social agreement, because they are de facto valued by groups of people. As de Saussure (1916/1978) put it:

> The arbitrary nature of the sign explains in turn why the social fact alone can create the linguistic system. The community is necessary if values that owe their existence solely to usage and general acceptance are to be set up; by himself the individual is incapable of fixing a single [linguistic] value. (p. 113)

With this analysis, the role of the individual user of language changes dramatically. Rather than choosing words to mean certain things, users in effect depend on contrasts in the system: they make meaning through invoking these contrasts that depend on de facto social agreements.[8] Think, for example, of a conversation among friends in which a term is used that one or two people do not recognize; that portion of the conversation is meaningless to them even though they may well know the thing to which the term refers in the world, but not know the term itself. So language depends on a speech community to create and sustain meanings. Access to those meanings, the linguistic contrasts to which that speech community gives value, comes through being a user of its language.

Given this foundation of meaning in social practice, it becomes problematic to think in terms of universal meanings. While it may make sense to conceive of certain general attributes in the world, such as gender, for example, we cannot be sure that the words capture through their arbitrary value the same universal quality for all who use them (see Butt, 1989, pp. 36–39). In other words, although there are people who "teach" in every society, the term "teacher" will have different meanings within those societies reflecting tacit, de facto social agreements about the boundaries of the term.

The challenge to the referential notion of meaning posed by the work of structural linguistics is a substantial one. I have argued that much of the research on teachers' knowledge is predicated on the notion that language data can stand for something outside itself, that talk can represent the inner world of the teacher. The concept of meaning as based in linguistic values that come to be shared by a speech community contradicts this view. Since it is virtually impossible to define the limits and member-ship of the speech community in which a particular meaning is shared, it is equally impossible to be certain that language data means the same things to researcher and teacher. In fact, regardless of their collaborative intent, it seems likely that researcher and teacher come from different speech communities. Therefore, the language data that is produced by their interactions — through interviews, stimulated recall, co-constructed narratives, and so on — must be viewed as unique to their relationship and not as representative of other speech communities that are not present or in-volved in the interaction.

This observation about the social basis of language data has been made before, al-though it has not been seriously heeded or examined. In an early article on teacher decisionmaking, Hargreaves (1977) noted:

> When teachers are asked to display their values (to researchers, parents, colleagues, etc.), they doubtless feel constrained by that situation to express their ideals and to assert a strong degree of coherence, consistency, and integration among those val-ues. Practice will not be a simple reflection of those values because practice arises in a very different situation which has a quite different structure and set of constraints. (p. 17)

Mishler (1986) has made a similar point in his analysis of the research interview:

> Questioning and answering are ways of speaking that are grounded in and depend on culturally shared and often tacit assumptions about how to express and under-stand beliefs, experiences, feelings, and intentions. . . . [This] ordinary language competence shared by investigators and respondents is a critical but unrecognized precondition for effective research practice. (p. 7)

Although structural linguistics presents a profound challenge to representational assumptions about language data, it also offers some potential solutions when its con-cepts are converted into methodological procedures. Qualitative researchers Maxwell and Miller (1991) argue that the concepts of paradigmatic and syntagmatic relation-ship are useful in analyzing data that often seem contradictory. They point out that paradigmatic relationships relate to the similarities among data, while syntagmatic re-lationships relate to its coherence. When researchers attend to similarity among vari-ous different pieces of data, a common process referred to as "categorizing," they are examining the paradigmatic dimension. When researchers attend to the ways in which various pieces of data fit together, often called "contextualizing" the data, they are examining the syntagmatic dimension. "The main argument of our paper," Maxwell and Miller (1991) write,

> is that researchers' attempts to analyze qualitative data by means of only one of these two approaches have led to serious distortions of our understanding. We be-lieve that there has been far too little recognition of the complementarity of para-digmatic and syntagmatic approaches to qualitative analysis, and of their joint util-ity as a form of triangulation. (p. 3)

However, in spite of this argument in favor of combining categorizing and contextualizing strategies in analysis of qualitative data, Maxwell and Miller persist in a representational view of language data; they draw on the perspectives of structural linguistics without truly taking them to heart. In approaching language data from a presentational standpoint, as both a fabric and an image, one cannot avoid the social world out of which the language is woven and which it pictures.

The Individual and Language as Relationship

The structural linguist's view of language — that it is systematic, that it is collective before it is individual, and that it gains meaning by presence or lack of contrast — all center on the notion of relationship. From a linguist's stance, the critical research issue is how particular language data contains such relationships; in other words, how it means. How is the individual user expressed in words? Much educational research and research on teachers' knowledge have turned to the concept of socially constructed voice to answer this question. The term *voice* principally seems to refer to three interrelated sets of ideas: voice as an epistemological stance about the source of knowledge and understanding (Britzman, 1991; Belenky et al., 1986; Gilligan, 1982); voice as a sociopolitical stance about who is doing the speaking and for what purpose (Freedman, Jackson, & Boles, 1983; Hargreaves, 1996); and voice as a methodological stance, where what lies in the data to be heard is recognized through analysis and advanced through the research process (Carter, 1993). These stances find their way into research on teachers' knowledge and have become inextricably interwoven, as Elbaz (1991) illustrates in the following statement:

> Thus the language we have to talk about teaching has been not only inadequate but systematically biased *["voice" as a sociopolitical stance]* against the faithful expression of the teacher's voice *["voice" as a methodological stance]*. Recognition of this has given rise to efforts to present teachers' knowledge in its own terms, as it is embedded in the teacher's and the school's cultures *["voice" as an epistemological stance]*. In a sense, the research on teacher thinking constitutes a developing conception of voice *[as an epistemological stance]* and an ongoing attempt to give voice to teachers *[as a sociopolitical stance]*. (p. 11, italic notations added)

The translinguistic view of voice, derived from the work of Bakhtin (1981) and more recently of cognitive psychologist Wertsch (1985, 1991), differs from these three stances. It takes as its starting point the fact that voice is social and not individual, thus individuals assume, participate in, and in a sense are made up of the various voices available to them. As Wertsch (1991) says, "In Bakhtin's view, the notion of sole, isolated authorship is a bogus one. An essential aspect of his construct of dialogicality is that multiple authorship is a necessary fact about all texts, written or spoken" (p. 49). In this view, voices, like language, exist in social communities and people take them on; they are mutually created:

> Throughout his analysis, Bakhtin stressed the idea that voices always exist in a social milieu; there is no such thing as a voice that exists in total isolation from other voices. . . . [M]eaning can come into existence only when two voices come into contact: when the voice of the listener responds to the voice of the speaker (which Bakhtin called "addressivity"). (Wertsch, 1991, pp. 51–52)

So in the translinguistic view, voices are not produced by individuals using words to say what they mean. Rather, voices are relationships created and sustained in and through language; they are interlinguistic relationships (see Cazden, 1989, p. 121). This social view of voice is clearly at odds with the idea of giving voice to teachers on epistemological, sociopolitical, or methodological levels, as argued for by Elbaz (1991) and other researchers in teachers' knowledge. Voices do not belong to individuals, and they cannot be sought out, acknowledged, or valued in that way. Voices exist in and as a social medium. To understand voice, researchers must accept that what they hear is a function of who they are as individuals within the social community.

The dialogical nature of voice means that it is always mutual. Bakhtin explains this notion in terms of the reciprocity of "words and counter words." What the hearer or reader understands is a result of the internal answers he or she "lays down" in response to speaker's or writer's words:

> For each word of the utterance that we are in the process of understanding, we, as it were, lay down a set of our own answering words. The greater their number and weight, the deeper and more substantial our understanding will be. Thus each of the elements of an utterance, and the entire utterance as a whole, are translated in our minds into another active and responsive context. . . . Understanding seeks to match the speaker's word with a counter word. (Voloshinov, 1973, p. 102)[9]

The researcher-teacher dyad, no matter how egalitarian its organization, creates one sort of voice that is unique and differs from other voices, such as those of the teachers' room or parent-teacher conferences, for example. While some of the research on narrative in teachers' knowledge has acknowledged the central role of this dyadic relationship (Connelly & Clandinin, 1990), this work generally claims it as the foundation of epistemological and sociopolitical voice. In the narrative view, the teacher-researcher dyad creates the possibility and the vehicle for the teacher to voice what might otherwise be unheard, and thus the teacher's inner world is brought out, through co-narration or co-construction, in the research process. The assumption is that the teacher's world is there to be revealed. In the view that Bakhtin proposes, however, that voice is created on and for the occasion of the researcher-teacher collaboration out of utterances — "words and counter words" — that each person borrows from existing social voices.[10]

In this social view, language is a fabric of relationships that links people, not a vehicle by which individuals communicate meanings. In his oft-cited statement, Bakhtin argues that:

> Language lies at the borderline between oneself and the others. The word in language is half someone else's. Language is not a neutral medium that passes freely and easily into the private property of the speaker's intentions. It is populated — over populated — with the intentions of others. (1981, p. 294)

Translinguistic voice is a statement about the relationships found in a portion of language. To understand language data from this point of view, the researcher must investigate where the words come from, their sources, and how they are blended together.

Bakhtin's dialogical view of language has proved easier to embrace on a theoretical level than to enact on a methodological one. There are many challenges, chief among them how to uncover and work with the relationship between "words and counter-words." This entails locating the sources of the language, in other words the social communities from which the language is drawn, as evidence of the intended relationship, or voice, created between users by the language.

The Individual and Sources of Language

Thus far, the linguist's stance has argued that language use is more than simply a matter of choosing words to express one's meaning; it involves creating mutual recognition among users. A person chooses words for social, not individual, purposes; the aim is to be recognized, not simply to communicate. Therefore, language that is not mutually recognizable by speaker and hearer is essentially meaningless; it goes "unheard" and unacknowledged because speaker and hearer are not participating in the same social community. The research issue then becomes how to identify these communities and how their relationship shapes the data. When words are taken as representations, these issues are overlooked.

In using the notion of speech community as a source of words, language is seen as social before it is individual. However, speech community is itself an extremely complex notion for three reasons: speech communities are not confined to a particular geographical place (consider the various speech communities among users of electronic mail), they are not confined to the present (think about using baby talk as an adult or slipping into the slang you used in high school), and people can and do participate in multiple speech communities simultaneously (for example, family, work, circles of friends, etc.). As sources of language, speech communities cannot be defined as specific groups in particular places or times. They are linked to the multiple social experiences we have with language throughout our lives.

One approach to defining speech communities has been to see them not as groups of language users, but as modes through which people participate in life. The speech community defines the form of participation to which people gain access through their increasingly proficient involvement in language. Cognitive psychologists Lave and Wenger (1991) have argued that such participation defines who an individual is:

> Activities, tasks, functions, and understandings do not exist in isolation; they are part of broader systems of relations in which they have meaning. These systems of relations arise out of and are reproduced and developed within social communities, which are in part systems of relations among persons. *The person is defined by and defines these relations.* Learning thus involves becoming a different person with respect to the possibilities enabled by these systems of relations. (p. 53, italics added)

Since, as we have said, people can and do participate in multiple forms of life, they take part in multiple speech communities.[11]

The idea that language is a system of contrasts expressing relationships among its users, relationships that are drawn from wider speech communities, provides the theoretical background for a different way to work with language data. This core idea, which I have called the linguist's stance, emphasizes the collective nature of language. It challenges, and indeed debunks, the notion that an individual's words have meaning because they refer to things in the inner or outer world. Instead, the linguist's stance argues that those words must be understood within the social fabric of the research process that produces them. Thus the researcher-teacher/participant dyad is critical to any analysis, since any reading of a passage of language data will depend, in large part, on the researcher's own experience.[12] The truth or accuracy of the data cannot simply be confirmed through a process of triangulation or reference to an external world. Instead, it is established in part by the understanding it triggers in those who hear or read it.[13] This perspective, however, leaves unaddressed the question of how the individual fits into such analysis. If language data is inherently social and interactive, how do we accommodate individual intentions, reasons, beliefs, and so on within the analysis?

In my own work, I have suggested the teacher's conception of practice (Freeman, 1992, 1996) as a way of thinking about this complex meeting of individual and collective that appears not only in research interactions, but also, as Hargreaves (1977) recognized, in any teaching situation. The idea of a conception of practice provides a bridge among individuals' internal sense-making, the socially constructed meanings that they use in that process, and the language and actions that are evidence of such sense-making in the world. The conception of practice offers a way to focus on the individual within the language data. In a presentational approach, language data is examined for how it means by analyzing the relationships created in the particular researcher/teacher dyad and the language sources from which those relationships are drawn. This is done by laying out the structure of syntagmatic and paradigmatic contrasts in the data and by identifying mutually accessible sources for the words that are used.

The strength of presentational analysis is that it can lay out in a passage of language data how thinking and reasoning is working; it leaves open, however, what such data can say about the participants' reasons for doing what they do. In a representational approach, teachers' reasons are taken as given in their words. In a presentational approach, the language data is studied in relation to itself so that the teacher's reasons are analyzed through the language in which they are expressed. The combination of both forms of analysis is crucial to gaining a fuller interpretation.

Combining Presentational/Representational Readings: Examples of Integrated Language Data Analysis

To illustrate integrated analysis of language data, I turn to two examples, each drawn from studies of change in teachers' conceptions of classroom practice. The first study (Freeman, 1991) examined the influence of formal teacher education on classroom teaching, specifically how an in-service teacher education program for practicing second-language teachers influenced their conceptions of practice. By adopting an integrated approach to language data analysis, I was able in the three-year study to document the shifting nature of the participants' thinking about their teaching. These changes, which began initially through the teachers' ways of using language to talk and write about their teaching, gradually took root in their classroom practices, through their conceptions of subject matter, teaching activities, classroom behaviors, and eventually the new professional roles they assumed in their schools (Freeman, 1992, 1996). In the second example, Zinn (1996) examines the influence of formal teacher education on classroom teaching. In the context of South African teacher education, Zinn is particularly interested in the role participants' prior knowledge of teaching plays in their learning. Her study, which is now under way, is a cross-sectional examination of how a particular South African in-service program shapes practicing teachers' views of teaching and learning within the context of educational transformation in South African society. In both studies, integrated analyses of language data have supported a closer and more finely detailed tracing of how teachers' knowledge develops and changes.

Ann: "What do you mean by 'success'? How do you gauge that?"

Ann, a high school Spanish teacher, was a participant in the first study (Freeman, 1991). The following excerpt is drawn from an interview that took place during her classroom practicum midway through the in-service teacher education program. At this point in the study, Ann has taken part in an intensive summer of course work and is now back at her school site where she is a second-year teacher. In the interview, which occurs toward the end of the school year, she talks about her teaching and how she feels the practicum year has gone for her as a teacher:

1]   DF: How would you describe your teaching over the course of this year?

Ann: I think it's worse. (laughs)

DF: Say more.

Ann: I thought I had a lot more . . . I don't know what . . . how I would term this . . .

5]   you were going to ask me . . . I thought I had more success last year. "What do you mean by 'success'? How do you gauge that?" I don't know how to gauge that. (pause) I don't know. Maybe I was more ignorant or something and I just thought all this was fine. This was fine.

DF: "This" meaning . . .

10]   Ann: The class. "Oh, that lesson was fine, that lesson was fine. Oh, so a lot of them failed, that's O.K. That's what students do sometimes." At least that's what they tell me, you know. Maybe I would have gotten upset that they were failing and it's like, "Oh, that's the way it is." They tell me, "Some students fail. You just let them go."

15]   DF: "They" meaning . . .

Ann: Other teachers.

On the surface, the excerpt is straightforward. Ann describes feeling conflicted about her teaching during the practicum year, that she has been less effective as a teacher, which seems odd since she is in the midst of an in-service professional development program. This paradox nags at her: It seems that when she was "more ignorant" [l. 7] she actually had more "success" as a teacher [l. 5ff]. Now, in the midst of this professional training, she feels she is not reaching some of her students; so, is her teaching better or worse now than it used to be? Previously such lessons would have been "fine" [ll. 7–10], but how can a lesson be "fine" [l. 10ff], she asks, when "some students fail" [l. 13]?

When a presentational reading is added, the resulting analysis becomes deeper and more complex. The excerpt shows Ann navigating a process of change through the interplay of voice and community. In Table 2, the text (on the left) is placed beside the presentational reading (on the right).

This exchange presents an intersection of communities as language sources caught in the two voices that Ann creates. The first voice, (A) through (C), is the supervisor-to-teacher-in-training voice from her teacher education experience; the second, (E) through (G), is a peer-to-peer voice from the local language, perhaps from her school's teachers' room conversation. Within the teacher education program, questions like (C) are a way of understanding classroom practice. Among Ann's colleagues in her high school, success is explained through the realization of what kids will and won't do (E). Both voices are intended to be supportive: the first as part of the teacher education experience and the second as part of experienced teachers comforting a novice colleague. These voices are relationships, presented by Ann in the words she uses. Each group of words, as explanations of success, come from a community for whom they articulate a way of making sense of the world. In this brief exchange, Ann is participating in two communities at once, and she is using the voice from the first to critique the second.

The integrated reading offers a more textured way to look at Ann's experience of change. When the two voices — of teacher education and of school — collide as they do here, they affect each other. Ann is clearly torn as she entertains two competing ways of thinking about "success." It is not a matter of one explanation simply replacing the other. Rather, the explanation in one voice actually creates the possibility of the other. Without the language of questioning, (B) and (C), Ann would not recognize or be able to evaluate the local language explanation she has heard and lived in her school: "Some students fail. You just let them go" (G). In shifting her thinking about success, Ann is renegotiating her allegiances. Where her colleagues' explanations for student failure (G) used to be adequate, they are now being called into question. In this process her sense of belonging to that community is also at question: they used to all be teachers; now Ann puts some distance between herself and the "other teachers."

The excerpt illustrates the critical role that belonging to communities plays in making conceptual change. The shifts in allegiance that map the change are captured in the language data of the interview and made visible through the presentational reading. Thus the integrated analysis actually unpacks the processes by which Ann is changing her mind about what constitutes "success" in her teaching.

Nozizwe: "You are only shy . . . why?"

Nozizwe is a Black South African teacher who is participating in the Further Diploma in Education (FDE) Program at the Centre for Continuing Education in Port Elizabeth, South Africa, which Zinn is studying.[14] Zinn's (1996) research has sought to better understand how these teachers may transform their experience of hierarchical education through participating in a learner-centered in-service program that focuses explicitly on collaboration and reflection. Nozizwe has completed the year-long FDE program when Zinn interviews her. Zinn writes in her notes of the interview:

> A striking feature of Nozizwe's manner is her shyness, which she points out herself. In fact, Nozizwe remarked to me before one of our interviews, "My mother said, 'Why would she want to interview you?'" It seems Nozizwe was cuing me into a

TABLE 2

Ann: Presentational Reading

Text	Presentational Reading
DF: How would you describe your teaching over the course of this year?	
Ann: I think it's worse. (laughs)	Ann responds with a global answer that seems to invite elaboration . . . which the interviewer asks for.
DF: Say more.	
Ann: I thought I had a lot more . . . I don't know what . . . how I would term this . . . ^A<u>you were going to ask me</u> . . .	She then constructs a conversation (**A**) between "you" (the interviewer) and "me" (Ann).
^B*I thought I had more success last year.* ^C*"What do you mean by 'success'? How do you gauge that?"* I don't know how to gauge that. (pause) ^D*I don't know. Maybe I was more ignorant or something and I just thought all this was fine. This was fine.*	Using these roles, she answers (**B**) and then queries herself (**C**) as her practicum supervisor might have. Her use of pronouns here is interesting. In the exchange Ann refers to herself from the outside in, using the second person "you" in the question, "What do <u>you</u> mean . . ." (**C**), and from the inside out using the first person in the answer, "Maybe <u>I</u> was more ignorant . . ." (**D**).
DF: "This" meaning . . .	
Ann: The class. ^E*"Oh, that lesson was fine, that lesson was fine. Oh, so a lot of them failed, that's O.K. That's what students do sometimes."* ^F*At least that's what they tell me,* you know. Maybe I would have gotten upset that they were failing and	As she continues, she shifts the dialogue to one with her fellow teachers at her school (**E**). Here again her positioning with pronouns is key. Using the most removed pronoun, the third person plural, "that's what <u>they</u> tell <u>me</u>," (**F**) she puts the greatest distance she can between herself and their opinion.
it's like, "Oh, that's the way it is." ^G*They tell me, "Some students fail. You just let them go."*	These comments address her directly, "they tell me" (**G**).
DF: "They" meaning . . .	
Ann: ^H<u>Other teachers.</u>	And when asked, she identifies the "they" as other people like herself — "other teachers" (**H**).

dominant feature of her personality, one that goes so deep, it involves all of who she is, in the way her mother knows her. In keeping, therefore, with the way Nozizwe uses her own learning process to understand what may be going on with her students, she focuses frequently on those learners who may be shy, and the ways in which her learning in the FDE can facilitate their learning.

Zinn notes that Nozizwe's comments are "extremely significant, because shyness in the South African context is not simply a personality trait; it has a political dimension." In their interview, Nozizwe herself alludes to this point:

1] I usually say to my kids at school, when I look, say, in the classroom for instance: "You take the White child and you take the Black child. You are only shy . . . why?" I don't want to say it's the upbringing. It's the way we were taught in our schools, right. At the top [the teachers], you like to say "No" . . . Same thing

5] applies with something like interviews, we are not used to that. Because we don't teach our kids. . . . We haven't got that confidence. I don't know whether it's myself or how I see it, because I'm not used to talking.

Reading the excerpt on the representational level, Zinn comments that

Nozizwe is conveying a complex set of ideas. First, she is prompting her students not to take their behavior at face value [ll. 2–3]. She asks them to look to sociopolitical factors and maybe racism for the reasons why they behave differently [ll. 3–4]. Second, she identifies the top-down, authoritarian approach in black schools [l. 4], which denies children the freedom to ask questions and be themselves, as one of the reasons students are afraid to talk up in class. This undermines the students' — and later adults' — confidence, and teachers do little to help build that confidence. At the same time, she is providing a rationalization for her own "shyness," maybe her reticence in answering some of the interview questions, when she says that "the same applies" to interviews [ll. 4–5], invoking all of the above reasons in her explanation of her own manner [ll. 6–7].

The presentational analysis of the same excerpt allows us to see more exactly how Nozizwe constructs her explanation of shyness as a personal and sociopolitical attribute.

As in Ann's excerpt, the shifts in pronouns trace how Nozizwe, as speaker, positions what she says in relation to Zinn, the interviewer. The syntagmatic unfolding of pronouns moves from "I" (A) to "you" (B), (C), to "we" (D), (F), to "I" (H), thus linking Nozizwe and Zinn as protagonists in different ways. Beneath these surface movements is a complex argument; as Zinn notes, "Nozizwe is helping me understand (A) how she asks the kids to step outside of themselves to look at themselves and try to understand their reluctance to speak up (B-C)." She locates this pedagogical discussion with Zinn within the larger framework of their common experience, as Zinn observes: "Nozizwe includes herself (and possibly me too) (D-E) in the membership of this group of teachers (F) [who have been similarly impacted by the hierarchical sociopolitical structure of apartheid] . . . helping to locate this idea [of the personal and sociopolitical roots of shyness] for us within this black community of practitioners (G-I)."

TABLE 3
Nozizwe: Presentational Reading

Text	Presentational Reading
[A]I usually say to **my** kids at school, when **I** look, say, in the classroom for instance:	The "I," (A), is Nozizwe speaking as the teacher to position herself in her classroom with her students.
[B]**"You** take the White child and **you** take the Black child.	Using "you," (B), she refers directly to her students, addressing the interviewer, Zinn, "You take . . ."
[C]*You are only shy . . . why?"*	But then the "you" changes and she is in the room addressing her Black students: "You are only shy . . . why?" (C).
I don't want to say it's the upbringing. It's the way [D]**we** were taught in **our schools,** [E]right. At the top [the teachers], you like to say "No"	In her answer, she places herself with Zinn, a South African of color (D), confirming their shared experience (E).
. . . [the] same thing applies with something like interviews, [F]**we** are not used to that.	Drawing the parallel to the interview situation, "we" changes (F) to the teachers interviewed by Zinn as part of the study.
[G]Because we don't teach our kids. . . . We haven't got that confidence.	She points out that it takes conscious intervention to change the status quo (G). She captures herself both as a product of that system (F), and possibly one who does not interrupt it (G).
[H]I don't know whether it's **myself** or how **I** see it, because [I]**I'm not used to talking.**	Then, reverting to first person (H), as an FDE student Nozizwe makes sense of herself as learner, wondering whether it is her nature, "myself," or the sociopolitical context that has rendered her "not used to talking" (I).

Source: Zinn (1996).

Voices and Their Language Sources in Presentational Analyses

To identify the voices and their language sources in presentational analyses, it is critical to know something about the backgrounds of the participants in the researcher-teacher dyad, for it is that dyad that generates the passage of language data. In these two instances, the researchers are "insiders" to the social communities on which the teacher draws to explain her thinking. In the first excerpt, I am Ann's interlocutor; I have also been a faculty member of the teacher education program and thus can recognize and hear the language of the practicum supervisor. Like Ann, I too have been a high school foreign language teacher and can recognize the language of peers in the teachers' room. Thus I can "hear" her conflicting explanations of "success." In the second excerpt, as a fellow South African, former classroom teacher, and woman of color, Zinn clearly shares the language sources of the experience as student and teacher that Nozizwe uses to explain her shyness.

These relationships come into play in elaborating the voices that are in each excerpt. Each voice is a mutual social construction that depends as much on being heard as it does on what is said. Thus, who the researcher is shapes what she or he can hear because it circumscribes the sources of language available to the researcher-teacher dyad. The sources from which the teacher — as Ann or Nozizwe do — "borrows" her words are shaped by who is listening. Thus rather than being implicated as a shadowy presence in the process, the researcher is firmly located within the analysis. Ann says what she does because she is talking to me; likewise Nozizwe says what she does because she is talking to Zinn. The presentational analyses make visible these relationships as the medium through which the meaning is expressed.

Herein lies the value of integrated analyses of language data. When language is treated as transparent data and Ann and Nozizwe are simply taken at their words, the resulting representational readings show only the broad sweep of their ideas. When the same language data is treated as language, and their words are taken as words, the resulting presentational analysis shows how each teacher is revising and building her way of thinking. Without a closer analysis of her words, the actual processes by which her knowledge and thinking are developing would be missed. The integration of representational and presentational analyses — what the data says and how it says it — is key to realizing these insights. The topic and the categories of meaning are established through the straight, representational reading of the data in each case, that is how we know what the teacher is talking about. However, the development of these ideas is charted through a close study of where her words come from, their sources in the language of particular communities, how these words are combined to invoke specific voices, or relationships.

When, as it often does in research on teachers' knowledge, analysis of language data means simply reading what is there and taking the teacher at her word, processes of change and development in knowledge and thinking — like those we see in Ann and Nozizwe — can be claimed, but they cannot be seen. However, when that same data is also viewed from the linguist's stance, as language, and the words are taken for themselves, then new possibilities arise and it becomes feasible to examine *how* the data means.

Integrating Representational/Presentational Analyses in the Study of Language Data

When representational and presentational analyses are integrated, we can trace, in the data itself, how teachers are constructing their knowledge of teaching. We can move beyond simply documenting teachers' "mental lives" to mapping out how their lives evolve and what influences the development of those lives. We can also study much more closely what creates change in teachers' knowledge and the processes by which such change is happening.

This opens new possibilities to focus on the actual processes of learning and change in such diverse areas as teacher socialization, teacher learning, the influences of teacher education on teaching, teacher thinking, teachers' experiences in school restructuring, mentoring, among others. It becomes possible, for example, to study teacher socialization as the acquisition by new teachers of the social fabric of the school: How does language data express the relationships, tensions, and conflicts between these new arrivals' personal backgrounds and professional training, and the conceptions of teaching, learning, and work in the school as a social/language community? Similarly, mentoring can be studied as the meeting of language sources: the mentor and the apprentice. What is the new voice created in that relationship as one teacher learns from another within the social community of the school? Because presentational analysis can trace the intersections, conflicts, and melding of different sources of language out of which the voices in the data are created, researchers can amplify the ways in which these crucial processes work.

The integration of these two forms of analysis affirms the epistemological and sociopolitical agenda in the study of teachers' knowledge, namely, to feature the teacher centrally in such work. However, it does so with greater justice to the complex processes through which teachers' knowledge develops and is displayed. The generally intuitive and naive treatment of language data in such research has usually made arguments for shared teacher/researcher participation a matter of ethics and politics rather than of actual procedure. With the addition of presentational analysis, shared participation becomes a practical necessity for achieving comprehensive understanding. The presentational analysis of voice, for example, calls for an intimate knowledge of where particular words in the data come from and why they have been chosen to express what they say. Although the researcher can have some access to this information through immersion in the language of the research setting, or by studying settings in which he or she is a resident participant as Zinn and I did, the analytical work is greatly enhanced by the teachers' full participation. Learning to recognize and identify voices, and their sources in the data, can make teachers full and genuine collaborators in the research process since the knowledge of the sources and structure of linguistic information may belong only to them.

Revisiting Dichotomies as Oppositions:
"The weather in words and words in sounds of sound"

The dichotomies inherent in "taking teachers at their word" and "language data" — the notion that they are either/or — are meant as heuristics to propel new thinking about forms of analysis of language data. I do not want to leave them intact as dichotomies, but rather as useful oppositions, for I believe the productive use of language data in the study of teachers' knowledge depends on their integration. The view I have outlined here treats language data in ways that are complex and more appropriate to its character as language. It is not easy, however, and perhaps for that reason alone it may be resisted. Writing about the similar difficulties in anthropological linguistics, Doe (a pseudonym) (1988) summarizes the challenges this way:

> The task is to understand this dramatic teetering interaction of *reality, experience,* and *expression.* This task . . . is complicated by the fact that two of its three objects of study are invisible. *Expression* can be heard and seen, measured, and calculated.

. . . However *reality* can only be approached through experience: there is no objective standpoint outside of experience from which to view reality. . . . And *experience* can only be revealed through a telling. Perceptions are, after all, invisible mental processes which are revealed only through speech. Hence the task of exploring the interaction between reality, experience, and expression runs into the problem of the inaccessibility of both reality and experience. (p. 193, emphasis added)

What is left, as Doe notes, is expression, and this becomes the focus of a presentational study of language data: How are teachers' experiences, and thus their versions of reality, told? How do their words mean?

This brings us full circle to where we began, with Wallace Stevens's poem, in which he traces everything to the abstraction of words:

> The day in its color not pretending time,
> Time in its weather, our most sovereign lord,
> The weather in words and words in sounds of sound.

This, it seems to me, is the challenge of any study of what people know or think: How to work with their words while not letting those words get in the way or become things in themselves. It is not a challenge to be ignored or avoided, as we have largely done to date in the study of teachers' knowledge. It is one that promises the productive blending of the linguist's stance towards the participants' words and intentions, within the frameworks, tools, and values of interpretative research.

Notes

1. Clark and Peterson (1986, pp. 259–260) offer a detailed discussion of various such data-gathering procedures in their review of teacher-thinking research.
2. In discussing how knowledge develops, Shannon (cited in Rivers, 1991, p. 287) makes a distinction between presentational, as the "process of acquisition of knowledge," and representational, as the "product established in the mind." While I have recently discovered that we are using the same words, my meaning differs from his and is strictly linguistic.
3. Dunkin and Biddle (1974) outlined four types of variables that influenced these processes: presage or background variables, context variables (about the community, school, and classroom), process variables (behaviors and changes in the classroom), and product variables (short and longer term effects on student learning and achievement).
4. The major literature reviews in these domains (e.g., Clark & Peterson, 1986; Shavelson & Stern, 1981), along with major collections of published research (Calderhead, 1987), cite the NIE and SSRC panels as articulating the focus that evolved into research on teachers' knowledge and cognition.
5. Clark and Peterson commented in the third edition of the *Handbook of Research on Teaching* (1986) that the second edition, some thirteen years earlier, contained no formal mention of teacher thinking as an area of research (p. 292). Shavelson and Stern (1981) also noted teacher thinking's relatively recent emergence as a research concern, referring to Shavelson's article, "What is *the* Basic Teaching Skill?" (1973), which proposed decisionmaking as a lens through which to analyze teaching, as the precursor to this area of research. The reviews, and most of the other literature, argue that the mid-1970s, with both the NIE (1975) and SSRC (Eggleston, 1979; Sutcliffe, 1977) reports, created an important change in how teachers and teaching were viewed by the research community.
6. Mackay and Marland (1978) write that the concept of teacher as decisionmaker was popularized in the early 1970s before any substantial research on it had been carried out. The early ar-

ticulations make no reference to medical problem-solving and diagnosis (see Shavelson, 1973, as an example).

7. The apparent envy with which researchers on teaching have looked to medicine for constructs to lend teaching legitimacy is intriguing. It is particularly evident in discussions of professionalization (see Labaree, 1992).

8. Perhaps the clearest example of the function of shared linguistic value in created meaning lies in phonology. If, for instance, a speech community does not value vowel length as between a single vowel sound and a diphthong, then the contrast that is used in English between such words as "slip" and "sleep" does not exist. Similarly, if a community does not differentiate among categories of tone, then distinctions such as those made in Mandarin Chinese, Cantonese, or Thai are not readily available to those speakers.

9. There continues to be some discussion about the relationship between Bakhtin and Voloshinov (see Wertsch, 1991, pp. 48–50; also Cazden, 1989, p. 117) and whether, in fact, they may have been the same person. This is interesting, given the place of mutuality in Bakhtin's conceptual framework.

10. Willinsky (1989) makes a related observation, suggesting that, even in narrative research that proceeds collaboratively, the researcher-dyad generates "the press for narrative unity," which may not be actually present in the data or felt by the teacher.

11. Gee's concept of Discourses (1989, 1990) suggests a way to make visible participation in a speech community. Through examining language data for evidence of the Discourses within it, the researcher can begin to identify the sources of the data — the speech communities from which it comes. Each Discourse is, as Gee says, "an identity kit which comes complete with [ways] to act, talk, and often write, so as to take on a particular social role that others will recognize" (1990, p. 142); language reflects that identity.

12. Siddle-Walker (1993) has made a similar point in arguing for the need to examine what she has called the "authenticity" of data, which differs from the generally acknowledged category of face or descriptive validity (Maxwell, 1992). "Authenticity" arises in large part out of the researcher-participant relationship, whereas face validity can be a matter of reference to the objective world.

13. A similar argument has been advanced by Mishler (1990) in his discussion of "trustworthiness" as the central criterion for validity in narrative. See also Connelly and Clandinin (1990, p. 7) on validity in narrative research.

14. The data and analyses in this section are drawn from Zinn's (1966) ongoing research and used with her permission.

References

Bakhtin. M. (1981). *The dialogic imagination.* Austin: University of Texas Press.

Belenky, M., Clinchy, B., Goldberger, N., & Tarule, J. (1986). *Women's ways of knowing: The development of self, voice, and mind.* New York: Basic Books.

Bjerstedt, A. (1969). Critical decision situations on videotape: An approach to the exploration of teachers' interaction tendencies. *Didakometry and Sociometry, 1,* 54–76.

Bowers, C. A. (1987). *Elements of a post-liberal theory of education.* New York: Teachers College Press.

Britzman, D. (1991). *Practice makes practice: A critical study of learning to teach.* Albany: State University of New York Press.

Bruner, J. (1990). *Acts of meaning.* Cambridge, MA: Harvard University Press.

Butt, D. (1989). *Talking and thinking: The patterns of behaviour.* Oxford, Eng.: Oxford University Press.

Butt, R., & Raymond, D. (1987). Arguments for using qualitative approaches in understanding teacher thinking: The case for biography. *Journal of Curriculum Theorizing, 7*(1), 62–93

Calderhead, J. (1987). *Exploring teacher thinking.* London: Cassell.

Carter, K. (1993). The place of story in the study of teaching and teacher education. *Educational Researcher, 22*(1), 5–12, 18.

Cazden, C. (1989). Contributions of the Bakhtin circle to "communicative competence." *Applied Linguistics, 10,* 116–127.

Clandinin, D. J . (1986). *Classroom practice: Teacher images in action.* London: Falmer Press.

Clandinin, D. J., & Connelly, M. (1987). Teachers' personal knowledge: What counts as "personal" in studies of the personal. *Journal of Curriculum Studies, 19,* 487–500.

Clark, C., & Peterson, P. (1986). Teachers' thought processes. In M. Wittrock (Ed.), *Handbook of research on teaching* (3rd ed., pp. 255–297). New York: Macmillan.

Connelly, M., & Clandinin, D. J. (1986a). On narrative method, personal philosophy, and narrative unities in the study of teaching. *Journal of Research in Science Teaching, 3,* 293–310.

Connelly, M., & Clandinin, D. J. (1986b). *On narrative method, biography, and narrative unities in the study of teaching.* Ontario: University of Calgary, Ontario Institute for Studies in Education.

Connelly, M., & Clandinin, D. J. (1990). Stories of experience and narrative inquiry. *Educational Researcher, 19*(5), 2–14.

de Saussure. F. (1978). *A course in general linguistics* (C. Bally & A. Schehaye, Trans.). Glasgow, Scotland: Fontana/Collins. (Original work published 1916)

Doe, J. (1988). *Speak into the mirror: A story of linguistic anthropology.* Lantham, MD: University Press of America.

Dunkin, M., & Biddle, B. (1974). *The study of teaching.* New York: Holt, Rinehart, and Winston.

Eggleston. J. (1979). Editorial introduction: Making decisions in the classroom. In J. Eggleston (Ed.), *Teacher decisionmaking in the classroom: A collection of papers* (pp. 1–7). London: Routledge & Kegan Paul.

Elbaz, F. (1983). *Teacher thinking: A study of practical knowledge.* New York: Nichols.

Elbaz, F. (1987). Response to Clandinin and Connelly. *Journal of Curriculum Studies, 19,* 501–502.

Elbaz, F. (1991). Research on teacher's knowledge: The evolution of a discourse. *Journal of Curriculum Studies, 23*(1), 1–19.

Feiman-Nemser, S., & Floden, R. (1986). The culture of teaching In M. Wittrock (Ed.), *Handbook of research on teaching* (3rd ed., pp. 505–526). New York: Macmillan.

Freedman, S., Jackson, J., & Boles, K. (1983). Teaching: An imperiled "profession." In L. Shulman & G. Sykes (Eds.), *Handbook of teaching and policy* (pp. 261–299). New York: Longman.

Freeman, D. (1991). *"The same things done differently": A study of the development of four foreign language teachers' conceptions of practice.* Unpublished doctoral dissertation, Harvard University.

Freeman, D. (1992). To make the tacit explicit: Teacher education, emerging discourse, and conceptions of teaching. *Teaching and Teacher Education, 7,* 439–454.

Freeman, D. (1996). Renaming experience/reconstructing practice: Developing new understandings of teaching. In D. Freeman & J. C. Richards (Eds.), *Teacher learning in language teaching* (pp. 221–241). New York: Cambridge University Press.

Gee, J. (1989). Literacy, discourse, and linguistics: Introduction. *Journal of Education, 17,* 5–17.

Gee, J. (1990). *Social linguistics and literacies: Ideology in discourses.* Philadelphia: Falmer Press.

Gilligan, C. (1982). *In a different voice: Psychological theory and women's development.* Cambridge, MA: Harvard University Press.

Halkes, R., & Olson, J. (1984). *Teacher thinking: A new perspective on persisting problems in education.* Lisse, Netherlands: Swets & Zeitlinger.

Hargreaves, D. (1977). A phenomenological approach to classroom decisionmaking. *Cambridge Journal of Education, 7*(1), 12–20.

Hargreaves, A. (1996). Revisiting voice. *Educational Researcher, 25*(1), 12–19.

Jackson, P. (1968). *Life in classrooms.* New York: Holt, Rinehart and Winston.

Kagan, D. (1988). Teaching as clinical problem-solving: A critical examination of the analogy and its implications. *Review of Educational Research, 58,* 482–505.

Labaree, D. (1992). Knowledge, power, and the rationalization of teaching: A genealogy of the movement to professionalize teaching. *Harvard Educational Review, 62,* 123–154.

Lave, J., & Wenger, E. (1991). *Situated learning: Legitimate peripheral participation.* New York: Cambridge University Press.

Lortie. D. (1975). *Schoolteacher: A sociological study.* Chicago: University of Chicago Press.

Lowyck, J. (1986). Post-interactive reflections of teachers: A critical appraisal. In M. Ben-Peretz, R. Bromme, & R. Halkes (Eds.), *Advances of research in teacher thinking* (pp. 172–185). Lisse, Netherlands: Swets & Zeitlinger.

Mackay, D., & Marland, P. (1978). *Thought processes of teachers.* Paper presented at the annual meeting of the American Educational Research Association. (ERIC Document Reproduction Serivce No. ED 151-328)

Maxwell, J. (1992). *Understanding and validity in qualitative research. Harvard Educational Review, 62,* 279–300.

Maxwell, J., & Miller, B. (1991). *Two aspects of thought and two components of qualitative data analysis.* Unpublished manuscript.

Mishler, E. (1986). *Research interviewing: context and narrative.* Cambridge, MA: Harvard University Press.

Mishler, E. (1990). Validation in inquiry-guided research: The role of exemplars in narrative studies. *Harvard Educational Review, 60,* 415–442.

Munby, H. (1986). Metaphor in the thinking of teachers: An exploratory study. *Journal of Curriculum Studies, 18,* 197–209.

National Institute of Education [NIE]. (1975). *Teaching as clinical problem-solving* (Report of Panel No. 6, National Conference on Studies in Teaching). Washington, DC: Author.

Rivers, W. (1991). Psychological validation of methodological approaches and foreign language classroom practices. In B. Freed (Ed.), *Foreign language acquisition research and the classroom* (pp. 283–294). Lexington, MA: D.C. Heath.

Shavelson, R. (1973). What is *the* basic teaching skill? *Journal of Teacher Education, 24,* 144–151.

Shavelson, R., & Stern, P. (1981). Research on teachers' pedagogical thoughts, judgments, decisions, and behaviors. *Review of Educational Research, 51,* 455–498.

Shulman, L. (1986). Paradigms and research programs in the study of teaching. In M. Wittrock (Ed.), *Handbook of research on teaching* (3rd ed., pp. 3–36). New York: Macmillan.

Siddle-Walker, V. (1993, May). *What does it mean to* do *the research? What does it mean to* be *the researcher?* Paper presented at the meeting of the National Academy of Education, Stanford, CA.

Stevens, W. (1982). *The collected poems of Wallace Stevens.* New York: Alfred A. Knopf.

Strauss, A. (1987). *Qualitative analysis for social scientists.* New York: Cambridge University Press.

Suppes, P. (1978). *Impact of research on education.* Washington, DC: National Academy of Education.

Sutcliffe, J. (1977). Introduction to the "volume on classroom decisionmaking." *Cambridge Journal of Education, 7*(1), 2–3.

Voloshinov, V. (1973). *Marxism and the philosophy of language.* New York: Seminar Press.

Walberg, H. (1977). Decision and perception: New constructs for research on teaching effects. *Cambridge Journal of Education, 7*(1), 33–39.

Wertsch, J. (1985). The semiotic mediation of mental life: L. S. Vygotsky and M. M. Bakhtin. In E. Mertz & R. Parmentier (Eds.), *Semiotic mediation: Sociocultural and psychological perspectives* (pp. 49–71). New York: Academic Press.

Wertsch. J. (1991). *Voices of the mind: A sociocultural approach to mediated action.* Cambridge, MA: Harvard University Press.

Willinsky, J. (1989). Getting personal and practical with personal practical knowledge. *Curriculum Inquiry, 19,* 247–264.

Zinn, D. (1996). *"Becoming ourselves as we teach": A study of South African teachers in transition.* Manuscript in preparation, Harvard Graduate School of Education, Cambridge, MA.

Reporting Ethnography
to Informants

REBA N. PAGE
YVETTE J. SAMSON
MICHELE D. CROCKETT

The idea that scholars should report the results of research projects to the people who participate in them has become commonplace in the last ten to fifteen years (Whyte, 1981). Sometimes such reporting is regarded as a courtesy, even a kind of recompense, to people who have given generously of their time to an investigation; at other times, particularly in interpretive inquiries, it may be deemed a validity check; at still other times, the process is expected to provide information and recommendations that will spark improvements in local conditions, possibly by empowering local actors in their struggles for resources.

However, we know little about what actually happens when researchers and participants in research come together to discuss the results or how they react when their representations of social practices diverge. As a result, we primarily have only prescriptions for how researchers should proceed and assumptions about the value (usually wholesome) of such interchange. Our lack of knowledge is particularly significant in an applied discipline such as education, where scholars, as well as practitioners and policymakers, increasingly expect that the studies they participate in should prove useful in resolving some of the perplexing issues of schooling. However, the record of the impact of research on practice, or of practice on research, can hardly inspire their confidence.

Perhaps the most that can be said about encounters between researchers and educators is that they tend to be volatile. One compelling explanation traces this volatility to differences between the cultures of the university and the school (Bloor, 1983; Emerson, 1983; Hargreaves, 1996; Kliebard, 1993; Lampert, 1985; Schwab, 1969). From this perspective, university researchers and school people value different kinds of knowledge, engage in different modes of inquiry, and bring different roles and statuses to discussions of schooling. Teachers are said to value practical, particular knowledge, for example, while researchers value theoretical abstractions, which they also have the resources to generate and disseminate. Given these cultural differences, teachers and researchers will struggle over knowledge about schooling without quite realizing why. They may find themselves dismissing rather than learning from the perspective of the

Harvard Educational Review Vol. 68 No. 3 Fall 1998, 299–333

other, with the result that the gap between educational research and practice remains unbridged, and the status quo unchanged (Boostrum, Jackson, & Hansen, 1993).

Ethnography is sometimes hailed for moderating the differences between the two cultures. Like teachers, educational ethnographers are characteristically interested in the details of life in classrooms and corridors, the meaning-making of school participants, and the influence of local circumstances. In addition, the methods and reports of ethnography are typically less technical than traditional studies and, therefore, deemed more accessible to teachers. These characterizations notwithstanding, asymmetries in academic and social relations characterize ethnographic projects, too. They may be especially potent between researchers and practitioners precisely because ethnography appears to be so "democratic" or "friendly" that the asymmetries are rendered invisible (Page, 1997). Teachers may not realize that researchers write down otherwise casual conversations, for example, and researchers may forget that showing an interest in others can also be an invasion of their privacy.

This article will not disclose a formula for successfully sharing research. We wish we had such a formula, but we do not. We do have, however, an intriguing case that has made us wonder about what reporting research means to teachers as well as researchers. Particularly, what kind of knowledge do teachers want and expect from research projects, and how do they want it represented? What kind of knowledge do we researchers gather, and how do we represent it?

Research Design

This case is one component of a larger ethnographic research project we have pursued in California off and on since 1993, called "High School Science: What Is It, Who Decides, and How Does It Matter?" The central orientation of the larger project is the politics of representing high school science (Clifford & Marcus, 1986; Edelman, 1995; LaTour & Woolgar, 1979, 1986; Rabinow, 1996). As the word "representation" suggests, the science that schools teach is both an aesthetic and political construction. Thus, two questions have guided our inquiry. First, what representations, or versions, of school science are proposed by the many and diverse constituents of school science, including teachers, students, administrators, parents, scientists, and policymakers? Second, for whom and in what circumstances is any particular representation of school science representative, or legitimate? Put another way, we have studied science curriculum as symbolic action (Burke, 1966; Edelman, 1995; Geertz, 1973; Kliebard, 1990), asking how people in classrooms, schools, and communities use words and other signs to construct and conjoin definitions of school science and make them consequential. For example, when and how are teachers able to persuade students to memorize the phyla of biology, develop sound environmental practices, or forgo creationist science?

Integrated Science

To understand the politics of representing high school science, we focused on the particular case of integrated science. Integrated science is one version of school science —

a quite ambitious version—now recommended by policymakers in California's State Department of Education (1990), as well as by various national associations of science educators (American Association for the Advancement of Science, 1989; National Science Teachers Association, 1988).[1] According to the state's department of education, California schools have a double task: they should integrate the natural sciences and they should integrate students (Crockett, Page, & Samson, 1997). That is, high schools should discontinue the traditional tracked, "layer-cake" curriculum in science, with its separate years of biology, physics, and chemistry, or general science. Instead, all students, particularly ninth and tenth graders, should be grouped heterogeneously in integrated science courses where they should engage in "hands-on," "relevant" lessons with all of the natural sciences brought to bear on themes such as earthquakes, the universe, evolution, and so forth. Done right, the integrated courses should satisfy the admission requirements of the University of California, so that all students are ensured access to high-status, college preparatory science.

"High School Science" has worked to trace how the policy recommendation for integrated science came to life in two large, public, comprehensive high schools in a diverse urban school district in southern California. Fieldwork began when the district's high schools piloted a few sections of Integrated Science 1 in 1993–1994, and continued through 1995–1996, as the schools discontinued general science courses and sections of biology, fully launched Integrated Science 1, and piloted and then fully implemented Integrated Science 2 (See Appendix for chronology of the study).

We chose Westridge and Endeavor High Schools as research sites.[2] Both are located in Orangetowne, a long-established working- and middle-class city of 250,000 in southern California, now part of the sprawl of Los Angeles. Westridge is the oldest of the city's five high schools and until the late 1950s was the city's only high school. Although the two schools are similar in size, faculty characteristics, formal resources, and administrative policies, they differ in their histories and student bodies.[3] Therefore, we thought that they might also differ in their cultures, or meaning systems (Metz, 1978, 1986; Page, 1989; Sarason, 1971), so that the "same" subject, such as biology or integrated science, might be differently meaningful and differently structured.

Since 1993, we have collected data about school science. We have used extended and intensive participant-observation, conducted interviews, collected documents, and video- and audio-taped various events at Westridge and Endeavor High Schools. For instance, we observed and participated regularly in the Integrated Science 1 and Integrated Science 2 classes and in traditional science classes, such as honors and regular biology and chemistry. Among other things, we talked with students, took part in lab work, did homework, and helped teachers with papers.

To understand the contexts in which the science classes were embedded, we attended classes in other subjects, extracurricular activities, and informal events at the two high schools; we also attended events in the wider community, such as school board meetings. To deepen and check our understanding of school events, we conducted interviews with all of the science teachers and about a dozen other teachers at each high school. We also interviewed scores of students from the science classes, some parents, school administrators and district staff members, school board members, and state policymakers. To document formal discourse systems (Greenblatt, 1991), we collected written documents, including classroom worksheets and tests, department memos and school bulletins, in-service materials, curriculum guides (from the two high school science departments, the school district, and the state), and national, state, and local media reports about science and education.

In brief, our research suggests that California's two-pronged revolution in science curriculum is not yet realized in these two schools. Considering the magnitude of the proposed change and the minimal and uncertain resources provided to teachers, this was hardly a surprise. What was surprising, however, were some negative, and not just negligible, consequences of the reform effort. For example, rather than promoting the integration of the natural sciences, the recommended reform has prompted a hodge-podge curriculum, with lessons so confused that at times there seems to be a virtual absence of science in science classes (Page, 1995). Further, the effort to de-track school science has been paralleled by re-tracking. The schools redifferentiated the new heterogeneous classes almost immediately by adding within them a special "embedded honors" option, which provided selected students extra, harder assignments and added credit. The reform notwithstanding, honors biology continued to be an option for some ninth graders.[4]

Teacher Seminars

Another focus of the research project was what we called teacher seminars. Tellingly, we on the research team did not originally think these seminars would prove so central to the study. They took place in spring 1996, when members of the research team met with the teachers in the two science departments to present some of the data and interpretations from the research project and to listen to teachers' responses.

We proposed a seminar format for sharing the research, chiefly because neither a brief report at a general faculty meeting nor an executive summary mailed to the district office seemed appropriate. For one thing, like most ethnographers, we had gathered a lot of material and we did not want to oversimplify it. For another, we appreciated the generosity the science departments had shown the research project and we wanted to reciprocate. Most important, some of our data were troubling, with uncertain implications for policy and practice. We wanted a setting in which we researchers could engage with teachers in sustained conversation over the data. We thought such discussion might be of use to both the university research project and school practice, and saw reporting the research in the seminars as a "research intervention." As researchers, we would gain more and different data, including teachers' responses to our emerging analysis. Teachers would have access to new information, as well as a public forum in which to discuss science curriculum, specifically integrated science, with their colleagues.[5]

The teacher seminars took place in March and April of 1996. The research team met with teachers from the science departments once a week for 90 minutes at the end of the school day, for a total of six meetings at each high school. Participation was voluntary; eight teachers at each school signed on, for a participation rate of about 70 percent.[6] Participants received stipends of $300. For each meeting, the research team prepared a "lesson," so that the group had research data and interpretations to use as a basis for beginning discussion. The weekly topics moved from general school and community data to classroom data. For example, we began with portraits of each high school, moved to teacher voice in curriculum, and concluded with reflections on the research and seminar experience.[7]

A Case of Reporting Research to Teachers

For the research team, the key puzzle of the teacher seminars was their meaning. What did the teacher seminars mean for teachers and what did they mean for us as researchers?

The question arose with particular force because we had planned the seminars at the two schools to be quite similar, but reactions to them differed. In brief, the Westridge teachers told us we had gotten everything right, but because some of our data and interpretations were critical, we were unsure what to make of their positive assessment. Meanwhile, the same materials prompted outrage and rejection (and almost ejection) at Endeavor, where teachers told us we had gotten everything wrong.

In the last of the six meetings of the teacher seminars, we asked the teachers to comment on their participation in the seminars and the research project. We report the discussion that ensued in narratives constructed by using large chunks of talk transcribed from the videotapes. We have edited the transcripts somewhat for clarity and conciseness; we also intersperse occasional interpretive comments to indicate tone and context, as well as how topics evolved.[8] In general, though, we leave the data relatively unmediated. As a result, readers will encounter strips of talk that are quite long, even by qualitative standards. This representational strategy asks readers to discern the unfolding story without many explicit cues,[9] but it provides a quite direct encounter with the data, allowing readers to assess the teacher seminars, evaluate our interpretations of them, and develop their own interpretations.[10]

Reporting Research at Endeavor High School

The last teacher seminar at Endeavor High School, like the previous five, takes place in a rather dark room with low ceilings just off the main cafeteria, with snatches of conversations among the cooks and lingering smells of school lunch in the background. The two members of the research team who led the teacher seminars, Yvette Samson and Lily Rivera, meet with six of the eight science teachers who volunteered to participate in the seminars. The group is seated around several large tables pushed together to make a square. The food we brought is in one corner and people have helped themselves to it. The video cameraman is in another corner.

Lily opens the last part of the teacher seminars, which will occupy the final minutes of the sixth meeting. Briefly and rather solemnly, she reviews the history of the seminars at Endeavor. She then notes that the concluding topic for discussion is "your experience in the research project." It has both "selfish and altruistic" aspects, she says:

> Selfishly, we want to be better people, better researchers, better reporters of data. Altruistically, we hope what you say may be useful to future researchers and practitioners. So, with that in mind, I'd like to ask you to comment on - your experience in the entire research project, your comments on the data we reported, - your comments on the seminars themselves. I urge you to be honest - - because I don't think it is an easy thing to do. But, I believe it is the only way we can improve. So -

The first response to Lily comes from Margaret, a teacher who is especially vocal, engaged, and assertive, both in the seminars and the science department. She seems to have been waiting for Lily to finish the review because she begins speaking very rapidly, in a kind of pent-up outburst:

> The only positive thing I can say, you guys have been very nice, and I did appreciate when Reba came and spent the time with us, and I've enjoyed getting to know you better. And, the rest of this - - it's been a very frustrating, uh, disappointing - - possibly developing paranoia, uh - just a real negative experience. It's sad because the first two-and-a-half or three years were very positive, but the way it all came together at the end, nehhh! [makes a face and shakes her head]. . . . And I thought that you weren't going to generalize, that you were still developing a hypothesis. I thought that this was still the preliminary groundwork that you were setting so that you could study other research questions, but it doesn't come across that way. It sounds like it's case cut, sealed, this is it.

Taken aback by the emotion in Margaret's response, Lily reassures her and the other teachers that the analysis the research team has presented is indeed "preliminary" and that the research team will be "reconsidering its interpretations" in light of teachers' comments. However, Margaret interrupts Lily's reassurances:

> Then, [if the analysis is truly "preliminary"] I would have thought that you would have presented your findings possibly as a newscaster would, that "This is the news," and you really don't know how the newscaster feels about it. We knew how the writer of that first document [the portrait of Endeavor's culture, presented in the first teacher seminar] felt. It lent a slant to it so that it wasn't credible anymore.

Another teacher, Sue, joins the conversation. Equally vocal and active in the seminars and department affairs, Sue moderates somewhat her colleague's criticism, recalling that the research team's interest is in the meanings of events, as well as facts:

> Well, I felt better when Reba came and explained it [the school portrait], in terms of being ethnography, and what that meant and so on and so forth. It wasn't necessarily accurate, it was how people viewed - uh, it's one way of viewing the school. I could see it.

Gesturing to Margaret, however, Sue agrees that the research experience has not been a happy one, and even though "it never bothered me to have anyone in my room," Sue doubts she will agree to participate in future research projects.

Sue then explains what "bothers" her about the research: It is "not just what [the research team] said, because I just don't really give a lot of credence to this type of research anyway, because outside of the bounds of this high school, it does not have a lot of broad, wide-range application because it's so specific." However, before Sue can say specifically what "bothers" her, Margaret interrupts to corroborate Sue's criticism that the project's findings will not generalize. She notes that the research is doubly flawed: If published, it will "harm" teachers in the department because it is so specific that Endeavor High will be recognizable and the specificity means the research will not be of any use to other high schools.

Picking up on "the harm this [research] could do to Endeavor," Yvette asks Margaret for clarification. In a rare moment, Margaret seems at a loss for words. She hesitates, looks around the table, and then proceeds:

> Uh -, eh -, ah - - - Anybody want to help me here? - - Uh, the negativism. The, uh, how bad we do everything. Uh, how single-minded the students are. How all we do is compete with Westridge High School, uh-

Yvette interrupts Margaret's list to "re-ask" the question, focusing explicitly now on the school: "I'm hearing Endeavor is going to be harmed by this research project - - how is Endeavor going to be harmed?" Margaret replies:

> First, we have already been harmed, teachers themselves. Instead of feeling that we're being supported by you, we don't feel we are being supported by you . . . so that's a harm. And number two, once you destroyed that initial trust - - I don't know where this is going [exasperated]. I don't know if I believe one or the other, and if this "book" or "article" or whatever is published anywhere in this area, anybody would know who you're talking about. It is written so - - I don't know, that, that competition thing with Westridge [with a slight, wry grimace], I see it doing harm. There are a lot of students at Endeavor who still are fighting this — "We're not as good because we're not at Westridge" — and their friends are at Westridge, and then to read something like this? What good can come of it?

Yvette responds directly to Margaret's worries about confidentiality. She notes first that "it's not the general public that reads articles, it's other academics." Further, she reminds Margaret and the other teachers that pseudonyms will be used for all names. Finally, she adds, "If you want to bring up the competition thing, well, most schools do have a competition, so the characteristics that we are describing [for Endeavor] could describe numerous schools."

Again, Sue intervenes to explain the research to Margaret: "I have to say, it is what they are describing, and then some. There's all sorts of competition. It's sick - but I saw it in San Diego when I student taught." Then, reiterating that she is "not worried about the publishing - that's not my area of concern," Sue returns to the point she began earlier, about what she gained from being a participant and what in the research reports "disappointed" her:

> What I wanted to say, what I got out of the teacher seminars? - - God, this sounds so shallow - - but I'm getting - - a stipend - - and it's something to do and I talk with my colleagues. But, to be honest with you, that's it. As far as being more reflective, I think I'm already extremely reflective - and you didn't tell me something that I didn't already know about me. And I didn't really see myself in a lot of the research - - I saw a couple of people represented a lot, a couple of styles represented a lot. But things have changed here, so that's what disappointed me. Because I think our department has come a long way, there are three new people and the teacher styles now are not represented. Most of your data was gathered early on. It doesn't represent us.

One of the new additions to the science faculty, Pat, joins the discussion, agreeing with Sue that the research is not representative:

Actually, from that first writing that we got about the school [the school portrait], that was not my idea of what an ethnographic study would be all about. It was too - colorful. I guess it's because we were looking more toward facts, or something that has foundation. And, to me, and to most of us new to this department, it was not factual. We don't see that communication as an issue - er, I mean, competition [with Westridge] - as an issue. And, I don't know what it was like three years ago, but maybe it seemed more prevalent then, but -

Lily responds to Pat:

From our conversations, Pat, from this [the teacher seminars], we will be seeing that your views are incorporated because that was one portrait and you pointed out some things that we need to reconsider. I just want to add, too, some of your comments have been extremely helpful. It hasn't been something like, "Oh, my god, they didn't like this session," or whatever. Everything you've said has been valuable to us, it's part of the ethnographic effort. We thought, "This is what we see." You're giving us disconfirming evidence. We have taken a lot from this - - we just hope you took something from it too.

Again, Margaret provides the first rejoinder. Voicing unhappiness with the way the research team has shared the data and findings, she asks: "Are we going to see the finished product? It would be nice to mail it to us." Lily replies mildly, "Your request is noted and valid - - we have it on camera." But Margaret continues, and other teachers join her critique. They offer the "suggestions for improvement" that Lily and Yvette request:

You shouldn't have waited three years to get together like this. Even if you had to make up questions that we had to sit around and discuss together. It would have helped develop some type of community. We don't have any with you guys. Even if you two had been here for three years, you wouldn't have what we should have for a fair exchange to go back and forth. We should have met every year, maybe every six months. That should have been built in, so that we're not surprised.

Lily acknowledges the teachers' concern, but notes, too, the research team's dilemmas:

Well, see, that is a problem in ethnography. You've got long-term stuff and you're very cautious because you can make a conclusion, and go back to observe, - and you were way off the bat. I know Reba feels she needs to be careful about presenting an analysis prematurely and I understand her position. And, we also didn't want to take more time from your busy schedules than we already were. But I also understand the need to present some tentative reports to you.

Changing the subject, Pat then asks, "How did the idea of an ethnographic study come up - - versus another type of study?" Yvette explains that "generally, it's a result of a person's interest in particular questions, it's an individual thing." Pat probes further, suggesting that there was something about Endeavor itself that called for ethnographic research: "It seems that Reba felt there was a need for this type of study - here?" Yvette responds again, clarifying that the research design arose from questions about school science, not because of any peculiarities at Endeavor:

From my conversations with Dr. Page, she feels that we have lots of numbers - - how many students, how many times girls are called on, that kind of thing. But what is lacking in education is understanding what really happens in classrooms, and it's not just about teachers, but how classrooms are shaped by the community and by the district and the state. She tries to get at that, to understand the big picture of what makes things happen in classrooms, and you can't do that quantitatively.

With about five minutes remaining in the meeting, Margaret indicates it is time to conclude by asking the members of the research team a personal question: "With the semester ending, have both of you finished your data collection part of your thesis?" Surprised, Lily and Yvette respond simultaneously that their work on the research project is not related to either's thesis. It is a job. Yvette adds:

> But, I have to say, too, while I considered this my job, this year I've learned so much. It's been like a hands-on course for me about ethnography, which I hope to teach someday. So, yes, it was a job, but I would never have learned as much about ethnography from a course.

Equally surprised to learn that Yvette and Lily are not deriving their theses from the research project, Margaret then offers "another suggestion" for improving the seminars. Speaking softly and tentatively for the first time during the meeting, she says:

> Maybe it's my fault because I didn't pay attention or whatever, but if - - For some reason, I thought you were more involved than you are. If you had come up at the first teacher seminar and said, "This is my job. I have nothing to do with this research. I don't even really care about this research," - - It might have changed the climate - just slightly. I don't know, made it more candid? For some reason, up until this point I thought you were just a little bit more involved than what you just described.

Now Lily asks for clarification: "We don't want you to think the study hasn't meant a great deal to us - but you mean, that would have made a difference?" Margaret explains:

> I think it could have made a little bit of difference. Maybe in a positive way. Possi- and maybe we were hurting your feelings. I know some of the times my responses - - I kinda thought, you know - - But if I'd known from the very start that you were earning money, just like we are, I would not have been so worried.

Lily overlaps Margaret's last words, murmuring: "Maybe we didn't think it was important to tell you about ourselves." Sue has the final word:

> You know, I would say, it's not just this research project or seminar. It's just, teachers are so heavily criticized by everybody outside this room that doesn't really understand how the school works, like a parent or like an administrator or like anyone, that we're all kinda, a little paranoid about letting other people in our rooms - - whether it's other teachers or - - - You're always like, "Now why did the vice-principal just walk in my room?" [group laughter]. But, so, it's not just this [the research project]. This is just one more thing on top. I wish it wasn't like that. You know, you see certain images on television, and you think, "That's not the way it is."

Needless to say, the predominantly negative response from the Endeavor teachers was not the outcome the research team had hoped for when planning the teacher seminars. We knew we had data and interpretations that would trouble teachers — they troubled us, too — but we hoped the seminars might provide a chance to explore the complicated issues. Instead, as the Endeavor teachers told us, the reporting process operated negatively, spawning what eventually seemed a succession of mutual accusations.[11] As Margaret put it, we and the teachers did not "develop some type of community . . . for a fair exchange to go back and forth."

Reporting Research at Westridge High School

The final of the six teacher seminars held at Westridge High introduced some complicating data that throw a rather different light on reporting research than the experience at Endeavor. They suggest that the idea of teacher seminars is not totally naive, our skills in reporting research are not inherently flawed, and that antagonism between members of the cultures of the university and school is not inevitable.

At Westridge, the last teacher seminar, like the previous five, takes place in a bright, sedate conference room just off the school library. As at Endeavor, there are food and video cameras. Eight of the department's ten teachers, along with the two members of the research team, are sitting around several tables pushed together. Again, Lily poses the topic for the last half hour of the final meeting: teachers' assessments of the seminar and research experience. Here, though, her tone is less strained, even jovial:

> For our last portion of this last session - - and, oh yes, before I forget, your stipends are in the mail. Harvard has finally gotten itself organized! [group laughter] - - Anyway, the last portion we devote to what one might call an evaluation of the entire experience. I have two questions I'd like you to give us feedback on. Number one, what has the experience been like for you - - of having people observe you, the seminars, the information? - - And secondly, how would you suggest that researchers conduct this kind of research, how might what we have done be improved?

June begins, and her opening comment sets the tone and topic for the assessments that follow:

> Well, I, - I particularly liked the way Yvette gathered her data without interrupting the class time. [Turning to Yvette] It was kinda like you were just a part of the class [group laughter]. And my students sort of like, expected you to be there, you were not a distraction, they got used to having you there [group laughter]. [Looking around the table to the other teachers] They were looking for her - - and they found out she was not a high school student [group laughter]![12]

Other teachers follow June's lead, taking turns to chime in with their praise. Jack "agrees with June" that "you guys were just - - kinda part of the room," adding that he had to "fight this tendency to want to go talk to you." Dorothy commends the seminars themselves, particularly their "openness":

> HERE [pointing to the group around the table] - - is what I like. We got around in a group and we talked about what's been going on, differently than from the usual way when we're planning Integrated Science or something. You allowed us to open

up and be critical about things that happened and how they're connected with the history of California - - and political systems - - and that's good.

William, too, "agree[s] with all the comments made so far," and adds "three other things I liked":

> First, you know, the project gave kids a chance to see an experiment in real life. We talk about science too theoretically. Even science fair is more theory than reality. This was science in action. The other thing I appreciated was the really interesting contrast between Dr. Page's description of what Westridge is like and our description of the culture of the school that we did for the WASC accreditation. Our description is to some extent our "vision" [sarcastically], and it's interesting to see the difference between a report that a group makes that has a particular "ax" - uh - to sharpen, or whatever, versus one that's an individual who's just trying to do an experiment and make a description, so that was good.
>
> Also, I got some insight as to our kids, 'cause I'd been frustrated at various times, and that another person had a view of the kids that explained their behavior in ways that helped me understand, that was good.

Summarizing the positive commentary, June notes: "Well [group laughter], it's, - it's just pleasurable having you come to visit with us [group laughter]."

At this point, the research team begins working to redirect the teachers' attention. "Let me ask you," Lily says, "can you point out anything that was troublesome to you about the research, that caused a problem, or that you feel definitely needs some improvement?" Dorothy begins, asking whether the research team "can tell us what you're gonna do from here with what you have, because we still don't, I'm not sure I know exactly what you are going to do yet?" Dick, a new teacher at Westridge, adds: "Yeah, is, - have you made, uh, what you were doing this year was making hypotheses, that was your main objective?"

Responding to both Dorothy and Dick, Lily concurs that the research team was interested in making hypotheses and testing them in "a continual process: From day one, you're always coming up with hypotheses and testing them, looking for confirming information and finding new ones to test - and so forth." Yvette elaborates:

> And, we have team meetings every week, and when Reba is here we get together too. And we say, "I see this," and someone else says they see something else, and - - they're not huge arguments or anything, we work very well together I think - - but we compare and we play devil's advocate and throw our ideas off on each other. And then we go back and observe again. And we ask if we see the same thing at Endeavor that we see at Westridge. So, that's what our process has been - - a kind of ongoing process of constant analysis - and eventually, we have to do some writing, some articles, journal articles, and I think Dr. Page plans a book - -

Dorothy interrupts, excited perhaps by the mention of a book about her alma mater: "Oh, might we ever see it - the book - or the article?" When her colleagues laugh, she clarifies that she is not making a demand. "I don't mean, they're sending it to us. I mean, if we were reading a book sometime, might we see it?" Voicing some anxiety, Jack quips, "Imagine what would be written about department meetings!" Again, amid group laughter, Dorothy explains, "I didn't mean like that. I meant it positively [group laughter]. I meant it positively. Not like I'm afraid."

Without waiting for a response to Dorothy's question, Dick directs attention back to Lily's query about "problems" with the research project: "I'm not, uh, to be honest with you, I'm not real clear about what the objectives of the research were. It seems very, very subjective to me." Lily and Yvette concur, pointing out that "it is - because it involves guessing at what things mean, for you - and in the entire context of the culture. So, yeah. But the subjectivity, the interpretation, is always based on consideration of ample data."

Persisting in clarifying the nature of the ethnographic project, Dick asks further: "You gather data and then analyze it?" Before Lily or Yvette can reply, William, a veteran at Westridge, jumps in to speak directly to Dick: "They are all trying to reach a consensus." Then, Yvette explains: "Yes, we do debate. We don't always see the same thing and so we go back and look at the evidence again - - 'Why do I think I see this?'" But Dick interrupts: "Did you have a data collection format or do you all just basically write down things that you observed?" Lily picks up the explanation:

> We had an idea of certain things we wanted to include each time - - for example, what students were in different classes, seating arrangements, and, of course, what assignments you gave. We took down lots of your words because teachers talk a lot, but also kids' too, and what they said back, as you saw here in the teacher seminars — [Dick nods and concurs, "Uh-huh"] — and what the context of those conversations was. So, a very comprehensive kind of notetaking.

Other teachers chime in to "answer" Dick's questions and elaborate on Lily's and Yvette's responses. For example, June commends the notetaking: Mimicking a person writing, she says, "I just feel that Yvette did not miss a thing, she was always writing." Al counters Dick's implicit criticism that the project was vague, noting that he "think[s] it's good we didn't know what you were looking for because, uh, we would taint your study. There's a tendency to teach to the observer, not to the class. This was okay, I just went on and did what I had to do - and tried not to make a complete fool of myself." Amid more group laughter, Lily mentions the uncertainty of ethnographic studies:

> It wasn't that we knew either, actually. We didn't know what we were seeing at the time. It was only later, when we reviewed and talked about it. Like, one of the things we first questioned - Are we seeing you teaching science or are you busy also teaching safety and explaining course requirements to such an extent that you don't have much time for science at the beginning of the year? Later on, we were asking: What kind of engagement in science are we seeing? We had to look a lot to really see what we were seeing.

Teachers nod, there is a pause, and again Lily prompts: "Other suggestions for improvement?" Again, teachers express their satisfaction with the experience. Dorothy notes that she "thought it was kinda neat, the way you created some sense of anonymity, so that if I did read an article later, I would recognize my school, but I wouldn't, someone couldn't say, 'Oh, her, I know her!'" Laughing with the others, the researchers tease, "No, we've masked your identity, Dorothy, we changed it so that we're gonna say you were here twenty-five years instead of twenty-eight."

Finally, the department chair suggests that there should be more feedback to individual teachers and, possibly, to parents:

One thing I was thinking about, in terms of improving. Dr., er, Dr. Page initially started off observing some people and one day - just by accident - she sat down with another teacher, somebody in social studies, and they just talked about what she was observing about Westridge and that's probably the one thing that most teachers would like to have. Or, maybe - it might be useful, we got some calls last week from parents questioning why the Golden State Exams are so low - all five high schools are low, very low for us compared to the rest of the state, just awful! Of course, I didn't have an answer. But, maybe parents would like to get this feedback: "This is what we're observing; your kids want to do this and that's the reason why they perform the way they do in science - - there's not that love or interest, they just want the credits." It might be very beneficial.

Perhaps with Endeavor's reactions to the teacher seminars in mind, Lily commends the Westridge teachers while asking them about their reactions to the research: "You know, you were exceptionally willing to open your classrooms to us and you accepted some of our observations without taking them negatively. You gave us reasons why we were right and why we were wrong, but you didn't take it personally. Why is that?" Al begins, linking his comment to Lily's query:

Personally, I would say, because of your approach. There was really nothing, no standard to teach to, so there's no pressure, and so we just went about what we did and let you do what you needed to do. That put us more at ease when we got together to find out what you'd been doing - - so there was anticipation. We wanted to know and then compare.

Dorothy repeats the value she places on getting together with colleagues and speaking openly:

I also felt good to be talking to each other about some of these things. I felt comfortable talking to you about that and I felt, "Gee, we're open about that," and sometimes in faculty meetings, we're not as open.

Jack concurs, "That's right. And, I've just got to add, too, we just like you guys." He adds another thought:

You know, there's also kind of an aura here at Westridge, a kind of friendliness type thing. For a lot of you guys [looking at his colleagues] who have been here a lot of years and not on other campuses, you - - I've been subbing and I've seen some places where you need to dress like Mad Max to survive. People are just outright after each other - and that doesn't exist here that way. We have our differences but I don't have that feeling of non-safety here.

Dick qualifies Jack's description of Westridge "friendliness": "You mean among colleagues - - because we have it [non-safety] with students!" As teachers laugh together, the chair adds one final explanation for the department's equanimity — the teachers are scientists:

One other thing I see, as far as our response to what was written down, there was really agreement in many instances and some disagreement and we offered our suggestions and we're realizing, because of our background, our science background, that it's an experiment and so there is a certain amount of data where there's interpretation. We know that there's always a humanity aspect about it all. But, if you were trying to do a report like this in, say, an English or math department where things are a little more fixed one way or the other, you might get a bigger, uh, or negative response.

A First Interpretation of the Two Responses: Different School Cultures

As these two sketches indicate, teachers at the two high schools presented quite different responses to the "same" teacher seminars — almost blanket approval at Westridge, but broad disapprobation at Endeavor. How might we understand the different reactions at the two schools?

The research team looked first at the teachers. For example, listening to the Endeavor teachers, we heard them dismiss the research as too "colorful," biased, outdated, and inaccurate. What they wanted from research was something "with foundation." In almost direct contrast, the Westridge teachers commended the research as being careful and informative description, contrasting it particularly with the "ax-grinding" description the school had just completed for accreditation.

Teachers at both schools commented on the belated feedback we provided. At Westridge, however, teachers remained unconcerned about eventual publications, whereas at Endeavor, teachers worried that detailed accounts would leave them and the school dangerously recognizable.

Finally — and most difficult for us to hear — Endeavor teachers said the research team had proved as "unsupportive" as everyone else teachers encounter, including other teachers, parents, and administrators, and that even if Lily and Yvette had been in the school for three years, there would not have been a basis "for a fair exchange to go back and forth."[13] By contrast, the Westridge teachers characterized the seminars as sociable encounters: "We just like you" and "It was pleasurable to have you come and visit with us."

In considering these different responses, we first explained them as manifestations of the distinctive cultures of the two high schools. That is, we hypothesized that the different teacher talk in the two seminars was congruent with the distinctive ethos, or meaning system, of each of the high schools. As Waller (1932, p. 106) puts it, however diverse a school's participants, all "drink from its cultural stream" and, in their actions, including talk, they both reflect its particular "we-feeling" (p. 13) and recreate it. We may have begun with this explanation of the teachers' reactions because school culture was an important focus in the research project.

Thus, the unremitting criticism from the Endeavor teachers seemed to make sense, given what we saw as the all-or-nothing boosterism pervading and distinguishing the high school. You were either for Endeavor or you were against it. There was little room for ambivalence and no time for debate about purpose. The point was to work hard to make Endeavor "Number 1." Accordingly, the meetings of the science department we attended were always a mile-a-minute race through the chair's agenda. If teachers had reservations about integrated science, they failed to air them; when two teachers finally went public with their concerns in 1994, they did so in an appearance before the school board, after which the chair called their action "a betrayal."

The research project, too, made explicit some of the usually tacit and complicated cultural politics surrounding curriculum, a subject that Endeavor rarely addressed directly. When we documented some of the contextual factors that had contributed to Endeavor's living in Westridge's shadow for three decades, such as the school's larger proportion of poor and minority students, we "betrayed" Endeavor by calling attention to some of the very real constraints on its ability to pull itself up by its bootstraps into the position of the district's best high school.

Equally troubling for the teachers was our hypothesis that student diversity presented the school with an element of unpredictability that prompted its tight discipline. Teachers criticized our reporting of the percentages of students from different ethnic groups as "stereotyping" and "negative." Our description of the school's differentiated curriculum, which included an International Baccalaureate (IB) program, offended many, too. Many of the administrators, parents, students, school board members, and teachers in the district whom we interviewed saw Endeavor's IB program drawing mostly White, socially advantaged, and academically motivated students from the other high schools, including Westridge. The program also absorbed more than its share of resources within Endeavor; when we reported the perception that resource distributions across classes and students were skewed, teachers decried our misplaced emphasis on Endeavor's "competitiveness."

By contrast, the persistently positive assessment of the research project among Westridge teachers seemed to us to be congruent with a school context of congeniality and kickbacks (Page, 1996). The school's "aura of friendliness" and its long-established reputation as the district's "college-prep" high school were maintained by the principle, "You scratch my back, I'll scratch yours." The principle worked in two ways, conveying both being relaxed and being on the take. For example, students, including many whom one would expect to be serious about schooling, were intent on bargaining for lower academic demands in exchange for good classroom behavior (see Powell, Farrar, & Cohen, 1985, regarding this "treaty"). As they told us, they had worked hard earlier in their school careers, and they deserved to "kick back" and have time for parties, jobs, the beach, and other activities. At the same time, the school accommodated students when they or their parents complained: grades or test scores might be raised, absences excused, or disciplinary exceptions granted. Dissatisfied families had the means to raise a ruckus or, if that failed, they could take their business elsewhere. If enough of these parents did take their children out of Westridge, the school would be left with a larger proportion of lower-status and, in general, lower-achieving students, jeopardizing Westridge's reputation for excellence.

Operating in a system of kickbacks, then, Westridge teachers knew how to schmooze with high-status outsiders, including a research team from the University of California. Even though we documented practices that were at least as troubling as any we saw at Endeavor, teachers glossed over the texts we furnished or reinterpreted them so that their classroom practices were exempted. Sometimes the Westridge seminars seemed like "venting" sessions in which teachers only blamed others for their troubles and their sense of powerlessness. For example, teachers read our analysis of the twists and turns of integrated science in the district and the state as confirmation that they were indeed victims of larger social forces and, consequently, could not successfully implement the recommendations. Similarly, Westridge teachers noted the insights we had given them into kids' lack of interest and achievement in science and added that maybe we could tell that to parents, too, so that they would quit indulging their children and blaming teachers for the kids' failure.

In sum, our first analysis linked the teachers' different assessments of the seminars with the distinctive traditions and values of the two high schools. The lid on deliberating over problems fit with Endeavor's individualistic, can-do ethos, while whitewashing problems fit with the worldly wise system of kickbacks at Westridge.

A Second Interpretation: The Research Team's Role

Despite our confidence in our characterizations of the cultures of the two high schools, at some point we became uneasy with the initial analysis. We could see that it was remarkably self-congratulatory. No matter how teachers responded to the seminars — whether critically or positively — their comments simply confirmed our representation of the way things were at the two schools. Thus, if teachers said the research was inaccurate, as teachers at Endeavor did, we could say, "See how defensive they are." If teachers said the research was accurate, as teachers did at Westridge, we could say, "See how they schmooze."

The first analysis also cast the teachers as "cultural dopes" (Goffman, 1961), implying that they were caught in school cultures and unable to see through them. But this analysis contradicted the political and sociocultural theory guiding the research project. We did not assume that culture causes people's actions. Rather, culture furnishes them resources and constraints that they will mobilize in ways that are sensible or understandable, given their particular circumstances.

Finally, on both counts, our initial analysis did not acknowledge the role that we researchers played in the production of the different reactions to the teacher seminars. If meaning is a social construction, then teachers' actions in the teacher seminars are not attributable simply to them. They are also responses to us, so our actions also need to be taken into account.

Embroiled in such reflections, we began to appreciate Geertz's (1973) characterization of ethnography as "thick description" and saw that the seminars operated on several levels. The politics of representing high school science, which the seminars constituted and were constituted in, is not a unidimensional or linear process. Hence, we began a second line of analysis, looking this time at our presence in the seminars. We focus here on the opening minutes of the first teacher seminar at the two schools in which we introduced the seminars.

Setting the Stage at Westridge High

At both high schools, we began the teacher seminars with a brief introduction. We reminded teachers of the purposes of the seminars, described the seminars' place in the larger research project, and suggested how we hoped they would proceed. In planning this introduction, we thought that the opening remarks should be brief so as not to contradict the dialogic format we had advertised; that they should emphasize the confidentiality we had promised to assure teachers about participating in a public forum; that they should remind teachers of key assumptions of fieldwork without becoming overly technical so that possible debates about method or design could proceed from those assumptions; and that they should reiterate our indebtedness to department members for their generosity in allowing the research to take place in their classes.

Lily opened the first session at Westridge on a Tuesday in March 1996, speaking informally, but deliberately, occasionally checking her notes. Her words are cadenced, and warmth, sincerity, and enthusiasm permeate her welcome:

> Welcome - to this, the first of the teacher seminars. And I'd like to also express our appreciation to all of you guys, very very sincerely, for letting us into your classrooms - - for giving us MOUN-tains of papers [group laughter] - for sharing numerous hours with us, and, in short, letting us into your lives. [Uh-huh]

Speaking even more personally — "not just as a researcher" — Lily thanks the teachers a second time:

> We also want you to know that - and not just as researchers, but as parents and teachers ourselves - - and Jack well knows this [she reaches over and touches Jack on the arm, everyone laughs] - - we value what you do immensely. So, thank you. [Uh-huh]

Throughout Lily's introduction, and later in Yvette's, a teacher's murmured "Uh-huh" punctuates the remarks of the researchers and indicates the group's attentiveness. So does frequent laughter. Both vocalizations make the introduction of the teacher seminars at Westridge a kind of mutual, participatory call-and-response, rather than a monologue or lecture delivered to a quiescent audience. They contribute, too, to evoking the relaxed, congenial tone that will pervade all the seminars at Westridge.

After welcoming the teachers, Lily turns to her next point — the format of the teacher seminars. Promising confidentiality and asking for candor, she also puts mutual responsiveness at the forefront when she specifies that "the ethical considerations the teachers expect" are "truly important" to the researchers too:

> We want to assure you of TOTAL - confidentiality. Anything you say in this room, anything we've observed in the past, is NOT to be shared with anyone outside the research project itself. We intend - sincerely, to abide by all ethical considerations that you would want us to abide by, but that we too hold truly important - - and so, [rapidly] I hope you will speak with us candidly today.

Lily concludes her remarks with a brisk "review of the two purposes of the seminars":

> Number one, as you know, we wanted to give you a chance to see some of the data we've collected and some of the interpretations we've come up with so that you can give us feedback. Secondly, we want to give you an opportunity to discuss topics that you may not have had a chance to discuss in your own meetings because, I know, you guys are very busy people. [Uh-huh]

She then asks the teachers to introduce themselves for the camera, she and Yvette introduce themselves, and she turns the floor to Yvette.

Like Lily's, Yvette's introduction is informal and carefully organized, but her style is lighter and faster. She stipulates that her "job is to discuss a little bit about the type of research that we do." She begins by distinguishing the social and natural sciences, and the work of the research team and the science teachers:

> We understand that you are science - people, but your version of science is just a lit-
> tle bit different than ours. We consider ourselves doing field research, and, um, the
> "king" of field research, Robert Emerson, says it is "the study of people acting in the
> natural course of their daily lives. The field worker ventures into the worlds of oth-
> ers in order to learn firsthand about how they live . . . and tries to understand the
> meanings that activities have for those engaged in them" [1983, p. 1].

Elaborating further, Yvette emphasizes that the object of field research is not frequency counts or distributions but "meanings":

> We didn't come into your class - although it may have looked like it - and count
> how many times you called on males and how many times you called on females; we
> didn't count how many posters you had that had White Americans on them versus
> how many had African Americans or how many Hispanic Americans. So, we didn't
> count, we weren't into counting. Our purpose was to try to get at the meaning.

Pausing momentarily, Yvette puts a rhetorical question to the group to make her
point: "If we counted how many times you called on people in class and how many
posters, and we put it on this table, do you think that that would represent what happens in your classes?" A teacher jokes conspiratorially — "Thank you for not doing
that" — and everyone laughs.

Buoyed perhaps by the group's laughter and attentiveness, Yvette launches into a
brief introduction of a complex series of concepts — ethnography, culture, behavior,
inference, and differences in points of view. The exposition is succinct yet fluent, and
Yvette even has the presence of mind to offer a somewhat risqué dramatization of "the
difficult process" of inferring meaning from behavior:

> We wanted to create a picture of what was happening in class. The word that we
> like to throw around is "ethnography." Ethnography is describing a culture, it's un-
> derstanding another way of life from the native's point of view - - and, you are -
> kind of - [heh] the natives. Uh-, we were interested in the teacher's point of view,
> but also the student's point of view, the administrator's, the community around
> you.
>
> Uh, it's considered that people display their culture through their behavior. But
> their behavior itself does not say what the meaning is. It has to be inferred. I can go
> like this [she moves her arm up and down] and you might think I'm waving to you
> [Uh-huh] but actually I'm really hot - and trying to air things out. [Uh-huh, uh-
> huh] So, we need to infer - from all the data that we've collected. And, as you can
> well guess, it's a very difficult process. ["That's for sure," a teacher chimes in.]

Yvette turns then to "the focus of the first seminar on the school culture" and how
school culture "sets the parameters within which you live a great deal of your life in
the classroom." However, she emphasizes that culture "doesn't tell you what to do,
but it gives you a foundation for what's appropriate, what's not appropriate [Uh-huh]
- - not necessarily consciously, but - it guides you. . . . So, school culture is very much
a part of what you teach, and how you teach, and that's one of the things we want to
discuss today." She points out, too, that the teachers probably intuitively recognize
differences in the cultures of high schools: "Those of you who have taught at other

schools probably can very much relate to the culture of the school, because Westridge is probably very different. And if you come from a different state, as you know I do — there's a very BIG difference in the cultures. [Uh-huh]"

Finally, Yvette comments on the "struggles" entailed in field research, both for teachers and researchers. She speaks empathetically and personally, emphasizing particularly how the Westridge teachers made the project easier for her.

> I do want to stress some of our personal - - our struggles, I think, as ethnographers. Being in your classes - - and I'm sure, I can only speak for myself, but when I teach, and someone comes to observe, I get really nervous, and so I can imagine that possibly, at first, we made you a little nervous. Well, we were nervous too and, I think that was, for me, - I was terrified - coming in here, and I just want to thank you because you all made me feel so comfortable and I never imagined I'd feel as comfortable as I do in your classes today. [group laughter]

She identifies part of the "struggles" as deriving from the tensions of ethnographic research — tensions that may be masked by the method's otherwise casual aspects:

> It was kind of like invading your privacy. There were meetings where I felt like, "I shouldn't be here, I'm censoring what they're saying, I'm making them nervous, I'm making me nervous." We also, we kind of struggled between a role of investigator - and confidante [Uh-huh, uh-huh]. There were a lot of times when things were said that were like, "Well, just between you and me." So, we're in this kind of, like, tug of war with ourselves observing - - you're supposed to be totally objective, yet we're also human beings. As Lily said, we care about what you do, we care very much about teaching, it's a part of our lives.

Yvette concludes her introduction of field research with "an analogy," likening the representations of ethnographers to the portraits that artists compose. She indicates that there may be disagreements in the teacher seminars over how Westridge should be represented, but that conflict can also be positive by generating new insights for both the represented and representors:

> And so, in presenting this today, how we can resolve our struggle, it's an analogy of a portrait. We're the artists - and we've developed this portrait of the culture of your school. And, if you've ever had a portrait taken, for me, whenever anyone takes my picture, I think when I first look at it that it doesn't look anything like me, or I question its resemblance of me. But then as I look at it, it might pick up some things that you don't notice about yourself, and "oh yeah," or about your surroundings, uh, and as you study it, each time you might see something new.

Asking for teachers' "feedback" on the portrait of Westridge, she specifies: "What you liked, what you agree with, what you think we may have missed. We very much want your input."

The teachers spend ten minutes reading a four-page description and analysis of the "kickback" culture at Westridge. Lily opens the floor for discussion, and a teacher begins: "Well, this sounds very close to me. I mean, comparing what other teachers tell me and lunch conversations and stuff like that, and my personal experience, I'd say you've got us!"

Succeeding comments mirror the first teacher's in both their topic and tenor. In general, teachers express little disagreement with the representation of the high school's ethos. Like their comments in the last of the six seminars, those in the first confirm the research as fair and accurate.

Setting the Stage at Endeavor High

Two days later, Lily and Yvette present the "same" introductory remarks, guided by the same purposes, in the first seminar at Endeavor. As at Westridge, the topics include expressions of thanks to the teachers, promises of confidentiality, a brief explanation of ethnography, and so forth. Again, Lily leads off. At Endeavor, however, her demeanor is somewhat guarded, she smiles less than at Westridge, and she seems less certain or confident in what she is saying. As a result, even though the topics and some of the phrases are identical to those Lily used at Westridge, here they are qualitatively different in their significance.

Lily begins haltingly, she bids (unsuccessfully) for confirmation that the teachers are following her remarks, and her expression of gratitude to the teachers is unembellished with the personal asides and humor that gave it such resonance at Westridge:

> This is the first of six sessions that we'll be having. And, I want very much to express our appreciation for letting us walk into your classrooms - uh, at leisure - for letting us share your lives for, what has the project been? - three years now? - for sharing materials - and, most of all, for allowing us your very valuable time. We appreciate that, but even more important, we honestly and sincerely value what you do. We don't think there is a more important task in the world.

Moving on hurriedly, Lily reminds teachers of the "two-fold purpose of the seminars": to present data and explications for teachers' "feedback" and to provide "a forum" in which to discuss curricular issues teachers usually have little time for. At Endeavor, however, Lily anticipates dissension when she adds that if the teachers are not interested in some of the topics the research team has scheduled, the topics can be changed: "If you decide something isn't of interest to you, this is your seminar, we can change the schedule."

Lily turns then to Yvette — "Yvette is going to tell us a little about the ethnographic effort" — but she has forgotten to affirm that the seminars are confidential. She backtracks, giving the appearance perhaps of being disorganized. She appeals to "ethics" as she did at Westridge, but here they signal distance rather than collegiality; the researchers do not so much share the "standards in [the teachers'] profession" as they will comply with them:

> Oh! I forgot. I don't want you to be concerned about anything, uh, going out from us - to any administrator, er, - or community people. We intend to abide by the same ethical standards that you abide by in your profession. Only the research team sees the data we have and, in the write-ups later, we will assure anonymity completely. So, we wanted to be sure you understood that.

Lily then asks the teachers to introduce themselves to the camera. Yvette joins in, but Lily does not, and Lily turns the floor to Yvette.

Like Lily, Yvette is visibly tense, and she speaks more rapidly than usual. As the introduction progresses, the pace increases even more, she begins repeating herself, and topics overlap each other in confused fashion.

Yvette begins as she did at Westridge, by comparing the social and natural sciences and by quoting from Robert Emerson's Contemporary Field Research. At Endeavor, however, she emphasizes specific differences between the work of the researchers and that of the science teachers. Some of the differences come close to disparagement.

For example, Yvette begins by noting, "We know you are all science people. And so, our view of science is a little bit different." She indicates that teachers "may have noticed" some differences: "We didn't come into your classroom and count - the number of time you called on students or the number of females you called on . . . . We kind of had a different approach." She poses the task of understanding social interactions as more difficult than understanding chemical interactions: "As scientists, you're probably - - two chemicals come together, this is what happens, and that's great. But, when you watch people, it's not so easy . . . we're trying to understand the meaning of what we see in your classrooms." She states, rather than asks, that she doesn't think the teachers "would want numbers" anyway, because "you would understand - that that wouldn't really tell much about teaching. So, we're really trying to come in and give a different picture from the numbers and statistics that are very often cited."

Receiving few encouraging gestures from the Endeavor teachers with whom she is also not well-acquainted, Yvette begins speaking even faster and shifting topics abruptly. She races through the series of concepts — ethnography, culture, school culture, behavior, divergent interpretations. Because she hurries, the exposition is jumbled, and she omits examples that might ground the concepts, such as the demonstrative arm-waving or her personal background as a newcomer to California culture:

> They call it "ethnography," which means basically describing a culture. Now, a culture can be types of behavior. But the behavior itself does not give you the meaning. We have to infer the meaning. And that's why, we kind of want to make sure that you are here when we give you a picture of the school, because we may think it means one thing but you may tell us it means something totally different. And, so, we want to make sure we get it right.
>
> A school culture, as you probably know - it's different from school to school. It doesn't tell you what to do on a daily basis, but it sets parameters as far as what's appropriate, what's not appropriate. So, basically, your curriculum is a translation of the culture and how you teach can also be something that's based in the culture. So, today, what we want to focus on is the culture of the school.

Speaking yet more rapidly and disjointedly, Yvette turns to the tensions of ethnographic research. In one long, run-on sentence, she commingles nervousness in having her teaching observed, the researchers' apparently general nervousness, their gratitude and appreciation for Endeavor's welcome, their K–12 teaching experience, and the difficulties of being an objective observer:

> Um - I thought it was important to let you know, we're in your classes and I, know, I've taught, and I'm always nervous when someone comes in the room and watches me and it makes me very nervous, and so, I also think it's important to tell you that - we're very nervous too, and we're also very grateful, and we appreciate that you

welcomed us in, because we know what it's like to have someone, we've both taught, and it's very uncomfortable and basically, I want to thank you again.

So, we also struggle - because as Lily mentioned, we're both teachers and very much interested in teaching and so we have an interest here and if we sit in your classroom, it's very difficult for us to be objective.

Yvette begins to discuss the "struggle between being objective or being a confidant," but falls again into expressing the researchers' gratitude. The repetitions may have suggested to the teachers that the researchers "doth protest too much."

Almost breathlessly, Yvette arrives at the analogy between ethnography and portraiture. Here, as at Westridge, she points out that perspectives may differ, but that differences can enhance understanding. However, she also demurs, noting that the research team "is not here to get a pat on the back. . . . We really want your - er, honest input [about] what did we get right, what did we get wrong." Lily reiterates Yvette's anticipation of differences when she hands out the four-page portrait of the school: "This is an unfinished portrait, and we want you to read it primarily by asking yourselves, 'How does this fit with the way I see teaching, how does this fit with the way I see students, how does this fit with the way I see teaching at this school?'"

The teachers read for about ten minutes, and Lily then opens the floor for discussion, saying, "So, let's begin. Comments! Questions!" Margaret responds: "Who wrote this?" Lily answers that "Reba did, but it represents input from every member of the research team." Margaret continues: "Well, when I say, 'What does she mean by this?' will you be able to tell me?" Lily replies, "Not always — but we are in contact with Reba by phone and we should be able to usually, because it does represent the team's general consensus." Margaret then turns to her colleagues and sets the focus: "Well, would it be okay to start on page one? Does anyone have a problem about paragraph one?"

The Second Interpretation

For all the similarities in our introductions at the two schools, they are also marked by differences that, if seemingly minuscule, made for big differences in the significance of the seminars. Put simply, we researchers brought different expectations into the two seminars; as we expressed our different expectations, we set the conditions for their fulfillment. Our excitement and anxiety at beginning the seminars were present in both introductions, but anxiety predominated at Endeavor and excitement at Westridge. Seen from this angle, the different responses from the teachers are social constructions, produced, in part, on account of our differences.

For instance, we hear ourselves joke with the Westridge teachers, and they reciprocate with laughter and jokes of their own. We smile more and are more lighthearted in our demeanor. We add asides that interject a personal as well as professional relationship, as when Lily says she respects teachers, not just as a researcher, but as a parent and fellow teacher. The introduction is also considerably longer, less hurried, and more coherent at Westridge. We pause to give examples that elaborate some of the abstract concepts. Often, we appeal to teachers to remember events that happened during the research project; for example, Yvette assumes that teachers will remember personal information that she has told them, such as that she is a newcomer to

California. Through such seemingly trivial references, our introduction at Westridge recalls the affiliations we and other teachers established during the lengthy fieldwork and evoke the possibility of continuing affiliation in the teacher seminars. Even though disagreements over the research may arise, having things in common will modulate differences and keep discussions civil.[14]

By contrast, at Endeavor we are serious, even a bit grim. There are no jokes. No teacher ventures a collegial aside to the researchers, and there is no responsive undercurrent of "uh-huh's." Our introduction is more tentative, disjointed, and hurried, and it becomes even more hurried and disorganized as it continues. At Endeavor, we emphasize that teachers' perspectives may differ from ours, as when Lily instructs teachers to consider, "How does this [portrait of the school] fit with how I see teachers, ... students, ... [and] teaching in this school?" Before the teachers say a word, we anticipate potential disagreements. We also make allowances for these anticipated disagreements, as when Lily asserts that the seminars belong to the teachers and the schedule can be changed if it does not suit them. Notably, we did not feel it necessary to make such a disavowal at Westridge.

In this second interpretation, we see three factors differentiating the two introductions. First, while we entered the seminars as researchers from the culture of the university, we did not bring immutable researcher or university roles or values to the seminars. Rather, like the teachers', our own participation was shaped by the local school contexts — that is, we had been partially socialized to the high schools during the long process of studying in them. As a result, we found ourselves seduced by the congeniality at Westridge and somewhat put off by the contentiousness at Endeavor. Our different reactions had arisen occasionally as topics in our team meetings. In the teacher seminars, the differentiated responses became even more pronounced and influential. For instance, as we found ourselves more and more beleaguered at Endeavor, we quit pushing hard at Westridge to get teachers to acknowledge critical issues in the data. In retrospect, we must have felt we had as much critique on our hands as we could handle. Our reactions were more complicated than this suggests, too, because we found that we were not only appreciative of the approval at Westridge but sometimes vexed by teachers' insouciance, whereas we admired the fervor with which Endeavor teachers scrutinized our presentation of the materials we presented, even as we also thought them defensive.

Second, the differences in our introductions were shaped by events we could not have foreseen when we planned for the teacher seminars. As ethnographers point out in justifying the open-ended research designs they favor, events in school sites are often serendipitous and beyond the control required in traditional designs. They less often acknowledge the contingencies that permeate ethnographic projects themselves.

In this case, members of the research team who had worked extensively at Endeavor were not present for the seminars. Reba Page, the principal investigator for the research project, was teaching at Harvard, having accepted a two-year position there in the summer of 1995, just as the project received funding from the National Science Foundation. Ellen Longo, who had a long association with Endeavor and was hired in the summer as liaison for the California fieldwork, had to quit the research project in December because of health problems. Yvette's primary assignment was at Westridge, so she had met the Endeavor teachers only briefly at the beginning of the school year and at several district in-services. Lily's assignment had included both high schools, and she had spent as much time during the year observing in Endeavor classes as Ellen, but the strong relationships she established with teachers did not extend to the two most powerful and vocal teachers in the department. Furthermore, the teachers with whom Lily established close relations were unable to participate in the seminars.

Hence, before the seminars began, the research team worried that credibility would be a problem at Endeavor. Yvette and Lily feared they would be seen only as "Reba's flunkies." Their worries were confirmed when the first questions in the Endeavor seminars were who had written the portrait and whether Lily and Yvette would be able to talk meaningfully with Endeavor teachers about its representations.

The third factor influencing differences in the introductions involved tensions in ethnography itself. Ethnography muddies traditional notions of research because it mixes categories more often kept separate. For example, Yvette noted in the introductions that ethnographers are intent on documenting behavior, but that they are equally intent on inferring its meaning. She pointed out that ethnography is an art akin to portraiture (Lightfoot, 1983), yet it is also a science; still, it is a human science that is not like the natural sciences (Hammersley, 1992).

Less explicit in our introductions, however, is the point that expertise and authority are unerringly ambiguous in ethnography. The point became pivotal in the differentiation of interactions and meaning in the seminars at the two schools. On the one hand, ethnography assumes that the members of cultures are the experts. After all, they know what researchers do not; they are experts on their own cultural knowledge, and scholars are dependent on them for access to it (Spindler, 1983). Participants in research may also feel particularly free to comment on ethnographic studies because data and interpretations are not usually represented in a highly technical format. The close attention that educational ethnographers pay to life in classrooms may also make the research endeavor seem closer to the kind of knowledge that practitioners have and value. In these practices and assumptions, then, ethnography appears "friendlier" and more egalitarian than traditional research.

On the other hand, ethnography also assumes that much of what members know about their culture is tacit, and that a culture maintains itself precisely through mechanisms that keep its precepts below members' explicit awareness (Geertz, 1983). Therefore, members may be blind to that which would be most obvious to an outsider. Ethnographers are such outsiders — and, like the young child who mentions that the emperor is not wearing any clothes, their insights are not necessarily going to be countenanced or appreciated within the culture (Varenne, 1986).

Because we did not address the ambiguities of expertise in our introductions, they played a double, perhaps we should say duplicitous, tune. Both qualities may have been particularly salient to no-nonsense teachers of the natural sciences.[15]

For example, in the structure of the seminars, we set ourselves apart as experts with research findings to report. We conveyed a view of research that the schools and teachers relied on — that is, that we as researchers must have discovered things that, if shared, would directly improve teaching practices. Moreover, for all our disavowals about "preliminary analysis," we had considerable confidence in the data and interpretations because we had drawn them over three years of fieldwork. We also felt we owed the teachers forthright reports of our data and conclusions. In short, we presented ourselves as experts with valuable knowledge to report.

Yet we also downplayed our authority and appealed to teachers' expertise. We knew that our analysis, like all analyses, was partial and that we both needed and valued teachers' feedback. We fully expected that we would revise our understanding of school science based on teachers' comments in the seminars. We also tried to moderate asymmetries in the teacher-researcher relationship by citing our own backgrounds as teachers, our respect for teaching, and some of the contradictory imperatives we felt in doing fieldwork. At the same time, we knew that the story we had to tell was a disturbing one and were worried about hurting and angering teachers we had come to know and like. Accordingly, our assertions about the importance of teacher feedback also functioned as moves to ingratiate ourselves with teachers so they would not be too hard on us when we presented "the bad news."

The ambiguities surrounding expertise, particularly in a society that prides itself on being egalitarian, emerged as the seminars unfolded. At Westridge, we researchers could moderate these ambiguities, and teachers could excuse them because all participants could appeal to a shared history and school norms that placed a premium on sociability and kickbacks. In the different circumstances at Endeavor, however, it may have seemed to teachers that we were not to be trusted because we did not understand "real research" or because we were talking out of both sides of our mouths.

A Third Interpretation: Teacher Power

We on the research team eventually became dissatisfied with this second interpretation, too. Whereas it highlighted how we researchers contributed to the different responses at the two schools, it still cast teachers as rather passive or reactive participants. The teachers acted as they did, the analysis suggests, in response to our presentations of the research. Like the first analysis, this interpretation also failed to consider that the drama in the seminars was not just going on between researchers and teachers; teachers there were also watching and performing for each other.

Our first and second analyses exhibited the conventional wisdom about reporting research to practitioners — that is, researchers should take measures to shift their power and privilege so that teachers are empowered. The conventional wisdom, however, neglects the fact that teachers already have power. Researcher agenda notwithstanding, teachers can appropriate a research project and use it for their own local purposes. Pursuing this tack, we began a third interpretation that looked at the teacher seminars as solidarity-building rituals for the two science departments (Collins, 1988; Samson, Page, & Crockett, 1997).

Seen from this perspective, the science teachers at Endeavor reacted to the teacher seminars by casting the research project as a common enemy and accordingly closed ranks against it. For example, alarmed by the "negativity" in the materials presented during the first seminar meeting, the department chair went immediately to the principal, reported that a document had been written that was unfair to the school, and asked him to stop the seminars. This move not only may have helped the chair maintain a leadership position with the other science teachers by offering them protection, but also demonstrated her loyalty to Endeavor (where loyalty counts). Further, it repaired a rather bitter, year-long feud the chair had been having with the principal.

In the seminars themselves, Endeavor teachers united with a solidarity we had not seen before. They followed the chair's lead, some often repeating the chair's comments almost verbatim. Their reading of the materials we provided was almost always negative, even when we pointed out some of their effective practices. When we explicitly noted that teachers seemed to be avoiding a discussion of the positive teacher-student relations we had documented, the Endeavor teachers still would not talk about them. Similarly, Endeavor teachers seemed to consider some of our efforts to reciprocate their generosity to be bribes — snacks, stipends, and the care we took in preparing "lessons" became targets in the move to discount the seminars, as when Sue said the stipend was what she "got out of" the seminars. In all of the seminars at Endeavor, only one teacher agreed publicly and explicitly with some of the research. When she did, she always followed her remarks with conciliatory gestures toward her colleagues.

By contrast, Westridge teachers maintained a unified front in support of the research. They affiliated with the university project, using the association to enhance the department's status in a community that included a large number of professionals, including university professors, and to ward off parents and administrators who were increasingly critical of the department. From the first seminar, Westridge teachers adopted the vocabulary of the research team, talking easily about "ethnography," "culture," "participant-observation," "experiments," and so forth. As the chair pointed out, they were at ease with the project and its reports because, like the research team, they too were "scientists."

Furthermore, like the teachers at Endeavor, the Westridge teachers read the data and findings in a way that was consistent with local school politics. For instance, they consistently interpreted the research as validating their status as victims. When negative comments about the research occasionally surfaced, they almost always came from teachers who were new to Westridge, and veteran teachers often took it upon themselves to corral the criticism. When Dick criticized the research as ill-defined, for example, a veteran in the department corrected him, noting that it was not good for teachers to know the research focus lest it "taint" the experiment by prompting teachers to teach as they thought researchers wanted.

In short, at both schools teachers were not passive consumers of university research. Nor, however, were they victims. They appropriated the research project for their own internal political purposes, defused external threats from within the two school communities, and built solidarity within the departments, whether by defending against the research project as a common enemy, as at Endeavor, or by uniting around it as a sacred object, as at Westridge.

Conclusion

These three interpretations of the different reactions to the teacher seminars are not inconsistent with each other. All show how the seminars were shaped by, and themselves shaped, our and teachers' encounters in the schools and the science departments. Taken together, the three readings begin explicating the multiple "strata of meaning" (Geertz, 1973, p. 9) that were the teacher seminars and aim to do justice to the complex, human experience of reporting research to the people who agree to participate in it. In particular, the three readings moderate theories that suggest that there are cultures of the university and school that will determine how teachers and re-searchers can engage over research about schooling. They suggest that participants think with "cultural facts," not simply because of them (Varenne & McDermott, 1998). People do not construe meanings of self, other, and knowledge in irrevocable or formulaic fashion, but in ways that are understandable, given the particular local and larger circumstances in which they act. Therefore, we may say that university scholars and schoolteachers are at risk of conflict over knowledge about schooling. The cultures of the university and school provide resources for conflict, but people will have to select them and use them in locally coherent ways. Conflict or consensus will not emerge in the readily predictable fashion suggested by conventional explanations based on stable cultural differences.

The three interpretations that we make of the teacher seminars are not the only possibilities either. For example, other approaches might consider the internal politics of the research team, where doctoral students were responsible to each other and to the principal investigator who, in some cases, was the students' major professor; conflict as well as solidarity within the high school science departments where some teachers, particularly at Endeavor, sought to be singled out for excellence or seemed uneasy about engaging in public discussions about curriculum with colleagues; differences in the two "school portraits" that may have influenced the teachers' different responses; the emergence of distinctive roles for participants as the seminars evolved; and how extraordinarily "strange," or unfamiliar, the work of university scholars may be to many school teachers, whereas members of the research team had themselves all worked in public schools. Additional interpretations of the teacher seminars continue to "thicken" our characterization of the process of discussing research with practitioners.

We researchers learned a great deal in the teacher seminars, but we worry that our gain was too much at the expense of the teachers (see Whyte, 1981, Appendix A). Some teachers said that they gained little knowledge of value, others that the experience only further disheartened them about public school teaching. As a result, we now question rather than assume that reporting research to participants is obligatory, inherently valuable, crucial to validity, or tantamount to progressive action. Instead, the pertinent question seems to be, in whose interest is sharing research? Or, to pose the matter more ethically than politically, how shall we "be attentive to existing 'minor' practices . . . and virtues . . . that escape the dominant discursive trends of theorists of modernity and postmodernity alike . . . [so as to make them] more visible, more available, [and] thereby contribut[e] to their reinvention" (Rabinow, 1996, p. 7; see also Jackson, Boostrum, & Hansen, 1993)? From this perspective, social research might aim both to render the intricacy and contingencies of the encounters in which people actually negotiate definitions of their roles and relationships, and to do so in accounts that themselves are "self-consciously tentative" (Edelman, 1977) rather than peremptory. Interpretative research is neither objective detachment nor relativism, but "a particular [analytic] form of involvement. . . . This is a way of classifying situations, not a contrast between concerned people and detached people. Everyone is involved in both ways in some degree at different times and in some situations. But the phenomenological contrast is profound" (Edelman, 1985, p. 209).

Having only begun to mull over such questions, we conclude with three comments. First, in the weeks following the seminars, several Endeavor teachers mentioned privately to Lily that the seminars had made them think differently about their teaching, even though in the seminars themselves they said that they had learned little or nothing. This makes us remember and hope that in reporting research, as in teaching school, effects may be less immediate or direct than our assessments usually assume. It also recalls the suggestion for improvement that the department chair at Westridge offered: Teachers may want to hear about research findings individually and privately, rather than in a public format.

Second, we and the teachers did complete the series of six teacher seminars. Despite temptations to abandon them, we all persevered, even when the going got tough at Endeavor or when meetings seemed to be nothing but venting sessions at Westridge. That seems a worthy outcome in what may be an increasingly fragmented society and profession.

Finally, we hope to propose to the two science departments at Westridge and Endeavor yet another phase of research that will extend our three-year relationship. We will try to secure support for the teachers to engage in the nuts and bolts of developing an integrated science curriculum — a support that they have so far lacked and that has hindered their best intentions. They, in turn, will let us return to their classrooms for further participation and observation. We pursue this option because sustained discourse over knowledge about curriculum and teaching may be an essential means of moving toward respectful relations between researchers in universities and practitioners in schools. However haltingly, we gain clearer pictures of what it means to respect one another rather than to dissect, disregard, denounce, or minister to the misguided. Discourse is action. In it, we produce, specifically and complexly, how we differ, what we have in common, and how we may begin to reimagine how we may live together.

Notes

1. *Integrated science* has a long pedigree, dating back to progressive proposals for general education in the early decades of the twentieth century; see Kliebard (1988, 1995).
2. The school names are pseudonyms, as are all names except those of the members of the research team.
3. *Composition of Student Populations*

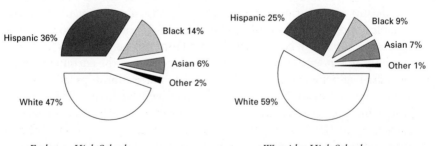

Endeavor High School
49% eligible for free lunch
Dropout rate: 9.4%
SAT Verbal: 43% above 450
SAT Math: 44% above 450
AP Exam Scholars: 26

Westridge High School
26% eligible for free lunch
Dropout rate: 2.9%
SAT Verbal: 47% above 450
SAT Math: 56% above 450
AP Exam Scholars: 26

Note that enrollments total more than 100 percent. *Source:* School Report Cards, 1992-1993, Orangetowne School District.

4. For a description and analysis of this characteristic cycle of tracking in U.S. schools, in which moves to integrate curriculum and de-track are followed by moves to differentiate curriculum and provide for students' particular abilities, needs, and/or aspirations, see Page (1991).

5. The research interventions differ from collaborative, or action, research in at least two important respects. First, teachers were not formally co-researchers; they did not collaborate in setting research topics or collecting data. Second, researchers were not formally co-practitioners; we did not try to influence practice directly, but sought to establish structures within which teachers, with us and each other, could choose to deliberate over practice.

6. At Endeavor, two teachers who volunteered to participate in the seminars were unable to attend because coaching schedules conflicted with the time designated by the chair of the department.

7. The same seminar materials were used at both high schools, except for the portraits of the cultures of the high schools, presented at the first meetings of the seminars. The portraits were similar in length, descriptiveness, and amount of data displayed, but the Westridge document had gone through more drafts and was probably more clearly written.

   The schedule of topics for the six teacher seminars was as follows: Week 1, The culture of the school; Week 2, The history of implementing *integrated science;* Week 3, Curriculum in *integrated science 1 and 2* classes; Week 4, Teacher voice in curriculum; Week 5, Teaching strategies, including student talk and tests; and Week 6, Teacher advice regarding the research team offering a summer course for students ("Doing the Ethnography of High School Science") and teacher evaluation of their experiences in the seminars and the research project.

8. We render speech in writing using these conventions: short, untimed pauses by -, slightly longer pauses by - -, and timed pauses by (seconds); emphasis by *italics* and greater emphasis by CAPITAL LETTERS; elongated pronunciation by repetitions of letters, as in *repetiiitions;* descriptions or explanations of the situation by [brackets]; and ellipsis by . . . .

9. Some scholars, including some ethnographers, report that they pay little attention to the data reported in field studies, moving instead to authors' summaries and conclusions (see Hammersley, 1992).

10. A version of this article was presented as a "performance" at the annual meeting of the American Educational Research Association (AERA) in Chicago, March 24–28, 1997. We presented the transcripts as dramatic "interpretive readings" (see Clark & Moss, 1996, regarding Readers Theatre). The medium proved very effective: Audience members were attentive, readily grasped the situation of the teacher seminars, and, when we asked them to interpret the data, they could cite specific instances we had read. We are grateful to members of the audience at AERA for their participation, including helpful comments about the analysis. We also acknowledge the helpful suggestions of a group of colleagues during a "dress rehearsal" prior to AERA.

11. For another instance in which reporting research to teachers developed as "mutual accusation," see Page (1994).

12. Yvette is young (28) and looks even younger. Early in the project, campus security guards stopped her when she was leaving the high school campus before the final bell.

13. The research project spanned three school years, but Lily and Yvette worked on it only during 1995–1996.

14. What we call affiliations are termed "co-participation structures" by Erickson and Schultz (1982).

15. As Rabinow (1996) remarks in a compelling essay about ethnography as an ethical enterprise, ethnographers may establish co-participation with subjects by acknowledging the deep uncertainties in their own work and knowledge, as well as in the participants'. We voiced those uncertainties inadequately in our introduction.

References

American Association for the Advancement of Science. (1989). *Science for all Americans.* Washington, DC: Author.

Bloor, M. (1983). Notes on member validation. In R. Emerson (Ed.), *Contemporary field research* (pp. 156–172). Prospect Heights, IL: Waveland Press.

Boostrum, R., Jackson, P., & Hansen, D. (1993). Coming together and staying apart: How a group of teachers and researchers sought to bridge "the research/practice gap." *Teachers College Record, 95,* 35–44.

Burke, K. (1966). *Language as symbolic action.* Berkeley: University of California Press.

California State Department of Education. (1990). *The science framework for California public schools, K-12.* Sacramento: Author.

Clark, C., & Moss, P. (1996). Researching with: Ethical and epistemological implications of doing collaborative, change-oriented research with teachers and students. *Teachers College Record, 97,* 518–548.

Clifford, J., & Marcus, G. (1986). *Writing culture: The poetics and politics of ethnography.* Berkeley: University of California Press.

Collins, R. (1988). *Theoretical sociology.* San Diego: Harcourt Brace Jovanovich.

Crockett, M., Page, R., & Samson, Y. (1997, March). *Integrated science: Old wine in old bottles.* Paper presented at the annual meeting of the American Educational Research Association, Chicago.

Edelman, M. (1977). *Political language: Words that succeed and policies that fail.* New York: Academic Press.

Edelman, M. (1985). *Symbolic uses of politics.* Urbana: University of Illinois Press.

Edelman, M. (1995). *From art to politics: How artistic creations shape political conceptions.* Chicago: University of Chicago Press.

Emerson, R. (1983). *Contemporary field research: A collection of readings.* Prospect Heights, IL: Waveland Press.

Erickson, F., & Schultz, J. (1982). *The counselor as gatekeeper: Social interaction in interviews.* New York: Academic Press.

Geertz, C. (1973). Thick description: Toward an interpretive theory of culture. In *The interpretation of cultures: Selected essays* (pp. 3–30). New York: Basic Books.

Geertz, C. (1983). Commonsense as a cultural system. In *Local knowledge: Further essays in interpretive anthropology* (pp. 73–93). New York: Basic Books.

Goffman, E. (1961). *Encounters.* Indianapolis, IN: Bobbs-Merrill.

Greenblatt, S. (1991). *Marvelous possessions: The wonder of the New World.* Chicago: University of Chicago Press.

Hammersley, M. (1992). *What's wrong with ethnography?* New York: Routledge.

Hargreaves, A. (1996). Transforming knowledge: Blurring the boundaries between research, policy, and practice. *Educational Evaluation and Policy Analysis, 18,* 105–122.

Jackson, P., Boostrum, R., & Hansen, D. (1993). *The moral life of schools.* San Francisco: Jossey-Bass.

Kliebard, H. (1988). The liberal arts curriculum and its enemies: The effort to redefine general education. In I. Westbury & A. Purves (Eds.), *Cultural literacy and the idea of general education* (pp. 29–51). Chicago: University of Chicago Press.

Kliebard, H. (1990). Vocational education as symbolic action. *American Educational Research Journal, 27,* 9–28.

Kliebard, H. (1993). What is a knowledge base, and who would use it if we had one? *Review of Educational Research, 63,* 295–303.

Kliebard, H. (1995). *The struggle for the American curriculum, 1893–1958* (2nd ed.). New York: Routledge.

Lampert, M. (1985). How do teachers manage to teach? *Harvard Educational Review, 55,* 178–194.

Latour, B., & Woolgar, S. (1986). *Laboratory life: The construction of scientific facts.* Princeton, NJ: Princeton University Press. (Original work published 1979)

Lawrence-Lightfoot, S. (1983). *The good high school: Portraits of character and culture.* New York: Basic Books.

Metz, M. (1978). *Classrooms and corridors: The crisis of authority in desegregated secondary schools.* Berkeley: University of California Press.

Metz, M. (1986). *Different by design: The context and character of three magnet schools.* New York: Routledge.

National Science Teachers Association. (1988). Report of the NSTA task force on scope, sequence, and coordination of secondary school science. Washington, DC: Author.

Page, R. (1989). Cultures and curricula: Differences between and within schools. *Educational Foundations, 4,* 49–76.

Page, R. (1991). *Lower-track classrooms: A curricular and cultural perspective.* New York: Teachers College Press.

Page, R. (1994). Do-good ethnography. *Curriculum Inquiry, 24,* 479–502.

Page, R. (1995). Who systematizes the systematizers? Policy and practice interactions in a case of state-level systemic reform. *Theory Into Practice, 34,* 21–29.

Page, R. (1996, April). *What is relevant school knowledge?* Paper presented at the annual meetings of the American Educational Research Association, New York.

Page, R. (1997). Teaching about validity. *International Journal of Qualitative Studies in Education, 10,* 145–156.

Powell, A., Farrar, E., & Cohen, D. (1985). *The shopping mall high school: Winners and losers in the educational marketplace.* Boston: Houghton-Mifflin.

Rabinow, P. (1996). *Essays on the anthropology of reason.* Chicago: University of Chicago Press.

Samson, Y., Page, R., & Crockett, M. (1997, March). *Solidarity rituals: How subjects respond to research.* Paper presented at the annual meeting of the American Educational Research Association, Chicago.

Sarason, S. (1971). *The culture of the school and the problem of change* (2nd ed.). Boston: Allyn & Bacon.

Schwab, J. (1969). The practical: A language for curriculum. *School Review, 78,* 1–23.

Spindler, G. (1983). *Doing the ethnography of schooling.* New York: Holt, Rinehart & Winston.

Varenne, H. (Ed.). (1986). *Symbolizing America.* Lincoln: University of Nebraska Press.

Varenne, H., & McDermott, R., with Goldman, S., Naddeo, M., & Rizzo-Tolk, R. (1998). *Successful failure: Education as cultural fact.* Boulder, CO: Westview Press.

Waller, W. (1932). *The sociology of teaching.* New York: John Wiley & Sons.

Whyte, W. (1981). *Street corner society: The social structure of an Italian slum* (3rd ed.). Chicago: University of Chicago Press.

Appendix

The chart sketches the evolution of *High School Science: What Is It, Who Decides, and How Does It Matter?* in the two high schools, 1993–1996, as well as the responsibilities of the various members of the research team.

Year	Endeavor High	Westridge High
1993-1994*	Reba Page: half-time fieldwork, Sept.-Feb.; intermittent fieldwork, Mar.-June. Beth Allan: half-time fieldwork, Sept.-June. Ellen Longo: volunteer fieldwork, Nov.-April.	Reba Page: half-time fieldwork, Sept.-Feb.; intermittent fieldwork, Mar.-June.
1994-1995*	Reba Page: occasional contact, Sept.-June. Ellen Longo: full-time fieldwork (dissertation), Feb.-June.	Reba Page: occasional contact, Sept.-June.
1995-1996	Ellen Longo: team leader and liaison; half-time fieldwork, Aug.-Dec. Lily Rivera: quarter-time fieldwork, Aug.-June.	Ellen Longo: leader and liaison, Aug.-Dec. Lily Rivera: quarter-time fieldwork, Aug.-June. Yvette Samson: half-time fieldwork, Aug.-June.
1995-1996	Reba Page: supervision of fieldwork in California and policy research in Cambridge, Massachusetts, with Nina Arschavsky and Julie Pearson Stewart.	
Summer, 1996	Reba Page, Michele Crockett, Lily Rivera, and Yvette Samson: data analysis.	

*Support for the research conducted during 1993-1994, continued in 1994-1995, was provided by the National Center for Science Teaching and Learning, Grant No. R117Q00062, Office of Educational Research and Innovation, U.S. Department of Education.

The preparation of this article and the research reported in it are supported in part by the National Science Foundation, under RED 9550761. The findings and conclusions are our own and do not reflect the view of the sponsoring agency.

PART SIX

The Uses of Research

Lessons from Students
on Creating a
Chance to Dream

SONIA NIETO

> How does it come about that the one institution that is said to be the gateway to opportunity, the school, is the very one that is most effective in perpetuating an oppressed and impoverished status in society? (Stein, 1971, p. 178)

The poignant question above was posed in this very journal almost a quarter of a century ago by Annie Stein, a consistent critic of the schools and a relentless advocate for social justice. This question shall serve as the central motif of this article because, in many ways, it remains to be answered and continues to be a fundamental dilemma standing in the way of our society's stated ideals of equity and equal educational opportunity. Annie Stein's observations about the New York City public schools ring true today in too many school systems throughout the country and can be used to examine some of the same policies and practices she decried in her 1971 article.

It is my purpose in this article to suggest that successfully educating all students in U.S. schools must begin by challenging school policies and practices that place roadblocks in the way of academic achievement for too many young people. Educating students today is, of course, a far different and more complex proposition than it has been in the past. Young people face innumerable personal, social, and political challenges, not to mention massive economic structural changes not even dreamed about by other generations of youth in the twentieth century. In spite of the tensions that such challenges may pose, U.S. society has nevertheless historically had a social contract to educate *all* youngsters, not simply those who happen to be European American, English-speaking, economically privileged, and, in the current educational reform jargon, "ready to learn."[1] Yet, our schools have traditionally failed some youngsters, especially those from racially and culturally dominated and economically oppressed backgrounds. Research over the past half century has documented a disheartening legacy of failure for many students of all backgrounds, but especially children of Latino, African American, and Native American families, as well as poor European American families and, more recently, Asian and Pacific American immigrant

Harvard Educational Review Vol. 64 No. 4 Winter 1994, 392–426

students. Responding to the wholesale failure of so many youngsters within our public schools, educational theorists, sociologists, and psychologists devised elaborate theories of genetic inferiority, cultural deprivation, and the limits of "throwing money" at educational problems. Such theories held sway in particular during the 1960s and 1970s, but their influence is still apparent in educational policies and practices today.[2]

The fact that many youngsters live in difficult, sometimes oppressive conditions is not at issue here. Some may live in ruthless poverty and face the challenges of dilapidated housing, inadequate health care, and even abuse and neglect. They and their families may be subject to racism and other oppressive institutional barriers. They may have difficult personal, psychological, medical, or other kinds of problems. These are real concerns that should not be discounted. But, despite what may seem to be insurmountable obstacles to learning and teaching, some schools are nevertheless successful with young people who live in these situations. In addition, many children who live in otherwise onerous situations also have loving families willing to sacrifice what it takes to give their children the chance they never had during their own childhoods. Thus, poverty, single-parent households, and even homelessness, while they may be tremendous hardships, do not in and of themselves doom children to academic failure (see, among others, Clark, 1983; Lucas, Henze, & Donato, 1990; Mehan & Villanueva, 1993; Moll, 1992; Taylor & Dorsey-Gaines, 1988). These and similar studies point out that schools that have made up their minds that their students deserve the chance to learn do find the ways to educate them successfully in spite of what may seem to be overwhelming odds.

Educators may consider students difficult to teach simply because they come from families that do not fit neatly into what has been defined as "the mainstream." Some of them speak no English; many come from cultures that seem to be at odds with the dominant culture of U.S. society that is inevitably reflected in the school; others begin their schooling without the benefit of early experiences that could help prepare them for the cognitive demands they will face. Assumptions are often made about how such situations may negatively affect student achievement and, as a consequence, some children are condemned to failure before they begin. In a study by Nitza Hidalgo, a teacher's description of the students at an urban high school speaks to this condemnation: "Students are generally poor, uneducated and come from broken families who do not value school. Those conditions that produce achievers are somewhere else, not here. We get street people" (Hidalgo, 1991, p. 58). When such viewpoints guide teachers' and schools' behaviors and expectations, little progress can be expected in student achievement.

On the other hand, a growing number of studies suggest that teachers and schools need to build on rather than tear down what students bring to school. That is, they need to understand and incorporate cultural, linguistic, and experiential differences, as well as differences in social class, into the learning process (Abi-Nader, 1993; Hollins, King, & Hayman, 1994; Lucas et al., 1990; Moll & Díaz, 1993). The results of such efforts often provide inspiring examples of success, because they begin with a belief that all students deserve a chance to learn. In this article, I will highlight these efforts by exploring the stories of some academically successful young people in order to suggest how the policies and practices of schools can be transformed to create environments in which all children are capable of learning.

It is too convenient to fall back on deficit theories and continue the practice of blaming students, their families, and their communities for educational failure. Instead, schools need to focus on where they *can* make a difference, namely, their own instructional policies and practices. A number of recent studies, for example, have concluded that a combination of factors, including characteristics of schools as opposed to only student background and actions, can explain differences between high- and low-achieving students. School characteristics that have been found to make a positive difference in these studies include an enriched and more demanding curriculum, respect for students' languages and cultures, high expectations for all students, and encouragement for parental involvement in their children's education (Lee, Winfield, & Wilson, 1991; Lucas et al., 1990; Moll, 1992). This would suggest that we need to shift from a single-minded focus on low- or high-achieving students to the conditions that create low- or high-achieving schools. If we understand school policies and practices as being enmeshed in societal values, we can better understand the manifestations of these values in schools as well. Thus, for example, "tracked" schools, rather than reflecting a school practice that exists in isolation from society, reflect a society that is itself tracked along racial, gender, and social-class lines. In the same way, "teacher expectations" do not come from thin air, but reflect and support expectations of students that are deeply ingrained in societal and ideological values.

Reforming school structures alone will not lead to substantive differences in student achievement, however, if such changes are not also accompanied by profound changes in how we as educators think about our students; that is, in what we believe they deserve and are capable of achieving. Put another way, changing policies and practices is a necessary but insufficient condition for total school transformation. For example, in a study of six high schools in which Latino students have been successful, Tamara Lucas, Rosemary Henze, and Rubén Donato (1990) found that the most crucial element is a shared belief among teachers, counselors, and administrators that all students are capable of learning. This means that concomitant changes are needed in policies and practices *and* in our individual and collective will to educate all students. Fred Newmann (1993), in an important analysis of educational restructuring, underlines this point by emphasizing that reform efforts will fail unless they are accompanied by a set of particular commitments and competencies to guide them, including a commitment to the success of all students, the creation of new roles for teachers, and the development of schools as caring communities.

Another crucial consideration in undertaking educational change is a focus on what Jim Cummins (1994) has called the "relations of power" in schools. In proposing a shift from coercive to collaborative relations of power, Cummins argues that traditional teacher-centered transmission models can limit the potential for critical thinking on the part of both teachers and students, but especially for students from dominated communities whose cultures and languages have been devalued by the dominant canon.[3] By encouraging collaborative relations of power, schools and teachers can begin to recognize other sources of legitimate knowledge that have been overlooked, negated, or minimized because they are not part of the dominant discourse in schools.

Focusing on concerns such as the limits of school reform without concomitant changes in educators' attitudes toward students and their families, and the crucial role of power relationships in schools may help rescue current reform efforts from simplistic technical responses to what are essentially moral and political dilemmas. That is, such technical changes as tinkering with the length of the school day, substituting one textbook for another, or adding curricular requirements may do little to change student outcomes unless these changes are part and parcel of a more comprehensive conceptualization of school reform. When such issues are considered fundamental to the changes that must be made in schools, we might more precisely speak about *transformation* rather than simply about reform. But educational transformation cannot take place without the inclusion of the voices of students, among others, in the dialogue.

Why Listen to Students?

One way to begin the process of changing school policies and practices is to listen to students' views about them; however, research that focuses on student voices is relatively recent and scarce. For example, student perspectives are for the most part missing in discussions concerning strategies for confronting educational problems. In addition, the voices of students are rarely heard in the debates about school failure and success, and the perspectives of students from disempowered and dominated communities are even more invisible. In this article, I will draw primarily on the words of students interviewed for a previous research study (Nieto, 1992). I used the interviews to develop case studies of young people from a wide variety of ethnic, racial, linguistic, and social-class backgrounds who were at the time students in junior or senior high school. These ten young people lived in communities as diverse as large urban areas and small rural hamlets and belonged to families ranging from single-parent households to large, extended families. The one common element in all of their experiences turned out to be something we as researchers had neither planned nor expected: they were all successful students.[4]

The students were selected in a number of ways, but primarily through community contacts. Most were interviewed at home or in another setting of their choice outside of school. The only requirement that my colleagues and I determined for selecting students was that they reflect a variety of ethnic and racial backgrounds, in order to give us the diversity for which we were looking. The students selected self-identified as Black, African American, Mexican, Native American, Black and White American (biracial), Vietnamese, Jewish, Lebanese, Puerto Rican, and Cape Verdean. The one European American was the only student who had a hard time defining herself, other than as "American" (for a further analysis of this issue, see Nieto, 1992). That these particular students were academically successful was quite serendipitous. We defined them as such for the following reasons: they were all either still in school or just graduating; they all planned to complete at least high school, and most hoped to go to college; they had good grades, although they were not all at the top of their class; they had thought about their future and had made some plans for it; they generally enjoyed school and felt engaged in it (but they were also critical of their own school experiences and that of their peers, as we shall see); and most described themselves as successful. Although it had not been our initial intention to focus exclusively on academically successful students, on closer reflection it seemed logical that such students would be more likely to want to talk about their experiences than those who were not successful. It was at that point that I decided to explore what it was about these students' specific experiences that helped them succeed in school.

Therefore, the fact that these students saw themselves as successful helped further define the study, whose original purpose was to determine the benefits of multicultural education for students of diverse backgrounds. I was particularly interested in developing a way of looking at multicultural education that went beyond the typical "Holidays and Heroes" approach, which is too superficial to have any lasting impact in schools (Banks, 1991; Sleeter, 1991).[5] By exploring such issues as racism and low expectations of student achievement, as well as school policies and practices such as curriculum, pedagogy, testing, and tracking, I set about developing an understanding of multicultural education as antiracist, comprehensive, pervasive, and rooted in social justice. Students were interviewed to find out what it meant to be from a particular background, how this influenced their school experience, and what about that experience they would change if they could. Although they were not asked specifically about the policies and practices in their schools, they nevertheless reflected on them in their answers to questions ranging from identifying their favorite subjects to describing the importance of getting an education. In this article, I will revisit the interviews to focus on students' thoughts about a number of school policies and practices and on the effects of racism and other forms of discrimination on their education.

The insights provided by the students were far richer than we had first thought. Although we expected numerous criticisms of schools and some concrete suggestions, we were surprised at the depth of awareness and analysis the students shared with us. They had a lot to say about the teachers they liked, as well as those they disliked, and they were able to explain the differences between them; they talked about grades and how these had become overly important in determining curriculum and pedagogy; they discussed their parents' lack of involvement, in most cases, in traditional school activities such as P.T.O. membership and bake sales, but their otherwise passionate support for their children's academic success; they mused about what schools could do to encourage more students to learn; they spoke with feeling about their cultures, languages, and communities, and what schools could do to capitalize on these factors; and they gave us concrete suggestions for improving schools for young people of all backgrounds. This experience confirmed my belief that educators can benefit from hearing students' critical perspectives, which might cause them to modify how they approach curriculum, pedagogy, and other school practices. Since doing this research, I have come across other studies that also focus on young people's perspectives and provide additional powerful examples of the lessons we can learn from them. This article thus begins with "lessons from students," an approach that takes the perspective proposed by Paulo Freire, that teachers need to become students just as students need to become teachers in order for education to become reciprocal and empowering for both (Freire, 1970).

This focus on students is not meant to suggest that their ideas should be the final and conclusive word in how schools need to change. Nobody has all the answers, and suggesting that students' views should be adopted wholesale is to accept a romantic view of students that is just as partial and condescending as excluding them completely from the discussion. I am instead suggesting that if we believe schools must provide an equal and quality education for all, students need to be included in the dialogue, and that their views, just as those of others, should be problematized and used to reflect critically on school reform.

Selected Policies and Practices and Students' Views about Them

School policies and practices need to be understood within the sociopolitical context of our society in general, rather than simply within individual schools' or teachers' attitudes and practices. This is important to remember for a number of reasons. First, although "teacher bashing" provides an easy target for complex problems, it fails to take into account the fact that teachers function within particular societal and institutional structures. In addition, it results in placing an inordinate amount of blame on some of those who care most deeply about students and who struggle every day to help them learn. That some teachers are racist, classist, and mean-spirited and that others have lost all creativity and caring is not in question here, and I begin with the assumption that the majority of teachers are not consciously so. I do suggest, however, that although many teachers are hardworking, supportive of their students, and talented educators, many of these same teachers are also burned out, frustrated, and negatively influenced by societal views about the students they teach. Teachers could benefit from knowing more about their students' families and experiences, as well as about students' views on school and how it could be improved.

How do students feel about the curriculum they must learn? What do they think about the pedagogical strategies their teachers use? Is student involvement a meaningful issue for them? Are their own identities important considerations in how they view school? What about tracking and testing and disciplinary policies? These are crucial questions to consider when reflecting on what teachers and schools can learn from students, but we know very little about students' responses. When asked, students seem surprised and excited about being included in the conversation, and what they have to say is often compelling and eloquent. In fact, Patricia Phelan, Ann Locke Davidson, and Hanh Thanh Cao (1992), in a two-year research project designed to identify students' thoughts about school, discovered that students' views on teaching and learning were remarkably consistent with those of current theorists concerned with learning theory, cognitive science, and the sociology of work. This should come as no surprise when we consider that students spend more time in schools than anybody else except teachers (who are also omitted in most discussions of school reform, but that is a topic for another article). In the following sections, I will focus on students' perceptions concerning the curriculum, pedagogy, tracking, and grades in their schools. I will also discuss their attitudes about racism and other biases, how these are manifested in their schools and classrooms, and what effect they may have on students' learning and participation in school.

Curriculum

The curriculum in schools is at odds with the experiences, backgrounds, hopes, and wishes of many students. This is true of both the tangible curriculum as expressed through books, other materials, and the actual written curriculum guides, as well as in the less tangible and "hidden" curriculum as seen in the bulletin boards, extracurricular activities, and messages given to students about their abilities and talents. For instance, Christine Sleeter and Carl Grant (1991) found that a third of the students in a desegregated junior high school they studied said that *none* of the class content related to their lives outside class. Those who indicated some relevancy cited only current events, oral history, money and banking, and multicultural content (because it dealt with prejudice) as being relevant. The same was true in a study by Mary Poplin and Joseph Weeres (1992), who found that students frequently reported being bored in school and seeing little relevance in what was taught for their lives or their futures. The authors concluded that students became more disengaged as the curriculum, texts, and assignments became more standardized. Thus, in contrast to Ira Shor's (1992) suggestion that "what students bring to class is where learning begins. It starts there and goes places" (p. 44), there is often a tremendous mismatch between students' cultures and the culture of the school. In many schools, learning starts not with what students bring to class, but with what is considered high-status knowledge; that is, the "canon," with its overemphasis on European and European American history, arts, and values. This seldom includes the backgrounds, experiences, and talents of the majority of students in U.S. schools. Rather than "going elsewhere," their learning therefore often goes nowhere.

That students' backgrounds and experiences are missing in many schools is particularly evident where the native language of most of the students is not English. In such settings, it is not unusual to see little or no representation of those students' language in the curriculum. In fact, there is often an insistence that students "speak only English" in these schools, which sends a powerful message to young people struggling to maintain an identity in the face of overpowering messages that they must assimilate. This was certainly the case for Marisol, a Puerto Rican girl of sixteen participating in my research, who said:

> I used to have a lot of problems with one of my teachers 'cause she didn't want us to talk Spanish in class, and I thought that was like an insult to us, you know? Just telling us not to talk Spanish, 'cause they were Puerto Ricans and, you know, we're free to talk whatever we want, . . . I could never stay quiet and talk only English, 'cause sometimes . . . words slip in Spanish. You know, I think they should understand that.

Practices such as not allowing students to speak their native tongue are certain to influence negatively students' identities and their views of what constitutes important knowledge. For example, when asked if she would be interested in taking a course on Puerto Rican history, Marisol was quick to answer: "I don't think [it's] important. . . . I'm proud of myself and my culture, but I think I know what I should know about the culture already, so I wouldn't take the course." Ironically, it was evident to me after speaking with her on several occasions that Marisol knew virtually nothing about Puerto Rican history. However, she had already learned another lesson well: given what she said about the courses she needed to take, she made it clear that "important" history is U.S. history, which rarely includes anything about Puerto Rico.

Messages about culture and language and how they are valued or devalued in society are communicated not only or even primarily by schools, but by the media and community as a whole. The sociopolitical context of the particular city where Marisol lived, and of its school system, is important to understand: there had been an attempt to pass an ordinance restricting the number of Puerto Ricans coming into town based on the argument that they placed an undue burden on the welfare rolls and other social services. In addition, the "English Only" debate had become an issue when the mayor had ordered all municipal workers to speak only English on the job. Furthermore, although the school system had a student body that was 65 percent Puerto Rican, there was only a one-semester course on Puerto Rican history that had just recently been approved for the bilingual program. In contrast, there were two courses, which although rarely taught were on the books, that focused on apartheid and the Holocaust, despite the fact that both the African American and Jewish communities in the town were quite small. That such courses should be part of a comprehensive multicultural program is not being questioned; however, it is ironic that the largest population in the school was ignored in the general curriculum.

In a similar vein, Nancy Commins's (1989) research with four first-generation Mexican American fifth-grade students focused on how these students made decisions about their education, both consciously and unconsciously, based on their determination of what counted as important knowledge. Her research suggests that the classroom setting and curriculum can support or hinder students' perceptions of themselves as learners based on the languages they speak and their cultural backgrounds. She found that although the homes of these four students provided rich environments for a variety of language uses and literacy, the school did little to capitalize on these strengths. In their classroom, for instance, these children rarely used Spanish, commenting that it was the language of the "dumb kids." As a result, Commins states: "Their reluctance to use Spanish in an academic context also limited their opportunities to practice talking about abstract ideas and to use higher level cognitive skills in Spanish" (p. 35). She also found that the content of the curriculum was almost completely divorced from the experiences of these youngsters, since the problems of poverty, racism, and discrimination, which were prominent in their lives, were not addressed in the curriculum.

In spite of teachers' reluctance to address such concerns, they are often compelling to students, particularly those who are otherwise invisible in the curriculum. Vinh, an eighteen-year-old Vietnamese student attending a high school in a culturally heterogeneous town, lived with his uncle and younger brothers and sisters. Although grateful for the education he was receiving, Vinh expressed concern about what he saw as insensitivity on the part of some of his teachers to the difficulties of adjusting to a new culture and learning English:

> [Teachers] have to know about our culture. . . . From the second language, it is very difficult for me and for other people.

Vinh's concern was echoed by Manuel, a nineteen-year-old Cape Verdean senior who, at the time of the interviews, was just getting ready to graduate, the first in his family of eleven children to do so:

> I was kind of afraid of school, you know, 'cause it's different when you're learning the language. . . . It's kind of scary at first, especially if you don't know the language and like if you don't have friends here.

In Manuel's case, the Cape Verdean Crioulo bilingual program served as a linguistic and cultural mediator, negotiating difficult experiences that he faced in school so that, by the time he reached high school, he had learned enough English to "speak up." Another positive curricular experience was the theater workshop he took as a sophomore. There, students created and acted in skits focusing on their lived experiences. He recalled with great enthusiasm, for example, a monologue he did about a student going to a new school, because it was based on his personal experience.

Sometimes a school's curriculum is unconsciously disrespectful of students' cultures and experiences. James, a student who proudly identified himself as Lebanese American, found that he was invisible in the curriculum, even in supposedly multicultural curricular and extracurricular activities. He mentioned a language fair, a multicultural festival, and a school cookbook, all of which omitted references to the Arabic language and to Lebanese people. About the cookbook, he said:

> They made this cookbook of all these different recipes from all over the world. And I would've brought in some Lebanese recipes if somebody'd let me know. And I didn't hear about it until the week before they started selling them. . . . I asked one of the teachers to look at it and there was nothing Lebanese in there.

James made an effort to dismiss this oversight, and although he said that it didn't matter, he seemed to be struggling with the growing realization that it mattered very much indeed:

> I don't know, I guess there's not that many Lebanese people in . . . I don't know; you don't hear really that much . . . Well, you hear it in the news a lot, but I mean, I don't know, there's not a lot of Lebanese kids in our school. . . . I don't mind, 'cause I mean, I don't know, just I don't mind it. . . . It's not really important. It *is* important for me. It would be important for me to see a Lebanese flag.

Lebanese people were mentioned in the media, although usually in negative ways, and these were the only images of James's ethnic group that made their way into the school. He spoke, for example, about how the Lebanese were characterized by his peers:

> Some people call me, you know, 'cause I'm Lebanese, so people say, "Look out for the terrorist! Don't mess with him or he'll blow up your house!" or some stuff like that. . . . But they're just joking around, though. . . . I don't think anybody's serious 'cause I wouldn't blow up anybody's house — and they know that. . . . I don't care. It doesn't matter what people say. . . . I just want everybody to know that, you know, it's not true.

Cultural ambivalence, both pride and shame, were evident in the responses of many of the students. Although almost all of them were quite clear that their culture was important to them, they were also confronted with debilitating messages about it from society in general. How to make sense of these contradictions was a dilemma for many of these young people.

Fern, who identified herself as Native American, was, at thirteen, one of the youngest students interviewed. She reflected on the constant challenges she faced in the history curriculum in her junior high school. Her father was active in their school and community and he gave her a great deal of support for defending her position, but she was the only Native American student in her entire school in this mid-size city in Iowa. She said:

> If there's something in the history book that's wrong, my dad always taught me that if it's wrong, I should tell them that it is wrong. And the only time I ever do is if I know it's *exactly* wrong. Like we were reading about Native Americans and scalping. Well, the French are really the ones that made them do it so they could get money. And my teacher would not believe me. I finally just shut up because he just would not believe me.

Fern also mentioned that her sister had come home angry one day because somebody in school had said "Geronimo was a stupid chief riding that stupid horse." The connection between an unresponsive curriculum and dropping out of school was not lost on Fern, and she talked about this incident as she wondered aloud why other Native Americans had dropped out of the town's schools. Similar sentiments were reported by students in Virginia Vogel Zanger's (1994) study of twenty Latinos from a Boston high school who took part in a panel discussion in which they reflected on their experiences in school. Some of the students who decided to stay in school claimed that dropping out among their peers was a direct consequence of the school's attempts to "monoculture" them.

Fern was self-confident and strong in expressing her views, despite her young age. Yet she too was silenced by the way the curriculum was presented in class. This is because schools often avoid bringing up difficult, contentious, or conflicting issues in the curriculum, especially when these contradict the sanctioned views of the standard curriculum, resulting in what Michelle Fine has called "silencing." According to Fine, "Silencing is about who can speak, what can and cannot be spoken, and whose discourse must be controlled" (1991, p. 33). Two topics in particular that appear to have great saliency for many students, regardless of their backgrounds, are bias and discrimination, yet these are among the issues most avoided in classrooms. Perhaps this is because the majority of teachers are European Americans who are unaccustomed, afraid, or uncomfortable in discussing these issues (Sleeter, 1994); perhaps it is due to the pressure teachers feel to "cover the material"; maybe it has to do with the tradition of presenting information in schools as if it were free of conflict and controversy (Kohl, 1993); or, most likely, it is a combination of all these things. In any event, both students and teachers soon pick up the message that racism, discrimination, and other dangerous topics are not supposed to be discussed in school. We also need to keep in mind that these issues have disparate meanings for people of different backgrounds and are often perceived as particularly threatening to those from dominant cultural and racial groups. Deidre, one of the young African American women in Fine's 1991 study of an urban high school, explained it this way: "White people might feel like everything's over and OK, but we remember" (p. 33).

Another reason that teachers may avoid bringing up potentially contentious issues in the curriculum is their feeling that doing so may create or exacerbate animosity and hostility among students. They may even believe, as did the reading teacher in Jonathan Kozol's 1967 classic book on the Boston Public Schools, *Death at an Early Age,* that discussing slavery in the context of U.S. history was just too complicated for children to understand, not to mention uncomfortable for teachers to explain. Kozol writes of the reading teacher:

She said, with the very opposite of malice but only with an expression of the most intense and honest affection for the children in the class: "I don't want these children to have to think back on this year later on and to have to remember that we were the ones who told them they were Negro." (p. 68)

More than a quarter of a century later, the same kinds of disclaimers are being made for the failure to include in the curriculum the very issues that would engage students in learning. Fine (1991) found that although over half of the students in the urban high school she interviewed described experiences with racism, teachers were reluctant to discuss it in class, explaining, in the words of one teacher, "It would demoralize the students, they need to feel positive and optimistic — like they have a chance. Racism is just an excuse they use to not try harder" (p. 37). Some of these concerns may be sincere expressions of protectiveness toward students, but others are merely self-serving and manifest teachers' discomfort with discussing racism.

The few relevant studies I have found concerning the inclusion of issues of racism and discrimination in the curriculum suggest that discussions about these topics can be immensely constructive if they are approached with sensitivity and understanding. This was the case in Melinda Fine's description of the "Facing History and Ourselves" (FHAO) curriculum, a project that started in the Brookline (Massachusetts) Public Schools almost two decades ago (Fine, 1993). FHAO provides a model for teaching history that encourages students to reflect critically on a variety of contemporary social, moral, and political issues. Using the Holocaust as a case study, students learn to think critically about such issues as scapegoating, racism, and personal and collective responsibility. Fine suggests that moral dilemmas do not disappear simply because teachers refuse to bring them into the schools. On the contrary, when these realities are separated from the curriculum, young people learn that school knowledge is unrelated to their lives, and once again, they are poorly prepared to face the challenges that society has in store for them.

A good case in point is Vanessa, a young European American woman in my study who was intrigued by "difference" yet was uncomfortable and reluctant to discuss it. Although she was active in a peer-education group that focused on such concerns as peer pressure, discrimination, and exclusion, these were rarely discussed in the formal curriculum. Vanessa, therefore, had no language with which to talk about these issues. In thinking about U.S. history, she mused about some of the contradictions that were rarely addressed in school:

It seems weird . . . because people came from Europe and they wanted to get away from all the stuff that was over there. And then they came here and set up all the stuff like slavery, and I don't know, it seems the opposite of what they would have done.

The curriculum, then, can act to either enable or handicap students in their learning. Given the kind of curriculum that draws on their experiences and energizes them because it focuses precisely on those things that are most important in their lives, students can either soar or sink in our schools. Curriculum can provide what María Torres-Guzmán (1992) refers to as "cognitive empowerment," encouraging students to become confident, active critical thinkers who learn that their background experiences are important tools for further learning. The connection of the curriculum to real life and their future was mentioned by several of the students interviewed in my study. Avi, a Jewish boy of sixteen who often felt a schism between his school and home lives, for instance, spoke about the importance of school: "If you don't go to school, then you can't learn about life, or you can't learn about things that you need to progress [in] your life." And Vanessa, who seemed to yearn for a more socially conscious curriculum in her school, summed up why education was important to her: "A good education is like when you personally learn something . . . like growing, expanding your mind and your views."

Pedagogy

If curriculum is primarily the *what* of education, then pedagogy concerns the *why* and *how*. No matter how interesting and relevant the curriculum may be, the way in which it is presented is what will make it engaging or dull to students. Students' views echo those of educational researchers who have found that teaching methods in most classrooms, and particularly those in secondary schools, vary little from traditional "chalk and talk" methods; that textbooks are the dominant teaching materials used; that routine and rote learning are generally favored over creativity and critical thinking; and that teacher-centered transmission models prevail (Cummins, 1994; Goodlad, 1984; McNeil, 1986). Martin Haberman is especially critical of what he calls "the pedagogy of poverty," that is, a basic urban pedagogy used with children who live in poverty, which consists primarily of giving instructions, asking questions, giving directions, making assignments, and monitoring seat work. Such pedagogy is based on the assumption that before students can be engaged in creative or critical work, they must first master "the basics." Nevertheless, Haberman asserts that this pedagogy does not work and, furthermore, that it actually gets in the way of real teaching and learning. He suggests instead that we look at exemplary pedagogy in urban schools that actively involves students in real-life situations, which allows them to reflect on their own lives. He finds that good teaching is taking place when teachers welcome difficult issues and events and use human difference as the basis for the curriculum; design collaborative activities for heterogeneous groups; and help students apply ideals of fairness, equity, and justice to their world (Haberman, 1991).

Students in my study had more to say about pedagogy than about anything else, and they were especially critical of the lack of imagination that led to boring classes. Linda, who was just graduating as the valedictorian of her class in an urban high school, is a case in point. Her academic experiences had not always been smooth sailing. For example, she had failed both seventh and eighth grade twice, for a combination of reasons, including academic and medical problems. Consequently, she had had both exhilarating and devastating educational experiences. Linda had this to say about pedagogy:

> I think you have to be creative to be a teacher; you have to make it interesting. You can't just go in and say, "Yeah, I'm going to teach the kids just that; I'm gonna teach them right out of the book and that's the way it is, and don't ask questions." Because I know there were plenty of classes where I lost complete interest. But those were all because the teachers just [said], "Open the books to this page." They never made up problems out of their head. Everything came out of the book. You didn't ask questions. If you asked them questions, then the answer was "in the book." And

if you asked the question and the answer *wasn't* in the book, then you shouldn't have asked that question!

Rich, a young Black man, planned to attend pharmacy school after graduation, primarily because of the interest he had developed in chemistry. He too talked about the importance of making classes "interesting":

> I believe a teacher, by the way he introduces different things to you, can make a class interesting. Not like a normal teacher that gets up, gives you a lecture, or there's teachers that just pass out the work, you do the work, pass it in, get a grade, good-bye!

Students were especially critical of teachers' reliance on textbooks and blackboards, a sad indictment of much of the teaching that encourages student passivity. Avi, for instance, felt that some teachers get along better when they teach from the point of view of the students: "They don't just come out and say, 'All right, do this, blah, blah, blah.' . . . They're not so *one-tone voice*." Yolanda said that her English teacher didn't get along with the students. In her words, "She just does the things and sits down." James mentioned that some teachers just don't seem to care: "They just teach the stuff. 'Here,' write a couple of things on the board, 'see, that's how you do it. Go ahead, page 25.' " And Vinh added his voice to those of the students who clearly saw the connection between pedagogy and caring: "Some teachers, they just go inside and go to the blackboard. . . . They don't care."

Students did more than criticize teachers' pedagogy, however; they also praised teachers who were interesting, creative, and caring. Linda, in a particularly moving testimony to her first-grade teacher, whom she called her mentor, mentioned that she would be "following in her footsteps" and studying elementary education. She added:

> She's always been there for me. After the first or second grade, if I had a problem, I could always go back to her. Through the whole rest of my life, I've been able to go back and talk to her. . . . She's a Golden Apple Award winner, which is a very high award for elementary school teachers. . . . She keeps me on my toes. . . . When I start getting down . . . she peps me back up and I get on my feet.

Vinh talked with feeling about teachers who allowed him to speak Vietnamese with other students in class. Vinh loved working in groups. He particularly remembered a teacher who always asked students to discuss important issues, rather than focusing only on learning what he called "the word's meaning" by writing and memorizing lists of words. The important issues concerned U.S. history, the students' histories and cultures, and other engaging topics that were central to their lives. Students' preference for group work has been mentioned by other educators as well. Phelan et al. (1992), in their research on students' perspectives concerning school, found that both high- and low-achieving students of all backgrounds expressed a strong preference for working in groups, because it helped them generate ideas and participate actively in class.

James also appreciated teachers who explained things and let everybody ask questions because, as he said, "There could be someone sitting in the back of the class that has the same question you have. Might as well bring it out." Fern contrasted classes where she felt like falling asleep because they're just "blah," to chorus, where the teacher used a "rap song" to teach history and involve all the students. And Avi, who liked most of his teachers, singled out a particular math teacher he had had in ninth grade for praise:

> 'Cause I never really did good in math until I had him. And he showed me that it wasn't so bad, and after that I've been doing pretty good in math and I enjoy it.

Yolanda had been particularly fortunate to have many teachers she felt understood and supported her, whether they commented on her bilingual ability, or referred to her membership in a folkloric Mexican dance group, or simply talked with her and the other students about their lives. She added:

> I really got along with the teachers a lot. . . . Actually, 'cause I had some teachers, and they were always calling my mom, like I did a great job. Or they would start talking to me, or they kinda like pulled me up some grades, or moved me to other classes, or took me somewhere. And they were always congratulating me.

Such support, however, rarely represented only individual effort on the part of some teachers, but rather was often manifested by the school as a whole; that is, it was integral to the school's practices and policies. For instance, Yolanda had recently been selected "Student of the Month," and her picture had been prominently displayed in her school's main hall. In addition, she received a certificate and was taken out to dinner by the principal. Although Linda's first-grade teacher was her special favorite, she had others who also created an educational context in which all students felt welcomed and connected. The entire Tremont Elementary School had been special for Linda, and thus the context of the school, including its leadership and commitment, were the major ingredients that made it successful:

> All of my teachers were wonderful. I don't think there's a teacher at the whole Tremont School that I didn't like. . . . It's just a feeling you have. You know that they really care for you. You just know it; you can tell. Teachers who don't have you in any of their classes or haven't ever had you, they still know who you are. . . . The Tremont School in itself is a community. . . . I love that school! I want to teach there.

Vanessa talked about how teachers used their students' lives and experiences in their teaching. For her, this made them especially good teachers:

> [Most teachers] are really caring and supportive and are willing to share their lives and are willing to listen to mine. They don't just want to talk about what they're teaching you; they also want to know you.

Aside from criticism and praise, students in this study also offered their teachers many thoughtful suggestions for making their classrooms more engaging places. Rich, for instance, said that he would "put more activities into the day that can make it interesting." Fern recommended that teachers involve students more actively in learning: "More like making the whole class be involved, not making only the two smartest people up here do the whole work for the whole class." Vanessa added, "You could have games that could teach anything that they're trying to teach through notes or lectures." She suggested that in learning Spanish, for instance, students could act out the words, making them easier to remember. She also thought that other books should be required "just to show some points of view," a response no doubt to the bland quality of so many of the textbooks and other teaching materials available in schools. Avi thought that teachers who make themselves available to students ("You know, I'm here after school. Come and get help") were most helpful.

Vinh was very specific in his suggestions, and he touched on important cultural issues. Because he came from Vietnam when he was fifteen, learning English was a difficult challenge for Vinh, and he tended to be very hard on himself, saying such things as "I'm not really good, but I'm trying" when asked to describe himself as a student. Although he had considered himself smart in Vietnam, he felt that because his English was not perfect, he wasn't smart anymore. His teachers often showered him with praise for his efforts, but Vinh criticized this approach:

> Sometimes, the English teachers, they don't understand about us. Because something we not do good, like my English is not good. And she say, "Oh, your English is great!" But that's the way the American culture is. But my culture is not like that. . . . If my English is not good, she has to say, "Your English is not good. So you have to go home and study." And she tell me what to study and how to study and get better. But some Americans, you know, they don't understand about myself. So they just say, "Oh! You're doing a good job! You're doing great! Everything is great!" Teachers talk like that, but my culture is different. . . . They say, "You have to do better."

This is an important lesson, not only because it challenges the overuse of praise, a practice among those that María de la Luz Reyes (1992) has called "venerable assumptions," but also because it cautions teachers to take into account both cultural and individual differences. In this case, the practice of praising was perceived by Vinh as hollow, and therefore insincere. Linda referred to the lesson she learned when she failed seventh and eighth grade and "blew two years":

> I learned a lot from it. As a matter of fact, one of my college essays was on the fact that from that experience, I learned that I don't need to hear other people's praise to get by. . . . All I need to know is in here [pointing to her heart] whether I tried or not.

Students have important messages for teachers about what works and what doesn't. It is important, however, not to fall back on what Lilia Bartolomé (1994) has aptly termed the "methods fetish," that is, a simplistic belief that particular methods will automatically resolve complex problems of underachievement. According to Bartolomé, such a myopic approach results in teachers avoiding the central issue of why some students succeed and others fail in school and how political inequality is at the heart of this dilemma. Rather than using this or that method, Bartolomé suggests that teachers develop what she calls a "humanizing pedagogy" in which students' languages and cultures are central. There is also the problem that Reyes (1992) has called a "one-size-fits all" approach, where students' cultural and other differences may be denied, even if teachers' methods are based on well-meaning and progressive pedagogy. The point here is that no method can become a sacred cow uncritically accepted and used simply because it is the latest fad. It is probably fair to say that teachers who use more traditional methods but care about their students and believe they deserve the chance to dream may have more of a positive effect than those who know the latest methods but do not share these beliefs. Students need more than such innovations as heterogeneous grouping, peer tutoring, or cooperative groups. Although these may in fact be excellent and effective teaching methods, they will do little by themselves unless accompanied by changes in teachers' attitudes and behaviors.

The students quoted above are not looking for one magic solution or method. In fact, they have many, sometimes contradictory, suggestions to make about pedagogy. While rarely speaking with one voice, they nevertheless have similar overriding concerns: too many classrooms are boring, alienating, and disempowering. There is a complex interplay of policies, practices, and attitudes that cause such pedagogy to continue. Tracking and testing are two powerful forces implicated in this interplay.

Tracking/Ability Grouping/Grades and Expectations of Student Achievement

> It is not low income that matters but low status. And status is always created and imposed by the ones on top. (Stein, 1971, p. 158)

In her 1971 article, Annie Stein cited a New York City study in which kindergarten teachers were asked to list in order of importance the things a child should learn in order to prepare for first grade. Their responses were coded according to whether they were primarily socialization or educational goals. In the schools with large Puerto Rican and African American student populations, the socialization goals were always predominant; in the mixed schools, the educational goals were first. Concluded Stein, "In fact, in a list of six or seven goals, several teachers in the minority-group kindergartens forgot to mention any educational goals at all" (p. 167). A kind of tracking, in which students' educational goals were being sacrificed for social aims, was taking place in these schools, and its effects were already evident in kindergarten.

Most recent research on tracking has found it to be problematic, especially among middle- and low-achieving students, and suggestions for detracking schools have gained growing support (Oakes, 1992; Wheelock, 1992). Nevertheless, although many tracking decisions are made on the most tenuous grounds, they are supported by ideological norms in our society about the nature of intelligence and the distribution of ability. The long-term effects of ability grouping can be devastating for the life chances of young people. John Goodlad (1984) found that first- or second-grade children tracked by teachers' judgments of their reading and math ability or by testing are likely to remain in their assigned track *for the rest of their schooling.* In addition, he found that poor children and children of color are more likely to face the negative effects of tracking than are other youngsters. For example, a recent research project by Hugh Mehan and Irene Villanueva (1993) found that when low-achieving high school students are detracked, they tend to benefit academically. The study focused on low-achieving students in the San Diego City Schools. When these students, mostly Latinos and African Americans, were removed from a low track and placed in college-bound courses with high-achieving students, they benefited in a number of ways, including significantly higher college enrollment. The researchers concluded that a rigorous academic program serves the educational and social interests of such students more effectively than remedial and compensatory programs.

Most of the young people in my study did not mention tracking or ability grouping by name, but almost all referred to it circuitously, and usually in negative ways. Although by and large academically successful themselves, they were quick to point out that teachers' expectations often doomed their peers to failure. Yolanda, for instance, when asked what suggestions she would give teachers, said, "I'd say to teachers, 'Get along more with the kids that are not really into themselves. . . . Have more communication with them.' " When asked what she would like teachers to know about other Mexican American students, she quickly said, "They try real hard, that's one thing I know." She also criticized teachers for having low expectations of students, claiming that materials used in the classes were "too low." She added, "We are supposed to be doing higher things. And like they take us too slow, see, step by step. And that's why everybody takes it as a joke." Fern, although she enjoyed being at the "top of my class," did not like to be treated differently. She spoke about a school she attended previously where "you were all the same and you all got pushed the same and you were all helped the same. And one thing I've noticed in Springdale is they kind of teach 25 percent, and they kinda leave 75 percent out." She added that, if students were receiving bad grades, teachers did not help them as much: "In Springdale, I've noticed if you're getting D's and F's, they don't look up to you; they look down. And you're always the last on the list for special activities, you know?"

These young people also referred to expectations teachers had of students based on cultural or class differences. Vanessa said that some teachers based their expectations of students on bad reputations, and she found least helpful those teachers who "kind of just move really fast, just trying to get across to you what they're trying to teach you. Not willing to slow down because they need to get in what they want to get in." Rich, who attended a predominantly Black school, felt that some teachers there did not expect as much as they should from the Black students: "Many of the White teachers there don't push. . . . Their expectations don't seem to be as high as they should be. . . . I know that some Black teachers, their expectations are higher than White teachers. . . . They just do it, because they know how it was for them. . . . Actually, I'd say, you have to be in Black shoes to know how it is." Little did Rich know that he was reaching the same conclusion as a major research study on fostering high achievement for African American students. In this study, Janine Bempechat determined that "across all schools, it seems that achievement is fostered by high expectations and standards" (Bempechat, 1992, p. 43).

Virginia Vogel Zanger's research with Latino and Latina students in a Boston high school focused on what can be called "social tracking." Although the students she interviewed were high-achieving and tracked in a college-bound course, they too felt the sting of alienation. In a linguistic analysis of their comments, she found that students conveyed a strong sense of marginalization, using terms such as "left out," "below," "under," and "not joined in" to reflect their feelings about school (Zanger, 1994). Although these were clearly academically successful students, they perceived tracking in the subordinate status they were assigned based on their cultural backgrounds and on the racist climate established in the school. Similarly, in a study on dropping out among Puerto Rican students, my colleague Manuel Frau-Ramos and I found some of the same kind of language. José, who had dropped out in eleventh grade, explained, "I was alone. . . . I was an outsider" (Frau-Ramos & Nieto, 1993, p. 156). Pedro, a young man who had actually graduated, nevertheless felt the same kind of alienation. When asked what the school could do to help Puerto Ricans stay in school, he said, *"Hacer algo para que los boricuas no se sientan aparte"* (Do something so that the Puerto Ricans wouldn't feel so separate) (p. 157).

Grading policies have also been mentioned in relation to tracking and expectations of achievement. One study, for example, found that when teachers deemphasized grades and standardized testing, the status of their African American and White students became more equal, and White students made more cross-race friendship choices (Hallinan & Teixeira, 1987). In my own research, I found a somewhat surprising revelation: although the students were achieving successfully in school, most did not feel that grades were very helpful. Of course, for the most part they enjoyed receiving good grades, but it was not always for the expected reason. Fern, for instance, wanted good grades because they were one guarantee that teachers would pay attention to her. Marisol talked about the "nice report cards" that she and her siblings in this family of eight children received, and said, "and, usually, we do this for my mother. We like to see her the way she wants to be, you know, to see her happy."

But they were also quick to downplay the importance of grades. Linda, for instance, gave as an example her computer teacher, who she felt had been the least helpful in her high school:

> I have no idea about computer literacy. I got A's in that course. Just because he saw that I had A's, and that my name was all around the school for all the "wonderful things" I do, he just automatically assumed. He didn't really pay attention to who I was. The grade I think I deserved in that class was at least a C, but I got A just because everybody else gave me A's. . . . He didn't help me at all because he didn't challenge me.

She added,

> To me, they're just something on a piece of paper. . . . [My parents] feel just about the same way. If they ask me, "Honestly, did you try your best?" and I tell them yes, then they'll look at the grades and say okay.

Rich stated that, although grades were important to his mother, "I'm comfortable setting my own standards." James said, without arrogance, that he was "probably the smartest kid in my class." Learning was important to him and, unlike other students who also did the assignments, he liked to "really get into the work and stuff." He added,

> If you don't get involved with it, even if you do get, if you get perfect scores and stuff . . . it's not like really gonna sink in. . . . You can memorize the words, you know, on a test . . . but you know, if you memorize them, it's not going to do you any good. You have to *learn* them, you know?

Most of the students made similar comments, and their perceptions challenge schools to think more deeply about the real meaning of education. Linda was not alone when she said that the reason for going to school was to "make yourself a better person." She loved learning and commented that "I just want to keep continuously learning, because when you stop learning, then you start dying." Yolanda used the metaphor of nutrition to talk about learning: "[Education] is good for you. . . . It's like when you eat. It's like if you don't eat in a whole day, you feel weird. That's the same thing for me." Vanessa, also an enthusiastic student, spoke pensively about success and happiness: "I'm happy. Success is being happy to me; it's not like having a job that gives you a zillion dollars. It's just having self-happiness."

Finally, Vinh spoke extensively about the meaning of education, contrasting the difference between what he felt it meant in the United States and what it meant in his home culture:

> In Vietnam, we go to school because we want to become educated people. But in the United States, most people, they say, "Oh, we go to school because we want to get a good job." But my idea, I don't think so. I say, if we go to school, we want a good job *also,* but we want to become a good person.
>
> [Grades] are not important to me. Important to me is education. . . . I not so concerned about [test scores] very much. . . . I just know I do my exam very good. But I don't need to know I got A or B. I have to learn more and more.
>
> Some people, they got a good education. They go to school, they got master's, they got doctorate, but they're just helping *themselves.* So that's not good. I don't care much about money. So, I just want to have a normal job that I can take care of myself and my family. So that's enough. I don't want to climb up compared to other people.

Racism and Discrimination

The facts are clear to behold, but the BIG LIE of racism blinds all but its victims. (Stein, 1971, p. 179)

An increasing number of formal research studies, as well as informal accounts and anecdotes, attest to the lasting legacy of various forms of institutional discrimination in the schools based on race, ethnicity, religion, gender, social class, language, and sexual orientation. Yet, as Annie Stein wrote in 1971, these are rarely addressed directly. The major reason for this may be that institutional discrimination flies in the face of our stated ideals of justice and fair play and of the philosophy that individual hard work is the road to success. Beverly Daniel Tatum, in discussing the myth of meritocracy, explains why racism is so often denied, downplayed, or dismissed: "An understanding of racism as a system of advantage presents a serious challenge to the notion of the United States as a just society where rewards are based solely on one's merits" (Tatum, 1992, p. 6).

Recent studies point out numerous ways in which racism and other forms of discrimination affect students and their learning. For instance, Angela Taylor found that, to the extent that teachers harbor negative racial stereotypes, the African American child's race *alone* is probably sufficient to place him or her at risk for negative school outcomes (Taylor, 1991). Many teachers, of course, see it differently, preferring to think instead that students' lack of academic achievement is due solely to conditions inside their homes or communities. But the occurrence of discriminatory actions in schools, both by other students and by teachers and other staff, has been widely documented. A 1990 study of Boston high school students found that while 57 percent had witnessed a racial attack and 47 percent would either join in or feel that the group being attacked deserved it, only a quarter of those interviewed said they would report a racial incident to school officials (Ribadeneira, 1990). It should not be surprising, then, that in a report about immigrant students in California, most believed that Americans felt negatively and unwelcoming toward them. In fact, almost every immigrant student interviewed reported that they had at one time or another been spat upon, and tricked, teased, and laughed at because of their race, accent, or the way they dressed. More than half also indicated that they had been the victims of teachers' prejudice, citing instances where they were punished, publicly embarrassed, or made fun of because of improper use of English. They also reported that teachers had made derogatory comments about immigrant groups in front of the class, or had avoided particular students because of the language difficulty (Olsen, 1988). Most of the middle and high school students interviewed by Mary Poplin and Joseph Weeres (1992) had also witnessed incidents of racism in school. In Karen Donaldson's study in an urban high school where students used the racism they experienced as the content of a peer-education program, over 80 percent of students surveyed said that they had perceived racism to exist in school (Donaldson, 1994).

Marietta Saravia-Shore and Herminio Martínez found similar results in their ethnographic study of Puerto Rican young people who had dropped out of school and were currently participating in an alternative high school program. These adolescents felt that their former teachers were, in their words, "against Puerto Ricans and Blacks" and had openly discriminated against them. One reported that a teacher had said, "Do you want to be like the other Puerto Rican women who never got an education? Do you want to be like the rest of your family and never go to school?" (Saravia-Shore & Martínez, 1992, p. 242). In Virginia Vogel Zanger's study of high-achieving Latino and Latina Boston high school students, one young man described his shock when his teacher called him "spic" right in class; although the teacher was later suspended, this incident had left its mark on him (Zanger, 1994). Unfortunately, incidents such as these are more frequent than schools care to admit or acknowledge. Students, however, seem eager to address these issues, but they are rarely given a forum in which such discussions can take place.

How do students feel about the racism and other aspects of discrimination that they see around them and experience? What effect does it have on them? In interviews with students, Karen Donaldson found three major ways in which they said they were affected: White students experienced guilt and embarrassment when they became aware of the racism to which their peers were subjected; students of color sometimes felt they needed to overcompensate and overachieve to prove they were equal to their White classmates; and students of color also mentioned that discrimination had a negative impact on their self-esteem (Donaldson, 1994). The issue of self-esteem is a complicated one and may include many variables. Children's self-esteem does not come fully formed out of the blue but is *created* within particular contexts and responds to conditions that vary from situation to situation, and teachers' and schools' complicity in creating negative self-esteem certainly cannot be discounted. This was understood by Lillian, one of the young women in Nitza Hidalgo's study of an urban high school, who commented, "That's another problem I have, teachers, they are always talking about how we have no type of self-esteem or anything like that. . . . But they're the people that's putting us down. That's why our self-esteem is so low" (Hidalgo, 1991, p. 95).

The students in my research also mentioned examples of discrimination based on their race, ethnicity, culture, religion, and language. Some, like Manuel, felt it from fellow students. As an immigrant from Cape Verde who came to the United States at the age of eleven, he found the adjustment difficult:

> When American students see you, it's kinda hard [to] get along with them when you have a different culture, a different way of dressing and stuff like that. So kids really look at you and laugh, you know, at the beginning.

Avi spoke of anti-Semitism in his school. The majority of residents in his town were European American and Christian. The Jewish community had dwindled significantly over the years, and there were now very few Jewish students in his school. On one occasion, a student had walked by him saying, "Are you ready for the second Holocaust?" He described another incident in some detail:

> I was in a woods class, and there was another boy in there, my age, and he was in my grade. He's also Jewish, and he used to come to the temple sometimes and went to Hebrew school. But then, of course, he started hanging around with the wrong people and some of these people were in my class, and I guess they were . . . making fun of him. And a few of them starting making swastikas out of wood. . . . So I saw one and I said to some kid, "What are you doing?" and the kid said to me, "Don't worry. It's not for you, it's for him." And I said to him, "What?!"

Other students talked about discrimination on the part of teachers. Both Marisol and Vinh specifically mentioned language discrimination as a problem. For Marisol, it had happened when a particular teacher did not allow Spanish to be spoken in her room. For Vinh, it concerned teachers' attitudes about his language: "Some teachers don't understand about the language. So sometimes, my language, they say it sounds funny." Rich spoke of the differences between the expectations of White and Black teachers, and concluded that all teachers should teach the curriculum *as if they were in an all-White school,* meaning that then expectations would be high for everybody. Other students were the object of teasing, but some, including James, even welcomed it, perhaps because it at least made his culture visible. He spoke of Mr. Miller, an elementary teacher he had been particularly fond of, who had called him "Gonzo" because he had a big nose and "Klinger" after the *M.A.S.H.* character who was Lebanese. James said, "And then everybody called me Klinger from then on. . . . I liked it, kind of . . . everybody laughing at me."

It was Linda who had the most to say about racism. As a young woman who identified herself as mixed because her mother was White and her father Black, Linda had faced discrimination or confusion on the part of both students and teachers. For example, she resented the fact that when teachers had to indicate her race, they came to their own conclusions without bothering to ask her. She explained what it was like:

> [Teachers should not] try to make us one or the other. And God forbid you should make us something we're totally not. . . . Don't write down that I'm Hispanic when I'm not. Some people actually think I'm Chinese when I smile. . . . Find out. Don't just make your judgments. . . . If you're filling out someone's report card and you need to know, then ask.

She went on to say:

> I've had people tell me, "Well, you're Black." I'm not Black; I'm Black and White.
> I'm Black and White American. "Well, you're Black!" No, I'm not! I'm both. . . . I
> mean, I'm not ashamed of being Black, but I'm not ashamed of being White either,
> and if I'm both, I want to be part of both. And I think teachers need to be sensitive
> to that.

Linda did not restrict her criticisms to White teachers, but also spoke of a Black
teacher in her high school. Besides Mr. Benson, her favorite teacher of all, there was
another Black teacher in the school:

> The other Black teacher, he was a racist, and I didn't like him. I belonged to the
> Black Students Association, and he was the adviser. And he just made it so obvious:
> he was all for Black supremacy. . . . A lot of times, whether they deserved it or not,
> his Black students passed, and his White students, if they deserved an A, they got a
> B. . . . He was insistent that only Hispanics and Blacks be allowed in the club. He
> had a very hard time letting me in because I'm not all Black. . . . I just really wasn't
> that welcome there. . . . He never found out what I was about. He just made his
> judgments from afar.

It was clear that racism was a particularly compelling issue for Linda, and she
thought and talked about it a great deal. The weight of racism on her mind was evident when she said, "It's hard. I look at history and I feel really bad for what some of
my ancestors did to some of my other ancestors. Unless you're mixed, you don't know
what it's like to be mixed." She even wrote a poem about it, which ended like this:

> But all that I wonder is who ever gave
> them the right to tell me
> What I can and can't do
> Who I can and can't be
> God made each one of us
> Just like the other
> the only difference is,
> I'm darker in color.

Implications of Students' Views for the Transformation of Schools

Numerous lessons are contained within the narratives above. But what are the implications of these lessons for the school's curriculum, pedagogy, and tracking? How can
we use what students have taught us about racism and discrimination? How can
schools' policies and practices be informed through dialogue with students about
what works and doesn't work? Although the students in my study never mentioned
multicultural education by name, they were deeply concerned with whether and in
what ways they and their families and communities were respected and represented in
their schools. Two implications that are inherently multicultural come to mind, and I
would suggest that both can have a major impact on school policies and practices. It is

important that I first make explicit my own view of multicultural education: It is my understanding that multicultural education should be *basic for all students, pervasive in the curriculum and pedagogy, grounded in social justice, and based on critical pedagogy* (Nieto, 1992). Given this interpretation of multicultural education, we can see that it goes beyond the "tolerance" called for in numerous proclamations about diversity. It is also a far cry from the "cultural sensitivity" that is the focus of many professional development workshops (Nieto, 1994). In fact, "cultural sensitivity" can become little more than a condescending "Band-aid" response to diversity, because it often does little to solve deep-seated problems of inequity. Thus, a focus on cultural sensitivity in and of itself can be superficial if it fails to take into account the structural and institutional barriers that reflect and reproduce power differentials in society. Rather than promoting cultural sensitivity, I would suggest that multicultural education needs to be understood as "arrogance reduction"; that is, as encompassing *both* individual *and* structural changes that squarely confront the individual biases, attitudes, and behaviors of educators, as well as the policies and practices in schools that emanate from them.

Affirming Students' Languages, Cultures, and Experiences

Over twenty years ago, Annie Stein reported asking a kindergarten teacher to explain why she had ranked four of her students at the bottom of her list, noting that they were "mute." " 'Yes,' she said, 'they have not said one word for six months and they don't appear to hear anything I say.' 'Do they ever talk to the other children?' we asked. 'Sure,' was her reply. 'They cackle to each other in Spanish all day' " (Stein, 1971, p. 161). These young children, although quite vocal in their own language, were not heard by their teacher because the language they spoke was bereft of all significance in the school. The children were not, however, blank slates; on the contrary, they came to school with a language, culture, and experiences that could have been important in their learning. Thus, we need to look not only at the individual weaknesses or strengths of particular students, but also at the way in which schools assign status to entire groups of students based on the sociopolitical and linguistic context in which they live. Jim Cummins addressed this concern in relation to the kinds of superficial antidotes frequently proposed to solve the problem of functional illiteracy among students from culturally and economically dominated groups: "A remedial focus only on technical aspects of functional illiteracy is inadequate because the causes of educational underachievement and 'illiteracy' among subordinated groups are rooted in the systematic devaluation of culture and denial of access to power and resources by the dominant group" (1994, pp. 307–308). As we have seen in many of the examples cited throughout this article, when culture and language are acknowledged by the school, students are able to reclaim the voice they need to continue their education successfully.

Nevertheless, the situation is complicated by the competing messages that students pick up from their schools and society at large. The research that I have reviewed makes it clear that, although students' cultures are important to them personally and in their families, they are also problematic because they are rarely valued or acknowledged by schools. The decisions young people make about their identities are frequently contradictory and mired in the tensions and struggles concerning diversity that are reflected in our society. Schools are not immune to such debates. There are numerous ways in which students' languages and cultures are excluded in schools: they are invisible, as with James, denigrated, as in Marisol's case, or simply not known, as happened with Vinh. It is no wonder then that these young people had conflicted feelings about their backgrounds. In spite of this, all of them spoke about the strength they derived from family and culture, and the steps they took to maintain it. James and Marisol mentioned that they continued to speak their native languages at home; Fern discussed her father's many efforts to maintain their Native American heritage; Manuel made it clear that he would always consider himself first and foremost Cape Verdean. Vinh spoke movingly about what his culture meant to him, and said that only Vietnamese was allowed in the home and that his sisters and brothers wrote to their parents in Vietnamese weekly. Most of these young people also maintained solid ties with their religion and places of worship as an important link to their heritage.

Much of the recent literature on educating culturally diverse students is helping to provide a radically different paradigm that contests the equation *education = assimilation* (Trueba, 1989). This research challenges the old assumptions about the role of the school as primarily an assimilationist agent, and provides a foundation for policy recommendations that focus on using students' cultural background values to promote academic achievement. In the case of Asian Pacific American youth, Peter Kiang and Vivian Wai-Fun Lee state the following:

> It is ironic that strengths and cultural values of family support which are so often praised as explanations for the academic achievement of Asian Pacific American students are severely undercut by the lack of programmatic and policy support for broad-based bilingual instruction and native language development, particularly in early childhood education. (Kiang & Lee, 1993, p. 39)

A study by Jeannette Abi-Nader of a program for Hispanic youth provides an example of how this can work. In the large urban high school she studied, students' cultural values, especially those concerned with *familia,* were the basis of everyday classroom interactions. Unlike the dismal dropout statistics prevalent in so many other Hispanic communities, up to 65 percent of the high school graduates in this program went on to college. Furthermore, the youth attributed their academic success to the program and made enthusiastic statements about it, including this one written on a survey: "The best thing I like about this class is that we all work together and we all participate and try to help each other. We're family!" (Abi-Nader, 1993, p. 213).

The students in my research also provided impassioned examples of the effect that affirming their languages and cultures had on them and, conversely, on how negating their languages and cultures negated a part of them as well. The attitudes and behaviors of the teachers in Yolanda's school, for example, were reflected in policies that seemed to be based on an appreciation for student diversity. Given the support of her teachers and their affirmation of her language and her culture, Yolanda concluded, "Actually, it's fun around here if you really get into learning. . . . I like learning. I like really getting my mind working." Manuel also commented on how crucial it was for teachers to become aware of students' cultural values and backgrounds. This was especially important for Manuel, since his parents were immigrants unfamiliar with U.S.

schools and society, and although they gave him important moral support, they could do little to help him in school. He said of his teachers:

> If you don't know a student there's no way to influence him. If you don't know his background, there's no way you are going to get in touch with him. There's no way you're going to influence him if you don't know where he's been.

Fern, on the other hand, as the only Native American student in her school, spoke about how difficult it was to discuss values that were different from those of the majority. She specifically mentioned a discussion about abortion in which she was trying to express that for Native Americans, the fetus is alive: "And, so, when I try to tell them, they just, 'Oh, well, we're out of time.' They cut me off, and we've still got half an hour!" And Avi, although he felt that teachers tried to be understanding of his religion, also longed for more cultural affirmation. He would have welcomed, for example, the support of the one Jewish teacher at school who Avi felt was trying to hide his Jewishness.

On the contrary, in Linda's case, Mr. Benson, her English teacher, who was also her favorite teacher, provided just that kind of affirmation. Because he was racially mixed like Linda, she felt that he could relate to the kinds of problems she confronted. He became, in the words of Esteban Díaz and his colleagues, a "sociocultural mediator" for Linda by assigning her identity, language, and culture important roles in the learning environment (Díaz, Flores, Cousin, & Soo Hoo, 1992). Although Linda spoke English as her native language, she gave a wonderful example of how Mr. Benson encouraged her to be "bilingual," using what she referred to as her "street talk." Below is her description of Mr. Benson and the role he played in her education:

> I've enjoyed all my English teachers at Jefferson. But Mr. Benson, my English Honors teacher, he just threw me for a whirl! I wasn't going to college until I met this man. . . . He was one of the few teachers I could talk to . . . 'cause Mr. Benson, he says, I can go into Harvard and converse with those people, and I can go out in the street and "rap with y'all." It's that type of thing. I love it. I try and be like that myself. I have my street talk. I get out in the street and I say "ain't" this and "ain't" that and "your momma" or "wha's up?" But I get somewhere where I know the people aren't familiar with that language or aren't accepting that language, and I will talk properly. . . . I walk into a place and I listen to how people are talking and it just automatically comes to me.

Providing time in the curriculum for students and teachers to engage in discussions about how the language use of students from dominated groups is discriminated against would go a long way in affirming the legitimacy of the discourse of *all* students (Delpit, 1992). According to Margaret Gibson (1991), much recent research has confirmed that schooling may unintentionally contribute to the educational problems of students from culturally dominated groups by pressuring them to assimilate against their wishes. The conventional wisdom that assimilation is the answer to academic underachievement is thus severely challenged. One intriguing implication is that the more students are involved in resisting assimilation while maintaining their culture and language, the more successful they will be in school. That is, maintaining culture and language, although a conflicted decision, seems to have a positive impact on academic success. In any case, it seems to be a far healthier response than adopting an oppositional identity that effectively limits the possibility of academic success (Fordham & Ogbu, 1986; Skutnabb-Kangas, 1988). Although it is important not to overstate this conclusion, it is indeed a real possibility, one that tests the "melting pot" ideology that continues to dominate U.S. schools and society.

We know, of course, that cultural maintenance is not true in all cases of academic success, and everybody can come up with examples of students who felt they needed to assimilate to be successful in school. But the question remains whether this kind of assimilation is healthy or necessary. For instance, in one large-scale study, immigrant students clearly expressed a strong desire to maintain their native languages and cultures and to pass them on to their children (Olsen, 1988). Other research has found that bilingual students specifically appreciate hearing their native language in school, and want the opportunity to learn in that language (Poplin & Weeres, 1992). In addition, an intriguing study of Cambodian refugee children by the Metropolitan Indochinese Children and Adolescent Service found that the more successful they became at modeling their behavior to be like U.S. children, the more their emotional adjustment worsened (National Coalition, 1988). Furthermore, a study of Southeast Asian students found a significant connection between grades and culture: in this research, higher grade point averages correlated with the *maintenance* of traditional values, ethnic pride, and close social and cultural ties with members of the same ethnic group (Rumbaut & Ima, 1987).

All of the above suggests that it is time to look critically at policies and practices that encourage students to leave their cultures and languages at the schoolhouse door. It also suggests that schools and teachers need to affirm, maintain, and value the differences that students bring to school as a foundation for their learning. It is still too common to hear teachers urging parents to "speak only English," as my parents were encouraged to do with my sister and me (luckily, our parents never paid attention). The ample literature cited throughout this article concerning diverse student populations is calling such practices into question. What we are learning is that teachers instead need to encourage parents to speak their *native* language, not English, at home with their children. We are also learning that they should emphasize the importance of family values, not in the rigid and limiting way that this term has been used in the past to create a sense of superiority for those who are culturally dominant, but rather by accepting the strong ethical values that all cultural groups and all kinds of families cherish. As an initial step, however, teachers and schools must first learn more about their students. Vinh expressed powerfully what he wanted teachers to know about him by reflecting on how superficial their knowledge was:

> They understand something, just not all Vietnamese culture. Like they just understand something *outside*. . . . But they cannot understand something inside our hearts.

Listen to Students

Although school is a place where a lot of talk goes on, it is not often student talk. Student voices sometimes reveal the great challenges and even the deep pain young people feel when schools are unresponsive, cold places. One of the students participating in a project focusing on those "inside the school," namely students, teachers, staff, and parents, said, "This place hurts my spirit" (Poplin & Weeres, 1992, p. 11). Ironically, those who spend the most time in schools and classrooms are often given the least opportunity to talk. Yet, as we saw in the many examples above, students have important lessons to teach educators, and we need to begin to listen to them more carefully. Suzanne Soo Hoo captured the fact that educators are losing a compelling opportunity to learn from students while working on a project where students became coresearchers and were engaged with the question, "What are the obstacles to learning?" a question that, according to Soo Hoo, "electrified the group" (1993, p. 386). Including students in addressing such important issues places the focus where it rightfully belongs, said Soo Hoo: "Somehow educators have forgotten the important connection between teachers and students. We listen to outside experts to inform us, and consequently, we overlook the treasure in our very own backyards: our students" (p. 390). As Mike, one of the coresearchers in her project, stated, "They think just because we're kids, we don't know anything" (p. 391).

When they are treated as if they do know something, students can become energized and motivated. For the ten young people in my study, the very act of speaking about their schooling experiences seemed to act as a catalyst for more critical thinking about them. For example, I was surprised when I met Marisol's mother and she told me that Marisol had done nothing but speak about our interviews. Most of the students in the study felt this enthusiasm, and these feelings are typical of other young people in similar studies. As Laurie Olsen (1988) concluded in an extensive research project in California in which hundreds of immigrant students were interviewed, most of the students were gratified simply to have the opportunity to speak about their experiences. These findings have several implications for practice, including using oral histories, peer interviews, interactive journals, and other such strategies. Simply providing students with time to talk with one another, including group work, seems particularly helpful.

The feeling that adults do not listen to them has been echoed by many young people over the years. But listening alone is not sufficient if it is not accompanied by profound changes in what we expect our students to accomplish in school. Even more important than simply *listening* is *assisting* students to become agents of their own learning and to use what they learn in productive and critical ways. This is where social action comes in, and there have been a number of eloquent accounts of critical pedagogy in action (Peterson, 1991; Torres-Guzmán, 1992). I will quote at length from two such examples that provide inspiring stories of how listening to students can help us move beyond the written curriculum.

Iris Santos Rivera wrote a moving account of how a Freirian "problem-posing" approach was used with K–6 Chicano students in a summer educational program of the San Diego Public Schools in 1975 (Santos Rivera, 1983–1984). The program started by having the students play what she called the "Complain, Moan, and Groan Game." Using this exercise, in which students dialogued about and identified problems in the school and community, the young people were asked to identify problems to study. One group selected the school lunch program. This did not seem like a "real" problem to the teacher, who tried to steer the children toward another problem. Santos Rivera writes: "The teacher found it hard to believe in the problem's validity as an issue, as the basis for an action project, or as an integrating theme for education" (p. 5). She let the children talk about it for awhile, convinced that they would come to realize that this was not a serious issue. However, when she returned, they said to her, "Who is responsible for the lunches we get?" (p. 6). Thus began a summer-long odyssey in which the students wrote letters, made phone calls, traced their lunches from the catering truck through the school contracts office, figured out taxpayers' cost per lunch, made records of actual services received from the subcontractors, counted sandwiches and tested milk temperatures, and, finally, compared their findings with contract specifications, and found that there was a significant discrepancy. "We want to bring in the media," they told the teacher (p. 6). Both the local television station and the major networks responded to the press releases sent out by the students, who held a press conference to present the facts and answer reporters' questions. When a reporter asked who had told them all this, one nine-year-old girl answered, "We found this stuff out. Nobody had to tell us anything. You know, you adults give yourselves too much credit" (p. 7). The postscript to this story is that state and federal laws had to be amended to change the kinds of lunches that students in California are served, and tapes from the students in this program were used in the state and federal hearings.

In a more recent example, Mary Ginley, a student in the doctoral program at the School of Education at the University of Massachusetts and a gifted teacher in the Longmeadow (Massachusetts) Public Schools, tries to help her second graders develop critical skills by posing questions to them daily. Their responses are later discussed during class meeting time. Some of these questions are fairly straightforward ("Did you have a good weekend?"), while others encourage deeper thinking. The question posed on Columbus Day, "Was Columbus a hero?" was the culmination of much reading and dialogue that had previously taken place. Another activity she did with her students this year was to keep a daily record of sunrise and sunset. The students discovered to their surprise that December 21 was *not* the shortest day of the year. Using the daily almanac in the local newspaper, the students verified their finding and wrote letters to the editor. One, signed by Kaolin, read (spelling in original):

Dear Editor,

Acorting to our chart December 21 was not the shotest day of the year. But acorting to your paper it is. Are teacher says it happens evry year! What's going on?

As a result of this letter, the newspaper called in experts from the National Weather Service and a local planetarium. One of them said, "It's a fascinating question that [the pupils] have posed. . . . It's frustrating we don't have an adequate answer"(Kelly, 1994, p. 12). Katie, one of the students in Mary's class, compared her classmates to Galileo, who shook the scientific community by saying that the earth revolved around the sun rather than the other way around. Another, Ben, said, "You shouldn't always believe what you hear," and Lucy asserted, "Even if you're a grown-up, you can still learn from a second grader!"

In the first part of this article, I posed the question, "Why listen to students?" I have attempted to answer this question using numerous comments that perceptive young people, both those from my study and others, have made concerning their education. In the final analysis, the question itself suggests that it is only by first listening *to* students that we will be able to learn to talk *with* them. If we believe that an important basis of education is dialogue and reflection about experience, then this is clearly the first step. Yolanda probably said it best when she commented, "'Cause you learn a lot from the students. That's what a lot of teachers tell me. They learn more from their students than from where they go study."

Conclusion

I have often been struck by how little young people believe they deserve, especially those who do not come from economically privileged backgrounds. Although they may work hard at learning, they somehow believe that they do not deserve a chance to dream. This article is based on the notion that all of our students deserve to dream and that teachers and schools are in the best position for "creating a chance" to do so, as referred to in the title. This means developing conditions in schools that let students know that they have a right to envision other possibilities beyond those imposed by traditional barriers of race, gender, or social class. It means, even more importantly, that those traditional barriers can no longer be viewed as impediments to learning.

The students in my study also showed how crucial extracurricular activities were in providing needed outlets for their energy and for teaching them important leadership skills. For some, it was their place of worship (this was especially true for Avi, Manuel, and Rich); for others, it was hobbies (Linda loved to sing); and for others, sports were a primary support (Fern mentioned how she confronted new problems by comparing them to the sports in which she excelled: "I compare it to stuff, like, when I can't get science, or like in sewing, I'll look at that machine and I'll say, 'This is a basketball; I can overcome it' "). The schools' responsibility to provide some of these activities becomes paramount for students such as Marisol, whose involvement in the Teen Clinic acted almost like a buffer against negative peer pressure.

These students can all be characterized by an indomitable resilience and a steely determination to succeed. However, expecting all students, particularly those from subordinated communities, to be resilient in this way is an unfair burden because privileged students do not need this quality, as the schools generally reflect their backgrounds, experiences, language, and culture. Privileged students learn that they are the "norm," and although they may believe this is inherently unfair (as is the case with Vanessa), they still benefit from it.

Nevertheless, the students in this research provide another important lesson about the strength of human nature in the face of adversity. Although they represented all kinds of families and economic and social situations, the students were almost uniformly upbeat about their future and their lives, sometimes in spite of what might seem overwhelming odds. The positive features that have contributed to their academic success, namely, caring teachers, affirming school climates, and loving families, have helped them face such odds. "I don't think there's anything stopping me," said Marisol, whose large family lived on public assistance because both parents were disabled. She added, "If I know I can do it, I should just keep on trying." The determination to keep trying was evident also in Fern, whose two teenage sisters were undergoing treatment for alcohol and drug abuse, but who nevertheless asserted, "I succeed in everything I do. If I don't get it right the first time, I always go back and try to do it again," adding, "I've always wanted to be president of the United States!" And it was evident as well in the case of Manuel, whose father cleaned downtown offices in Boston while his mother raised the remaining children at home, and who was the first of the eleven children to graduate from high school: "I can do whatever I want to do in life. Whatever I want to do, I know I could make it. I believe that strongly." And, finally, it was also clear in the case of Rich, whose mother, a single parent, was putting all three of her children through college at the same time. Rich had clearly learned a valuable lesson about self-reliance from her, as we can see in this striking image: "But let's not look at life as a piece of cake, because eventually it'll dry up, it'll deteriorate, it'll fall, it'll crumble, or somebody will come gnawing at it." Later he added, "As they say, self-respect is one gift that you give yourself."

Our students have a lot to teach us about how pedagogy, curriculum, ability grouping, and expectations of ability need to change so that greater numbers of young people can be reached. In 1971, Annie Stein expressed the wishes and hopes of students she talked with, and they differ little from those we have heard through the voices of students today: "The demands of high school youth are painfully reasonable. They want a better education, a more 'relevant' curriculum, some voice in the subject matter to be taught and in the running of the school, and some respect for their constitutional and human rights" (1971, p. 177). Although the stories and voices I have used in this article are primarily those of individual students, they can help us to imagine what it might take to transform entire schools. The responsibility to do so cannot be placed only on the shoulders of individual teachers who, in spite of the profound impact they can have on the lives of particular students, are part of a system that continues to be unresponsive to too many young people. In the final analysis, students are asking us to look critically not only at structural conditions, but also at individual attitudes and behaviors. This implies that we need to undertake a total transformation not only of our schools, but also of our hearts and minds.

Notes

1. I recognize that overarching terms, such as *European American, African American, Latino*, etc., are problematic. Nevertheless, *European American* is more explicit than *White* with regard to culture and ethnicity, and thus challenges Whites also to think of themselves in ethnic terms, something they usually reserve for those from more clearly identifiable groups (generally, people of color). I have a more in-depth discussion of this issue in chapter two of my book, *Affirming Diversity* (1992).

2. The early arguments for cultural deprivation are well expressed by Carl Bereiter and Siegfried Englemann (1966) and by Frank Reissman (1962). A thorough review of a range of deficit theories can be found in Herbert Ginsburg (1986).

3. "Critical thinking," as used here, is not meant in the sense that it has come to be used conventionally to imply, for example, higher order thinking skills in math and science as disconnected from a political awareness. Rather, it means developing, in the Freirian (1970) sense, a consciousness of oneself as a critical agent in learning and transforming one's reality.

4. I was assisted in doing the interviews by a wonderful group of colleagues, most of whom contacted the students, interviewed them, and gave me much of the background information that helped me to craft the case studies. I am grateful for the insights and help the following colleagues provided: Carlie Collins Tartakov, Paula Elliott, Haydée Font, Maya Gillingham, Mac Lee Morante, Diane Sweet, and Carol Shea.

5. "Holidays and Heroes" refers to an approach in which multicultural education is understood as consisting primarily of ethnic celebrations and the acknowledgment of "great men" in the

history of particular cultures. Deeper structures of cultures, including values and lifestyle differences, and an explicit emphasis on power differentials as they affect particular cultural groups, are not addressed in this approach. Thus, this approach is correctly perceived as one that tends to romanticize culture and treat it in an artificial way. In contrast, multicultural education as empowering and liberating pedagogy confronts such structural issues and power differentials quite directly.

References

Abi-Nader, J. (1993). Meeting the needs of multicultural classrooms: Family values and the motivation of minority students. In M. J. O'Hair & S. Odell (Eds), *Diversity and teaching: Teacher education yearbook 1* (pp. 212–236). Fort Worth, TX: Harcourt Brace Jovanovich.

Banks, J. A. (1991). *Teaching strategies for ethnic studies* (6th ed.). Boston: Allyn & Bacon.

Bartolomé, L. (1994). Beyond the methods fetish: Toward a humanizing pedagogy. *Harvard Educational Review, 64,* 173–194.

Bempechat, J. (1992). *Fostering high achievement in African American children: Home, school, and public policy influences.* New York: ERIC Clearinghouse on Urban Education, Teachers College, Columbia University.

Bereiter, C., & Englemann, S. (1966). *Teaching disadvantaged children in the preschool.* Englewood Cliffs, NJ: Prentice Hall.

Clark, R. M. (1983). *Family life and school achievement: Why poor Black children succeed or fail.* Chicago: University of Chicago Press.

Commins, N. L. (1989). Language and affect: Bilingual students at home and at school. *Language Arts, 66,* 29–43.

Cummins, J. (1994). From coercive to collaborative relations of power in the teaching of literacy. In B. M. Ferdman, R-M. Weber, & A. G. Ramírez (Eds.), *Literacy across languages and cultures* (pp. 295–331). Albany: State University of New York Press.

Delpit, L. (1992). The politics of teaching literate discourse. *Theory into Practice, 31,* 285–295.

Díaz, E., Flores, B., Cousin, P. T., & Soo Hoo, S. (1992, April). *Teacher as sociocultural mediator.* Paper presented at the Annual Meeting of the AERA, San Francisco.

Donaldson, K. (1994). Through students' eyes. *Multicultural Education, 2*(2), 26–28.

Fine, M. (1991). *Framing dropouts: Notes on the politics of an urban public high school.* Albany: State University of New York Press.

Fine, M. (1993). "You can't just say that the only ones who can speak are those who agree with your position": Political discourse in the classroom. *Harvard Educational Review, 63,* 412–433.

Fordham, S., & Ogbu, J. (1986) Black students' school success: Coping with the "burden of acting White." *Urban Review, 18,* 176–206.

Frau-Ramos, M., & Nieto, S. (1993). "I was an outsider": Dropping out among Puerto Rican youths in Holyoke, Massachusetts. In R. Rivera & S. Nieto (Eds.), *The education of Latino students in Massachusetts: Research and policy considerations* (pp. 143–166). Boston: Gastón Institute.

Freire, P. (1970). *Pedagogy of the oppressed.* New York: Seabury Press.

Gibson, M. (1991). Minorities and schooling: Some implications. In M. A. Gibson & J. U. Ogbu (Eds.), *Minority status and schooling: A comparative study of immigrant and involuntary minorities* (pp. 357–381). New York: Garland.

Ginsburg, H. (1986). The myth of the deprived child: New thoughts on poor children. In U. Neisser (Ed.), *The school achievement of minority children: New perspectives.* Hillsdale, NJ: Lawrence Erlbaum.

Goodlad, J. I. (1984). *A place called school.* New York: McGraw-Hill.

Haberman, M. (1991). The pedagogy of poverty versus good teaching. *Phi Delta Kappan, 73,* 290–294.

Hallinan, M., & Teixeira, R. (1987). Opportunities and constraints: Black-White differences in the formation of interracial friendships. *Child Development, 58,* 1358–1371.

Hidalgo, N. M. (1991). *"Free time, school is like a free time": Social relations in City High School classes.* Unpublished doctoral dissertation, Harvard University.

Hollins, E. R., King, J. E., & Hayman, W. C. (Eds.). (1994). *Teaching diverse populations: Formulating a knowledge base.* Albany: State University of New York Press.

Kelly, R. (1994, January 11). Class searches for solstice. *Union News,* p. 12.

Kiang, P. N., & Lee, V. W-F. (1993). Exclusion or contribution? Education K–12 policy. In *The State of Asian Pacific America: Policy Issues to the Year 2020* (pp. 25–48). Los Angeles: LEAP Asian Pacific American Public Policy Institute and UCLA Asian American Studies Center.

Kohl, H. (1993). The myth of "Rosa Parks, the tired." *Multicultural Education, 1*(2), 6–10.

Kozol, J. (1967). *Death at an early age: The destruction of the hearts and minds of Negro children in the Boston Public Schools.* New York: Houghton Mifflin.

Lee, V. E., Winfield, L. F., & Wilson, T. C. (1991). Academic behaviors among high-achieving African-American students. *Education and Urban Society, 24*(1), 65–86.

Lucas, T., Henze, R., & Donato, R. (1990). Promoting the success of Latino language-minority students: An exploratory study of six high schools. *Harvard Educational Review, 60,* 315–340.

McNeil, L. M. (1986). *Contradictions of control: School structure and school knowledge.* New York: Routledge & Kegan Paul.

Mehan, H., & Villanueva, I. (1993). Untracking low achieving students: Academic and social consequences. In *Focus on Diversity* (Newsletter available from the National Center for Research on Cultural Diversity and Second Language Learning, 399 Kerr Hall, University of California, Santa Cruz, CA 95064).

Moll, L. (1992). Bilingual classroom studies and community analysis: Some recent trends. *Educational Researcher, 21*(2), 20–24.

Moll, L., & Díaz, S. (1993). Change as the goal of educational research. In E. Jacob & C. Jordan (Eds.), *Minority education: Anthropological perspectives* (pp. 67–79). Norwood, NJ: Ablex.

National Coalition of Advocates for Students. (1988). *New voices: Immigrant students in U.S. public schools.* Boston: Author.

Newmann, F. M. (1993). Beyond common sense in educational restructuring: The issues of content and linkage. *Educational Researcher, 22*(2), 4–13, 22.

Nieto, S. (1992). *Affirming diversity: The sociopolitical context of multicultural education.* White Plains, NY: Longman.

Nieto, S. (1994). Affirmation, solidarity, and critique: Moving beyond tolerance in multicultural education. *Multicultural Education, 1*(4), 9–12, 35–38.

Oakes, J. (1992). Can tracking research inform practice? *Educational Researcher, 21*(4), 12–21.

Olsen, L. (1988). *Crossing the schoolhouse border: Immigrant students and the California public schools.* San Francisco: California Tomorrow.

Peterson, R. E. (1991). Teaching how to read the world and change it: Critical pedagogy in the intermediate grades. In C. E. Walsh (Ed.), *Literacy as praxis: Culture, language, and pedagogy* (pp. 156–182). Norwood, NJ: Ablex.

Phelan, P., Davidson, A. L., & Cao, H. T. (1992). Speaking up: Students' perspectives on school. *Phi Delta Kappan, 73,* 695–704.

Poplin, M., & Weeres, J. (1992). *Voices from the inside: A report on schooling from inside the classroom.* Claremont, CA: Claremont Graduate School, Institute for Education in Transformation.

Reissman, F. (1962). *The culturally deprived child.* New York: Harper & Row.

Reyes, M. de la Luz (1992). Challenging venerable assumptions: Literacy instruction for linguistically different students. *Harvard Educational Review, 62,* 427–446.

Ribadeneira, D. (1990, October 18). Study says teen-agers' racism rampant. *Boston Globe,* p. 31.

Rumbaut, R. G., & Ima, K. (1987). *The adaptation of Southeast Asian refugee youth: A comparative study.* San Diego: Office of Refugee Resettlement.

Santos Rivera, I. (1983–1984, October–January). Liberating education for little children. In *Alternativas* (Freirean newsletter from Río Piedras, Puerto Rico, no longer published).

Saravia-Shore, M., & Martínez, H. (1992). An ethnographic study of home/school role conflicts of second generation Puerto Rican adolescents. In M. Saravia-Shore & S. F. Arvizu (Eds.), *Cross-cultural literacy: Ethnographies of communication in multiethnic classrooms* (pp. 227–251). New York: Garland.

Shor, I. (1992). *Empowering education: Critical teaching for social change.* Chicago: University of Chicago Press.

Skutnabb-Kangas, T. (1988). Resource power and autonomy through discourse in conflict: A Finnish migrant school strike in Sweden. In T. Skutnabb-Kangas & J. Cummins (Eds.), *Minority education: From shame to struggle* (pp. 251–277). Clevedon, Eng.: Multilingual Matters.

Sleeter, C. E. (1991). *Empowerment through multicultural education.* Albany: State University of New York Press.

Sleeter, C. E. (1994). White racism. *Multicultural Education, 1*(4), 5–8, 39.

Sleeter, C. E., & Grant, C. A. (1991). Mapping terrains of power: Student cultural knowledge vs. classroom knowledge. In C. E. Sleeter (Ed.), *Empowerment through multicultural education* (pp. 49–67). Albany: State University of New York Press.

Soo Hoo, S. (1993). Students as partners in research and restructuring schools. *Educational Forum, 57,* 386–393.

Stein, A. (1971). Strategies for failure. *Harvard Educational Review, 41,* 133–179.

Tatum, B. D. (1992). Talking about race, learning about racism: The application of racial identity development theory in the classroom. *Harvard Educational Review, 62,* 1–24.

Taylor, A. R. (1991). Social competence and the early school transition: Risk and protective factors for African-American children. *Education and Urban Society, 24*(1), 15–26.

Taylor, D., & Dorsey-Gaines, C. (1988). *Growing up literate: Learning from inner-city families.* Portsmouth, NH: Heinemann.

Torres-Guzmán, M. (1992). Stories of hope in the midst of despair: Culturally responsive education for Latino students in an alternative high school in New York City. In M. Saravia-Shore & S. F. Arvizu (Eds.), *Cross-cultural literacy: Ethnographies of communication in multiethnic classrooms* (pp. 477–490). New York: Garland.

Trueba, H. T. (1989). *Raising silent voices: Educating the linguistic minorities for the twenty-first century.* Cambridge, MA: Newbury House.

Wheelock, A. (1992). *Crossing the tracks: How "untracking" can save America's schools* New York: New Press.

Zanger, V. V. (1994). Academic costs of social marginalization: An analysis of Latino students' perceptions at a Boston high school. In R. Rivera & S. Nieto (Eds.), *The education of Latino students in Massachusetts: Research and policy considerations* (pp. 167–187). Boston: Gastón Institute.

Researching Change
and Changing the Researcher

CONCHA DELGADO-GAITAN

Over the past twenty years or so, anthropological researchers in education have employed interpretive ethnographic theories and research tools to study learning processes from a cultural perspective. Their primary task has been to provide an adequate contextualization of the cultural phenomena related to education.

More recently, interpretive anthropology has been enriched by the convergence of such approaches as phenomenology, structuralism, transformational linguistics, semiotics, critical theory, and hermeneutics (Marcus & Fischer, 1986). This cross-fertilization has been especially useful in providing a new perspective on the "native point of view," and on the problem of depicting cultural realities in social interaction. Through critical theory analysis in particular we find a language of possibility to understand change. Critical theory allows for discussion regarding the interaction between researcher and researched in the context of the researched community. Discussion about the researcher's viewpoint has in turn been important in raising questions regarding the outsider/insider position of researcher/researched (Hirschkind, 1991; Thomas, 1991).[1]

How we perceive our role in the communities we study matters greatly because it impacts the nature of the research we conduct (Elliott, 1988; Peshkin, 1982; Podermaker, 1967). The way we, as researchers, relate to ourselves and to the people we study was the focus of Dorinne Kondo's (1990) ethnography of the Japanese company as a family. She describes how notions of her identity as a Japanese American woman anthropologist changed throughout her research. Kondo's thesis is that the researcher shapes his or her research and is, in turn, shaped by it. Smadar Lavie's (1991) anthropological study with the Mzeina people, a Bedouin tribe in the South Sinai Desert, also illuminates how the researcher's identity is changed through her work. In her study, Lavie depicts the Bedouin struggle with the military occupation as she tries simultaneously to define her own identity vis-à-vis the Mzeinis, who were like family to her, a Jewish Arab woman trained as a Western anthropologist at the University of California, Berkeley. Based on critical inquiry of the Mzeina, she composes a written ethnography that retraces the process by which the Bedouin identity emerged through the performances of seven allegory-telling characters; within the ethnography, Lavie's own identity is fused with the personas of these characters. Both Kondo

Harvard Educational Review Vol. 63   No. 4   Winter 1994, 389–411

and Lavie use their ethnic identities as a tool for participating in the cultural communities that they studied, in order to involve the research participants in constructing their ethnographies.

In the United States, Michael Apple (1993) expands the discourse of the researcher's role in local communities by building and rebuilding a space where the researcher and the participants collectively raise questions about the meaning and power of knowledge through text. Apple emphasizes the importance of the researcher/researched relationship in questioning the source of knowledge in established canons. His role in the communities he researched exemplifies the possibilities of conducting research with socially disenfranchised groups in the United States.

I am a woman of Mexican immigrant heritage. My working-class family valued education and provided me with a strong foundation for learning and succeeding in school. My ethno-cultural identity was a key motivation for my studying family-school interconnections in the Spanish-speaking community of Carpinteria, California, where I engaged myself as a researcher. I set out to understand the nature of Latino family interactions involving literacy. The question of family literacy led me to further explore family-school relationships, including communication between family and school, and community empowerment.

In this article, I describe the Carpinteria study in order to discuss my role as an ethnographic researcher. I reflect on my evolving role as an observer of the people's daily interactions; as an active participant in family, school, and community activities; and as a facilitator in a conscious, reflective process undertaken by community members and between the researcher and the community.

The Participant Researcher: A Relational Perspective

Sharing the same ethnic background as the participants does not necessarily make the researcher more knowledgeable about the meanings of the participants' feelings, values, and practices. Researchers often hold misperceptions about participants' feelings, values, and practices based on influences such as assumed cultural knowledge. Therefore, interpretive fieldwork strategies that bring together theory and process through dialogue between research participants and researcher promise to yield a more complete interpretation (Delgado-Gaitan, 1987; Heath, 1983; Macias, 1987; Moll & Díaz, 1987; Spindler, 1970, 1974; Spindler & Spindler, 1970; Spradley, 1979; Suárez-Orozco, 1989).[2]

Given that basic tenets of critical theory presuppose a commitment to the emancipation of groups that have been socially, economically, and politically disenfranchised in society, researchers espousing this theoretical orientation enter the field with a notion about the insider-outsider relationship that includes a commitment to change. Henry Trueba and I have developed a framework called the Ethnography of Empowerment, which provides a broad sociocultural premise and possible strategy for studying the process of disempowerment and empowerment of disenfranchised communities (Delgado-Gaitan & Trueba, 1991). I understand empowerment as an ongoing, intentional process centered in the local community, involving mutual respect, critical reflection, caring, and collective participation (Barr, 1989; Barr & Cochran, 1991). Through this process, people become aware of their social conditions and strengths: they determine their choices and goals, and thus unveil their potential to act on their own behalf. Implicit in this process is a conscious responsibility on the part of disenfranchised communities for their own behavior and a willingness to shape their behavior as they desire through social processes. The Ethnography of Empowerment framework calls for the construction of knowledge through the social interaction between researcher and researched, with the fundamental purpose of improving the living conditions of the communities being researched. Thus, this kind of ethnography redefines the fundamental priorities of anthropological, educational, and social science research.

Consistent with Paulo Freire's critical theory premise, our construct of Ethnography of Empowerment establishes the process of ethnography as a theory and method applied in disenfranchised communities that addresses the question of the insider/outsider perspectives (Delgado-Gaitan & Trueba, 1991).[3] Ethnography of Empowerment rests on two fundamental premises about the nature of learning. First, learning among humans occurs across cultures, primarily in the home or in sociocultural units in which individuals are socialized. Second, learning ideally is purposive, and should ultimately be directed to the enhancement of cultural values. This ideal is possible when learning is embedded in the context of the learning community (Delgado-Gaitan & Trueba, 1991). These notions of social and cultural self-awareness attempt to develop a description of the ethno-historical and cultural context that makes it possible to understand the nature of oppression experienced by disenfranchised people and communities. This kind of context and description can be developed when ethnographic researchers practice dialogical research processes.

In the Ethnography of Empowerment framework, not only does the ethnographer effect and/or affect change in the communities as a result of being a participant-observer, but he or she is also influenced by the community being studied, such that the direction and orientation of his or her research may be changed.

It is within this theoretical orientation that I discuss my role as an ethnographic researcher in Carpinteria.[4] Central to this discussion is my relationship with the participants — in particular, how that relationship helped me understand myself, and how it informed my role in crafting the study and influencing change in the Carpinteria community.

Action: Establishing a Relationship

During the first five years of the Carpinteria study, I was a professor at the University of California, Santa Barbara, and lived twenty minutes from Carpinteria. My initial interest in the Carpinteria Latino community was as an extension of research that I had conducted in other Latino communities in northern California and Colorado. In particular, I wanted to observe a setting that provided successful educational programs for Latino students.

My eight years of research in Carpinteria began with an ethnographic study on family literacy in the Spanish-speaking Latino community. It evolved to encompass the parent involvement process in the Carpinteria school, which had been one of shared power between families and the school. The parent-school empowerment process, through the Comité de Padres Latinos (COPLA), illustrated a difficult but doable approach taken by a community interested in Latino children's education.

Part of the impetus for this study was my reaction to much of the research literature that focused on devastating educational conditions in culturally different communities. My observations of children and their families in ethnically diverse California communities where I had been an elementary school teacher and principal
convinced me that Latino people could be more than the helpless victims characterized in many studies of school failure. I observed members of the Latino community
being active participants in the day-to-day shaping of their lives, which convinced me
that active participation is for them a source of strength and empowerment.

This optimism impelled my study on family literacy (involving oral, reading, and
written text in daily family life) in Carpinteria, and encouraged me to try to shatter
the monolithic portrayal of Mexicans as ignorant, powerless failures in U.S. schools.
My own background as an immigrant from Mexico, who grew up in California from
age eight and attended school in various Los Angeles communities, further impelled
me to understand the complexity of these immigrant families' lives and their relations
with the schools.

I negotiated my initial entry into the Carpinteria community through the school
district in order to observe literacy abilities in the Latino households and in the community, including the schools. This topic was of serious concern to the schools because many Latino students were reading at levels below school expectations. The issue of literacy was especially important for me in that literacy occupies a far more
complex and important place in the Mexican community than schools sometimes understand. This discrepancy between the place of literacy in the Mexican community
and the schools' understanding of its place is not unique to Carpinteria; it has, in fact,
been documented by various researchers (Ada, 1988; Delgado-Gaitan, 1990; Goldenberg, 1987; Moll & Díaz, 1987). School personnel, however, often do not have the
time to examine family and community literacy practices. I am familiar with school
personnel time constraints through personal experiences in the schools and through
interviews in the Carpinteria study.

I collected data through systematic ethnographic observations of literacy activities
in the household, school, and community, and through interviews of family members
over a two-year period. I recorded these observations in written field notes, and in
video and audio recordings. I found that although families shared common literacy
activities, such as oral storytelling by parents to younger children, letter writing to relatives in Mexico, and storybook reading of popular trade books in Spanish, variation
existed in parent-child interaction around homework-type literacy tasks (Delgado-
Gaitan, 1990). Observations showed that children who were placed in novice reading
groups in the classroom generally faced stricter rules in the home and received more
direct instructional assistance from parents. These parents believed that their children
needed supervised assistance, since the teachers' reports stressed negative behavior and
low performance. Children who were placed in the advanced reading groups in the
classroom tended to enjoy more freedom in the way they did their homework because
parents usually assisted them only indirectly by assuring completion of the task.
These parents seemed to trust their children and to believe that they were responsible
and knowledgeable enough to do their work; they also communicated more frequently with the teachers and received pointers on ways to assist their children.

Part of the ethnographic method I employed involved sharing data with nearly one
hundred Latino families to elicit their input and insight about their own literacy prac-

tices in the home and in relation to the school. The intent of the data-sharing sessions was to solicit the insider's perspective and to make meaning of their experiences. An unanticipated outcome of this relational process (which I will discuss later) altered the course of my research, while forcing participants and myself to reexamine our perceptions. Friday evening meetings at the Aliso Elementary School were the setting where the families and I analyzed their experiences; these meetings eventually redirected the study.

In Carpinteria, every noon during lunchtime, the tables in the Aliso Elementary School auditorium were filled with children who swallowed their lunches as quickly as possible before running outside to play. On some Friday nights, many Latino families came together in that same school auditorium to discuss topics related to family education as part of the Migrant Education Program. The meetings were held on a monthly basis (occasionally more often) and were already taking place when my study began. The purpose of the program was to share information with families about immigration laws, AIDS, and other pertinent issues, such as health care for preschool children. For example, on one particular Friday evening, over seventy people, including men, women holding young children on their laps, and older children, listened attentively to a guest speaker who discussed legal rights for immigrants.

I selected those Friday night meetings as the forum to share with the families the ethnographic data on literacy activities that I had collected in their homes. At six consecutive monthly meetings, I spent over one hour of their two-hour meeting sharing my data and soliciting comments from the parents. The data included findings about parents telling stories to children, reading to children at home, and assisting with schoolwork. I presented my findings while attempting to maintain a warm and friendly, yet somewhat distant, posture; generally, parents who attended the meetings talked with me about the study findings. Their insights and meaning provoked my interest and, periodically, both confirmed and challenged my interpretations.

I began my first presentation by commending the parents for their commitment to and interest in their children's education. However, I also pointed out that some parents did not read much to their children, even in Spanish, and that a connection existed between parents who read to their children and the school's expectations and perceptions about Latino children's performance. The issue that I intended to raise with parents was diversity in family literacy practices; I believed that parents' familiarity with such ideas would provide insights about their children's performance in schools.

In presenting my data to this group, I wanted them to recognize that literacy practices at home — particularly their interaction with written text — affected their children's school performance. I was not, however, advocating that they change their reading practices as a result of my data. At that point, I merely wanted to share my findings with them and to solicit their perspective about my data. When I began studying literacy activities in the homes, my understanding of literacy practices in the Latino community conformed to those of the schools in that I believed literacy to be primarily the act of decoding written text. As the study unfolded, my understanding of literacy transcended those of the school. I expanded my understanding of literacy to include oral literacy activities, as well as the critical interpretation of the "word" (Freire & Macedo, 1987). During the process of data collection, I learned that parents demonstrate their concern for their children's success in school in ways other than reading to their children in the households. The following parent's comment illustrates one of the alternative ways in which parents expressed their concern for their children's success: "My husband and I remind our children that they have a great opportunity to go to school and they should take advantage of it so they can have the opportunities we did not have."[5]

At these meetings, parents listened attentively to the speakers, even when distracted by their young children, who often ran in and out of the auditorium. I talked about the stories that some parents read to their children. The question I posed to them was "Do you read to your children, and if so, what kind of stories do you read?" Parents raised their hands enthusiastically and related their experiences:

> I never read to my older children, although I did encourage them to read to each other. When we moved to Carpinteria, my youngest daughter went to preschool and the teacher always told us to read to our children in Spanish so that they would learn to read in their own language. It didn't make sense to me, but I did it anyway, and now that my daughter is in the second grade I see that she likes reading much more than my other children. I think it has to do with the fact that I still read to her.

Other comments were made:

> I think it's good to read to our children like the teacher has told us, but neither my husband nor I read either in Spanish or English so it's hard to help our children. What we do is to encourage our children to stay in school and to learn. They can be educated in a way that we never could.

At the Friday meetings, during my exchange with the community, parents generally shared information about their literacy activities with their children. They reported on a variety of interactions, which included adults and children reading popular storybooks such as *Snow White,* analyzing legal documents, and writing letters to their relatives in Mexico. Occasionally, parents helped their children with particular homework assignments.

Combing through piles of field notes and tape transcripts, I identified types and contexts of literacy activities in the home and in the classroom. I analyzed videotapes to define further the nature of the literacy events. Who, when, and how parents helped their children with schoolwork emerged as an unexpected salient issue in what began as an exploration of literacy in the Latino community. This issue emerged in the process of data analysis about a month before I began to meet with parents on Friday nights, and convinced me of the need to reflect with them. The parents' immediate purpose, which was to have their children succeed in school, dominated most of their literacy practices.

I pursued the theme of the home-school connection because I was perplexed by the differences in participation of parents in their children's education that emerged during my Friday night discussions with the families. Some parents interacted more actively with their children to help them complete their homework, while some felt less able to assist their children. Regardless of the parents' level of engagement with their children's homework, most parents felt incompetent in communicating with the school. Most of them had received only a fourth-grade education in Mexico, and they blamed their lack of formal education for their *ineffective exchanges* with the school, by which I mean those attempts parents made to relate to the school, but which in fact left them more confused. For example, in one case a boy was being retained in the first grade and the mother went to the school to talk to the teacher. The teacher told her that the reason for the child's retention was his low reading ability, and that the parents needed to help him read at home. Without further clarification, the mother assumed that her son's failure in school was her fault. Essentially, this example indicates that some parents did not know what questions to ask because of their lack of familiarity with the school system. Parents repeatedly explained this problem to me; moreover, when they did know the questions they wanted to ask, they did not know how to ask them or of whom. Led by the developments of this phase of the analysis, I probed further into the question of how parents learned to help their children do their homework. Most of the parents who were active in the school responded that they had been taught by the preschool teacher to communicate with educators. The undereducated parents, whether or not they were active in the schools, felt isolated because they believed that as a result of their limited formal schooling, their children might not have access to the best education.

As they responded to my research questions about parental participation in schools and in their children's schooling, angry emotions flared as some parents told of going to the school to make an appointment to talk with their child's teacher, and finding that they could not communicate with anyone in the office. Not knowing how to connect with the schools had clearly traumatized some of these parents. The identification of this issue expanded my research focus from describing literacy in the Latino community to understanding its meaning to the parents, including their communication with schools.

Change: Redirected Role of the Researcher

At the third Friday night meeting with the parents at Aliso Elementary School, a father, Mr. Reyes, stood up and said that he had been listening to me present information about the Latino families in Carpinteria over the prior weeks. In his opinion, many families felt isolated, not because they did not care, but because they did not have the necessary experience to communicate with the schools. He proposed that those parents who had more contact with the schools should organize and teach those who needed it. At that point, as a I stood in front of the parents, I found myself fighting to remain in the "neutral" research role. I tried to resist the temptation to advocate for forming the parent leadership group that Mr. Reyes proposed, which I could see would be instrumental in achieving their cultural adjustment goal — that is, effective, cooperative, family-school relationships. It was clear to me that some type of support group could benefit the families in their communication with the schools.

Following the meeting, I approached Mr. Reyes and asked him about his intent to organize the parents. He lamented that most administrators did not have the time to work with the community, and that those who were interested, like the Migrant Education director, had quite an overload of work imposed on them. I asked him what might prevent him from organizing the group himself, and he responded that he could not because he didn't have a list of people to call. He questioned his own skills in organizing the group. He said that he knew other people's names, but did not have their phone numbers. Mr. Reyes looked around as if he were looking for someone, and then he said that possibly the director of Migrant Education had a list. Instinctively, I wanted to persuade him to ask the director for a list of parents' names and phone numbers, but I refrained. Mr. Reyes indicated that he wanted to get the parents together if their phone numbers were available. His response made me question again the nature of my role as a researcher. I evaluated the appropriateness of my intervening, and I contemplated the possibility of suggesting to him how to obtain the list of parents' names and organize a meeting.

At this point, I remembered the voices of some of my teachers, who had reminded me that the ethnographer's work entails only observing and describing. However, another voice resounded even more loudly and defended the role of the researcher as politically weighted. Such a position seemed to obligate the researcher, me, to intervene when it might lead to favorable results for the participants or even when it involves a question of the researcher's moral conscience. Freire (1970) advocates for direct intervention as a way to learn about the communities' needs. These internal voices intensified my quandary about whether or not to intervene directly as an advocate. Paulo Freire's work in community organizing for literacy and empowerment had long governed my research pursuits. Now I had to determine if my intervening in these families' *concientizaçao* (consciousness raising) would influence the integrity of their process of change, as well as my process of traditional "objective" research, which seemed necessary to protect, given my academic training.[6] The decision to refrain from encouraging Mr. Reyes was a difficult one.

Traditional ethnographic methodology asserts the researcher's privileged position, leading one to participate in the culture in covert ways for the mere purpose of obtaining data. Under this premise, we are still led to believe that the research process can be removed from any human contamination (Schatzman & Strauss, 1973; Strauss, 1987). Thus, I confronted an ethical question as to what my real intent would be if I participated as a facilitator in the parents' emerging organization. By now I was convinced by praxis that no research is neutral, yet the realization was academic in that I still had to consider what it meant in the context of this setting, with real human beings who were working to change their lives.

At a subsequent parent meeting, I approached Mr. Reyes and asked him about the progress that he had made in convening a meeting of Latino parent leaders. After pondering the question during the previous two weeks, I had decided to initiate this topic with Mr. Reyes. By the time of this meeting, I had reconciled my intervention with my role as a researcher. He shrugged his shoulders and said that he had not mobilized parents because he did not have their phone numbers. I asked, "Why don't you ask the Migrant Education director to provide you with a list of parents you can call to a meeting?" I then suggested to him that if he called together a meeting of parents, I would like to attend. I invited myself to the meeting with the understanding that I would not act as their leader, because it was their community. I did, however, offer to share my data with the parents at their leadership meetings. By this time, I had collected a large amount of data on the literacy activities and learning contexts in the home and the schools in this research site, data ranging from bedtime stories to superintendent administrators' meetings.

The following week, Mr. Reyes called me at my home and announced that he had reached several parents who were interested in attending a meeting to discuss how they could support each other on issues of educating their children. He had arranged with the director of Special Programs (the Migrant Education Program was part of these Special Programs) to have the meeting take place in the faculty room of Aliso Elementary School that coming Friday, when there was no Migrant Education Program meeting scheduled.

On that Friday evening, I made it a point to arrive at the site on time to observe how the event unfolded. Although I normally arrived on time, it had never been as crucial as this night, since now — with my decision to intervene — my purpose included studying the process of the meeting. Eleven parents gathered in front of the school's faculty room, which apparently had not been unlocked as the parents had requested. One of the parents went to the public phone to call the district director of Curriculum. He learned that there had been a misunderstanding about the time at which the door had to be opened, since the school's regular custodian was out ill. Evidently no one had keys to a classroom, so a couple of the men moved a large lunch table with benches from the playground to the inner courtyard. People sat and talked about their concerns as Mexican immigrants raising children in Carpinteria.

Mr. Reyes convened the meeting by asking people to introduce themselves. He explained that the purpose of the meeting was to try to get some Latino parents together to see how they could help other Spanish-speaking parents who needed to communicate with the school about their children. He emphasized that they had been called together because of their experiences with the schools so that they could share ideas on how to organize Latino families to support each other.

At that point, I began to notice a shift in my research focus from concerns with literacy activities and processes in home and school to the process of empowerment. Parents took turns talking about their heartfelt desire to have their children get a good education so that they would have greater economic security than their parents experienced as Spanish-speaking immigrants from a low socioeconomic level. Their primary concern was with their perceived distancing of the children from the family culture. This distancing was created as children learned American values that were different from their family traditions. Mrs. Ortiz was choked by her words as she disclosed her ordeal with her daughter, who did not want to speak Spanish to them because she felt ashamed:

> Our insistence to have her speak to us in Spanish is overshadowed by her need to be liked in school. She's just in the sixth grade, but English is more important to her and her friends. We need to speak Spanish, that's the language of our family. There's nothing wrong with English, but the school's not teaching them Spanish, so we should, because we will always speak it.

Such words captured me. I was also captured by the support that participants in the meeting gave each other, which in turn created a safe environment that permitted them to express their feelings. Parents' love for their children was mixed with fear and frustration because, in their efforts to help, they were still faced with unknown results and expectations. The parents shared their experiences in relating to the White, European American community and the schools, and also told their stories of challenge and commitment to their families. Their contact with the school had been more active than that of other Latino parents in the Carpinteria community, yet these parents felt the pressure of not meeting the school's expectations, such as speaking English and being familiar with the way the school operated. As Mr. Soto noted:

I always go to the school when my son's teachers call me and want to talk to me about his problematic behavior. One day the school called me, and as usual I had to leave work and take a pay cut for that release-time to help out my son. When I got there [to the school] I waited almost an hour and no one knew where my son was or what the problem was. As it turned out, it was not my son who had been in the fight. I was quite upset and I didn't even get an apology from the school. I find this degrading and humiliating. I don't think they would do it to someone who could defend himself in English.

Mr. Soto's humiliation was addressed by others in the group who believed that although he did not know English, Mr. Soto certainly deserved more respect than the school had extended.

Stories such as the one shared by this parent consumed much of the time during this initial meeting. The underlying message to each other seemed to be that they, as parents, tried very hard to do the best for their children, and that they had the desire and commitment to support their children in their education both at home and at school. The fact that they cared about their children and their education was understood by them to mean that they were "good parents."

Mrs. Mora, who would later become the group leader for the Latino parents, stressed that the parents' life experiences were of much value and should be shared with their children. For example, Mrs. Mora was a part of the Latino Spanish-speaking immigrant community. Her educational experience was somewhat more advanced than most Latino immigrants in Carpinteria, whose formal education in Mexico did not exceed elementary school. Mrs. Mora's words — "We came because *we can*, not to see *if* we can" — frame the quintessential statement for this study of family and community, since her statement reflects the perceived reality of power by Latino families. The meaning of this claim became clear as the process of community organization unfolded. Mrs. Mora's reminder to parents of their responsibility to communicate pride and struggle to their children resonated in her statement, "Many of us do not have the formal education necessary to help our children with their demands in school, but we value and respect the family. Through our family we help our children value their own lives and education."

Her words impressed me as being important, but still left me doubting how knowledgeable parents were in actually helping their children succeed in school. My findings had shown that parents who actively communicated with the school had children who were more advanced readers. But here were parents who perceived their own experience as the power base of their family and, in spite of their limited schooling, recognized the importance of transmitting their cultural values and beliefs to their children. Given this opportunity to listen to parents represent their views of what education means to them, I questioned my initial analysis of the family-school relationship study, which minimized the parents' experience as a value transmitted to children and its importance to their children's overall attitude about schooling beyond their placement in the classroom reading groups (Delgado-Gaitan, 1989).

At a subsequent meeting, parents agreed to select a leader for their group. Their approach to selecting a leader demonstrated their respect for each others' abilities while recognizing their need for a person to help them make contact with the schools. The choice of a president of this parent group occupied most of the discussion. Parents described a person who could speak at least some English because she or he would have to talk with administrators who might not speak Spanish. This criterion was subsequently dismissed, as they decided that someone could have leadership skills without being English-speaking. Another practical qualification desired in their leader was that the person be able to drive a car so that she or he could attend meetings at the schools. That notion was also readily dismissed because parents felt that if the person who assumed the position of president had good communication skills and wanted the position but did not drive, she or he could find transportation.

Their expectations for leadership qualifications were defined by the collective group through a process of turn-taking, in which each person shared his or her views. The person in the leadership role had to commit to the group's position. Pragmatic qualifications such as bilingualism, knowledge about the schools, availability of time, and transportation became secondary as the commitment to the group became the primary factor that the Latino parents wanted upheld.

Mrs. Mora was nominated by a parent, and the nomination was supported unanimously. It was noted that she had been a teacher in Mexico, and that her expertise in working with schools could assist the group in their communication with the schools. Mrs. Mora was also the eldest member of the parent group and no longer had children in the school district. Although she did not drive a car or speak fluent English, parents recognized her experience as an educator in Mexico and sought to utilize her skills.

It was unclear to me why they dismissed their need for people who could communicate more effectively with the schools through the use of English. Although their recognition of Mrs. Mora's teaching experience made sense from their point of view, it seemed impractical to me to have a leader who could not communicate with school personnel. However, her position as a teacher and the group's respect for her knowledge were considered high priorities by the group. Recent interviews with the group's leadership have clarified this question for me further. Their decision to select Mrs. Mora as their leader was not a disqualification of individuals who were more competent in English, but rather an affirmation of their interest in being represented by someone who would articulate their values and vision as concerned Latino parents.

Parents took turns complimenting Mrs. Mora's strong and positive spirit that so inspired them all. As Mr. Soto stated, "Mrs. Mora shares our vision of how we view our responsibility to communicate with our children and with the schools. We want to put our best foot forward because we know how much it matters." The group believed that the way she spoke about family cohesiveness, interdependence, and the motivation for education reflected the Mexican community's goals for their children.

The selection of a president clearly held a different meaning for this parent group from what I had expected, given my general concepts of leadership, which were based on a model of organization and participation that was different from that which oriented this group. I was under the impression that the parents would elect a president for the purpose of attending to logistical tasks, such as scheduling meetings with the principals. My teaching, administrative, and academic experience had taught me that the president's role in an organization meant representing the group, deciding the agenda, and defining the membership of the group by its voting privileges. Yet, how this organization — eventually named Comité de Padres Latinos (COPLA) — was organized revealed an obvious cultural difference between me and the Latino families.[7] However, this difference became apparent only after I discussed my observations with them. For example, the data on family systems and interaction that I shared with them at the Friday night meetings indicated a strong sense of unity and respect for one another that transcended the immediate nuclear family and extended to relatives and other members of the community. Yet, as the parent organization evolved, I failed to account for the cultural linkages between family values and those shaping the organization.

COPLA parents' division of labor at the Canalino Elementary School — the first school they approached — showed that as organizers they wanted every participant to have an active voice in the process. COPLA parents spoke to the issue of wanting more input from a larger group of Latino parents about this new organization.

During this initial part of their organizing efforts, Mrs. Mora, now COPLA president, called me. She wanted me to address the group about the overall structure and curricular programs in the Carpinteria schools, so that I could begin to show the parents how to initiate organizational contact with the schools. I had offered my facilitator services to the parents as a way of sharing the data that I had collected, but I continued to experience a great deal of consternation about moving away from my role as researcher. I asked Mrs. Mora what it was that the group wanted to know and why they believed I could help. She said that COPLA parents considered me knowledgeable about the schools, and that they trusted me and considered me to be an advocate for them. Furthermore, I was qualified to inform and teach them, in Spanish, about the way that schools worked in the United States, enabling them to communicate better with school personnel.

The parents' request for my services forced me to delineate my role as a researcher and focus on whether I could participate in COPLA and maintain my role of observer without compromising the integrity of the research. Would I abandon the study and just act as a facilitator? Was it possible to act as an advocate, or broker, while researching the change process? If I was going to educate parents about schooling in Carpinteria, how would it change the direction of the study? Could I, as Rosalie Wax (1971) says, "step in and out"? Again these questions surfaced, forcing me to clarify how to participate without interfering with the parents' process.

Driven by the work of Freire and the Cornell University Empowerment Group (Allen, Barr, Cochran, Dean, & Greene, 1989; Freire, 1970, 1973), I transcended my qualms and decided to involve myself as the parents requested. In Freire's work, the principles of community empowerment recognize the researcher as an active participant who acts as a facilitator in the community's change process. One week after Mrs. Mora's request, I called her and committed my services to the group. I made my position clear to the group — I would be an informant to them, but I would not be responsible for COPLA's goals and direction.

Mrs. Mora instructed me to inform the group about the way the schools operated. I asked her what the parents knew about the schools. Although I knew something about their knowledge of the education system by having sat in on the initial COPLA meetings, it was nevertheless important to hear it from her. Mrs. Mora felt that the parents wanted to learn about school programs and about how they could help their children succeed in school.

I considered how I would share my data with them regarding the schools' organization and the classroom learning setting. We first met in the teachers' room at Aliso Elementary School. About thirty parents were present, including the eleven members of the original district-wide COPLA group. I outlined the structure of the Carpinteria school system, from preschool to high school level, as well as the academic expectations at each grade level. I described what the schools expected of children, with particular emphasis on methods to achieve high grades, and presented data that I had collected in their homes and schools. In relation to parental tasks in the home, the data that I presented illustrated that as students got to the upper grades, parents lacked the language or formal academic preparation to be able to help their children directly.

During the second COPLA meeting, I assumed that Mrs. Mora, as group president, would identify the eleven formal COPLA members as those who would make the decisions. However, when it came time to vote on questions such as whether to continue to organize COPLA at Canalino Elementary School, Mrs. Mora called for a vote from all thirty people present. Everyone raised his or her hand, and I found that everyone's vote was recognized. No distinction was made between members of the COPLA group and the parents who were attending for the first time. By doing this in her role as president, Mrs. Mora defined the importance of all the people's voices, not just COPLA members'. Everyone in the room seemed satisfied with the decisionmaking process. Mrs. Mora entertained comments from non-COPLA members about the need for an organization like COPLA, then one member parent circulated a sign-up sheet and invited parents to participate in the organization. The president's message, as well as that of other COPLA members, encouraged the other parents to learn together and to accept the challenge of this new experience for themselves and for the benefit of their children. Everyone present signed on as a new COPLA member.

The COPLA group continued inviting me to their subsequent weekly meetings to talk to them more about education in Carpinteria. A slightly different group of parents attended each meeting.[8] Twenty-five parents attended the fourth meeting of the district-wide COPLA meeting. The original eleven-member COPLA cohort was present, along with five parents who were present for the first time and nine who had attended the previous meeting. Mrs. Mora opened the meeting and introduced me. She told the gathering that COPLA parents were trying to learn how to better help their children in school by having the parents support each other, which made these meetings very important. All parents present concurred, and talked about the need to spread their message to more Latino parents.

I presented what I perceived to be a distance between the school's academic demands and what the parents provided for their children. The group then discussed the ways in which they had worked with their children. As one parent recounted, "I never know whether helping my son benefits him because there's much I don't know." Another parent recommended having a dialogue with school district administrators about their needs, so that they could agree on the best way to educate Latino children. As in previous meetings, when a vote was taken to decide whether to invite school administrators to subsequent meetings, Mrs. Mora counted everyone's vote. Consistent with COPLA's concept of inclusion, she made no distinction between parents who had attended previous meetings and those who were attending for the first time. They agreed to invite school administrators to the following meeting. I juggled feelings of optimism and apprehension. I was optimistic that the empowerment process was advancing because they had plans to include educators in COPLA. On the other hand, I was apprehensive about the sharing of power between parents and school personnel. My optimism was rooted in my belief that involving school personnel seemed to indicate progress, in that families and educators could begin a dialogue to improve learning conditions for Latino students. My apprehension, however, had to do with my knowledge and experience in communities where schools try to work with families, but often ultimately distort the power relations so that the school dictates the agenda and goals for the group.

Even though parents had voted to invite an administrator, the strategy for extending the invitation was not addressed, and they did not decide who would contact the administration. Before Mrs. Mora closed the meeting, she invited everyone to return the following week to continue the discussion about the children's education, and encouraged them to bring a neighbor or friend since these topics were important. One COPLA member pointed out that COPLA could not speak on behalf of all Latino families unless it had the whole community's support. As people were leaving, Mrs. Mora asked for a volunteer to accompany her to the district office to speak to the director of Special Programs. Mrs. Alonso, a member of the original COPLA group, volunteered to go because she knew the director and she spoke more English than Mrs. Mora. I was impressed with their commitment to negotiate their needs and combine their strengths in order to communicate in a different language and culture.

Interpretation: A Question of Perception, Reflection, and Voice

My relationship with COPLA as a facilitator haunted me. I feared that what I shared with them would inevitably define the direction of their organization, regardless of how neutral I intended to be. I experienced deep concern as I realized that I had abandoned my neutral, noninfluential position. In reality, what I had to do was to interpret my actions along with theirs in the change process.

I constantly reminded COPLA of their progress as a group. I consciously made my presentations at their meetings less didactic and more reflective by raising questions to the group. For example, when discussing bilingual programs, I suggested to the members that they think about questions that were important to them. They wanted to know why Spanish-speaking children did not have teachers who spoke in their language, but taught in bilingual programs. They also wanted to know why schools did not send out communications in Spanish to Latino families and why their children learned limited English in bilingual programs. These concerns provided a framework for discussing with them the observational data I had regarding the district's bilingual program. I suggested that they invite the director of Special Programs to their meeting to deal with the part of the programs I could not address. COPLA members did invite administrators and teachers to talk to them about the district's bilingual program and other curricular matters.

To make sure that the school district was aware of my extended role as a facilitator with COPLA, I informed the administration of my changing status. My emerging role as a facilitator became a test of the community's and the school district's trust in me. The school administration felt that my role as a facilitator with the Latino families could support the district's educational goal of forging closer communication with the Spanish-speaking Latino community. The administration became even more supportive of my role in COPLA when the district director began attending the meetings and witnessed the power of the organization.

COPLA's continued practice of acknowledging all parents who attended the meetings, without defining or limiting membership, illustrated the organization's egalitarian character and its commitment to involve everyone in the discussion. When the group and I reflected on my observations of their organizational meetings, they clarified to me the importance of the collective voice in their decisionmaking process, as expressed by one parent in this statement: "We cannot be an authoritarian elite group making decisions for others."

This attitude revealed to me a cultural gap between the parents' analysis of the situation and my own. I offered information about the way the dominant school culture might expect this parent organization to operate; that is, that a formal organization meant that the leader of the group had authority over the rest of the group. COPLA in fact had a different dynamic, one rooted in more egalitarian ways of relating to each other.

At an early COPLA meeting held to organize Latino parents at Canalino School, the parents suggested that they should meet with the principal as a group. That way they could support each other, and they would present a strong united force. COPLA parents then strategized their mobilization of the school's Latino community. I felt that their efforts were designed to involve as many parents as possible in their meetings with the school administration, and that their need to involve a large number of parents represented fear about their lack of experience. I later learned that my interpretation was clearly based on my expectation of how an effective organization should operate.

The parents interpreted their behavior during meetings in two significant ways: 1) their interactions at the meetings showed respect for each other's voice and viewpoint while minimizing the authority of the leader, and 2) their collective effort to solicit input from as many families as possible represented a commitment to a democratic voice among Latino parents. Respect and democracy defined their interaction with each other and shaped COPLA.

How was I to reconcile the difference between my insider/outsider interpretation of their mode of relating to one another and their reality? Following several meetings with the parents in which we analyzed their process, I recognized that it was not fear or ignorance of the school system that motivated their mode of organizing. Rather, it was their respect for each other's opinions, insights, and experience that defined their interactions. Even though I had observed the parents empowering themselves through the process of sharing their experience as Spanish-speaking immigrant families in Carpinteria, my outside academic and social perspectives biased my interpretation. These parents' interactions with each other were not as I had initially perceived them; that is, as "ignorant" of the mainstream ways of organizing and communicating with the schools. Rather, the parents joined forces democratically in order to resolve their problems with the school system.

Building on this sense of empowerment, and despite the insider/outsider relationship, both I as the researcher and the parents as the researched moved toward change in Carpinteria. In the dilemma of being a member/nonmember of the ethnic group, I recognized that I had to remain conscious of the insiders' perspectives since, even though I belonged to the same ethnic group as the subjects of this study, I could not ensure true understanding of the culturally bound practices of the parent group. My lack of understanding was due to both my acculturation into the dominant culture and my academic training.

Once I understood their way of constructing meaning in their organization, I came to understand and respect the particular process and perspective that gave their organization credibility. As an outsider, I had relied on empowerment theories advanced by Freire and the Cornell Empowerment Group to guide my facilitator activities. Those theories dictated that I could not intervene in the participants' change process unsolicited (Delgado-Gaitan & Trueba, 1991). Although my involvement in their meetings unquestionably influenced their orientation and knowledge base about the schools, the COPLA parents themselves defined their organizational goals and their sociopolitical awareness and identity. My interpretation of the empowerment process in COPLA, in which I was a participant and observer, an insider and outsider, underwent its own transformation. The experience strengthened my connection with the families. The insights I gained about the process of empowerment reframed what I initially thought to be merely a set of activities conducted by a group of Latino immigrant families who were ignorant of the dominant institutional culture. I came to see these activities as a meaningful construction of literacy that included their ability to read not only written text, but also their world as text (Freire & Macedo, 1987).

Some Final Reflections on Research for Empowerment

The Ethnography of Empowerment framework, supported by critical theory principles, involves methodological strategies that engage the community in the research analysis. The researcher participates concurrently in the transformation of the setting being studied. Conducting the Carpinteria study taught me that a researcher can only be an outsider; however, with insight, the researcher can encourage and foster the relational process between researcher and researched. In the Carpinteria study, the reflective analysis between the parents and the researcher impacted the direction of the study; the researcher provided the community members with specific data to develop their organization, while the parents changed the researcher's perception of the meaning of their activities.

The concepts of enduring self and situated self, introduced by Spindler and Spindler (in press), provided me with a psychosocial framework to look at the nature of change experienced by the COPLA parents and myself. The concept of the enduring self permits us to understand the continuity that exists in our lives, and the way in which our beliefs, values, and practices are constructed through our cultural communities. The situated self is a conception of the self that evolves, develops, and transforms, given specific contexts and activities.[9] Our situated self represents the shifting of those values, beliefs, and practices as a result of new knowledge and new contexts. These constructs are interconnected, not dichotomous.

The relational nature of change between myself as the researcher and the researched was characterized by steps that revealed the cultural center of the enduring self of those involved by: 1) transcending fear, 2) liberating our voices through self-acceptance, and 3) transforming the situation through the situated self; that is, the self that shifts from context to context given new knowledge. In the case of the Latino parents who felt fearful and insecure because they did not know how to interact with the schools, I noticed how honest and sincere they were in sharing their feelings and confronting their fears by going beyond the perceived limitations — in other words, in how they encountered their enduring selves. They confronted their enduring selves through continuity with their social history. The Latino parents realized that they were whole and complete as they shared their life experiences with each other. Thus, they found continuity in the midst of a fractured immigrant experience. As parents discovered their strengths and developed new ones, they became more capable of articulating their situated selves in their new contexts, as evidenced by their formation of COPLA.

In my own case, I believed initially that COPLA parents' collective organizational behavior was based on their ignorance of political organizations. I subsequently revised my interpretation as I understood how they shared power and voice among themselves. Essentially, COPLA parents interacted with one another in ways familiar to them based on mutual respect for each other's opinions and experiences in the traditions of their own culture. I learned how important self-reflection was to COPLA parents through my own introspection about my role in their organization. Simultaneously, my personal need forced me to understand my gestalt while reevaluating my learned methods. I learned that there were no guaranteed outcomes and no fail-safe methods to achieve objectives. I then understood what the process of organization meant to COPLA members, which enabled me to interact in their discourse of change. COPLA moved from conceptualizing change as a list of outcomes, to a list of books they could read to their children, to interacting with each other, to learning the process by which to inquire and access information that would lead them to obtain the resources they desired.

The relational nature of the study was evident in practice. For example, when COPLA's first president had to leave the organization, members called me to help them decide how to select another president. I met with them to reflect on why they chose a president for COPLA the first time and they thought about the reasons they needed a president. I asked them what leadership meant to them, and they were able to assess their needs in the new situation and make their own decision accordingly.

The tension between the insider/outsider perceptions raised questions about diversity and the need to understand the phenomenon in its specific context. A key lesson for me was that, as a researcher, the way I perceive the world of education is shaped by the culture in which I mainly participate, and thus is based on European American cultural constructions of self, research, and education. A broader question that emerges from this tension is, What happens when the ethnographer participates in the change influenced by the research?

When the setting is transformed in some way, as occurred in Carpinteria, empowerment is effected in favor of the community if and when the researcher can reconcile the duality between the researched and the researcher. Conceivably, a danger for the underrepresented community would exist if the researcher failed to recognize the needs of a different culture when the cultures and perceptions of the researcher and researched interact. If this is the case, we need to examine just how the value system of the researcher influences the study. Ethnographers have entered communities as participant-observers with seemingly well-grounded theories for conducting research. Knowledge of the people's language and culture may facilitate research; the researcher's own cultural background, however, may conceal biases that shape ethnographic insights about a given community. As Alan Peshkin (1982) reminds us, a close association exists among four aspects of research: the researcher, the actual research, the act of researching, and the results. To counter our own ignorance and biases as researchers, we must integrate into our research rigorous and systematic joint analysis with our participants.

The role of the researcher in relation to the researched is particularly significant when disenfranchised communities are attempting to exercise their own power. Disenfranchised groups in the United States are being rediscovered through ethnographic study, which enhances our understanding of people's real conditions in their respective communities. These groups deserve a voice as the architects of their own changing historical circumstances. Ethnography of Empowerment connects the researcher to the insider's point of view in constructing new paradigms for explicating change in the education of culturally different, underrepresented groups in our post-traditional and postmodern world.

Notes

1. The term *position* is used in academic discourse to refer to the oppositional role we researchers assume as we conduct ethnographic research. Cast in this binary oppositional framework, the researcher is considered the outsider while the participants — the researched — are the insiders.

2. Interpretive fieldwork strategies have, nevertheless, been criticized regarding researcher bias from several different epistemological paradigms. Questions of objectivity have been a continuing point of contention between positivists and qualitative researchers, including ethnographers. Positivists have argued that if the ethnographer becomes involved with the group he or she is studying, the ethnographer ceases to identify with the professional subgroup as his or her dominant reference group. The conventional premise here is that the ethnographer has to maintain an interpretive stance congruent with the professional group he or she represents. In contrast, the relational position attempts to depict the complexity of the relationship between the participant and the researcher. For further discussion on this aspect of interpretive research, see Chow, 1986; Geertz, 1973; Spindler and Spindler, 1987; and Wolcott, 1981.

   A criticism against participant observation is that the participant and the researcher usually belong to different cultures. Critics argue that through researcher participation, such as the researcher engaging in community activities, the setting may be transformed and the goals of an "objective" field study may be altered by changing the power relations in favor of the subordinate group or of the dominant groups. Critical theorists refute this criticism by maintaining that value-neutral theories and research are nonexistent (Habermas, 1974).

3. A central theme in Paulo Freire's work with Brazilian indigenous groups is his portrayal of community learning, in which the relationship between educators and students is a phenomenon involving a certain permanent, although not antagonistic, tension. It is this same tension — which exists between theory and practice, and between authority and freedom — that renders teaching and learning inseparable. I have extended Freire's relational thesis about learning and critical practice into my research methodology framework. Freire would assert that, through active involvement of the learner, critical theory seeks practical solutions for structural problems that are social and cultural constructions. For additional discussion on Freire's critical theory, see Freire, 1985; Shor and Freire, 1987.

4. Except for Carpinteria, all names used in this article are pseudonyms. The real name of the school district is used because I received permission from the school district to use it in publications.

5. All of the participants' quotations in this article have been translated by me from Spanish.

6. My academic training was rich in ethnography; I learned to structure rigorous and systematic observations and interviews that did not include intervention in changing the setting I was studying.

7. Space limitations prevent me from expanding fully on more recent developments of COPLA. The organization has continued to mobilize in Carpinteria. It has now been active for five years, and has established a structure in each school by which one teacher provides systematic linkages between the school and the parents. With formally written by-laws, COPLA has organized a district-wide committee, as well as satellite school-site groups in all of the elementary, junior high, and high schools. COPLA holds monthly meetings for their district-wide committee on the first Friday of each month. The school-site COPLA meetings are held on alternate Fridays so as not to conflict with those of the district COPLA. Each school has two parent representatives on the district committees, who report to the group about their activities. For additional information about more current developments in the organization and its role as a community support group, see Delgado-Gaitan, 1991.

8. Essentially, every Latino parent in the Carpinteria community was a COPLA parent by virtue of the name of the organization. There were no formal requirements to become a member. As the Central District leadership committee began to organize satellite COPLA groups in every school, school personnel seemed to identify only those parents in the leadership as COPLA parents, distinguishing them from parents who only attended meetings. However, the COPLA leadership stressed that every Latino parent was part of COPLA and thus needed to become actively involved.

9. The concepts of enduring and situational self seem appropriate in this analysis, because both the Latino parents and I seemed to test our notions of self and perceptions of personhood. For a discussion of these theoretical representations, see Spindler and Spindler, 1990 and in press.

References

Ada, A. F. (1988). The Pajaro Valley experience: Working with Spanish-speaking parents to develop children's reading and writing skills in the home through the use of children's literature. In T. Skutnabb-Kangas & J. Cummins (Eds.), *Minority education: From shame to struggle*. Philadelphia: Multilingual Matters.

Allen, J., Barr, D., Cochran, M., Dean, C., & Greene, J. (1989). Empowerment through family support: The empowerment process. *Networking Bulletin, 1,* 2–6.

Apple, M.W. (1993). *Official knowledge: Democratic education in a conservative age.* New York: Routledge.

Barr, D. (1989). *Power and empowerment.* Ithaca, NY: Cornell University, College of Human Ecology.

Barr, D., & Cochran, M. (1991) Preparation for the empowerment process: Identifying competencies and developing skills. Networking Bulletin, 2(1), 26.

Chow, R. (1986). Rereading Mandarin ducks and butterflies: A response to the "postmodern condition." *Cultural Critique, 5,* 69–71.

Delgado-Gaitan, C. (1987). Traditions and transitions in the learning process of Mexican American children: An ethnographic view. In G. Spindler & L. Spindler (Eds.), *Interpretive ethnography of education at home and abroad* (pp. 333–362). Hillsdale, NJ: Lawrence Erlbaum.

Delgado-Gaitan, C. (1989). Classroom literacy activity for Spanish-speaking students. *Linguistics in Education, 1*(3), 285–297.

Delgado-Gaitan, C. (1990). *Literacy for empowerment: The role of parents in children's education.* London: Falmer Press.

Delgado-Gaitan, C. (1991). Linkages between home and school: A process of change for involving parents. *American Educational Journal, 100,* 20–46.

Delgado-Gaitan, C., & Trueba, H. (1991). *Crossing cultural borders: Education for immigrant families in America.* London: Falmer Press.

Elliott, J. (1988). Educational research and outsider-insider relations. *International Journal of Qualitative Studies in Education, 1,* 155–166.

Freire, P. (1970). *Pedagogy of the oppressed.* New York: Continuum.

Freire, P. (1973). *Education for critical consciousness.* New York: Continuum.

Freire, P. (1985). *The politics of education: Culture, power, and liberation.* South Hadley, MA: Bergin & Garvey.

Freire, P., & Macedo, D. (1987). *Literacy: Reading the word and the world.* New York: Bergin & Garvey.

Geertz, C. (1973). *The interpretation of cultures.* New York: Basic Books.

Goldenberg, C.N. (1987). Low-income Hispanic parents' contributions to their first grade children's word-recognition skills. *Anthropology and Education Quarterly, 18,* 149–179.

Habermas, J. (1974). Introduction. In *Theory and practice.* London: Heineman.

Heath, S. B. (1983). *Ways with words: Language, life and work in communities and classrooms.* New York: Cambridge University Press.

Hirschkind, L. (1991). Redefining the "field" in fieldwork. *Ethnology, 30,* 237–250.

Kondo, D. (1990). *Crafting selves: Power, gender, and discourses of identity in a Japanese workplace.* Chicago: University of Chicago Press.

Lavie, S. (1991). *The poetics of military occupation.* Berkeley: University of California Press.

Macias, J. (1987). The hidden curriculum of Papago teachers: American Indian strategies for mitigating cultural discontinuity in early schooling. In G. Spindler (Ed.), *Doing the ethnography of schooling: Educational anthropology in action.* Prospect Heights, IL: Waveland Press.

Marcus, G. E., & Fischer, M. J. (1986). *Anthropology as cultural critique: An experimental moment in the human sciences.* Chicago: University of Chicago Press.

Moll, L., & Díaz, S. (1987). Change as a goal of educational research. *Anthropology and Education Quarterly, 18,* 300–311.

Peshkin, A. (1982). The researcher and subjectivity: Reflections on an ethnography of school and community. In G. Spindler (Ed.), *Doing the ethnography of schooling: Educational anthropology in action* (pp. 48–67). Prospect Heights, IL: Waveland Press.

Podermaker, H. (1967). *Stranger and friend: The way of an anthropologist.* New York: Norton.

Schatzman, L., & Strauss, A. (1973). *Field research strategies for natural sociology.* Englewood Cliffs, NJ: Prentice Hall.

Shor, I., & Freire, P. (1987). *A pedagogy for liberation.* South Hadley, MA: Bergin & Garvey.

Spindler, G. (Ed.). (1970). *Fieldwork in eleven cultures: Being an anthropologist.* New York: Holt, Rinehart & Winston.

Spindler, G. (Ed.). (1974). *Education and cultural process: Toward an anthropology of education.* New York: Holt, Rinehart & Winston.

Spindler, G., & Spindler, L. (1970). *Being an anthropologist: Fieldwork in eleven cultures.* Prospect Heights, IL: Waveland Press.

Spindler, G., & Spindler, L. (Eds.). (1987). *Interpretive ethnography of education at home and abroad* (pp. 363–384). Hillsdale, NJ: Lawrence Erlbaum.

Spindler, G., & Spindler, L. (1990). The self and the instrumental model in the study of culture and change. *Proceedings of 1987 meetings of the Kroeber Anthropological Society* (pp. 97–124). Berkeley, CA: Kroeber Anthropological Society.

Spindler G., & Spindler, L. (in press). The process of culture and person: Multicultural classes and cultural therapy. In P. Phelan & A. Davidson (Eds.), *Cultural diversity and educational policy and change.* New York: Teachers College Press.

Spradley. J. (1979). *Participant observation.* New York: Holt, Rinehart & Winston.

Strauss, A. (1987). *Qualitative analysis for social scientists.* New York: Cambridge University Press.

Suárez-Orozco, M. (1989). *Central American refugees and U.S. high schools: A psychological study of motivation and achievement.* Stanford, CA: Stanford University Press.

Thomas, N. (1991). Against ethnography. *Cultural Anthropology, 6,* 306 –319.

Wax, R. (1971). *Doing fieldwork: Warnings and advice.* Chicago: University of Chicago Press.

Wolcott, H. (1981). Teaching fieldwork to educational researchers: A symposium [special issue]. *Anthropology and Education Quarterly, 14.*

I am indebted to Carpinteria community members who provided insights about the theme and the text of this article. I am also grateful to Marc Blanchard, Nancy Hornberger, Ellen Lubic, and George and Louise Spindler for their critical feedback on earlier versions of this manuscript. Parts of the project and the preparation of this manuscript were also partially supported by grants from the Spencer Foundation and the Johns Hopkins Center for Social Organization of Schools.

Good Readers, Good Teachers?
Subject Matter Expertise as a Challenge
in Learning to Teach

DIANE HOLT-REYNOLDS

The past decade has been marked by a renewed interest in and focus on questions of how best to educate teachers. Landmark publications such as *A Nation at Risk* (National Commission, 1983), a series of reports on the nation's high schools (Boyer, 1983; Powell, Farrar, & Cohen, 1985; Sizer, 1984), and the seminal *A Nation Prepared: Teachers for the 21st Century* (Carnegie Forum, 1986) positioned teacher educators to examine once more the ways we structure and support prospective teachers' learning. These documents led to an agenda for the 1990s: find ways to improve what schoolchildren have the opportunity to explore, master, and learn by improving the quality of the teaching they encounter.

The calls for reform in the late 1980s were by no means novel. Klausmeier (1990) has pointed out the "almost cyclical" (p. 23) nature of the nation's interest in questions of how to prepare teachers. His review of reform movements, beginning in 1950, demonstrated that, while a variety of issues emerged in each decade, calls for improved scholarly, academic, or subject matter preparation of teachers repeatedly headed the list (see Bestor, 1955; Conant, 1963; Howsam, Corrigan, Denemark, & Nash, 1976; Koerner, 1963; Smith, 1980). The Holmes Group added its voice in 1986 and so helped to place the reform of teachers' subject matter preparation at the forefront of the reform discourse in the 1990s.

Of the various domains of teacher knowledge (Shulman, 1986), subject matter expertise might appear to be the most easily addressed. Approaches to this domain have included adjusting teacher education programs to require disciplinary majors for all K–12 teachers, developing admissions standards to favor prospective teachers with high grade point averages in their disciplinary majors, and/or moving course work in pedagogy to a fifth year in order to leave undergraduates ample time to pursue course work in their majors as suggested by The Holmes Group (1986). All of these represent programmatic attempts to respond to almost five decades of calls for stronger, more substantive disciplinary preparation of new teachers.

Agreeing that prospective teachers need to be knowledgeable about the subjects they teach is easy. Finding ways to shape the quantity of time prospective teachers spend in academic departments is practical and tenable. However, defining or articu-

Harvard Educational Review Vol. 69 No. 1 Spring 1999, 29–46

lating what we, as teacher educators, mean by "knowledgeable about subject matter" is a far more complex maneuver. Berliner (1986) has made a helpful distinction between *knowing that* and *knowing how*. *Knowing that*, he maintains, is the more general of the two knowledge types. It is represented by an ability to perform a skill or demonstrate comprehension of a discipline's facts, principles, or theories. A prospective teacher might know, for example, that Shakespeare wrote many plays, lived at a particular time, and influenced literature profoundly. She might demonstrate a thorough recall of the plots of Shakespeare's plays, describe the form of his sonnets, and recite dominant critical views on his work. However, Berliner also argues for a second kind of knowledge that transcends knowing that Shakespeare is an important figure in literature and that there are standard rationales for defending his prominence in literary circles and high school curricula. *Knowing how*, Berliner explains, includes an ability to articulate the personal strategies that a teacher would use to approach Shakespeare, to tell another how she reads his work, and what she does in her mind to understand and respond to it. Shulman (1986) argues similarly. His premise, those who *understand* teach, parallels Berliner's argument. Thinking about expertise as "understanding," like thinking of it as "knowing how," points teacher educators interested in improving the subject matter knowledge of prospective teachers toward a kind of teacher knowledge or expertise that extends beyond the level of general mastery required for degree status. This knowledge includes an ability to transform disciplinary knowledge so that novice learners can participate in discipline-specific ways of understanding the world around them.

What sorts of criteria might help teacher educators distinguish teacher candidates who have rich subject matter preparation and a genuine knowledge of how their own expertise functions from others who do not? What guidelines might help to identify those who have completed required courses in their majors, accumulated above-average grades there, and yet are unable to understand their own expertise well enough to do more than merely tell others the factual contents of their disciplines? Assessing what teachers know (National Board, 1991; Shulman & Sykes, 1986) and improving their knowledge base through preservice teacher preparation is a concern not only of the teacher education community, but of the public as well (Barnes & DeRoche, 1994). And yet, as Grossman and Stodolsky (1994) noted, the research data available to focus teacher education reform on this critical issue — especially in terms of secondary teachers — are sparse.

A Disciplinary Example

Subject matter preparation for teaching literature in secondary schools is one potentially useful and informative area for a case study. The language arts have historically been tolerant of and enriched by multiple definitions, perspectives, and traditions (Applebee, 1974; Elbow, 1990; Graff, 1987) for articulating what counts as expertise within the discipline. At the most sophisticated disciplinary levels, those of us who think about the teaching of high school English live with, and perhaps even cherish, multiple and various responses to seminal questions such as, "What do truly expert readers do when they read literature?" The scholarly, defensible, and well-regarded discourse within the discipline frames its answers in various ways. In fact, enduring questions about what readers should/could/ought to do when performing a quality act of reading a text constitute the intellectual center of the discipline, yet critical theories have yet to exhibit consensus. In fact, it is not clear that consensus is even a desired disciplinary objective. Informed participation in this ongoing debate about what expert readers do and why they do it is actually one important way to signal mastery of the discipline.

Study Design

At the National Center for Research on Teacher Learning, a team of researchers consisting of this author, three graduate students in the College of Education, and another education professor invited twelve undergraduate literature majors enrolled in a teacher education program to talk with us about what literature is, why and how they read it, what literature they hope to share with future adolescent readers, and, especially, to explain to us the reading actions they intend to teach to those future students. By reading actions, we mean those particular mental processes prospective teachers believe good readers use when they read. We wanted to learn how successful literature majors transfer their own disciplinary expertise — that is, their abilities as readers — into an understanding of the school subject "literature" and project a subject-specific pedagogical role for themselves as teachers. Several lines of inquiry informed our design and guided our direction.

Purpose of the Study

Drawing on the work of Grossman (1990), we were curious about how these prospective literature teachers would see and understand the role of a reader and the purposes for reading as they neared completion of a bachelor's degree, but before they participated in a teacher education program or real classrooms as student teachers or interns. We wanted to understand how they talked about and drew on their own actions as readers when attempting to transform that personal knowledge into a knowledge for teaching others. Our question paralleled that of Zancanella (1991), in that we wanted to trace the connections prospective literature teachers might make between their personal practices as readers and the actions they most valued as they envisioned their work as teachers. Like Zancanella, we made no attempt to critique their knowledge on the basis of its viability. We were not looking to see whether their knowledge "worked" or would stand up in the act of teaching real students in real high schools. Nor did we have any interest in making a critique of the quality of the education they received as English majors. We were, rather, curious about the character and content of their subject matter knowledge at the point when they would begin course work designed to help them transform that knowledge for teaching. We hoped to use these data as a springboard for a theoretical exploration of the potential interactions between knowledge of subject matter and the yet-to-be-developed knowledge of subject-specific pedagogical practices (Shulman, 1986).

Design Features

We selected participants from a pool of volunteers at a large midwestern university according to three criteria: participants had to anticipate becoming secondary school literature teachers; they needed to be sophomores or juniors so we could be relatively certain of the stability of their selection of English as a major; they could not be seniors, because prospective literature teachers spend significant numbers of hours in schools early in their senior year, and we wanted to have ample opportunity to talk with participants before they modified their positions to accommodate field experiences. We spoke with each participant at the end of each semester between the time they volunteered for the study and the time they enrolled in the teacher certification course sequence. This meant that, in addition to the entrance and exit interviews, we interviewed the participants at the end of each of three semesters, for a total of five interviews each. We video- and audiotaped each interview. Interviewers had no previous connections with any study participants and saw them exclusively in the context of the formal interview sessions.

Entrance and Exit Interviews

The most extensive of these interviews was the entrance interview, a 119-question protocol in four parts (see Appendix A). Part one solicited participants' histories as readers by asking them to recall early reading experiences at home and at school, favorite books, and memories of family events where stories — oral or textual — figured prominently. Part two invited participants to define "literature" and to talk about their values for genre and text types.

This portion of the protocol included asking participants to examine twenty-five different texts and to decide whether to classify each as literature. Samples ranged from *The Complete Shakespeare* to a romance novel complete with steamy front cover to rap lyrics to instructions for operating a coffee maker to a child's wordless picture book. Part three elicited participants' current theories about critical perspectives widely recognized within the discipline of literary studies. We provided participants with a one-page position paper written from each of four critical perspectives — New Criticism, deconstructionism, reader response theory, and postmodern structuralism (see Appendix B). Each untitled position paper focused on the role of readers, critics, authors, and the printed text in the development of meaning, given each particular perspective. Participants were asked to evaluate each position paper and to talk about elements within the paper with which they either agreed or disagreed.

Part four moved into participants' projections about the role of a literature teacher. They were asked to select books for an imaginary class and to talk about the rationales guiding their selections; they were asked to read Edgar Allan Poe's "The Raven," a highly controversial narrative poem easily read during the time of the interview, and to talk about what they did as a reader to understand the poem. We also asked participants to look at a short paper on Poe's life, and then to talk about how/whether the biography informed their reading and whether they might use it to inform future students. We then asked participants to construct a test on *Romeo and Juliet* for tenth graders by choosing test items from among a set of twenty-five questions we had written. Finally, we asked them to talk about what they might learn from students' answers to those questions, especially from "wrong" answers. (A more extensive discussion of the entrance interview protocol is available; see McDiarmid, 1993.)

We returned to this protocol eighteen months later when we conducted exit interviews with each participant. This exit interview repeated many items from parts two, three, and four of the entrance interview protocol. Our purpose was to record and acknowledge any shift in position that may have resulted from maturation or the effects of three semesters of university course work. While some participants evidenced slight variations from entrance to exit interviews, no one reported radical or extensive revisions in their beliefs. Variations were limited to selecting different texts for imaginary classrooms due to increased familiarity with the texts from which we asked them to choose, or offering more liberal definitions of literature. Some of these students recalled the task from the entrance interview and explicitly claimed, "I've been thinking about this!"

Other Interviews

We were able to conduct interviews with participants at the end of each of three semesters. These were brief interviews in which participants told us about course work they had taken that semester and texts they had read, and shared any ideas they had formed that semester about themselves as readers. None of these interviews became powerful data sources in the study, but they did serve to maintain rapport and contact across time with participants.

Data Analysis

Each participant's data were read as a whole text at the end of the study by all five researchers. During this reading, each researcher also focused on one piece of the larger research question, read the participant's data with that one subquestion in mind, and prepared an issue paper reflecting the participant's position on the question/issue. We chose issues to parallel the four parts of the entrance/exit interview protocols: personal history and biography, definition of literature, theory of reading, and perspective on teaching. The research team then met to build the case around each participant's data. Consensus of analysis was reached by repeated hypothesis creation and tested by re-reading the data. Beach and Marshall (1991) provided a framework for thinking about participants' personal ways of understanding the purposes of reading and describing the ways readers think about or mentally act on and around texts.

The orientations these prospective literature teachers took toward their own actions as readers tended to reflect disciplinary positions and perspectives quite poorly. Most participants cobbled together bits and pieces of standard critical perspectives when describing their own actions as readers. When shifting to discuss what they imagined high school readers might do with texts, those participants who were themselves talented readers were most likely to set strict boundaries on the range of teacher actions they projected. These talented readers believed that teachers should set no goals for students' reading. They believed that teachers might legitimately ask, "What do you think?" but treated any guided questioning or direct modeling of possible ways a reader might interpret or respond to a text as suspect, a potential misuse of authority.

Their projections about what literature teachers should do suggested that they held thinly understood versions of reader response theories of reading and the teaching strategies that reflect this theory of reading. A richer understanding of reader response theories of reading and pedagogy would have included a sense of how teachers use classroom conversations about texts as opportunities to help adolescent readers see additional possible meanings, engage with textual elements, envision characters and events, enter the world of the text, or make judgments about it. Those participants most enamored of reader response theories for use in classrooms were also least likely to recognize the potential utility of textual forms of reader response (see Beach, 1993) or teaching strategies that might be based in New Criticism. For example, they passionately rejected the idea that an author has an intended meaning or that reading includes an effort to discover that intended meaning. Therefore, they rejected teaching strategies that would focus readers on the author, her life, or the context in which she wrote.

Mary: A Knowledgeable Subject Matter Major

Mary gave us an especially clean, clear, and counterintuitive case. The connections that reform-minded teacher educators might assume between genuine expertise in a subject area like literature and a conscious appreciation of the underpinnings of that expertise did not help Mary see an instructional role for herself. Despite her status as a skilled reader — a subject matter expert — she demonstrated little accompanying ability to recognize the processes she used in a way that might lead her to imagine how she could share reading process information or model it with high school readers. In the first conversation we had with her, Mary described herself as "average," but, as the research sequence progressed, we learned that she had been valedictorian of a large, urban high school; had a 4.0 in every literature course she took; and was an avid, lifelong reader with a fondness for poetry. We came to see Mary was anything but an "average" reader.

Evidence of Expertise

Our interview questions were not designed explicitly to "test" prospective literature teachers' knowledge of criticisms, theories, or individual texts in any way. However, we did invite study participants to talk to us about their ways of classifying some texts as either literature or not literature. This open-ended, general probe proved to be a rich source of information about how study participants thought about literature. It was the point within the interview sequence where we began to see how Mary understood the activities of reading.

The interviewer showed Mary twenty-five different sorts of texts, including "standards" such as *The Complete Shakespeare*, less typical story-based texts such as a Calvin and Hobbes cartoon, nonstory texts such as Darwin's *On the Origin of Species*, and texts that might challenge her definition of reading, such as a child's wordless picture book. In response, Mary talked with the interviewer about her criteria for classifying something as "literature." She consistently made her decision about whether something was or was not literature by analyzing the sample text's potential for inviting a reader to develop multiple meanings or interpretations, its ability to provoke abstract thinking, and its power to elicit a reader's passion. She was quick to dismiss such items as newspapers, a history textbook, and a memo as "not literature":

> I consider literature anything not just written for the purpose of information. Literature, I think, takes on a lot of different aspects. A newspaper is just purpose writing; it gives information. It doesn't evoke any other feelings. Literature is something [that gives you] different ways that you can read and interpret it. It's not just written for one purpose.

In each of her decisions about a sample text, Mary estimated whether that text might invite or allow a reader to use sophisticated mental processes for understanding or interacting with it. She determined whether a text was literature by telling the interviewer what she believed a reader would need to do in order to understand it. If she estimated that a reader would need to engage in the act of interpreting in order to understand the text, Mary classified that text as literature.

Given a magazine advertisement for an automobile, Mary classified it as literature because, she said, "It's creating an image for your own interpretation." She followed this same logic to decide that a Calvin and Hobbes cartoon strip is literature: "I never thought of a cartoon as literature, but I guess by the images that it creates, it's an opinion."

The interviewer then asked Mary to clarify the concept she was trying to articulate. In the following interview excerpt, Mary explains how a text that intentionally opens itself to reader interpretation is more literary than a text written by an author who has one idea or point she wants a reader to find:

> I think the reader can choose what you want to do with [something that is] literature. When Emily Brontë wrote *Wuthering Heights*, I don't think she meant it to be read the different ways that people read it. She might have, but there are different ways that people can interpret that story. . . . Like Mary Shelley when she wrote *Frankenstein*. There was a lot of social disorder going on, and revolution and change. But you can look at the different angles of the story. She may have intended them, but she was young, nineteen. So I don't think that she had everything [in mind] that other people read into it. Literature is something you can read into, look for something on your own, create your own interpretation.

Wuthering Heights and *Frankenstein* were not texts the interviewer brought into the interview as samples to be classified. Instead, Mary brought these texts into the discussion. Her citing them suggests that she was able to recall and use intertextual references to support her theory-making. Her argument above is a scholarly one, based on rules of evidence that represent one way of thinking about the relationship between authors' meanings and interpretations. Mary argued that literature is text that is by design open to reader interpretations. As Mary explained, "purpose writing" (her term) differs from literature in that the author intends to transmit particular information, and the text is meant to be read as the author intended, rather than to be open to a reader's personal interpretation. Mary's was a sophisticated argument about what readers do, what authors do, and how literary texts differ from other types of text. We heard many less powerful or discipline-based ways of discriminating among the samples in this portion of the interview with other subjects. Other study participants classified everything with words as literature, everything with a plot as literature, everything fictional as literature, or anything that was published as literature. Mary's rationales were consistently far more sophisticated than those offered by other study participants, and were rooted in the literary theories that define the discipline.

For example, Mary was quite capable of referencing these theories by name. In this same portion of her entrance interview, she introduced critical theory into the conversation, though the protocol would not explicitly take her to these theories until later in that interview session. Her spontaneous use of theory was another marker of Mary's skill as a literature major:

> It depends on how you read [*Frankenstein*] — if you read it at the scientific level, if you read it from the woman's point of view or from Marxism, or if you just want to read it on the Gothic level. I don't know if [by] just looking at it or reading it you can guess what you thought Mary Shelley had in mind when she wrote it, because I think you bring your own interpretations in.

When asked to look again at the same texts eighteen months later, Mary advanced the same argument. "What makes it [the history textbook] not literature is because I don't think that when you read something just for facts, when you search for information, I don't think that counts as literature."

In the exit interview, we were able to see that Mary's expertise included an awareness of the multiple and varied purposes for which readers read:

> *Native Son* is literature because it stimulates thought. I mean, I read Shakespeare just to think. A lot of his themes are powerful and it is something that I can think about and move on from there. [Literature] can make you think about other things; it stimulates thought. The history text is facts and you memorize it. That is where the difference is. . . .The romance novel [*Sunder, Eclipse and Seed*] is literature because it is something you read to escape. It takes you to a different level of thinking. Anything you can get lost in and see yourself and move on from there I would classify as literature.

Mary also knew a lot about the theoretical underpinnings of the discipline. As a standard part of the entrance and exit interviews, we gave each participant one-page position papers, as described above in the protocol. As part of her discussion of these papers, Mary indicated her familiarity with these four theoretical positions. She volunteered the name of the position summarized in three of the four pieces, though we did not ask her to do this. She had not prepared in advance of our interview; the interviewer showed her the position pieces for the first time when he sat down with her in the entrance interview context. She simply added the formal names to her critique of these ideas. We found this interesting and treated it as evidence of Mary's expertise in her discipline. Only one other study participant out of the twelve volunteered his recognition and knowledge of the names of these theoretical schools of thought.

Finally, Mary gave us some indication of her own ability to read with sophistication. When the interviewer asked in the exit interview why she would want to teach literature in college or high school, Mary responded:

> I want to teach literature because I like it. I want to read it. If I take a class, I want to learn more about reading. . . . As a reader, you could be a superficial reader without getting down to the depth of it. You could read a book and totally miss all of the symbolism. . . . I want to be able to pick up a book and get more out of it than I would have. I [first] read *Romeo and Juliet* and thought it was a nice love story. I

read it this week and thought it was an example of bad parenting. I don't believe they were ever in love. It was infatuation.

Mary had been reading *Romeo and Juliet* as an assignment in an English class she was taking. As she told the interviewer what she was noticing about the possible directions a teacher might take the play, she revealed her own ability to read and locate potential interpretations:

> When you pick *Romeo and Juliet* apart, you find that it is just packed. . . . There are a lot of different things you can support. The Friar. Some people say he was just scheming; others say he was just doing it for the kids or because he wanted to end a family feud. I say he wasn't doing it to end the feud because he was going to send Juliet secretly away [to Romeo] and they weren't ever going to come back. That was in his mind. Nobody can get into the Friar's mind or Shakespeare's mind and say what he was thinking exactly. It [the play] is vague enough that there are different interpretations you can have. [The question] is which one fits the play? They all fit; it just changes how you look at *Romeo and Juliet*. It's not that these interpretations are wrong, it's just that they are not standard, not what you're used to hearing. . . . If you can support it, then it's a valid point.

Connecting Personal Expertise and Teaching Others

Mary had substantial expertise in her discipline, as evidenced by her knowledge of how to read for interpretation. What's more, she knew how to use that disciplinary knowledge as a framework for deciding which of multiple interpretations were most valid. Hers would be a "poster" case study for the advantages of recruiting skilled subject matter majors into the profession, were it not for one critical plot twist: Mary did not see that her skills as a reader were learned. She did not treat the mental processes and actions she knew how to use when reading as anything special. There is no evidence in the data to suggest that she regarded herself as an unusually skilled reader. Rather, Mary told her interviewer that she was "average." We could read her interviews and see in them evidence of her expertise; Mary held no similar view of herself. Her expertise was invisible to her, a tacit set of skills she could use but did not directly identify as belonging in the category Shulman (1986) has called subject-specific pedagogical knowledge. She had not identified her use of a rich array of reading processes and actions as a knowledge important enough to share with the adolescent readers she imagined she would one day teach. In Berliner's words, Mary knew that she read in particular ways, but she did not give evidence of *knowing how* those reading actions contributed to her expertise or how they might be useful to less experienced or less skilled readers.

Mary was, however, conscious of some ways in which her personal history as a reader had served her well. First, she was often clear about what she *learned* by reading. The quotations above include her references to her own learning, and she also reported that she felt she had never been *taught* anything as a reader. We discovered how strong this feeling was when her interviewer asked her to draw a representation — an open-ended prompt that she interpreted as a request for a picture or model — showing the relationship between a text, an author, a reader, and a meaning or interpretation. She explained:

I think the author writes the text and the text helps the reader create the meaning. The author becomes a part of what you are reading. That is why it is all connected to meaning. This is how I read. I cannot draw it for anybody else except myself.

When the interviewer asked her to insert a teacher into her representation, Mary responded:

The teacher doesn't fit into the picture for me when I read. I get the book and I consider the author and I consider the period and the text. So that is a private experience for me. For somebody else, I can't say what the teacher would do. I can't say what I'm going to do. A teacher is not an influence when I read. I can't include her or him in this circle.

The interviewer then asked her whether she meant that there is nothing she could gain from a teacher's perspective. Mary replied, "I am not saying that. I'm saying when I read, I don't read for a teacher. I read for myself. The teacher is not in my circle because it is a private experience." Mary's logic reflects her own experiences as a talented learner and skilled reader. She had experienced high school teachers in particular as interfering with her reading by seeming to ask that she hold the same interpretations they held and that she agree with their readings of a text:

We as readers have the choice to see [our teachers'] perspective but it should not be forced on us. We don't want it. We shouldn't be guided to reach their interpretation. It should be an option. . . . I don't think that a reader necessarily needs help to understand. I think readers are quite capable of getting out of it what they want. . . . The teacher or a critic is just a different opinion, it's a separate opinion. You may not agree with the teacher. Does that mean that you are wrong? I don't think so.

Mary powerfully rejected a conception of the teacher as a directive force. In its place she put value on a teacher who would honor any and all valid interpretations. She remarked, "You can talk to [students] and ask, 'What do you think?' . . . The reader is going to find [his] own meaning. I think the reader's role is to discover whatever he wants." Pressed by her interviewer for an imaginary example to clarify her idea, Mary explained:

[A teacher should] ask for general reactions and then ask [students] why they felt that. And if they can't answer, [I'd] ask other people where they might draw their conclusions from and just talk about the poem and about theories behind that poem. You can draw a bunch of different things into it. . . . Ask them to form their opinions why they think anything is significant. Then tie that back into the literature to make them feel they answered the question. Students need to think for themselves rather than be told an answer.

Mary's scenario reveals the importance she placed on student thinking; it is silent about what she believed a teacher might do to foster that thinking beyond inviting students to demonstrate what they already know how to do. How readers might be taught more than they already know about making personal interpretations was simply not apparent to Mary. She seemed unable to envision it as a problem that might require an instructional response.

Mary's interviewer regularly invited Mary to talk about what kinds of instructional input she thought might inform a reader's ability to develop an interpretation. As a research group, we were curious about whether Mary might then work backward to talk about how she as a teacher would help a reader learn to arrive independently at meaning. Nothing emerged. Instead, Mary talked about "understanding the language" as the only prerequisite a reader might need in order to develop an interpretation. Her earliest statement of this type came in the entrance interview as she talked about her own study of Shakespeare: "With Shakespeare, part of it is interpretation. [Our professor] taught us how to get over the confusion point about the language. . . . If you don't understand it, you are going to interpret it to mean what you think and that may not always be right." Mary never enriched or expanded on this fairly simplistic stand; in her mind, if a reader understands the language, a valid interpretation is unproblematic. Yet she herself was able to bring critical theory, personal experiences, knowledge of authors' devices like symbolism and alternative viewpoints to her own work as a reader and interpreter of literature.

The Teacher's Role

Over the eighteen months and more than sixteen hours of interview time, we were able to invite all study participants to tell us what they thought their role as a teacher might include. The most revealing responses were to our questions about teaching particular texts to imaginary students. Invited to talk about what might cause a group of tenth graders to have difficulty with Poe's poem "The Raven," Mary cited lack of maturity as the most likely culprit: "I think experience colors how you read things. If you don't have any experience because of your age, then you're not going to be quite as knowledgeable as the mature reader is. So I think the older you are, the better."

While I would not argue with Mary's underlying premise — that readers bring life experiences to texts and that it is an advantage to have lots of experiences on which to draw — a student's chronological maturity is not something a teacher can affect. However, a teacher might help readers compensate for lack of experience by attempting to provide background and help readers build a base of experience. But these are my ideas about roles for a teacher, not Mary's. Mary-as-Teacher imagined simply reserving a text until students become old enough to read it. She went on to recall how she "didn't like it" when she read Shelley's poetry in high school, but then she "read it in college and liked it a lot. So, I think once you get older, you just learn more." She said her own development occurred outside any instructional experiences and that her expertise was a function of getting older. It is altogether reasonable that she would assume her students would also become better readers as they matured. As stated above, Mary believed that "the teacher doesn't fit into the picture."

Other evidence points to Mary's sense that Mary-as-Teacher would have, both on principle and by definition, a limited role. She believed that readers are best left alone: "I think the reader's role is to discover whatever he wants. . . . I don't think that everybody can have the same interpretation, but I believe that somebody can find a constant theme that runs through a book for themselves." Given a set of questions from an anthology that included "The Raven" and asked whether they might help readers understand the poem, Mary responded:

> I can look at these and say, "What a joke." . . . These questions require regurgitation of facts. They don't focus on discussion. When you answer these questions, you are basically going to critique the question's statement and try to prove [that the ques-

tion's premise] is right. That is what the anthology wants to hear. If you are open to your own interpretation, these questions don't give you room to explore. . . . I don't want to present students with an anthology question and I don't want to present them with my own question because with my own question they are going to answer what they think I want to hear. If I present them with their own questions, then they feel free to argue what they raise.

Mary apparently imagined that all readers are replications of herself — naturally capable of reading texts for personal meaning and frustrated by teaching that either silences them or forces them to adopt interpretations other than their own. Granted, we talked with Mary before she had any authentic field experiences; she had not been in a high school classroom since she left as class valedictorian. Perhaps, we thought, a few weeks in an eighth-grade classroom would radically alter Mary's sense of the relationships possible between teachers, students, and texts, but the point here remains. As a successful, well-prepared literature major just ready to enter professional study, Mary was unprepared to see a teacher's use of personal reading expertise as anything other than misuse of authority. She believed that all readers are able to develop valid personal interpretations of text with no tutoring, schooling, or teaching: "I think that most teachers go in with expectations that the kids don't know very much. And students, knowing that's what the teacher thinks about them, fall into that trap and let them believe that and then they don't try as hard."

Mary did have a projected game plan. She had a list of attributes good teachers need in order to be effective literature teachers. She told her interviewer that her best teachers had been those who demonstrated that they cared about students, who were personable, yet could retain class control — all attributes to which we feel prospective teachers should aspire. Yet, in spite of being asked "What does it take for someone to teach *literature* in schools?" she gave no response that was in any way literature-specific:

> Knowledge, patience, flexibility. They have to bridge the generation gap. They have to be good storytellers. They have to be good listeners. There are so many characteristics. They have to share; they have to give the student a chance to speak and use their own voice and create a good class community so that students feel they can share without being ridiculed. I mean, anything you would think a good teacher would have to do would be applied to a teacher of literature, except the most important thing with literature is that students make sure they're safe because nobody wants to be made a fool of. Teachers must be open-minded, flexible, and able to keep [students] on task because students can go off on a tangent and teachers have to be able to incorporate that tangent back into the original plan, but at the same time make students feel worthwhile.

Pushed by her interviewer to say how a good literature teacher would be different from, for example, a good math teacher, Mary added, "Well-read would be the only difference I can think of. In order to teach literature, you have to have a solid background in literature."

There is absolutely nothing "wrong" with Mary's list. Teachers indeed need to be generous individuals with strong interpersonal and communications skills. We certainly hope to attract flexible, open-minded, smart individuals into the profession, and everything Mary has named would be beneficial in a teacher of literature. What is striking here, however, is that Mary knew so much about how to read, how to interpret, how to think about text, that she could use the skills she valued to her own reading advantage, and yet she offered none of that expertise as a valuable trait for a literature teacher.

Mary and Teacher Education

Mary completed her undergraduate major saddled with an ironic challenge. The potential problems she brought to her study of teaching were not the outgrowth of deficiency; they had their roots in the very expertise she had so easily cultivated. Mary "knew" a lot about reading, and knew a lot about her discipline, but she did not know that her expertise was learned. Treating her learned skills as merely a function of maturation, Mary could not talk to us about a "teacher self" who *taught* those skills to others. Instead, she imagined only extending opportunities to her students to display full-blown personal expertise at an earlier age than she had been allowed that freedom. Her apparently egalitarian belief in the innate and untutored skill of others positioned her to reject most teacher actions designed to make the mental processes of reading for personal meaning explicit for inexperienced readers. She saw these actions as oppressive, silencing, and patronizing.

Conscious Expertise

Mary's case suggests that at least some prospective teachers may come to teacher education unaware of their own expertise. They may be unable to recall or be unaware of how they have learned the processes they use and that render them expert. Unaided by their disciplines in locating the underpinnings (see Graff, 1992) of their expertise, these skilled, talented, and desirable recruits to teaching may easily become, ironically, those who can *do* but who cannot *teach* (Shulman, 1986). Our work as teacher educators would then include helping them recognize and claim as *learned* expertise the skills and abilities that they take for granted as unlearned. A definition of subject matter expertise needs to include awareness of that expertise as learned, earned, or developed.

Anticipating a Teacher's Role

However sharply it violates our intuitive senses, it is also possible that highly expert subject matter majors may, like Mary, aggressively avoid imagining an active, instructional role for themselves as they face the transition from university student to schoolteacher. Mary's sense that interpretations are constructed, rather than given, marks her as a sophisticated reader and interpreter of literature. It was this same sophisticated commitment to the generation of personal interpretations that also led her to see any and all instructional actions as nothing more than a veiled preferencing of a teacher's interpretation. Truly expert subject matter majors like Mary may arrive in teacher education passionately committed to a model of Self-as-Teacher in which the teacher has little instructional responsibility in the classroom. Therefore, a definition of subject matter expertise must also include an awareness of concepts, ideas, and dispositions that must be actually taught to others.

Discussion

The reform rhetoric calls for better subject matter preparation of prospective teachers; however, that call is not grounded in a research-based model that predicts the relationship between exemplary subject matter expertise and the disposition to adopt an active role as a teacher. Those of us actively engaged in teacher education hear little or nothing about what challenges we might face if we successfully recruit into the profession genuinely expert disciplinary majors. While I would certainly *not* argue the counter point, I suggest that we use the case of Mary as a point of departure. Admittedly, Mary is only one case. Without overextending these data, it is fair to worry about whether prospective teachers like Mary will be able to sustain themselves in the profession. Mary's case projects at least the possibility of a teacher who will find herself unable to have a noticeable or personally satisfying impact on her learners. What would prompt a teacher who never sees student improvement to remain in the profession? Her case suggests a teacher who is prepared to frame student nonengagement exclusively as a function of her choices of texts and their current level of maturation. What happens to adolescent readers when they encounter teachers who read well and know a lot about texts, but who have no sense of how they learned to read well or how to show others how to behave in a like manner?

An Afterword

The research in which Mary was a formal participant ended one year before she entered her internship year in her university's Teacher Certification Program. Because the research team members remained interested in Mary and because our team knew she was progressing to an internship, we arranged to informally observe her work there. As one of the principle investigators on the research team, I elected to be the team member who would visit Mary's classroom. There, Mary's extensive expertise as a reader was invisible. Instead, I saw her working hard to explain to eighth graders how to make a collage, how to fill out question sheets, how to staple pages of a personal poetry collection book in order, how to create its cover page. Fostering students' completion of assignments appeared to have become Mary's entire role as a teacher.

Following one such lesson, I asked Mary whether she had meant to teach the poem students read that day or to teach the worksheet she coaxed them to fill out. Her blue eyes met mine and grew large as she affirmed her desire to teach the poem, not the worksheet, and recognized that she had in fact done just the opposite. She was surprised when I asked her whether these younger readers might benefit more from hearing her talk about what she does with her mind when she reads poetry — what she notices, what makes her smile or satisfies her, what other ideas and texts she brings to the poem as she reads. It was an idea she had not considered.

Few experiences in my life as a teacher educator and researcher have moved me more. Mary's case shows me vividly that unidentified, unclaimed, and untapped subject matter expertise has little power. It lies dormant and useless in a classroom. Helping talented, sophisticated prospective teachers identify their expertise, value it, and imagine ways to share and model it with their students may be a challenge teacher educators had not anticipated when we set out to recruit more subject matter experts into teaching. Shulman was right: those who can must also understand. The surprise for teacher education is that we may need to work hard to help prospective teachers identify their expertise and transform it into effective instruction.

References

Applebee, A. N. (1974). *Tradition and reform in the teaching of English: A history.* Urbana, IL: National Council of Teachers of English.

Barnes, D., & DeRoche, E. F. (1994). What do newspaper editorials have to say about teacher education programs? *Teacher Education Quarterly, 21,* 111–114.

Beach, R. (1993). *A teacher's introduction to reader-response theories.* Urbana, IL: National Council of Teachers of English.

Beach, R., & Marshall, J. (1991). *Teaching literature in the secondary school.* New York: Harcourt Brace Jovanovitch.

Berliner, D. C. (1986). In pursuit of the expert pedagogue. *Educational Researcher, 15*(7), 5–13.

Bestor, A. (1955). *The restoration of learning.* New York: Alfred Knopf.

Boyer, E. L. (1983). *High school: A report on secondary education in America.* New York: Harper Colophon.

Carnegie Forum on Education and the Economy. (1986). *A nation prepared: Teachers for the 21st century.* New York: Author.

Conant, J. B. (1963). *The education of American teachers.* New York: McGraw-Hill.

Elbow, P. (1990). *What is English?* New York: Modern Language Association of America.

Graff, G. (1987). *Professing literature: An institutional history.* Chicago: University of Chicago Press.

Graff, G. (1992). *Beyond the culture wars: How teaching the conflicts can revitalize American education.* New York: Norton.

Grossman, P. L. (1990). *The making of a teacher: Teacher knowledge and teacher education.* New York: Teachers College Press.

Grossman, P. L., & Stodolsky, S. S. (1994). Considerations of context and the circumstances of secondary school teaching. In L. Darling-Hammond (Ed.), *Review of research in education* (pp. 179–221). Washington, DC: American Educational Research Association.

Holmes Group. (1986). *Tomorrow's teachers.* East Lansing, MI: Author.

Howsam, R., Corrigan, D., Denemark, G., & Nash, R. (1976). *Educating a profession.* Washington, DC: American Association of Colleges of Teacher Education.

Klausmeier, R. L., Jr. (1990). Four decades of calls for reform of teacher education: The 1950s through the 1980s. *Teacher Education Quarterly, 17*(4), 23–64.

Koerner, J. D. (1963). *The miseducation of American teachers.* Boston: Houghton Mifflin.

McDiarmid, G. W. (1993, April). *Studying prospective teachers' views of literature and teaching literature.* Paper presented at the annual meeting of the American Educational Research Association, Atlanta.

National Board for Professional Teaching Standards. (1991). *Toward high and rigorous standards for the teaching profession* (3rd ed.). Washington, DC: Author.

National Commission on Excellence in Education. (1983). *A nation at risk: The imperative for educational reform.* Washington, DC: U.S. Government Printing Office.

Powell, A. G., Farrar, E., & Cohen, D. K. (1985). *The shopping mall high school: Winners and losers in the educational marketplace.* Boston: Houghton Mifflin.

Shulman, L. S. (1986). Those who understand: Knowledge growth in teaching. *Educational Researcher, 15*(2), 4–14.

Shulman, L. S., & Sykes, G. (1986). *A national board for teaching? In search of a bold standard.* Paper presented before the Task Force on Teaching as a Profession, Carnegie Forum on Education and the Economy, San Diego.

Sizer, T. R. (1984). *Horace's compromise: The dilemma of the American high school.* Boston: Houghton Mifflin.

Smith, B. O. (1980). *A design for a school of pedagogy.* Washington, DC: U.S. Department of Education.

Zancanella, D. (1991). Teachers reading/readers teaching: Five teachers' personal approaches to literature and their teaching of literature. *Research in the Teaching of English, 25*(1), 5–32.

Appendix A

Description of Understanding Literature Interview Protocol

Part One: Personal History

Example Questions:

- Tell me about how your interest in reading and literature developed.
- Tell me what you remember about reading and literature in elementary school.
- What about English or American literature classes in high school? Which did you take? When you think back to that class, what stands out for you?
- Tell me about why you decided to major in English. . . . When did you make this decision?
- What's the best English or literature course you've taken?
- What made it so good?
- What about the flip side — what's the worst English or literature course you've taken?
- What made it bad?
- In college, have you found that literature is treated differently than it was in high school?

Part Two: Defining Literature; Knowing Literature

Example Questions:

- Could you tell me what texts or books or works you think of when you hear the word "literature"?
- Now I want to present you with a bunch of different texts and I want you to tell me whether or not you consider each of them literature. As we are most interested in *how* you think about this issue, please think aloud and say whatever comes to your mind as you look at each text.
- Can you tell me how you decided? What influenced your decisions and ideas about this classification? Why is a particular text literature and another text isn't?
- Is there anything that you want to comment about? Is there anything else that you want me to know? Anything else you want to say?
- I'd like for you to take a moment and think of something you've read or a writer that has meant a lot to you. Then, I'd like for you to tell me about when you think about what it means to know or understand literature, what sort of ideas come to mind? How did you come to think that way?
- As you probably know, we are trying to find out more about how people think about literature and what it means to say someone knows literature. Can you think of someone who you would say knows literature?
- How did you come to believe that this person knows literature?

Part Three: Critical Theories

Examples:

- Here is what someone has said about literature. Take some time to read it. When you feel ready, I want you to tell me what you think of it.
- How would you compare these different views?
- Which is closest to your idea of literature? Why?
- What do you find in the others that you don't agree with?
- Is there a theory of literature that you prefer that we haven't included? [If yes:] How does it differ from these four?
- Are there things about literature that you believe but that these authors left out?
- How do you think it happens that people disagree about literature?
- What experiences have you had reading about or studying literary theory?

Part Four: Teacher Roles

Examples:

- Here is a copy of "The Raven." Read it, and when you're finished we'll talk a little about what you think is going on in this poem.
- I'm eager to understand "The Raven" the way you do without biasing you too much. So, I'd really like to know what you think of this poem. Tell me about it.
- If you think of this poem from your perspective as an English major, is there anything you'd add? Anything about your original analysis you'd especially want to highlight or explain differently? Is there anything you feel would be less important or not important at all?
- What do you know about Poe's life? The reason I'm asking this is because sometimes what we know about an author's life influences how we read and think about his or her work. Is that important for you when you're reading "The Raven"?
- "The Raven" is a poem you could find yourself teaching one day. Would you choose to teach it if you found it in the anthology your students had been assigned? Could you explain what factors might affect your decision? Anything else?
- Let's assume for a moment that this poem is important to teach in a high school curriculum. Think about grades 9 through 12. Where do you think this poem could best be included? Would this be a difficult poem for students? What helps you decide? How do you predict students will react to this poem?
- Imagine that you were going to "teach this poem": what would you focus on?
- If I were a visitor in your classroom when you were teaching this poem, what would I likely see you doing? How about the students — what would they likely be doing? From the first moment that students see the poem through to the last time they talk, think, or write about it, what might be going on in your classroom?
- Why do you think we teach literature in college? How about in high schools? And in elementary schools?

Appendix B

Summary of Theoretical Positions

Theory #1: Postmodern Structuralism

A **work of literature** is a self-contained world. The meaning is found within the text itself. The various parts of the text may conflict or be in tension. The form or structure of the work pulls these parts together into a coherent whole. The form *is* the meaning.

Since a literary work contains its own reality and its form is its meaning, knowledge of the intentions or the life and times of the **author** is *not* important for understanding what the work means.

Similarly, since the work exists in and is its own world, **society** has little influence on the meaning of a text.

The **reader** must experience the meaning of the work. However, experiencing the meaning is not simply a matter of responding subjectively and/or affectively to the work. Experiencing the meaning requires hard-nosed, rigorous, objective analyses of the text.

This is where the **critic** comes in. The critic cannot merely paraphrase the meaning for the reader. Indeed, since the meaning of a work is its form, it cannot be paraphrased. "Close" reading — attention to the use and meaning of words, symbols, metaphors, and structure — is required. The critic helps the reader learn to do this close reading.

Theory #2: Reader Response

The reader largely determines the meaning of a **work of literature**. Nevertheless, the text sets constraints on the meaning that the reader can find because its language and structure elicit certain common responses rather than others.

One group of critics who adhere to this idea claim that all **authors** necessarily have an intended audience in mind when writing. Other critics argue that meaning is created by reading; thus the reader is really the **author**.

The **reader** plays the central role in both of these views. If the author writes for an intended reader (audience), the reader effectively controls the meaning of the text. If the reader is the author, then the reader creates whatever meaning the text has through the act of reading.

Forces within **society** affect the backgrounds that authors and readers bring to a text. Similar backgrounds and perspectives lead author and reader to create meanings for a text that are compatible.

The **critics** define and write about the respective roles of the text, author, reader, society, and critics. Some critics primarily describe how and why these roles developed and are the way they are; other critics attempt to demonstrate how the reader functions as author of what is read.

Theory #3: New Criticism

A **work of literature** exposes the reader to other points of view, other imaginations, other emotions and actions, and enables the reader to see more and further and, hence, to become a better person. The traditions and cultural values found in the greatest literature represent some of the finest sentiments and achievements of the species: particular notions of the True and Beautiful and of enduring moral and aesthetic values; an affinity for the "eternal" human truths; a sense of a shared humanity and a deep and abiding awareness of the importance of democratic ideals.

The **author**, particularly the author of a great work, creates a world so powerful and alive that a reader actually experiences themes that are ageless and comes to understand universal truths.

The **reader**'s role is to discover the meaning of the text, a meaning that transcends the time and circumstances in which it was written. In discovering this meaning, the reader also learns about her or his own existence and shared humanity as well as his or her individuality and distinctive heritage. A reader reads to become a more complete and better person.

The ideals and truths depicted in literature can only imperfectly be realized in **society**. But by reading and becoming a better person, the individual contributes to the improvement of society as a whole.

The **critic** helps the reader to learn to read critically, to find the meaning more readily. The reader thus becomes capable of experiencing the meaning more deeply and intensely and, hence, gains increased pleasure and understanding from reading.

Theory #4: Deconstructionism

A **work of literature** has no fixed or constant meaning. A single word can be defined in multiple ways, and each definition of a given word is a definition of that word by default; that is, because it is *not* the definition of a different word. Each of the myriad words, separately and strung together, imparts to the text an uncertainty and indeterminableness. Other texts, past and future, entwine with a work. Also present in any work are faint suggestions of alternative texts that are absent only because the author chose to write the one written.

The words used and the meaning the **author** wants cannot coincide; notions about the author's intention and original meaning are merely empty phrases.

The **reader** will find at most an ebb and flow of shadowy meanings that fade, reform, fade again.

What is true of a single work is true of Literature as a whole; and if Literature cannot capture and hold meaning, can there be any ultimate meaning in **society**?

The role of the **critic** is to "defamiliarize" the text: to enable the reader to see that the appearance of meaning is but illusion; to expose as rhetoric claims that the traditional moral and cultural values transmitted by "Great Literature" are immutable and eternal truths. It is through this rhetoric that traditional authority and privilege perpetuates itself.

About the Authors

Adrienne Alton-Lee is Director of the Understanding Learning and Teaching Institute in Wellington, New Zealand. Her current work involves the development of collaborative classroom research case studies in the ERUDITE (Educational Research Underpinning Development in Teacher Education) Program. She is coauthor of "Inclusive Practice within the Lived Cultures of School Communities: Research Case Studies in Teaching, Learning, and Inclusion" in *International Journal of Inclusive Education* (forthcoming), and "Predicting Learning from Student Experience of Teaching: A Theory of Student Knowledge Construction in Classrooms" in *American Educational Research Journal* (with G. A. Nuthall, 1993).

Joan Kernan Cone teaches English at El Cerrito High School in El Cerrito, California. She is also a doctoral student at the University of California, Berkeley, where her research focuses on school reform from the perspective of teacher leaders. Her publications include "Reconfirming a Commitment to Untracking" in *California English* (1996), and "The Key to Untracking: Learning to Teach an Untracked Class" in *College Board Review* (1994).

Michele D. Crockett is an Assistant Professor at the University of Southern California's Rossier School of Education. Her areas of interest include mathematics teaching and learning, and curriculum. She is coauthor of "Teachers' Shifting Assessment Practices in the Context of Educational Reform in Mathematics" in *Teaching and Teacher Education* (with G. Saxe, M. Gearhart, M. Franke, and S. Howard, 1999).

Concha Delgado-Gaitan is a writer and former professor of sociocultural studies. Her research interests are lifestory narrative, community historical archiving, and applied anthropology. She is author of *Protean Literacy: Extending the Discourse of Empowerment* (1996) and "School Matters in the Mexican-American Home: Socializing Children to Education" in *American Educational Research Journal* (1992).

Donald Freeman is Professor of Second Language Education and Director of the Teacher Knowledge Project at the Graduate School for International Training, Brattleboro, Vermont. His current work focuses on documenting development and change in practitioners' knowledge, and its impact on student learning. He is author of *Doing Teacher-Research: From Inquiry to Understanding* (1998) and coeditor of *Teacher Learning in Language Teaching* (with J. C. Richards, 1996).

Andrew David Gitlin is Professor of Educational Studies at the University of Utah. His research interests include teacher research, school change, and issues of culture, schooling, and inequality. He is coauthor of *Becoming a Student of Teaching: Methodologies for Exploring Self and School Context* (with R. Bullough, 1995) and author of *Power and Method: Political Activism and Educational Research* (1994).

Lorie Hammond, Assistant Professor in Teacher Education at California State University at Sacramento, is interested in teacher research and teacher education, and school community relations in multicultural settings. Her publications include "Making Science Accessible to Language Minority Students" in *Multicultural Education* (with B. Merino, 1998), and "Teaching and Learning through Mien Culture: A Case Study in School-Community Relations" in *Education and Cultural Process: Anthropological Approaches* (edited by G. Spindler, 1997).

Shirley Brice Heath is Professor of English and Linguistics at Stanford University. Her current research interests are language, learning, and culture/organizational contexts. Her recent published works include "Discipline and Disciplines in Education Research: Elusive Goals?" in *Issues in Education Research: Problems and Possibilities* (edited by E. C. Lagemann and L. S. Shulman, 1999) and "Imaginative Actuality: Learning in the Arts during the Nonschool Hours" in *Champions of Change* (with A. A. Roach, 1999).

Diane Holt-Reynolds is Assistant Professor of Teacher Education at Michigan State University in East Lansing. Her professional interests center around prospective teacher learning. Her published works include "Did the Teaching Change the Thinking? An Examination of One Teacher Educator's Pedagogical Theory for Responding to Prospective Teachers' Beliefs" in *Teacher Education Quarterly* (in press), and "Preservice Teachers and Course Work: When Is Getting It Right Wrong?" in *Educating Teachers for Leadership and Change: Teacher Education Yearbook III* (edited by M. J. O'Hair and S. J. Odell, 1995).

Peter H. Johnston is Professor and Chair, Department of Reading, State University of New York, Albany, and Senior Scientist at the university's National Research Center on English Learning & Achievement. He is interested in assessment, reading and writing difficulties, and the development of a democratic literacy. His publications include "Unpacking Literate 'Achievement'" in *Stirring the Waters: A Tribute to Marie Clay* (edited by J. Gaffney and B. Askew, 1999), and *Knowing Literacy: Constructive Literacy Assessment* (1997).

Magdalene Lampert is Professor of Educational Studies at the University of Michigan School of Education in Ann Arbor. Her professional interests center around research on teaching and teachers' professional learning. She is coauthor of *Teaching, Multimedia, and Mathematics: Investigations of Real Practice* (with D. Ball, 1998), and coeditor of *Talking Mathematics: Studies of Teaching and Learning in School* (with M. Blunk, 1998).

Mary Haywood Metz is Professor of Educational Policy Studies at the University of Wisconsin–Madison. She is interested in school organization, teachers' working lives, and the effects of a community's social class on both of these. Her publications include "Desegregation as Necessity and Challenge" in *Journal of Negro Education* (1994), and *Different by Design: The Context and Character of Three Magnet Schools* (1986).

Elliot G. Mishler is Professor of Social Psychology at the Harvard Medical School. His professional interests include narrative research, clinical and research interviews, craftwork and identity, and the process of trauma and recovery among survivors of sexual abuse and domestic violence. His recent publications include *Narratives of Identity* (1999), *Research Interviewing: Context and Narrative* (1996), and *Ethnography and Human Development: Context and Meaning in Social Inquiry* (1996).

Sonia Nieto, Professor of Language, Literacy, and Culture at the University of Massachusetts Amherst, is interested in multicultural education, Puerto Rican children's literature, and the education of Latinos in the United States. She is editor of *Puerto Rican Students in U.S. Schools* (2000) and author of *Affirming Diversity: The Sociopolitical Context of Multicultural Education* (3rd ed., 2000) and *The Light in Their Eyes: Creating Multicultural Learning Communities* (1999).

Graham Nuthall is Professor of Education at the University of Canterbury in Christchurch, New Zealand. His research interests include learning and teaching, internalization of cognitive processes, and designing effective inclusive classroom activities. His recent related publications include "The Role of Memory in the Acquisition and Retention of Knowledge in Science and Social Studies Units" in *Cognition and Instruction* (2000), and "Learning How to Learn: The Evolution of Students' Minds through the Social Processes and Culture of the Classroom" in *International Journal of Educational Research* (1999).

Reba N. Page is Professor of Education at the University of California, Riverside. Her major professional interests focus on curriculum, interpretive research methods, and the social and cultural foundations of education. Her publications include *Lower-Track Classrooms: A Curricular and Cultural Perspective* (1991) and *Curriculum Differentiation: Interpretive Studies in U.S. Secondary Schools* (coedited with L. Valli, 1990).

John Patrick, prior to his retirement, was a Senior Lecturer at the Christchurch College of Education, Christchurch, Aotearoa New Zealand, where his research focus was teaching skills and the influence of learners' self-concepts on learning. He is coauthor of "Take Your Brown Hand Off My Book: Racism in the Classroom" in *SET: Research Information for Teachers* (with A. Alton-Lee and G. Nuthall, 1987).

Annie G. Rogers is Associate Professor in Human Development and Psychology at the Harvard Graduate School of Education. Her research addresses gender and psychological development, particularly the effects of trauma on memory and relationships. She is interested in girls' and women's writing as a key to sustaining voice and psychological health. Her publications include "An Interpretive Poetics of Languages of the Unsayable" in *The Narrative Study of Lives* (with M. Casey, J. Ekert, J. Holland, V. Nakkula, and N. Sheinberg, 1999), and *A Shining Affliction: A Story of Harm and Healing in Psychotherapy* (1995).

Yvette J. Samson is Assistant Professor at Bloomsburg University in Bloomsburg, Pennsylvania. Her areas of professional interest are emotions, race, and education.

Wendy Schoener is a judicial clerk on the Indiana Court of Appeals. Her professional goal is to combine her interest in education and immigration with the practice of law. She is author of "Were They Prepared? College ESL Students in Content Classes" (1992) and "What Do Good Writing Teachers Do?" (1991), both in the newsletter of the Massachusetts Association of Teachers of Speakers of Other Languages.

George Spindler is Professor Emeritus in Anthropology and Education at Stanford University. His research interests center around anthropology and education. His extensive published works include "The Processes of Culture and Person: Cultural Therapy in Culturally Diverse Schools" in *Native North American Cultures: Four Cases* (coedited with L. Spindler, 1977), and *The American Cultural Dialogue and Its Transmission* (with L. Spindler, 1990).

Polly Ulichny is a Research Associate in the Rural Trust Research and Evaluation Program at the Harvard Graduate School of Education. Her present areas of professional interest are rural and urban school renewal, and literacy. She is author of *Living and Learning in Rural Schools and Communities: A Report to the Annenberg Rural Challenge* (1999), and "When Critical Ethnography and Action Collide" in *Qualitative Inquiry* (1997).

Sofia Villenas is a Visiting Assistant Professor of Education at the Harvard Graduate School of Education. Her research centers on investigating Latino home and community education within the dynamics of racial/cultural community politics. Her present areas of professional interest include anthropology of education, Latino education, and Chicana feminist social theory. She is coeditor of *Race Is . . . Race Isn't: Critical Race Theory and Qualitative Studies in Education* (with L. Parker and D. Deyhle, 1999), and coauthor of "Critical Race Theory and Ethnographies Challenging the Stereotypes: Latino Families, Schooling, Resilience, and Resistance" in *Curriculum Inquiry* (1999).

About the Editors

Jennifer Garvey Berger is a doctoral candidate at the Harvard Graduate School of Education (HGSE). She also works with preservice and in-service teachers, is a teaching fellow at HGSE, and teaches at the Bard Institute for Writing and Thinking. Her research examines the connection between adult development and teacher professional development. She is a former middle and high school English teacher.

Bárbara M. Brizuela is a doctoral candidate at the Harvard Graduate School of Education. She is a teaching fellow at HGSE in the areas of teaching and learning. Her research examines the ideas that young children develop about the number system, especially focusing on their understandings and learning of notations. She is a former kindergarten and seventh-grade teacher.

Romina G. Carrillo is a doctoral candidate at the Harvard Graduate School of Education. She is also a clinical professor at Brown University, where she teaches an introductory course in qualitative research methods. Her current research examines the role of professional development in the student-teacher and mentor-teacher relationship. She previously taught in bilingual elementary classrooms.

Julie Pearson Stewart is a doctoral candidate at the Harvard Graduate School of Education, where she works as a teaching fellow in classes on qualitative methodology. She also works for an educational research firm in Cambridge, Massachusetts. Her research is on the intersection of politics, history, curriculum, and language. She previously taught secondary English and humanities.